EUROPEAN INDUSTRIAL POLICY

POLICY

The Twentieth-Century Experience

Edited by

JAMES FOREMAN-PECK and
GIOVANNI FEDERICO

OXFORD
UNIVERSITY PRESS

OXFORD

UNIVERSITY PRESS

Great Clarendon Street, Oxford OX2 6DP

Oxford New York
Athens Auckland Bangkok Bogotá Buenos Aires Calcutta
Cape Town Chennai Dar es Salaam Delhi Florence Hong Kong Istanbul
Karachi Kuala Lumpur Madrid Melbourne Mexico City Mumbai
Nairobi Paris São Paulo Singapore Taipei Tokyo Toronto Warsaw
and associated companies in Berlin Ibadan

Oxford is a registered trade mark of Oxford University Press

Published in the United States
by Oxford University Press Inc., New York

British Library Cataloguing in Publication Data
Data available

Library of Congress Cataloging in Publication Data
European industrial policy : the twentieth-century experience / edited
by James Foreman-Peck and Giovanni Federico.
p. cm.
Includes bibliographical references (p.).
1. Industrial policy—Europe—History—20th century. 2. Europe—
Politics and government—20th century. 3. Europe—Commercial
policy. 4. Europe—Economic policy. 5. Europe—Economic
conditions—20th century. I. Foreman-Peck, James. II. Federico,
Giovanni, 1954– .
HD3616.E8E872 1999 338.94′009′04—dc21 98–44962
ISBN 0–19–828998–7 (alk. paper)

1 3 5 7 9 10 8 6 4 2

Typeset in 10/12pt Times
by Graphicraft Ltd, Hong Kong
Printed in Great Britain
on acid-free paper by
Biddles Ltd,
Guildford & Kings Lynn

PREFACE

A big plant is going to close. Thousands will lose their jobs. A government minister steps in with a massive subsidy. Thousands breathe sighs of relief. So perhaps does the minister, facing re-election in the next few months. Financing details can be left until later.

The government miraculously reduces borrowing without raising taxes or cutting expenditure. At the same time it boasts of an economy rejuvenated by sales of state enterprises. Former government ministers find themselves advising banks on the next wave of privatizations.

If we accept that both these examples should be covered by the broad definition of 'industrial policy', there is no surprise that the subject provokes strong reactions. During the great economic boom after 1945, European governments were widely believed to be benevolent, powerful, and informed helmsmen of national industries. More commonly today industrial policy is irrevocably linked with wasteful state intervention. Despite these polarized positions, what is contentious is often unclear. The definition and scope of 'industrial policy' differs not only between European countries (with Germany taking the broadest option) but also within their boundaries. Some regard competition policy as an element of industrial policy, others consider it to be separate and distinct.

The present study takes the wider view. The aim is to contribute to an understanding of European industrial policy, broadly interpreted, by introducing a historical perspective. We show the remarkable continuity in European national institutions, cultures, and societies, despite the traumas of world wars, revolutions, and foreign occupations. 'Liberal' France at the end of the nineteenth century was far more interventionist than liberal Britain. Later in the twentieth century, British expenditure on industry as a proportion of national income tended to converge with France's. But in the 1980s 'economic liberalism' resurfaced in Britain earlier and more prominently than elsewhere in Western Europe. Continuity offers some explanations for the instruments and objectives of national policies and for comparative industrial performance. Differences in the competitiveness of national industries often take a considerable time to emerge. They also persist for lengthy periods. In such cases a long-term perspective on the effectiveness of policy intervention is helpful. The quite extraordinary growth of Italian industrial productivity in the decades after 1945, radically narrowing the productivity gap with the United States, contrasts with the considerable but less spectacular performance of the more interventionist Spanish economy over the same period.

Conventional European historiography distinguishes 'the long nineteenth century' ending in the slaughter of the First World War. Here instead we are concerned with 'the long twentieth century', beginning with (fairly) liberal late nineteenth-century Europe, including the two world wars, the world economic crisis of the 1930s, great boom after the second war, the Cold War, and culminating in the widening and deepening of the European community.

Comparative study is helpful in judging the effectiveness of one national industrial policy in contrast with others. That is a reason for including so many case studies of European economies. Of course we consider the four big Western European economies, Germany, France, Italy, and Britain, but more unusually we offer chapters on smaller countries as well. Even though small countries may have little impact on the European economy as a whole, they can broaden the range of evidence of policy effectiveness and policy causation. Moreover, as we argue in the concluding chapter, world economic development increasingly makes formerly 'large' economies 'small', when measured by their policy independence. An additional novel feature of this book is the inclusion of the largest European economy. Russian industrial policy is of great interest, both because Soviet Russian policy represents an extreme case of state interventionism and because Russia experienced two transitions, towards and away from, this polar position.

The country chapters provide a synthesis of a great deal of literature unavailable in English. A multi-authored volume, such as this one, is the only way the project could be undertaken. No single author can hope to command the necessary range of languages and detail of national experiences. After publication of this collection the task of writing a history of European industrial policy will be more manageable.

Each of the country authors was asked to write their chapter according to two general principles. The first was that authors should obtain from secondary sources an outline of national policies over the last century or so, and analyse policy towards particular industries, and in particular issue areas. The second was that the studies should discuss as far as possible the following aspects of industrial policies:

(*a*) pressures behind the formation of policy;
(*b*) the objectives and possible benefits of policy;
(*c*) the recipients of those benefits;
(*d*) the instruments or tools of policy; and
(*e*) the effectiveness of the link between objectives and instruments.

The editors recognized that countries were sufficiently different from each other to make rigid adherence to these principles sometimes problematic. In any case, we concluded that reading a dozen studies all following exactly the same pattern would be monotonous. The contributors have therefore been granted considerable latitude. The last two sections of Chapter 10 make European comparisons for the three industries on which the essay focuses especially, and offer a concluding discussion of the implications for industrial policy of the theory of dictatorship. The availability of literature differs markedly between the big four economies in the West and Russia, on the one hand, and the rest of Western Europe. So the detail that can be included in the most deeply ploughed fields of these 'large' countries is limited by the space available.

In order to interpret historical experience we need organizing concepts and theory. We offer a brief conceptual survey in the introductory chapter and in the penultimate Chapter 14 there is a synthesis of European experience based on a cultural theory of industrial policy. This conception of industrial policy is at a higher level of generality than almost all the theories considered in Chapter 1, which have a strong neoclassical or new classical flavour. The concluding chapter attempts a more conventional summary of the European experience of industrial policy over the last century or more.

We are grateful for financial support from the EC SPES fund and for a grant from the Italian Consiglio Nazionale delle Ricerche for a seminar at Pisa. We have relied heavily on the good will of the many scholars who have commented on early chapter drafts. Leslie Hannah's assistance with the project in its early stages is much appreciated, as were Chris Davis's comments and Elisa Boccaletti's preparation of the final draft.

J. F. P. and G. F.

CONTENTS

LIST OF TABLES

LIST OF FIGURES

1

Industrial Policies in Europe: Introduction

GIOVANNI FEDERICO AND JAMES FOREMAN-PECK

Universita di Pisa, University of Oxford

At the end of the twentieth century, Europe confronts a range of industrial challenges. The integration of Eastern Europe with the West, indeed the very definition of 'European' and the boundaries of Europe, are perhaps the most fundamental in the long run. But more immediate are the potential consequences of a core group of states linked by a common currency, while industry in other Union states gains competitive advantages from exchange-rate depreciation. Divergences between 'regional' European economies within or outside such a currency area could be equally problematic. Moreover slow industrial growth coupled with real wage rigidity has allowed unemployment in all Member States to reach levels not experienced since the 1930s.

Policy responses at the European level can be distinguished as either concerned with 'widening' or with 'deepening'. 'Deepening' is advancing legal and regulatory changes to create a genuine domestic market for European companies and workers. 'Widening' the European market entails spreading the benefits of economic integration to cover new applicants to the Union and the reform countries of Central Europe. Global economic cooperation—avoiding trade wars—must also find a place on the agenda of 'widening'.

Among 'deepeners', interventionist industrial policies are often presented as remedies; under the Maastricht Treaty for the first time the European Union was granted industrial policy powers. Yet for others concerned with policy, they are part of the problem. In particular, the recent drive for a European Single Market has exacerbated concerns about the fairness of competition between firms in participating states. Long-standing differences in national industrial policies have made for conflict in the past and make agreement difficult today. Businesses question why competitors should be supported by subsidies, by national standards to which products and services must conform, or by a depreciated exchange rate, merely because they are located in a particular region of the European market. They contend that the 'playing field' should be levelled either upwards, by giving the same support to all competing European companies, or downward, by removing the props from them all. Simultaneously the European growth miracle has faded, amid concerns of techological backwardness, labour costs above even those in the United States and de-motivatingly high tax rates.

Ironically Europe, broadly interpreted to include the East and Russia, is now returning to the market economies that were the rule until 1917. A century ago we see a substantially integrated European market, in which passports were not needed, where national exchange rates were virtually locked together by membership of the gold standard, and where industrial policies were less important than today. Despite far higher real transport and communications costs, European economies were tightly enmeshed by trade, capital movements, and migration. Much of the great boom between 1945 and 1973 was reaping the harvest of returning to the 1913 level of integration.

In the intervening years, wars, revolutions, and economic crises shattered the unity of the European economy. This period offers sobering lessons of the need for policies that create prosperity and international harmony. Over the longer term the divergence between the east and west of Europe by 1989 added prestige to market economies. Progress towards freeing the regulated markets of the west of Europe, where states own a considerable proportion of industrial assets, has nonetheless been slow, in part because of the difficulties of plausibly estimating the policy impacts of doing so.

The economic analysis of industrial policy still relies largely either on a descriptive approach, or upon entirely theoretical reasoning, both of which are less than satisfactory. A possible solution is to compare similar countries in order to isolate the effects of different policies. The present book adopts this approach, following, for example, Adams and Klein (1983) and Duchene and Shepherd (1987). We offer twelve case studies of national European industrial policies over a much greater span of time than is usual, followed by syntheses. An innovative aspect of this book is the inclusion of small country policies. Although Portugal, Ireland, and Greece have relatively small populations, their histories provide a good deal of information about the causation and impact of independent industrial policies. A third feature is the introduction of Russia. Until now Russian industrial policy has not usually been evaluated by reference to Western Europe, nor have Western European policies been assessed explicitly against a Russian standard. In short a historical comparative analysis of European experience will throw light on the contribution of industrial policy (positive or negative) to industrial growth—a matter of undoubted interest for developed and less developed countries, as well as for transition economies.

As an introduction to the studies of national policy, the present chapter discusses what exactly industrial policy is and justifies the broad definition adopted in the national studies. The next section briefly summarizes the debate over interventionist versus (liberal) market industrial policies, throughout the century. State intervention has been widespread and persistent, so the third section considers suggestions as to why that should be. The fourth section gives an account of some pitfalls in assessing the impact of industrial policies. We are then ready for the individual country studies.

1.1. WHAT IS INDUSTRIAL POLICY?

Industrial policy is an elusive concept, which can cover almost everything bearing on industry. Most authors favour a definition based on objectives: Adams and Klein (1983: 3) include 'everything which is useful to improve growth and competitive performance'.[1] This definition is both too limited and too all-embracing. On the one hand, it excludes policies for 'structural adaptation'—to manage industrial crises and protect jobs, on the other, it might include macro-economic management. In 1992, a publication of the European Commission stated that 'industrial policy concerns the effective and coherent implementation of all those policies which impinge on the structural adjustment of industry with a view to promoting competitiveness' (quoted in Ferguson and Ferguson 1994: 137). Ha-Joon Chang (1994: 66) proposes that an industrial policy is one 'aimed at particular industries (and firms as their components) to achieve the outcomes that are perceived by the state to be efficient for the economy as a whole'.

All these recent definitions exclude the most important historical motivation for promoting industry—the desire to enhance military capabilities. From the seventeenth century onwards, a large industrial sector, both to produce weapons and to earn gold from exports, was deemed indispensable for any self-respecting power. Mercantilism as an economic doctrine was largely discredited by the end of the eighteenth century, but defence and nationalism remained powerful justifications for interventionist industrial policy.

Considerations such as these suggest we should not refer to any specific policy objective in the definition: industrial policy will be defined as 'every form of state intervention that affects industry as a distinct part of the economy'. The category is very broad, excluding only macroeconomic policies with the final qualification ('as a distinct part of the economy'). The 'state' is meant to cover not only central government, local authorities, and the EC but also all independent agencies following government directives primarily with public funds (such as the now terminated 'Cassa per il Mezzogiorno' in Italy). 'Industry' includes manufacturing and also utilities.[2] 'Intervention' describes the official endorsement of private agreements such as cartels among firms (as in Germany and Italy in the 1930s) and all measures which affect industry even if not primarily intended to do so ('involuntary' or 'implicit' industrial policy). We must note that the conventional use of the term 'policy' implies clearly identifiable policy-makers, who choose policy instruments to achieve explicit objectives. In practice many consequences of action are unforeseen or unintended,[3] policy-makers may be institutions rather than individuals, and, above all, policies may be implicit, and hardly, if at all, articulated.[4] An example is the Greek tariffs of the 1880s–1890s, which

---

[1] While the meaning of growth is clear, that of competitiveness is somewhat ambiguous. Porter (1990: 6) identifies it with high productivity and technical progress, which enables countries to produce innovative, high-quality goods. Dollar and Wolff (1993: 3) focus on success in exports, stating that 'a competitive nation is one that can succeed in international trade via high technology and productivity, with accompanying high income and wages'. This formulation sits uncomfortably with the principle of comparative advantage that demonstrates mutual gains from trade.

[2] We might quite reasonably define industry as any source of employment, including agriculture, education, and insurance for instance. Our excuse for not doing so is that state policies towards these sectors have been different from those towards industry more narrowly defined, and we need to limit our field of enquiry if it is to be manageable.

[3] Sir Karl Popper's (1976) definition of the task of social science is to explain the unintended consequences of human action.

[4] As Thomas (1994) represents policy towards the pharmaceutical industry.

were imposed for fiscal purposes and ended up fostering the development of previously non-existent industrial activities.

The definition can be elaborated by distinguishing three levels of industrial
policy: (*a*) 'creating a landscape' (a legal and institutional framework); (*b*)
'modifying the ecological environment' (the technology and the markets for inputs
and output); and (*c*) 'changing the fauna' (the relative importance of the industries and firms, or 'species').[5] Policy at each level can be implemented with a
different set of tools.

(*a*) The essential component of a suitable 'landscape' is the existence of clearly
defined and rigorously enforced private property rights. This minimal condition
was by and large met in all European countries by the end of the nineteenth century (in some of them for many centuries)—even if enforcement was not everywhere perfect. In Eastern European countries, however, private property rights
were later abolished by the communist regimes, and are now being laboriously
re-established. The details of legislation defining property rights may matter a
great deal, for they have to reconcile conflicting needs. Patent laws should capture all the possible profits for innovation without stifling competition by other
firms; company law should be flexible enough to encourage entrepreneurship
but also to provide protection for investors. The environment has to be protected
without excessively restricting freedom of property rights. For a long time, each
country devised its own compromises, but in recent decades, national differences
have been reduced by the steady adoption of common European legislation. In
Eastern Europe continuing 'landscape' problems deter investment from home and
abroad.

(*b*) Industrial policy might 'modify the ecology'; foster technical progress by
supporting innovation or the diffusion of existing techniques, possibly imported
from abroad. To this end, the state can directly undertake Research and Development (R & D) (usually for military purposes) or simply subsidize the R & D
of firms (often by granting tax reductions). The state can make the available technology known through the specialist press, training projects, and so on. The relative importance of these two methods depends on the level of development of
the country: support for innovation is clearly more useful in advanced countries,
while import and adaptation of foreign technology are essential in backward ones.
Industrial policy can enhance competition in the market for products. But until
recently, the evidence for the desirability of competition was impressionistic,or
historical, especially the ultimately poor performance of Soviet-style economies
which excluded competition. In favour of competition is that it may give more
precision to incentives based on relative managerial performance. When there
are a number of comparable firms, there are yardsticks for identifying how well
managers do their job, despite the buffeting of market forces. In a truly competitive economy only the fittest businesses survive, it is asserted. Against competition, more monopolistic firms might be better able to fund research and

---

[5] The 'green' metaphor is inspired by Lindbeck (1981).

development, facing less market uncertainty and receiving a larger and more stable cash flow (Levin, Cohen, and Mowery 1985).

In the 1990s most governments and the European Commission tried, at least nominally, to prevent the creation of monopolies and to increase competition. In the past, however, European policy-makers frequently took the opposite view, promoting mergers to achieve scale economies and sometimes, especially in the 1930s, the creation of cartels. The state can also change the geographical desti-nations of particular exports by granting privileged status to some trading part-ners (such as former colonies) or by restricting foreign commerce (for instance during trade wars). Technical or quality standards have been used to favour national firms, reducing competition by handicapping foreign businesses.

Policies for capital and labour markets are usually quite different. Those for capital tend to make investments easier. To this end governments may provide incentives for savings, reduce taxes on investment funds, and offer low-interest loans. Governments have also indirectly supported investment by increasing stocks of human capital, by financing education, and of infrastructure (though pub-lic investment may crowd out private projects). On the other hand, labour market policies to protect workers' rights may have had the opposite effect: limits on the minimum age for work and on the maximum duration of work, reduce the supply of labour, and a minimum wage may increase the cost. Some states (the communist countries, Italy in the 1930s) have also hampered the occupational or geographical mobility of workers for political reasons. Governments can regulate the price of inputs such as energy and water to support industry at the expense of utility companies or of private consumers. This policy gave rise to the problem of negative value added among some enterprises in the USSR (see Chapter 13). In addition, the efficiency with which the state supplies infrastruc-ture services that it has selected for itself, such as those of roads and sometimes utilities, and the volume that it provides, may substantially influence the busi-ness environment (Lynde and Richmond 1993).

'Ecological environment' is an encompassing concept, referring to policies which target all firms (general industrial policies), and/or specific activity such as R & D (activity-specific policies). The definition could also be extended to policies targetting particular areas (regional development schemes), and/or firms of a given size. In these cases, however, policies are often disguised support for specific industries in an area or to a size class of firms.

(*c*) Measures to 'change the fauna', to redistribute resources among indus-tries and firms, are the core of classical industrial policy. With some exceptions (notably the attempts at general planning of the 1950s–1960s) these policies have targetted single firms or industries according to two different criteria. One is 'picking winners'—those industries or businesses that seem to have bright pro-spects for future development, or that are deemed necessary for whatever reason (including military requirements). The stars of the nineteenth century were the iron and steel industries and shipbuilding. Nowadays they are the so-called hi-tech industries (computers, aircraft, biotechnology). French support for the computer manufacturer Bull in the 1950s (Chapter 3) is only one of many possible examples. The other criterion is 'helping losers', firms and industries which are in trouble. In theory, the government should support them temporarily, either to help them to restructure and survive in the long run or to avoid a too sudden demise, and to assist an orderly reallocation of the workers to other firms and industries. Many 'winners' of the nineteenth century have become 'lame ducks', to be protected in the late twentieth century.

These policies favouring particular sectors can use all the tools of general industrial policy, simply by restricting their application. Tariffs can and usually are differentiated by product, and tax incentives can be given only to selected industries. But the state can support an industry in many other ways. It can subsidize output, offer soft bank loans, promote exports, impose quotas on competing imports, or buy the products. These measures may be used to assist all the firms of the industry, or only some companies or even just a single product. Government procurement policies have been widely used to support national defence industries or other strategic suppliers, such as telecommunications. The ultimate policy instrument is state ownership—often after a financial crisis. State-owned companies are usually supposed to follow the government's instructions, whether they make losses or profits.

1.2. THE EUROPEAN INDUSTRIAL POLICY DEBATE

By the 1990s, European government intervention in industry was not popular as a principle, though in practice matters were often rather different. Privatization and price-cap regulation, spreading outwards from Britain during the 1980s became the basis of much new industrial policy, at least as recommended. An OECD survey notes that, since the 1980s, industrial policy 'has gradually moved from . . . measures in support of industries in decline or aiming at stimulating promising activities by "picking the winners" . . . [to] measures which do not interfere with the market process directly and instead attempt to improve its mechanism . . . [though] it is also true that the practice of policy has often lagged behind the rhetoric' (OECD 1992: 11). The World Bank's *World Development Report* (1997) takes a similar position. But of course, the tide may change, and more interventionist policies might become fashionable again. Periods of (relative) restraint have been the exception in history—and active involvement has been the rule. This feature contrasts starkly with prevailing opinion among the majority of contemporary economists—contributors to the *American Economic Review* and authors of World Bank, OECD, and International Monetary Fund reports. These economists tend to be suspicious about any state intervention, although the position is not unanimous (Geroski 1989 is an example of dissent). They believe markets operate efficiently—at least compared with the alternatives. One of the basic principles of neoclassical economics is that normally (perfectly competitive) markets direct the available resources into the sectors where they yield the greatest returns. This makes society as a whole as well off as possible (at least if we define 'social welfare' as merely the sum of the preferences of the 'individuals' in society—there is no greater good, such as an abstract state being 'the manifestation of our higher selves').[6] The state should therefore create the conditions for the market to work (a suitable 'landscape' and 'environment' in the language of the previous section) and then leave well alone.

Since the beginning of their profession most Anglo-American economists have consistently argued against state intervention (except under very special circumstances), but their advice has been more often ignored than followed.[7] Alfred Marshall at the University of Cambridge in the late nineteenth century deduced the theoretical proposition that 'increasing returns' industries should be subsidized, but remarked this did not necessarily warrant 'government interference'. On the continent, excluding Scandinavia, the pattern of thought was rather different. In the nineteenth century the German historical school, with disciples in Britain and the United States, took over the task of explaining the need for national interventionist industrial policies from mercantilism. Friedrich List favoured infant industry protection, and Gustav von Schmoller, Professor of Economics at the University of Berlin, the most enthusiastic organizer of support for von Tirpitz's naval expansion programme in the 1890s, was an advocate of historical laws of development that were certainly not derived from Anglo-American economics (Barber 1991). The British economic historians William Cunningham and W. J. Ashley gained some popularity from their rejection of many of the propositions of neoclassical economics on the basis of history. Although Jules Dupuit favoured free trade, he formulated an analysis of the ideal amount of 'public goods' that should be supplied under government ownership where there was an overriding 'public interest'. This formulation is consistent with Dupuit's membership of the corps of eminent French engineer-economists employed by the state (Ekelund and Hebert 1975: 217–30).

On the European continent then theory and practice were often in harmony, but from 1931 that was not true of Britain (or of the United States for most of its history). The principal explanation for Anglo-American economists' limited success in influencing their governments has surely been the pressure of the vested interests. But this is not the only reason. These economists have not been entirely convincing in presenting their case.[8] They admit that markets may fail. This can happen in three well-defined cases. The first is when increasing (static

---

[6] This condition (or, in the terminology of economics, Pareto optimality) implies that no one in the society can be made better-off without reducing the welfare of someone else—that is, without a redistribution of income. If the distribution of income is undesirable, it can be changed more effectively by direct measures—by taxation—than by policy aimed at industry.

[7] Genuine evidence of how consensual were British economists' views is supplied by Brittan (1973). In microeconomics academic economists agreed but not in macroeconomics. Probably that consensus has spread to macroeconomics since then.

[8] Evidence of the uncertain scientific status of industrial policy is the lack of a proper category in the *Journal of Economic Literature*: the works on it are scattered among classes F ('international economies'), H ('national governments, expenditures and related policies'), and O ('economic development, technological change and growth'). Another is the conspicuous absence of the term from the index of Auerbach and Feldstein (1985).

or dynamic) returns and/or high entry costs confer advantages on large firms, which can charge prices above their marginal costs. A particular example of this first instance is the doctrine of 'excessive' entry to an industry creating 'too much' competition. Portuguese industrial policy at one stage licensed industrial entrants to prevent such an outcome, which is undoubtedly possible theoretically. If firms have to cover certain fixed costs, and can influence the prices at which they sell (face downward sloping demand curves for their products), new entrants who 'steal' their business will raise the unit costs of these established businesses by more than they cut industry output prices (Mankiw and Whinston 1986). Apparently reducing such entry could therefore be socially beneficial. The second case arises when incomplete or asymmetric information, or externalities, such as technological spillovers, cause social returns to inputs to exceed private ones.[9] The knowledge created by one company's research and development may lower another company's costs of production. But if the first company gains nothing from that, it may undertake less than the socially desirable amount of R & D, if only because the business lacks the revenue to finance the research. A third type of failure theoretically occurs in markets where the seller has more information about what is being sold than the buyer. The buyer may therefore pay too much or acquire an unwanted product. When the seller is in business for more than one sale, the cultivation of a reputation for fair dealing is worthwhile, for buyers can recognize reputation even if they do not have much information about what is being sold. In principle reputation might prevent the market failure. There are then cases where intervention might be useful, provided the state can identify the failure and devise appropriate intervention to tackle it.

Neither condition is easily satisfied. States do not necessarily have better information than private firms, and they do not necessarily succeed in exploiting it. There is abundant evidence of 'government failure' (Krueger 1990). Many would-be 'winners' proved to be costly losers, such as the nuclear industry. Governments may pinpoint the wrong educational qualifications to support. And they are prone to use the 'wrong' tools to address real failures—a typical case being the subsidies to production instead of to R & D to capture technological spillovers (Grossman 1990). An industrial policy may be designed in the public interest yet be captured by better informed special interests closer to the points of implementation (Laffont 1996). Government departments and firms often face only soft budget constraints, and therefore lack incentives for efficiency.

These arguments however fail to convince the supporters of an active industrial policy. One position is to accept the above reasoning but argue that market failures are so widespread as to make government intervention indispensable. In Eastern European transition economies, where markets are rather poor, this stance is more warranted than in Western Europe. Another line is to object that

---

[9] Externalities exist because information is incomplete and there are transaction costs. They would disappear if information were perfect and transaction costs negligible (Coase theorem). For example if social value of skills exceeded the private return to entrepreneurs in hiring and training manpower, the same workers would be willing to borrow the funds for their training and the banks would be willing to finance them.

the whole neoclassical approach is flawed. The real problem supposedly is not how to make the best use of existing inputs but how to increase future endowments and to devise new ways to exploit them. In short, the objective should be to maximize the growth rate and not current welfare. Radicals argue that the example of high-income countries shows that this objective can be achieved only if industry is modern and competitive. Therefore the state should push industrialization in backward countries (according to Wade 1990), and support the development of strong innovative firms in advanced countries. In both cases, success tomorrow is allegedly worth the price of the short-term welfare losses inflicted by an apparent misallocation of resources today.

Another strand of 'neo-mercantilist' thought emphasizes that hi-tech industries supplying civilian uses in effect subsidize military projects. Without these industries a state becomes vulnerable to foreign boycotts or has to invest much more in military R & D, in computers, advanced materials, and machine tools (for instance Zysman 1991; Zysman and Cohen 1987; Stowsky 1992).

Whereas mercantilists and neo-mercantilists emphasize export expansion, from a traditional neoclassical perspective the destination of production does not matter by itself, for in an efficient market exports and domestic consumption yield exactly the same returns to inputs at the margin. Moreover, export-expansion policies can distort specialization away from the ideal distribution of resources among industries and markets (guaranteed by free trade) if successful, or waste resources if unsuccessful. A failure is more likely the larger is the number of countries competing for the same markets (they are more likely to adopt 'beggar my neighbour' strategies), and the lower is the elasticity of world demand for the products (because price will be driven down further by a given increase in exports).

Thinking of European states as merely European regions, we can invoke neoclassical location theory. In a free market, according to this theory, businesses and industries decide where to base themselves, or survive and flourish in particular places rather than others, by weighing proximity to markets against accessibility and suitability of materials and labour. Transport and communication costs and land rents play a vital part in this balancing exercise. Free trade Belgium in the 1830s showed what railways could do for the prosperity of a small country by successfully planning the economy's main lines to capture the Rhine–Channel trade. Expensive domestic labour in the 1990s encouraged German companies to locate new plants elsewhere in Europe, especially in relatively low wage Britain. What other manufacturers and transport suppliers have done offer advantages and disadvantages that pull firms towards particular locations or push them away. Transport networks built to service existing industrial locations will enhance their benefits, for new arrivals can share the overheads of transport infrastructure with established businesses, rather than bear the full costs themselves.

Falling transport costs can favour either concentration or dispersion. If transport costs become low, and 'footloose' industry share high economies of scale, then a single industrial core may emerge. Policy might influence where it is and whether there is one major industrial centre, or two or more. On the other hand, where there are few advantages from size or concentration, lower transport costs reduce the pull of markets or raw materials and allow industrial dispersion (Krugman 1991). Over the last century the shift away from coal as the fundamental source of power and heat in European regions with the spread of electricity distribution networks, should have increased industrial dispersion. Information costs and availability changes exercised comparable locational pressures in information-intensive service industries, such as banking and insurance, in the later twentieth century. Governments may feel justified in interfering with this process if there are a number of equally profitable locations around Europe. Then chance, or a state subsidy, may be enough to tip the locational balance, to the possible benefit of employment, technology, and exports in the successful country.

Recent developments in industrial economics and international trade theory have not solved theoretical or policy differences. Both strains explore oligopolistic firms' behaviour and the effects of increasing returns, technological spillovers and learning by doing (Fagenberg 1994; Romer 1994). Unfortunately, the research is still very far from yielding operationally conclusive results. Some game-theoretical models do include the state as a player (Basu 1994: 208–14) but on the whole research has not emphasized policy applications (Martin 1993: 566). The main exception is the debate on strategic trade policy (Laussel and Montet 1994). It has been shown that active support for the development of national firms might be justified if they can extract rents from foreign consumers. However, the argument refers to a very special case and rests on too many assumptions (on the model of oligopolistic behaviour, on the size of the rents, on the opportunity cost of resources, and on the absence of retaliation from other states) to be really convincing (Krugman 1989). Meanwhile, a common opinion among present-day economists is that 'competitive market forces do an imperfect job but one that the instruments of industrial policy are unlikely to improve upon' (Neven and Vickers 1992: 194).

1.3. WHY DO COUNTRIES ADOPT INDUSTRIAL POLICIES?

The reply to the question should be straightforward in an ideal world. An industrial policy would be adopted as soon as its merits were established, possibly thanks to the enlightened advice of economists, subject to the proviso that the country is ruled by 'benign politicians, whose concerns go beyond using state power to support the affluence of a small group' (Wade 1990: 350). The question is more complex if the industrial policy is not self-evidently beneficial and/ or politicians are not 'benign'. In such cases we may turn to economists of the 'public choice' school. They analyse decisions as the outcome of the interaction between firms and politicians, both rationally pursuing their own interests (Magee 1994). Firms seek rents, to earn more than the 'normal' return to their inputs (that gained in a competitive market); politicians want to stay in power and sometimes to improve their personal circumstances—by becoming rich or by guaranteeing themselves a lucrative private sector job after retirement from state employment (*pantouflage*). This unholy alliance reduces society's well-being. Successful rent-seeking distorts the ideal use of resources by dissipating them in lobbying. The risk of successful rent-seeking suggests a need to be cautious in adopting policies which might be sensible if only temporary, because lobbying may make them permanent. A straightforward extension includes among those interested in adopting an interventionist industrial policy bureaucrats who are responsible for the implementation of the projects entrusted to them.

The extent of rent-seeking behaviour probably depends on the type of policy and on the nature of the political system. Lobbying is the more likely the smaller the interest group because of the risk of free-riding (Olson 1965). Therefore, rent-seeking is encouraged by sector- or firm-specific policies, for each industry or firm can potentially gain directly from state support. Lobbying for the broader types of policies is usually less common. The recent development of environmental and consumers' associations as effective lobbyists shows it cannot be ruled out, even when they face tough opposition from large monopolies, such as public utilities. A plausible explanation for the inefficiency of state firms is that they pursue the objectives of politicians rather than the market. Holding on to employment and raising wages is electorally popular. An apparent corollary is that privatization breaks the subservience of managers to politicians and hence brings efficiency gains, as conventionally defined (Boycko, Shleifer, and Vishny 1996). However the Czech Republic's difficulties with voucher privatization and wider experience in Russia during the 1990s casts some doubt on the conclusion; privatization is apparently not a sufficient condition for efficiency gains.

Governments often try to temper the winds of competition to the shorn industrial region, because losing an industry typically seems to hurt more than the gain to the winning area. At least the losers protest and the winners keep quiet. What policy is adopted may depend upon whether losers and gainers belong to the same jurisdiction. A state may put up trade barriers in an attempt to stave off the decline of one industry only if the replacement activity is establishing itself beyond the national frontiers. If the industry has merely shifted regions within the state, then external trade barriers will be ineffective, and the beneficiary region may well lobby to prevent discriminatory policy measures. Certainly European governments have continued to ensure that their state has certain industries, or that some national 'industrial champions' survive the ravages of market forces. These imperatives may have influenced the location and spatial distribution of output and employment, along with traditional raw materials and markets. A plausible hypothesis then is that the smaller the number of industrial policy jurisdictions in a given geographical area, the fewer will be the restrictions on industrial growth and development, and hence the higher will be industrial productivity.

Theoretical discussion of the influence of the political system is not easy to summarize. Most public choice literature refers to democratic states, where politicians need votes to stay in power. But the basic principles can be applied to authoritarian states as well (Tullock 1987). Personal motives may loom larger in the dictators' aims, but the main difference is that they need the consensus of special groups much more than that of the whole voting population. From their point of view, the single most important organization is surely the army and therefore dictators are more likely than democratic leaders to adopt nationalistic and aggressive industrial policy. It is also likely that dictators will use civil service and managerial jobs as rewards for their cronies instead of appointing qualified people (Brough and Kimenyi 1986). Both factors would make an authoritarian state less efficient than a democratic one. This conclusion cannot however be generalized. A controversial point made by Wade (1990) is that in backward countries a strong state may be necessary to quash the traditional elites' opposition to modernization. And the weight of Olson's (1982) 'distributional coalitions' is almost certainly greater in democratic than in authoritarian states.

1.4. WHAT DO COUNTRIES GAIN FROM INDUSTRIAL POLICY?

Neoclassical economics provides a clear rule for establishing the gains from a policy. First, there has to be a market failure and second, the social benefits of the policy must exceed the opportunity costs of the necessary resources. Unfortunately, these conditions are very difficult to satisfy. It is not easy to prove the existence of a market failure, a divergence between social and private returns.[10] And it is difficult to measure how serious any failure is; that is, by how much its eradication would increase welfare. There are some well-established techniques for measuring the effects of trade policies (tariffs, quotas, customs unions) such as computable general equilibrium models for competitive markets or game-theoretic models for oligopolistic ones (Laussel and Montet 1994; Srnivasan, Whalley, and Wotoon 1993). But the quantitative analysis of the returns to other policies, such as subsidies to R & D, is still in its infancy. It is often not possible to assess the efficiency of an overall strategy involving several measures. The same reasoning applies to costs: the real opportunity cost of a policy is equal to the money outlay only if there are no other market failures (a demanding assumption).

These objective difficulties can at least partly explain the limited appeal of the efficiency rule outside the economic profession. Politicians, managers, journalists, and public opinion quite often disregard costs (if not disproportionately large) and assess industrial policy on the basis of the direct apparent results. In this way, they adopt a different standard, that of effectiveness. A policy is deemed

---

[10] Possible evidence of market failure is the strong positive correlation between investment in equipment and growth rate in output (De Long and Summers 1991, 1993).

effective if it succeeds in achieving its aim, whatever it may be. So measures
to support an industry are considered effective if the industry develops, and a
great success if it is competitive on the world market. The overall success of
industrial policy is judged on the basis of the country's rate of growth. French
industrial policy after 1945 is praised because France grew very fast (for example Wilkinson 1984), whereas British policy is blamed because the long-run
performance of the national industry is judged disappointing. Japanese interventionist industrial policy in the 1950s and 1960s was supposedly a success because
output and exports grew so rapidly. (However many unsubsidized industries—
sewing machines, cameras, bicycles, motorcycles—performed at least as well
as the supported ones (Komiya, Okuno, and Suzumura 1988).) The limitation of
the principle is particularly apparent when the last stage of central planning in
the USSR is considered as a model of effective industrial policy.

Even ignoring the extreme last case, this type of reasoning suffers from two
drawbacks. First, it often neglects the details of implementation. The same set
of measures may be quite effective if properly managed by an honest and competent civil service or a total waste of resources if applied by ignorant or corrupt
bureaucrats. As the following chapters show, there is ample evidence of collusion between bureaucrats and the firms they were supposed to control. Second,
popular judgements on the effectiveness of industrial policy are typically *post hoc
propter hoc* arguments—the cock that crowed and caused the dawn—neglecting
other factors, notably resource endowments and entrepreneurship.

The pitfalls of assessing the effect of industrial policy, never mind about
the efficiency, can be illustrated by 'the world's favourite industrial policy instrument'—protection of domestic industries from the competition of imported
goods. Even estimating protection is problematic, yet a suitable measure must
be found before the impact of tariffs, quotas, and prohibitions can be discovered.
The simplest index is the ratio of tariff revenue to the value of imports. But if
a tariff on a product is so high that imports are completely excluded, no tariff
revenue will be earned and no evidence of protection will appear in the numer-
ator of the index. Moreover a steel industry in a country dependent on imports
of coal subject to a tariff will receive negative protection, unless the policy-
induced higher coal costs are compensated for by a steel tariff. What is needed
is a measure of effective protection that takes into account these higher input
costs (Federico and Tena 1998). But industries with few interdependent firms
will raise prices (and therefore costs of the firms to which they sell) by amounts
dependent on the responsiveness of demand faced by these businesses, which is
typically difficult to establish. Anderson and Neary (1992, 1994) have suggested
a 'trade restrictiveness index' (TRI)—the uniform tariff which would have the
same effect as the structure of tariffs and quotas in place. The level of TRI depends
not only on the structure of protection but on the structure of the protected economy. In a comparison of protection in nineteenth-century Britain and France, the
level of the TRI indices, and therefore the conclusion that Britain was more protectionist than France, depends on wine and beer being close substitutes in Britain

(O'Rourke 1997).[11] This is a foretaste of the challenges of making correct judgements about even relative levels of protection.

1.5. THE CASE STUDY MENU

The next four chapters deal with the industrial policies of the largest Western European states. As the earliest—and latest—market-oriented practitioner of industrial policy, concerned with the 'landscape', Britain is placed first. By way of contrast, the French case study follows, showing how a much more corporatist style of industrial policy operated. The most powerful economy in Europe, Germany, is the subject of the next case study. Compared with France or Britain, Germany is something of a newcomer to national industrial policy formation and implementation, retaining a considerable regional independence. It is second only to Russia in the intensity and multiplicity of shocks and divisions to which our case study nations have been subject. Italy is the last of the big four, a mere ten years older than Germany, but with very different economic and political cultures. Italian industrial performance since the Second World War is a rarely noted European 'economic miracle'. The part played by industrial policy in this extraordinary achievement must be of fundamental interest.

The second group of nations are small, liberal, and highly productive for most, if not all, of our period. Sweden heads this collection, having bred a number of world-class multinationals, almost certainly as a consequence of an industrial policy largely devoted to 'landscaping'. Swedish business suffered less than most European industry thanks to the long-established and cohesive Swedish state remaining neutral in the two world wars. Belgium and the Netherlands have different endowments of natural resources, which is reflected in their industrial structures and thus in the industrial policies adopted. Dutch writers used to lament the lack of coal, but Belgian coal mines were a policy headache from the 1930s.

The Republic of Ireland, geographically on the European periphery, and largely rural when an independent industrial policy became possible, at first appears to fit in to 'group three', along with Portugal, Spain, and Greece. In recent decades rapid development and less of a tendency to intervene with industry, shifts the Irish case study into the second group.

Spain and Portugal have a long tradition of state industrial regulation and ownership. Like the rest of Europe they participated in the great boom after 1945. Both were under authoritarian rule for much of the boom. Both then made transitions to democracy and attempted some economic liberalization. Spain attracted considerable foreign direct investment. But when European growth slowed down, their economies turned out to be too inflexible. Greece fits in with this group, being predominantly rural at the beginning of the period of study and with a heavily regulated industry during the great boom.

---

[11] Although O'Rourke's source for his TRI calculations ignores some of the protection in the 1870s shown in Ch. 3.

Finally there is the huge Russian economy, supporting a population larger than those of our 'big four' combined. For all of our period, Russian industrial policy and performance have deeply concerned Western Europe. That is unlikely to change in the immediate future.

REFERENCES

ADAMS, F. G., and KLEIN, L. (1983) (eds.). *Industrial Policies for Growth and Competitiveness*. Lexington, Pa.: Lexington Books.

ANDERSON, J. E., and NEARY, J. P. (1992). 'Trade reform with quotas, partial rent retention and tariffs'. *Econometrica*, 60: 57–76.

—— —— (1994). 'Measuring the restrictiveness of trade policy'. *World Bank Economic Review*, 8: 151–69.

AUERBACH, A. J., and FELDSTEIN, M. S. (1985) (eds.). *Handbook of Public Economics*. Amsterdam: North-Holland.

BARBER, W. J. (1991). 'Attempts to comprehend the nature of war 1910–20', in C. D. Goodwin (ed.), *Economics and National Security: A History of their Interaction*. Durham, NC and London: Duke University Press.

BASU, K. (1994). *Lectures on Industrial Organization Theories*. Oxford: Blackwell.

BOYCKO, M., SHLEIFER, A., and VISHNY, R. W. (1996). 'A theory of privatisation'. *Economic Journal*, 106: 309–19.

BRITTAN, S. (1973). *Is There an Economic Consensus? An Attitude Survey*. London: Macmillan.

BROUGH, W. T., and KIMENYI, M. S. (1986). 'On the inefficient extraction of rents by dictators'. *Public Choice*, 48: 37–48.

CHANG, H.-J. (1994). *The Political Economy of Industrial Policy*. New York: St Martin's Press.

DE LONG, B., and SUMMERS, L. H. (1991). 'Equipment investment and economic growth'. *Quarterly Journal of Economics*, 106: 415–502.

—— —— (1993). 'How strongly do developing economics benefit from equipment investment?'. *Journal of Monetary Economics*, 32: 395–415.

DOLLAR, D., and WOLFF, E. (1993). *Competitiveness, Convergence and International Specialization*. Cambridge, Mass.: MIT Press.

DUCHENE, F., and SHEPHERD, G. (1987) (eds.). *Managing Industrial Change in Western Europe*. London-New York: Pinter.

EKELUND, R. B., and HEBERT, R. F. (1975). *A History of Economic Theory and Method*. Tokyo: Kogakusha: McGraw-Hill.

FAGENBERG, J. (1994). 'Technology and international differences in growth rates'. *Journal of Economic Literature*, 32: 1147–75.

FEDERICO, G., and TENA, A. (1998). 'Was Italy a protectionist country?' *European Review of Economic History*, 2: 73–97.

FERGUSON, P., and FERGUSON, G. (1994). *Industrial Economics: Issues and Perspectives*, 2nd edn. London and Basingstoke: Macmillan.

GEROSKI, P. (1989). 'European industrial policy and industrial policy for Europe'. *Oxford Review of Economic Policy*, 5/2.

GROSSMAN, G. (1990). 'Promoting new industrial activities: A survey of recent argument and evidence'. *OECD Economic Studies*, 14: 87–121.

KOMIYA, R., OKUNO, M., and SUZUMURA, K. (1988) (eds.). *Industrial Policy of Japan*. Tokyo, San Diego, London: Academic Press.

KRUEGER, A. O. (1990). 'Government failures in development'. *Journal of Economic Perspectives*, 4: 9–23.

KRUGMAN, P. R. (1989). 'Industrial organization and world trade', in R. Schamlensee and B. Willing (eds.), *Handbook of Industrial Organization*, ii. 1181–1223. Amsterdam: North-Holland.

—— (1991). *Geography and Trade*. Cambridge, Mass.: MIT Press.

LAFFONT, J. J. (1996). 'Industrial policy and politics'. *International Journal of Industrial Organisation*, 14: 1–27.

LAUSSEL, D., and MONTET, C. (1994). 'Strategic trade policies', in D. Greenaway and L. A. Winters (eds.), *Surveys in International Trade*, 177–205. Oxford: Blackwell.

LEVIN, R. C., COHEN, W. M., and MOWERY , D. C. (1985). 'R & D appropriability, opportunity and market structure: New evidence on some Schumpeterian hypotheses'. *American Economic Review*, 75: 20–4.

LINDBECK, A. (1981). 'Industrial policy as an issue of economic environment'. *World Economy*, 4.

LYNDE, C., and RICHMOND, J. (1993). 'Public capital and long-run costs in UK manufacturing'. *Economic Journal*, 103: 880–93.

MAGEE, S. (1994). 'The political economy of trade policy', in D. Greenaway and L. A. Winters (eds.), *Surveys in International Trade*, 139–76. Oxford: Blackwell.

MANKIW, N. G., and WHINSTON, M. D. (1986). 'Free entry and social inefficiency'. *Rand Journal of Economics*, 17: 48–58.

MARTIN, S. (1993). *Advanced Industrial Economics*. Oxford: Blackwell.

NEVEN, D. T., and VICKERS, J. (1992). 'Public policy towards industrial restructuring: Some issues raised by the Internal Market program', in K. Cool and J. Walter (eds.), *European Industrial Restructuring in the 1990s*, 162–98. London and Basingstoke: Macmillan.

O'ROURKE, K. H. (1997). 'Measuring protection: A cautionary tale'. *Journal of Development Economics*, 53: 169–83.

OECD *ad annum* (since 1988). *Industrial Policy in OECD Countries*, Annual. Paris: OECD.

OLSON, M. (1965). *The Logic of Collective Action*. Cambridge, Mass.: Harvard University Press.

—— (1982). *The Rise and Decline of Nations*. New Haven: Yale University Press.

POPPER, K. (1976). *Unended Quest: An Intellectual Autobiography*. London: Fontana.

PORTER, M. (1990). *The Competitive Advantage of Nations*. London and Basingstoke: Macmillan.

ROMER, P. (1994). 'The origins of endogenous growth'. *Journal of Economic Perspectives*.

SRNIVASAN, T. N., WHALLEY, J., and WOTOON, I. (1993). 'Measuring the effects of regionalism on trade and welfare', in K. Anderson and R. Blackhurst (eds.), *Regional Integration and the Global Trade System*. New York: Harvester.

STOWSKY, J. (1992). 'From spin-off to spin-on: Redefining the military's role in American technology development', in W. Sandholtz *et al.* (eds.), *The Highest Stakes: The Economic Foundations of the Next Security System*. New York: Oxford University Press.

THOMAS, L. G., III (1994). 'Implicit industrial policy: The triumph of Britain and the failure of France in global pharmaceuticals'. *Industrial and Corporate Change*, 3/2: 451–90.

TULLOCK, G. (1987). *Autocracy*. Dordrecht: Kluwer.

WADE, R. (1990). *Governing the Market*. Princeton: Princeton University Press.

WILKINSON, C. (1984). 'Trends in industrial policy in the EC: Theory and practice', in A. Jacquemin (ed.), *European Industry: Public Policy and Corporate Strategy*. Oxford: Clarendon Press.

World Bank (1997). *World Development Report*. Washington, DC.

ZYSMAN, J. (1991). 'US power trade and technology'. *International Affairs*, 67: 81–106.

—— and COHEN, S. S. (1987). *Manufacturing Matters*. New York: Basic Books.

2

Britain: From Economic Liberalism to Socialism—And Back?

JAMES FOREMAN-PECK AND LESLIE HANNAH

University of Oxford, City University Business School

Much of early European industrial policy was concerned to promote industrialization, often to support defence industries deemed essential to national security. British policy in the nineteenth century was rather different. Economic liberalism required that, as Prime Minister Gladstone said, money should be left to fructify in the pockets of individuals. But the state's embrace of British industry progressively tightened over the following century. Government expenditure and taxation as a proportion of national output rose, while firm size and concentration grew, technology became far more sophisticated and productivity soared. Adjustments of the policy framework to changed economic circumstances depended on electoral and other political contingencies, among which the two world wars have been considered the most prominent causes (Tomlinson 1994).

As early as 1886, the Royal Commission on the Depression of Trade and Industry complained of 'a falling off of energy' amongst manufacturers. Despite this and other concerns, the gap between what might reasonably be achieved by industry, and what was accomplished, did not become substantial until perhaps the Edwardian years. The Boer War and the First World War both shook the complacency of British nineteenth-century liberal approaches to industrial or supply-side policy, already threatened by the rise of the economies of Imperial Germany and the United States. From 1916 the focus of policy shifted first under the stimulus of the perceived demands of national security. After the war new political forces and changes in the world economy ensured the reorientation persisted. Novel policy goals were added, addressing the industrial costs of 'an early start', and old objectives assumed greater prominence. By comparison with other economies, British industrial policy between the world wars seems to have performed tolerably well; manufacturing productivity growth was not below that of other advanced industrial economies, except those of North America.

After 1945, state ownership and control of industry was greatly extended by a variety of measures, including rationing of credit and raw materials, and artificially low input prices became pervasive. Physical controls, apart from those on imports, were abandoned at the beginning of the 1950s, though bank credit rationing persisted. Huge state-owned corporations, electricity, gas, telecoms, in transport and in mining, absorbed great volumes of capital; their rate of productivity improvement was comparable with the manufacturing sector, though inferior to that of similar industries abroad. British industry as a whole rode the wave of the great post-war expansion of the world economy from 1950 to 1970, raising productivity at rates unprecedented in peacetime. Increasing openness of the economy triggered a number of spectacular collapses in the 1970s, such as British Leyland and Rolls Royce, to which both Conservative and Labour governments responded with state ownership. Industrial concentration in the private sector grew, especially through mergers, at least partly by explicit state encouragement of mergers and a more aggressive state policy towards cartels and restrictive agreements. These were the years when industrial policies aimed to keep British productivity up with that of its competitors. But the policies adopted were not obviously successful. The 1980s saw an abandonment of state ownership and direction of industry. A much smaller manufacturing sector broadly matched the performance in other European economies by the end of the decade, apparently vindicating the policy shift.

Such supposed policy effects are problematic, because so many influences cause variations in industrial performance and in other goals of industrial policy. Less controversial is the focus on labour productivity as the simplest measure of policy impact or of the need for a more effective policy. Even defence-orientated industrial policies cannot ignore this index because it determines the resources available for security. The change in British manufacturing labour productivity relative to one or more 'standard' economies indicates how well British policy has counterbalanced or supported institutional and other changes. If other influences on productivity have been favourable, then policy does not have to be so effective. There are obvious difficulties with the criterion though. A 'satisfactory' performance is not the same as 'ideal'. And any one economy is not necessarily an appropriate standard of comparison in every period, or in any.

Less controversial is the record of industrial growth to which policy responded and by which it was perhaps influenced. Figure 2.1 shows steady, but hardly rapid, expansion when Britain was the 'workshop of the world' and population growth was high in comparison with rates in the twentieth century. From 1856 to 1913, the average annual compound growth rate of industrial production was 2.2%. War conditions distorted and reduced production between 1914 and 1918. Then a boom and deep slump, together with the boundary change that removed the very small industrial output of the republic of Ireland from the series, reduced 1921 output below that of 1918. From the 1920 peak to the peak of 1937 just before the Second World War, industrial output beat the nineteenth-century growth rate, averaging an annual rate of 3.0%. The loss of output during the Second World War was soon compensated for by even higher growth rates of industrial production. The 3.5% per annum averaged from 1946 to 1973 was more than half as much again as Victorian growth, yet this is a period of policy failure, according to many commentators.

Figure 2.1 clearly identifies the periods of most acute concern for industrial policy, the oil crisis years of 1974–5 together with the slumps of the early 1980s

FIG. 2.1. UK industrial production, 1856–1995

and early 1990s. In 1996 industrial output was more than three times the level achieved in 1937, but only 7% above the previous peak in 1989. In turn the 1989 pinnacle was merely 9% higher than that of 1979. Although output did not indicate that 'de-industrialization' had set in, certainly the growth pattern of the economy had changed. Knowledge-based business services may have become as important for manufacturing output as fixed capital (Tomlinson 1997). Perhaps new definitions of industrial output are needed now, but for much of the century the old one will suffice for understanding industrial policy.

2.1. THE INDUSTRIAL POLICY OF NINETEENTH-CENTURY LIBERALISM

Late Victorian industrial policy was concerned primarily to improve the operation of the market, by remedying failures stemming from inadequately defined or enforceable property rights, in education and in innovation especially. Creation of a legal structure conducive to capital-intensive economic development, in the form of joint stock limited liability companies, and their regulation, were vital components of policy. Health and safety, and natural monopoly concerns also triggered state intervention in industry. Only just before the First World War did national defence—a guaranteed oil supply for the Royal Navy—prompt the British government to acquire a 51% stake in Anglo-Persian Oil (later BP).

As the first industrial nation, Britain was also the first to consider shoring up her established position. Whenever depression or retardation strikes, there is a tendency to reach for an industrial policy. So it was in 1886 when a Royal Commission was appointed 'to inquire into the nature and extent and probable causes of the depression in the various branches of trade and industry'. The Commission heard complaints of German competition, excess supply, low prices, and railway rates that favoured importers, but made few definite recommendations. It highlighted the need for better technical education, which was followed up (Sanderson 1994). It also identified the desirability of better knowledge of foreign languages, and of checking the creation of unsound limited liability companies. Neither of these recommendations was pursued.

In the provision of technical education, policy followed the lines of Adam Smith's classical economic liberalism. But pressures of foreign competition and the localized public good features of, for example, university science, threatened to subvert the market framework. Anglo-German trade rivalry provoked increasingly strident exchanges (Kennedy 1982). Some Liberal Unionists and Conservatives supported protection against foreign competition but the Liberal victory in the election of 1906, and the rise of the free trade Labour party, prevented Britain from copying the world's favourite industrial policy. Free trade, exemplified by the 1860 Cobden–Chevalier Treaty with France and the most favoured nation clause, remained the central plank of British industrial policy. Tariffs on sugar, wine, tobacco, tea, and spirits maintained the British tariff revenue to imports ratio above that of France until 1880 (Nye 1991), but most manufactured goods and most agricultural produce were free of duties. Competition and specialization supposedly would ensure the survival of the fittest businesses in each country, and the benefits of this selection would raise British, and world, industrial output.

2.1.1. Competition Policy

Competition went hand in hand with free trade as tenets of nineteenth-century industrial policy. In practice this required the government to prevent mergers in natural monopoly or network industries, especially in railways. As the only significant medium- and long-haul inland transport in the nineteenth century, railways aroused strong emotions in the business community, who expressed their concerns to the legislature. In 1852 a London & North-Western Railway and Midland Railway merger was blocked, and in 1872 a LNW and Lancashire and Yorkshire merger was prevented. Even so, before the First World War the British considered but rejected an explicit general antitrust policy (Freyer 1992).

At first, regulation of established railways, or other businesses, was perceived as breaking a contract (retrospectively changing it without consent), and thus violating the rights of private property. Hence the 1844 Railway Act only regulated new railways.[1] Subsequently British governments showed they were prepared to

---

[1] By 1844 some 2,200 miles of railway were open in the UK. By 1910 the figure for Great Britain was approximately 20,000.

'break contracts' if there was a demonstrated public interest. Users increasingly demanded regulation on the grounds that they were being exploited, or made uncompetitive by railway charges; railway companies, in their turn, aimed to ensure regulatory legislation did not work. Price discrimination on British railways was outlawed under an 1873 Act, though this failed to resolve the conflict between the companies and their customers. The Railway and Canal Commission, created at the same time, dealt with many more cases than the previous regime but was not an ideal regulatory body (Foster 1992; Foreman-Peck and Millward 1994: 87). In this special tribunal railways found little difficulty in justifying charging different rates by showing there was some difference in circumstances. They were helped by having no obligation to publish their rates. More effective was the 1888 Railway Rates Commission, a division of the High Court. Cases were argued by barristers before a judge and two lay assessors. Railways were required by the new Commission to bring down some rates. In 1893, when they decided to raise other rates, which were below the maxima permitted by statute, there was a public outcry. Another bill in 1893, reaching the statute book in the following year as the Railway and Canal Traffic Act, shifted the burden of proof of discrimination in a rate change from the objector to the railways. Since the offence was not clearly defined, railways eventually became committed to holding down rates under any circumstances. The 1894 Act also breached the principle that private statutes (by which railways were established) were sacrosanct contracts.

An alternative policy, adopted in the USA, was to construct cost categories and artificially allocate costs, making a more workable, though inefficient, solution. Superior US railway performance is very striking, though the contribution of the two regulatory arrangements is hard to measure precisely.

Regulation was also blamed for the high capitalization of British railways (Foster 1992: 30). But since the rate of return constraint imposed by statute was not binding, greater capitalization was not necessary to pay higher profits in the late nineteenth century, unlike earlier in the century. High capital costs are more correctly attributed to the form taken by competition and to inadequate accounting. Before the building of branch lines to capture traffic from rivals, railways were sufficiently profitable to pay 8–9% dividends, compared with the 10% maximum specified under the Act of 1844. By 1865 competition ensured that railway capital was yielding only 4% on average.

2.1.2. Company Law and Limited Liability

Railways were the most prominent of the increasing number of businesses needing great volumes of capital which could not be provided by partnerships nor accumulated from retained profits. 'Widows and orphans'—and other passive investors—could not be expected to evaluate the risk of investments accurately and share the risks fully in partnerships. Yet the minimalist state provided an insufficient supply of low-risk government bonds for them to hold. Limited liability status opened the way for the development of large, capital-intensive enterprises, using their savings but not requiring them to assume risks beyond that of the capital they advanced.

Mid-Victorian Britain extended the privilege of joint stock, limited liability to almost anybody who applied, under Acts of 1855, 1856, and 1862. The original intention behind the 1856 Act had been to increase the disclosure obligations of joint stock companies, but Parliament actually reduced requirements to very little. Reporting obligations imposed on banks and railways (under an Act of 1868) and utilities were rather greater (Napier 1995). Stock exchange quotation in Britain imposed additional reporting requirements, but these were still minimal, especially considering how great were the payoffs from a stock market quotation. Victorian businesses changed hands at 6–10 years purchase (or a price-earnings ratio of 6–10). If such an enterprise could be sold on the stock exchange, then a price-earnings ratio of 12–20 became possible (Hannah 1994*a*). We know little about how this market worked. There were clear inefficiencies; with such margins of profits, entrepreneurs of easy virtue such as Terah Hooley, Harry Lawson, and Horatio Bottomley were available to encourage flotations with excessive capitalizations, and to take their cut. But some information was available to push markets towards efficient allocations. Dun & Co., Bradstreets, Seyd & Co., and the Manchester Guardian Society for the Protection of Trade used trade and other sources (such as county court judgments against directors), to assess creditworthiness. Insider dealing by directors—then perfectly legal— helped steer stock market prices to the right level. Provincial exchanges may have been better informed of the real value of the assets they traded because of their smaller size and local knowledge relative to London. The active markets in insurance shares, in steel and coal, in shipbuilding, cycles, gas, and telecommunications were in the provinces, for that is where the major shareholders in these sectors lived.

Even with limited liability, each shareholder is still liable for a portion of the downside risk over which they can have little control in a large enterprise. Directors and managers typically have better access to information about the firm than either shareholders or outsiders. The lack of legal or stock exchange obligations to reveal the state of the company in these years may have encouraged unscrupulous directors to expropriate shareholders' capital for themselves. They could establish fraudulent companies with no genuine assets or earnings prospects, as the distribution of early company failures under the 1856 Act implies (Shannon 1932, 1933; Cottrell 1980). Finance, insurance, and banking showed very high failure rates, while coal, iron, and engineering, which needed physical industry-specific assets to be credible, were much more likely to be genuine enterprises. Limited liability continued to offer opportunities for the morally flexible. An Act of 1890 laid down that company officials guilty of misconduct, misinformation, or trading while insolvent, could be required to pay full compensation to those affected. But the Comptroller-General for bankruptcies for 1895 reported that this provision was not in general implemented (Board of Trade 1895). Many liquidations still occurred solely because joint stock companies provided the opportunity to defraud creditors, his report complained.

For this reason, the possibility that more stringent bankruptcy laws might have deterred entrepreneurs from innovating did not concern Victorians. Creditors defrauded were the focus of legislation. Ninety per cent of company failures were due to their circumstances of promotion, formation, or management (Markham 1995: 3). Statistical evidence suggests that limited liability both increased investment and also reduced the productivity of investment. Liberal company legislation did not supply the ideal mix of information about company performance and incentives for efficient management (Foreman-Peck 1990).

2.1.3. Patent Protection

Like company law, the patent system is an instrument of industrial policy which can stimulate capital accumulation and technical progress. A patent confers a temporary monopoly right either to license or exploit an invention. This right may offer an incentive to invest in research and development greater than merely trying to keep profitable techniques or products secret while exploiting them commercially. On the other hand, there is a divergence of interests between the patentee and the users of the invention. The greater the monopoly reward of the patentee, the greater also is the price paid by the users. Both the charges levied to register patents and the duration of the rights influence the balance between the incentive to innovate and the gains to society from innovation.

The mid-Victorian patent system conferred benefits without a user charge on third parties as well. Founded in 1854, the Patent Office Library was concerned with the dissemination of technological information. In 1912 there were 159,000 readers, more than in 1964 (Boehm 1967). Under the patent system in operation between 1852 and 1883, patent fees were 18.5 times more expensive relative to national income per person, than in 1965 (Sullivan 1994). The greater expense meant that 90% of patents were allowed to lapse before their eighth year in the period 1852–76 ('the age of patentless invention') compared with 40% for the period 1950–76. Patenting was facilitated by the 1883 Act. Whether or not the arbitrary monopoly period of two apprenticeships, 14 years, which was allocated to a patentee, was excessive from society's viewpoint has yet to be determined.

Britain's interests as an innovator were that other countries should respect her inventors' rights, and enhance her income stream from abroad. Hence Britain was obliged to honour other national patents. This respect for innovators' property rights was one of mid-Victorian Britain's attractions for William Siemens, whose electrical and steel-making innovations certainly made a substantial contribution to industrial technology. And this despite the expense of patenting. As Britain imported more high technology products at the beginning of the twentieth century, the balance of advantages was less obvious. Where foreign competition in synthetic chemicals and pharmaceuticals was concerned, the late nineteenth-century patent system was a particular bone of contention.

Because Germany was not at first a signatory to international patent agreements, before 1877 German organic chemical firms were able to imitate freely products invented in Britain and France. Once Britain had lost its technological lead in this sector to Germany, its patent legislation may have exacerbated the lag. Foreign firms taking out patents in the UK were not required to use them in any way. Between 1891 and 1895, 600 patents for coal tar dyes were granted to foreigners, but not one was worked in Britain (Reed 1992). German manufacturers were thereby enabled to block innovation in Britain. The Patent Amendment Act of 1907, obliging foreigners to work or license patents in Britain, demonstrated the impact of earlier legislation by the response the Act evoked. Hoechst set up an indigo plant at Ellesmere Port (Lucius & Bruening), BASF assigned 270 of its patents to the new Mersey Chemicals Co., and Bayer began production on a small scale in Liverpool. Two years later a court decision effectively nullified the law. Whether the 1907 Act enhanced British well-being remains an open question. Internationally 'footloose' industries might be attracted to Britain, once blocking patents were removed. But industries which were not footloose incurred higher production costs, merely to protect their investment in research and development. These costs are likely to have been passed on to the industries' customers.

Even when patent holders were prepared to license, all-embracing patents could discourage experimentation at a vital stage in an industry's development. Harry Lawson's patent on the motor car allegedly discouraged at least one early motor innovator, Herbert Austin, who abandoned development of the first Wolseley he built. A second unsatisfactory feature of the patent system could arise from its 'self-enforcing' form. An innovator whose property rights were infringed was obliged to finance legal action. A small business could therefore be threatened with bankruptcy by a large infringing corporation. Harry Ricardo maintained that he was placed in this position as a result of his 1933 action against Humber-Hillman over the high turbulence cylinder head.

A few anecdotes do not constitute a major data set, and it is possible to supply other examples of the patent system apparently working well. Sebastian de Ferranti was enabled to continue his electrical research, financed by royalties from the Belgian and French rights to his 1885 meter, sold to Compagnie Générale d'Électricité (Wilson 1988: 26–7). Charles Parsons would have been unable to license his steam turbine to General Electric in the USA, and to Brown Boveri on the European continent, without an international patent system. Britain also did well as a licensee; Brunner Mond, for example, was a more effective licensee of the Belgian Solvay company's patents than its American or German equivalents.

Before 1852 patenting was rare, for the next thirty years it was expensive, and after 1883 it was easier. If patenting becomes cheaper or easier, we expect more patents to be taken out, a once and for all increase. If there is an alteration in the pace of technical progress in the economy, we expect a change in the growth rate of patenting technology. Suppose there was a change of trend, as well as of level, at the 'break points' when legislation transformed the terms of patenting. Then the patent laws may have changed the rate of technical progress. An increase in the growth of patenting, responding merely to the internationalization of technical knowledge and the sealing of blocking patents, would not occur merely because patenting was made easier; acceleration—if it occurred—could begin at any point in the later nineteenth century.

Inspection of the time path of the log of patents (Figure 2.2) clearly shows the two Victorian legislative changes in jumps upwards of patent numbers. To deduce anything more from the series, formal statistical methods are required.[2] They reveal that patenting did indeed accelerate after new legislation. This evidence therefore does suggest the patent reforms raised the rate of technical progress (potential or actual) in the economy.

2.1.4. Determinants of Policy

The basis of nineteenth-century policies towards industry was a middle-class (male) electorate supporting a laissez-faire doctrine in which even the institutions necessary to improve the operation of markets were to be privately provided. An older English tradition, embodied in the 1688 'Glorious Revolution', emphasized the ability of a strong interventionist government to oppress the people. Laissez-faire reduced that danger. Nineteenth-century liberalism maintained that adult males were the best judges of their own well-being and that their choices should not be restricted by law any more than essential. Women and children were in a different category. They did need protecting from the rigours of economic life by Factory and Mines Acts. Safety was another reason for regulation, especially in mines and on railways, although in both cases it was not until towards the end of the century that much was required by law.

Paradoxically laissez-faire policies predicated on competitive, market institutions, could lead to lobbying for government interference with other firms, as they did in setting railway rates or in creating the state telegraph monopoly. Moreover the British did not believe that all government 'meddling' was inefficient; by the 1860s the Post Office's service was highly regarded. Key lobbyists in the nationalization of the telegraph industry in Acts of 1868 and 1869 were newspapers. At the level of local government, from the 1880s there was increasing municipalization of basic industries—water, gas, tramways, and eventually, electricity supply. By 1907 state industrial employment accounted for 7.4% of total Census of Production jobs (Table 2.1).

---

[2] The following regression equation was estimated by ordinary least squares for the years 1779–1912:

$$\Delta(\log \text{ patents}) = -23.37 + 0.01(\text{time}) - 0.42(\log \text{ patents lagged one year}) + 0.50(\text{step dummy } 1852) +$$
$$(-4.30) \quad (4.37) \quad\quad (-4.92) \quad\quad\quad\quad\quad\quad\quad\quad\quad\quad (4.20)$$
$$0.61(\text{impulse dummy } 1852) + 0.25(\text{step dummy } 1884) + 0.84(\text{impulse dummy } 1884)$$
$$(5.88) \quad\quad\quad\quad\quad\quad\quad (4.23) \quad\quad\quad\quad\quad\quad (8.06)$$

DW = 2.20 R^2 = 0.51 n = 134. t statistics in parentheses are calculated from White robust standard errors. The positive step dummies indicate an increase in the growth of patenting.

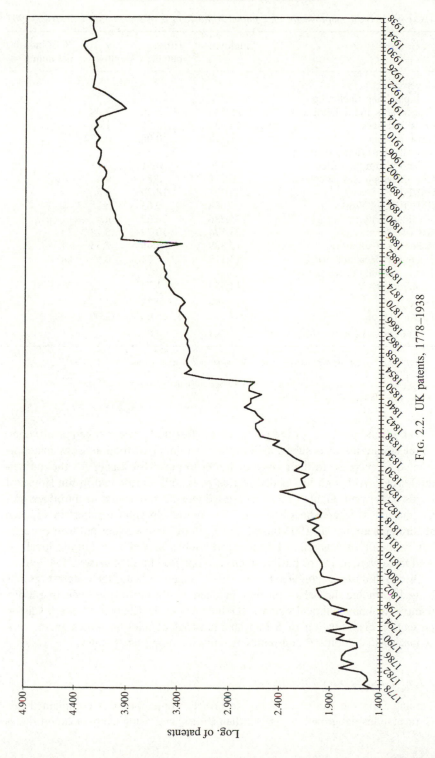

FIG. 2.2. UK patents, 1778–1938

TABLE 2.1. *State employment and output in the Census of Production industries, 1907*

	Employment	Gross output	Net output	% of industry net output
Government shipbuilding (including dockyards and lighthouses)	25,580	6.46	2.49	
Royal ordnance	14,533	3.36	1.45	
Naval ordnance	1,118	0.083	0.077	
Miscellaneous (army clothing factory, army bakeries, etc.)	2,329	0.51	0.18	
HM Telegraph and Telephone	10,171	2.87	n.a.	
HM Post	202,193[a]	18.70[b]	n.a.	
HM Office of Works	5,668	0.63	n.a.	
Local authority (building)	185,286	20.02	n.a.	
Gas (local authority)	28,574	10.77	5.73	33
Water (local authority)	17,389	8.46	7.35	81
Electricity (local authority)	14,119	5.73	3.59	64
Trams and light railways (local authority)	12,434	1.74	n.a.	57[c] (73)
TOTAL	519,394	79.33		
TOTAL NATIONAL	6,984,976	1,765.00	712.00	
STATE PERCENTAGE OF THE TOTAL	7.4	4.5		

[a] 1910 total for post and state telecom minus 1907 state telecom employment.
[b] 1910.
[c] Proportion of gross output. Figures in brackets indicate proportion of employment. Values in £m.
Source: Foreman-Peck and Millward 1994: 5.

　　The second principle of the liberal creed, free trade, was altogether different. An electorate that was substantially reliant on imported food and raw materials wanted no increase in their costs of living to make life easier for the agricultural sector. Although the landed interest was well represented in the House of Lords, they were unable to persuade governments and voters to introduce protection against cheap wheat from the 'New World'. Joseph Chamberlain's speech at Birmingham in May 1903 turned 'tariff reform' into a major political concern, but essentially it was still a businessman's lobby spiced with Empire loyalists. And there were plenty of businessmen who opposed him (Marrison 1996: ch. 1).

　　British industrial policies before 1914, together with the interest groups behind them and the behaviour they induced, might be seen as reflecting a distinctive national 'political culture' (Dobbin 1994). In Chapter 14 Mark Casson presents a classification of European industrial policies in which nineteenth-century British 'culture' and policy is unusual among large states.

2.1.5. *Overall Policy Effectiveness*

Turning from the causes of policy to effects, contemporaries complained that German industrial growth was faster than British, and rising German export shares

TABLE 2.2. *Manufacturing output per person employed* (UK = 100)

	US/UK	Germany/UK		US/UK	Germany/UK
1869	203.8		1937	208.3	99.9
1875		100	1950	262.6	96.0
1879	187.8		1958	250.0	111.1
1889	195.4	94.7	1968	242.6	120.0
1899	194.8	99.0	1975	207.5	132.9
1907	190.0	106.4	1980	192.8	140.2
1913	212.9	119.0	1985	182.3	121.5
1920	222.8		1987	188.8	107.8
1925	234.2	95.2	1989	177.0	105.1
1929	249.9	104.7	—	—	—

Source: Broadberry 1994.

were hurting British trade. German unification in 1870 was bound to create a German domestic market sufficient to encourage German industry to catch up Britain, as well as to develop distinctive specialisms. Nonetheless, in the last quarter of the nineteenth century British manufacturing output per person remained better than or equal to Germany's (Broadberry 1994). Only in the decade before the First World War did Germany begin to pull ahead (Table 2.2). US labour productivity, on the other hand, was apparently almost double Britain's in the later nineteenth century, with some sign of increasing the lead just before 1914. Both competitors were, like Britain, market-orientated economies, though the scale and access to natural resources of the United States were far greater. If Germany is the only appropriate comparator, then until 1900 or so British industrial policy must be judged satisfactory.

2.2. BETWEEN THE WARS: RATIONALIZATION AND NATIONAL SECURITY

The rise of the Labour party, constitutionally committed to state ownership of industry, together with the extension of the franchise in 1918, transformed industrial policy, but probably less so than Britain's new position in the world of the 1920s. The Labour party saw nationalization as a means of controlling the economy and redistributing income; industrial policy was an instrument. On the other hand, both Conservative and Labour inter-war governments also regarded private industry as an objective of economic policy, in need of rationalization that market forces failed to achieve.

Although deficiencies in the human capital necessary for national defence or offence were highlighted by the Boer War, it was not until the First World War that military objectives were judged to be constrained by industrial shortcomings. International specialization might maximize well-being, but that was no help when trading partners began fighting each other. Synthetic dyestuffs, magnetos, and selected pharmaceuticals were products in which Britain could not afford to be dependent on Germany. With the founding of the Department of Scientific and Industrial Research in 1916, British policy attempted to prevent such reliance as well as to extend the scientific base of British industry.

In the same year the now contentious term 'industrial policy' was coined, with the broad meaning, including competition policy, with which it is used in the present discussion. The report of the Committee on Commercial and Industrial Policy after the War, published in 1917, considered the potentially harmful impact of combinations and proposed they be registered (Balfour Committee 1928: pt. 1, p. 90).

Post-war reconstruction was soon swamped by boom and slump and persistent heavy unemployment, especially in the traditional export industries. Proposals for legislation against monopolies were put to one side. Of greater official British concern was unemployment and over-capacity in industry, neither of which competition appeared capable of eliminating over an acceptable timescale. After the expiry of the Profiteering Acts in 1921, British courts increasingly enforced restrictive agreements (Freyer 1992).

A new round of official concern with employment and competitiveness was initiated by the first minority Labour government in 1924. The Committee on Industry and Trade they appointed did not offer explicit recommendations, but it discussed state measures for meeting post-war difficulties of industry, including such matters as transport costs, the marking of goods, import duties, and export credits. With the election of the second Labour government of 1929, the Bank of England felt obliged to pursue mergers and rationalization policies in the export industries (cotton, shipbuilding, and steel) that suffered most from the shifts of the international economy. Otherwise the government would have undertaken more drastic intervention itself (Marrison 1996: 404). Conservative/National governments resisted nationalization (pressures were strong for dealing with coal in this way) but were willing to promote new public interest corporations for constructing and operating a national electricity grid and for radio broadcasting.

2.2.1. General Industrial Policies

Breaking the tradition of almost a century, tariff protection was a new general industrial policy introduced during the inter-war years. Throughout the 1920s, with the exception of one year, the motor industry had been protected by a $33\frac{1}{3}\%$ duty. As a competitive infant industry with scale and learning economies, a protected motor vehicles sector probably benefited the economy as a whole. But general protection in 1931/2 was a different matter and may anyway have been unnecessary in view of the abandonment of the fixed exchange rate in 1931. General protection was actually intended as balance of payments support, but industry tariffs were subsequently employed to encourage industrial restructuring (for instance in the case of steel). Disruption of international trade by misaligned exchange rates is likely to have been more decisive than tariffs in reducing the intensity of competition, though either separately could have cut industrial efficiency (Broadberry and Crafts 1990).

More original was the new policy to encourage exports. Eventually in the 1930s this proved profitable, suggesting that a state initiative had created a missing market. During the 1920s successive governments retained the Export Credit Guarantee scheme for its usefulness in paying off politically influential lobbies and also for temporarily assisting industries in difficulties (Aldcroft 1962). In these years, take-up of guarantees was very limited and even on that business the scheme lost money. From 1930 a small executive committee of businessmen with board of directors' powers took over the management of the department. From this date net premiums received exceeded claims and expenses. By the first half of 1937 over £2 million of profits had been earned on the more than £35 million of credit cover extended. However the proportion of exports guaranteed remained small because of emphasis on short-term credit.

Direct state research subsidies were also very limited. From 1916 the Department of Scientific and Industrial Research partly funded industrial research associations, which remained of modest dimensions, if they survived at all. Many of the largest spenders on R & D in inter-war Britain were foreign-owned or members of international cartels, with outlays quite independent of government support. ICI easily dominated the league. R & D as a percentage of GDP in major industrial economies, like the USA and Germany, probably remained somewhat greater than Britain's (Edgerton and Horrocks 1994).

State attempts to improve resource allocation by tightening corporate accounting obligations had no greater impact than R & D policy. Company financial reporting became less informative during the First World War in attempts to conceal profitability. It continued to be prone to manipulation by directors during the 1920s and even when an Act of 1929 required particular assets be shown separately. The inadequacies of regulation by the state and the stock exchange were exposed when Britain's largest shipping combine, the Royal Mail Group, collapsed. In 1926, a typical year of the 1920s for the Group, the company had converted an operating loss of half a million pounds into a reported surplus of the same figure, by drawing on hidden reserves and consolidating the accounts of subsidiaries (Napier 1995).

2.2.2. Human Capital Formation and Industrial Policy

Attempts to improve the supply of human capital to industry, such as they were, had impeccable market justifications. In the absence of considerable state finance, a laissez-faire market economy could well under-invest in education. Investors in somebody else's education or training cannot legally enforce a claim upon the extra income the person earns as a result. So a market in investment in education and training will at best be very imperfect. Other bonds, in particular family ties, are usually necessary to link investor with recipient. If families lack the capital, then there will be insufficient spending on education unless the state or another non-profit institution provides support.

Apprenticeship at one time modified this dilemma by binding the trainee to the employer who was contributing to his on-the-job training. Some training costs could then be recouped towards the end of the contract period, when wages were less than productivity. But at best it was only a partial solution; moreover, as the Balfour Committee lamented in the later 1920s, apprenticeship had been in decline for some years, and had never taken hold in some industries, such as textiles and clothing.

Corelli Barnett, among others, alleges that, by comparison with Germany, there was massive educational underprovision in inter-war Britain and earlier (Barnett 1986). Broadberry and Crafts (1992*a*) reach a similar conclusion by a different approach. Pollard (1989) noted such criticism sometimes stems from a failure to appreciate the extent and diversity of what was provided. Also the effectiveness of tuition should be considered as well as inputs to education. Unfortunately that is extremely difficult. A minimal indicator, literacy, was slightly higher in Germany and in Northwestern Europe than in the UK throughout the nineteenth century (Cipolla 1965). What can be said is that state willingness to pay for education does show a commitment which was apparently far stronger in Germany than in the UK. In 1936 only one in four British school leavers attended any evening class and of those that did, only a very small minority studied technical subjects (Gollan 1937: 246–7). There were few employer-run continuation day schools even in the inter-war years and some of these were minimal in their curriculum provision (PEP 1935*b*: app. II). In university students Britain apparently lagged behind much of developed Europe in 1900 and 1910, including Italy. Perhaps these patterns merely represent different styles of investment in human capital, not necessarily different efficiencies. British engineers, for example, were often 16-year-old school leavers trained in a demanding premium apprenticeship rather than at university. Their training in total lasted as long as a university graduate and was almost certainly more practical.

Laggardly investment in formal education might be traced to a correct appreciation of the returns—possibly due to on-the-job acquisition of professional or vocational qualifications, to an unwillingness to impinge upon traditional church roles, or to a desire not to spend public money lest taxes be raised. Official discussions about raising the school-leaving age in the inter-war years invariably cited the costs and other priorities, as well as parental resistance, as reasons for holding back. On the benefit side the impact on the unemployment figures was considered. Lord Irwin in 1934 maintained the way to proceed was to keep children between the ages of 14 and 15 at school until they found jobs (von Mayenberg 1996: 226). But changes over the first half of the twentieth century were radical; from around 1% of national income in 1900, state spending on education rose to 3 or 4% by the mid-century (Sanderson 1987: 112).

2.2.3. Sector-Specific Policies

State ownership, local or national, was an alternative to an active competition policy for avoiding private monopoly in particular sectors. In the electricity supply industry, both privately owned and municipally owned generating stations persisted, in an administered market structured by the Central Electricity Board (CEB) and regulated by the Electricity Commissioners. There were however no significant differences in the efficiency of the two types of station supplying the CEB's grid (but for non-suppliers, local authorities were less efficient) (Foreman-Peck and Hammond 1997). Nor were differences apparent earlier between enterprises with municipal and private ownership in the gas industry (Foreman-Peck and Millward 1994). Since these forms of state ownership apparently did not create higher costs than private enterprise, they might have been a means of avoiding monopoly pricing, or of convincing the public that they were protected from exploitative private prices, without efficiency losses.[3]

Sector-specific restructuring policies were pursued with varying success. About 60 railway companies were merged into four (Great Western, Southern, London & North Eastern, and London, Midland & Scottish), under an Act of 1921. Cross-hauling was reduced, and therefore so were operating costs, as experience of unified operation during the war had suggested. Through the Securities Management Trust/Bankers Industrial Development Co., the Bank of England and the commercial banks developed a rationalization policy. They devised schemes to re-equip and merge companies in industries with excess capacity. One of their creations was the Lancashire Cotton Corporation which absorbed almost one hundred firms but within two years experienced difficulties in managing the new agglomeration. Much Bank effort went into steel reorganization. In return for restructuring, the industry was promised tariff protection. But the resulting cartel did not behave as its sponsors hoped. In shipbuilding rationalization produced similarly unsatisfactory results. The National Shipbuilders Security scheme closed down yards and, in doing so, devastated the shipbuilding town of Jarrow, as well as reducing capacity below the unexpectedly high demand for ships to be experienced in the 1940s.

The inter-war years saw the discrediting of private ownership of coal mining, though not for especially cogent economic reasons (Greasley 1995). John Singleton (1995) notes that the coal miners were the only trade union sufficiently politically influential to engage in 'rent-seeking' through nationalization. The union pressed for nationalization after the war and resisted strong downwards pressure on wages from foreign competition. These industrial relations problems culminated in the General Strike of 1926 and the miners remained out after other workers. The Coal Mines Act of 1930 was intended to introduce a compulsory industry-wide

---

[3] Possibly more important for national well-being was the voluntarism in the re-regulation of the electricity supply industry. Unexploited gains from the new system amounted to half as much again as the cost reductions actually achieved (Foreman-Peck and Hammond 1997).

cartel (Supple 1988). This would have restricted output by assigning production quotas, raised coal prices, and permitted a reduction in the working day without wage cuts. The Act only partially achieved its objectives, because of hostility of the mineowners and union opposition to rationalization that would lose jobs. In 1938 the government nationalized ownership of the coal seams in an attempt to remove the supposed brake of mixed ownership on cost-reducing local mine rationalization.

The newer industries were more tractable. In radio broadcasting, an Act of 1922 established the British Broadcasting Corporation, a non-profit state-sponsored monopoly organization with some independence. There was subsequently a high degree of customer satisfaction with the quality of the BBC's service, and extraordinary growth in radio sets licensed, doubling to 6 million between 1929 and 1933, and reaching 9 million six year later.

Electricity supply was a crucial element in the modernization of inter-war industry and households, yet at the end of the First World War Britain lagged well behind Germany and the United States in the application of this power source. The industry was fragmented into a large number of excessively small suppliers, each jealously guarding their territory. Ineffective legislation in 1919 was followed by an Act of 1926 which established the (non-profit) Central Electricity Board, empowered to build a national electricity distribution grid and to negotiate contracts with suppliers of electricity to this grid (Hannah 1979; PEP 1935*a*). Built during the world depression, the grid was the instrument that virtually closed the British industry's power station total productivity gap with the Americans by 1937, massively increased electricity output and greatly reduced costs. Reorganization of distribution, where costs were unnecessarily high, was deferred.

Civil aviation gained support thanks to its potential contribution to imperial communications and military security. Subsidized French competition on the London–Paris route immediately after the war almost eliminated the nascent British industry. To maintain a capability in this field, the government countered with more extended civil aviation subsidies throughout most of the inter-war years (Lythe 1995). The culmination of the policy was nationalization of the British Overseas Airways Corporation in 1939.

State buying was another encouragement to the aircraft industry and to a few other advanced technology sectors as well. As with all other national aircraft industries between the wars, the British state was by far the largest buyer of British aircraft. The Air Ministry maintained a ring of approved firms in order to keep design teams in existence and to stimulate technical progress through competition. The success of this policy may be judged by the fact that Britain was probably the single largest exporter of aircraft until the mid-1930s (Edgerton 1991). Naval communications demands brought the Marconi Co. to life in the face of the Post Office monopoly before the First World War (Pocock 1988). During the 1920s Marconi developed short-wave beam (microwave) radio for telephone communication with the other side of the world and in the 1930s made the transmitter arrays for radar stations (Baker 1970: 219–25, 303). Government procurement exercised a greater influence over industry after rearmament began seriously, with the 'Statement Relating to Defence' of March 1935, which also initiated the 'shadow factories' of the later 1930s.

Rather similar in the impact on specific domestic industries was the state purchase and finance of road services. In a period when motor transport was soaring, the government was responsible for road building and maintenance. Roads were paid for by a vehicle tax graduated according to the horsepower of the car. In practice the tax provided protection for the British motor industry against imports of larger engine American cars. When the horsepower loading of the tax was reduced in 1935, North American imports flowed in (Foreman-Peck, Bowden, and McKinlay 1995: 73–6).

Despite the greater industrial role of government, for much of the period inter-war industrial policy clung to the Victorian liberal precepts of minimum state expenditure and 'self-regulation'. Any assessment of policy effectiveness in these years must recognize that British and German manufacturing productivity were broadly similar (Table 2.1). The United States pulled further ahead in the 1920s, but fell back almost to the later nineteenth-century margin of superiority in the depressed 1930s. Again with Germany as the standard, British industrial policy in these years can hardly be condemned, especially in view of the relative performance over the Edwardian years. On the other hand, the political disorders of inter-war Germany mean the yardstick is rather undemanding.

2.3. POST-1945: THE PERVASIVE STATE

Much closer continued government direction of the economy after 1945 may be explained in part by the macroeconomic strains produced by the war, and the discrediting of market economies by the world depression that began in 1929. Nationalization in particular stemmed from the supposed lessons of the war economy, and from the belief that governments knew best and markets were not to be trusted. These ideas persisted for a generation or more after 1945. Industrial policy, necessarily highly interventionist in the war, remained so afterwards.

The share of civil employment in manufacturing peaked in 1955 at 36%, an all time historical high. German manufacturing output by then had just returned to 1929 levels, but British manufacturing produced more than half as much again as in 1929. This policy-induced expansion, to pay for war debt and to finance the balance of payments, supported by the temporary elimination of German and Japanese competition and the world's 'dollar shortage', was historically unique and could not persist.

Manufacturing employment in total reached a pinnacle around 1966 and thereafter fell, amid worsening industrial relations and rising inflation. Of the 2.9 million decline in manufacturing jobs from 1966 to 1983, perhaps three-fifths was due to rising incomes and the higher income elasticity of demand for services (the 'maturity' effect) (Rowthorn and Wells 1987). The specialization effect (in service exports, helped by cheaper food and raw materials and eventually by North Sea oil) explained an additional fall in employment of 900,000. So 200,000 jobs were lost through an unnecessarily poor performance of the manufacturing sector, Rowthorn and Wells calculate. In an international context there is no doubt that productivity growth was poor; GDP per person hour rose only 3.2% per annum 1950–73 compared with 4.5% for the OECD countries as a whole (Maddison 1989: table 7.2).

2.3.1. New Policies for Manufacturing Industry

Compared with the years before 1939, industrial policy acquired new instruments, direct controls, information provision and discriminatory taxation, and used most traditional tools more vigorously. Post-war rationing of raw materials, in particular steel, aimed to direct manufacturing resources into the export sector. Overseas debts accumulated in paying for the war made some such diversion essential. But selected prices were held down, so that energy, building materials, and capital were artificially cheap and incentives to economize were reduced. Many physical controls were abandoned in the early 1950s but issues of new capital were restricted until 1958. Bank credit was rationed through the 1950s and 1960s to favour manufacturing, reducing the total amount lent. Japanese attempts to restrict lending appear to have been far less effective (Hannah 1994*a*).

From 1948, 'as with guests who have outstayed their welcome, a question increasingly asked about post-war controls was, when would they be gone?' (Chick 1998: 197). Yet import controls, in the form of quotas, remained an instrument of a barely articulated and harmful industrial policy throughout the 1950s. Quotas are far more restictive of trade than tariffs, for as demand expands and supply increases, trade volume is fixed by such direct controls, whereas tariffs do not prevent trade growth.

These import quotas radically improved Britain's balance of payments during the years 1945–1960 (Milward and Brennan 1996). Subsequently their abandonment allowed deterioration and crises. Government officials and policy-makers were formally committed to free trade but in practice 'the time was not ripe' for liberalization. They protected large sections of British manufacturing industry, for employment purposes, but also for defence. The herring canning industry, for instance, was supported to keep jobs in north-east Scotland and because the industry provided the Royal Navy with ships and men. Milward and Brennan (1996) estimate that in 1954 perhaps one-sixth of manufacturing output would have been lost without quantitative import controls. A comparison of the low imports of the UK with those of Switzerland, the most liberalized OEEC country, is instructive. Without quotas, Switzerland imported massively more in the post-war period compared with 1938. Without quotas, British industry would have been forced to become more competitive and/or sterling would have been devalued further.

Exhortation to greater efforts also were continued into the post-war years by the Anglo-American Council on Productivity. In a series of sectoral reports, the Council pointed out where and why US industries out-performed their British equivalents (Tomlinson 1994: 179–80). At the beginning of the 1960s, another attempt at improving information began under the influence of the French example. British industrial policy began an experiment with indicative planning. The Conservative Prime Minister Harold Macmillan established the National Economic Development Council (NEDC) in 1962, and a National Economic Development Office which worked out, independently of the government, a plan for industrial growth. Unlike French planning however, the British version lacked compulsion (NEDC 1963). The NEDC relied on their planned 4% growth between 1962 and 1966 being self-fulfilling, when announced; they assumed that a closer meshing of business expectations that the plan was to facilitate would boost performance.

With their election in 1964 the Labour government took planning further by establishing a new Ministry, the Department of Economic Affairs (DEA 1965). This new department quickly produced a plan for a 25% increase in output between 1964 and 1970. Although economic models of disequilibrium through mismatched expectations have been constructed, their relevance to British industry in the 1960s remains questionable, since neither NEDC's nor the DEA's plan apparently raised industrial growth. The uncharitable referred to the exercises as 'talking up the growth rate'. The NEDC proved more durable than the DEA; sector working parties continued to publish often excellent reports on problems in their particular industries.

As import penetration increased, the Labour government of 1964–70 conducted an experiment that tested whether favouring the manufacturing sector, because of its supposed greater productivity potential, was an effective industrial policy. A Selective Employment Tax (SET) explicitly discriminated in favour of manufacturing industry. The great jump in industrial policy expenditure in Figures 2.3 and 2.4, to more than 5% of GDP at the end of the 1960s, is largely due to SET rebates (included in the 'national' category of Figure 2.4). As a proportion of GDP, and absolutely, Figures 2.3–2.5 make clear that industrial policy spending, for civil aircraft, shipbuilding, regional and industrial (sector) as well as 'national' (including investment grants), took off under the 1964–70 Labour government (calculated from Wren 1996). Had the discrimination in favour of manufacturing worked, we might expect that labour productivity in manufacturing would grow consistently over the heavy spending period. It did not, although in 1967 and 1968 expansion was rapid. On the other hand, conceivably performance would have been worse without SET. As we see below, there was also the impact on the service sector to take into account.

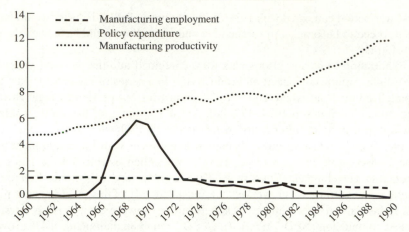

FIG. 2.3. UK industrial policy and performance, 1960/1–1990/1

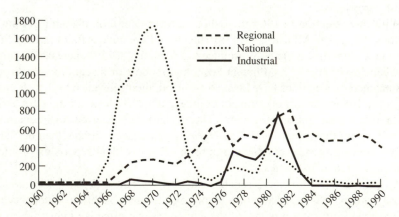

FIG. 2.4. Components of UK industrial policy expenditure, 1960/1–1990/1

2.3.2. Nationalized Industries

State ownership was not a new industrial policy instrument but it was undoubtedly employed more energetically when the Labour government with a massive parliamentary majority in 1945–51 proceeded to nationalize 'the commanding heights' of industry. Yet, aside from the coal industry, a strong case can be made that most of the nationalizations (such as gas, electricity, and railways), if not the form they took, were consensus measures to rationalize under-performing industries. That is not necessarily to concede that the consensus was correct or that more effective reforms were impossible. Inaction over the water industry may be

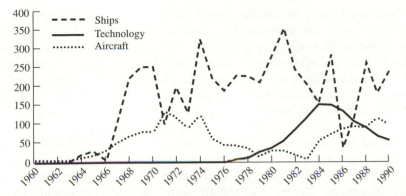

FIG. 2.5. UK industrial policy expenditure on shipbuilding, technology, and aircraft, 1960/1–1990/1

traced to the absence of a supply crisis and the variety of lobbying opportunities open to parties concerned to block nationalization (Millward and Singleton 1995).

After these nationalizations, the proportion of state-owned industry was comparable with other Western European economies, though significantly more than in the USA or Japan. Subsequent Conservative governments broadly accepted the nationalizations, except for steel and road haulage, which were privatized. The steel industry showed how damaging was political controversy about ownership (Rowley and Yarrow 1981). Under-investment in British steel was partly caused by the threat of re-nationalization. After returning to state ownership in 1968, investment in the later 1970s was managed so inefficiently that much was wasted.

During the 1970s came a new reliance on nationalization as a response to industrial bankruptcy. A Conservative government undertook the first of these acquisitions, Rolls Royce, though the greater part (aerospace, shipbuilding, and motor vehicles) was taken over after the first oil crisis by the Labour government of 1974–9. This was not so much an industrial policy of 'picking winners' but of (large) losers picking government support, for fear of the unemployment that would otherwise result. In short, it was an employment policy in which industry was the policy instrument.

How well the newly nationalized sectors performed might be judged against a private sector standard. Labour productivity gains in the utilities and other nationalized industries averaged more than 3% per annum over the years 1951–64, compared with 2.5% in private manufacturing (Foreman-Peck and Millward 1994: 310). The proximate source was labour shedding by the largest employers, coal and railways. With a slightly different choice of years, including more of immediate post-war years, the period 1948–58, the picture is rather different. (Private) manufacturing labour productivity growth fell to 1.9% a year, but that was more than double what was achieved in nationalized road freight and coal, and more than six times the productivity growth of nationalized railways. Lack of administrative and managerial resources compromised productivity performance in the 1950s. Co-ordination of transport was never achieved. On the other hand, labour productivity in capital-intensive state-owned electricity supply averaged 4.6% (Hannah 1994*b*). Peak performance by both sectors was reached in the 1960s, but state-owned industry labour productivity growth was ahead.

Worried that cheap capital, boosting labour productivity growth in the capital-intensive nationalized industries, was crowding out private sector investment, the Treasury in 1961 raised the target rate of return. In 1967 price targets based on long-run marginal costs were set and discounted cash flow investment appraisal was required. These were often inconsistent; there were too many constraints on most nationalized industries for them to pursue consistent policies. But on occasion, cost-cutting and revenue-raising became the order of the day. British Railways was placed under the management of Dr Beeching from ICI, who raised productivity by shutting branch lines. The economist Ronald Edwards at the Electricity Council introduced off-peak pricing earlier than in other economies.

Both private and public sectors were unable to raise productivity so rapidly in the turbulent 1970s, though the decline was greater in the state-owned businesses. Price-capping of nationalized industries in the 1970s as an anti-inflationary policy, by both Conservatives and Labour governments, removed efficiency incentives and demanded huge subsidies.

2.3.3. The Supply of Capital to Industry

The inter-war state initiative to boost exports expanded so that by 1959–60 the Export Credit Guarantee department insured 18.4% of total UK exports. Persistent criticism that the financial services of the City left a gap in the supply of funds to small- and medium-sized businesses was at least partly met with the setting up in 1945 of the Industrial and Commercial Finance Corporation (ICFC) (Coopey and Clarke 1995). Both this and the sister Finance Corporation for Industry (FCI) were too redolent of socialism for the City's nose; they employed industrial (as well as financial) investment assessment criteria, opting for long-term investment, latterly often in equity. Clearing banks, who were shareholders of ICFC, were generally hostile, but Bank of England support ensured survival. During the 1960s ICFC expanded by establishing regional branches. Total assets rose from £11 million in 1948 to £2.8 billion in 1994. Half of the investments of 3i, the successor organization,[4] were in manufacturing. In 1991 some 10% of all manufacturing workers in Britain were employed by companies financed by 3i.

---

[4] In the 1970s ICFC merged with Finance Corporation for Industry (originally insurance fund financed) to become Finance for Industry. The organization was relaunched in the 1980s as Investors in Industry or 3i's.

Investment allowances and subsidies were new instruments that affected the supply of capital to industry from the beginning of the Labour government's period of office (Tomlinson 1994: 170, 226). Labour taxed distributed profits heavily, reaching a 50% rate in 1951, on top of which income tax at 47.5% was levied, because of the government's dislike of 'unearned' income and inequality. The policy encouraged businesses to retain profits for expansion, and capitalized these retentions in share prices. Investment allowances then reduced the impact of profit taxes, for firms that made profits.

These measures were introduced and withdrawn in the 1950s as determined by macroeconomic considerations. As with the frequent redrawing of boundaries for regionally-specific investment subsidies, policy uncertainty confused and deterred investors. In any case subsidizing capital began to look increasingly odd by the 1970s. Moore, Rhodes, and Taylor (1986) estimated that regional investment subsidies led to a loss of 28,000 jobs in the chemicals industry, as more capital-intensive production methods were introduced in response to the higher relative price of labour.

Despite new institutions and policies, complaints continued that British finance was 'short-termist', sought quick returns, and avoided profitable investment that required long gestation periods. In the later 1970s the Wilson Committee (1980) pondered the problem at great length but no policy emerged from the deliberations. Between 1970 and 1984 British industry was over-financing itself from retained profits, whereas economies with faster growth rates, France, Germany, the USA, and Japan, drew substantially upon loans and short-term securities (Mayer 1988). The unanswered question is whether there was a causal link between finance and investment, and if so in which direction. Instead of industrial investment and productivity being constrained by the unwillingness of banks and stock markets to lend to British industry, it is no less probable that such inhibitions should be attributed to poor productivity performance and lack of profitable investment opportunities in British industry. High sterling dividends were necessary because lack of industrial competitiveness depreciated the sterling exchange rate. Whether industry required policy intervention in the operation of financial markets thus remains unproven. The success of 3i and ancestors suggests however that in 1945 there was at least one genuine gap in the market's provision and that it was filled by a state initiative.

2.3.4. The Supply of Human Resources and Management

Another such initiative was the Robbins expansion of the universities in the early 1960s. This increased the supply of high-grade researchers and may explain the increasing interest of multinational pharmaceutical companies in locating research laboratories in the United Kingdom.

Nonetheless skill deficiencies compared with the USA are not hard to find. There were far fewer engineers and more technicians in Britain relative to the USA in 1959 in electrical engineering, chemical and mineral oil refining, plant and machinery, and in metal manufacture (Caves 1968). But the comparison of more relevance is with Europe. In the mid-1950s, Britain produced more science and technology graduates than Germany, France, or Italy (Edgerton 1996). In the 1960s, 4.6% of the 20–24 year-old age group graduated in science and technology, whereas the figure for Germany was 2.2%. Britain's stock of science graduates was larger than that in any other European country and a larger proportion of them were employed in industry.

A deficiency is more obvious at lower skill levels. The cause of poor British productivity performance was inadequate human capital accumulation (coupled with a bargaining environment that inhibited growth), according to Broadberry and Crafts (1992b).[5] Apprentices accounted for some 3% of British manufacturing employment in the 1960s, whereas in Germany the figure was 5% (Broadberry and Wagner 1996). By 1968 the labour productivity lead of German industry over Britain's was from 20 to 30%. By the 1980s both gaps had widened. Prais (1993) estimated that intermediate qualifications were the most significant education variables in predicting industrial performance by countries. In the 1970s and 1980s, a clear skills lag behind Germany had emerged (O'Mahony and Wagner 1994).

Defence continued to absorb a much greater proportion of national resources than before 1939. Perhaps half of the high level of British R & D was defence-related and a great deal of scientific manpower was employed by defence-related industry, especially aerospace and nuclear power (Ergas 1992). In 1962 aircraft alone absorbed one-third of British industrial R & D.

Concern that skill deficiencies were induced elsewhere in industry, in particular in management, has been warranted by the observation that US subsidiaries earned higher rates of profits between 1950 and 1964 (15.4% after tax on net assets) than competitor UK companies (which averaged returns of 8.7%). Part of the difference was due to US research. US subsidiaries may have benefited from their parents' research without fully paying for it. But other comparative data does not favour British management in these years. US subsidiaries maintained higher ratios of capital to labour to create higher labour productivity. They spent a smaller proportion on administration than the British, but more on marketing and distribution. Wholly-owned US subsidiaries performed better than partly-owned subsidiaries. British business leaders were apparently more liable to problems than German, French, or Italians as well, perhaps because market forces were rather sluggish in penalizing poor British decisions (Geroski and Jacquemin 1988).

As a remedy for the perceived shortage of competent top managers, the Industrial Reorganization Corporation was established in 1966 to encourage the

---

[5] They reach this conclusion in a comparison of British with US productivity by industry in 1950 and from a cross-British industry analysis of labour productivity growth for the years 1963–73. In the first model they find relative capital, both physical and human, are significant contributors to Britain's productivity lag. Unionization was not, nor was industry concentration in two of the three regression equations reported. The second model finds significant capital/labour ratio growth, output growth, import penetration, and decline in employment growth in the five years preceding the estimation period. Neither collective bargaining nor industry concentration were significant, although the best estimates of their impacts on productivity growth were negative.

more successful managers to take over the businesses of less satisfactory per-
formers. The upshot was no improvement in the case of British Leyland, or perhaps even for the GEC/AEI takeover (Hague and Wilkinson 1983).

2.3.5. Competition Policy and Business Performance

Full employment in the 1940s and 1950s created an increasingly propitious environment for competition policy. At the same time there was a continuing tension
with the belief in economies of scale, and with the managerial hubris, that great
managers could control organizations of any size.

The 'landscape' was created by the 1948 reform of company law, which required
greater transparency in company financial reporting. Perhaps not coincidentally,
a few years later came the first contested takeover bids (Hannah 1974; Wilson
1995: 203). Threats of such takeovers should have encouraged management to
focus their minds on maximizing the returns on their assets. Competition law
also made its debut in 1948, when the Monopolies Commission was established.
Economists criticized the three strands of competition policy—monopolies regulation, restrictive practice legislation, and merger controls—for being weak and
ineffective. Monopoly policy for instance was inconsequential until 1956 for a
number of reasons:

(1) the Board of Trade was unwilling to press its recommendations;
(2) references to the Monopolies Commission were political, they could only
be made by the Secretary of State who might ignore some or all of the
Commission's recommendations;
(3) the opportunities for lobbying by business to avoid adverse judgements
were—and in some cases remain—considerable.

But in historical perspective, what is surprising is that such general policies
were implemented at all, for the first time. The Monopolies and Mergers Act of
1965 introduced stronger powers against large companies and mergers. Between
1950 and 1987 the Monopolies and Mergers Commission reported on 78 monopoly positions—an average of two reports a year. But only 4 monopoly positions
out of 45 references were found unambiguously against the public interest and
7 cases were judged to show no adverse conduct or performance (Gribbin and
Utton 1986). The thrust of the recommendations was to reduce entry barriers,
for dominant firm groups on average had 3 entry barriers per market.

Apparently more radical was the second strand of competition policy. The
Restrictive Trade Practices Act of 1956 required a wide variety of trade association practices be registered. The Act empowered the Registrar to refer agreements to the Restrictive Practices Court. By 1966, 2,550 practices had been
registered and 1,875 abandoned. Prices were cut where agreements were dropped,
but mergers enabled some firms to reinforce market control. A particular restrictive practice was addressed by the 1964 Resale Prices Act, which prohibited manufacturers from stipulating resale prices and enforcing these prices by

withholding supplies from retailers not adhering to the manufacturer's conditions. Such a restriction of competition keeps up the number of small and inefficient shops and strengthens price agreements among manufacturers. Filtering out the impact of Resale Price Maintenance abolition is hindered by the 1966 introduction of Selective Employment Tax that discriminated between manufacturers and their distributors. One estimate of the impact on retailing productivity of the SET–RPM jointly was cumulatively between 4 and 6% by 1968 (George 1971: 169–87).

Merger regulation, the third element of competition policy, in principle might prevent the emergence of dominant positions, but also could preclude exploitation of scale economies and synergies. In practice merger control was weak. If two firms wished to merge and thereby increase their market share above 25%, they faced a 2–3% chance of referral to the Monopolies and Mergers Commission between 1965 and 1988 (Walshe 1991: 367). If they were referred, there was a 40–45% chance that they would be forbidden to proceed. Putting these probabilities together, there was a one in 80 chance of a horizontal merger being prohibited, whereas in 3 cases out of 4, mergers may have worsened performance.

Government policy and public opinion until the 1980s were still prone to conclude that Britain needed to become more like the United States in the scale of its industrial businesses: the USA was after all richer than Britain even though its productivity was growing more slowly. However, faster growing economies —France, Germany, Japan, Italy—all had distinctly smaller firms and thus faith in scale was perhaps misplaced. Moreover, by the 1960s Britain's poor industrial relations militated against the success of large firms (Davies and Caves 1987). Disruption of one section of an integrated business could bring all the other departments and processes to a standstill. The larger the enterprise, or the greater the likelihood of industrial action, the greater the risks (Prais 1976).

By 1970 the 100 largest British companies produced a greater share of output than in any other major economy. These big firms were not necessarily very efficient. ICI was too much of an industrial dinosaur. As this realization dawned on the company, in the 1960s it demerged Imperial Metals Industries (20% of its assets). In 1993 ICI's pharmaceutical division was separated into an independent company, Zeneca (of more than half the company's stock market value). So ICI eventually voluntarily achieved a split of the size which the Allies imposed on the German equivalent, IG Farben, in 1945. Competitive pressure on ICI also came from US entry into the British market by Dow Chemicals and Monsanto, and by British oil companies, Shell and BP.

Britain was not alone in the misconception that 'big was beautiful'; 'national champions', huge flagship businesses, were the focus of many industrial policies in the 1960s (Hayward 1995). But Britain was unusual in her ability to pursue such policies. During the 1960s the British Ministry of Technology and the Japanese Ministry of International Trade and Industry held similar views. But whereas Japanese policy to concentrate the motor industry on Toyota and Nissan was thwarted by other lively competitors and Honda's new entry, the British government's support for the Leyland–BMH merger tipped the balance towards a unified British-owned motor industry. Within a few years, British Leyland was saved from bankruptcy only by government support and import restrictions, coming to depend on technology from Honda, a company that had barely entered motor car manufacture at the time BL was the second largest car maker in Europe.

Sometimes those who created giant monopolies by mergers received unpleasant shocks. After GEC took over AEI in 1967, GEC discovered that AEI's profit statement showing £10 million should have recorded a loss of £5 million. Effective cartelization in allocation of orders for power station equipment featherbedded the industry in the 1950s. The merger itself was not then responsible for the subsequent employment shrinkage in the electrical engineering industry, but equally, it did nothing to prevent it.

Occasionally Britain made correct policy decisions on industrial structure. Boots, Beecham, and Glaxo argued in 1972 that Britain needed a national pharmaceutical champion to compete with the German, Swiss, and American giants. Glaxo then ranked 16th and Beecham 42nd in the world pharmaceutical league tables. A combination of Glaxo's research capabilities with Beecham's marketing skills would, it was maintained, be particularly effective. The then Conservative government refused permission for the merger, so Beecham improved its research skills and took over an ailing US pharmaceutical company, Smith Kline. Glaxo developed its marketing skills, particularly in the USA. Boots recently sold off its pharmaceutical arm and concentrated on retailing. In 1995 Britain had in Smith Kline Beecham and Glaxo, two of the four largest pharmaceutical firms in the world and in Boots a focused and profitable retail chain.

2.3.6. Sector-Specific Industrial Policy

In aerospace and computers, government policy and market size were especially vital. British Aerospace and Rolls Royce remained the largest aircraft and aero-engine manufacturers in Europe. Yet they lacked a very profitable history largely because of industry learning effects and scale economies which conferred an advantage on subsidized and protected US producers. Only Britain and France in the 1950s were in a position to waste resources competing with the world leader (Hayward 1983). Much the same was true in computers, where again Britain had the largest European output but no chance of competing with IBM by the 1960s (Hendry 1989). High-tech military R & D was a Second World War 'winners' curse' which medium-sized countries were better without.

One solution to the enormous expense of aircraft development was sharing the overheads with another national industry. The Anglo-French supersonic Concorde passenger aircraft project did just that, but cost overruns and the commercial conception of the project ensured that British state expenditure was still enormous.

Other features of government policy or the broader British environment may well have contributed to the unique success of pharmaceuticals in British manufacturing industry. The state interest in holding down the costs of the National

Health Service created a competitive market for pharmaceuticals in which foreign companies were welcome—in contrast to French policy affecting the pharmaceutical industry (Thomas 1994). British businesses that could learn from competitors would also be competitive in the world market.

The telecommunications equipment industry revealed the obverse of this coin; that a comfortable 'ring' of manufacturers supplying a government departmental monopoly would not make any world beating products. The electronic telephone exchange, System X, was designed to be modular so that each manufacturer could make different components. Unfortunately coordination difficulties were enormous, and the project was massively delayed, so that other electronic exchanges launched earlier, were able to capture most of the markets that were not 'tied'. One estimate of the excess costs of the System X procurement policy was £5 billion, doubling the expense of this digital system (Grindley 1987). Not surprisingly then, when the British telecommunications equipment industry was opened to competition by the liberalization policies of the 1980s, much of their business was lost.

2.3.7. Explaining Performance

Relatively poor British business performance from 1950 to 1980 is not to be explained by a failure to imitate US managerial hierarchies (Chandler 1990) or research and development (Mowery and Rosenberg 1989). British managerial hierarchies were much deeper than Italy and possibly larger than France or Germany's. Britain's big companies also had both higher levels and a faster rate of adoption of the multidivisional management structure. On indices such as science Nobel prizes per head, US patenting, and R & D expenditure, Britain led Europe in this period. In absorbing new technology, Britain generally appears ahead of continental Europe in introduction during the 1950s and only slightly behind France and Germany in diffusion in the 1960s (Nabseth and Ray 1974). Yet British productivity grew more slowly than the economies of continental Europe. The Common Market was not the principal reason, both because the effects that must be explained antedate the Six's first serious tariff reductions and because Britain's output and trading patterns responded, at least in the short and medium term, in different ways (Milward 1992). However Britain's improving relative performance after 1979 is certainly consistent with a delayed positive effect of 1973 entry.

There is a large literature arguing that France and Japan had effective industrial policies because shared backgrounds and training of civil servants and industrialists created shared values and identification with agreed national goals (Shonfield 1965; Johnson 1982). Such writers are wrong to argue this did not exist in Britain, where its peak was reached in the 'white heat of technology' enthusiasms for industrial intervention of the Labour government of 1964–70. Establishment values were easily transmitted through elites because the British economy was one of the most concentrated in the world. Judged by the divergence of British manufacturing productivity from that of its major competitors (Table 2.1), this style of industrial policy was apparently inadequate.

2.4. THE 1980S: THE RETURN OF THE MARKET

The pro-manufacturing policy of the years 1945–79 was reversed in the 1980s when the state shifted from a directly interventionist industrial policy to a more market-centred approach. Productivity then rose rapidly, as the manufacturing sector shrank. By 1976, the costs of industrial support were becoming impossibly high, if the exchange rate was to be maintained at a reasonable level. At the same time Britain's industrial performance—productivity, delivery times, and quality—had deteriorated badly relative to her principal competitors.

A severe monetary squeeze massively raised unemployment and radically contracted manufacturing at the beginning of the 1980s. The process was reinforced by the impact on the exchange rate of British self-sufficiency in oil and rising oil prices during the second oil crisis. Industrial productivity began to grow strongly as less efficient firms were eliminated. Populist Thatcherism (boosted by victory in the Falklands War) supplied the political support to pursue a radical redirection of industrial policy towards private ownership and markets. This reorientation was at first gradual. It is no surprise that, when told the consequences of shutting down British Leyland in 1982, Mrs Thatcher's government continued the support policy of the preceding administration. Cambridge Econometrics estimated that unemployment would rise by more than 200,000, GDP would fall by 0.6%, the balance of payments would deteriorate by £0.7 billion, and the public sector borrowing requirement would rise by £0.2 billion (Wilks 1988: 221).

2.4.1. Privatization and Re-regulation

Structural industrial policy, 'creating a landscape', returned for the first time for many decades in the form of privatization and liberalization. Financial markets were re-regulated. A project such as the Channel tunnel, which formerly almost certainly would have attracted state support, was entirely funded by the private sector on the British side, even though it proved a poor investment in the medium term. Given clear and simple objectives for the first time, nationalized industries, massively improved productivity before privatization. By the late 1980s British Steel (BSC) productivity overtook US and German levels for the first time in a century. BSC became the lowest cost producer in the world, with POSCO of South Korea.

The deregulation movement in the United States during the 1970s undoubtedly influenced British Conservative policy-makers in the early 1980s. Essentially technological change pressed upon US regulatory institutions, in form dating from the nineteenth century. This was especially apparent in telecoms, where the

TABLE 2.3. *The regulatory reform of state industries, 1984–1997*

Enterprise	Privatized	Main changes to competitive environment
British Airways	Jan. 1987	Routes liberalized; North Atlantic (1977); UK (1982); Europe (1984 forwards)
BAA	July 1987	—
British Coal	Jan. 1995	Quasi-competitive contracts for supply to electricity generators (1989)
British Gas	Dec. 1986	Gas Act (1985); partial competition in supply to industrial customers
British Rail	Mar. 1994–Mar. 1997	Separation of track ownership, rail service provision, rolling stock leasing and track maintenance
British Steel	Dec. 1988	Unwinding of EC steel quotas (1980 forwards)
British Telecom	Nov. 1984	Liberalization of apparatus supply (1981); value added services (1981); and second fixed link carrier (1982)
Electricity supply	Dec. 1990/Spring 1991	Energy Act (1983); partial competition in supply. Electricity Act (1986); competition in supply (1990 forwards)
Post Office	—	Courier services deregulated (1981)

Source: primarily Bishop, Kay, and Mayer 1994: 355.

ensuing massive cross-subsidies between services triggered initial US deregulatory moves. The difference between Britain and the USA was that the apparent gains from deregulation apparently could not be achieved in Britain without the more radical policy of privatization. Privatization then turned out to yield other substantial political benefits as well. So ownership, and in some cases organization, of British network industries increasingly resembled those in the USA, but with innovative regulatory institutions, dependent much more on regulator discretion than the court-based nineteenth-century style still favoured in the United States.

Beginning with British Telecom, a series of huge sell-offs reduced the size of the state sector. Only the Post Office was left in state ownership (detailed sector surveys are to be found in Bishop, Kay, and Mayer 1994 and 1995). Allowing for inflation, the sums raised in privatization only matched the costs of nationalization of 1945–51, suggesting the massive investment in the intervening period was not well spent. A novel form of price regulation and regulatory agencies was introduced to control the newly privatized industries. Although the earlier privatizations entailed no break-up of the monolithic state corporations, regulation soon encouraged more competition (Table 2.3). Electricity supply was actually reorganized so that generation and distribution could be separated. Railway restructuring involved even greater, and more controversial, separation of competing and complementary entities—legal set-up costs amounted to £70 million. Because the state-owned railways had incurred substantial losses, a new form of subsidy was paid to the private train operating companies. In most cases, the subsidies were 'tapered' so that they gradually fell to zero by the end of the operating franchise, while the franchise contract specified that a substantial proportion of the railway services should be continued.

Privatized industries obtained more freedom to pursue commercial policies and therefore could be expected to perform better, judged by that criterion. British Steel would have found the closure of the Ravenscraig plant in Scotland difficult if it had still been state-owned.

2.4.2. General Market-Orientated Industrial Policies

Industrial policies in the 1980s aimed to follow the grain of the market and to reduce expenditure. Liberalization and exhortation fitted this strategy, but ideology and the heavy unemployment of the 1980s sometimes required more intervention and outlays. Expenditures on industrial and regional subsidies by the Department of Trade and Industry peaked at £3.2 billion in 1981/2 but were down to about £1 billion by the early 1990s (Figs. 2.4 and 2.5), a return to the level of 1960 (calculated from Wren 1996). Since prices were rising all the time, the decline in real terms was considerably greater. Policy towards investment, implemented by capital allowances reduced from 100% to 25% after 1984, might be justified on the grounds that such allowances distort resource use. The former policy of making capital cheaper relative to labour might have discouraged employment and so raised unemployment, at least in the short term. The fundamentals of the British economy were given more scope to assert themselves under the new regime.

On the shopfloor, work flexibility and decentralized bargaining became flavours of the decade, supported by legislation reducing the power of trade unions, while training schemes attempted to remedy shortcomings in the match of skills to jobs (Gospel and Palmer 1993). Encouragement of small businesses proved expedient as support for 'enterprise' and as a means of mopping up some of the unprecedentedly heavy unemployment of the 1980s. A loan guarantee scheme and investment grants were targetted at 'Small and Medium Sized' enterprises. The 'Business Links' scheme was intended to provide supporting services for them and to encourage networking relations to capture external economies of scale. At the time of writing the scheme is receiving mixed reviews (Oughton and Whittam 1997).

Active policies to attract foreign investment in manufacturing policies were pursued with success. Between 1993 and 1996 more than 1,300 direct investment projects came to Britain. The largest was announced in 1996 when Korea's largest business, Lucky Goldstar, chose Newport, a former steel and coal town in South Wales as the site for a £1.7 billion electronics plant employing 6,000 people. The British government agreed to pay the Korean firm a subsidy, rumoured to

TABLE 2.4. *Sectoral labour productivity divergences: Six large industrial countries, 1960 and 1987* (% by which service sector value added per employee exceeded manufacturing sector value added per employee at local factor cost)

	1960	1987
USA	−4%	−5%
Japan	−36%	−17%
Germany (W)	+11%	+8%
France	+18%	+11%
Italy	+17%	+5%
UK	+35%	+20%

Source: calculated from OECD 1994: 41, 63.

amount to £200 million, or £30,000 for each job. Foreign direct investment was one element in the recovery of British industrial productivity by the mid-1990s from the slippage of the 1970s. British productivity also by then compared favourably with that of most other European economies. Another probable contributor to this transformation was the considerable improvement in the educational qualifications of top managers (Hannah 1993).

The shift in predominant economic ideas was noticeable in the Competition Act of 1980, which switched attention to 'anti-competitive practices' that might be referred to the Monopolies and Mergers Commission, away from the 'market structure' focus of earlier legislation. Insofar as the policies of the 1980s increased competition, there is reason to believe they improved industrial performance. Analysis of a panel of UK manufacturing companies for the years 1972–86 shows that productivity of firms facing more competition in product markets did grow significantly faster (Nickell 1996). Additional evidence that market-orientated solutions of the 1980s were apparently better at raising industrial efficiency than the highly interventionist policies of the previous generation is the closing of the productivity gap (Table 2.1).

Policy from 1945 to 1981 was effective at diverting resources into manufacturing but not efficient. Services were a much better bet. Table 2.4 shows British service sector productivity in 1960 was extraordinarily high compared with manufacturing. Reducing commitment to lower productivity manufacturing and increasing commitment to services—what happened in the 1980s—made sense. Overall productivity was raised as fewer resources were devoted to resisting market pressures.

Of more dubious merit was the series of government White Papers on 'competitiveness' beginning in 1994 (DTI 1994). These identified ten policy areas that influenced competitiveness: (1) the macroeconomy, (2) education and training, (3) labour market, (4) innovation, (5) management, (6) fair and open markets, (7) finance for business, (8) communications and infrastructure, (9) the commercial framework, and (10) the business of government and public procurement. The wide-ranging nature of industrial policy was highlighted by the 300 measures to improve performance that were proposed. The present study of industrial policy, broadly interpreted, excludes the first and third areas, but is concerned with the others. We prefer the term 'productivity' to 'competitiveness', but acknowledge that the signs of competitiveness may be easier to detect than high productivity, as well as the utility of many forms of competition in raising productivity.

2.4.3. Lacunae in British Industrial Policy

Even though the redirection of economic activity seems to have radically improved the performance of the British economy, the precise reallocation was not necessarily ideal. Infrastructure investment, much of which remained in the state sector, remained a significant contributor to industrial productivity, and was typically neglected during the 1980s. According to one estimate, until 1979 public capital contributed about as much as private capital, around 17% of productivity growth (Lynde and Richmond 1993). During the 1980s the contribution was negligible or even negative. A higher rate of infrastructure investment, sufficient to maintain the public capital contribution at its pre-1980 average, could have increased the growth of labour productivity in UK manufacturing from around 4% to about 4.5% per annum, if these calculations are correct.

In an economy where the industrial use of knowledge was increasingly vital, some commentators found even more ominous the relative decline of Britain's research effort—the proportion of GDP devoted to R & D expenditure lagged well behind the USA and Germany at the end of the 1980s (OECD 1990). Britain's ratio was close to the OECD average in fact, but, as we noted for an earlier period, a large proportion continued to be devoted to defence and the remaining civilian R & D was concentrated in one industry—pharmaceuticals (Oughton 1997). During the 1980s the aerospace industry spent 30% of gross value added on research and development—but only depended on the British government for an average of one-third of sales, thanks to a falling trend over the decade. Wages and salaries per R & D employee were lowest in aerospace, which Hartley, White, and Chaundy (1997) believe refute the claim that defence industry crowds out R & D employment. Pharmaceutical companies, depending much more on sales to a government agency (the NHS), employed a higher proportion of their workforce in R & D (21% compared with 14%) and spent 25% of gross value added on R & D. Unlike much aerospace expenditure, the pharmaceutical industry paid for this outlay itself.

A government initiative established Technical Foresight Programme panels for industrial sectors to identify areas for future research and so to improve innovation. The similarity with the technology-driven programmes 'picking winners' in the 1950s and the 1960s does not increase confidence in the policy's likely success, but at least the sums of money wasted are likely to be smaller.

Probably most fundamental were the skill and learning deficiencies that began with English secondary education (or earlier). English schools, according to Prais

(1995), were far less capable than those in the rest of Western Europe of delivering the basic requirements of industry. The British 'system' was very good for the few and unacceptably poor for the many. Admissions to the elite University of Oxford undergraduate programmes from UK schools make the point clearly. Teenagers from fee-paying schools account for some 5% of the age cohort but for about half the admissions. In 1990/1, 27% of British 16 year olds passed GCSEs in maths and the national language compared with 62% in Germany, 66% in France, and 50% in Japan achieving comparable qualifications (Green and Steedman 1993). With unchanged policies, the longer term consequences for the productivity and competitiveness of increasingly knowledge-based industry are perhaps less favourable than those over the next few years.

2.5. CONCLUSION

National security, new technology, and political pressures, all markedly increased the extent to which the state intervened in industry or established the operating framework by the 1970s, compared with the mid-Victorian years. The very fact that there was a Balfour Committee investigating industrial efficiency and policy in the 1920s shows how the wind had changed after the First World War. Although not concerned with 'picking winners', rationalization by the Bank of England accompanied the shutting off or collapse of export markets in the 1930s. But the greatest policy shift of all occurred for the period of the great boom after 1945, when the powers of central government to direct industry beneficially were overestimated. Nationalization, credit-rationing, import controls, industrial subsidies, and discriminatory taxation, all attained unprecedented levels. Productivity performance relative to other countries deteriorated until the policy reversal of the 1980s. These outcomes are consistent with British mid-nineteenth century pre-eminence being attributable to the liberal market policies pursued then, as is Britain's recovery in the 1980s and 1990s. Those European economies that most closely approached British income per head before the First World War often also adopted liberal policies. The reduction of Britain's lead (in sectors where there was one) by 1914 may be explained by 'catching up', by the diffusion of techniques in a liberal international economy.

Nonetheless there are many institutions and ways of defining rights and obligations consistent with a market economy and some may well encourage better performance than others. In particular those institutions concerned with the generation and transmission of knowledge differ substantially between economies and may explain a good deal of the variations in productivity. There is no reason to suppose that the improved policies of the 1980s, or those in other market-orientated periods, were necessarily ideal. The links between institutions and economic efficiency are still not well understood, and these policies remain among the most controversial determinants of the institutional framework within which business operates.

REFERENCES

ALDCROFT, D. H. (1962). 'The early history and development of export credit insurance in Great Britain 1919–39', *Manchester School*, 30: 69–84.

BAKER, W. J. (1970). *A History of the Marconi Company*. London: Routledge.

Balfour Committee (1928). *Committee on Industry and Trade*. London: HMSO.

BARNETT, C. (1986). *The Audit of War: The Illusion and Reality of Britain as a Great Nation*. London: Macmillan.

BISHOP, M., KAY, J., and MAYER, C. (1994) (eds.). *Privatization and Economic Performance*. Oxford: Oxford University Press.

—— —— —— (1995) (eds.). *The Regulatory Challenge*. Oxford: Oxford University Press.

Board of Trade (1895). *12th Annual Report of the Board of Trade into s131 of the Bankruptcy Act of 1883*. London: HMSO.

BOEHM, K. (1967). *The British Patent System*. Cambridge: Cambridge University Press.

BROADBERRY, S. (1994). 'Technological leadership and productivity leadership in manufacturing since the Industrial Revolution: Implications for the convergence debate'. *Economic Journal*, 104: 291–302.

—— and CRAFTS, N. F. R. (1990). 'Explaining Anglo-American productivity differences in the mid-twentieth century'. *Oxford Bulletin of Economics and Statistics*, 52: 375–402.

—— —— (1992*a*). 'Britain's productivity gap in the 1930s: Some neglected factors'. *Journal of Economic History*, 52: 531–58.

—— —— (1992*b*). 'British industrial policy and performance in the early postwar period'. Dept of Economics Working Paper. University of Warwick.

—— and WAGNER, K. (1996). 'Human capital and productivity in manufacturing during the twentieth century: Britain, Germany and the United States', in Bart van Ark and N. F. R. Crafts (eds.), *Quantitative Aspects of Post-War European Economic Growth*. Cambridge: Cambridge University Press.

CAVES, R. E. (1968). 'Market organization, performance and public policy', in R. E. Caves (ed.), *Britain's Economic Prospects*. London: Allen & Unwin.

CHANDLER, A. (1990). *Scale and Scope*. Cambridge, Mass.: Belknap Press.

CHICK, M. (1998). *Industrial Policy in Britain 1945–1951: Economic Planning, Nationalisation and the Labour Governments*. Cambridge: Cambridge University Press.

CIPOLLA, C. M. (1965). *The Rise of Literacy in the West*. Harmondsworth: Penguin.

COOPEY, R., and CLARKE, D. (1995). *3i: Fifty Years Investing in Industry*. Oxford and New York: Oxford University Press.

COTTRELL, P. L. (1980). *Industrial Finance 1830–1914*. London: Methuen.

DAVIES, S. W., and CAVES, R. E. (1987). *Britain's Productivity Gap*. Cambridge: Cambridge University Press.

DEA (Department of Economic Affairs) (1965). *The National Plan*. Cmnd 2764. London: HMSO.

DOBBIN, F. (1994). *Forging Industrial Policy: The United States, Britain and France in the Railway Age*. Cambridge: Cambridge University Press.

DTI (Department of Trade and Industry) (1994). *Competitiveness*. White Paper, Cmd 2563. London: HMSO.

EDGERTON, D. E. H. (1991). *England and the Aeroplane: An Essay on a Militant and Technological Nation*. London: Macmillan.

—— (1996). *Science, Technology and the British Industrial 'Decline' 1870–1970*. Cambridge: Cambridge University Press.

—— and HORROCKS, S. M. (1994). 'British industrial research and development before 1945'. *Economic History Review*, 47/2: 213–38.

ERGAS, H. (1992). 'A future for mission-oriented industrial policies? A critical review of developments in Europe'. OECD, unpublished.

FOREMAN-PECK, J. S. (1990). 'The 1856 Companies Act and the birth and death of firms', in P. Jobert and M. Moss (eds.), *The Birth and Death of Companies: An Historical Perspective*. Carnforth, Lancs.: Parthenon.

—— and HAMMOND, C. J. (1997). 'Variable costs and the visible hand: The re-regulation of electricity supply 1932–37'. *Economica*, 64: 15–30.

—— and MILLWARD, R. (1994). *Public and Private Ownership of Industry in Britain 1820–1980*. Oxford: Clarendon Press.

—— BOWDEN, S., and MCKINLAY, A. (1995). *The Motor Industry*. Manchester: Manchester University Press.

FOSTER, C. D. (1992). *Privatisation and Public Ownership and the Regulation of Natural Monopoly*. Oxford: Blackwells.

FREYER, T. (1992). *Regulating Big Business: Antitrust in Great Britain and America 1880–1990*. Cambridge: Cambridge University Press.

GEORGE, K. D. (1971). *Industrial Organization: Competition Growth and Structural Change in Britain*. London: George Allen and Unwin.

GEROSKI, P. A., and JACQUEMIN, A. (1988). 'The persistence of profits: A European comparison'. *Economic Journal*, 98: 375–89.

GOLLAN, J. (1937). *Youth in British Industry*. London: Gollancz.

GOSPEL, H., and PALMER, G. (1993). *British Industrial Relations*, 2nd edn. London: Routledge.

GREASLEY, D. (1995). 'The coal industry: Images and realities on the road to nationalization', in R. Millward and J. Singleton (eds.), *The Political Economy of Nationalization in Britain 1920–1950*. Cambridge: Cambridge University Press.

GREEN, A., and STEEDMAN, H. (1993). 'Educational provision, educational attainment and the needs of industry: A review of research in Germany, France, Japan, USA and Britain'. *National Institute Economic Review*, Report Series no. 5.

GRIBBIN, J., and UTTON, N. A. (1986). 'The treatment of dominant firms in UK competition legislation', in H. W. De Jong and W. G. Shepherd (eds.), *Mainstreams in Industrial Organisation*. Dordecht: Kluwen Academic Publishers.

GRINDLEY, P. (1987). 'System X: The failure of procurement'. Centre for Business Strategy, London Business School Working Paper, 29.

HAGUE, D., and WILKINSON, G. (1983). *The IRC: An Experiment in Industrial Intervention*. London: George Allen and Unwin.

HANNAH, L. (1979). *Electricity Before Nationalization*. London: Macmillan.

—— (1993). 'Cultural determinants of economic performance: An experiment in measuring human capital flows', in G. D. Snooks (ed.), *Historical Analysis in Economics*. London and New York: Routledge.

—— (1994a). 'Joint stock company concentration and the state'. Unpublished.

—— (1994b). 'The economic consequences of state ownership of industry 1945–1990', in R. Floud and D. N. McCloskey (eds.), *The Economic History of Britain since 1700*, 2nd edn. Vol. iii. Cambridge: Cambridge University Press.

—— (1995). 'Effects of monopoly and credit rationing in UK retail banking 1945–1979 and their elimination 1980–1993'. Unpublished.

HARTLEY, K. R., WHITE, J., and CHAUNDY, D. (1997). 'Government and industry performance: A comparative study'. *Applied Economics*, 29: 1227–37.

HAYWARD, J. (1995). *Industrial Enterprise and European Integration: From National to International Champions in Western Europe*. Oxford: Oxford University Press.

HAYWARD, K. (1983). *Government and British Civil Aerospace: A Case Study in Post-War Technology Policy*. Manchester: Manchester University Press.

HENDRY, J. (1989). *Innovating for Failure: Government Policy and the Early British Computer Industry*. Cambridge, Mass.: MIT Press.

JOHNSON, C. (1982). *MITI and the Japanese Miracle: The Growth of Industrial Policy 1925–1975*. Stanford, Calif.: Stanford University Press.

KENNEDY, P. (1982). *The Rise of the Anglo-German Antagonism 1860–1914*. London: Allen and Unwin.

LYNDE, C., and RICHMOND, J. (1993). 'Public capital and long-run costs in UK manufacturing'. *Economic Journal*, 103: 880–93.

LYTHE, P. J. (1995). 'The changing role of government in British civil air transport 1919–49', in R. Millward and J. Singleton (eds.), *The Political Economy of Nationalisation in Britain 1920–1950*. Cambridge: Cambridge University Press.

MADDISON, A. (1989). *The World Economy in the 20th Century*. Paris: OECD.

MARKHAM, L. V. (1995). *Victorian Insolvency: Bankruptcy, Imprisonment for Debt and Company Winding-up in Nineteenth Century England*. Oxford: Clarendon Press.

MARRISON, A. (1996). *British Business and Protection 1903–1932*. Oxford: Clarendon Press.

MAYER, C. (1988). 'New issues in corporate finance'. *European Economic Review*, 32: 1–17.

MILLWARD, R., and SINGLETON, J. (1995). *The Political Economy of Nationalisation in Britain 1920–1950*. Cambridge: Cambridge University Press.

MILWARD, A. (1992). *The European Rescue of the Nation State*. London: Routledge.

—— and BRENNAN, G. (1996). *Britain's Place in the World: A Historical Enquiry into Import Controls 1945–1960*. London: Routledge.

MITCHELL, B. R. (1982). *European Historical Statistics 1750–1980*. London: Macmillan.

MOORE, B., RHODES, J., and TYLER, P. (1986). *The Effects of Government Regional Economic Policy*. Department of Trade and Industry. London: HMSO.

MOWERY, D. C., and ROSENBERG, N. (1989). *Technology and the Pursuit of Economic Growth*. New York: Cambridge University Press.

NABSETH, L., and RAY, G. F. (1974). *The Diffusion of New Industrial Processes*. Cambridge: Cambridge University Press.

NAPIER, C. (1995). 'The history of financial reporting in the UK', in P. Walton (ed.), *European Financial Reporting: A History*. London: London Academic Press.

NEDC (National Economic Development Council) (1963). *Growth of the United Kingdom to 1966*. London: HMSO.

NICKELL, S. J. (1996). 'Competition and corporate performance'. *Journal of Political Economy*, 104/4: 724–45.

NYE, J. V. (1991). 'The myth of free-trade Britain and fortress France: Tariffs and trade in the nineteenth century'. *Journal of Economic History*, 51: 23–46.

OECD (1990). *Main Technology Indicators*. Paris: OECD.

—— (1994). *Economic Outlook, June*. Paris: OECD.

O'MAHONY, M., and WAGNER, K. (1994). 'Changing fortunes: An industry study of British and German productivity growth over three decades'. Report Series no. 7, National Institute of Economic and Social Research. London.

OUGHTON, C. (1997). 'Competitiveness policy in the 1990s'. *Economic Journal*, Sept.: 1406–1503.

—— and WHITTAM, G. (1997). 'Competition and cooperation in the small firms sector'. *Scottish Journal of Political Economy*, 44: 1–30.

PEP (Political and Economic Planning) (1935*a*). *Report on Electricity Supply*. London: PEP.

—— (1935*b*). *Entry to Industry*. London: PEP.

POLLARD, S. (1989). *Britain's Prime and Britain's Decline*. London: Edward Arnold.

PRAIS, S. J. (1976). *The Evolution of Giant Firms in Britain*. Cambridge: Cambridge University Press.

—— (1993). 'Economic performance and education: The nature of Britain's deficiencies'. NIESR Discussion Paper, 52.

—— (1995). *Productivity Education and Training: An International Perspective*. Cambridge: Cambridge University Press.

REED, P. (1992). 'The British chemical industry and the indigo trade'. *British Journal for the History of Science*, 25: 113–25.

ROWLEY, C. K., and YARROW, G. K. (1981). 'Property rights, regulation and public enterprise: The case of the British steel industry 1957–1975'. *International Review of Law and Economics*, 1: 63–96.

ROWTHORN, R. E., and WELLS, J. R. (1987). *De-Industrialisation and Foreign Trade*. Cambridge: Cambridge University Press.

Royal Commission (1886). *On the Depression in Trade and Industry*, Parl.P., 23/ Cmnd. 4893.

SANDERSON, M. (1987). *Educational Opportunity and Social Change in England*. London: Faber and Faber.

—— (1994). *The Missing Stratum: Technical School Education in England 1900–1990s*. London: Athlone Press.

SHANNON, H. A. (1932). 'The first five thousand limited companies and their duration'. *Economic History*, 2: 396–424.

—— (1933). 'The limited liability companies of 1886–1893'. *Economic History Review*, 4.

SHONFIELD, A. (1965). *Modern Capitalism: The Changing Balance of Public and Private Power*. London: Oxford University Press.

SINGLETON, J. (1995). 'Labour, the Conservatives and nationalization', in R. Millward and J. Singleton (eds.), *The Political Economy of Nationalization in Britain 1920–1950*. Cambridge: Cambridge University Press.

SULLIVAN, R. J. (1994). 'Estimates of the value of patent rights in Great Britain and Ireland 1852–1876'. *Economica*, 61: 37–58.

SUPPLE, B. (1988). 'The political economy of demoralisation'. *Economic History Review*, 566–91.

THOMAS, L. G., III (1994). 'Implicit industrial policy: The triumph of Britain and the failure of France in global pharmaceuticals'. *Industrial and Corporate Change*, 3/2: 451–90.

THOMAS, M. (1983). 'Rearmament and economic recovery in the late 1930s'. *Economic History Review*, 552–79.

TOMLINSON, J. (1994). *Government and the Enterprise since 1900: The Changing Problem of Efficiency*. Oxford: Clarendon Press.

TOMLINSON, M. (1997). 'The contribution of services to manufacturing industry: Beyond the de-industrialisation debate'. CRIC Discussion Paper, no. 5. University of Manchester.

VON MAYENBERG, D. (1996). *Schule, Bewfsschule, Arbeitsmarkt: Die Englische Debatte um die Elementarschulreform 1914–1939*. Frankfurt am Main: Peter Lang.

WALSHE, J. (1991). 'Industrial Organization and Policy', in N. F. R. Crafts and N. Woodward (eds.), *The British Economy since 1945*. Oxford: Oxford University Press.

WILKS, S. (1988). *Industrial Policy and the Motor Industry*. Manchester: Manchester University Press.

WILLIAMS, G. (1957). *Recruitment to Skilled Trades*. London: Routledge & Kegan Paul.

—— (1963). *Apprenticeship in Europe: The Lessons for Britain*. London: Chapman and Hall.

Wilson Committee (1980). *Committee to Review the Functioning of Financial Institutions*. London: HMSO.

WILSON, J. F. (1988). *Ferranti and the British Electrical Industry 1864–1930*. Manchester: Manchester University Press.

WREN, C. (1996). 'Gross expenditure on UK industrial assistance: A research note'. *Scottish Journal of Political Economy*, 113–26.

3

France: The Idiosyncrasies of Volontarisme

University of Montpellier

3.1. THE MATRIX OF COLBERTISM

The French ordinarily claim precedence in inventing the concept of industrial policy. The roots of dirigisme, the control by the political authority of the development of the national economy, can be traced back to Jean-Baptiste Colbert, Louis XIV's eminent minister. Henceforth national economics, the idea that 'national economic strength is measured by productive capacity and that productive capacity can be increased by state aid' (Clough 1939: 324) permeated French political and economic life. The imperative for the active involvement of the state in the deployment of industrial potential may have originated with the mercantilist theories of Montchrestien and Richelieu. Certainly the emphasis on national defence had mercantilist inspirations. But, as Charles W. Cole emphasized, the ambition of Colbertism was also to attain full employment—to stave off mass poverty, as well as strengthen national industrial champions, necessary for national *grandeur*.

In the nineteenth century, Colbert's ambitions were revived by the Saint-Simonian ideology adopted by Napoléon III in his effort to boost French industrial fortunes. Unlike mercantilism, however, St Simonianism advocated free trade and is usually credited with having sustained the major industrial spurt of the century. Under the parliamentary regime established after the Franco-Prussian war of 1870–1, relations between the business community and politicians became more intricate. A restrained rate of economic growth made entrepreneurs more dependent on the political decision-makers. Thus, the Colbertist ambition never entirely left the corridors of French political power until it again became obvious under President De Gaulle.

One way of assessing the changing scope of the French government's involvement in industry is by observing the trends of the subsidies to government expenditure ratio over the long term (Figure 3.1). But interpretations of the data can differ, even in their basic outlines. One can stress the secular rise of the trend from about 12–15% in the 1870s to 25–30% in the 1970s (Delorme and André 1981: 727).[1] In such a perspective, the role assigned to the peaks observable in

---

[1] In the compilation, the author has aggregated all economic subsidies, therefore including agricultural as well as commercial subsidies. Industrial subsidies proper represented on average half of the total over the last century.

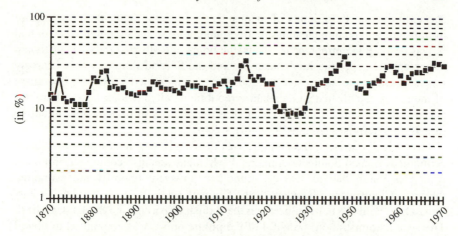

FIG. 3.1. Proportion of government subsidies to total expenditure, 1870–1970
Source: Fontvieille 1976: appendix.

the aftermath of wars (especially the two world wars) is particularly prominent. Or one can, alternatively, sustain the view of the overall stability across the century, arguing as the *école de la régulation* has, that certain types of public subsidies represent in fact transfers of costs from the private to the public sector (Fontvieille 1976). Far from moving towards a *Sozialmarktwirtschaft*, the French economy would have thus remained intrinsically 'capitalist'.

In both views, nevertheless, the positive correlation observed between the growth of public expenditure and subsidies, and economic performance, has been interpreted as a complete vindication of government intervention, especially for the post-1945 period.

As many historians have stressed, the *fil rouge* for such intervention goes back into the nineteenth century. The first section examines the selective measures taken by the Third Republic's governments that would qualify today as industrial policy. Some of them were to leave an enduring legacy. For the sake of clarity, the post-World War II experience is examined in the light of the various policy instruments used by successive governments.

3.2. INDUSTRIAL POLICY UNDER THE THIRD REPUBLIC

The Third Republic inherited from its predecessors an arsenal, albeit limited, of public policy tools designed to help government officials promote, encourage or else deter industrial ventures. Direct interventions in the country's industry by France's longest-lasting regime since the Revolution can hardly be equated with the concept of industrial policy as we know it today. During this period some politicians supported the idea of the need for the state to give impetus to industrial projects; but treasury officials usually put a break—though not always successfully—on these bouts of inconsiderate spending. Outside infrastructure in transport and communications, entrepreneurship, so the common wisdom had it, was best left to entrepreneurs. Thus, the bouts of Colbertist industrial activism —perceptible under the July Monarchy and the Second Empire—were scarcely repeated under the successive regime. But the ingrained economic liberalism of the newly established parliamentary republic entailed neither laissez-faire nor perfect competition: 'it merely resulted in the abdication of economic initiative to private enterprise' (Adam 1989: 48).

Ideologically at least, the republic was decisively non-interventionist: liberal economists shaped dominant opinions. Parliament was also committed to liberal principles but it had to also accommodate powerful regional and economic interests. Clemenceau (President of the Council 1906–9) saw it the duty of Parliament to 'hold the balance between the industrial barons and the landed ones'. The state administration, watchful of the public purse, was committed to liberal ways and neutrality in economic affairs. Politicians and bureaucrats alike saw it their duty to preserve what they perceived as a 'balanced economy' where agriculture should play an important role and which should aim at providing for the basic needs of the population. Méline, the promoter of the protectionist reform of 1892 himself spoke of a 'static economy' and advocated, as the title of one of his books makes clear, '*le retour à la terre*'. The Radicals who gained control of the House in 1898 emphasized the anti-big business bias already present under the Opportunists' administration and solidified what became one of the tenets of economic policy for fifty years: the government should seek to avoid dramatic economic changes and to cushion, subsidize, or else salvage hard-pressed activities.

This clear preference expressed in speech and deed by political decision-makers of the period for 'stability' as opposed to 'growth' has lent them to accusations of having in fact deliberately 'retarded' the process of industrialization and modernization. Alfred Sauvy coined the expression of 'Malthusianism' to describe the consensus among entrepreneurs, politicians, and civil servants to maintain the status quo. Later, Stanley Hoffmann and Michel Crozier dissected the ideology of the 'stalemate society'. Government activism after 1945, intent on promoting economic growth, seems with hindsight to justify the accusations against the political leaders of the Third Republic.

3.2.1. *Erratic Support for Industry*

If anything, the regime lacked the resources necessary for the task of launching or supporting large-scale industrial projects. Contemporary and more recent critics have pointed to the inadequacy of the tax system which failed to provide the right incentives to industrial entrepreneurs. New ventures and mergers were typically discouraged—by legislation if necessary. Indirect taxation inherited from the Revolutionary period put a brake on consumption and grew in importance throughout the period. After the introduction of the income tax in 1916 and of

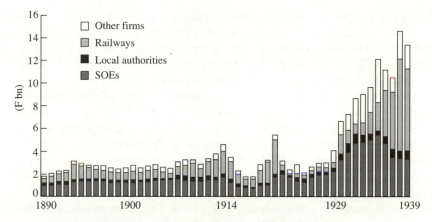

FIG. 3.2. Distribution of government industrial subsidies, 1890–1940
Source: Fontvieille 1976: table xlii.

the turnover tax in 1919, the government was able to increase its revenues by 50%. Furthermore, from its beginnings, the Republic was encumbered by an unusually heavy debt burden. The Franco-Prussian war of 1870 had multiplied it by a factor of three to F 33 billion and indebtedness showed no sign of abating up to 1913.[2] By that date interest payments represented 30% of the budget compared to 20% in the UK and 10% in Germany (Lévy-Leboyer, Lescure, and Straus 1991: 250). After the First World War, the servicing of the huge debt accumulated in wartime as well as the priorities of reconstruction limited the freedom of action of the government.

A narrow tax base as well as a heavy debt burden therefore restrained public spending. Between 1890 and 1939, the government typically devoted between 6.2 and 8.6% of its budget to economic programmes. Most of it was used to pay salaries of public servants and only 5% of the total contributed to national capital formation. An independent Ministry of Commerce and Industry had been set up in 1886 which, with a F 350 million annual endowment, had the responsibility for promoting French exports, organizing international exhibitions, supervising the Chambers of Commerce, and selecting businessmen for awards and medals. Commercial policy in fact depended on the all-powerful Ministry of Finances while the Ministry of Public Works was in charge of implementing the mining code and of regulating utilities and transport. The government could moreover consult the *Conseil des Arts et Manufactures* for advice and relied on the *Conseil d'État* for drafting new legislation and settling disputes.

Under these circumstances, government support to industrial firms could only be superficial and uncoordinated. However insignificant as a percentage of GDP (less than 1%), industrial subsidies experienced a long-term rise. According to

---

[2] Between 1871 and 1873 alone the government 'purged' Frenchmen's savings to the level of F 7.9 billion, doubling the servicing of the debt (most of it short term) to F 865 million per annum from 1874 onwards.

Fontvieille (1976) the advances of budget spending tended to be countercyclical. Several schemes (*Grands travaux*) increased transfers to industry in response to deteriorating business conditions: after the Freycinet plan at the onset of the Great Depression (1878–82), the Baudin Plan after the downturn of the business cycle in 1903 and during the worldwide depression of the 1930s.

The First World War brought about a renewed advance of government intervention in industry. The German invasion of 1914 had deprived France of 60% of its iron and steel production capacity, 30% of its Martin furnaces as well as much of its textile mills. This amputation made it somewhat easier for the government to extend controls. But the decisive steps towards organized production were not taken until 1916: it was only gradually that the liberal republic eased towards *dirigisme*. Wartime governments concentrated their efforts on two objects: imports (obviously substitutes had to be found for missing raw materials and intermediate goods) and armament supply.

Arsenals and firms already under contract proved inadequate to satisfy wartime needs. In July 1915, a year after the beginning of the war, the government transferred massive resources to stimulate output of artillery and small arms (Jèze 1927: 160). The architects of France's wartime 'rearmament' were Albert Thomas, a 'Socialist *Normalien* turned munition-maker' (Kuisel 1981) and Etienne Clémentel who transformed the Ministry of Commerce into the 'first real ministry of national economy', a laboratory for post-war economic planning. As such, the latter was in charge of organizing the requisition of the merchant fleet, the prohibition of manufacturing exports, the control over imports and the centralization of purchasing and distribution of scarce supplies (Godfrey 1974).

Clémentel and his directors (among whom was Jean Monnet) implemented industrial wartime mobilization with two main policy instruments. The first was the enforcement of strict import regulations which were ultimately coordinated for strategic goods by the interallied purchasing boards (where Monnet convinced himself of the necessity of European unity). When the American expeditionary force landed in France in the Spring of 1918, it was jointly armed by the British armament industry (providing heavy guns and armoured vehicles) and its French counterpart (providing ammunition and light artillery). The second instrument was the organization of production under the supervision of the pre-war cartels —quite a bold move for an avowed Socialist. The Consortiums, created in March 1917, were made single purchasing agents for major raw materials; they grouped importers and manufacturers who submitted together lists of required materials to the Ministry of Commerce (MoC). MoC officials acted as intermediaries to purchase and ship the desired commodities. The Consortiums then paid for shipment and freight and distributed the goods to their members at a price fixed by the government. Profits were limited to a 6% return (Plutino 1969). By early 1918, consortiums were established for about every major raw material and many manufactured products and virtually all branches of manufacturing were under government control. In spite of Clémentel's and Thomas's ambitions there is little evidence that the consortiums, beyond successfully channelling resources, advanced either the concentration or modernization of French industry. As is often the case in similar circumstances this arrangement gave the illusion to industrialists that they could make good from the windfall brought about by the war: they substituted their products for German exporters and built new capacity, exploited shortages and maximized profits at consumers' and taxpayers' expense (Godfrey 1987).

After the first war's extravaganza (military operations—excluding destruction —cost a staggering F 150 billion—equivalent to 385% of pre-war GNP), return to normality and retrenchment of expenditures were the order of the day. But for all the proclamations, the restoration of the pristine 'liberal' order did not occur. Again expediency imposed hard choices.

Debt repayments took precedence and, until the de facto devaluation of 1926, pre-empted any advance in government intervention. Reconstruction, spanning over a decade, took place so as to rebuild industrial structures to their pre-war standard (Delorme and André 1981: 229). In 1921, expenditure on trade and industry increased to 6.5% of budget spending, to 10% on transport, and 5% on housing. Ten years later, in 1931, 7,700 factories had been rebuilt (out of 9,330 destroyed), 300 minepits had been recovered, 61,000 km of roads, more than half a million homes, and 250,000 farm buildings (Ogburn and Jaffé 1929: 180). Because of the initial guidelines, structural dispersal and decentralization still dominated the French industrial landscape. France at the end of the 1920s was still characterized by '*la poussière industrielle*'. Only in the 1930s was the government ready to leave free rein to cartels and ententes. The role of the state had been more conservatory than innovative, so that whatever industrial renovation may have occurred in the 1920s, did so in private rather than public companies.

The Popular Front (1936–8) was the first manifestation of the public service elite's new-found commitment to 'planism' and strategic government intervention. For the first time US industry was presented as a model to emulate and many 'young turks' of rationalization crossed the Atlantic for inspiration. But inertia took its toll and instead of bold pro-growth measures, traditional recipes prevailed first up to 1935 in the context of a deflationary policy and then after 1936 under a heavy countercyclical expansionary strategy that ultimately led to a return of conventional fiscal rigour.

On repeated occasions, successive governments fell back on the politically safer practice of scattering subsidies, budget permitting. After 1936 subsidies were thus 'freely extended to an assortment of petitioners ranging from civil servants to shipbuilders' (Kuisel 1981: 96). Léon Blum's 'New Deal' amounted in this respect to the multiplication of trade and industry subsidies by a factor of nine (in an endemic inflationary context though). An Act passed in the summer of 1936 prescribed temporary financial assistance to businesses in difficulty to fend off closures.[3] Payment facilities were extended through the *Caisse des Dépôts* who could turn to the *Banque de France* which was partly nationalized. Together with

---

[3] This was the Treasury's rationale when it decided to salvage Citroën in 1934.

the *Caisse Nationale des Marchés de l'État*, it offered subsidized loans and official guarantees.

3.2.2. Improving Infrastructure

On repeated occasions, the government used public works programmes as a lever to raise demand for 'key' industries. Directly involving building and construction firms, such ventures had repercussions on upstream producers of semi-finished goods, especially steelmakers and the engineering industry.

The first of these was the *Plan Freycinet* which set a pattern for successive schemes. Voted in 1879, it originally assigned F 4 billion to finance transport infrastructure: three-quarters were allocated to the building of the 'secondary' railway network and the remainder to navigable rivers, canals, and ports. Following the financial crash of 1882, the Plan had to be discontinued. At this date its cost had already doubled. The government's ambition had been to make railway transport a universal service, accessible all over French territory. But, in addition to crowding out other forms of private investment for several years, the Plan tended to stimulate traditionally organized activities (foundries, shipyards, and sawmills) at the expense of the newer industries and to increase dramatically the state's indebtedness. The public debt had risen to 125% of GNP (or 13% of private wealth) by 1890 and remained around this mark until the outbreak of the first war (Lévy-Leboyer, Lescure, and Straus 1991: 255). It has been argued also, that the public works strategy served as a delaying tactic—albeit unavowed—for the introduction of welfare measures for the benefit of the industrial working classes (as in contemporary Germany and in the UK). The government seemingly preferred to subsidize France's myriad of small entrepreneurs rather than a still peripheral minority (hence the industrial activism of the working-class movement in the *Belle Epoque*).

Twenty years later in 1903, the *Plan Baudin* took the same path. Again, the initiative was conceived as a countercyclical policy measure, this time towards the end of the Great Depression. In addition to establishing the first trans-Alpine connection through the Mont-Cenis as well as several others in Algeria (then integrated with the Republic), it extended the home network by a further 10% to 40,000 kms. The government first concluded 'Conventions' in which it promised to insure all the 'excess expenses' for the building of local lines, Delorme and André (1981) reckon, to the extent of 90% of all new investment, in exchange for an obligation by companies to standardize passenger fares and freight charges. The interest guarantee clause alone represented on average an annual F 50 million subsidy. But soon the government took over the establishment and management of a public railway network.[4] The embryonic state network, estab-

---

[4] It has been rightly noted that from the beginning, railway building and operation was a civil service business given the interest lawmakers gave to this innovation: ever since the 1842 convention, government officials 'designed the trunk line, built the roadbeds, insured dividends for investors, controlled rates and shared in overall management' (Kuisel 1981: 9).

lished in 1878, was extended by the purchase, in 1908, of the *Compagnie de l'Ouest*, one of the six major national operators. Together these measures allowed for the large and rich companies (PLM, Compagnie du Nord) to maintain levels of efficiency and profitability comparable to those of their Continental counterparts, but inferior to the British and American. By contrast, the perceptible over-capacity had detrimental effects on the management of others and generated diseconomies, the financial burden of which became heavier as time went by. By 1908 average gross receipts per km represented only 54% of the British and 70% of the German levels—the lag in terms of net product being even larger (Lévy-Leboyer, Lescure, and Straus 1991: 160).

The network extension yielded mixed fortunes for the supplying industries as well. Rail manufacturers enjoyed a reprieve, but the supply of rolling stock slipped partially into the hands of foreigners: 30% of engines by 1906 (Crouzet 1977: 200). Paradoxically, the countercyclical timing of government's handouts inevitably caught mechanical engineering firms as their capacity had contracted. Furthermore, the Third Republic's railway policy seems to have slowed down urbanization by making it viable for villagers to remain in the countryside (Lévy-Leboyer, Lescure, and Straus 1991: 161). The building of railway overcapacity thus had far-reaching effects on the path of economic development as a whole.

A similar conservative role on the part of the state is perceptible in water transport. The merchant marine received some 56% of the subsidies throughout the period after 1882. The aim of such an intervention was to preserve jobs on the canals and in the ports and its rationale was the compensation paid by the government for insuring mail carrying to unprofitable destinations. By 1913 all major Atlantic and Mediterranean companies (the *Messageries Maritimes*, *Compagnies Générale Transatlantique*, *Sud-Atlantique*, and *Fraissinet*) would have gone bankrupt without these subsidies. There again such financial support had negative effects: for instance 'it allowed more sailing than steam ships to be built up to as late as 1904' (Delorme and André 1981: 150).

In the field of public utilities the central government offered essentially the regulatory framework for the building of the networks. Two ministerial decrees in 1882 and 1889 had established the norms for water canalization and lighting, respectively. The Berthelot Act of 1906 drafted the network for the electricity supply. The government's financial participation in these ventures was minimal. They were almost entirely supported by the municipalities; government subsidies actually decreased over the whole period in nominal, as in actual, terms (see Figure 3.2).

Only in communications was the government directly involved. As in the case of the telegraph in 1850, the telephone companies were nationalized in 1889. The rationale for such intervention had more to do with national defence than with provision of universal public service. Obsessed with the recurrence of revolutionary movements and coups, officials saw the 'propagation of news' as as dangerous as the 'transport of explosives'. State management of the telephone service resulted in inadequate provision in response to needs. For lack of investment, the network remained for a long time (indeed up to the 1970s) under-developed in comparison to neighbouring countries (Foreman-Peck 1989). Up to 1939, it never reached the dimensions that would have made the telephone a profitable activity (Dormois 1992: 501–2) and indeed its service, like that of the telegraph, was in fact run thanks to transfers drawn on the profits of their twin activity, the postal service. For Henri Fayol, an engineer, the telephone service was 'living proof of the government's incompetence in industrial matters' (Fayol 1921).

World War I destructions made it if anything more imperative for the government to upgrade, at least temporarily, its support to transport and other infrastructure and extend its control over public utilities. The railways, already targetted for nationalization by the mainstream labour unions, faced in the postwar, an aggravated situation. Some companies, already threatened by bankruptcy before the war, faced awesome reconstruction costs. The Act of 1919 provided for the latter. The *Compagnie du Nord* and the *Compagnie de l'Est* received the bulk of state aid for rebuilding tracks and stations; the pre-war rolling stock was reconstituted. The Alsatian network was incorporated in the State Railways. Once the network could again operate normally, the annual flow of subsidies did not stop. The government tried as a first step to foster the rationalization of management by creating a *Fonds Commun* which paid compensations to loss-making companies. But overcapacity and competition from the nascent trucking industry were taking a heavier and heavier toll. In order to even out profits and costs, the government set up the *Conseil Supérieur des Chemins de Fer* to standardize fares and coordinate implementation of technological improvements. But very soon, the Treasury had to pick up the companies' heaviest debts; only in 1926 and 1928–9 did the private networks run a surplus. These measures, however, did not resolve the railway companies' financial situation which had continued to amass deficits while bondholders still received handsome dividends.

In the name of public interest and national security, aircraft manufacturers Latécoère, Breguet, and Farman likewise enjoyed public subsidies to the level of 70–90% of their receipts on the pioneering connections between Toulouse and national destinations.

In the field of public utilities steps were taken in the direction of state-managed monopolies. Unwilling to take the whole energy sector into their own hands, conservative governments of the 1920s created a new legal business structure: the mixed company or *Société d'Économie Mixte*. Hitherto, the state had traditionally relied on the 'concession' system. This was not abolished, just completed by a financial stake in the newly established firms. This form of organization was applied to a number of former consortiums, the mining sector, confiscated German industrial interests in Alsace-Lorraine, and the public utilities. In electricity a number of companies were created for the production of hydroelectricity (*Compagnie Nationale du Rhône* and *Compagnie d'Énergie Électrique de la Moyenne Dordogne*) in 1921 and 1928, respectively, in addition to a soon monopolistic high-voltage transport licensee, the *Société de Trans-*

port de l'Énergie Électrique. Likewise for petroleum, two initiatives moved civil service engineers into the arena of industrial management. The *Compagnie Française des Pétrole* grew out of the confiscated German shares of the Turkish Petroleum Company in 1924. In 1927 and 1928 oil refining and distribution fell to the *Compagnie Française de Raffinage* and the *Compagnie Navale des Pétroles* in which the government held a 25% share of the capital. By 1939 they provided 88% of the country's needs. Other mixed company creations included former German concerns in Alsace, especially the *Compagnie des Mines de Potasses d'Alsace* for potash and the *Office National Industriel de l'Azote* for nitrogen. The government's management of reconstruction tended therefore to confirm the status quo, solidify the stronghold of traditional industries and protect existing structures.

After the return of financial and monetary stability, the government, under an avowed modernizer, André Tardieu, launched in 1929 the first of a series of public works programmes. This first post-war plan, designed on the model of its pre-war predecessors and grandly named 'Plan of National Retooling', intended to earmark 3% of foreseeable budget surpluses to the replacement of 'national equipment'. Thus, when it was passed in 1928, the government had allocated F 5 billion over a period of five years to invest in industrial infrastructure. Unfortunately, it was to peter out after the wave of bankruptcies brought forth by the 1931 slump. Several proposals were drafted to replace this programme, most notably by PMs Daladier in 1933 and 1938 and Blum in 1936. Of the four plans which were eventually passed by Parliament, none was completed. Up to 1935, a bare F 7 billion was spent and after 1936 another 10 billion, the bulk of which, however, went to the rearmament effort. The Blum plan of April 1936, allegedly modelled on FDR's NRA, was downgraded from F 20 billion to 4 billion. After much haggling between deputies and ministers, the funds were distributed among different departments: 38% went to public infrastructure, 18% to the agricultural sector (mainly for price support), 18% to technical training, 15% to health services, and 7% to public utilities. The cumulated effects of these plans were nevertheless limited. They hardly dampened unemployment—official unemployment[5] soared from 0.25 to 0.85 million from 1930 to 1936. Governments, even the left-wing government of the Popular Front, had been unable or unwilling to risk the further unbalancing of already retrenched public expenditure by running a full-scale deficit-spending policy (Saly 1980: 741).

A series of nationalizations in transport came as the natural development of the long-term investment of the state in this sector. With the Reform of 1933, the government had forced a merger between the *Chemin de Fer d'Orléans* and the *Compagnie du Midi* and imposed government representatives in all companies' boards of administrators. It decided in 1937 the nationalization of the five remaining railway companies and their merger into the state railways. For financial reasons, the compensations to shareholders were to be paid at annual

---

[5] i.e. subsidized, which represented only a fraction of total unemployment.

intervals so as not to destabilize the budget. Furthermore, civil service engineers were to take over control of the companies gradually. The government pledged to keep subsidizing equipment in exchange for a *droit de regard* on prices. In air transport, after the receivership of the *Aéropostale* in 1930, the government merged the more heavily subsidized companies into a new state company, Air France, in 1933 and turned the remaining private two (*Air Bleu* and *Air Transatlantique*) into mixed companies with an overwhelming share majority. A similar solution was adopted in maritime transport with the CGT and the energy sector. The state reinforced its technical and financial participation in coal mining and oil refining by the creation of the *Régie Autonome des Pétroles*. As of 1935, a government licence was mandatory to produce electrical power, thereby granting the existing SEMs a virtually monopoly on production. Thus 'a combination of widening government intervention and resurgent cartelisation all but obliterated competition in an economy not known for its vigorous market' (Kuisel 1981: 94).

3.2.3. *The Industrial Military Complex*

As successor to the Colbertist and Napoleonic tradition, the Third Republic was also responsible for managing industrial activities. Aside from being the country's first employer by the number of employees and the size of its transactions, the state had also inherited from previous regimes various artistic workshops, arsenals (64 altogether), as well as several monopolies (tobacco, matches, and explosives). In addition, the upkeep of a conscription army of *c.* half a million men made it the major purchaser of bulk commodities as well as a provider of armaments and military equipment.

The civilian industrial state sector was until the 1930s, and by present standards, limited in scope. It included the prestigious *manufactures* (manufactories) of Sèvres (porcelain), Les Gobelins and Beauvais (tapestries). Several smaller government workshops like the Imprimerie Nationale (printing office), the Monnaie (Mint), the Mobilier National (furniture-making and repair) provided primarily for the needs of official business. The rationale for the establishment of these SOEs had been national security.

Assessment of the efficiency and proftability of these industries is difficult, because subsidies were incorporated in the operating costs (in addition, workers enjoyed public servant status). There is, however, ample evidence of the escalation of subsidies received by these industries: they increased fourfold between 1870 and 1913 (cf. Table 3.1).

In addition to these peacetime industrial activities, the government controlled important markets necessary for the maintenance of a standing army. Military expenditure (including the budgets of the War, Navy, and Colonial Departments) dwarfed all other categories of public spending during the whole period. However, a sizeable share of entitlements was used to pay wages and salaries

TABLE 3.1. *Gross turnover of state monopolies and other SOEs, 1872–1931*

(in F million)	1872	1890	1913	1922	1931
Matches	0	15	44	119	263
Tobacco	268	373	542	1,667	2,079
Gunpowder	9	11	25	53	204
Postal service	108	162	293	720	1,835
Telegraph	14	41	60	198	293
Telephone	0	0	59	199	898
Miscellaneous	0	10	13	16	529
TOTAL	399	612	1,036	2,972	6,101

Source: *Bulletin de statistique & législation comparée*, various years.

(Dormois 1992: 479). Only the War Department had less personnel expenditure than the other ministerial departments but spent more on material (Akriche 1994: 176). The Army and Navy, as rational consumers, set suppliers in competition so as to obtain the best purchasing conditions. '*Adjudications*' (auctions) were not always devoid of corruption, but very few suppliers enjoyed a monopolistic position. In 1913 they numbered 1,541 for the Army and 348 for the Navy; history recalls to this day one, a shoe-manufacturer, Alexis Godillot, who supplied shoes to 22 Army corps (out of a total of 23) so that his name became a byword for military footwear.

Procurement of weapons represented between 12 and 16% of military spending, and between 3.6 and 4.5% of the government budget. The cumulated effect of this type of equipment was of F 4.25 billion between 1870 and 1914. But, on the whole, military procurement failed to have a commanding role on the metal production. According to Delorme and André armament industries did sustain activity in some iron and steel factories up to 1896. On the whole, however, armaments played only a minor part in spurring economic growth. Even amid the pre-war tensions, 'an accelerating arms race . . . failed to widen defence appropriations significantly' (Crouzet 1974: 420) so that it was only under the threat of invasion and defeat that the 'business of war' significantly altered the structure and production of French industry.

The same pattern is observable twenty years later on the eve of World War II. Belated rearmament entitlements took precedence over some expansionary policy measures. After 1935 military procurement expenditure escalated dramatically and constrained the allocation of budget resources. As a share of the budget, procurement spending rose from 22 to 33% in 1938 to a staggering 60% in 1939. After the building of the Maginot line (supposedly to prevent any invasion from the East), military appropriations had fallen back to ordinary, i.e. insufficient, in view of the Nazi menace, levels. It was not only huge investments but the direct management by officials that was needed for the rearmament programmes to

Jean-Pierre Dormois

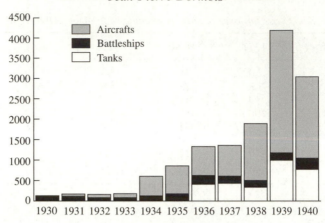

FIG. 3.3. French armament output, 1930–1940
Source: Frankenstein 1980: 751.

be completed. In 1937 subsidies originally assigned to civilian industrial support were redirected to armament factories. The financial effort was again upgraded with a F 9.5 billion scheme passed by the Renaud government in November 1938.

The expansionary effects on industry of increased government transfers to the military were however limited, because of the upstream bottlenecks in the production line. During the 1937 boom, the armament industry grew at a rate below that of the engineering sector as a whole and during the following recession, procurement orders failed to compensate for the contraction of civilian output. In fact, positive effects are perceptible, according to Alfred Sauvy, only on the eve of the outbreak of the hostilities in 1939 when the manufacturing sector increased its turnover by 10 billion representing the total of government transfers (Frankenstein 1980: 755). Several factors conspired to restrain the positive effects of the rearmament policy on either military or overall production. The *loi des 40 heures*, the Act limiting the working week to 40 hours, acted as a brake on expansion. Because of rigidities in the supply of semi-finished goods and shortages of skilled labour, of scanty and obsolete equipment, war equipment plants were unable to make full use of the funds allocated to them and grants had to be deferred from one year to the next. Confronted with the lethargy of the aeronautical industry, Industry minister Pierre Cot implemented a programme of forced mergers and partial nationalization with the creation of the six SNCA (*Sociétés Nationales de Construction Aéronautiques*) in which the government held two-thirds of the equity but did not replace the existing management. The mobilization, depriving factories of part of their workforce, dampened the escalation of output by the end of 1939 (Figure 3.3). There is no doubt, however, that the expansion of the French armament industry in the second post-war period owes its origins to the efforts deployed in these crucial years.

3.2.4. *Trade Discrimination as Industrial Policy*

Trade policy is without a doubt the area where government action had the farthest reaching effects on industrial structure and performance. Under the 1875 Constitution (abolished in July 1940), the President of the Republic was given extensive powers in the area of tariffs and trade as part of his foreign policy prerogative. It was only gradually that the initiative was reclaimed by Parliament. The protectionist lobby gained considerable support after the onset of the Great Depression in the late 1870s. Its frontman, Méline, introduced a new comprehensive tariff, passed by the Chamber on 11 January 1892. Intended to counterbalance France's 'natural handicaps' in industry vis-à-vis its competitors, the tariff represented a 'skilful accomodation of various interests' (Smith 1980: 90) who in fact dictated their will through the standing committee: a two-tier system of minimum and maximum tariff was elaborated, geared to discriminate against goods also produced domestically and to exempt those the country lacked. As a result, it is extremely complex and the listing is divided under 27 headings into 677 articles, some of them again broken down according to the size of shipments.

In the short term, the tariff did reduce imports drastically—it virtually stopped imports of food staples, grain, and cattle. But as competition upgraded, its impact diminished and duties had to be raised. The 1897 'padlock act' allowed the government to do so in an emergency without parliamentary consultation. On 30 March 1910, in face of increasing grain and other imports, Parliament raised tariffs yet again. By 1914, tariff revenues had increased over fivefold (while trade barely doubled) and doubled again by the beginning of the depression of the 1930s (for a comparable volume of trade). Such revisions are indicative of the failure of the tariff policy to achieve avowed aims of strengthening domestic industries.

Instead the policy encouraged many industries to stick to traditional and increasingly obsolete technologies, and meet demand with inadequate supplies as witnessed by the railway engine industry (cf. *supra*). As a result, new technology-intensive industrial goods continued to be imported or else manufactured under a foreign licence by franchised companies. This is revealed by an effective protection analysis (Dormois and Bardini 1993). Despite the many refinements introduced in the subsequent versions of the tariff, the semi-finished goods-bias always remained overwhelming. Designed to protect producers of staples of the first generation (basic iron bars, tin-plates, or chemicals) this strategy handicapped capital goods or semi-durables producers. Thus, in engineering and chemicals, domestic producers were placed at a disadvantage because their foreign competitors paid lower prices for their inputs.

Furthermore, there is evidence of a negative impact of Méline-style protection on industrial productivity performance. A comparison with UK industry reveals a persuasive negative correlation between protection rates and labour productivity (Dormois and Bardini 1993: 11). When the German high command

TABLE 3.2. *Nominal protection rates on manufactured goods, 1873–1931*
(at constant prices)

(in %)	1873	1911	1931
Metals	9.1	18.8	13.9
Mechanical engineering	7.0	15.5	18.0
Cottons and woollens	11.2	12.5	20.3
Manufacturing industries	e	7.3	13.7
Foodstuffs	1.2	7.0	21.5
Sugar	73.0	18.7	20.0
Wine	3.5	6.0	8.0
Manufactured tobacco	23.0	24.5	25.0
Coal	3.7	4.5	3.5
Petrol	72.5	53.4	84.4

e: negligible (less than to 0.5%).

Source: *Tableau général du commerce de la France*, selected years.

conducted in 1916 a survey of industrial plants in the French occupied territories, it was amazed at the sheer dominance of German machine-tools therein.

Renewed protectionist measures were adopted after World War I. In the fear
of German competition after the return to peace, the government was empowered
by Parliament to update and upgrade tariff duties without notice. As a result,
tariffs kept pace with international prices throughout the 1920s. The collapse of
world trade and export prices in 1930 prompted interest groups to call for the
raising of tariff duties in 1931. 'Exchange surtaxes' were created to counterbalance the effects of devalued currencies (France remained on the Gold Standard
until 1936). In addition, onerous internal duties and excises were levied on a plethora
of consumer goods. This plethora of indirect taxes represented, when added to
the profits of public monopolies, F 11.7 billion, or 42% of the government's
income.

The new tariffs failing to slow foreign import flows, volume quotas were imposed
from 1932 first on agricultural imports, then on chemicals and finally on most
manufactured goods. At the beginning of 1936, 65% of all imports were man-
datorily apportioned by the government. The strain eased somewhat after the
devaluation of the franc (duties were lowered to 20% on industrial raw materials) but the quota system was to be reinstated in 1937. As a result, colonial trade
(as for the UK) escalated in this period: colonial imports tripled their share in
French trade from 1931 to 1936 (from 12 to 33.6%).

The various and sometimes contradictory measures which can be loosely
described as pro-industry policy bear more resemblance to pre-war or even
nineteenth-century experiments (the epic of the *Ateliers Nationaux*[6] of 1848

---

[6] Workshops set up by the Republican government after the Revolution of February 1848 to give jobs to the
mass of workers laid off as a result of the slump of 1847–8.

served the propaganda of the Blum public works programme) than a preview of post-war attempts at a managed economy and industrial planning. Public policy was more defensive than offensive (as already noticed by Lauffenberger in 1939). The marginal expansionary measures of a countercyclical nature did not alter the global aims of insulating the economy, dampening foreign competition, compressing output, and favouring particularly vocal or powerful interest groups.

The 1930s witnessed a proliferation of political and economic programmes designed to cure 'capitalist ills' which precipitated into ambitious 'neocapitalist' projects from many corners of organized labour and political parties. Some historians see in the 'technocratic' movement the cradle of post-war economic expansion, as public servants wanted to extend the government's hand into industry: in face of the obvious failure of market forces and the business community, the government was supposedly the better equipped to solve problems of rationalization and organization of production that could ensure in the long run financial stability, productive expansion, and full employment.

3.3. VICHY'S PLANS FOR INDUSTRIAL RENOVATION

The Pétain camarilla which took over the administration in June 1940 came to power with a host of grand designs to regenerate the 'fibre' of the French nation. But these were often contradictory in terms; two main streams can be identified, one traditionalist in outlook which contemplated a return to patriarchal, agrarian values and a 'corporatist' organization of society modelled on Nazi Germany and Fascist Italy; the other involved plans to shake French industry out of its alleged lethargy. In their ambitions, Vichy modernizers resemble those of the previous decade and those who were to follow and implement to some extent some of their ideas.

With the suspension of Parliament, those public servants who remained in office and others lured by its glitter had all freedom to produce new schemes hoping to implement them in some way. 'Although the French found it difficult to produce goods and services during the war, they excelled at paper work' (Kuisel 1981: 133). Thus, the first Pétain government (under Laval) set off to reorganize the central government economic agencies. It revamped the statistical office (now renamed *Service National des Statistiques*) where Alfred Sauvy was able to launch its first enquiries. Darlan, named PM after Laval's fall and a committed member of the Redressement Français before 1939, was responsible for the creation of the DGÉN (*Délégation Générale à l'Équipement National*). Under its director, François Lehideux, the planning agency launched in May 1942 a ten-year Plan d'Équipement National aimed at replacing the machine and equipment stock of a number of factories and modernizing France's transport and communication infrastructure. In September industrialists were summoned to the *Conseil Supérieur de l'Économie Industrielle* which was supposed to coordinate the 'National Revolution's' enterprising efforts. But, on the one hand, 'Vichy's impulse towards economic catch up struggled against the social conservatism of official ideology' (its bias in favour of rural activities and ways of life) and, on the other hand, it was constrained by the needs of the Nazi war machine. The Germans had for one annexed Alsace, a major pre-war component of the French industrial system; factories in the Nord, Pas-de-Calais, and Lorraine departments were subjected to regulations from the Nazi government, and the Armistice agreement of June 1940 had forbidden France to operate any industries that could have strategic implications. What Vichy's industrial activism achieved in the absence of any reality test was to embed in the upper civil service the conviction that they should have their say—indeed that there was no other way—in the management of the country's industrial activities.

Vichy's real 'contribution' to the theory and practice of government intervention for the post-war experience was in its implementation of wartime controls. Under the strain of circumstances, dirigisme turned into a necessity and it fell upon the government to manage scarcity. The arsenal of controls introduced by the outgoing government at the declaration of war (strict controls over imports, prices and wages blocked) was further extended. Building on the first war's experience, Vichy resuscitated the Consortiums and extended their powers. A decree issued on 10 September 1940 organized the allocation office for industrial products (OCRPI), an overstaffed bureaucracy intended to rationalize and equalize rationing and divert as much as possible from German authorities (it seems to have worked in the end the other way around).

The *Comités d'Organisation* (COs), set up in August 1940 to manage rationed inputs, allocate the labour force, and fix production targets in each branch of industry, were a major step towards the establishment of a 'Corporatist' society (employers' associations and labour unions had hereby been dissolved). They turned out to be Vichy's major instrument of intervention. They overtook in 1941 the operations of the import consortiums and emerged soon afterwards as the real decision-makers for all industrial activity. First conceived as consultative bodies, they operated like cartels after their takeover by large company executives with special access to government planners and German officials. It is believed that 'the exigencies of war distorted the modernizing aims of the COs network' (26 in 1941, 1,929 in 1944!) but what it did was in fact ensure the survival of the largest and most modern production units (those more likely to swiftly fulfil German war contracts for instance) and sacrifice the least efficient. To some extent this practice fostered concentration and constituted a strong incentive to increase efficiency. To that end the efficacy of Vichy's dirigiste experiment is hard to judge. Germans occupiers, for whom 30% of French industrial plants operated and one-third of French workers toiled, were for the most part the beneficiaries of the system together with the war profiteers. 'In the end the Vichy regime had proved unable to control the controllers' (Kuisel 1981: 143).

3.4. INDUSTRIAL POLICY SINCE 1945

Government intervention in general and industrial policy in particular started off with a very high credibility rating and was upheld by the successive governments of the Fourth and Fifth Republics. Measured by the aggregate value of transfers from the public purse to enterprises, industrial policy did not abate until the beginning of the 1990s. Over the same period taxation, especially business taxes, escalated, reaching unprecedented heights in the 1980s. In a way government entrepreneurship and transfers to industry can be perceived as a counterpart to the burden of restrictive regulations and excessive taxation to such an extent that 'few companies could have survived without the selective exemptions that in turn rendered them dependent on the good will of industrial policy makers' (Hall 1986: 153).

In the immediate aftermath of war prevailing economic conditions demanded that the government supervised and financed, as it had done after World War I, the reconstruction of the economy. The effort bore essentially on the country's infrastructures (transport, utilities, capital goods, heavy industry). The second phase started under General de Gaulle's presidency, in the mid-1960s, which set priorities in industrial development with the launching of several ambitious programmes: it was the 'golden age' of industrial policy and the one experts have in mind when they refer to 'French' industrial policy. The onset of the worldwide oil crisis forced policy-makers to adjust the aims and means during Giscard d'Estaing's presidency (1974–81): this period witnessed the 'redeployment' of policy instruments. The coming of the Socialists to power in 1981 ushered in a third phase, a new impetus to *volontarisme* in industrial organization: many policies were reversed and complex schemes for a strategy of niches and subsequently 'vertical streams' were implemented. The return of the Right to power in 1986 signalled a return to financial orthodoxy, budget cuts, and large-scale privatizations which have since considerably weakened the scope and strength of industrial policy instruments.

This chapter will review in turn the goals pursued and the technical aspects of these policies and attempt to assess their effects in the short and long run. Most coexisted throughout the period but, at the same time, in each time period, certain actions were given priority over others. These actions can be sorted under three headings: substitution strategies whereby the government substituted itself for the market, sector-specific policies grouping both 'reactive' and 'proactive' policies, and finally so-called 'influence tactics' where government intervention was more indirect and more sporadic, more 'selective'.

3.5. SUBSTITUTION STRATEGIES

Under this heading is grouped a bundle of global policies which included the takeover by government agencies of the decisional procedure of large firms, the creation of public monopolies or operations that affected the structure of a whole industry.

3.5.1. Rebuilding the Infrastructure

After the end of hostilities, the responsibility, in a country drained of its resources for five years, for financing and coordination of reconstruction fell on the government. The greatest part of infrastructure on French territory was out of order: not one bridge over the Loire had survived and the aggregate industrial production index was down to 38 in 1944 from 100 in 1938 (and 132 in 1929). In the face of massive currency depreciation, it was foreign aid, mainly American, which provided the bulk of reconstruction expenditure. After a first loan in January 1946 (Blum–Byrnes agreement), aid under the Marshall Plan provided a total of $4.6 billion from 1948 on (representing 43% of the balance of payments current deficit over a period of 12 years). All in all reconstruction expenditure on trade and industry was roughly multiplied by a factor of ten compared with the pre-war years and accounted for 23% of the budget between 1947 and 1952.

The reconstruction, which continued until the mid-1950s, established the pattern for aid-granting that lasted until the 1980s. The government chose to rely on direct subsidization rather than on tax credits.[7] The management of aid was left to Treasury officials through the *Fonds de Modernisation et d'Équipement* (FMÉ) set up in 1947.

3.5.2. Indicative Planning

In order to coordinate the reconstruction effort and supervise the modernization of French industrial structure, the first post-war government set up the *Commissariat Général au Plan* (CGP) in 1946 under the headship of its initiator, Jean Monnet. Having served on the Interallied Supply Board during World War I, Monnet, who nurtured a great admiration for US production methods, was intent on bringing 'fordism' and modern firm management to outmoded French capitalism. The main *raison d'être* of the new agency was to foster economies of scale through a global concentration strategy; it intended through the elimination of the 'industrial dust' (the myriads of small-size firms) to build up French industries capable of sustaining France's restoration as a world power. Under an initially small permanent staff, the CGP set priorities for selected branches of industry, fostered cooperation, set up tripartite commissions (of officials, employers, and unions), and circulated relevant information to producers. Planners sometimes displayed creativity and foresight. But the decisions for grants and subsidies always remained firmly in the hands of the Treasury.[8] At best it seems,

---

[7] Which it is now by contrast increasingly favouring.

[8] The Treasury commanded a minimum 80% of financial interventions over the whole period.

'officials' ability to alter market decisions . . . might not have been commensurate with their appetite for and rhetoric of intervention' (Adam 1989: 47). From the start, planning whereby the government sought to compensate for ingrained risk-aversion by reducing perceived levels of risks, was meant to be indicative. But at the same time, plans rarely met their targets and frequently had to be redesigned in mid-stream, sometimes following a change of majority in Parliament. As French industry became more integrated in an increasingly competitive world economy, the Plan has seemingly lost some of its original purpose. Thus, the early diagnosis that 'official planning served to some extent to reduce uncertainty for entrepreneurs' (Carré, Dubois, and Malinvaud 1975: 583) might no longer hold true.

3.5.3. Nationalizations

In the immediate post-war period, the extension of the public sector was a widely accepted policy solution endorsed not only by Socialists, but also higher civil servants, and supported by large sections of public opinion. The consensus lasted until the second major wave of nationalizations in 1981 after which the tide turned. The first one took place in 1944–5 as the interim government launched a wave of acquisitions by the state of major financial institutions (including the *Banque de France* placed until 1993 under direct Treasury supervision). Nationalizations affected primarily energy, utilities, and transport. Confiscation of two car-makers, Renault and Gnôme & Rhône, charged with collaboration with Nazi Germany, substantially increased the government's stake in manufacturing industry (as well as its payroll). In addition two government agencies were created: the nuclear energy agency (CÉA) and the centre for space research (CNES) who were to supervise and set objectives for the nuclear and aircraft industry.

Nationalization in energy and transport was a change to the extent, rather than in the nature of government intervention; it was the outcome of decades of rampant subsidization and regulations, especially those brought about during wartime. Thus in energy, after having issued mandatory deliveries from the collieries, the government proceeded in 1946 to force mergers and full-scale nationalization in one single entity, *Charbonnages de France*. The same pattern is observable in the creation that same year of two nationwide public utilities: *Électricité de France* (ÉDF) soon supplied 40% of output and provided 100% of distribution of electricity; *Gaz de France* (GDF) was created by the merger of 251 independent producers representing 94% of output. As the government was taking over the bulk of reconstruction costs and operations for road and rail transport, it completed the acquisition by Air France, already a mixed company, of its two transatlantic competitors. In 1948, it purchased equity in CGT (*Compagnie Générale Transatlantique*) and the *Messageries Maritimes* which made it a majority shareholder. The government's quasi-monopoly on maritime transport was completed in 1960 by the creation of the SNCM (*Société Nationale de la Corse et de la Méditerranée*). Throughout the 'Thirty Glorious years' (1945–75)[9] the French government had therefore a powerful leverage in key sectors of the economy and made further additions to the public sector by controlling (through mixed companies) the transport and refining operations for imported oil.

TABLE 3.3. *Share of SOEs in industrial output, 1962* (%)

Natural gas	100
Electricity	100
Tobacco, matches	100
Miscellaneous minerals	65
Military goods	62
Aircraft	47
Vehicles	40
Health services	37

Source: INSEE 1962.

3.5.4. Restructuring the Economy

With the return of General de Gaulle as head of state in 1958, industrial policy took a decisive turn towards *volontarisme*. In the late 1960s and 1970s the government encouraged mergers and fostered concentration in iron and steel, chemicals, and electrical appliances. In 1978 the Plan Acier merged iron and steel prodution under a duopoly Usinor-Sacilor. Concentration operations led to the grouping of basic chemicals under a SOE, CDF-Chimie (a parent company of the nationalized collieries CDF) and fine chemicals, pharmacy under the leadership of Rhône Poulenc and Péchiney (PUK).[10]

In 1981–2, in part to reverse the contraction of employment brought about by these groupings, the newly elected Socialist government embarked on an ambitious nationalization programme. In addition to bringing 98% of financial institutions under government control (36 commercial and two investment banks), an assortment of large firms were purchased in fine chemicals and pharmaceuticals (Sanofi, Rhône Poulenc, Roussel-Uclaf), in bulk chemicals (CMF, Elf, Péchiney), in electronics and electric engineering (CGÉ, Thomson, Matra, and CII-Bull), St-Gobain (a glass-making to food-processing conglomerate), and the still debt-ridden steel-maker Usinor-Sacilor. No sooner had they fallen into public ownership than they needed immediate infusions of equity. The cost was huge: 130 billion were invested between 1981 and 1984 (of which 54 billion alone was for the newly nationalized firms). It was believed these groups would become

---

[9] An expression coined by the economist Jean Fourastié in reference to the 'Three Glorious Days' of the July revolution of 1830.
[10] In 1967 the Nora Report revealed that the SOEs were the main recipients of government procurement orders and subsidies.

TABLE 3.4. *Distribution of cumulated equity endowment to SOEs, 1981–1985*

	(Fbn)	(%)
Iron and steel making (Usinor, Sacilor)	19.9	40.0
Chemicals (Rhône Poulenc, CDF, EMC, PUK)	13.2	26.5
Electronics (CGE, Thomson, Bull, CGCT)	8.9	18.0
Vehicles (Renault)	6.8	13.5
Others (St-Gobain, etc.)	1.0	1.7

Source: Coletis 1991: 863.

leading sectors which would carry with them the rank and file of French industry. But initial ambitious designs of R & D sharing arrangements with subcontracting medium-size firms (PME) in fact never materialized and, if the large groups managed to maintain their market share, the former were facing defeat. By 1984, after the initial bouts of largesse and three devaluations, the government was forced to tighten the strings of the purse and conduct painful 'restructuring' anew by massive lay-offs of workers. Slimming down did not reach the upper-management layers, though. Still, leftist critics argue, the government never tried hard enough. Between 1981 and 1985 when government assistance to SOEs was at its peak, their total funding was always 'lower than their cumulative losses' (Cohen 1995: 41).

3.5.5. Denationalization

The Right returning to power in 1986 (the so-called first '*cohabitation*') started to deregulate the financial sector and return reflated large industrial conglomerates to the private sector. After an interlude of five years following President Mitterrand's re-election (1988–93) during which the Socialists froze state ownership, the Right's programme resumed so that by 1995 the regime of company ownership was probably the most liberal the country had known since the war. However, privatizations have been cautiously monitored so as to ensure the survival of government control in some form or other and prevent SOEs from falling prey to 'hostile' takeovers. The privatization of Renault, the flagship of government enterprise in consumer durables which has only been out of the red in 1995 and 1996, has been postponed. Thus, the argument runs, the government in fact only nationalized large industrial firms, hard-bitten by the new world market conditions prevailing after the oil crisis in order to release them after having sponged up their losses and upgraded their facilities. However, to fend off accusations of 'underselling the silverware of the Republic', the government designed transaction procedures which reserved a significant share of the stock of privatized SOEs to a '*noyau dûr*' (hard core) of institutional investors to make sure that the company would not fall prey to either speculators or hostile takeovers.

The French version of stakeholder capitalism has resulted in a complicated network of cross-ownership between banks, SOEs, and private conglomerates. This practice had the added effect of maintaining management and its privileged access to high public officials. By most independent accounts it is responsible for limited internal reorganization, and therefore strategy adaptation (the age structure in French big business is much higher than elsewhere) as well as increased instances of graft and insider dealing, which were referred to the COB (*Commission des Opérations de Bourse*), the French equivalent of the SEC. Somehow while advocating openness and urging adaptation to worldwide standards for the business sector at large, a consensus still dominates among political decision-makers and high public servants of the alleged superiority of the '*modèle français*' of large industrial companies with preferential access to government without whose help they are deemed unable to capture domestic as well as foreign markets.

3.5.6. A Contrasted Balance Sheet

The role of government as entrepreneur and corporate manager is not easily assessed due to the complexity (and sometimes secrecy) of the financial operations involved.

The gas and electricity utilities (ÉDF-GDF) have seemingly fared better than the other SOEs, although from a business point of view they, as all others, 'have tended to spend substantially more on tangible assets than they generated in cash flows' (Adam 1989: 70). In addition to water distribution on which the government exercised a certain leverage, utilities have registered since the 1980s improving performance (see Table 3.5).[11]

While their share in investment has markedly dropped due mainly to the completion of the nuclear plant building programme,[12] the public utilities contribute substantially to French exports. According to its management, ÉDF-GDF is now

TABLE 3.5. *Annual productivity growth by branch, 1980–1994*

	1980–4	1985–9	1990–4
Gas, water, electricity	5.5	5.8	2.4
Food processing	−0.2	2.7	2.0
Textiles	3.7	1.5	5.3
Paper	2.9	−2.2	1.1
Chemicals	5.6	0.2	5.6
Metals	1.1	2.1	8.3
Machines and equipment	2.0	1.0	2.0
Manufacturing	2.0	1.6	3.1

Source: OECD 1995: 170.

[11] Today dominated by an oligopoly, the Lyonnaise des Eaux.
[12] As of 1995 there are 56 reactors in 18 nuclear sites in operation. See below.

managed like a private enterprise with the sole restriction of the obligation of public service, which implies a certain laxity towards defaulting consumers. The serious problems will start with the forthcoming decommissioning of a number of nuclear plants in the next decade; the efficiency and reliability of the system will then ultimately be tested.

With the return of the old tobacco and match monopoly (SEITA) to the private sector in 1995 and the drastic closures of most coal mines, the government has ridden itself of its most burdensome lossmakers. Despite the halving of employment, the dwarfed mining sector still lags behind in terms of productivity (−2.9% in 1993−4).[13] An identical scenario applies to iron and steel-making. After twenty years of haggling with the unions and a last injection in 1995 of equity (F 17.5 billion), the government finally privatized Usinor-Sacilor and put the decimated cohorts of the steel-producing areas (Lorraine essentially) under the care of regional assistance schemes (retraining etc.): Cohen calls it 'playing stretcher-bearer'.

The diagnosis is bleaker for transport despite impressions to the contrary and the much publicized TGV and Airbus contracts. In air transport the government-managed Air France and Air-Inter (merged in early 1996) cope with persistent losses, dismal performance, and a shrinking market share. Of all the major European airlines, Air France is the only one able to afford steady losses above 5% of gross turnover (17% in 1993).[14] Servicing its cumulated deficit absorbs annually 30% of it in financial charges. At the same time productivity growth has been the slowest in Western Europe (AF pilots receive salaries 20% on average above those of their US colleagues). The government has tried to cut over-manning since 1991 but so far has run into the effective industrial activism of a very corporatist profession which is resisting the implementation of the last scheme to date ('Plan Blanc') to cut the payroll by 5,000 in exchange for a F 20 billion subsidy. By most informed accounts, the privatization of Air France could take up to ten years.

Likewise the rail operator (SNCF) faces a deteriorating financial situation and seems unable to master escalating financial costs stemming from the upgrading of the network in the 1980s. In 1994 its cumulated debts (inflated by generous retirement benefits) reached a total equivalent to 2.5% of GNP and the government had to inject a F 48 billion subsidy (including 15 billion for the pension scheme). In terms of performance, however, the SNCF fares better: it has kept a larger market share for both passenger and freight than any other national operator and its productivity by employee is likewise the highest when measured in relation to the size of the network. This is the result of compression of the workforce from 253,000 to 192,000 between 1982 and 1992, matched by productivity growth of 1.5% per annum. Since then however, the reorganization effort has stalled: the government's attempts to close lines and suppress railwaymen's

---

[13] Between 1950 and 1980, output had already been divided by a factor of 2.5 and employment by 5.
[14] Which corresponds to between one-third and two-fifths of net earnings.

'privileges' have met with harsh opposition from the unions, culminating in the all-out strike of December 1995.[15]

Similar trends are perceptible for the SNCM, the SNCF's much smaller sister for sea transport in the Mediterranean. Wild-cat strikes in 1995 and 1996, sometimes cutting off Corsica from mainland ports, have further endangered its financial position. But after over a century of continuous subsidizing, the French government has virtually withdrawn from shipbuilding. Unions should therefore beware: with the perspective of a F 520 billion PSBR for fiscal year 1997, it is unlikely the government will be able to indulge its rail and sea operators for much longer.

3.6. SECTOR-SPECIFIC POLICIES

3.6.1. Subsidy Scattering

After the completion of the First (Reconstruction) Plan (also referred to as the 'Monnet Plan') (1947–53) and as both infrastructure and industrial production reached their pre-war levels, the successive governments of the Fourth Republic (1946–58) turned progressively towards a more general approach to industrial development. In fact, the strong legislature of the Fourth Republic fostered the emergence of influential interest groups which in return encouraged the scattering of subsidies and the multiplication of assistance schemes. Government aid meanwhile moved gradually from the modernizing imperatives, which had been the hallmark of the Monnet Plan to salvage operations of hard-pressed sectors and regions.

First engaged on a path of systematic support of public utilities, transport, and basic industries (all supposed to have strong positive externalities), the Fourth Republic kept investment flowing to the SOEs also referred to as GENs (*Grandes Enterprises Nationales*). In exchange it required SOEs and other recipients of aid to adopt favourable price schedules for 'collective consumers', i.e. firms. Between 1954 and 1968 the price of electricity fell through regulation by 2.5% in real terms, the price of gas by 0.2% and SNCF freight charges by 0.6% per annum.

The evidence indicates that this policy strengthened the position and standing of the large conglomerates (either SOE or private firms) in their respective field. Moreover, tariffs and import controls reinforced until the mid-1960s the latter's dominant position. However, the build-up of national champions created overcapacity and crowded out resources (especially equity) for other industries (especially consumer and capital goods). Table 3.6 shows that among major sectors, public utilities, transport, and the telecoms, as well as agriculture and semi-finished goods, received a disproportionate share of government grants compared to their share of the overall capital stock.

---

[15] Retirement age is typically at 50 for travelling agents.

TABLE 3.6. *Credit allowances to major sectors, 1956* (in billions of [old] Francs[a])

	(1)	(2)	(3)	(4)	(5)
Agriculture	176.7	340.6	517.4	11.6	9.5
Agro-industries	156.8	—	128.1	3.2	7.0
Public utilities	319.2	1,056.2	260.7	18.4	14.9
Semi-finished goods	442.3	202.0	361.3	11.3	9.8
Capital goods	420.8	—	343.7	8.6	8.5
Consumption goods	336.9	0.3	275.2	6.9	7.7
Building and construction	167.7	—	137.0	3.4	3.3
Transport and telecommunication	142.5	209.2	1,780.8	24.0	20.1
Trade and services	607.5	21.3	496.2	12.6	19.1
TOTAL	2,770.4	1,829.6	4,300.4	100.0	100.0

[a] The monetary reform of 1958 replaced the old franc by the new franc (NF) on the basis 1 NF = 100 fr.

(1) bank loans   (4) total grants as a %
(2) FDES grants   (5) share of aggregate stock
(3) cumulated subsidies 1947–56

Source: Sicsic and Wyplosz 1996: 21.

Concurrently, the government assumed its traditional role of trade regulator and rescuer of declining industries. It thereby slowed down the very structural changes which its proactive policies were fostering. The Fourth Republic had thus inherited the arsenal of wartime controls on foreign trade and used it extensively. Until the implementation of the Treaty of Rome starting in 1961, import rationing and licences were still widespread (despite a brief repeal in 1955–7). Financial facilities for the payment of 'vital' or 'strategic' imports, as well as for defaulting foreign clients, were extended by the BFCE, set up in the aftermath of World War I, and the COFACE, two banks monitored by the Treasury.

Timid steps were concurrently taken to diffuse competitive behaviour. A government decree prohibited in 1952 ententes (cartels), extending the ban in 1953 on a wide array of discriminatory business practices.[16] But at the same time, the government multiplied regional and sectoral schemes designed to encourage business creation in peripheral areas. A myriad of *'fonds'*, committees, and bodies were set up to promote industrial 'reconversion', decentralization, retraining of redundant employees, and regional entrepreneurship. These schemes were engineered through subsidized loans (*bonification d'intérêts*). But despite all the publicity—to obvious political benefits—the final amounts remained negligible. Between 1955 and 1965 the *Caisse des Dépôts & Consignations* granted F 400 million in subsidized loans and a further F 450 million for regional 'equipment'. A total of 2,000 fragmented grants provided for the creation of a mere 200,000 jobs. Aid flowed in greater abundance to two branches which had been first boosted by reconstruction and found themselves wanting of customers in its aftermath: steel-making and shipbuilding. Their large workforce and supposed

---

[16] Decrees were bills issued on the sole responsibility of the cabinet without parliamentary discussion.

strategic importance ensured that they were kept afloat well past the moment any salvation was possible. 'In the absence of an ambitious long-term project, industrial policy was thus conducted short-sightedly and dispersed in many, often inconsistent, directions' (Levet 1988: 31).

The dispersion of aid grants seems to have done minimum harm but the massive diversion of resources, especially investment, handicapped the diversification of French industrial activities. Thus, the 'disappointing performance of post-reconstruction growth can be traced back to faulty allocation of productive investment' (Sicsic and Wyplosz 1996: 13).

3.6.2. 'Picking Winners'?

The creation of a much stronger executive under the 1958 constitution and the Treaty of Rome's pledge to open the French market to EEC partners apparently boosted French industrial expansion in the 1960s. On the eve of the oil crisis, France had not only overturned its traditional handicaps; it had also caught up in terms of output and productivity with its direct competitors. An annual growth rate of 5.1% throughout the 1960s enabled it to produce a share of world manufactures unseen since the mid-nineteenth century (8.5%). As long as De Gaulle remained at the helm (1958–69), the trend was definitely away from systematic government intervention towards market initiative and discipline, from automatic assistance to increased discrimination in the allocation of government aid (with of course a fair share of exceptions).

Under pressure from the Treasury to keep both budget deficit and inflation under control, trade and industry expenditure, at 23% of the budget in 1950, was scaled down to 14% in 1962 and 15.3% in 1971, divided equally between industry and transport. Once financial commitment to the SOEs is discounted (45% of the annual endowment) the remainder went through complicated management procedures by the FMÉ and the FDES. The aggregate allowance of the FDES was halved between 1959 and 1971 showing a clear retreat from 'reactive' operations. From that period onwards government assistance became 'locked in' to selective areas. Between 1959 and 1968 for instance most non-financial SOEs received no external equity except Air France, ÉDF, GDF, aircraft-makers, and the PTT (post office). By the end of the decade, an increasing portion of subsidies went

TABLE 3.7. *Main industrial assistance recipients, 1950–1968*

	1950	1962	1965	1968
FME	80.5	40.0	15.9	22.6
CEA	—	28.0	34.0	27.5
FDES and SOEs	10.7	11.3	13.3	23.6

Source: Delorme and André 1981: 261.

to telecoms via the PTT (for the completion of the telephone network) and the *Centre à l'Energie Atomique* (CÉA).

To undermine the reliance of the beneficiaries on public aid, the government introduced in the late 1960s the RCB, a French version of the American PPBS for the management of its agencies (in electronics, telecoms, and armament industries). Besides, a simple growth distribution matrix purchased from the Boston Consulting Group, an independent consultancy, helped planners sort out candidates. In any branch, typically only the 25 top firms would be eligible for government contracts and subsequent financial assistance. The infusion of new external equity was especially important between 1966 and 1973 when the programme was run, the SOEs relying heavily on government support.[17]

3.6.3. The 'Grands Programmes'

The Fifth Plan (1966–70) thus inaugurated a new approach to 'proactive' industrial policy. It defined activities of special significance to French industrial development in which the government intended to build up national champions capable of competing on a par with world leaders. The selected activities had to be nurtured on French soil thanks to a privileged diet of monopoly exemptions, public orders, fat operating subsidies, preferential tariffs, and public R & D financing, before being allowed to face foreign competition.

In the cluster of branches selected, three both belonged to 'sunrise' industries and had direct military applications and two, steel and shipbuilding, were the survivors of the previous set of priorities: the major concern behind their inclusion was that of employment. Also, the latter, because of its alleged military implications with defence, was continuously expanded, despite evidence of blatant overcapacity at great cost until 1977. The fall would be the harder: today France has the smallest merchant fleet of the major European sea powers. In steel, the building in the late 1960s of the gigantic coastal complex at Fos-sur-Mer on the Mediterranean (working therefore imported raw materials) never fulfilled its promises.[18]

The original F 12 billion envelope for '*grands programmes*' was upgraded to 13 in the following Plan (1971–5). Continuously lavishly supported through the 1970s and 1980s were the aeronautics and nuclear industries, both under the supervision of government research agencies, the CÉA (Atomic Energy Centre) and CNES (Spatial Study Centre).

In aeronautics both research and production were heavily dependent on military procurement. As a result, subsidies amounted to 37% of turnover on

[17] Adam who makes this remark (Adam 1989: 72), obviously counts the PTT, relabelled La Poste in 1988, a central government agency among the SOEs which it is not technically.

[18] In the same category fell the textile industry which the government was pressured to include as a priority action. But it took ten years before the first agreement on reduction of capacity could be presented (Accord multifibres, 1976).

TABLE 3.8. *Estimated returns from nuclear programme, 1982*

| | Value added (F bn) | | | Employment (000) | | |
	Direct	Induced	Total	Direct	Induced	Total
Construction	13.8	6.3	20.1	75	37	112
Equipment	4.3	1.5	5.8	20	8.2	28.2
Exploitation	8.0	2.3	10.3	17	12	29
Production	13.9	2.1	16.0	18	14.4	32.4
Military applications	5.3	3.1	8.4	12.6	16.6	29.2
Other	6.8	4.1	8.2	22.4	8.8	31.2
TOTAL	52.1	16.7	68.8	165	97	262

Source: *Revue d'Économie Industrielle* 1985: 31.

average in the 1970s. Recipients, mostly private manufacturers such as Dassault and Matra, as well as state-controlled SEMs, such as SNECMA and SNIAS, were encouraged to coordinate their operations and work in collaboration. Friendly foreign governments were invited to conclude agreements with or else pass orders to the national purveyors of fighter aircraft and more recently, passenger and freight carriers. While the building of Concorde was definitely a commercial flop, the 'Rafale', a fighter-jet and Airbus (fruit of multinational cooperation with Germany, Spain, and Belgium) managed to break into the civil aviation market and accounts today for a world market share of 20%, thus emerging as the only serious competitor to the US Boeing in aircraft manufacture.[19]

In the nuclear industry, de Gaulle's decision, soon after his return to power in 1958, to develop a French nuclear bomb had far-reaching repercussions and gave a long-lasting boost to the CÉA and its supplying industry.[20] Until 1969, the CÉA tried to implement its own technology from natural uranium; that year, as de Gaulle left the presidency, the government yielded to ÉDF's demand to adopt the US Westinghouse technology (based on enriched uranium) instead. As a complement to the military nuclear programme, the decision had been taken before the doubling of the oil bill in 1974, to develop the civilian applications of nuclear energy and build several reactors. The plan was carried out over the ensuing fifteen years and involved four large enterprises: two public agencies, the utility ÉDF and the CÉA which created with Empain-Schneider (the legendary gunmaker) a specialized subsidiary, Framatome in addition to Alsthom, itself a subsidiary of the *Compagnie Générale d'Électricité* (CGÉ).[21] The hopes of a plentiful windfall from the nuclear programme were partly misplaced and the anticipations shown in Table 3.8 did not entirely materialize.

[19] The merging of Boeing with MacDonnell-Douglas has of course been a blow to Airbus's aspirations.
[20] The first French A-bomb was tested in Reggane in the Sahara on 13 Feb. 1960.
[21] The two private operators were nationalized in 1982 (and privatized again in 1994).

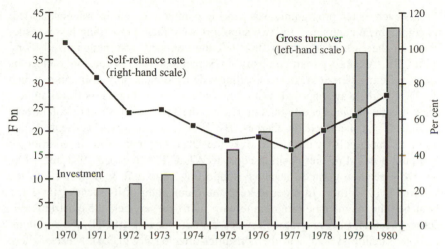

FIG. 3.4. Investment, turnover, and self-financing rate in telecoms, 1970–1980

3.6.4. Ventures in Communications

The Seventh Plan (1976–80) identified the development of telecommunications as a priority area. Up to 1970, France had one of the smallest and most outdated networks in Europe. Two subsidiaries of foreign ITT and L. M. Ericsson (the latter sole purveyor of handsets and equipment since the 1880s), enjoyed a cosy duopoly in supplying equipment to the *Direction Générale des Télécommunications* (DGT).[22] The Treasury progressively eased constraints on borrowing and the DGT (a Vichy creation) was given broader financial independence. Between 1975 and 1980, public investment was multiplied by a factor of three compared to the previous qinquennium (and ten compared to 1965–70) (Fig. 3.4).

Soon after, ITT and Ericsson were pressured by the DGT to license their technology to CIT, a structure staffed with a new generation of telecom engineers from the *Centre National d'Études des Télécommunications* (CNÉT). In January 1970, the CNÉT developed a new fully digital switch system (the so-called 'Platon project') at a direct R & D cost one-fifth less than the British 'System-X'. The DGT decided then to remove ITT and Ericsson and create a competitor to CIT (by then CIT-Alcatel). In 1976, it went further by transfering ITT and Ericsson's assets to Thomson. From then on, a large-scale catching-up process took place. In 1978, 10,000 new subscribers were connected every day; the number of main lines jumped from 7 to 25 million. In October 1985, new eight-digit numbering had to be introduced. 'By 1989, France had one of the most modern telecoms networks in the world' (Ergas 1992). Besides French firms had clearly strengthened their technological capabilities; as a result, their relative share of registered foreign patents in the USA doubled.

---

[22] ITT product managers used to refer to the French market as the 'gilded cage'.

However, as the programme was nearing completion, public orders subsided; as employment contracted, the two suppliers were facing mounting losses, especially in the case of Thomson. In 1982 the company was nationalized along with CGÉ, Alcatel's parent company; in September 1983, Thomson's telecoms assets were transferred to Alcatel creating a de facto monopoly—an option which the DGT had always opposed. With direct access to the highest political authorities, Alcatel obtained equity injections from the Treasury (instead of conditional subsidies) and increased its charges. By 1990, Alcatel was a well-entrenched domestic monopolist with a hold over the DGT's procurement; in addition, it had built a world market position equal to AT & T.[23] Between 1983 and 1990, the DGT acted as Alcatel financier, supporting various R & D projects to the level of F 100 billion. In order to keep the momentum of its success, the DGT launched the telematique programme with four new services: the electronic directory (Minitel), the Integrated Services Digital Network (ISDN), the communications satellite system, and the consumer-oriented fax (TGD). Most of these projects fell through due to the absence of interested customers.

By 1991, it had become clear that Minitel was not an export product and a report by Coopers & Lybrand assessed that commercial viability was unlikely to be reached before 1998; by then France Télécom, as the DGT is now known, would have spent F 45 billion on Minitel. As for the ISDN, customer take-up lagged behind initial projections and the number of primary rate services in operation are less than half the number achieved by British Telecom. The three other programmes were clear failures. In 1991, cable TV subscribers numbered 0.3 million (out of the 5 million anticipated), far below break-even point. The TGD (fax) never quite made it beyond the drawing board. In retaliation, France Telecom set obstacles to the exploitation of the fax market which had clearly failed to capture market anticipations; as a result, the present stock of fax machines in use in France represents one-third of the US's and half of Germany's. Conversely, it neglected the promising development of the cellular phone as well as the 'intelligent' voice-operated network services. Overall the public company appears to have 'greatly overestimated its capacity to shape its environment' (Ergas 1992: 10). Because of an insufficiently customer-oriented strategy, little marketing expertise at management level, and an inflated payroll, its operating costs are still 20–25% higher than its major counterparts. France Télécom (FT) which the government has heretofore sheltered from competition, is currently resisting liberalizing measures required by the Maastricht Treaty. Of the 90,000 jobs FT created in the expansion of the 1970s and 1980s, a minimum of 40,000 will have to be shed in the coming years.

---

[23] Thomson Multimédia was earmarked for privatization in 1996. With debts totalling over F 14 billion, the Juppé government decided to sell for a 'franc symbolique' to the Japanese Daewood but the deal was then suddenly called off (December 1996).

TABLE 3.9. *Government purchases as percentage of total sales, 1974*

T04 Coal	3.7	T14 Mechanical equipment	5.0
T05 Petroleum	4.9	T15 Electrical equipment	17.2
T06 Electricity, water	1.4	T16 Ground transport equipment	3.0
T07 Ferrous minerals and metals	2.8	T17 Ships and aircraft	38.4
T08 Non-ferrous minerals and metals	2.0	T18 Textiles, apparel	0.8
T09 Building materials	1.2	T19 Leather, shoes	0.7
T10 Glass	0.4	T20 Wood and miscellaneous	1.2
T11 Bulk chemicals	0.2	T21 Paper	0.7
T12 Chemicals, pharmaceuticals	2.0	T22 Printing, publishing	0.9
T13 Metallic products	2.9	T23 Rubber, plastics	1.1

Source: Mathieu and Suberchicot 1978.

3.7. INFLUENTIAL TACTICS

In addition to direct intervention in business operations, French governments have also resorted to more traditional forms of indirect assistance to firms in the shape of procurement, subsidies, and R & D financing. The telecoms industry, namely Thomson and Alcatel, were, as has just been explained, the main beneficiaries of this latter form of indirect aid.

Already in 1967, the Nora report had revealed that these forms of government assistance were heavily concentrated upon a handful of suppliers. In 1974, only two industries (out of twenty) had received orders which amounted to more than 5% of their turnover: electronics and electrical engineering (17%) and ship and aircraft manufacturing. Moreover, the government tended to spend its procurement funds in industries over which it already exercised most leverage. Procurement therefore had an effect on industrial structure: 36% of all contracts, representing 67% of the aggregate value of orders went to large corporations (those with over 2,000 employees).

In the provision of R & D the pattern of concentration is even more apparent. In 1975, 65% of public R & D went to aerospace, 24% to electronics, and 6% to office equipment and the R & D expenditure of the top twenty firms accounted for over 50% of all investment in industrial R & D (and 88% of government R & D aid). Two-thirds of the grants were handled by the Ministry of Defence, a quarter by the Ministry of Industry, and 7% by the telecom state agency PTT.

Among government departments, the Ministry of Defence has been the main purveyor of orders, from the armament and naval and aeronautical industries essentially. The military establishment has apparently managed until recently to keep the main suppliers in competition (Dassault, Matra, and Thomson CSF) which has resulted in France being able to claim the third rank among world arms exporters. The secrecy surrounding contract negotiations and the intermingling of officials with industrialists and experts makes any attempt at auditing the

TABLE 3.10. *Areas targeted by subsidies in computer industry, 1982–1986*

(in Fbn)	Amount	%	Recipients
Telecoms and electronics	80	57	CGE
Space and medical research	21	15	Bull, Thomson
Office equipment	19	13	Bull, Thomson, SEMS
Computer components	10	7	Thomson-CSF, Matra
Home computers	7	5	Thomson-MM
Robots	3	2	CGA (CGE subsidiary)
TOTAL	140	100	

Source: Shams 1990.

profitability of transfers to the arms industry extremely tentative. It is clear, however, that the decision by the government to scale down the size of its armed forces and consolidate the national arms industry will reduce employment, and increase profitability—perhaps . . .

While armaments have been a case of the strategy nicknamed 'industrial slotting' ('*politique des créneaux*') the policy developed towards electronics received in the 1980s the label of 'vertical stream strategy'. Originally set up in the Fifth Plan among the '*Grands Programmes*', the '*plan Calcul*' was designed to create a home-grown computer industry. The first company CII merged first with Bull and then, in 1976, with Honeywell. The government subsequently invested 1.2 billion in Bull, the first in a long series of government handouts to the company.

Upon its accession to power in 1981, the socialist government designed a grand plan to boost the ailing computer industry which, it was revealed, was an '*industrie industrialisante*' (the development of which was supposed to have a stimulating effect over other activities). In 1982, it employed 8% of the industrial labour force and had a gross turnover of F 114 billion, or 5% of world output in this sector. Moreover, it brought a trade surplus of some F 11 billion. The government earmarked F 140 billion over five years for priority areas with the aim of reconquering the home market. The French industry's strong points lay in space research, telecoms, and professional equipment; it had to catch up in components and home equipment. As Table 3.10 shows, however, the bulk of financing still went to the sectors where the French computer industry already had an advantage. Before the Chirac administration scaled down the project in 1986, its outcome was a contrasted one. True, the turnover had increased (from 116 to 167 billion), import coverage dwindled, and employment contracted (from 241,000 to 217,000). Outside public administration, especially the post office, Thomson proved unable to enlarge its clientele among non-institutional customers. After a last bail-out plan, Bull was forced to retreat into its stronghold (and shed a good deal of its payroll) and last but not least, Thomson, already split in two, was forced to merge its military branch (CSF) with Matra (from the Lagardère group) while the South Korean Daewoo put in a bid for its television and computer activities.[24]

3.8. RETREAT OR LOSS OF DIRECTION?

More powerful forces than a mere change of mood in public opinion (the so-called '1980s liberal wave') forced the Socialists to cut down their ambitious programmes of 're-industrialization': the dire situation of public finances. Between 1980 and 1985 the current budget deficit jumped from 30 to 153 billion (to reach 350 billion in 1992). After three devaluations, the operation of an independent national industrial strategy became nothing short of impossible. Industrial policy ambitions have gradually been surrendered as macroeconomic policy options have relegated them to the background.

Macroeconomic options (deflation, competition promotion, monetary stability) and the burden of public deficits have not only limited government activism, but also restricted the number of potential beneficiaries. Under these conditions, the choice was made to reserve subsidies to those firms 'which [could] demonstrate their need for substantial and risky investments' (Cohen 1995: 42). The newly privatized Thomson, Bull, and Air France received the bulk of government aid in 1992. For those who remained state-owned, or the public utilities, most had by now completed their cure and the Balladur government could in 1993 contemplate their future privatization. The privatization of Renault, former flagship of government enterprise, was then put on the agenda. In the wake of the December 1995 strike in the public sector, the government has put it on hold.

While resisting full-scale liberalization and its consequences for some privileged few (bail-out in 1994 of *Crédit Lyonnais*, and of Air France, followed by its forced merger with Air Inter), the Balladur right-wing government continued on the path opened up by the Socialist Bérégovoy. The reforms conducted since 1986 have gradually dismantled the government's watch over financial operations. Restrictions on foreign subsidiaries and imports have been repealed while labour markets underwent only timid reforms: the Socialist-introduced authorization that companies had to secure in order to lay off workers was repealed in 1988. By most accounts, the French labour market is still one of the most rigid in the OECD. Moreover, the government is tempted, under pressure from public opinion, to regulate dismissal procedures in a desperate effort to halt the rising tide of unemployment (now hovering around 12%).

The major breakthrough, and to some extent, the easier to conduct, was the deregulation of financial markets. There, the government had no choice but to follow the injunctions of the *Acte Unique* and the Maastricht Treaty. But in addition it eagerly embraced it in the expectation that domestic and foreign private investors would enlarge the French market for productive investment and public borrowing while keeping interest rates low. Already under the Socialist PM

---

[24] The deal was finally called off for political reasons in the first week of December 1996.

Rocard (1988–91), the proportion of capital injections from the public purse had fallen under 10% (9.7% for a total of F 104 billion). The old arsenal of subsidized loans, equity capital, and insurance provision managed by the state was replaced by another three-pronged business-conducive strategy. A first initiative was taken to authorize SOEs to issue 'investment vouchers' to boost their equity endowment. To make these attractive (since they did not entail voting rights), the government offered in addition the security of treasury bills, higher returns, and fiscal exemptions; Rhône-Poulenc, a chemical and pharmaceutical giant, used this device extensively before the outright flotation of its stock. The Treasury likewise, in order to limit the repeated injection of equity capital to manufacturers, authorized cross-financing among financial and non-financial SOEs including purchase and exchange of stock as well as holding agreements. There were several relationships of this kind between Roussel-Uclaf, Thomson, Rhône-Poulenc again, and *Crédit Lyonnais*; the latter's near bankruptcy in 1994—it was bailed out by the Treasury to the tune of 130 billion francs—cast doubt on the speculation-prone possibilities it created. Another initiative aimed at merging Renault (then still a SOE) and the Swedish Volvo failed utterly because of opposition from the latter's shareholders.[25] Finally the last device introduced was to allow SOEs to float their subsidiaries on the market. That was the case for Péchiney when it took over American Can in 1991.

Today, the French government seems still reluctant to expose French industry to the full blow of 'market forces' and international competition. Its strategy is mainly defensive and its attitude conservative: it aims at preserving '*les acquis*', a closely-knit association of world-class enterprises relying on political protection and/or advice. Not much thought is given to potential business creation. CEOs and top civil servants have shared much in the last century and have become accustomed to swapping directorships for government posts and vice-versa (the so-called '*pantouflage*'). As advocates (albeit mostly subconscious) of Galbraith's 'organized capitalism', French officials are wary that without the type of cooperation that seems to have 'made France what it is today', French industries might be heading for serious trouble. But at the same time, by allowing financial institutions into the game of investing freely, the government has let go of the levers it held for so long over firms and that gave it a say in the shape of the country's industrial future.

Because measuring the costs and benefits of industrial policy is so hard—not to mention the lack of adequate information because of intricate accounting procedures—it is difficult to issue a substantiated verdict on the issue. Like so many policies, it resembles the 'curate's egg': some parts of it are excellent. One can recognize the apparent successes—the TGV which has given a new lease of life to the public train operator, the building of Airbus, Boeing's only European rival, which today controls just under 30% of the market for passenger carriers, the space-shuttle Ariane in cooperation with German and Spanish sister companies. In Brussels, French envoys have been advocating the European-wide imple-

---

[25] The current socialist government has obtained to float 25% of Renault's capital.

TABLE 3.11. *Distribution of industrial labour employment, major industrial countries, 1985*

	US	Japan	FRG	France
'High tech' industries	16	12	12	8
Consumer goods	22	27	29	35
Machines and equipment	30	26	25	21
Heavy industry	32	35	34	36

Source: Levet 1988: 70.

mentation of originally French projects, or projects that would boost primarily French companies (the high-definition television, Minitel). But there are offsets that augur badly for the ambitions of French manufacturers in Europe.

Thirteen years into the TGV venture, the SNCF has still to get out of the red: its debt amounts to 2.5% of French GNP and annual losses to F 40 billion. Airbus is still dependent on the orders of 'friendly' governments; EDF (which has a cumulated debt greater than the SNCF) was given free rein to crowd France's major rivers with nuclear plants to the point where only one other country in the world derives as much of its electricity from a nuclear source (the Ukraine) and the operator sells at a loss its output to neighbouring countries. The forthcoming decommissioning of the first generation of nuclear plants in the first decade of the next century will prove extremely difficult to conduct, financially and otherwise.

Thus, it is probable that future research will find Sicsic and Wyplosz's conclusions for the 1950s apply to the later decades as well—with more damaging consequences. By most predictions Italy's industrial output will have overtaken France's by the end of this century. But also, the present structure of French industry and manufactured exports reflects the biases introduced by the favoured treatment offered during the past decades to selected industries to develop at the expense of the rank and file of French consumer-oriented manufacturing. Clearly this allowed those preferential access to government procurement and subsidies. Table 3.11 which gives figures for 1985 exemplifies the French emphasis on heavy industries and basic consumer goods while it is found wanting in the 'sunrise' breed of machines and equipment and high-tech industries where embedded value added, R & D, competition, etc. are higher. Of the latter, only the armament industry has continuously grown during the past decades, closing the gap with the leader, the United States.[26] Moreover the *franc fort* policy (made more stringent after the crisis of summer 1993) has further undermined French positions in 'standard' manufacturing industries where French firms are undersold by their European rivals for the most sophisticated kinds as well as by emerging industrializers in the Third World. The continuous surpluses of the trade balance in 1995 might thus be a blind alley: in addition to firm creation and output expansion being

---

[26] It has been revealed by the US Department of Commerce that French arms sales to LDCs overtook those of the US for 1994.

constricted by high real interest rates,[27] French industry is currently locked into a dangerous situation: a combination of world-class exporting firms, some of which still rely on some kind of government assistance and regulation, and the basic 'fabric' of French industrial structure which seems on the decline and for which the hitherto introduced reforms are obviously altogether inadequate.[28]

[27] Many economists suspect that 'disinflation' has in fact given way to real deflation, since the annual inflation rate which today hovers around 1.8% takes into account government-set public services prices which rise regularly.

[28] The extraordinary development of France's pharmaceutical industry rests in part on the generosity of its social security system which is currently being reformed.

REFERENCES

ADAM, W. J. (1989). *Restructuring the French Economy: Government and the Rise of Market Competition since World War II*. Washington, DC: Brookings Institution.

—— and SOFFAËS, C. (1986) (eds.). *French Industrial Policy*. Washington, DC: Brookings Institution.

AKRICHE, I. (1994). 'Le Complexe militaro-économique en France 1871–1913'. Ph.D. thesis, Université de Montpellier-III.

ASSELAIN, J.-C. (1974). 'Une Erreur de politique économique: La Loi des 40 heures de 1936'. *Revue Economique*, 25: 672–705.

—— and MORRISSON, C. (1983). 'Economic growth and interest groups: The French experience', in Dennis C. Mueller (ed.), *The Political Economy of Growth*, 157–75. New Haven: Yale University Press.

BALASSA, B. (1965). 'Whither French planning?'. *Quarterly Journal of Economics*, 79: 537–54.

—— (1975) (ed.). *European Economic Integration*. Amsterdam: North-Holland.

BARJOT, D. (1989). 'Innovations et travaux publics en France 1840–1940'. *Histoire, Economie, Sociétés*, 8/4: 403–14.

BAUM, W. C. (1958). *The French Economy and the State*. Princeton: Princeton University Press.

BAVEREZ, N. (1984). 'Chômage et marchés du travail en France dans les années 1930'. Ph.D. thesis, Université de Paris-I.

BELLON, B., and CHEVALIER, J.-M. (1983) (eds.). *L'Industrie en France*. Paris: Flammarion.

BERGER, S. (1981). 'Lame ducks and national champions: Industrial policy in the Fifth Republic', in William Andrews and Stanley Hoffmann (eds.), *The Fifth Republic at Twenty*. Albany, NY: SUNY Press.

BLOCH-LAINÉ, F., and BOUVIER, J. (1986). *La France restaurée, 1944–1954: Dialogues sur les choix d'une modernisation*. Paris: Fayard.

CARRÉ, J.-J., DUBOIS, P., and MALINVAUD, E. (1975). *French Economic Growth*. Stanford, Calif.: Stanford University Press.

CATHERINE, R., and GOUSSET, P. (1965). *L'État et l'essor industriel: Du dirigisme colbertien à l'économie concertée*. Paris: Berger-Levrault.

CAZES, B. (1991). 'Un demi-siècle de planification indicative', in M. Lévy-Leboyer and J.-C. Casanova (eds.), *Entre l'État et le marché*, 473–506. Paris: Gallimard.

CERNY, P., and SCHAIN, M. (1985) (eds.). *Socialism, the State and Public Policy in France.* London: Frances Pinter.

CHARLE, C. (1987). 'Le Pantouflage en France (1880–1980)'. *Annales ESC*, 42/5: 1115–38.

CLOUGH, SHEPARD B. (1939). *France: A History of National Economics 1789–1939.* New York: Scribners.

COHEN, E. (1995). 'France: National champions in search of a mission', in Jack Hayward (ed.), *Industrial Enterprise and European Integration.* Oxford: Oxford University Press.

COLETIS, G. (1991). 'Aides publiques et structure productive', in Richard Aréna (ed.), *Traité d'economie industrielle*, 858–75. Paris: Economica.

COTTON, J. (1969). 'Politics and economics in the 1930s: The balance-sheet of Blum's "New Deal" ', in Charles K. Warner (ed.), *From the Ancien Régime to the Front Populaire.* New York: Columbia University Press.

CROUZET, F. (1974). 'Recherches sur la production d'armements en France 1815–1913'. *Revue Historique*, 251: 409–22.

—— (1977). 'Essor, déclin et renaissance de l'industrie française des locomotives 1838–1914'. *Revue d'Histoire Économique & Sociale*, 75: 112–210.

DELORME, R., and ANDRÉ, C. (1981). *L'Etat et l'économie: Essai d'explication de l'évolution des dépenses publiques en France.* Paris: Le Seuil.

DESSIRIER, J. (1935). 'Secteur "abrité" et "non-abrité" dans le déséquilibre actuel de l'économie française'. *Revue d'Économie Politique*, 49/4: 1130–59.

DOBBIN, F. (1990). *Forging Industrial Policy: The United States, Britain and France in the Railway Age.* Cambridge: Cambridge University Press.

DORMOIS, J.-P. (1992). 'Performance et productivité des économies française et britannique à la veille de 1914'. Ph.D. thesis, European University Institute, Florence.

—— and BARDINI, C. (1993). 'Comparative levels of manufacturing productivity and their relation to the degree of commercial protection in Western Europe before 1914'. *Conference on 'Economic Growth and Cultural Change'.* Katholieke Universiteit Leuven.

DUSSAUZE, E. (1938). *L'Etat et les ententes industrielles: Quelques expériences.* Paris: Librairie Sociale & Économique.

EHRMAN, H. (1957). *Organised Business in France.* Princeton: Princeton University Press.

ENCAOUA, D., and JACQUEMIN, A. (1982). 'Organizational efficiency and monopoly power: The case of French industrial groups'. *European Economic Review*, 19/1: 25–52.

ERGAS, HENRY (1992). 'France Telecom: Has the model worked?', Seminar on 'The Interplay of Government, Industry and Research in France', Oslo, Jan.

ESTRIN, S., and HOLMES, P. (1983). *French Planning in Theory and Practice.* London: Allen & Unwin.

FAYOL, HENRI (1921). *L'Incapacité industrielle de l'État: Les P.T.T.* Paris.

FIÉRAIN, J. (1980). 'L'action de l'État dans les constructions navales 1866–1975', in J. Bouvier and J.-C. Perrot (eds.), *États, fiscalités, économies*, 271–82. Paris: Éditions de l'EHESS.

FONTAINE, A. (1926). *French Industry during the War.* New Haven: Yale University Press.

FONTVIEILLE, L. (1976). 'Évolution et croissance de l'État français de 1815 à 1969'. *Économies & Sociétés*, 10.

FOREMAN-PECK, JAMES (1989). 'L'État et le développement du réseau de télécommunications en Europe à ses débuts'. *Histoire, Economie, Sociétés*, 8: 383–99.

FOURASTIÉ, J. (1979). *Les Trente Glorieuses ou la Révolution invisible de 1946 à 1975*. Paris: Fayard.

FRANKENSTEIN, R. (1980). 'Intervention étatique et réarmement en France 1935–39'. *Revue Économique*, 31/4: 743–81.

FRANZMEYER, F. (1982). *Approaches to Industrial Policy within the EC and its Impact on European Integration*. Aldershot: Gower.

GALAMBERT, P. (1982). *Les Sept Paradoxes de la politique industrielle*. Paris: Le Cerf.

GILMET, M., and PROVENCE, J. (1992). *Politique industrielle: État, Europe, entreprise*. Paris: Hatier.

GODFREY, J. (1987). *Capitalism and War: Industrial Policy and Bureacracy in France 1914–18*. Leamington Spa: Berg.

GONJO, Y. (1972). 'Le Plan Freycinet (1878–1882): Un aspect de la Grande Dépression en France'. *Revue Historique*, 249/3: 49–86.

HALL, P. A. (1986). *Governing the Economy: The Politics of State Intervention in Britain and France*. New York: Oxford University Press.

HARDACH, G. (1977). 'La Mobilisation industrielle en 1914–1918: Production, planification, idéologie', in Patrick Fridenson (ed.), *1914–1918: L'Autre front*. Cahiers du Mouvement Social, 2: 81–109. Paris.

HAUDEVILLE, B. (1983). 'Politique industrielle et politique économique générale: Réflexion sur le cas français'. *Revue d'Économie Industrielle*, 23/1: 57–65.

HAYWARD, J., and WATSON, M. (1985) (eds.). *The State and the Market Economy: Industrial Patriotism and Economic Intervention in France*. Brighton: Wheatsheaf.

HILSHEIMER, J. (1973). *Interessengruppen and Zollpolitik in Frankreich*. Ph.D. thesis, Heidelberg.

HURET, E. *et al.* (1972). *Les Entreprises publiques de 1959 à 1969*. Paris: INSEE.

JEANNENEY, J.-M. (1959). *Forces et faiblesses de l'économie française*. Paris: Armand Colin.

JENNY, F., and WEBER, A.-P. (1983). 'Aggregate welfare loss due to monopoly power in the French economy: Some tentative estimates'. *Journal of Industrial Economics*, 32/Dec.: 113–30.

JÈZE, G. (1927). *War Finance in France*. New Haven: Yale University Press.

JOUVENEL, B. DE (1928). *L'économie dirigée: Le Programme de la nouvelle génération*. Paris: Librairie de Valois.

KUISEL, R. (1981). *Capitalism and the State in Modern France: Renovation and Economic Management in the 20th Century*. Cambridge: Cambridge University Press.

LANDES, D. (1951). 'French business and the businessman: A social and cultural analysis', in E. M. Earle (ed.), *Problems of the Third and Fourth Republics*, 334–53. Princeton: Princeton University Press.

LAUBER, V. (1983). *The Politics of Economic Policy: France 1974–1982*. New York: Praeger.

LAUFFENBERGER, H. (1939). *L'intervention de l'Etat en matière économique*. Paris: Presses Universitaires de France.

LE FOLL, J. (1985). 'Les Aides publiques à l'industrie: Eléments d'évaluation'. *Economie & Prévision*, 70/4: 7–39.

LEHOUCQ, T., and STRAUSS, J.-P. (1988). 'Les Industries françaises de haute technologie: Des difficultés à rester dans la course'. *Économie & Statistique*, no. 207: 15–23.

LEVET, J.-L. (1988). *Une France sans usines*. Paris: Economica.

LÉVY-LEBOYER, M. (1971). 'La Décélération de l'économie française dans la seconde moitié du XIXè siècle'. *Revue d'Histoire Économique et Sociale*, 49/4: 485–507.

—— (1980). 'La Dette publique en France au XIXè siècle', in *La Dette publique aux XVIIIè et XIXè siècles*. Brussels: Crédit Communal de Belgique.

—— Lescure, M., and Straus, A. (1991). 'L'intervention de l'État: Mythes et réalités', in M. Lévy-Leboyer and J.-C. Casanova (eds.), *Entre l'État et le marché*, 251–87. Paris: Gallimard.

McArthur, J. H., and Scott, B. R. (1969). *Industrial Planning in France*. Boston: Harvard University Business School (Fr. translation, 1970).

Mason, E. S. (1931). 'Saint-Simonism and the rationalization of industry'. *Quarterly Journal of Economics*, 45/Aug.: 640–83.

Mathieu, E., and Suberchicot, M. (1978). 'Marchés publics et structures industrielles'. *Économie & Statistique*, 96/Jan.: 43–54.

Ministère de l'Industrie (1977). *Les Marchés publics en 1974 dans l'industrie*. Paris: La Documentation Française.

Monfort, J.-A., and Vassille, L. (1985). *La Concentration des activités économiques: Les Établissements, les entreprises et les groupes*. Paris: INSEE.

Morvan, Y. (1983). La Politique industrielle française depuis la Libération: Quarante ans d'interventions et d'ambiguités'. *Revue d'Économie Industrielle*, 23/1: 19–35.

OECD (1974). *The Industrial Policy of France*. Paris: OECD.

—— (1995). *Études économiques de l'OCDE: France*. Paris: OECD.

Ogburn, W. F., and Jaffé, W. (1929). *The Economic Development of Postwar France: A Survey of Production*. New York: Columbia University Press.

Paxton, R. O. (1972). *Vichy France: Old Guard and New Order*. New York: Columbia University Press.

Piettre, A. (1936). *L'Évolution des ententes industrielles en France depuis la crise*. Paris: Sirey.

Plutino, B. (1969). 'Un aspect de l'intervention de l'État dans le secteur privé pendant la guerre de 1914–18: Les Consortiums'. MA thesis, Université de Paris-X.

Sachs, J. D., and Wyplosz, C. (1986). 'The economic consequences of President Mitterrand'. *Economic Policy*, 2/Apr.: 261–312.

Saint-Paul, G. (1993). 'Economic reconstruction in France, 1945–1958', in R. Dornbusch, R. Layard, and W. Nölling (eds.), *Post-War Economic Reconstruction: Possible Lessons from Europe*. Cambridge, Mass.: MIT Press.

Saly, P. (1980). *La Politique des grands travaux en France 1929–1939*. New York: Arno Press.

Sautter, C. (1982). 'France', in Andrea Boltho (ed.), *The European Economy: Growth and Crisis*. Oxford: Oxford University Press.

Shams, A. (1990). 'Les Politiques industrielles dans un système d'économie mixte: L'Exemple de la France'. Ph.D. thesis, University of Paris-Dauphine, mimeo.

Sheanan, J. (1963). *Promotion and Control of Industry in Postwar France*. Cambridge, Mass.: Harvard University Press.

Sicsic, P., and Wyplosz, C. (1996). 'France', in Nicholas Crafts and Gianni Toniolo (eds.), *Economic Growth in Europe since 1945*, 210–39. Cambridge: Cambridge University Press.

Smith, M. S. (1980). *Tariff Reform in France 1860–1900: The Politics of Economic Interests*. London: Cornell University Press.

Toutain, J.-C. (1976). *Les Transports en France de 1830 à 1965*. Cahiers de l'ISEA, AF Series, Sept.–Oct.

Ullmo, Y. (1974). *La Planification en France*. Paris: Dalloz.

4

Germany: The Invention of Interventionism

WILFRIED FELDENKIRCHEN
Friedrich-Alexander Universitat
Lehrstuhl für Wirtschafts, Sozial, und Unternehmensgeshicte

More than any other Western European nation, industrial development in Germany has been marked by political, economic, and social upheavals. The years between 1914 and 1990 included the First World War, inflation, the Weimar economic recovery, the Great Depression, National Socialist re-armament, the Second World War, the post-war occupation, the emergence of the Federal Republic of Germany, and the nation's reunification. These radical changes are reflected in Germany's GDP (Fig. 4.1). The question naturally arises whether and to what extent changes in the 'economic order' precipitated new directions in industrial policy. Alternatively, can continuities in industrial policy be observed despite this erratic economic growth (Jäger 1988: 5; Schremmer 1976: 122; Einem 1991: 11–19; Adams and Klein 1983: 187 ff.; Kokalj and Albach 1987)?[1]

After a short survey of the development of the economic order in Germany, the chapter explains the German conception of industrial policy and the relationship between private economy and the state since the end of the last century. It then discusses the central components of German industrial policy, cartel and competition policy, tariffs and subsidies, infrastructure policy, and public ownership.

4.1. CHANGES IN THE 'GERMAN ECONOMIC ORDER' SINCE THE LATE NINETEENTH CENTURY

Between 1871 and 1913 internal policies and external events profoundly changed the character of the German economic order. After the so-called *Gründerkrise* ('Founders' Crisis'), there was a turning away from the economic and political ideology of laissez-faire liberalism and a shift towards activist industrial policy and protectionism. The new tariffs of 1879 marked a shift from liberal trade policies by industrialists, agrarian noble landowners, and small farmers. The convergence of the economic and political interests of the great landowners of the east threatened by overseas imports of wheat, and of the great industrialists

---

[1] The German term *Wirtschaftsordnung* ('economic order') encompasses the political and organizational framework in which the economy operates as well as the institutions that shape the economic processes. Changes in Germany's political and economic order occurred swiftly and dramatically, and often by violent means.

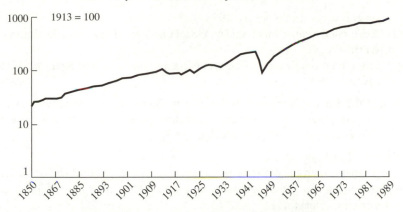

FIG. 4.1. Level of GDP in Germany, 1850–1989

in the west, threatened by English and Belgian iron and rail imports, has been called 'the marriage of iron and rye' (Feldenkirchen 1987*a*: 208 ff.; Henning 1988: 122 ff.). In addition to these tariffs, others were introduced, most notably on cotton, as the textile industrialists in the south-west feared the competition of Switzerland and France.

In the upheavals at the end of the First World War, the Weimar Republic introduced important reforms of Germany's economic order, along with the new democratic constitution. Parliament took control of economic policy. The central government gained financial sovereignty over the states in the Erzberger financial reform (Krohn 1974: 43; Witt 1982). A central finance ministry was formed. Public spending as a proportion of national product rose dramatically, as the modern welfare state began to appear in Germany (Borchardt 1982: 181; Abelshauser 1987: 18; Preller 1978).[2] When the tax burden on companies was increased, the unions saw it as a first step towards economic democracy, while most entrepreneurs considered it proof that the Weimar Republic was a 'Union State'. As the state often intervened in wage negotiations by decreeing new wage scales before and after the inflation period, this policy in the long run helped to undermine political support for the Republic. The Depression undermined the already weak support for Weimar's traditional parties, paving the way for extremist parties on the left and right, eventually leading to Hitler's rise to power (Blaich 1987: 170; Neebe 1981: 99; Weisbrod 1985; Grübler 1982).

Hitler's economic order was predicated on a war of expansion. Economic liberalism, or a system of private interest was not altogether abandoned, but it was subordinated to political goals. Private property was confirmed, as long as it oriented itself towards the goals defined by the party. It is possible to distinguish three periods in relations between the economy and the state:

---

[2] The public spending on social welfare (social security, supplementary benefit, health service, and housing programmes) per inhabitant rose from M 20,50 in 1913 to M 64,70 in 1925 and M 106,30 in 1932.

(1) general economic recovery 1933–6;
(2) accelerated rearmament under the 'Four-Year Plan' and beginning of World War II;
(3) massive rationalization of the war economy under Alfred Speer from 1942 onwards.

Within the existing economic order of a market system, instruments of Nazi industrial policy were taxes, subsidies, and direct orders in fields such as (Frank 1993: 175; Barkai 1977: 150–204; Erker 1993):

- raw material allocation;
- investment control and forced investments to achieve national self-sufficiency;
- promotion of further cartelization by a threat of mandatory cartelization;
- direction of workforce;
- direction of capital;
- price and wage control;
- control of foreign trade; and
- 'organization' of industry.

Industrial policy in Germany after 1933 was aimed at promoting German rearmament and war preparation. As chemicals, heavy industry, and automobiles were prime targets, consumer industries were seen as of lesser importance and fell behind capital goods industries (Hayes 1982: 81; Borkin 1986). As the example of National Socialist foreign trade proves, the reduction of imports through tariffs or non-tariff measures had the effect of boosting the value of the national currency and made exports more difficult. Exporting companies were thus protected by the so-called 'New Plan' of Reichsbank President Hjalmar Schacht introduced in 1934 (Barkai 1977: 163; Dengg 1986: 309; Döring 1969). In response to the New Plan, foreign economic relations became increasingly bilateral. Trade policy began to concentrate on northern and south-eastern European nations, as shown by the German–Soviet trade agreement and the Haavara agreement of 1933, rather than on Germany's traditional primary export partners (Teichert 1984: 19–21; Riemenschneider 1987: 202–5; Volland 1976).

After 1939 consumer industries came to a virtual standstill. Textile plants, for example, were often converted for use, say, in the electrical industry. In war-related industries production was concentrated in the 'best' plants, and companies had to waive their patent rights. The assignment of foreign forced labour to the armament industry after 1942 allowed production to increase until the autumn of 1944 (Hopmann and Spoerer *et al.* 1994: 104; Herbert 1985: 270–3). Prices and profitability increasingly lost their relevance as higher output became the only important consideration. To achieve this goal, research and investment were also directed only to war-related fields as for instance shown by the production of buna, synthetic rubber (Birkenfeld 1963: 56; Petzina 1968).

Under economics minister Ludwig Erhard the 'social market economy' was introduced simultaneously with currency reform in 1948. This concept combines aspects of a free market economy with the idea of 'the social state'. Prices and competition were supposed to be the primary means of order in the economy. The state should merely provide a framework to secure competitive practices in open markets without intervening in pricing policies, providing subsidies, or permitting monopolies or cartels. At the same time the state should block undue concentrations of power, support the weak, and prevent market excesses, as well as acting as a stabilizer by controlling money supply and implementing social reforms (Ambrosius 1977: 283 ff.; Buchheim 1990: 138 ff.). This apparent contradiction often led to unbalanced measures, which seemed to strengthen only one aspect of the policy.

Germany's strong export orientation proved to be a stabilizing factor in the economy. Policy encouraged expansion in the export sector particularly in times of stagnating domestic demand. To promote export business, the German government introduced a number of measures, including subsidization of the shipbuilding industry, tax advantages for exports (1951), government guarantees for export business and currency, and favourable rail shipping rates (Ambrosius 1984*b*: 283; Buchheim 1990: 138 ff.). On the other hand, a series of quantitative import restrictions, particularly in the agrarian sector as well as for textiles, were designed to protect domestic business sectors that were especially endangered by cheap international competitors. The post-war emphasis on free markets minimized, but did not eliminate, the use of tariffs and import controls as instruments of industrial policy. But the traditional German export orientation ensured that they gradually lost importance or became part of a supranational industrial policy (Sturm 1991: 26; Smeets 1989; Katzenstein 1989).

4.2. GERMAN CONCEPTS OF INDUSTRIAL POLICY

In Germany discussions about the concept and effects of industrial policy have been much more important than the actual implementation of industrial policy. In fact, there never has been a clear idea of what effects industrial policy should have. The closest approach to a realistic policy was in the period 1933–45, but even then long-term strategies were overtaken by immediate necessities (Hentschel 1980: 10; Fisher 1968).

The basic question has always been whether the state should initiate structural changes within the market economy, or whether its primary task lies in eliminating hindrances to the operation of market forces. In German party politics, as well as in economic theory, those who favoured structural planning maintained that the state should influence structural change to promote and accelerate the growth of promising industries and economic sectors, while quickly weeding out weaker sectors. In their view, this was the only way to boost overall economic growth in a country while creating more jobs and raising income. This active strategy was seen as positive structural adaptation, or simply 'picking the winners'. They claimed private investors did not think far enough in the future, were hesitant about taking risks, or unable to raise sufficient capital for large investment projects on the financial markets. Industrial policy measures and demands for them were often justified with the observation that certain industries received targeted support in other countries (Conrad 1987: 23 ff.; Rahmeyer 1989: 165).

Those who favoured market-oriented economic policies, on the other hand, maintained that successful structural planning was possible only if state institutions had better or earlier information about future economic developments than the private sector. Since this is not true in market economies, they claimed state planning activities necessarily distort a country's production structure and lead to an overall decline in economic efficiency. In the framework of the market approach, then, the primary task of industrial policy is to eliminate barriers to structural change. Seen from this point of view, it is impossible for the state to determine the optimal production structure for a national economy. State intervention was needed only when public goods needed to be financed or when external effects were involved. The goal of such measures must be to compensate for market failures, not to direct the production structure in a specific direction (Kokalj and Albach 1987: 246).

Industrial policies practised in Germany in the period between 1871 and 1990 generally fluctuated between these two poles. As economic policy is usually a result of compromises, it is hard to find periods in which either market or structural policies have been fully implemented. The political reality was that the two conceptions were put into practice in such a way that one of the two strategies prevailed, but one or another measure was borrowed from the opposite strategy. In this respect Eichengreen's view, adopting Charles Maier's idea of corporatism originating from a long-term party-political compromise between state, employers, and trade unions, is not tenable (Eichengreen 1994). The close cooperation between state and interest groups to support economic growth, significant for demand-side policies, is de facto only found in the 'concerted action' (*Konzertierte Aktion*) by state, trade unions, and employers which was initiated by Wirtschaftsminister Karl Schiller between 1967 and 1976. In contrast to this minor movement towards a Keynesian policy, the Federal government since the 1980s, along with, for example, Great Britain, has also tried to improve national economic conditions by means of a supply-side strategy. In particular, it has adopted the following measures:

- tax relief for enterprises by improved depreciation possibilities and lower trade taxes;
- higher levies on private households by increasing value added tax and other direct taxation;
- reduction of government expenditure and increasing social security contributions.

Although virtually every government, regardless of its political orientation, declared it was giving highest priority to improving the general framework for entrepreneurial activities, in fact, specific industries or companies were given targeted support. This was even true in the 1950s, when demand outpaced production for many years. Capital goods industries were given better tax breaks to promote their growth. Purely economic arguments were rarely used to support such actions; instead, so-called 'political necessity' was the general excuse. And here it is obvious that in most cases, pressure by interest groups actually precipitated the measures, as long as they were able to secure enough potential votes (Eickhoff 1989: 135; Schmal 1980).

Practical policy was not based on fully coherent industrial strategies, but instead was a bundle of more or less coordinated measures with differing objectives and competencies. If we leave out the period 1933–45 when other aims prevailed, there were three broad types of policies (Bletschacher and Klodt 1991; Conrad 1987; Eekhoff 1994):

1. In certain sectors of the economy, a certain minimal level of domestic production should be maintained. This usually serves to guarantee domestic supplies or military security (conservation policy).

2. Structural adaptations should be prolonged over a period of time to help alleviate social disruptions. This category is largely focused on declining industries and serves to preserve threatened jobs (structural adaptation policy). Lately this has been the policy in former East Germany.

3. Industries that appear to be promising for the future should be strengthened. The objective here is not to protect structurally weak sectors, but to target support of structurally strong sectors whose share of the total production should be increased (strategic industrial policy).

The first two policies—conservation and structural adaptation—have traditionally formed the core of industrial policy in Germany, while strategic policy has only recently assumed greater significance and even today is referred to as 'new industrial policy' (Conrad 1987: 26; Härtel 1986: 2; Bletschacher and Klodt 1991). The origin of strategic industrial policy in Germany, as in other countries, was the assumption that higher profits could be made in certain industries than in others. Above all, the example of Japan has prompted Germany to specialize increasingly on strategic industries in recent years in order to generate higher income in international competition than other countries. Industrial policy should provide targeted support for these industries to help them to achieve competitive advantages in the global market (Wartenberg 1991: 864; Seitz 1992; Narjes 1993). In 1962 the government established the Ministry for Scientific Research, which was transformed into the Federal Ministry for Research and Technology in 1972. Government policy had the primary objective of closing the technological gap with other countries and creating new incentives for innovation. The focal point of this strategic industrial policy in recent years has been research and technology policy, and above all the promotion of microelectronics as well as the aerospace industry through direct and indirect support measures. This support doubled in the years between 1974 and 1984 from DM 2.028 billion to DM 4.055 billion (Klodt 1992: 3 ff.; Ambrosius 1984a: 131).

Generally, research policy in Germany is more directed to pure research than to the development of products for certain markets. According to the principle of subsidiarity, the primary responsibility for R & D activities is given to industry. Compared to the numbers of patents, the German economy is meant to be less innovative than the US or Japanese economies. The number of patents declared by the German 'Patentamt' between 1913 and 1929 rose from 9,045 to 20,202, but decreased after World War II by almost 25% from totally 62,049 to 40,451 between 1961/5 and 1990 (IW 1994: 122; Statistisches Reichsamt). However, the question of how many of these patents found use in innovation processes still remains unanswered (Weyhenmeyer 1994: 150).

The training of employees plays an important role in an innovative economy. After World War II, new technology and processes triggered an increasing need to reform employee training. According to the trends in the labour market, the central ideas of German educational policy were geared towards increasing the proportion of qualified employees—for instance by strengthening of the so-called 'dual system' of practical training and training at school, and by upping the proportion of women by improving arrangements for combining work with the raising of a family. Thus, parents were able to take 'educational leave' for 18 months and benefited from greater flexibility in working hours.

In contrast, conservation industrial policy originated in Germany in the 1870s, when Bismarck's policy of customs protection was implemented to protect agriculture, and later, following the Second World War, protection was given to the mining and steel industries. In all three sectors, a certain self-sufficiency was considered crucial in order not to be fully dependent on foreign supplies, particularly in a crisis. Just as various programmes for supporting German agriculture were justified by the need to ensure a domestic supply of food for the population, today's argument in the mining sector is paradoxically that the industry preserves the nation's energy reserves. The iron and steel industry is considered by many to be indispensable for higher national policy reasons and from the standpoint of military strategy. It is generally in these three sectors that most industrial nations have been under pressure from less developed countries at different times. Policy aimed to protect agriculture since the late nineteenth century, and mining, and iron and steel industries in highly developed industrial nations such as Germany since the 1950s and 1970s, respectively. Increasingly, these protective policies have been instituted by the European Community, either through a common agricultural policy or in the framework of an iron and steel union. In addition to these EC measures, national programmes in Germany in the 1970s supported current investment (1974) and investment for the future (1977) (Gillingham 1991; Bührer 1986). One thing all these conservation policies had in common was their tendency to survive and thrive. Yet the significance of coal for producing energy had declined considerably since the end of the Second World War, or more precisely, since the end of the 1950s.

A second focal point of industrial policies in Germany in the twentieth century is support for declining industries. The primary concern has been to slow the loss of jobs in structurally weak industries. To this end, the government has relied on subsidy programmes for limited periods and often resorted to protective trade measures as well (Jàkli 1990: 100–3; Esser 1995: 55; Pilz 1983).

Among measures in the framework of structural adaptations are those conceived to restore the competitiveness of endangered industries. Such support is usually offered in the form of investment help for carrying out rationalization measures, for redesigning product ranges, or for modernizing production facilities. Often—and this is true above all for mining and heavy industry—such subsidies were linked to requirements voluntarily to reduce their capacities. In the period following the Second World War, structural adaptations were primarily prompted by international competitive pressure. Above all, labour-intensive industries and industries with standardized products, easily produced in developing countries, were most heavily subjected to competitive pressure. Consequently, structural adaptation policies in Germany after the Second World War focused on sectors such as the textiles and clothing or shipbuilding. As the crisis grew in the shipbuilding industry, government subsidies, often boosted by interest subsidies, had a stimulating effect (Suntum 1986: 103; Jàkli 1990; Jüttemeier 1984).

Although the social market economy originally was based on the elimination of subsidies in favour of market forces, industrial policies have been affected by problematic changes in the economic environment and the desire to protect small- and medium-sized companies with special credits, credit guarantees, tax advantages, and subsidies. The Investment Assistance Act of 1952 provided more than DM 4.5 billion to rebuild sectors that were in especially critical condition. The basic commodities, power and water supply utilities, as well as the German railroad authority, all benefited from this support.

4.3. CARTEL AND COMPETITION POLICY

Despite substantial changes in Germany's economic system over the last century, we nevertheless see some continuities, for example in competition policy. In contrast to the American antitrust laws, German governments or the judiciary never really opposed restraints of trade or ancillary restraints of trade up to 1945, although several phases in the governmental attitude towards cartelization can be distinguished. Prior to 1914 the governmental principle of laissez-faire prevailed, as cartels were widely perceived as legitimate instruments of 'economic order' (Pohl 1985: 12). The goals of the cartels, based on a broad political consensus, were:

- to ensure an 'adequate' return on investments by avoiding excessive competition;
- to coordinate supply and demand in the face of cyclical developments by introducing production or sales quotas;
- to help moderate and stabilize price fluctuations (Maschke 1964: 11, 24; Blaich 1973: 293).

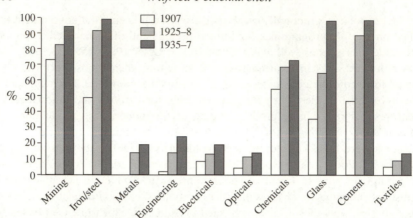

FIG. 4.2. Cartelized production in German industries
Source: König 1960: 311.

Legislation introduced by the Reichsgericht concerning the legitimacy of cartel agreements had a strong impact on the expansion of cartels around the turn of the century. In 1897 the highest German court ruled clearly in favour of cartels by confirming the civil law effectiveness of these arrangements also in cases of harmful competition. The conviction expressed in the judgment represented the widespread public opinion that absolute competition could be harmful for individual firms and that cartels and associations served a purpose for the national economy. Thus, in contrast to other countries, the number of German cartels rose steadily so that there were about 600 by 1911.

Favoured by the passivity of the state's economic policy, cartels and syndicates before World War I assumed an important function in the market order. The strong performance of the German economy up to World War I might therefore partly be explained by the widespread acceptance of cartels and syndicates as instruments of market order. At least economic growth was not greatly handicapped. Chandler (1991) attributes Germany's international economic success in this period to the internal organization of her firms, rather than to market conditions. German 'Organizational Capabilities' were supposedly greater than those of British firms and second only to the United States. If this contention is accepted, then it may be a piece of evidence that favours the correctness of German opinion of the period. Secure markets, achieved in the USA by monopolies and the entry barriers of distance and in Germany by cartels, perhaps encouraged professional and efficient business management.

After 1914 cartels were soon integrated into the war economy, sometimes becoming semi-governmental enterprises to guarantee the supply of raw material to the armament industry, and partly in order to forestall compulsory cartelization, as was the case in the cement and potash industries. Thus, increasing cartelization during World War I was due more to political than to economic considerations. Even though the first German cartel law of 1923 provided for the establishment of a special cartel court that had jurisdiction in all disputes between cartels and the government, the cartel decree was a failure, actually strengthening cartels, since it gave legal recognition to them and sanctioned boycotts and similar practices. Thus the number of cartels actually grew (Fig. 4.2) (Feldenkirchen 1992: 259; Pohl 1985). The Depression proved damaging to cartels as their pricing policy led to increasing criticism. In 1930, a Presidential Decree gave the Cabinet power to void cartel agreements or parts of them. In 1931 all cartel prices were reduced by 10% by emergency decree. These decrees and the Depression endangered the continuance of many cartels, but the coming to power of the Nazis saved the cartel system. The Zwangskartellgesetz passed already on 15 July 1933 gave them a chance for 'an industrial policy geared to the interest of the national economy if necessary with the help of compulsory cartels'. Cartels were allowed to oust 'unreliable competitors' from the market by declaring a boycott or by similar measures. De facto unreliability existed when a competitor sold below the 'justified' price, whether bound by price agreements or not (Feldenkirchen 1985: 148; Barkai 1977: 128).

The main reason that cartels could prosper in Germany until 1945 was that they were believed to be a form of economic organization far superior to unrestricted competition. The government at times only tried to influence the pricing situation, for instance in the widely cartelized heavy industry by buying up outsiders (Overy 1994: 144; Mollin 1988: 42–4; Riedel 1973: 155).

After 1945, free 'workable' competition in the 'social market economy' became the keynote of policy in West Germany. US pressure was the one coherent, driving force in the immediate post-war period leading to the Act Against Restraits of Competition in 1957. This pressure triggered a bitter dispute among protagonists of two very different conceptions of the economy (Satzky 1985: 232; Robert 1976: 106; Hoppmann 1988). Traditionally business associations were seen as a means of self-regulation to maintain order and reduce concentration. Supporters of the social market economy proposed a sovereign market regulated by state agencies to ensure similar goals. In the interest of compromise, the Act allowed exceptions in certain circumstances, particularly in periods of structural adjustments. In a second amendment of 1973, merger control was introduced which had the effect that concentration in the German economy—though increasing —seems to be fairly moderate in international perspective.[3] Several sectors of the economy have been exempt, i.e. agriculture, transportation, utilities, communications which are either seen as not fit for a market economy or are under strict government regulation. Moreover, the government is empowered to grant

---

[3] The influence of the banks and interlocking board memberships, however, led to a higher concentration than the relatively low rates of horizontal, vertical, conglomerate, or aggregate concentration seem to indicate. The aspect of limiting a bank's shareholdings in one company to 5% is being discussed again and again in Germany, as well as one bank sitting on the boards of competing industrial companies.

exceptions in merger cases in any industry for overriding economic reasons (Kokalj and Albach 1987: 245 ff.; Eickhof 1989: 135 ff.).

4.4. INDUSTRIAL POLICY INSTRUMENTS: TARIFFS AND SUBSIDIES

The targets of industrial policies were either production conditions for companies in Germany (domestic protection) or marketing conditions for competitors from abroad (foreign protection). The primary instrument used for domestic protection since the 1880s, when the agricultural sector profited from it, has been subsidies, that is, state financial benefits for companies that did not generate any— or enough—returns. Subsidies were offered in a wide variety of forms, whereby so-called financial aid, including direct payments by the state, comprised the largest part. Such subsidies included demobilization and reconstruction aid immediately following the First World War, or compensation for costs during the occupation of the Ruhr and the financing of the general strike, the so-called 'Ruhr Aid' in 1924 (Krohn 1974: 105–12).

Subsidies paid to German companies before 1914 amounted to less than DM 7 million per year or less than 0.01% of NNP. In the inter-war period subsidies had risen to RM 114 million already in 1925, but doubled again until 1928. In the 1930s every year more than RM 300 million were paid in subsidies, making up between 0.3 and 0.5% of NNP (Hoffmann *et al.* 1965: 802 ff.). In the post-war period this tendency continued, reaching more than 2% of NNP at times (Fig. 4.3).

Today coal mining is the most highly subsidized sector in the German economy as each job is subsidized annually with more than DM 100,000 within the

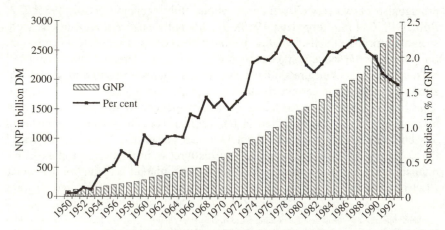

FIG. 4.3. NNP and share of subsidies in NNP
Source: Statistisches Bundesamt 1950–93.

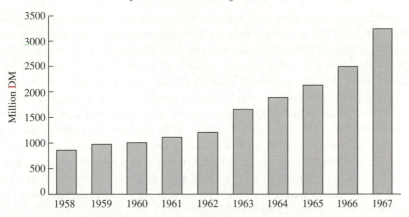

FIG. 4.4. Financial aid for Ruhr coal mining
Source: Jàkli 1990: 112.

last twenty years. These measures are justified by the fact that unfavourable mining conditions make the production of German lignite—almost DM 300 per ton—some three times more expensive than imported coal (Fig. 4.4). Yet coal mining is still subsidized because of employment and regional objectives and because the government is reluctant to give up domestic supplies completely. The use of German coal in producing electricity is guaranteed by law and by the so-called 'contract of the century'. Subsidies for energy in Germany are estimated to total nearly DM 10 billion a year. Of this total, roughly two-thirds are for the nation's coal subsidies, 17% is used to promote and subsidize district heating, rationalized energy supplies, and new sources of energy, 12% is earmarked for subsidizing nuclear energy—excluding support for basic research and development in this field—and 4% is used to support the country's oil policy.

In 1995 the Federal Constitutional Court declared the so-called 'coal penny', a form of taxation imposed on every consumer of electricity to help finance government subsidies of the coal industry, to be unconstitutional. Discussion in Germany no longer focuses on making long-overdue adjustments in the nation's coal policy, but on creating a new tax to fulfil the same purpose as the scrapped 'coal penny'. It is interesting to note that the same politicians that demand a reduction of air pollution because of environmental reasons at the same time asked for the increased use of German lignite for the production of electricity (Jàkli 1990: 104; Kokalj and Albach 1987: 264; Hohensee and Salewski 1993).

The iron and steel industry, which was regulated on a European level since the early 1950s, has long ceased to play a key role in the country's economic performance. The situation in the German steel industry nowadays, however, is such that structural measures have created an industry that is able to compete, at least as far as quality is concerned, with the highly subsidized French, Belgian, and Italian steel industries. As a result, subsidies for steel remain undiminished in Germany, similar to the situation in the agriculture and coal mining sectors (Kokalj and Albach 1987: 271; Albrecht and Wesselkock 1971; Jüttemeier 1984). Support for the iron and steel industry, above all in the Saar, Salzgitter, or Ruhr regions, was often designated as structural adaptation measures, so that their distinction from conservation industrial policy is difficult to determine. The fact is, however, that it is difficult to make a distinction between measures to retain structures and to adapt structures, because most adaptation support is provided over very long periods of time. If the adaptation problems were not solved at the end of the first subsidy phase, subsequent support programmes were always created. In the end, industrial policies that were originally designed to promote structural adaptation frequently ended up as measures for conserving structures (Wolfertz 1993: 24–30; Finking 1978: 156–80).

The three industries—coal, iron, and steel—number among the most heavily subsidized industries in the world. In fact each of these industries has got more government subsidies than for instance the German textile industry which has lost the most jobs of any German industry after World War II. The difference can be explained by the fact that the German textile industry has never been a big-scale industry nor has it been regionally concentrated. Thus the pressure on politics to soften the effects of structural change never had the same effect as in heavy industry (Rahmeyer 1989: 163–78).

Next to subsidies, tax relief and, finally, help in the form of conditional guarantees for structurally weak industries were important instruments of conservation policy. Among the financial support offered by the state was the provision of low-interest credit. Particularly during the Great Depression in the late 1920s and early 1930s, the state used such intervention to stabilize the situation in virtually all sectors of the economy (Roehl 1988: 96 ff.; Meister 1991; Plumpe 1985). It is more difficult to define the covert instruments for domestic protection, such as the preference for domestic suppliers in public procurement, or the mixture of commercial and political interests in state-owned companies. This is particularly true in the Third Reich, above all in the industries supplying the military (Overy 1994: 175 ff.; Riedel 1973).

Instruments for providing protection against foreign competition, that is, closing domestic markets to outside companies, were even more varied throughout the twentieth century. The classic instrument was tariffs imposed on foreign goods—a form of tax that could be raised to the point where imported products could no longer compete with domestic goods.

As already mentioned the first major step in this direction was made in 1880, when protective tariffs were introduced for raw iron and cotton products as well as for wheat. Following the First World War, Germany was first able to reintroduce tariffs in 1925, when it regained full sovereign rights in trade (Fig. 4.5). On the basis of the 1902 Bülow Tariffs, duties were imposed on agrarian and industrial products, above all on goods produced by heavy industry (Feldenkirchen 1987*b*: 338–40). Reflecting the international situation, the external

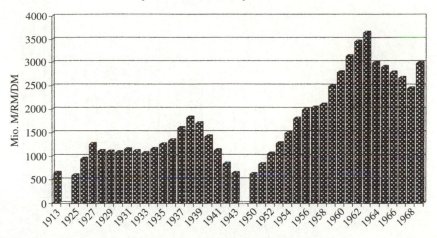

FIG. 4.5. Customs revenue in Germany
Source: Statistisches Bundesamt 1972: 233.

exchange of goods was increasingly divorced from the principle of open markets and elimination of trade barriers. Indeed, as the Depression intensified late in the 1920s, the country turned more and more to protectionist measures. Parallel to expensive subsidies for exports, imports were restricted by the regulation of currency exchanges and the imposition of high tariffs (Feldenkirchen 1987*b*: 352; Stegmann 1974: 502).

4.5. INFRASTRUCTURE

As an example of regional structural policy, one can cite the decentralization of production in major industrial regions, and the more balanced distribution of militarily relevant industrial potential throughout Germany during the Third Reich. Above all, the government promoted the so-called 'Middle German Industrial Centre' strategic plan. Enterprises as early as 1935 were told to disperse their regional concentration and to establish at least a second major plant in central Germany. This policy served a dual purpose: it helped to reduce unemployment in an area with an undeveloped infrastructure thus gaining additional support for the government and at the same time was part of the armament programme (Wagenführ 1963: 19 ff.). In the Federal Republic, regional structural policy is primarily aimed at balancing the regional differences between various parts of the country as best as possible. This was reflected by special promotion programmes for the zone along the border of East Germany and in West Berlin in effect up to the country's reunification. In addition, the government passed the Federal Regional Planning Act in 1965, which aimed at creating a framework of basic economic conditions (Steininger-Fetzer 1981: 118–21; Franz and Schalk

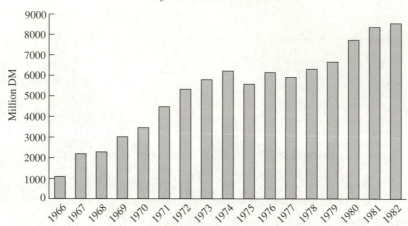

FIG. 4.6. Tax grants and regional policy

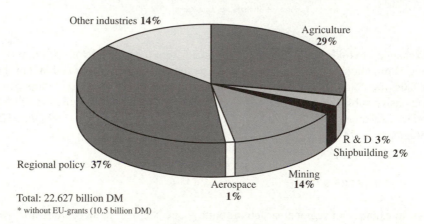

Total: 22.627 billion DM
* without EU-grants (10.5 billion DM)

FIG. 4.7. Financial aid of the central government to agriculture and industry in 1994

1989). From then until 1974, tax concessions for regional policy increased rapidly (Fig. 4.6). Regional policy in 1994 was the single most expensive component of German industrial and agricultural financial aid (Fig. 4.7).

Transportation objectives have been a major element in Germany's industrial policy. Policy concerning communications and the transportation of goods and persons was concerned with traffic planning, market regulations, and fare policy —that is, regulations governing market access, barriers to market exit, and fares, as well as controls for the process of cooperations and consolidations (Hoppmann 1988; Esser 1995). Germany's railroad system was taken over by the government before the First World War. The consolidation of the eight separate state railroad systems into the Reichsbahn, however, took place in March 1920. In 1924 the organization was transformed into the Deutsche Reichsbahn AG, which was supposed to function as an independent company on the basis of standard business principles (Voigt 1965: 581 ff.; Facius 1959: 106; Ambrosius 1984*a*: 77).

Looking at the government's transportation policy in the period after the Second World War, the main objective was first to repair war damages to the system and restore operations. Subsequent expansion of the rail network in Germany was almost exclusively oriented to the needs of the growing economy, and support for infrastructure in the zone along the East German border (Suntum 1986: 104).

Post-war fare policy was largely taken over from state regulations formulated in the period between the wars. The core of the policy was formed by the Long-Distance Freight Law of September 1949, the General Railroad Law of March 1951, the Federal Railroad Law of December 1951, the Freight Transportation Law of October 1952, and the Inland Waterway Shipping Law of October 1953. These laws were all essentially formulated with the protection of Deutsche Bundesbahn in mind. Although granted a special position, Deutsche Bundesbahn had long since lost its monopoly position in Germany, and could only operate at a deficit. Competitors of Deutsche Bundesbahn were subjected to hindrances and restrictions (Basedow 1990: 68–70). Railroads not owned by the state had to undergo an approval process and were forced to coordinate their fares. As for long-distance haulage, the government gave concessions and imposed restrictions, as well as setting freight rates without providing any legal possibility for industry participation. At the same time, the government established the Federal Office for Long-Distance Trucking as a controlling agency. A licensing procedure was introduced for highway haulage, and in 1959, margin rates had to be approved by the government. In inland waterway traffic, shipping associations were made mandatory for non-labour union or long-term contracted parties, a quota system was introduced for distributing freight among shippers, and unprofitable water routes were subsidized with compensatory payments and mandatory rates. For domestic passenger traffic, the Passenger Transportation Act of 1934 was taken over by the Federal government. Through all these measures, the transportation markets in the Federal Republic of Germany have been characterized by extensive market access restrictions and fare regulations controlled by the government (Hamm 1988: 254 ff.; Suntum 1986: 103 ff.; DIHT 1991: 18 ff.).

A second phase of market structuring and fare policy began in 1961. From this point onward, the aim was 'to adjust the competitive conditions of the traffic carriers, and make possible an economically practical distribution of tasks through remuneration in line with market trends and improved competitive conditions'. By loosening the rigid price structures, the intention was to allow limited price competition between traffic carriers. For the first time, all traffic carriers were given the right to set their own fares. The government only intervened in fare policy to prevent 'inequitable' competition, to prevent disadvantages of the agricultural sector, small- and medium-sized businesses and underdeveloped regions, as well as to ensure that public welfare was preserved. Despite these objectives, the traffic law of 1961 and its concept of 'controlled competition' brought no decisive loosening of the government's controls (Voigt 1965: 584; Esser 1995: 57).

From the 1980s there were intensive discussions about the possibilities and limitations of a general liberalization of the traffic markets. These discussions were prompted both by deregulation measures implemented outside Germany, and by the obvious flaws in the government's efforts to solve important problems in its traffic systems through controls. In the meantime, it has generally been accepted that true competition can be allowed in this sector as well, taking into consideration the heterogeneity of the objectives of differing traffic carriers as well as the historic and institutional separation of traffic routes and means of transportation. The basis of this conclusion was the recognition that the regulation of freight traffic markets ultimately served to protect Deutsche Bundesbahn, yet did not help slow the gradual weakening of this carrier's market position despite its efforts to conserve the old structure. From the point of view of German society, the hindrance to a true competitive environment, coupled with increased squandering of resources, was highly questionable. Policies towards Deutsche Bundesbahn and Lufthansa had the effect that air fares were considerably higher than railroad fares, and market access restrictions and fare surcharges for charter traffic simultaneously served to protect Lufthansa (Voigt 1965: 584; Ambrosius 1984a: 126 ff.; Esser 1995: 57, 62 ff.).

The government was particularly restrictive and dirigistic in the telecommunications sector. The sector was largely the domain of Deutsche Bundespost as a public authority. Even after the reform of the post office structure in 1989, Deutsche Bundespost Telekom retained its network monopoly as well as its telephone services monopoly. Competition was opened between Telekom and private suppliers in other telecommunication services as well as in communication terminals. The network monopoly is justified as a natural monopoly, and the telecommunications infrastructure is seen as an instrument of the government's obligation to ensure public services. Considering this situation, it should be noted that the post office structural reform has not yet exploited its full potential for liberalization (Esser 1995: 56, 58; Weyhenmeyer 1994: 159).

In general, it must be said that a step-by-step retreat by the German government to truly competitive conditions is absolutely necessary and more than overdue. This need not necessarily be coupled with fully giving up socio-economic duties. Socio-economic arguments and the obligation to ensure public services, however, should not hinder traffic carrier competition that meets the needs of the market. It must be possible to give transportation tasks to those traffic carriers and transportation industries that perform most efficiently.

4.6. PUBLIC OWNERSHIP

Prior to the First World War, the Imperial state, founded in 1871, possessed little land and few enterprises of its own, except in Alsace-Lorraine. Revenues for the Imperial state came from tariffs, indirect consumption and stamp taxes, redistributive transfers from the states, and inheritance taxes. The federal states and the municipalities retained the right of direct taxation. Yet, in Prussia, the most important German state, 75.4% of public income derived from the government's entrepreneurial activities, particularly the state railroads, in 1913 (Schremmer 1989: 457).[4]

Since the end of the First World War, the country's energy sector has remained one of the focal points of government intervention. The creation of a unified system of power, gas, and water supplies and the consolidation of telecommunication and transport systems led to the situation in 1929 in which 3,955 of the total 4,974 utilities in Germany were public (Hughes 1977: 160 ff.).

Beyond this, the large number of public enterprises can be ascribed to the numerous capital goods enterprises that suffered difficulties in the world economic crisis at the end of the 1920s. The United Steelworks AG (Vereinigte Stahlwerke), Germany's largest coal and steel group, founded in 1926 by a number of Ruhr enterprises, was put on its feet by the government's taking over a large part of the shares. Much the same happened in the banking sector: after one of the largest German banks, the Darmstädter and Nationalbank had become insolvent in 1931, a complete breakdown of the German credit sector could only be averted by a government takeover.

In addition, there were a number of companies with mixed ownership structures, such as Rheinisch-Westfälisches Elektrizitätswerk (RWE), founded in 1898 in which the cities still have the majority of voting rights due to their shares with multiple voting rights even though they own less than 50% of the capital (Esser 1995: 56; Pohl 1992: 21–36; Ambrosius 1984a: 71 ff.). Today 'public interest', which in the past used to be behind public utilities, seems to have become an empty phrase. Nevertheless, mixed or state ownership were seen for a long time as instruments of competition policy. The monopolistic status of these enterprises only began to dissolve in recent years, a process exemplified by the Post Office reform.

The period of the Weimar Republic can be seen as a liberal market economy. Yet, due to the hyperinflation until 1923 and the Depression after 1929, the state intervened to a much greater extent than the economic order would suggest. It is important to note, however, that there was no clear industrial policy (leaving aside the plans for nationalization of certain industries right after the war) but rather crisis management, which at first glance might appear to be industrial policy. As a result of difficulties or imminent bankruptcy, the government took over several enterprises, so that in 1928 the state controlled 1% of all businesses, which however employed 11% of the total workforce and held 20% of the combined share capital of German stock companies (see Table 4.1) (Knoche 1989: 132–5). In particular the cities had taken over most of the electric utilities, gas works,

---

[4] Cf. Schremmer: 'to put it in a nutshell, the population financed state expenditure by the purchase of railway tickets rather than by tax payments.'

TABLE 4.1. *Number of bankruptcies in Germany, 1897–1990*

Year	Number of bankruptcies
1895	7,111
1913	12,756
1929	13,180
1960	2,689
1990	13,271

Source: *Stat. Bundesamt* (Hrsg.), *Bevölkerung und Wirtschaft* 215; *Stat. Jahrbücher für das Reich*, several numbers.

and water utilities, these firms having been an important source of communal revenue were often combined with the cities' public transport system and ran great deficits. The German Lufthansa, founded by the fusion of Deutsche Aero Lloyd and Junkers Luftverkehr AG in 1926, counted as one of the biggest companies with mixed ownership. The Reich held 26% of the initial capital (Braunburg 1991: 18; Appel 1993).

Export-related industries were exempted from sales taxes, as exports were seen as absolutely necessary to pay for the country's reparations. During the Depression direct influence of the state on industry increased tremendously. Apart from price control and a fairly rigid anti-cartel policy, increased subsidization can be seen. Due to the difficulties of large German companies like Vereinigte Stahlwerke, the state at times was the major shareholder, a development which can also be seen in the banking sector. As this was only a temporary situation and reprivatization started already in 1932, it can be seen that this was no industrial policy, either, but rather clear-cut crisis management. Some of these holdings, however, persisted and today make up part of the government's holdings in industry (Ambrosius 1984*a*: 78 ff.).

In the 1960s and 1980s there were two major privatizations: VW and Veba. The state of Lower Saxony still holds 20% of Volkswagen capital and uses it as a lever when relocations of plants for cost reasons might endanger the state's economic performance or increase unemployment. In the last few years, some steps have been undertaken to reprivatize government holdings in enterprises. Perhaps the most notable recent step was taken by the Bavarian state government, which is selling a huge part of its holdings and is willing to spend the money on research. At the same time, however, the government is willing to increase its holding in the ailing steel mill Maxhütte, which has been running huge deficits due to outdated equipment and bad location. Here labour market considerations and regional policy indicate that industrial policy in Germany still is what it has always been: contradictory in itself and controversial. Expenditure of the state as percentage of GDP has been on the rise since the 1950s, recently peaking at 50%. Germany has thus reached the level of its Western European neighbours (Bletschacher and Klodt 1991: 33; IW 1994).

4.7. CONCLUSION

Germany's employment structure is still very much that of an industrial country, not that of a modern service-oriented economy. The share of the service sector is still quite small, not least because outdated industries, which actually have no chance of survival without ever-increasing subsidies, have been shepherded far too long, taking up money which should have been spent in promising sectors. The East German economy represents another problem child of industrial policy. Unsuitable conditions for investment and unclear private property rights still seem to hinder the economic reformation of the '*new Bundesländer*'.

The reunification of the two Germanies under a West German economic order apparently offers no patent remedy for a quick and successful economic integration. Even after the 'Treuhand' succeeded in creating a basis for a new economic start by shutting-down, rehabilitating, or returning to private ownership East German enterprises, the 'blossoming landscapes' predicted by Chancellor Helmut Kohl are still a long time in coming. Thus the main task of the governments's industrial policy continues to be to improve the location factors in the '*new Bundesländer*' in order to create the conditions for an economic upturn.

As far as an evaluation of industrial policies is concerned, there is a considerable gap between theory and practice. Economists continually point out that government industrial policies can seldom be justified theoretically, and that a worldwide reduction of domestic and foreign protective measures would ultimately benefit all countries (Wartenberg 1991: 869–72; Bletschacher and Klodt 1991: 3). Despite this view, however, government industrial policy intervention has been increasing in recent years. Public choice research has made it clear that deviations between economic theory and political reality can be explained by the laws of political and bureaucratic decision processes. For politicians, the public good is ultimately only one of many criteria taken into consideration in decisions. They tend to operate as coolly calculating seekers of votes on the political market, who offer selective protective measures in return for votes from interest groups. The effects of industrial policy on the decision process within companies is also increasingly attracting attention. The ultimate goal is to ease or completely eliminate the burden on companies adjusting to national or international structural changes. The more active a government is with its industrial policies, the greater the incentives for companies to participate in protected, but ultimately unproductive, activities. Thus structural policies oriented towards changing specific industries and regions, often have an eliminating, promoting, or slowing effect on structural transitions and adaptation processes (Seidenfus 1986: 13 ff.; Schmal 1980).

To conclude on the effectiveness of the German industrial policy, economic performance since the late nineteenth century shows that in contrast to the liberal view of Giersch, Paqué, and Schmiedinger, based only on development after World War II ('The Fading Miracle'), state interventionism and a positive economic performance are not incompatible at all. While these authors maintain that 'economic miracles emerge when spontaneity prevails over regulation, and they fade when corporatist rigidities impair the flexibility for smooth adjustment' (Giersch, Paqué, and Schmiedinger 1993: p. ix), the German example in the past demonstrates, that—in protecting competition—interventionism was connected with thoroughly acceptable economic development. Whether an interventionist German industrial policy will also provide adequate solutions in the future, especially in view of the challenges of the German reunification, remains to be seen.

REFERENCES

ABELSHAUSER, W. (1987). 'Die Weimarer Republik—ein Wohlfahrtsstaat?', in W. Abelshauser (ed.), *Die Weimarer Republik als Wohlfahrtsstaat: Zum Verhältnis von Wirtschafts- und Sozialpolitik in der Industriegesellschaft*, 9–23. Stuttgart: Steiner.

ADAMS, F. G., and KLEIN, L. (1983) (eds.). *Industrial Policies for Growth and Competitiveness*. Lexington, Pa.: Heath.

ALBRECHT, D., and WESSELKOCK, K. (1971). *Subventionen und Subventionspolitik: Eine Auswertung der bisherigen Subventionsberichte nach dem Gesetz zur Förderung der Stabilität und des Wachstums*. Bonn: Stollfuß.

AMBROSIUS, G. (1977). *Die Durchsetzung der Sozialen Marktwirtschaft in Westdeutschland 1945–1949*. Stuttgart: Dt. Verl.-Anst.

—— (1984a). *Der Staat als Unternehmer*. Göttingen: Vandenhoeck & Ruprecht.

—— (1984b). 'Europäische Integration und wirtschaftliche Entwicklung der Bundesrepublik Deutschland in den fünfziger Jahren', in H. Berding (ed.), *Wirtschaftliche und politische Integration in Europa im 19. und 20. Jahrhundert*, 271–94. Göttingen: Vandenhoeck & Ruprecht.

APPEL, B. M. (1993). *Entwicklungsbedingungen für die Luftverkehrsunternehmen in Deutschland 1919–1926*. Frankfurt/Main: Lang.

BARKAI, A. (1977). *Das Wirtschaftssystem des Nationalsozialismus: Der historische und ideologische Hintergrund 1933–1936*. Köln: Verl. Wissenschaft u. Politik.

BASEDOW, J. (1990). *Wettbewerb auf den Verkehrsmärkten—Eine rechtsvergleichende Untersuchung zur Verkehrspolitik*. Heidelberg: Müller.

BECKER, H. (1990). *Handlungsspielräume der Agrarpolitik in der Weimarer Republik zwischen 1923 und 1929*. Stuttgart: Steiner.

BIRKENFELD, W. (1963). *Der synthetische Treibstoff 1933–1945: Ein Beitrag zur nationalsozialistischen Wirtschafts- und Rüstungspolitik*. Göttingen: Musterschmidt.

BLAICH, F. (1973). *Kartell- und Monopolpolitik im kaiserlichen Deutschland*. Düsseldorf: Droste.

—— (1987). 'Staatsverständnis und politische Haltung der deutschen Unternehmer 1918–1930', in K. D. Bracher *et al.* (eds.), *Die Weimarer Republik 1918–1933: Politik, Wirtschaft, Gesellschaft*, 2nd edn., 158–78. Düsseldorf: Droste.

BLETSCHACHER, G., and KLODT, H. (1991). *Braucht Europa eine neue Industriepolitik?* Kiel: Institut für Weltwirtschaft.

—— —— (1992). *Strategische Handels- und Industriepolitik: Theoretische Grundlagen, Branchenanalysen und wettbewerbspolitische Implikationen*. Tübingen: Mohr.

BÖCKENHOFF, E. (1987). 'Die Agrarmarktordnungen nach 1945', in H. Pohl (ed.), *Die Auswirkungen von Zöllen und anderen Handelshemmnissen auf Wirtschaft und Gesellschaft vom Mittelalter bis zur Gegenwart*, 370–9. Stuttgart: Steiner.

BORCHARDT, K. (1982). 'Zwangslagen und Handlungsspielräume in der großen Weltwirtschaftskrise der frühen dreißiger Jahre: Zur Revision des überlieferten Geschichtsbildes', in K. Borchardt (ed.), *Wachstum, Krisen, Handlungsspielräume der Wirtschaftspolitik*, 165–82. Göttingen: Vandenhoeck & Ruprecht.

BORKIN, J. (1986). *Die unheilige Allianz der I. G. Farben: Eine Interessengemeinschaft im Dritten Reich*, 2nd edn. Frankfurt/Main: Campus.

BRAUNBURG, R. (1991). *Die Geschichte der Lufthansa*. Hamburg: Rasch & Röhring.

BUCHHEIM, C. (1990). *Die Wiedereingliederung Westdeutschlands in die Weltwirtschaft 1945–1958*. München: Oldenbourg.

BÜHRER, W. (1986). *Ruhrstahl und Europa*. München: Oldenbourg.

Bundesministerium Für Finanzen (1993). 14. Subventionsbericht v. 26.8.1993. Bonn.

CHANDLER, A. D. (1991). *Scale and Scope: The Dynamics of Industrial Capitalism*. Cambridge, Mass./London: MIT Press.

CONRAD, M. (1987). *Industriepolitik als wirtschaftspolitische Option in der Sozialen Marktwirtschaft: Ein ordnungskonformes industriepolitisches Konzept für die Bundesrepublik Deutschland*. Hamburg: Kovac.

DENGG, S. (1986). *Deutschlands Austritt aus dem Völkerbund und Schachts 'Neuer Plan': Zum Verhältnis von Außen- und Außenwirtschaftspolitik in der Übergangsphase der Weimarer Republik zum Dritten Reich (1923–1934)*. Frankfurt/Main: Lang.

DIHT (Deutscher Industrie- und Handelstag) (1991). *Verkehrspolitik in Deutschland*. Zukunftsaufgaben. Bonn.

DÖRING, D. (1969). *Deutsche Außenwirtschaftspolitik 1933–1935: Die Gleichschaltung der Außenwirtschaft in der Frühphase des nationalsozialistischen Regimes*. Diss. Berlin: Hilke.

EEKHOFF, J. (1994). 'Die ordnungspolitische Problematik der Industriepolitik', in P. Oberender (ed.), *Industriepolitik im Widerstreit mit der Wettbewerbspolitik*, 69–77. Berlin: Duncker & Humblot.

EICHENGREEN, B. (1994). 'Institutional prerequisites for economic growth: Europe after World War II'. *EER* 38: 883–90.

EICKHOFF, N. (1989). 'Soziale Marktwirtschaft und wettbewerbspolitische Ausnahmebereiche', in W. Fischer (ed.), *Währungsreform und Soziale Marktwirtschaft: Erfahrungen und Perspektiven nach 40 Jahren*, 135–48. Berlin: Duncker & Humblot.

EINEM, E. v. (1991). 'Industriepolitik: Anmerkungen zu einem kontroversen Begriff', in U. Jürgens and W. Krumbein (eds.), *Industriepolitische Strategien: Bundesländer im Vergleich*, 11–33. Berlin: Ed. Sigma.

ERKER, P. (1993). *Industrielle Eliten in der NS-Zeit*. Passau: Rothe.

ESSER, J. (1995). 'Germany: Challenges to the Old Policy Style', in J. Hayward (ed.), *Industrial Enterprise and European Integration*, 48–75. Oxford: Oxford University Press.

FACIUS, F. (1959). *Wirtschaft und Staat: Die Entwicklung der staatlichen Wirtschaftsverwaltung in Deutschland von 17. Jahrhundert bis 1945*. Boppard/Rhein: Boldt.

FELDENKIRCHEN, W. (1985). 'Das Zwangskartellgesetz von 1933: Seine wirtschaftliche Bedeutung und seine praktischen Folgen', in H. Pohl (ed.), *Kartelle und Kartellgesetzgebung in Praxis und Rechtssprechung vom 19. Jahrhundert bis zu Gegenwart*, 145–66. Stuttgart: Steiner.

—— (1987*a*). 'Zur Kontinuität der deutschen Agrarpolitik seit 1879: Bismarcks Schutzzölle und die Folgen', in H. Kellenbenz and H. Pohl (eds.), *Historia Socialis et Oeconomica: Festschrift für Wolfgang Zorn*, 205–23. Stuttgart: Steiner.

—— (1987*b*). 'Deutsche Zoll- und Handelspolitik', in H. Pohl (ed.), *Die Auswirkungen von Zöllen und anderen Handelshemmnissen auf Wirtschaft und Gesellschaft vom Mittelalter bis zur Gegenwart*, 328–57. Stuttgart: Steiner.

—— (1992). 'Competition policy in Germany', in W. J. Hausman (ed.), *Business and Economic History*, 257–69. Williamsburg, Va.: Business History Conference.

—— and HERRMANN, D. P. (1988). 'Das Gesetz über eine Altershilfe für Landwirte (GAL)'. *ZAA* 36: 78–97.

FINKING, G. (1978). *Grundlagen der sektoralen Wirtschaftspolitik*. Köln: Bund-Verlag.

FISHER, W. (1968). *Deutsche Wirtschaftspolitik 1918–1945*, 3rd edn. Opladen: Leske.

FRANK, H. (1993). 'Wirtschaftspolitik in der NS-Zeit', in R. Tilly (ed.), *Geschichte der Wirtschaftspolitik: Vom Merkantilismus zur sozialen Marktwirtschaft*, 148–98. München: Oldenbourg.

FRANZ, W., and SCHALK, H. J. (1989). 'Wie effizient ist die regionale Strukturpolitik', in W. Fischer (ed.), *Währungsreform und Soziale Marktwirtschaft: Erfahrungen und Perspektiven nach 40 Jahren*, 149–62. Berlin: Duncker & Humblot.

GESSNER, D. (1976). *Agrarverbände in der Weimarer Republik: Wirtschaftliche und soziale Voraussetzungen agrarkonservativer Politik vor 1933*. Düsseldorf: Droste.

—— (1977). *Agrardepression und Präsidialregierungen in Deutschland 1930 bis 1933: Probleme des Agrarprotektionismus am Ende der Weimarer Republik*. Düsseldorf: Droste.

GIERSCH, H., PAQUÉ, K. H., and SCHMIEDINGER, H. (1993). *The Fading Miracle: Four Decades of Market Economy in Germany*. Cambridge: Cambridge University Press.

GILLINGHAM, J. (1991). *Coal, Steel and the Rebirth of Europe*. Cambridge: Cambridge University Press.

GRÜBLER, M. (1982). *Die Spitzenverbände der Wirtschaft und das erste Kabinett Brüning*. Düsseldorf: Droste.

HAGERDON, K. (1992). 'Das Leitbild des bäuerlichen Familienbetriebes in der Agrarpolitik'. *ZAA* 40: 53–86.

HAMM, W. (1988). 'Verkehrspolitik', in Fisher *et al.* (eds.), *Handvörterbuch der Wirtschafts Wissenschaft* (*HdWW*), viii. 249–57. Stuttgart/New York: Fischer.

HÄRTEL, H.-H. (1986). *Neue Industriepolitik oder Stärkung der Marktkräfte? Strukturpolitische Konzeptionen im internationen Vergleich*. Hamburg: Verl. Weltarchiv.

HAYES, P. (1982). *Industry and Ideology: I. G. Farben in the Nazi Era*. New York: Cambridge University Press.

HENNING, F. W. (1988). *Landwirtschaft und ländliche Gesellschaft in Deutschland*. ii. *1750–1986*, 2nd edn. Paderborn: Schoeningh.

—— (1991). 'Soziale Marktwirtschaft und Landwirtschaft 1948/49', in D. Petzina (ed.), *Ordnungspolitische Weichenstellungen nach dem Zweiten Weltkrieg*, 101–21. Berlin: Duncker & Humblot.

HENTSCHEL, V. (1980). *Deutsche Wirtschafts- und Sozialpolitik 1815–1945*. Düsseldorf: Droste.

HERBERT, U. (1985). *Fremdarbeiter: Politik und Praxis des 'Ausländer-Einsatzes' in der Kriegswirtschaft des Deutschen Reiches*. Berlin/Bonn: Dietz.

HERTZ-EICHENRODE, D. (1969). *Politik und Landwirtschaft in Ostpreußen 1919–1930: Untersuchungen eines Strukturproblems in der Weimarer Republik*. Köln/Opladen: Westdeutscher Verlag.

HEUSS, E. (1988). 'Wettbewerb', in *HdWW*, viii. 679–97. Stuttgart/New York: Fischer.

HOFFMANN, W. G., *et al.* (1965). *Das Wachstum der deutschen Wirtschaft seit der Mitte des 19. Jahrhunderts.* Berlin: Springer.

HOHENSEE, J., and SALEWSKI, M. (1993) (eds.). *Energie—Politik-Geschichte: Nationale und internationale Energiepolitik seit 1945.* Stuttgart: Steiner.

HOPMANN, B., and SPOERER, M., *et al.* (1994). *Zwangsarbeit bei Daimler Benz.* Stuttgart: Steiner.

HOPPMANN, E. (1988). *Wirtschaftsordnung und Wettbewerb.* Baden-Baden: Nomos.

HUGHES, T. P. (1977). 'Technology as a force for change in history: The effort to form a unified electric power system in Weimar Germany', in H. Mommsen, *et al.* (eds.), *Industrielles System und politische Entwicklung in der Weimarer Republik*, i. 153–166. Düsseldorf: Droste.

IW (Institut der Deutschen Wirtschaft Köln) (1994). *Zahlen zur wirtschaftlichen Entwicklung der Bundesrepublik Deutschland 1994.* Köln: Dt. Instituts-Verlag.

JÄGER, H. (1988). *Geschichte der Wirtschaftsordnung.* Frankfurt/Main: Suhrkamp.

JÀKLI, Z. (1990). *Vom Marshallplan zum Kohlepfenning: Grundrisse der Subventionspolitik in der Bundesrepublik Deutschland 1948–1982.* Opladen: Westdt. Verl.

JÜTTEMEIER, K. J. (1984). *Deutsche Subventionspolitik in Zahlen 1973–1981.* Kiel: Institut für Weltwirtschaft.

KATZENSTEIN, P. J. (1989) (ed.). *Industry and Politics in West Germany.* Ithaca, NY/London: Cornell University Press.

KLODT, H. (1992). *Theorie der strategischen Handelspolitik und neue Wachstumstheorien als Grundlage für eine Industrie und Technologiepolitik.* Kiel: Institut für Weltwirtschaft.

KNOCHE, H. (1989). *Die Wirtschafts- und Sozialpolitik der Regierungen Brüning, Papen, Schleicher und Hitler in den Jahren der Weltwirtschaftskrise von 1928/30–1934.* Diss. Marburg.

KOKALJ, L., and ALBACH, H. (1987). *Industriepolitik in der Marktwirtschaft: Ein internationaler Vergleich.* Stuttgart: Poeschel.

KÖNIG, H. (1960). 'Kartelle und Konzentration unter besonderer Berücksichtigung der Preis- und Mengenabsprachen', in H. Arndt (ed.), *Die Konzentration in der Wirtschaft*, i. 303–32. Berlin: Duncker & Humblot.

KOOPS, T. P. (1974). 'Zielkonflikte der Agrar- und Wirtschaftspolitik in der Ära Brüning', in H. Mommsen, *et al.* (eds.), *Industrielles System und politische Entwicklung in der Weimarer Republik*, 852–68. Düsseldorf: Droste.

KROHN, C.-D. (1974). *Stabilisierung und ökonomische Interessen: Die Finanzpolitik des Deutschen Reiches, 1923–1927.* Düsseldorf: Bertelsmann.

MADDISON, A. (1991). *Dynamic Forces in Capitalist Development: A long-run Comparative View.* Oxford: Oxford University Press.

MASCHKE, E. (1964). *Grundzüge der deutschen Kartellgeschichte vor 1914.* Dortmund: Ardey-Verl.

MEISTER, R. (1991). *Die große Depression: Zwangslagen und Handlungsspieräume der Wirtschafts- und Finanzpolitik in Deutschland 1929–1932.* Regensburg: Transfer-Verl.

MOLLIN, G. (1988). *Montankonzerne und 'Drittes Reich': Der Gegensatz zwischen Monopolindustrie und Befehlswirtschaft in der deutschen Rüstung und Expansion 1936–1944.* Göttingen: Vandenhoeck & Ruprecht.

NARJES, K. H. (1993). 'Industriepolitik—eine europäische Aufgabe', in U. Steger (ed.), *Eine Antwort auf die japanische Herausforderung?*, 85–98. Frankfurt/Main/New York: Campus.

NEEBE, R. (1981). *Großindustrie, Staat und NSDAP 1930 bis 1933: Paul Silverberg und der Reichsverband der Deutschen Industrie in der Krise der Weimarer Republik.* Göttingen: Vandenhoeck & Ruprecht.

OVERY, R. (1994). *War and Economy in the Third Reich.* Oxford: Clarendon Press.

PETZINA, D. (1968). *Autarkiepolitik im Dritten Reich—Der nationalsozialistische Vierjahresplan.* Stuttgart: Dt. Verlags-Anstalt.

PILZ, F. (1983). *Die Investitionslenkung im Sozialstaat der Bundesrepbulik Deutschland: Merkmale, Funktionen und Kritikpunkte des sozialstaatsverpflichtenden Steuerungskonzepts.* Göttingen: Schwartz.

PLUMPE, G. (1985). 'Wirtschaftspolitik in der Weltwirtschaftskrise: Realität und Alternativen'. *Geschichte und Gesellschaft*, 11: 326–57.

POHL, H. (1985) (ed.). *Kartelle und Kartellgesetzgebung in Praxis und Rechtsprechung vom 19. Jahrhundert bis zur Gegenwart.* Wiesbaden: Steiner.

—— (1987) (ed.). *Kommunale Unternehmen in Geschichte und Gegenwart.* Stuttgart: Steiner.

—— (1992). *Vom Stadtwerk zum Elektrizitätsgroßunternehmen: Gründung, Aufbau und Ausbau der Rheinisch-Westfälischen Elektrizitätswerk AG 1898–1912.* Stuttgart: Steiner.

PRELLER, L. (1978). *Sozialpolitik in der Weimarer Republik.* Düsseldorf: Athenäum-Verlag.

PRIEBE, H. (1979). *Die agrarwirtschaftliche Integration Europas.* Baden-Baden: Nomos.

RAHMEYER, F. (1989). 'Sektorale Strukturpolitik als Anpassungs- und Gestaltungspolitik', in W. Fischer (ed.), *Währungsreform und Soziale Marktwirtschaft: Erfahrungen und Perspektiven nach 40 Jahren*, 163–78. Berlin: Duncker & Humblot.

RIEDEL, M. (1973). *Eisen und Kohle für das Dritte Reich: Paul Pleigers Stellung in der NS-Wirtschaft.* Göttingen: Musterschmidt.

RIEMENSCHNEIDER, M. (1987). *Die Deutsche Wirtschaftspolitik gegenüber Ungarn 1933–1944.* Frankfurt/Main: Lang.

ROBERT, R. (1976). *Konzentrationspolitik in der BRD: Das Beispiel der Entstehung des Gesetzes gegen Wettbewerbsbeschränkungen.* Berlin: Duncker & Humblot.

ROEHL, C. v. (1988). *Große Depression und Stagflation: Eine kritische Analyse der deutschen Wirtschaftspolitik 1927/33 und 1970/86.* Göttingen: Vandenhoeck & Ruprecht.

SATZKY, H. (1985). 'Grundsätze, Entstehung und Novellierung des Gesetzes gegen Wettbewerbsbeschränkungen', in H. Pohl (ed.), *Kartelle und Kartellgesetzgebung in Praxis und Rechtsprechung vom 19. Jahrhundert bis zur Gegenwart*, 229–40. Wiesbaden: Steiner.

SCHAUMANN, F., and HOFMANN, H.-G. (1990). *Bildungspolitischer Reformbedarf in der Bundesrepublik und in der DDR.* Köln: Dt. Inst.-Verl.

SCHMAL, E. (1980). *Die Ungleichbehandlung der Unternehmen durch Subventionen als wettbewerbspolitisches Problem.* Frankfurt/Main: Fischer.

SCHREMMER, E. (1976). 'Wirtschaftsordnungen 1800–1970', in H. Aubin and W. Zorn (eds.), *Handbuch der deutschen Wirtschafts- und Sozialgeschichte*, ii. 122–47. Stuttgart: Union.

—— (1989). 'Taxation and public finance: Britain, France and Germany', in P. Mathias and S. Pollard (eds.), *The Cambridge Economic History of Europe*, viii. 315–494. Cambridge: Cambridge University Press.

SEIDENFUS, H. (1986). 'Wettbewerbsbeeinträchtigungen als Folge der Kooperation von Staat und Wirtschaft', in B. Röper (ed.), *Der Einfluß des Staates auf den Wettbewerb*, 13–35. Berlin: Duncker & Humblot.

SEITZ, K. (1992). *Die japanisch-amerikanische Herausforderung. Deutschlands. Hochtechnologie-Industrien kämpfen ums Überleben*, 5th edn. München: mvg Verl.

SMEETS, H.-D. (1989). 'Freihandel im Widerstreit zu protektionistischen Bestrebungen', in W. Fischer (ed.), *Währungsreform und Soziale Marktwirtschaft: Erfahrungen und Perspektiven nach 40 Jahren*, 239–52. Berlin: Duncker & Humblot.

Statistisches Bundesamt (annual). *Statistisches Jahrbuch für die Bundesrepublik Deutschland*. Stuttgart: Kohlhammer, Metzler & Poeschel.

Statistisches Bundesamt (1972). *Bevölkerung und Wirtschaft 1872–1972*. Stuttgart/Mainz: Kohlhammer.

Statistisches Reichsamt (annual). *Statistisches Jahrbuch für das Deutsche Reich*.

STEGMANN, D. (1974). 'Deutsche Zoll- und Handelspolitik 1924/25–1929 unter besonderer Berücksichtigung agrarischer und industrieller Interessen', in H. Mommsen, *et al.* (eds.), *Industrielles System und politische Entwicklung in der Weimarer Republik*, 499–513. Düsseldorf: Droste.

STEININGER-FETZER, R. (1981). *Investitionslenkung als Konzeption zur Steuerung wirtschaftlicher Strukturen*. Frankfurt/Main: Campus.

STURM, R. (1991). *Die Industriepolitik der Bundesländer und die europäische Integration: Unternehmen und Verwaltung im erweiterten Binnenmarkt*. Baden-Baden: Nomos.

SUNTUM, U. v. (1986). *Verkehrspolitik*. München: Vahlen.

TEICHERT, E. (1984). *Autarkie und Großraumwirtschaft in Deutschland 1930–1939. Außenwirtschaftspolitische Konzeptionen zwischen Wirtschaftskrise und Zweitem Weltkrieg*. München: Oldenbourg.

VOIGT, F. (1965). *Verkehr*, ii/1. Berlin: Duncker & Humblot.

VOLLAND, K. (1976). *Das Dritte Reich und Mexiko: Studien zur Entwicklung des deutsch-mexikanischen Verhältnisses 1933–1942 unter besonderer Berücksichtigung der Ölpolitik*. Frankfurt am Main: Lang.

WAGENFÜHR, R. (1963). *Die deutsche Industrie im Kriege 1939–1945*, 2nd edn. Berlin: Duncker & Humblot.

WARTENBERG, L. v. (1991). 'Grenzen staatlicher Industriepolitik in einer Marktwirtschaft —Die Herausforderung neue Bundesländer und Japan'. *Wirtschaft und Wettbewerb*, 41: 863–72.

WEISBROD, B. (1985). 'Die Befreiung von den Tariffesseln: Deflationspolitik als Krisenstrategie der Unternehmer in der Ära Brüning'. *Geschichte und Gesellschaft*, 11: 295–325.

WEYHENMEYER, S. (1994). *Integrierte Unternehmensstrukturen in der Telekommunikation und staatliche Industriepolitik*. Baden-Baden: Nomos.

WITT, P. C. (1982). 'Staatliche Wirtschaftspolitik in Deutschland 1918–1923: Entwicklung und Zerstörung einer modernen wirtschaftspolitischen Strategie', in G. A. Feldman (ed.), *Die deutsche Inflation: Eine Zwischenbilanz*, 151–79. Berlin: de Gruyter.

WOLFERTZ, D. (1993). *Grundlagen und Probleme der indikativen sektoralen Planung in marktwirtschaftlich orientierten Systemen*. Berlin: Duncker & Humblot.

ZAVLARIS, D. (1970). *Die Subventionen in der Bundesrepublik Deutschland seit 1951*. Berlin: Ernst-Reuter-Ges.

ZINN, K. G. (1992). *Soziale Marktwirtschaft: Idee, Entwicklung und Politik der bundesdeutschen Wirtschaftsordnung*. Mannheim: BI-Taschenbuch-Verl.

5

Italy: Stalling and Surpassing

GIOVANNI FEDERICO AND RENATO GIANNETTI
Universita di Pisa, Universita di Firenze

5.1. INTRODUCTION

One hundred years ago, Italy was a backward agricultural country with a glorious past. Nowadays, it is the fifth or sixth industrial power in the world. How much did industrial policy contribute to this achievement? Unsurprisingly, the issue is highly controversial. Opinions cover almost the whole possible range, from (conditional) praise to harsh criticism. The differences depend on the period each author is dealing with and perhaps on his academic specialization. Historians, who take into account the long-run achievements, are on average more sanguine than economists, and among these latter the policies of the 1950s enjoy a much better reputation than those of the 1970s. Yet most authors share the common belief that the Italian state was very active. Vera Zamagni (1994: 154) reckons Italy to have been the 'most interventionist' country among advanced ones, alongside Japan and Germany. And this belief justifies the interest for industrial policy and its role in the overall debate on Italian development.

This chapter will outline the evolution of Italian industrial policy (according to the broad definition set forth in the Introduction), without providing a clear-cut, once-and-for-all answer. Policies were complex and manifold, and changed in time, while, as discussed more thoroughly in the Introduction, there is no simple way to assess the effects of any of them. Moreover, even the partial and incomplete methods available have hardly been applied to the Italian case. Therefore one has to rely on a descriptive approach, supplemented by some assessment of their effects whenever possible. The chapter is divided into sections, each of which focuses on one set of policies for the whole period of their implementation. It sketches the main decisions, without delving into too many details, and frames them into a wider discussion of the 'vision' of the policy-makers.

5.2. THE 1860S–1870S: A LIBERAL PRELUDE TO INDUSTRIAL POLICY

At the time of the Unification of the country (1861) the Italian landscape (to use the Introduction's jargon) was hardly favourable to industrialization, especially

The authors thank James Foreman-Peck, Gianni Toniolo, Vera Zamagni, and the participants in the conference 'Industrial Policy in Europe' (Oxford, 1992) and in a seminar held at the Fondazione ASSI (Milano) for their comments on an earlier version of this paper. G. Federico has written Sections 1–4, 6, and 11 and R. Giannetti Sections 5 and 7–10. The research benefited from a grant from the Ministero per l'Università e la Ricerca Scientifica, funds 40%.

in the South. Each state had its own legislation, and transaction costs were correspondingly high. The school system was underdeveloped and literacy rate nationwide did not exceed 25%. The infrastructures were in very poor condition: railways barely existed outside Piedmont and the whole communications network sorely needed investments.

The new state tackled boldly the immense task ahead. Primary education was made compulsory, even if the dearth of money caused the law to be largely ignored, especially in the South (Zamagni 1993). New French-style codes were approved, which protected in every possible way the property rights and the freedom of entrepreneurs (Rodotà 1995). And, above all, an extensive railways network was built in a relatively short time. The task was given the top priority because railways were regarded as the key to economic and political integration of the new state. The main North–South lines were built in the 1860s (in ten years the length of the network increased from 2,000 to 6,200 km) and the local ones in the 1880s (in 1890 there were more than 13,000 km). The railways were constructed and managed by private firms (including many foreign ones), lured into the very risky task by a promise of minimum guaranteed income (Papa 1973). At that time there was little alternative, as the new state could not afford to fund the construction. A hands-off policy was anyway totally consistent with the prevailing liberal ideology. This was proven at the beginning of the 1870s, when a series of circumstances (including the near-bankruptcy of many private companies) left the state the ownership of the railway network. Yet the government and the overwhelming majority of the Parliament turned down the possibility of direct management of it and renewed the concession with a different division of labour between the main companies. When this concession expired, in 1905, the railways were nationalized (Papa 1973). The move was not totally inconsistent with the previous liberal stance. The whole business community was favourable to nationalization, as the quality of the service was deteriorating because the railway companies could not afford the investments necessary to cope with the increase of traffic. The companies themselves were not hostile, as they looked forward to receiving the compensations and investing them in new lucrative businesses (mainly the electrical industry). Besides, nationalization appeared the only way to deal with the railway trade unions, which were then dominated by the aggressive Far Left.[1]

The Italian government in the 1860s–1870s did not provide any support to industrial activities. This entailed a relevant discontinuity with its predecessors, which had tried to foster their ailing industries with tariffs and sometimes incentives, usually with disappointing results. Actually, most states (save the Southern Regno delle Due Sicilie) had begun to liberalize trade before Unification. The movement was led by Piedmont which almost totally abolished protection in the 1850s. In 1861 its tariff was extended to the whole country by the stroke of a pen (an almost inconceivable move in the present-day world of wearisome and overcautious

---

[1] In those years, strikes among civil servants were forbidden. In fact the Socialist party voted against the law.

trade negotiations) and all the remaining duties were abolished two years later by the trade treaty with France.[2] Predictably, the industrialists complained loudly (Are 1965), but for many years they were ignored.

5.3. THE RETURN TO PROTECTION

The achievements of the 1860s–1870s should not be overlooked: the same survival of the newborn state was to some extent a success. Yet the economic growth in those years was decidedly inferior to the great hopes of the Risorgimento. This reinforced the appeal of a more interventionist (and less budget-conscious) policy, at least within the (very small) elite with voting rights. The parliamentary majority changed in 1876, and two years later the new government approved a new tariff. The importance of this decision should not be overemphazised. The tariff was mainly intended to be used in the future trade negotiation and anyway it imposed low duties on a limited range of industrial goods (mainly textiles). The protection was substantially increased in 1887, which was approved jointly with a duty on wheat (Del Vecchio 1978). The new tariff raised somewhat the duties on textiles but the great novelty was the duty on pig iron and steel products. The industry was then quite backward, so that protecting it was a bet on the future. Yet the government was ready to take the risk. The steel industry was in fact an essential component of that 'military-industrial complex' which was deemed indispensable to buttress Italy's political ambitions to the status of great power. In other words, as in Germany, industrial protection was largely inspired by nationalism, rekindled by a vociferous and aggressive propaganda (Lanaro 1979; De Rosa 1982). But the tariff would not have anyway been approved without the support of landowners, scared by competition from foreign wheat (Sereni 1966). Protectionism was to last officially until the trade liberalization of the 1950s–1960s. The level of aggregate protection peaked in the early 1890s and then it decreased until at least the second decade of the twentieth century, because the (specific) duties were reduced by trade treaties and their *ad valorem* equivalent was lowered by the increase in import prices. The layout of industrial protection changed somewhat in 1921, when a new tariff raised duties on chemicals, engineering goods, and steel products and lowered those on textiles. The trade policy is arguably the most controversial issue in the whole debate about Italian economic development. Very few—if any—people still believe, as did the nineteenth-century economists (Cardini 1981), that pure free trade would have been better. The debate concerns the choice of activities to protect. Some scholars defend the actual one, arguing that without protection industry would not have developed (Zamagni 1981; Sapelli 1992). Are (1974) criticizes the policy-makers for having made a choice at all, arguing that all industries deserved

---

[2] Cf. for more details on the history of the trade policy, IPSOA 1985; Calderoni 1961.

the same degree of effective protection. Many authors (Gerschenkron 1962; Fenoaltea 1993) point out that the duty on wheat lowered the real wages and increased the opportunity cost of labour, and therefore was inconsistent with the aim of fostering industrialization.[3] Gerschenkron (1962) criticizes the selection of industries to be protected, dismissing textiles as an 'old industry with limited possibility of technical progress' and suggesting that labour-intensive engineering would have been much more suited to Italy than resource-intensive steel production. Fenoaltea (1973) goes as far as arguing that, without duties on steel, Italian engineering could have started an export-led industrialization sixty years before it did.

Trade policy looms so large in the debate about industrialization because historians are convinced that it has deeply affected Italian development. They assume that duties were high and that they have been effective in shifting resources towards the protected activities. Both assumptions are however based on flimsy evidence. Duties are assumed to have been high because this was the prevailing opinion at that time, and they are assumed to have been effective because imports of many products diminished (cotton textiles are a textbook example of import substitution) and the Italian industrial output grew at an unprecedented rate from the late 1890s onwards. Actually, the duties were not that high (Federico and Tena 1998). The nominal duties on most manufactures were around or even less than 15%, and even those on steel and textiles hardly exceeded 25–30%. These figures are similar to French or German ones (Liepmann 1938; Capie 1994) and much lower than the duties raised by the LDCs in their ISI (imports-substitution industrialization) strategies in the 1950s–1960s. The effective rates were higher. The weighted averages for manufactures vary between 10% and 30% (according to the years and the input-output table), with peaks around 50–60% for steel products. Effective protection on manufacturing (steel apart) was anyway decidedly lower than that on other activities—notably wheatgrowing. This fact hardly tallies with the hypothesis that protection was instrumental to the development of industry. Also the evidence on trade flows and industrial growth is not convincing, if subject to a closer scrutiny. The implicit *post hoc propter hoc* argument is highly questionable, and duties did not always succeed in curbing imports. In some cases, there is evidence of a somewhat embarrassing delay before the development of the industries the tariff was supposed to foster. For instance, a modern pig iron production started only in 1899, and imports went on growing until the early 1900s.

One might therefore wonder whether protection was as important for industrialization as it is commonly believed. The losses of the protection on steel has been investigated by Toniolo (1977). He concludes that 'the maximum possible value of this handicap does not however support the claim that there would have been a radical change in long-term growth rate of Italian manufacturing

---

[3] Industrialists were well aware of this fact, but they realized how much the support of landowners was necessary to have the tariffs approved. Their leader A. Rossi (the owner of the largest wool company) campaigned for the duty on wheat.

... had a different tariff policy been introduced after the fall of Crispi [1896]' (1977: 672).[4] In other words, Italy may have not paid so dearly for its ambitions of having a steel industry. These partial equilibrium estimates are however likely to underestimate the total losses, and by definition a static approach cannot take into account the alleged dynamic effects of protection. Any conclusion on the effects of trade policy cannot be but provisional and tentative.

5.4. THE SUPPORT TO THE 'MILITARY-INDUSTRIAL COMPLEX'

The development of the 'military-industrial complex' was not pursued only with protection (actually, the duties on engineering goods were very low). In the early 1880s the government strongly encouraged the construction of a factory for the production of high-quality steel for guns and armour plates (Bonelli 1975).[5] The company ('Terni') and the whole affair of the production of weapons became a constant source of scandals, with widespread suspicions of bribery. Yet the government achieved its aim (Ferrari 1986, 1990). In the first decade of the twentieth century, the national industry supplied about 85% of total purchases of weapons (Zamagni 1978: tav. 15). Italy even succeeded in exporting warships to countries such as Turkey and Argentina. During World War I, Italian industry was able to supply the army with an increasing flow of weapons and ammunitions (Caracciolo 1969; Segreto 1997). This achievement was not trivial, even if it involved a lot of corruption, a huge waste of resources, and widespread inefficiency.

The government also supported the production of rolling stock. The railway concessions of the 1860s did not include any clause to favour national producers of rolling stock. The Italian firms were then rarely qualified to bid for sophisticated engineering goods, and so the foreign companies took the lion's share. For this reason Gerschenkron (1962) regards the first wave of railways construction as premature and hence a missed opportunity for development. Since 1882 national suppliers were given an automatic right of pre-emption on purchases, provided their bids did not exceed the lowest foreign offer by more than 5%. The preference was later much strengthened by subsequent laws (notably the railway law of 1905). The system worked. From 1885 to 1904 Italian companies supplied about three-quarters of railway equipment (Papa 1973), including most locomotives, which had previously been imported (Merger 1986). Italy had to pay a price: according to an estimate, on the eve of World War I, the national products cost 15–20% more than the foreign ones (Papa 1973).

[4] His counterfactual is not free trade, but an 'optimal' incentive policy of no duty and a subsidy to iron and steel industry. In 1911–13 the value added of engineering would have been 40% higher but the total GDP only 1% higher than the actual one, and the subsidy to the steel industry would have absorbed about 4% of total state revenues.

[5] The influence of the government did damage the economic viability of the undertaking. In fact it forced the firm to locate the factory in the city of Terni (Umbria) for military reasons, even if the choice was totally insane from an economic point of view. The city was in fact far from the sources of inputs (pig iron and coal) and the market for steel. It had only an abundant supply of hydraulic energy.

Finally, the state helped, directly or via the mixed banks, the companies of the 'military-industrial complex' when in trouble. In the late 1880s it averted an early bankruptcy of the 'Terni' by granting generous advances on future procurements. In 1911 the Banca d'Italia coaxed the main banks into organizing a rescue of the two major steel companies, the ILVA and the 'Piombino' (Confalonieri 1982). However, the real troubles began after the war, when the producers of weapons were not able to adjust to the sudden contraction in the public procurements. The worst case was the 'Ansaldo', a vertically integrated conglomerate which produced everything from iron ore to warships and owned the 'Banca Italiana di Sconto', the second largest Italian bank. The bank was allowed to fail, but the industrial activities were bailed out by an agency (the 'Sezione Speciale' of the 'Consorzio Sovvenzioni su Valori Industriali') owned by the Banca d'Italia (Doria 1989; Confalonieri 1992). Other companies (including, again, the ILVA) were bailed out by banks, which converted their loans into shares. This was to be the first step of a momentous process. In fact in the following years the banks rounded off their industrial portfolio by bailing out other companies and/or purchasing further shares (Confalonieri 1992; Ciocca and Toniolo 1984). On the eve of the Great Crisis the 'Banca Commerciale Italiana' and the 'Credito Italiano' owned most of the 'military-industrial complex' (100% of productive capacity for weapons, 90% for shipbuilding, 40% for steel, etc.) and much else. According to one estimate, the firms they controlled accounted for about two-fifths of the total capital of joint-stock companies (Toniolo 1980). The crisis drove the industrial companies, and hence the banks, to the edge of failure. Such a perspective was unthinkable, as it would have jeopardized the whole banking system, and the Fascist regime could not afford this.[6] At first the government tried to bail out industrial firms alone, but at the end was compelled to rescue banks as well (Cianci 1977; Toniolo 1980). The shares so acquired were transferred to a new holding, called 'Istituto per la ricostruzione industriale' (IRI). It was intended to be a temporary solution, waiting for an upturn of economic cycle which would have made a privatization possible. Some companies were indeed sold back in the following years, but very few buyers lined up to purchase the core of the rescued companies. State-ownership was made permanent in 1937.

It is thus undeniable that industrial policy was instrumental to the survival and growth of a 'military-industrial complex'. The obvious question is: how important was this latter for Italian industrialization? A satisfactory answer is very difficult, but there is at least some evidence to the contrary. First, the 'military-industrial complex' (including the production of rolling stock) was not so large. Fenoaltea (1982) has shown that railways procurements accounted for only 10% of total value added of engineering and steel production. He therefore judges 'relatively unimpressive' the effect of the increase in railway-related production for

---

[6] Actually bailing-out of banks was by no means a novelty. There had been at least two other major instances—those of the 'Società Bancaria Italiana' in 1907 and of the 'Banco di Roma' in 1922.

total growth of these industries. Unfortunately, there is no comparable study on military procurement. Anyway, according to Vitali (1992), in 1911 the state expenditure accounted for 25% of the value added and for 10% of the gross output of engineering and metallurgy. The figure is surely not negligible, but, even assuming that it consisted wholly in additional demand, without any crowding-out, it does seem difficult to conclude that state demand was essential for the development of these industries. A fortiori this holds true for Italian industry as a whole, as engineering and metallurgy were comparatively small: in 1911 they accounted for less than one-fourth of total manufacturing output (Fenoaltea 1992).

The 'military-industrial complex' might have been essential if and only if its existence had entailed substantial technological spillovers to other industries. In this case, the bailouts would also have been justified by the need to retain precious technical capabilities. The issue needs more research, but the scarce evidence available does not justify a sanguine assessment of the performance of these industries. Their productivity growth was far from impressive (Bardini 1996) and they did not exhibit a particular propensity to innovation (Giannetti 1994*a*). This may not be so surprising for highly supported industries.

5.5. THE POLICY TOWARDS NETWORK INDUSTRIES

The development of electrical technology in the 1890s was hailed in Italy with great enthusiasm, pretty much as the construction of railways thirty years before.[7] In fact the abundant waterfalls of the Alps seemed to offer the opportunity to escape from the traditional dependence on imported coal. This concept was popularized by many authors, including Nitti, who in a famous book (1905), defined electricity as 'white coal'. The growth of the electrical industry was indeed impressive, even if it never fulfilled the dreams of self-sufficiency (actually, since the late 1960s most of Italian energy has been produced by thermal sources). The contribution of the state was however minimal. The plants were built and managed by private regional companies and local authorities, especially at the very beginning. Unlike railways thirty years before, the state did not need to provide incentives, as prospective returns were extremely appealing. Neither did it plan the development of the network, the connections, etc. It simply granted the concessions to applicants on a first-come, first-served basis—and this was to cause some serious technical problems in the long run. The state did have a major direct role in the first phase of construction of the tiny telephone network (125,000 subscribers in 1925), but only because it was deemed of strategic importance in case of war. The local networks were privatized in 1923, but the state kept the control of the long-distance network.[8]

---

[7] Cf. on the history of electrical industry in Italy, the recent 5-volume official history (AA. VV. (1993–5)).

[8] The situation did not last for long because the telephonic companies returned back to public ownership (together with 30% of the electrical companies) in the great bailout of mixed banks in the 1930s.

Strictly speaking, state ownership or management is not a necessary condition for using utilities as a means of industrial policy. The government can regulate rates to favour industry as a whole over domestic consumption, or some specific productions and/or areas over the whole country. Or it can impose reservation clauses on purchase of equipment to favour national producers. Last but not least, it can set uniform technical standards to improve the efficiency of the service and/or to exploit scale economies in the production of equipment. The Italian state refrained from using any of these options, preferring to continue with a very liberal (some would say acquiescent) policy towards private companies until the 1950s.

The state did not interfere at all in the purchase of material (unlike for railways). Companies were left totally free to purchase whatever they wanted, wherever they wanted (provided they paid the duty, if applicable). At least for the electrical equipment, this was to some extent part of an implicit deal with the German suppliers of equipment, who financed many investments (Segreto 1992). Each utility company therefore adopted its own standard. In the 1920s there were four main regional electrical networks, each of which had its own 'system' (Giannetti 1993). In the late 1940s telephonic companies adopted four different standards (Siemens, Autelco, FACE, and Ericsson) for automatic switching (Bottiglieri 1987). In both cases, any interconnection, when it became technically feasible and necessary, was left to agreements among concessionaires or —in many cases—to the process of financial concentration. It is likely that this fragmentation caused Italy to lose external benefits in R & D and production of equipment—and possibly even the opportunity to exploit the scale economies in generation of electrical power.

The government had a substantial regulatory power, but used it very sparingly. Actually, the government seemed to be interested more in the use of its power for macroeconomic policy than for industrial policy. For instance it forbade the increase in electricity prices in 1921 and again in 1936 to fight inflation. In normal times the Ministery for Industry simply applied—in a quite approximate way—the average cost principle to overall tariffs, leaving each company free to fine-tune the rates for different classes of consumers. This resulted in a large cross-subsidization among consumers. At least until the 1920s, industrial rates were comparatively low, partly because the massive use of hydroelectric power caused marginal costs of off-peak supply to be very low and partly because the electric companies did not trust the possible development of a market for domestic consumption. This tariff structure brought about an excessive development of power-intensive industries and the adoption of power-intensive technologies such as the electrical furnaces for the production of steel. Such an outcome was hardly optimal in a country like Italy. Anyway, the tariffs and the quality of the service have always been criticized. The electrical companies were accused of reaping monopoly profits by charging high tariffs and of ignoring potentially unprofitable consumers (such as those in rural areas). Nationalization was demanded since the 1910s and, after a pause in the Fascist years, by a large campaign of opposition parties in the 1950s (Bottiglieri 1994).

5.6. FASCISM, AUTARKY, AND THE CORPORATE STATE:
A NEW COURSE?

The discussion so far has made no distinction between the so-called liberal period (until 1922) and the Fascist one, as if there were no difference either in the objectives or in the tools of industrial policy. In many respects, the continuity is evident. The aims of industrial policy remained largely the same, and its 'imperialistic' twist was greatly stressed, with a lot of rhetoric. As detailed before, the Fascist regime used all the 'traditional' tools, possibly on a greater scale (more money to public procurements, larger bailouts, etc.). The regime was not keen to stress this continuity. Actually, the official propaganda wanted to convey exactly the opposite view—that it had found a new, uniquely Fascist, way to organize the economy, which not only avoided the excesses of communism and unregulated capitalism but best enabled Italy to use its resources to prepare for war. The main innovation should have been the collaboration between employers and employees, of course under the enlightened guidance of the government. The tool was to be an organization (*corporazione*) of the representatives of all categories within each industry. The *corporazioni* were created in 1934 and a Camera dei Fasci e delle Corporazioni was substituted for the Lower House of Parliament four years later. However, these institutions remained pretty much debating chambers, with little or no power. This failure anyway does not mean that there were no innovations in Fascist industrial policy, especially in the 1930s. One can single out at least four of them—autarky, the local development schemes, and the regulation of markets for both labour and goods.

Autarky was the general heading for a wide range of policies which aimed at making Italy self-sufficient from imports and therefore not vulnerable in case of war. The government raised tariffs in the late 1920s and imposed quotas in the early 1930s, signing also several clearing agreements in 1933 (Tattara 1987). In 1935 imports were subject to licensing, which was granted by a newly created Ministry for Foreign Trade. The regime strictly controlled the balance of payments. Italians were forbidden to hold foreign currency (the prohibition was to last in part until the 1980s) and all the relative transactions had to be handled via a new branch of the Banca d'Italia, called 'Istituto Nazionale Cambi' (Zani 1988). The most innovative project was however the search for substitutes to imported raw materials. It entailed the exploitation of any possible source in the mainland or in the colonies and research and development for new 'autarkic' substitutes, both in universities and in private laboratories, such as the ISML for the aluminium or the 'Istituto Donegani' for chemicals (Zamagni 1990).

The development schemes consisted in various incentives (supplemented by moral suasion) to attract industrial settlements in some 'special industrial zones' (Petri 1990). The origin of the idea can be traced back to the law for Naples of 1904, which, *inter alia*, subsidized the construction of the Bagnoli steel plant (Dell'Orefice 1980). The practice was resumed in the late 1920s–early 1930s, giving the special status to harbours such as Venice and Leghorn, towns in the 'terre irredente' (the territories acquired after the war) such as Trieste and Bolzano, and finally particularly poor areas such as Massa and Ferrara. The criteria of selection were quite haphazard (why for instance Ferrara and not Mantua?), and there is wide suspicion that the choices were inspired by political considerations, such as the power of the local 'ras' (Fascist boss).

The interventions in the labour market were initially motivated by political reasons. In fact, as soon as they came to power in 1922, the Fascist party disbanded the socialist and Catholic trade unions, which it considered centres of potentially dangerous political opposition. In 1926–7 strikes, already strongly discouraged, were officially forbidden and the Fascist trade unions were given a monopoly of the right to represent workers (Acquarone 1965). Of course, the Fascist trade unions associations had no autonomy at all, and therefore the regime could manipulate wages for its macroeconomic policy. It imposed reductions in 1926, to deflate the economy in order to have the lira return to the gold standard, and again in the early 1930s to defend an overvalued exchange rate (Mortara 1978). Finally, the Fascist regime discovered that migration towards industrial cities threatened the rural character of Italy, and tried to discourage it, apparently without bothering about the effect on the industrial labour supply. At first, it tried, in vain, with propaganda, but later it had to resort to coercion. In 1931 migration to cities was subject to an authorization and since 1938–9 it was virtually forbidden.

Last but not least, the Fascist government attempted to restrict competition and to regulate the market for goods as much as possible. As early as 1926, mergers had been given a fiscal exemption and a law recognized the existence of cartels, which had existed since the late nineteenth century as purely private agreements. However, these interventions were stepped up after the Great Crisis. In 1936 participation in cartels was made compulsory, and two years later, there were 144 national and 111 local cartels in various branches of manufacturing (Gualerni 1976). They were supposed to allocate production and avoid competition among members. In the same years, the government tried to fight the creeping inflation by controlling prices, which were officially frozen from 1938 (Zamagni 1982). There were also some attempts to unify industrial standards—setting up special boards such as the UNI in 1936 (Locatelli 1938). The main innovation was however the attempt at regulatory planning. It began in 1935, when the construction of new mills or the increase of productive capacity of existing ones was subject to an official permit (but after 1939 factories of 'outstanding national interest' were exempted).

The Fascist industrial policy is, unsurprisingly, very controversial. The discussion has focused on the process of decision-making and on the vision which inspired it. On one hand, Gregor (1979) endorses the pretences of the regime. He argues that the Fascist government consistently aimed at modernizing the country, though he admits that it had borrowed many ideas from the nationalist movement during and after World War I. The regime disguised its plans until sure of its grip on power. On the other hand, radical and Marxist historians regard the Fascist government as somebody else's puppet. The puppeteer is vaguely identified with a coalition of landowners and big business. Some stress the influence of landowners, attributing to it the economic stagnation of the country (Rossi 1966). Others argue that the coalition was dominated by major companies, which did want a modernization of the country, but of course tailored to their own interests (Fano 1971; Grifone 1971). These somewhat simplistic views have now largely fallen out of favour, as many authors have noted that the Fascist economic policy was wavering and often contradictory. La Francesca (1973) blames Mussolini, who was notoriously ignorant of economic issues. Others, more realistically, stress the need for compromise between different lobbies and the habit of taking decisions on the spur of the moment (Cohen 1988; Toniolo 1980). A good example is the 1933 bailout, which was conceived and engineered by civil servants of liberal tradition, acting with Mussolini's direct approval. However its success (there was no run on the banks) was made possible by the control of the press by the totalitarian regime.

A look outside Italy raises further doubts about the originality of Fascist policies, as many of the allegedly 'new' tools were widely adopted elsewhere. Most countries sought to reduce imports in the 1930s and Italy did have partners to sign clearing agreements. Also the attempts to restrict domestic and foreign competition were widespread. In the second half of the 1920s, the international market for manufactures and raw materials was increasingly regulated by cartels which allocated the total demand among national producers (Liefmann 1932). Finally, non-binding planning was used, much more effectively, in Nazi Germany to prepare the country for the war (Hentschel 1989).

Though interesting and full of hindsight for political history, this discussion somewhat misses the main point: did the Fascist industrial policy foster or hamper industrialization, admittedly in very difficult circumstances? There is very little, if any, research on the issue. The (scarce) evidence casts many doubts on the effectiveness, let alone the efficiency, of most policies. All the qualitative analyses agree in defining planning a total failure. Day-to-day decisions were taken by civil servants, under the overwhelming influence of the largest companies (Gualerni 1976). Licensing became thus a further barrier to entry. Price control did not prevent the wholesale price index from rising by 30% from 1936 to 1939, and the restriction of internal migrations were largely evaded. Also the 'special areas' were not an unconditional success. Industrial employment did grow, but most areas failed to attract new firms beyond the initial ones. The most successful case was Porto Marghera, near Venice, which became a major centre for aluminium processing and the chemical industry. However the wisdom of locating these industries in such a fragile environment is highly questionable—and nowadays they are one of the worst environmental problems of the Lagoon.

Autarky was somewhat more effective, but far less so than the apparently impressive array of restrictions would suggest. From 1933 to 1938, imports in real terms fell by 2% only (Rossi, Sorgato, and Toniolo 1993: tab. 8), while the world trade increased by 12% (Vidal 1991: annexe 1). Anyway, self-sufficiency was unattainable because Italy's resource endowment was so poor. In 1939 only 21% of industrial raw materials were produced in Italy or in its colonies (Zamagni 1993). It is likely that, without autarky, some industries (chemicals, some branches of engineering, etc.) would not have developed, but the advantages of their existence for the welfare of the country and/or for its subsequent industrial development remain questionable. Sometimes, research on autarkic materials did bring valuable results. For instance the attempts to produce synthetic rubber led to the discovery of polypropylene, the main success of Italian chemical R & D in the 1950s (Petri 1996). Much more frequently, however, the pursuit entailed only a waste of precious financial resources in unsound projects, such as the substitution of aluminium for copper in electrical wiring.

The wage policy is a different matter altogether. It is believed to have contributed substantially to the stabilization of the lira at a high parity, belying Keynes's (1925) predictions that the exchange rate would not have obeyed castor oil.[9] But it had also important effects on the distribution of income and on the allocation of resources. The cuts should in principle have affected all incomes and prices, but the policy was much more effective on industrial wages than on agricultural ones (or other incomes). Besides the prohibition of trade unions surely prevented the workers from taking advantage of economic growth. Labour increased by about 50% from 1922 to 1938, while the real wages remained approximately constant (Zamagni 1995). This gap may have induced the companies to adopt more labour-intensive techniques and may have shifted the income distribution towards profits (Zamagni 1979–80). In turn this may have increased investments, if they were a function of profit, as suggested by the 'classical' models of Filosa, Rey, and Sitzia (1976) and Del Monte (1977). Anyway, the repression of civil liberties and the worsening of living standards were too high a price for any possible positive effect on the growth rate.

Summing up, the Fascist industrial policies did represent a discontinuity, but not as large as the regime claimed and decidedly not an original one (but for the wage control). Moreover their effectiveness is at best dubious. It may be useful to remember that the performance of the Italian industry in the 1930s was far from outstanding. From 1929 to 1939 the industrial output grew less than the total GDP, and Italy was outperformed by Japan and Germany.[10] On top of this, the Fascist regime failed in its own main avowed aim, the preparation for war. Italy was caught unprepared by the outbreak of World War II and its industrial performance during the war was decidedly unimpressive (Covino, Gallo, and Mantovani 1976; Gualerni 1982; Zamagni 1997). It is striking that the only permanent legacy of the Fascist policy was to be the state ownership of industrial companies, which was the unintended outcome of a 'traditional' bailout.

---

[9] The Fascist thugs used to compel their political foes to drink castor oil to humiliate them.

[10] The yearly growth rate of Italian industrial production was 1.7% (Ercolani 1969: tab. 1.1.A); GDP grew at 2.4% p.a., versus 0.1% in the United States, 0.3% in France, 1.6% in the United Kindgom, 3.7% in Germany, and 4.2% in Japan (Maddison 1991: tab. A.7).

5.7. THE 1950S: STATE-OWNED ENTERPRISES AND TRADE
LIBERALIZATION

The defeat in the war discredited forever the traditional 'imperialistic' reason
for an industrial policy, but not the need for state intervention. The legacy of
the Fascist period and of the war was heavy. Damage to the capital stock was
smaller than one would have expected, but the Italian industry was still small
and technically rather backward after many years of isolation. It badly needed
to be modernized, but without shedding too many jobs—as unemployment was
high. Besides, autarky and planning had left a lot of administrative and trade
restrictions.

The new democratic government was eager to mark the discontinuity with the
past regime, at least in economic policy. Amato (1972) argues that it returned
to the nineteenth-century practice of supporting private companies without interfering in their business decisions ('liberal protectionism'). So, in the 1940s the
government provided money for the reconstruction of the plants, especially in
the engineering industry. For instance Fiat got large sums from the European
Recovery Programme and the Eximbank, which were used to buy much-needed
modern American machinery (Bottiglieri 1984). On top of it, Fiat was granted
a supply of steel intermediate products at very low prices from state-owned companies (Ranieri 1985). Some engineering companies proved unable to pay the
state loans back. The state thus became their real owner. This situation was made
official in 1962, by setting up a new permanent holding, the EFIM ('Ente
Finanziamento Industrie Meccaniche').

Even without any proper industrial policy, in the 1950s the state-owned companies were quite active (Barca and Trento 1997). The IRI invested large sums
in the modernization of utilities (notably the telephone network) and manufacturing. The best-known success story is probably the steel industry. After the war
many experts questioned the wisdom of rebuilding the IRI factories, seriously
damaged during the war, suggesting that the demand for steel could be met by the
private producers or by imports. On the contrary, the president of Finsider (the
steel sub-holding of IRI), O. Sinigaglia, put forward a plan to increase their productive capacity (Balconi 1991; Ranieri 1993). It resumed the guidelines of a
plan which had been conceived by the same Sinigaglia and partially implemented
in the late 1930s. Its cornerstone was the construction of a new factory in
Cornigliano (Genoa) with American technology. Sinigaglia argued that the scale
economies were large enough to overcome the extra cost of imported coal and
iron ore, making protection unnecessary. In spite of the scepticism of the private
producers and of the American mistrust of state-owned enterprise, Sinigaglia
succeeded in having his plan approved and funded by ERP. He proved to be right.
The growth in demand even exceeded his expectations and in the 1950s the Italian
productive capacity was fully exploited. For the first time Italy had a large,
modern, and competitive steel industry, and was even a net exporter for some
time. Finsider acquired an undisputed price leadership and forced the private firms

to modernize. In other words, Sinigaglia's strategy was a resounding success. Finsider went on investing in the steel industry in the 1960s–1970s. It built a new plant in Taranto (Apulia), and then doubled it in size. This latter decision proved to be a costly mistake. The Taranto plant was too big, and caused Finsider to lose a lot of money.

In the 1950s another state-owned company, the AGIP, assumed a leading role in the energy industry (Sapelli *et al.* 1993). The company had been established in 1926 to search for oil, and during the war it had discovered substantial gas-fields in the Po Valley. Thanks to the intuition and political skill of its president, E. Mattei, AGIP was granted (after heated discussions) an exclusive right for further exploration (Colitti 1979). In the 1950s, it built a network of pipelines to distribute the gas, which cost less than other (imported) sources of energy. In 1953 the AGIP was subsumed in a new public holding, the Ente Nazionale Idrocar-buri or ENI, with the aim of providing Italy with an adequate supply of energy (Sapelli and Carnevale 1992). In the 1950s, ENI diversified into the market for fertilizers, which was a traditional monopoly of a leading private company, the 'Montecatini', and later, in the 1960s–1970s, into chemicals.

It seems therefore undeniable that the state-owned companies played a leading role in the modernization of the country in the 1950s and early 1960s. It is however doubtful to what extent their successes could be attributed to industrial policy in the usual meaning of the term (i.e. as a strategy of policy-makers). They would be more accurately described as the result of entrepreneurship of single managers who succeeded in having their plans approved by the government thanks to their personal links with prominent politicians—a 'privatization of state enterprises' in Ranieri's (1993) words. When their strategy clashed with the interests of private companies, the government often promoted collusive behaviour (Coombes 1971). For instance it brokered an agreement between Montedison and ANIC in the fertilizer war of the 1950s (Bottiglieri 1990).

The government however did take a very important decision, trade liberalization. After so many years (and the war inflation), the old 1921 tariff was clearly obsolete. Italy substituted it with a new one, approved in 1950, after long discussions in the GATT conferences of Annecy and Torquay (Fauri 1995). It entailed a return to the moderate protectionism of the 1920s, with average duties on manufactures around 20% (Pierucci and Ulizzi 1973). Behind this shield, Italy could afford to reduce drastically and eventually to abolish all quotas, well before any other country in the OECD. These were important steps forward, but the real milestone of liberalization was the decision to join the European Community for Steel and Coal in 1951 (Ranieri 1985). In spite of the industrialists' fears, the Italian steel industry sustained the foreign competition. The whole Italian industry (and especially textiles) proved to be very competitive in the 1950s. Therefore, in the following years, Italy could be extremely active in the foundation of the Common Market (Willis 1971), with little or no opposition from industrialists (De Cleva 1992). Anyway, the liberalization of imports was gradual, and duties were totally abolished in 1968. In the new environment, the Italian industry thrived. Indeed, some scholars have argued that the whole *'miracolo economico'* of the 1950s–1960s has been an example of export-led growth. The issue is still controversial, but the wisdom of the liberalization cannot be denied. It has been called 'the most important decision of industrial policy in the last forty years' (CER-IRS 1986: 141). Most scholars regard liberalization as a far-reaching strategic choice, attributed to the foresight and will of a few open-minded politicians such as the new Minister of Trade, La Malfa. A different view is put forward by De Cecco (1971), who maintains that it was just the effect of specific circumstances.

5.8. MACROECONOMIC PLANNING AND INDUSTRIAL POLICY IN THE 1960S

After the *'miracolo economico'* there could be no further doubt about Italy's status as an industrial country. The country was however still plagued by a host of social and economic problems—such as the North–South gap or a skewed income distribution. The government set itself the ambitious task to solve all these problems with a massive dose of macroeconomic planning (Pola 1967; AA.VV. 1981). There had been an unsuccessful attempt in 1955 (the so-called Schema Vanoni, named after the finance minister), but planning was officially adopted as the cornerstone of economic policy by the new Centre-Left government in 1962. The first plan was approved in 1967, after a long discussion in the Parliament. It was possibly the most ambitious one in the whole of Europe, with an endless list of reforms. None of them were implemented, partly for the opposition from outside and inside the ruling coalition, and partly for its technical shortcomings. The 'blueprints' of the plan lacked any serious technical base for a coherent intervention of industrial policy. The technical agencies were powerless, while all the power was wielded by ministerial committees (such as the Comitato per lo sviluppo dell'occupazione e del reddito) which more often discussed abstract models of planning than how to implement them (Momigliano 1986). To be sure, planning and the management of industrial policy was increasingly difficult because of proliferation of the different interests (Schmitter 1979). IRI and ENI wielded a substantial power thanks to their links with politicians. The private companies were less dependent on internal market (and hence on the government goodwill) thanks to the export boom. Finally, the government also wanted to involve the trade unions, which had previously been excluded from decision-making. Magnani (1992) has defined the 1960s as a 'missed opportunity' to elaborate a consistent model of industrial policy and frame it into a well-defined set of rules of the game.

Though planning failed, the new Centre-Left government did adopt some important measures. Possibly the most important single one was the nationalization of the electrical industry, in 1962. The decision was motivated by the shortcomings of the private companies and by rather mundane political considerations, but also by the belief that public ownership was essential to planning. Such belief is likely

TABLE 5.1. *Total resources for investment, 1964–1979* (billions of 1970 lire)

	(1)	(2)	(3)	(4)	(5)	(6)	(7)
1964	593.0	31.7	1,941.7	477.7	63.3	18.4	19.0
1965	589.6	22.7	2,248.5	417.6	66.3	21.8	21.2
1966	627.9	32.0	2,521.4	444.9	67.1	23.1	20.4
1967	1,039.4	33.9	3,163.6	801.7	69.1	56.3	32.4
1968	1,130.9	35.7	3,743.9	801.9	71.4	50.0	28.2
1969	1,093.2	38.9	4,144.8	758.3	72.5	66.2	24.2
1970	1,141.6	31.8	4,409.5	830.5	74.5	79.4	23.1
1971	1,726.6	24.1	5,379.8	1,371.5	74.9	28.7	34.1
1972	1,743.6	27.7	6,258.4	1,404.4	76.0	62.6	35.8
1973	1,300.5	35.0	6,024.0	1,011.5	68.1	66.1	23.4
1974	925.8	26.5	4,193.8	748.1	63.1	47.4	17.6
1975	1,040.2	28.2	4,704.3	862.4	61.4	91.6	24.3
1976	1,056.3	36.8	4,493.0	864.8	63.1	81.8	24.8
1977	1,004.9	31.2	4,329.0	690.5	60.8	72.4	20.1
1978	778.5	10.9	4,197.9	439.6	57.2	75.5	13.8
1979	713.1	4.1	3,813.4	451.3	54.9	94.3	13.4

(1) total soft loans ('credito agevolato') by year; (2) percentage of (1) to the small- and medium-sized industries; (3) total outstanding soft loans; (4) total soft loans for investment, col. (1) less credit to exports and to commerce; (5) outstanding soft loans as a percentage of total credit to manufacturing; (6) subsidies to investment ('contributi in conto capitale') in the South; (7) soft loans and subsidies (cols. 4 + 6) as a percentage of total investments in manufacturing.

Source: Silvestri 1983: tables 3.1, 3.2, 3.10; investment in manufacturing ISTAT 1985: table 8.29; implicit price index for investment goods from ISTAT 1987: tables 8.29 and 8.30.

to have made the very favourable settlement with private companies acceptable (Mori 1989). Besides, it was hoped that the ex-electric companies would use the compensation payments for investment in new industrial activities. From a technical point of view, nationalization was a success. The new agency, ENEL (Ente Nazionale Energia Elettrica), extended its network to all areas, rationalized it, and increased productivity thanks to systematic exploitation of scale economies. The real price of energy was lowered too much by the governments' decisions about tariffs, so that in the 1970s the ENEL was constantly in deficit. In other words, the electricity consumption was heavily subsidized.

The main tool for supply-side policy in the 1960s and 1970s was the subsidization of investment (Serrani 1971; Pontolillo 1980)—either with grants (*'contributi a fondo perduto'*) or soft loans (*'credito agevolato'*). As already said, the system had been experimental in the late 1940s, and in the 1950s the state had set up a network of financial institutions for medium- and long-term credit —the *'sezioni di credito speciale'* of some banks, the Mediocredito Centrale (and its regional branches), the ISVEIMER, IRFIS, etc. However, the funds had remained small until the end of the 1950s. By contrast, in the late 1960s and 1970s state subsidies accounted for about one-quarter of total investment in manufacturing (with peaks of up to one-third in some years) and for more than two-thirds of long-term credit for investment (Table 5.1). Most of these funds accrued to a specific class of projects, Southern-located plants in heavy industries. This was the, partially unintentional, consequence of the design of the incentives. In the late 1950s it had been decided, after a long discussion, that the '*questione meridionale*' could be solved only by industrializing the South, and this aim could be achieved only by a massive subsidization of investments. The initial idea was to reserve incentives only to small firms, but the clause was abolished in the early 1960s, in order to attract the investment by large Northern companies. The deal was particularly attractive for capital-intensive industries, such as metalworking, engineering, and chemicals, which received two-thirds of the total '*credito agevolato*' in 1964–73. The allocation of soft loans was characterized by several serious technical shortcomings. The banks tended to privilege the large projects, which increased their own commissions and interests, without bothering too much about the soundness of the projects and the companies' strategies. Consequently, they tried to hide as long as possible the bad loans and the ensuing losses. When this behaviour was no more possible, the banks protected their own investment by favouring purely financial solutions over strategies to improve efficiency or technical change (Filippi 1979).

One could not affirm that the subsidization had no results whatsoever. From 1951 to 1981, the number of industrial workers in the Southern regions increased by 2.5 times, or from 13% to 20.5% of the Italian total. The per-capita GDP in the South rose at 2.5% yearly—i.e. nearly as much as the national one. On the other hand, the highly capital-intensive industries were not suited to the Southern input endowment, and their settlement had little or no diffusion effect on the local entrepreneurship (the large chemical or steel plants were nicknamed 'cathedrals in the desert'). In 1973 the state-owned enterprises and the two largest private groups, FIAT and Montedison, accounted for about two-thirds of Southern industrial output and employed more than 70% of the workers (Del Monte and Giannola 1978: tab. 8.11). Therefore, one could define the policy for the South as effective but hardly an efficient one.

Summing up, the industrial policy of the 1960s did leave some positive legacy, but the costs were extremely high. Besides, it missed the opportunity of setting up an institutional framework for further development, including adequate financial markets, an anti-monopolistic legislation, and a coherent system of rules to plan public finance for the new goals.

5.9. THE FAILURE OF THE 'NATIONAL CHAMPIONS' STRATEGY IN THE 1970S

Many countries in Europe faced the crisis of the early 1970s by developing cooperation between government and private enterprises (Curzon Price 1981). In Italy this approach was implemented by setting up multilateral negotiations on different issues, including the investment policies of enterprises. The outcome was however disappointing. There were too many actors—private and public big firms, small- and medium-sized innovative firms operating in international markets, small- and medium-sized firms working in segmented markets with the help of public support, national, local, and industry trade unions, etc. (Valli 1979). Each subject pursued its own interests and had its own links with national and local politicians. These problems were common to other countries (Jessop 1979), but nowhere were they as serious as in Italy.

The government was unable to choose among these conflicting interests and tried to reconcile them by increasing the subsidies. The (all-inclusive) total grew from 1.2% of GDP in 1964 to 4.6% in 1975 to an all-time peak of 8.9% in 1984 (Ranci 1987). The growth is impressive but even more impressive is the change within the aggregate. In fact in the 1970s investment subsidies remained constant in real terms. The whole increase is accounted for by the growth in other types of subsidies—such as the exemption from welfare payments on current employees, and the subsidies for temporary lay-off of workers. Both measures were initially granted as a temporary relief for limited categories of workers in the South. They were later extended to all industrial workers in 1977 and/or made permanent. Therefore the expenditure soared from 5% to over 60% of the total subsidies and to 90% in the 1980s. In other words, most of the money was spent for short-term goals, such as preventing social unrest or easing the financial situation of the firms.

Some 'strategic' branches such as steel-making, energy, and petrochemicals were granted specific measures—notably Law no. 675 of 1977 for the '*ristrutturazione industriale*' (Compagna Marchini 1981). The policy was inspired by the then common idea of creating large, internationally competitive 'national champions' (Adams 1986). This approach did not work. First, it was not easy to fine-tune policies for diversified productions within the same industry (for instance, primary and secondary chemicals). Second, the sectoral plans often contradicted macro-oriented industrial policies to improve technical change and competitiveness. Last but not least, the actual choices were very often inspired by more mundane concerns—such as rescuing industrial companies (together with the state-owned banks which had financed them) from bankruptcy and defending employment at any cost.

As previously said, bailing-out had been a tradition in Italy, but it had been to some extent shelved as unnecessary during the '*miracolo economico*'. The practice was resumed in the late 1960s, and turned into a 'generalized right to public aid' (Compagna Marchini 1981). In the 1970s, the state felt obliged to bail out practically every company with a sizeable number of workers, and to buy loss-making subsidiaries of private companies. In 1971, all the mining activities of Montedison were transferred to a state holding company created for the purpose, the EGAM ('Ente gestione aziende minerarie'). The small- and medium-sized companies were cared for by the GEPI ('Gestione partecipazioni industriali'). Unlike IRI, ENI, or EGAM, it should have provided only temporary relief, with an innovative formula of partnership with private entrepreneurs. However, the partnership worked only in very few cases, and most firms never returned to the private sector. These massive bailouts caused the number of employees in manufacturing by state-owned companies to increase from 185,000 in 1953 to 236,600 in 1968 to 451,500 in 1974.

On the whole, the supply-side policy of the 1970s was a total disaster. Just to give an example, let us consider the case of the chemical industry. Its previous performance had been lacklustre at best, but the worldwide development of petrochemical production seemed to offer it a great opportunity for a new start. There were four main players, ANIC (owned by ENI), and three private companies, Montedison, SIR, and Liquichimica. They were in fierce competition (aptly known as the 'chemical war'), and they wanted to have an integrated production cycle from oil to plastics and fibres. Unfortunately, the Italian market was not large enough to accommodate three integrated companies, simply because the optimally-sized output of ethylene (the first intermediate product) was too great. The optimal solution would have been some sort of agreement to share it and a specialization in different intermediate products. However all the attempts failed, including one brokered by the government in 1971. Each company went on with its plans, and obtained the state subsidies thanks to its ties with prominent politicians of the ruling parties. The result was an inordinate rush to build new factories—and a serious problem of excess capacity. The second oil crisis in 1979 caused the bankruptcy of SIR and of Liquichimica. They were bailed out by ENI with public money, which in due time closed some plants (Giannetti 1996). Montedison was practically bailed out twice and then privatized again, and in the meantime it transferred to ENI most of its plants producing basic chemicals (Marchi and Marchionatti 1992).

In the 1970s, when stagflation endangered the profits and sometimes the very survival of the large companies, the small- and medium-sized enterprises and the 'industrial districts' flourished. Their growth is often regarded as a radical alternative to the strategy of the 'national champion'. The small firms specialized in traditional, labour-intensive activities, allegedly unsuited to an advanced industrialized country, and they developed flexible institutional arrangements totally different from the centralized hierarchy of big business. It would be tempting to add to this list of differences the lack of state support, but this would not be accurate. In fact the small- and medium-sized firms also received soft loans, granted by several ad hoc laws. The amount was anyway proportionally lower than their 'fair' share—measured for instance by their percentage on industrial value added. In fact the subsidies to small and medium enterprises accounted for about one-third of the total funds for investments (Table 5.1) and they received very little other subsidies. The contribution of state money to the development of small industry is thus controversial. Prodi and De Giovanni are rather sanguine, attributing to it 'the initial development of thousands of enterprises' (Prodi and De Giovanni 1993; Scognamiglio 1979). Others pinpoint the unnecessary amount of red tape involved and the lack of a proper technical assessment of the applications, substituted by a purely bureaucratic check of the respect for the procedures (Bianchi 1993).

TABLE 5.2. *Total transfers to manufacturing, 1964–1979*

	(1)	(2)	(3)	(4)	(5)	(6)
1964	128.3	7.8	—	—	136.1	1.24
1965	141.9	9.5	—	—	151.4	1.34
1966	133.1	10.1	—	—	143.2	1.17
1967	259.0	14.0	—	—	272.9	2.03
1968	254.0	23.4	4.1	4.8	286.3	1.97
1969	283.7	24.1	72.4	1.4	381.6	2.49
1970	353.5	21.5	113.1	1.8	489.9	2.95
1971	377.2	33.2	148.2	32.1	590.7	3.58
1972	456.8	24.9	185.8	39.6	707.1	4.07
1973	306.2	12.4	196.8	9.6	525.0	2.77
1974	220.8	7.2	250.0	22.9	500.9	2.71
1975	387.2	15.7	333.2	77.6	813.7	4.61
1976	388.1	28.3	300.1	60.3	776.8	4.06
1977	371.1	59.0	356.8	27.3	814.2	4.20
1978	301.1	59.2	386.1	77.9	824.3	4.03
1979	327.6	43.1	428.5	32.7	831.9	3.77

(1) resources for investments (direct subsidies and subsidization on soft loans); (2) credit to exports; (3) exemptions on welfare payments ('fiscalizzazione degli oneri sociali'); (4) net subsidies to temporary layoffs ('Cassa integrazione guadagni'); (5) total transfers; (6) percentage on manufacturing value added.

Sources: (1) and (2) 1964–9 estimates of the author from Table 5.1; (3) and (4) 1968–9 Brosio 1983; other Brosio and Silvestri 1983: table 2.1; implicit price index for investment goods ISTAT 1985: tables 8.29 and 8.30; value added ISTAT 1985: tables 8.18 and 8.19 (adjusting for the change in definition according to the new series).

5.10. THE INDUSTRIAL POLICY OF THE 1980S: FROM NATIONAL CHAMPIONS TO REGULATION

The costly failure of the policy of subsidization of the 1970s forced the state to rethink its approach. The emphasis of the industrial policy began to shift towards the support of R & D as a means to increase Italy's competitiveness. Public intervention in this field had begun sporadically in the late 1960s with interventions to support the diffusion of new machine tools (Law Sabatini 1965) and had been increased since the late 1970s, with a specific focus on applied research (Laws no. 675 of 1977 and no. 46 of 1982). In the early 1980s government expenditure in R & D increased more than in other advanced countries (Table 5.3), and Italy improved its position in comparison with all the major industrial countries, except Japan (Table 5.4). The effectiveness of this effort was however jeopardized by the lack of defined aims, by the narrow range of tools and by complex bureaucratic procedures. And in fact, Italy's performance was not brilliant, as shown by standard criteria such as the technological balance of payment, the percentage of Italian patents in the USA, and the competitiveness in high R & D branches (Malerba 1992).

Unlike other European countries, Italy did not implement any substantial liberalization and privatization policy in the 1980s. There were even some further

TABLE 5.3. *Total public expenses in R & D* (real rate of growth)

	1981–3	1983–4	1984–5
Italy	10.4	10.8	19.7
Germany	0.6	1.2	4.4
France	5.9	5.5	4
UK	0.3	−1.1	−1.1
USA	4.5	7.4	8.1
Japan	2	2	5.6

Source: Malerba 1992.

TABLE 5.4. *Indices of national R & D expenditure* (Italy = 100)

	1975	1985
Italy	100	100
Germany	341	269
France	237	197
UK	282	183
USA	1,821	1,503
Japan	475	537

Source: Malerba 1992.

bailouts. The only major exception was the sale of Alfa Romeo to Fiat in 1987. In spite of its reputation, Alfa Romeo was then in deep trouble (also because of serious managerial blunders), and needed to be integrated into a larger group. The decision to sell it was triggered by an offer from Ford, which wanted to expand its range of high-quality cars and needed a plant for the production of engines. Fiat did not need to buy Alfa, but feared the presence of such a strong competitor on its domestic turf. The government chose Fiat—though its offer entailed less favourable payment terms. So Italy had its own national champion —even if at a sizeable cost for the state. Only after the financial crisis of 1992 did privatization begin to be considered as a solution to the serious budget problems of state-owned companies and of the state itself. In 1992–3 the state dissolved EFIM (then practically bust) and sold some of its companies, and two major banks, the 'Credito Italiano' and the 'Banca Commerciale'. Since then, privatization has been comparatively slow, because of political resistance (often fuelled by the managers of the interested companies), and of the uncertainty between two alternative strategies—a British-style policy of widespread shareholding to reduce the too high concentration of power in the economy (Brioschi, Buzzacchi, and Colombo 1990; Barca 1994) or a French-style policy of creation of a *noyau dur* of shareholders to strengthen national industry and its financial independence. As usual, the result is a contradiction between the law and its implementation. For example, the legislation allegedly favours the public company, but the practice has been different. In spite of public offer and a statutory limitation of each shareholder's stake to 3% of the total capital, Mediobanca has succeeded in setting up a *noyau dur* to control both the 'Credito Italiano' and the 'Banca Commerciale'. The pace seems to have increased in 1995–6, but the future of several key operations, such as ENEL, ENI, is still uncertain. These difficulties confirm how the Italian state is unable to implement any kind of strategic intervention (including regulation) while industrial and financial enterprises are mainly interested in acquiring market power (Ranci 1995).

5.11. CONCLUSION

The above outline has highlighted a remarkable continuity in the aims of Italian industrial policy in the long run. They changed only twice in more than a century—in the 1880s and after World War II. The same aims were however pursued by an ever-changing mix of tools. As available resources were increasing thanks to economic growth (and of the rise in expenditure/GDP ratio), the state became more and more ambitious. In the nineteenth century, it limited itself to the railway policy, tariffs, and public procurements, then it progressively added bailouts, planning, regulation, subsidization, and the use of state-owned enterprises.

The evolution of industrial policy in Italy did not differ very much from that of other European countries. There were indeed some differences in emphasis. For instance, since the nineteenth century, bailouts were more widespread and frequent than elsewhere (and hence the state-owned companies played a larger role)—and the relationship between big business and the state was a little more intimate. In the 1960s–1970s Italy used financial incentives and banking intermediation more than other countries. But on the whole these differences do not seem so radical. Therefore one might doubt that the Italian state was so exceptionally active—especially if one takes into account also the very liberal policy towards utilities. The evidence is however not conclusive. The reputation of activism might still be vindicated if Italy had spent proportionally more than other countries. Such a hypothesis has however to be supported by quantitative comparison of the expenditures, which is not yet available but for the last twenty years. A simple description is not enough.

One can search for Italy's peculiarity in its institutions and hence in the implementation of its industrial policy. As a rule, institutions in Italy work worse than elsewhere in Europe. The civil service has a reputation for being bloated and inefficient, the political system for being corrupt and unable to take decisions, and it can be argued that big business (or at least a part of it) is no better. These reputations are likely to have been at least partly deserved. Therefore Italian industrial policy has been much less effective than it may have been given the large resources allocated to industrial promotion. The difficulties have been growing in the last decades, as both the underlying institutional problems and the ambitions of industrial policy were growing. There are now signs of improvement, but it is too early to say whether Italy has overcome its problems.

REFERENCES

AA. VV. (1981). *Sulla Programmazione: Una Parola Chiave della Politica Italiana*. Bari.
—— (1993–5). *Storia dell'Industria Elettrica in Italia*, 5 vols. Bari.
ACQUARONE, F. (1965). 'La politica sindacale del fascismo', reprinted in Acquarone and Vernassa (a cura di) (1974), *Il Regime Fascista*, 233–57. Bologna.
ADAMS, P. (1986). 'State policy and the chemical industry in the Western Europe', in A. Martinelli (ed.), *International Market and Global Firms: A Comparative Study of Organized Business in the Chemical Industry*. London.
—— and ORSENIGO, L. (1986). 'Tecnologie emergenti e la politica industriale in Italia', *Rivista Trimestrale di Scienza dell'Amministrazione*, 2.
AMATO, G. (1972). *Il Governo dell'Industria in Italia*. Bologna.
ARE, G. (1965). *Lo Sviluppo Industriale Italiano nell'età della Destra*. Pisa.
—— (1974). *Alle Origini dell'Italia Industriale*. Napoli.
BALCONI, M. (1991). *La Siderurgia Italiana*. Bologna.
BARCA, F. (1994). *Imprese in Cerca di Padrone*. Bari.
—— and TRENTO, S. (1997). 'La parabola delle partecipazioni statali: una missione tradita', in F. Barca (a cura di), *Storie del Capitalismo Italiano*, 186–234. Roma.
BARDINI, C. (1996). *Labour Productivity in Manufacturing: The UK and Italy in the 20th Century*, Nota di Lavoro no. 96.18 Dipartimento di Scienze Economiche Università Cà Foscari, Venice.
BIANCHI, P. (1993). 'Industrial policies for small and medium firms and the new direction of European commodity policies', in M. Baldassarri (ed.), *Industrial Policy in Italy 1945–1990*, 161–88. Basingstoke and London.
BONELLI, F. (1975). *Lo Sviluppo di una Grande Impresa in Italia: La Terni dal 1884 al 1962*. Torino.
—— (1978). 'Il capitalismo italiano. Linee generali di interpretazione', *Annali della Storia d'Italia*, i. 1126–1255. Torino: Einaudi.
BOTTIGLIERI, B. (1984). *La Politica Economica dell'Italia Centrista*. Milano.
—— (1987). *STET*. Milano.
—— (1990). 'Una grande impresa chimica tra stato e mercato: La Montecatini degli anni '50', in F. Amatori and B. Bezza (a cura di), *Montecatini, 1888–1966, Capitoli di Storia di una Grande Impresa*, 309–56. Bologna.
—— (1994). 'L'industria elettrica dalla guerra agli anni del miracolo economico', *Storia dell'Industria Eletrica Italiana dal Dopoguerra alla Nazionalizzazione 1945–1962*, 4: 61–87.
BRIOSCHI, F., BUZZACCHI, L., and COLOMBO, M. G. (1990). *Gruppi di Imprese e Mercato Finanziario*. Roma.
BROSIO, G., and SILVESTRI, P. (1983). 'Uno sguardo d'assieme', in P. Ranci (ed.), *I Trasferimenti dello Stato alle Imprese Industriali negli Anni Settanta*, 17–34. Bologna.
CALDERONI, U. (1961). *I Cento Anni della Politica Doganale Italiana*. Padova.

CAPIE, F. (1994). *Tariffs and Growth*. Manchester.

CARACCIOLO, A. (1969). 'La crescita e la trasformazione della grande industria durante la prima guerra mondiale', in G. Fuà (a cura di), *Lo Sviluppo Economico in Italia*, iii. 198–240. Milano.

CARDINI, A. (1981). *Stato Liberale e Protezionismo in Italia*. Bologna.

CASSESE, S. (1974). 'Corporazioni ed intervento pubblico nell'economia', in Acquarone and Vernassa (a cura di), *Il Regime Fascista*, 327–55. Bologna.

CER-IRS (1986). *Quale Strategia per l'Industria: Rapporto sull'Industria e la Politica Industriale Italiana*. Bologna.

CIANCI, E. (1977). *Nascita dello Stato Imprenditore in Italia*. Milano.

CIOCCA, P., and TONIOLO, G. (1984). 'Industry and finance in Italy 1918–1940'. *Journal of European Economic History*, 13 (Special Issue): 113–36.

COHEN, J. S. (1972). 'The 1927 revaluation of the lira: A study in political economy'. *Economic History Review*, 25.

—— (1988). 'Was Italian fascism a developmental dictatorship? Some evidence to the contrary'. *Economic History Review*, 41: 95–113.

COLITTI, M. (1979). *Energia e Sviluppo in Italia: La Vicenda di Enrico Mattei*. Bari.

COMPAGNA MARCHINI, L. (1981). *Nel Labirinto della Politica Industriale*. Bologna.

CONFALONIERI, A. (1982). *Banca ed Industria in Italia dalla Crisi del 1907 all'Agosto 1914*. Milano.

—— (1992). *Banche Miste e Grande Industria in Italia 1914–1933*, i. Milano.

COOMBES, D. (1971). *State Enterprise: Business or Politics?*. London.

COVINO, R., GALLO, G., and MANTOVANI, E. (1976). 'L'industria dall'economia di guerra alla ricostruzione', in P. L. Ciocca and G. Toniolo (a cura di), *L'Economia Italiana nel Periodo Fascista*, 171–270. Bologna.

CURZON PRICE, V. (1981). *Industrial Policies in the European Community*. London.

DE CECCO, M. (1971). 'Lo sviluppo dell' economia italiana e la collocazione internazionale'. *Rivista internazionale di scienze economiche e sociali*, 13: 10–35.

DE CLEVA, E. (1992). 'Integrazione europea e "iniziativa privata": Gli ambienti milanesi e la nascita del MEC (1955–1957)', in E. Di Nolfo, R. Rainero, and B. Vigezzi (eds.), *L'Italia e la Politica di Potenza in Europa*, 439–81. Milano.

DELL'OREFICE, A. (1980). 'Un'occasione mancata: La legge speciale per Napoli', *Cahiers Internationaux d'Histoire Economique et Sociale*, 18: 159–266.

DEL MONTE, A. (1977). 'Profitti e sviluppo economico negli anni 1881–1961, con particolare riferimento al periodo fascista'. *Rivista Internazionale di Scienze Sociali*, 75: 241–66.

—— and GIANNOLA, A. (1978). *Il Mezzogiorno nell'Economia Italiana*. Bologna.

DEL VECCHIO, E. (1978). *La Via Italiana al Protezionismo*. Roma.

DE ROSA, L. (1982). 'Economics and nationalism in Italy'. *Journal of European Economic History*, 11: 537–74.

DORIA, M. (1989). *Ansaldo*. Milan.

ERCOLANI, P. (1969). 'Documentazione statistica di base', in G. Fuà (a cura di), *Lo Sviluppo Economico in Italia*, iii. 378–470. Milan.

FANO, E. (1974). 'La Restaurazione antifascista liberista: Ristagno e sviluppo economico durante il fascismo', in Acquarone and Vernassa (a cura di), *Il Regime Fascista*, 281–305. Bologna.

FAURI, F. (1995). 'La fine dell'autarchia: I negoziati commerciali dell'Italia dal 1947 al 1953'. *Rivista di Storia Economica*, 12: 331–66.

FEDERICO, G., and TENA, A. (1998). 'Was Italy a protectionist country?'. *European Review of Economic History*, 1.

FENOALTEA, S. (1973). 'Riflessioni sull'esperienza industriale italiana dal Risorgimento alla prima Guerra Mondiale', in G. Toniolo (a cura di), *Lo Sviluppo Economico Italiano (1861–1940)*, 121–55. Bari.

—— (1982). 'Railways and the development of the Italian economy to 1913', in Patrick O'Brien (ed.), *Railways and the Economic Growth of Western Europe*, 49–120. London.

—— (1992). 'Il valore aggiunto dell'industria', in G. M. Rey (ed.), *I Conti Economici dell'Italia*, iii. *Una Stima del Valore Aggiunto per il 1911. Serie Statistiche*, i/2: 105–90. Bari.

—— (1993). 'Politica doganale, sviluppo industriale, emigrazione: Verso una riconsiderazione del dazio sul grano'. *Rivista di Storia Economica*, 10: 65–77.

FERRARI, P. (1986). 'La produzione di armamenti in età giolittiana'. *Italia Contemporanea*, 162: 113–39.

—— (1990). 'Amministrazioni statali ed industria nell'età giolittiana'. *Italia Contemporanea*, 180.

FILIPPI, E. (1979). 'I problemi dei piani di settore', in A. Cassone (a cura di), *Politica Industriale e Piani di Settore*. Milano.

FILOSA, R., REY, G. M., and SITZIA, B. (1976). 'Uno schema di analisi quantitativa dell'economia italiana durante il fascismo', in P. L. Ciocca and G. Toniolo (a cura di), *L'Economia Italiana nel Periodo Fascista*, 51–101. Bologna.

GERSCHENKRON, A. (1962). 'Observations on the rate of industrial growth of Italy (1881–1913)', in id., *Economic Backwardness in Historical Perspective*, 98–127. Harvard.

GIANNETTI, R. (1993). 'Vecchi e nuovi sistemi territoriali', in L. De Rosa (ed.), *Storia dell'Industria Elettrica in Italia*, ii. 235–317. Bari.

—— (1994a). 'Mutamento tecnico e sviluppo 1880–1980', in P. L. Ciocca (ed.), *Il Progresso Economico dell'Italia*, 47–80. Bologna.

—— (1994b). 'La politica degli investimenti e delle tariffe', in L. De Rosa (ed.), *Storia dell'Industria Elettrica in Italia*, iv. 148–217. Bari.

—— (1996). 'Imprese e politica industriale: La petrolchimica italiana negli anni '70', in L. d'Antone (a cura di), *Radici Storiche ed Esperienze dell'Intervento Statale nel Mezzogiorno*, 499–524. Rome.

GRASSINI, F. A. (1979). 'Le imprese pubbliche', in F. A. Grassini and C. Scognamiglio (eds.), *Stato ed Industria in Europa: L'Italia*, 79–114. Bologna.

GREGOR, J. (1979). *Italian Fascism and Developmental Dictatorship*. Princeton.

GRIFONE, P. (1971). *Il Capitale Finanziario in Italia*. Torino.

GUALERNI, G. (1976). *Industria e fascismo*. Milano.

—— (1982). *Lo Stato Industriale in Italia*. Milano.

HENTSCHEL, V. (1989). 'German economic and social policy', in P. Mathias and S. Pollard (eds.), *The Cambridge Economic History of Europe*, vol. viii (Cambridge), 752–806.

IPSOA (1985). *Annali dell'Economia Italiana*. Milano.

ISTAT (1987). *Sommario di Statistiche Storiche 1926–1985*. Rome.

JESSOP, B. (1979). 'Corporatism, parliamentarism and social democracy', in E. Schmitter and G. Lehmbruch (eds.), *Trends toward Corporatist Intermediation*. London.

KEYNES, J. M. (1925). *A Tract on Monetary Reform*. London.

KUDO, A., and HARA, T. (1992) (eds.). *International Cartels in Business History*. Tokyo.

LA FRANCESCA, S. (1973). *La Politica Economica del Fascismo*. Bari.

LANARO, S. (1979). *Nazione e Lavoro*. Padova.

LIEFMANN, R. (1932). *Cartels, Concerns, and Trust*. London.

LIEPMANN, H. (1938). *Tariff Levels and the Economic Unity of Europe*. London.

LOCATELLI, M. (1938). *Problemi dell'Unificazione*. Roma.

MADDISON, A. (1991). *Dynamic Forces in Capitalistic Development*. Oxford.

MAGNANI, M. (1992). 'L'appuntamento mancato degli anni '60', in P. L. Ciocca (a cura di), *Il Progresso Economico dell'Italia*, 161–76. Bologna.

MALERBA, F. (1992). 'R & D: Growth in Italian industry in an international perspective', in G. Dosi, R. Giannetti, and P. A. Toninelli (eds.), *Technology and Enterprise in a Historical Perspective*. Oxford.

MARCHI, A., and MARCHIONATTI, R. (1992). *Montedison (1966–1989)*. Milano.

MERGER, M. (1986). 'Un modello di sostituzione: la locomotiva italiana dal 1850 al 1914'. *Rivista di Storia Eonomica*, 3/1: 66–108.

MOMIGLIANO F. (1986) (cura di). *Le Leggi della Politica Industriale in Italia*. Bologna.

MORI, G. (1989). 'La nazionalizzazione in Italia: Il dibattito politico-economico', in *La Nazionalizzazione dell'Energia Elettrica: L'esperienza Italiana e di Altri Paesi Europei*, 34–57. Bari.

MORTARA, A. (1978). 'Osservazioni sulla politica dei "tagli salariali" del 1929–1934', in G. Toniolo (a cura di), *Industria e Banca nella Grande Crisi*, 65–71. Milano.

NITTI, F. (1905). *La Conquista della Forza*. Bari.

PAPA, A. (1973). *Classe Politica e Intervento Pubblico nell'Eta' Giolittiana*. Napoli.

PEDONE, A. (1969). 'La politica del commercio con l'estero', in G. Fuà (ed.), *Lo Sviluppo Economico in Italia*, ii. 241–59. Milano.

PETRI, R. (1990). *La Frontiera Industriale*. Milano.

—— (1996). 'Scienziati e tecnologia: Giulio Natta e la petrolchimica', in R. Giannetti (a cura di), *Nel Mito di Prometeo*, 100–23. Firenze.

PIERUCCI, C. M., and ULIZZI, A. (1973). 'Evoluzione delle tariffe doganali italiane dei prodotti manufatti nel quadro della integrazione economica europea', in Banca d'Italia (ed.), *Contributi alla Ricerca Economica*, 269–82. Roma.

POLA, G. (1967). 'La storia della programmazione economica italiana'. *Il Programma Economico Italiano, 1966–70*. 112–97. Milano.

PONTAROLLO, E. (1978). 'Le politiche di ristrutturazione industriale in Italia dal 1961 al 1977'. *L'Industria*, 3–47.

PONTOLILLO, V. (1980). *Il Sistema del Credito Speciale in Italia*. Bologna.

POSNER, M. V., and WOOLF, S. (1967). *Italian Public Enterprises*. London.

PRODI, R., and DE GIOVANNI, D. (1993). 'Forty-five years of industrial policy in Italy: Protagonists, objectives and instruments', in M. Baldassarri (ed.), *Industrial Policy in Italy 1945–1990*, 31–54. Basingstoke and London.

RANCI, P. (1987). 'Italy: The weak state', in F. Duchene and G. Shepherd (eds.), *Managing Industrial Change in Western Europe*, 110–43. London and New York.

—— (1995). 'La via italiana alle privatizzazioni', in CER/IRS (ed.), *7° Rapporto sull'Industria e la Politica Industriale: La Politica per l'Industria dopo l'Impresa Pubblica, le Imprese dopo la Crisi*, 107–51. Bologna.

RANIERI, R. (1985). 'La siderurgia italiana e gli inizi dell'integrazione europea'. *Passato e Presente*, 4/7.

—— (1993). 'La grande siderurgia in Italia', in G. L. Osti (ed.), *L'industria di Stato dall'Ascesa al Degrado*, 9–98. Bologna.

RODOTA, S. (1995). 'Le libertà ed i diritti', in R. Romanelli (a cura di), *Storia dello Stato Italiano dall'Unità ad oggi*, 219–45. Roma.

ROSSI, E. (1966). *Padroni del Vapore e Fascismo*. Bari.

ROSSI, N., SORGATO, A., and TONIOLO, G. (1993). 'I conti economici italiani: Una ricostruzione statistica'. *Rivista di Storia Economica*, 10: 2–47.

RUFFOLO, G. (1973). *Rapporto sulla Programmazione*. Bari.

SAPELLI, G. (1992). 'Technical change, microeconomic evolution and growth: An introductory view of Italian industrial development', in G. Dosi, R. Giannetti, and P. Toninelli (eds.), *Technology and Enterprise in a Historical Perspective*, 291–313. Oxford.

—— and CARNEVALE, F. (1992). *Uno Sviluppo tra Politica e Strategia: ENI 1953–1985*. Milano.

—— ORSENIGO, L., TONINELLI, P. A., and CORDURAS, C. (1993). *Nascita e Trasformazione d'Impresa: Storia dell'Agip Petroli*. Bologna: Il Mulino.

SCHMITTER, P. (1979). 'Still the century of corporatism', in E. Schmitter and G. Lehmbruch (eds.), *Trends toward Corporatist Intermediation*. London.

SCOGNAMIGLIO, C. (1979). 'Strategia industriale e programmazione', in F. A. Grassini and C. Scognamiglio (a cura di), *Stato ed Industria in Europa: l'Italia*, 29–78. Bologna.

SEGRETO, L. (1992). 'Imprenditori e finanzieri', in G. Mori (a cura di), *Storia dell'Industria Elettrica in Italia*, i. *Le Origini, 1882–1914*, 249–337. Bari: Laterza.

—— (1997). *Marte e Mercurio*. Milano.

SENGERBERGER, W., and PYKE, F. (1992). *Industrial Districts and Local Economic Regeneration*. Geneva.

SERENI, E. (1966). 'Il nodo della politica granaria', in id., *Capitalismo e Mercato Nazionale*, 101–278. Roma.

SERRANI, D. (1971). *Lo Stato Finanziatore*. Milano.

SILVESTRI, P. (1983). 'Agevolazioni sul credito e contributi in conto capitale (1964–1979)', in P. Ranci (ed.), *I Trasferimenti dello Stato alle Imprese Industriali negli Anni Settanta*, 35–82. Bologna.

TATTARA, G. (1987). 'An example of countertrade: The Anglo-Italian clearing'. *Rivista di Storia Economica*, 2: 115–54.

TONIOLO, G. (1977). 'Effective protection and industrial growth: The case of Italian engineering'. *Journal of European Economic History*, 6: 659–73.

—— (1980). *L'Economia dell'Italia Fascista*. Bari.

VALLI, V. (1970). *Programmazione e Sindacati in Italia*. Milano.

—— (1979). *L'Economia e la Politica Italiana dal 1945 a Oggi*. Bologna: Il Mulino.

VIDAL, J. P. (1991). *Les Fluctuations Internationales de 1890 à nos Jours*. Paris.

VITALI, O. (1992). 'Gli impieghi del reddito nell'anno 1911–1992', in G. M. Rey (ed.), *I conti economici dell'Italia*, iii. *Una Stima del Valore Aggiunto per il 1911. Serie Statistiche*, i/2: 283–326. Bari.

WILLIS, R. (1971). *Italy Chooses Europe*. Oxford.

ZAMAGNI, V. (1978). *Industrializzazione e Squilibri Regionali*. Bologna: Il Mulino.

—— (1979–80). 'Distribuzione del reddito e classi sociali nell'Italia fra le due guerre'. *Annali Feltrinelli*, 10: 17–50.

—— (1981). *Lo Stato Italiano e l'Economia*. Firenze.

—— (1982). *La Distribuzione Commerciale in Italia fra le due guerre*. Milano.

—— (1990). *Dall'Ammoniaca ai Nuovi Materiali*. Bologna.

—— (1993). 'L'offerta di istruzione in Italia 1861–1987: Un fattore guida dello sviluppo o un ostacolo'. Working paper, Università di Cassino Dipartimento Economia e territorio, serie Economia e storia no. 4.

—— (1994). 'Alcune tesi sull'intervento dello stato in una prospettiva di lungo periodo', in P. L. Ciocca (a cura di), *Il Progresso Economico dell'Italia*, 151–60. Bologna.

—— (1995). 'Una ricostruzione dell'andamento mensile dei salari industriali e dell'occupazione 1919–1939', in *Ricerche per la Storia della Banca d'Italia*, vi. 349–78.

—— (1997). *Come Perdere la Guerra e Vincere la Pace*. Bologna.

ZANI, L. (1988). *Fascismo, Autarchia, Commercio Estero*. Bologna.

6

Sweden: The Rise and Fall of the Swedish Model

JAN BOHLIN

School of Economics and Commercial Law
Göteborg University

Industrial policy as a separate branch of economic policy gained prominence in Sweden in the late 1960s. Conscious efforts to influence industrial growth and its pattern were an important part of economic policy-making in this period. If by industrial policy we understand not only selective interventions (subsidization of various sorts, nationalizations, etc.) but also general efforts to facilitate and stimulate industrial growth, then there was of course an industrial policy also before the 1960s.

In the following outline of industrial policy in Sweden since the late nineteenth century we confine ourselves to specific policies aimed at the manufacturing industry and general policies, such as infrastructure policy, that have contributed by providing the framework for its growth. We distinguish four separate periods, each with its own distinctive traits. In the first period, stretching from approximately the 1880s to the First World War, the state made large investments in the development of a national system of infrastructure and also tried to foster national industry by means of a protectionist commercial policy. After a brief 'liberal interlude' in the 1920s, the next period stretches from the 1930s to the middle of the 1960s. In this period the legitimacy of state interventions in order to stabilize the economy was recognized. Proposals for and discussions regarding selective industrial policy interventions were frequent, especially in the 1930s and 1940s, but on the whole industrial policy in this period relied on general instruments. In the third period, from the late 1960s to the early 1980s, industrial policy became much more selective and ambitious. Developments since the middle of the 1980s can be seen as a fourth distinct period in Swedish industrial policy, characterized by the return of market solutions.

6.1. INDUSTRIAL POLICY BEFORE WORLD WAR I: INFRASTRUCTURAL INVESTMENTS AND TARIFFS

Sweden entered the phase of rapid modern economic growth sometime between 1850 and 1870. Recent interpretations have stressed the liberal institutional reforms in the middle of the nineteenth century as a prerequisite for this take-off into self-sustained growth (Myhrman 1994). Though economically backward compared to many other nations on the European continent Sweden had none-theless a quite advanced institutional set-up exemplified by a modern and stable banking and financial system. Once economic growth gained momentum Sweden was not hampered by institutional obstacles and its rich stock of human capital could be put to use (Sandberg 1978, 1979).

The role of the state in the Swedish industrialization process was, however, not limited to the creation of liberal economic institutions. As long as the state did not favour certain individuals, companies, or sectors of the economy, state interventions to better the general conditions for economic growth were con-sidered appropriate (Kilander 1983, 1991). From this perspective it was natural for the government to launch programmes of public investments for a nation-wide extension of infrastructural utilities such as railway transportation, telephony, and electrical energy. Infrastructural investments commanded a sizeable share of national income in the period leading up to the First World War. At its peak in 1879 railway investments alone accounted for 6.3% of national income (Hedin 1972: 127). To finance these investments the government placed loans in other countries, after 1880 mainly in France, before that in England and Germany. The resulting state foreign debt was finally paid back by means of inflation and a surplus in Sweden's current account during the First World War (Schön 1989: 46). Private investments also played a considerable role in the construction of a national infrastructure system, but the activities of the private companies were regulated by state policy, as shown in the following account.

The building of railways in Sweden gained pace after a decision by the Parlia-ment in 1853–4 to build main lines to connect the various parts of the country (Andersson-Skog 1993: 38–9). The construction of local and regional lines, on the other hand, was left to private and municipal initiatives. Stimulated by the foundation of a railway mortgage institute, the privately built railways expanded rapidly in the late nineteenth century. Measured in constructed mileage the pri-vately and municipally owned railways had in fact more extensive coverage than the state railways in the late nineteenth century. In 1913 the state-owned railway company accounted for 33% of the railway mileage but 60% of the transporta-tion of goods (Mårtensson 1994: 48).

While state-owned railways were built according to a national communica-tion plan, the private railways arose more spontaneously in response to local and regional needs, which does not mean that they were completely outside govern-mental control. Before construction of a private railway was commenced it had to be approved by the government to make sure it fitted in with the nationwide plan for railway communications (Mårtensson 1994: 46). After 1882 the private railway companies were also obliged to keep the same tariffs as the state com-pany in order to gain concessions for building railways. During the late nineteenth and early twentieth century a national railway policy was formulated, whose stated goals were to give every part of the country access to railway transport at rea-sonable prices, which implied that lines that were profitable implicitly subsidized the unprofitable lines in the sparsely populated (mainly northern) regions of the country (Andersson-Skog 1993: 37–8). This regional policy aspect was made evident in the period 1910–30 when the state constructed several railway lines in the interior parts of northern Sweden.

The telegraph network in Sweden had been built by the state for administrative and military reasons, but when the first telephone lines emerged in the 1880s, private capital took an active part in the process, especially in the Stockholm area. Competition between private companies led to falling prices and a fast growth of subscribers, but the local networks were not connected.

When technical change in the 1880s made it possible to interconnect regional and local networks the state-owned Telegrafverket took a more active role in the spread of telephony. The objective of Telegrafverket was to control every local line in the country and to connect them into a nationwide network. This would bring about a unification of standards and lowered costs. Towards the close of the century Telegrafverket already controlled 97% of the telephone lines outside the Stockholm area. Stockholm, on the other hand, was dominated by the private company Stockholm allmänna AB. In 1890 an agreement to link their networks had been reached between this company and Telegrafverket. When the agreement terminated in 1900, it was not renewed by Telegrafverket on the ground that it was too expensive. In 1903 the connection between the two networks was cut off and a fierce competition, the so-called 'telephone war', broke out in Stockholm. Finally in 1918 Stockholm allmänna was bought up by Telegrafverket. Although it was not a legal monopoly Telegrafverket had gained a de facto monopoly position in 1918 (Kaijser 1994: 107–27; Waara 1980: 113).

Initially the state adopted a passive attitude towards the spread of electricity, but when technical development made it possible to transmit electricity over long-range distances it became a matter of state policy. New legislation was needed concerning the right to use waterfalls for electricity generation and the right to construct high-voltage wires on land for electricity distribution, which previously could be blocked by the landowners. Furthermore the question of ownership of many waterfalls needed clarification (Jakobsson 1995: 60–1; Kaijser 1994: 162–3).

Since many of the waterfalls were situated on state property, it was suggested that the state should take up the generation of electricity. The government's interest in the matter was also stimulated by the potential use of electrical energy in railways. In 1905 Trollhätte kanal- och vattenverk was formed to exploit the Trollhätte waterfalls. This company was transformed in 1911 to a nationwide state-owned corporation, Vattenfallsverket. While the state engagement in electricity generation was substantial, most of the power plants at this time were constructed by private companies. Regional electricity systems emerged where the state-owned Vattenfall and large private joint-stock companies (in which large municipalities and energy-intensive industrial corporations were important owners) produced energy that was distributed by municipal electricity works.

The regional energy systems were unified into a nationwide system in the inter-war period when energy consumers in southern Sweden were connected to the water power resources in northern Sweden. Technically speaking the Swedish energy system was unified already before World War II. Organizationally the relationship between Vattenfall and the private producers was not clarified until 1946, when it was decided that Vattenfall should build, own, and operate every new main line. Three years later an agreement was reached between Vattenfall and the private owners of main lines that Vattenfall should henceforward oper-ate also their lines. Vattenfall now got a new role in the Swedish electricity sys-tem. From being the most important producer (it accounted for about 35% of the Swedish electricity generation in the middle of the 1940s), it now held respons-ibility for the general functioning of the nation's electricity production and dis-tribution (Kaijser 1994: 156–78).

The national system for the production and distribution of electrical energy that matured after the Second World War can be seen as an example of a typ-ical 'Swedish infrastructure model' (Kaijser 1994: 179–84). It was characterized by a mixture of state, private, and municipal ownership, where state enterprises were responsible for the building and operation of the main lines, while local lines in many instances were left to private initiatives. The state enterprises were operated on a non-profit basis, i.e. tariffs were set so that the revenues should cover costs but not yield any profit. Eventual surpluses were transferred to the state budget. The capital needed for investments was also supplied over the state budget. After an organizational reform in 1911, these and other public com-panies, such as the postal services, were called *Affärsdrivande verk*. This term is untranslatable and we shall henceforward use 'public quasi-corporation', a term borrowed from present-day national accounts, to denote these companies.

One aspect of the Swedish infrastructure model has been the close coopera-tion in the twentieth century between state quasi-corporations and large Swedish firms. The quasi-corporations were cost-minimizing organizations and were not in any way obliged to buy equipment from Swedish firms (and in many cases they did not). For companies such as LM Ericsson (telephony) and ASEA (rail-way equipment and electrical engineering), the long-range technical cooperation with the state enterprises were nevertheless instrumental in the evolution of these companies into successful multinational firms (Glete 1983; Kaijser 1994: 182).

The relationship between the state and the economy was gradually altered in a more interventionist direction in the final decades of the nineteenth century (Kilander 1983, 1991). We have seen this already in the monopolist aspiration of the state company in the telephone market around the turn of the century. The most visible change in industrial policy, and the one most debated among con-temporaries, however, was the protectionist turn in trade policy.

Since the 1850s commercial policy had developed in a free trade direction. In 1857 most custom duties on foodstuffs, raw materials, and machines were abolished and the tariffs were lowered on many other goods as well. This development towards free trade continued in 1865 when Sweden concluded a commercial treaty with France, prolonged in 1882, which implied further lowering of the custom duties on many (especially manufactured) goods (Ohlin 1965: 220).

The free trade policy was reversed in the late 1880s. In Sweden as in other countries the 'long depression' in the last quarter of the nineteenth century brought falling prices and sinking profit rates for many producers. Under the influence of protectionist currents in other countries, demands for higher tariffs were raised, especially from agricultural producers facing tough price competition on imported corn from foreign producers. Following several years of intense political debate, the protectionists finally won the majority for their demands in the Swedish Parliament in 1888. After having been free of duties, the tariff on imported corn was now raised to approximately 20% of the imported value. Custom duties on other foodstuffs were raised as well. Tariffs on most industrial goods could not be raised until 1892, since Sweden was bound by its commercial treaties with France and Spain. At the same time, duties on imported corn and foodstuffs were lowered, but this was only temporary, since they were raised again in 1895.

The turn to protectionism in 1888 raised the average tariff rate (custom duties divided by the value of imports) from about 9–10% in the 1870s to 11–12% in the 1890s (Gårestad 1987: 239). The 20% increase in average custom duties in the 1890s might seem surprisingly low in view of the heated political debate that preceded the protectionist legislation, but one has to bear in mind that many manufactured goods, such as textiles, glassware, and potteries were already sheltered by high custom duties during the 'free trade' era (Montgomery 1947: 164). The modest increase in the aggregate nominal tariff rate can also be explained by the declining importance of purely 'fiscal' tariffs (Gårestad 1987: 99) and by the presumably lesser weight in total imports of goods with increased custom duties. A better view of the effects of the protectionist turn is gained if we look at Table 6.1 showing the average custom duties for selected years in agriculture and manufacturing industries. The highest level of protection was given to agricultural goods, foodstuffs, pottery, and glasswares. Other industries that received a markedly higher rate of protection were the paper, clothing, and rubber goods industries. The most important change in commercial policy in the beginning of the 1890s, however, concerned the steep increase in custom duties imposed on iron goods, metal goods, and machines and tools (Montgomery 1921: 178).

The level of protection in various industries was clearly motivated by considerations on how much was 'needed' to meet foreign competition. In general the argument was that only already existing industries should be given support, but the infant industry argument was also heard. If we exempt agricultural commodities raw materials were in general duty-free. Higher up in the manufacturing chain tariffs increased since the tariff system was supposed to be based on solidarity, i.e. one branch was not to be protected at the cost of another. The consequence of this was that tariffs on imported inputs to a certain branch led to compensatory tariffs in that branch (Gårestad 1987: ch. 4; SOU 1924: 37: 11–18).

TABLE 6.1. *Average custom duties, selected years, 1888–1913*
(custom revenues divided by value of imports) (%)

	1888	1892	1906	1913
Agriculture				
Corn	20.7	9.1	27.6	27.0
Meat	15.7	13.4	11.6	10.1
Pork	27.9	12.0	19.0	10.4
Manufacturing and mining				
Iron- and steelworks	20.6	40.1	15.9	15.8
Metal works	0	0	0	0
Iron and metal manufacturing	6.4	12.4	11.4	14.4
Machine and engineering industry	12.3	17.7	18.2	17.4
Electrical engineering	—	9.3	11.8	15.3
Shipbuilding	0	0	0	0
Mining	0	0	0	0
Glassworks	15.8	22.6	22.7	24.1
Cement factories	11.5	12.7	20.5	20.0
Brick works	1.3	1.3	8.9	10.8
Stone quarrying and stone works	0	0	0	0
Potteries and earthenware works	27.1	32.8	28.0	27.7
Sawmills	0	0	0	0
Furniture and wooden-fittings factories	22.7	23.9	17.5	15.6
Pulp mills	0	0	0	0
Paper mills	18.1	21.4	30.0	35.3
Printing and allied industries	1.8	4.3	3.5	8.4
Slaughter-houses, etc.	21.5	12.0	15.1	13.2
Dairies	15.9	14.6	13.2	12.4
Fat factories	28.6	26.1	20.0	13.3
Flour mills	29.8	15.8	39.9	36.4
Bakeries	25.2	17.0	32.7	27.5
Sugar factories	119.3	112.8	49.0	34.9
Sugar refineries	59.3	65.4	60.7	71.6
Chocolate and sweets factories	39.7	41.5	41.7	37.3
Liquor factories	50.3	37.9	83.5	72.8
Breweries	30.1	42.5	46.2	57.0
Tobacco factories	43.4	43.4	39.9	36.6
Other food industries	23.2	25.5	25.7	25.9
Textile factories	9.7	9.9	9.2	13.2
Clothing and garment factories	12.1	20.2	20.0	21.1
Boot and shoe factories	7.0	7.5	15.0	15.5
Tanneries	7.6	10.4	11.3	10.6
Rubber goods factories	18.1	24.0	22.7	21.9
Chemical industries	10.4	12.1	16.2	16.4
Manufacturing and mining	16.8	19.4	18.4	19.0

Remark: Most Swedish tariffs were specific. Their *ad valorem* equivalents have been calculated from index numbers on the weighted average of custom duties for groups of commodities, average custom duties 1913 for the same groups and price indices. The figures in the table are accordingly approximations.

Source: Bohlin 1996.

Some industries that were not protected by tariffs, such as shipbuilding, were reimbursed for the custom duties they had paid on imported inputs.

In the 1890s Swedish industrialization entered a phase of fast growth and diversification (Jörberg 1961: ch. 3). An intriguing question is what effects the protectionist turn in trade policy had on economic development in the decades preceding World War I. The protectionist system was evaluated by a public invest-igation committee in the early 1920s. Among its conclusions were that tariffs indeed contributed to the comparatively strong growth of home market indus-tries in the two decades preceding World War I, but on the other hand also led to an inefficient firm structure in these industries (i.e. too many small firms) and facilitated the formation of cartels. The general assessment was that the protec-tionist trade system led to allocative inefficiencies (SOU 1924: 37) and thus had 'a slightly dampening effect on overall economic growth' (Heckscher 1957: 278–9), but this seems to be derived more from neoclassical economic theory than empirical investigations. The protectionist trade regime has not been evaluated by later economic historians.

Protectionism was the principal method by which the state tried to foster national industry in this period, but there were also some attempts to support industries by other means. We have already mentioned the mortgage institute that provided loans to private railway companies. A similar loan institute was set up in 1900 to provide loans for the shipping companies. Small companies also gained easier access to credits through the formation of loan institutes (Iveroth 1943: 193 ff.). There were also some cases of outright subsidies to industry. A much debated subsidization scheme was the support for some shipping companies running inter-continental lines considered beneficial for Swedish exports as a whole (Kilander 1991: 187 ff.). In the years preceding the First World War, there were also plans to subsidize the shipbuilding industry, but these were never realized (K. Olsson 1983: 45–8).

The general attitude during this period was that the state should stay away from goods production. There are nevertheless some early examples of state-owned companies engaging in goods-producing activities. The state was a substan-tial owner of woodlands and it was thus natural for Domänverket, the quasi-corporation managing state-owned forests, to start up sawmills. In the 1870s the share of the state in the Swedish sawmill industry was 2%, in 1900 it was 5% and by 1920 it had grown to 10%. The state also became the owner of some joint-stock companies. In 1917 the tobacco monopoly, AB Svenska Tobaks-monopolet, and the wine and liquor monopoly, AB Vin- och Spritcentralen were formed. The motives behind the formation of these state monopolies were fiscal and in the case of the wine and liquor monopoly social political concerns also played a role (Waara 1980). Of greater interest from the point of view of industrial policy is the state takeover of the iron-ore mining company LKAB in 1907 when the state bought 50% of the shares and secured the option to buy the other 50% as well. The relationship between the state and the northern min-ing fields had been intensely debated since the 1890s, as part of a more general debate concerning state actions to promote economic development in the northern regions. The call for nationalization of the mining fields had united quite different political currents: protectionists wanting to preserve the Swedish iron ore for home producers, regional interests who saw the nationalization of the mining fields as part of a general policy towards a comprehensive development of the regional economy, the Social Democrats since nationalization of the mining fields fitted in with their programme of socialization of the principal means of production. The parliamentary majority had resisted nationalization on the ground that the state should not interfere with the market. What finally tipped the scale in favour of nationalization seems to have been a perceived threat of German capitalists buying up LKAB. The financial interests behind LKAB now also favoured a state takeover, since they wanted a fast turnover of the invested capital (Jonsson 1969: 366–73; Nordlund 1989: 115–22; Waara 1980: 132–4).

A sign of the increased interest in industrial policy matters around the turn of the century was the perennial debate on the formation of a ministry for trade and industry. Finally the formation of such a department was proposed in 1913 after a public investigation (Kilander 1991: 154–64), but after the First World War the interest in an active industrial policy had diminished and the proposal was never carried out.

6.2. THE FORMATION AND MATURATION OF THE SWEDISH MODEL: FROM THE INTER-WAR PERIOD TO THE POST-WAR GOLDEN AGE OF CAPITALISM

The tendencies towards increased state interventionism that had typified the period leading up to the First World War came to a temporary halt in the 1920s. The overriding concern of economic policy in the early 1920s was to obtain price stability and the return of the Swedish currency to the gold standard. This was achieved by a very sharp deflation that involved rapidly increasing unemployment in 1921–2. In 1924 Sweden was the first country returned to the gold standard. The remaining part of the 1920s was characterized by rapid economic growth (4% per year in GDP), but unemployment never fell short of 10% of the unionized workers.

The crisis in the beginning of the 1930s is generally regarded as making a fundamental change in Swedish economic policy. In 1932 the Social Democrats entered the government. The government was broadened in 1933 after an agreement between the Social Democrats and the agrarian party. In return for adopting a new agricultural policy that involved trade regulations on agricultural products and subsidization of the domestic producers, the Social Democrats gained parliamentary support for a new unemployment policy. The new government inaugurated a long era of Social Democrat rule in Sweden. From 1932 until 1976 the Social Democrats stayed in power, between 1933–46 and 1952–9 in coalition with other parties, for the rest of the time on their own. The long era of Social Democrat governmental rule has obviously left its imprint on Swedish society and the 1930s can be seen as the initial phase of an economic-political model that matured after the Second World War.

To counter unemployment the government started public work projects at going market wages. After the economy had recovered from the depression in 1931–3, growth rates were impressive. If we take the period 1929–39 as a whole, the growth in real GNP was 4% per year (Lundberg 1983: 90–1). Unemployment diminished but was still around 10% towards the end of the decade. Sweden's remarkable economic performance in the 1930s was, however, hardly due to any expansionist effects of the new unemployment policy (Gustafsson 1993). By and large state budgets were balanced in the 1930s, only in 1933/4 did the budget run a small deficit (Bergström 1969: 48–9). Of greater importance than fiscal policy was another Keynesian prescription, namely a low rate of interest, which encouraged a home-market based upswing in the investment rate, especially in housing construction, in the 1930s. The low rate of interest was made possible by the dissociation of the Swedish currency from the gold standard in 1931 and its pegging to the British pound in 1933 at 19.40, which was clearly an under-valuation. Stimulated by an undervalued currency, Swedish exports also did well in the 1930s. For the remainder of the decade, Sweden ran a permanent trade surplus (Lundberg 1983: 100–8). Another factor behind Sweden's relatively successful trade performance was the favourable commodity composition of its exports. To a large extent Sweden's export was based on raw materials that were difficult to substitute for its trading partners. The main items were wood products, pulp, paper, iron ore, and products from the engineering industry.

In contrast to many other countries, the depression in the 1930s did not lead to a fundamental reversal of trade policy. Towards the end of the 1930s only Denmark and the Netherlands had lower custom duties than Sweden in Europe. Except in the case of agricultural products, trade regulation was not used by Sweden (Ohlin 1965: 224, 238–45). In the 1920s governments had resisted most of the demands for higher tariffs and custom duties remained basically the same as before World War I. This implied a reduced rate of protection, since the First World War inflation had lowered the protection provided by primarily specific tariffs.

In the 1930s the Social Democrats had abandoned the long-range socialist goal of a comprehensive nationalization and adopted a pragmatic attitude towards the question of ownership of the means of production. The 'socialization question' had been relegated to a public investigation committee, Socialiseringsnämnden (the socialization board), already in 1920 by the first post-war Social Democrat government. The committee published several reports but the practical results of its work were nil, as far as socialization was concerned, and in 1935 it was dissolved. What mattered for the Social Democrats was not ownership per se but how efficiently the firms were run. In practice this meant a preference for private ownership. There was only one example of a state takeover on a large scale in the inter-war period; the nationalization of the remaining private railways in 1939. The state-owned railway company had gradually expanded in the inter-war period through acquisitions of private railways that were in economic distress because of the competition from car and lorry transports (Mårtensson 1994: 105–8). The motive behind the decision seems to have been that it was considered easier to rationalize the railway net if it had a single owner (Waara 1980: 119–20). Some new state enterprises were also started. Of these, the formation in 1939 of the steel plant Norrbottens Järnverk (NJA) in northern Sweden was the most important quantitatively (Waara 1980: 149–52).

The Social Democrats' abandonment of the socialization doctrine was coupled to an optimistic attitude regarding the possibilities of influencing economic development by means of policy. Downturns in the business cycles could be mitigated by a counter-cyclical fiscal policy and it was also suggested that it might be possible to avoid these crises altogether if an element of planning was introduced into the capitalist economy. The main weakness of the capitalist market economy was considered to be its lack of coordination between individually efficient firms, as this implied a waste of resources. By means of industrial policy the state should further an increased 'coordination of economic life' (Lewin 1967: 69–71). This idea seems to lie behind the rudiments of macroeconomic planning that was introduced in the 1930s. In order to provide the government with short- and long-range forecasts a special investigation unit, the Business Cycle Institute, Konjunkturinstitutet, was set up in 1937. It was considered especially desirable to receive forecasts on future investments (Wickman 1980: 69–75). In order to clarify the possible fields of action for industrial policy, several public investigations of industrial branches were initiated in the latter half of the 1930s (Lewin 1967: 99–102). Some sectors received support as a result of these investigations (Lewin 1967: 155–6), but on the whole subsidies were unimportant at this time.

In most cases the branch investigations did not lead to any practical results, but the government also introduced industrial policy measures of a more general nature. In order to stimulate exports an export guarantee, financed by premiums paid by exporters, was introduced. Credit institutes were also founded in order to supply long-range loans to firms (Lewin 1967: 154–5, 168; Waara 1980: 147). These institutes were quite insignificant in relation to the credit market as a whole (Dahmén 1950: 333). Nevertheless the initiatives of the government in this area in the 1930s signalled a renewed interest in stimulating industrial development. This was also shown by the reform of company taxation in 1938. The tax reform implied substantial tax reductions for profitable firms and was accomplished in order to stimulate investments (Gustafsson 1993: 63; Lewin 1967: 154).

The Second World War brought increased state intervention in the economy. The production in many sectors was regulated by wartime planning. To administer the regulations an extensive administration was put into place (Lewin 1967: 176–80; U. Olsson 1982: 64–71). After the war the government appointed a postwar planning commission to facilitate the transition to a peace economy. In 1944 the commission of post-war planning, also named the Myrdal Commission after its chairman Gunnar Myrdal, started its work. The commission suggested that most of the wartime regulations in the economy should be removed but it nevertheless foresaw an increased role for the state and more planning in economic life, as did the post-war programme of the labour movement (Lewin 1967: 214–56; Lindbeck 1975: 37–9). Only in the credit market did the programme call for state ownership; its most controversial proposition was that the insurance companies should be nationalized. For the manufacturing industry the programme underlined the importance of industrial rationalization and restructuring under state guidance. A series of motions in the Parliament led to the formation of numerous public investigations on conditions in different manufacturing branches. The practical results of these were very meagre. The post-war years did not lead to an extensive increase in state ownership in Sweden as was the case in many other European countries. The idea of socializing the insurance companies never made its way to a government bill and there were no instances of nationalizations in the manufacturing industry. A state-owned commercial bank was formed though, but its share of the credit market was quite small.

In the late 1940s the Social Democrat government retreated from the planning ambitions of the post-war programme. To a certain extent this was probably caused by the united resistance from the non-socialist parties and the employers' organizations against any step towards a planned economy, but real economic development also played its role. The prognoses of a post-war depression that had guided earlier programmatic formulations proved unfounded, and instead combating inflation became the predominant concern of economic policy. To curb inflation some of the wartime regulations that had been released in 1945–6 were reinstated in 1947–8 (Lindbeck 1975: 39–40). Most of these regulations were gradually removed in the first half of the 1950s. The important exceptions to this liberalization of economic policy were, besides the agricultural sector, the credit market, constructions, and the housing sector. Rationing in the credit market was an instrument for the government to steer credits to high-priority sectors such as housing construction (Bladh 1991: 226–7; Lindbeck 1975: 124–5). The regulations in the credit market were eased in the latter half of the decade and the principle of a low rate of interest was gradually abandoned as a target for monetary policy. Economic policy in the 1950s relied on general instruments. Of special interest is the investment fund system, initiated in 1938, that was changed and extended in 1955. Firms were allowed to deduct 40% of profits to investment funds. By doing so the firms could diminish accounted profits and thus reduce or defer their tax payments. When the business cycle turned down, the government could decide to 'free' the investment funds. If the firms decided to use investment funds without permission taxes would have to be paid, though after five years 30% of the funds could be used without tax payment (Lindbeck 1975: 111–13). The investment fund system was created as an instrument of stabilization policy and is not normally regarded as an industrial policy instrument. By putting the funded money at the discretion of governments it could nevertheless be used for industrial policy purposes, which was also the case in regional policy from the late 1960s onwards. The taxable profits could also be diminished by utilizing the liberal rules with respect to inventory valuation and depreciation allowances. While nominally the corporate tax rate was raised from 40 to 50% in 1955, the real tax rate was much lower at about 15–20% (Södersten 1977: 147–9). The company taxation system was constructed so that its implicit tax subsidization had the biggest effect on the most prosperous companies, but only if profits were reinvested within the firm.

The economic policies followed by Social Democrat governments in the 1950s and 1960s has been described as the application of a typical 'Swedish model' (Hedborg and Meidner 1984; A. L. Johansson 1989; Mjøset 1986: 123 ff.). Its characteristic features have been: a commitment to full employment, secured by demand management and an ambitious labour market policy; a highly developed class compromise which secured orderly wage increases in centralized wage negotiations, and the construction of tax-financed public welfare systems. The functioning of the model presupposed high growth rates. Social Democrat governments in the 1950s and 1960s did not rely on investment steering, sectoral planning, and selective industrial policies to promote economic growth. On the contrary, the structural change spontaneously created by competitive pressures in the market economy was to be reinforced by general policies. From this perspective it is understandable that Swedish governments were enthusiastic supporters of attempts to reduce tariffs and other trade barriers (Katzenstein 1985: 39 ff.). In the 1950s and 1960s Swedish exports gradually became less dependent on the traditional raw material based products and more refined goods from the engineering industry gained in importance. With a limited home market a liberalized world economy was necessary for large Swedish firms in order for them to achieve economies of scale. International competition was also seen as a necessary corrective to monopolistic tendencies in the domestic market.

The openness of the economy presupposed a system of wage formation so that wages did not become 'excessive'. In Sweden highly organized and centralized trade unions and employers' organizations succeeded in negotiating orderly wage increases without open conflicts in a spirit of 'social partnership'. In the ideology of the trade union movement, wage formation was in fact considered an instrument to stimulate structural transformation, as was demonstrated by the writings of two trade union economists, Gösta Rehn and Rudolf Meidner. The 'Rehn–Meidner model' was originally worked out in the early post-war years as a means to combat inflation in a full employment society. In order to achieve noninflationary wage increases, it was necessary, according to Rehn and Meidner, that wage negotiations were centralized and guided by a 'solidarity wage policy'. The latter concept, meaning equal wage for equal work irrespective of where it was performed, would lead to an equalization of the wage structure. The consequence of such a wage policy would be low profitability or losses for companies with below average productivity increases and labour would have to be transferred to high productivity sectors. There is some econometric evidence for the 1960s, that the stimuli to structural change given by solidarity wage bargaining indeed acted to enhance labour productivity growth within manufacturing as a whole, as predicted by the Rhen–Meidner model (Locking 1996; Hibbs and Locking 1997).

To stimulate the necessary mobility in the labour market, the government had to embark on an ambitious 'selective' labour market policy. By increased spending on manpower education and retraining, job matching, subsidization of geographical mobility costs, etc., the functioning of the labour market should be improved and the 'Phillips curve' shifted inwards. The 'natural unemployment' resulting from structural transformation was not to be combated by general economic policies that were used in recessions, since this would only lead to inflation. The goal of full employment was given an ambitious interpretation in Sweden, but it was not allowed to stand in the way of technical change and structural transformation.

Solidarity wage policy also implied wage restraint in high productivity sectors. This was considered acceptable by the trade unions and Social Democrats, as long as the resulting 'excess profits' were reinvested. The investment incentives built into the system of corporate taxation as well as later schemes of collective capital formation should be seen in this context. The introduction of general pension funds in the late 1950s, financed by charges on the wage sum paid by employers, was a first step in this direction. An enlarged share of the credit market now came under public control. Since contributions to the pension funds initially were much larger than disbursements, the funds grew very fast in the 1960s. Most of the capital was placed in long-range loans that financed a vast housing construction programme in the 1960s. Starting in the late 1960s attempts were also made to reallocate part of the funds to the risk capital market.

Economic policy in the 1950s had primarily relied on general policy instruments. The recession in 1958–9 signalled a change in focus. Inspired by the Rehn–Meidner model economic policy now to an increasing extent relied on 'selective' measures (Bergström 1969; Lindbeck 1975). The primary example is increased expenses on labour market policy. While in 1955 1.1% of the state budget or 0.2% of GNP was allocated to labour market policy the corresponding figures in 1960 were 3.7% and 0.9%. The ambitions of labour market policy were raised not only to counter unemployment but also to reinforce structural change in the economy. Consequently the expenses on labour market policy increased in the beginning of the 1960s despite diminishing unemployment (Axelsson, Löfgren, and Nilsson 1987: 80–4). The principal industrial policy document in the early 1960s was '*Samordnad näringspolitik*' (Co-ordinated industrial policy) adopted by the central organization of blue-collar workers in 1961 (Lewin 1967: 427 ff.). The main task of industrial policy was, according to this document, to remove the obstacles to the ever-present structural change. The 'development forces' should be freed not only from detailed state regulations but also from the 'inherent inertia' in the economic system. Labour market policy was seen as the principal policy instrument, but the programme also called for a more radical free trade policy and an easing of regulations in the credit market, so that capital could be channelled to the most efficient firms. The main tenet of the programme was that industrial policy should lubricate the structural change spontaneously generated by the market economy, but it also resurrected the ideas of active branch restructuring from the 1930s and 1940s. To give direction to a structural adaptation policy, the planning efforts had to be increased, i.e. prognoses over which sectors of the economy that were the most likely to expand should be formulated (Lewin 1967: 432–7).

In practice direct efforts to influence the direction of structural change in manufacturing industry had to wait another decade, but the call for more planning efforts was partially realized. In the autumn of 1962 the Economic Planning Council (Ekonomiska planeringsrådet) was formed with participation of representatives from the government, the employers' and trade union organizations and economic experts. Its task was to follow economic development and chart tendencies. At the same time, work with the five-year long-term forecasts that had begun in the late 1940s was institutionalized through the setting up of a special unit for this purpose within the Ministry of Finance.

Direct industrial policy interventions were few in this period but the government nevertheless took initiatives in the credit market, where new institutes were set up. Two of these were formed in order to extend long-range credits to companies in the agricultural sector and small firms, respectively. The most important of the new institutes was AB Export Kredit, founded in 1962 in order to help Swedish firms to finance export credits. Jointly owned by the state (50%) and the commercial banks (50%), the new institute was primarily financed by loans from the general pension funds. Its formation has to be seen against the background of the sharpened competition in the world market in the beginning of the 1960s, which in many branches made the possibility to extend credits to customers mandatory (Waara 1980: 159–60). Most of its lending went to the shipbuilding firms to refinance their customer credits. The shipbuilding industry was also supported by a loan guarantee system that was initiated in 1963. In contrast to the situation in many other countries, the loans extended to the shipbuilding industry were, however, given on commercial terms and no loan guarantee had to be redeemed before the middle of the 1970s (Bohlin 1989: 166 ff.).

6.3. FROM OFFENSIVE TO CRISIS MANAGEMENT (1960–1980)

Outwardly economic developments in the 1950s and 1960s had been successful, but in the middle of the 1960s it was also clear that cracks had begun to appear in the Swedish model. In order for the growing sectors to absorb the labour released by declining sectors, increased investments were called for in a situation of declining ability of self-financing in many firms. Several branches in the manufacturing industries were in need of restructuring and a public investigation had shown that concentration and monopolization were widespread. At the same time many voices criticized the adverse effects of economic growth such as bad working environments and regional imbalance. To address these problems, the Social Democrat government put industrial policy at the top of the agenda and started an 'industrial policy offensive' in the second half of the 1960s. The ideas of the 1930s and 1940s about influencing the direction of structural change through a programme of 'branch rationalization' was put forward again. At the same time the ambitions of industrial policy were widened to not only promote structural change and growth but also to channel this growth into 'socially acceptable forms' (Schäfer 1984: 47).

The heightened ambitions of industrial policy were clearly shown by increased efforts to redress the regional balance in Sweden. The middle of the 1960s had witnessed the breakthrough for a regional policy. In order to stimulate firms to set up businesses in certain 'support areas', a programme of state loans and subsidies was started. It has been estimated that the regional support policy could cover 20–25% of the investment costs in the support areas (J. Johansson 1991; Wibble 1971: 66). In 1970 the new regional policy that had been started in 1965 was evaluated in positive terms. New policy instruments were initiated, such as employment support (i.e. wage subsidization of companies), subsidization of transports and regional loan guarantees. The utilization of investment funds was practically freed from restrictions in the support areas. In the latter half of the 1970s companies in these areas received further tax concessions when employment taxes were lowered (J. Johansson 1991; Wibble 1971).

The increased priority given to industrial policy issues can be seen in the formation in 1969 of a special 'Ministry of Industry' in the government to take care of industrial policy issues. In order to gain a more detailed knowledge of different manufacturing branches a new investigation unit, Statens industriverk, which operated under the Ministry of Industry, was formed in 1973 (Schäfer 1984: 124 ff.).

The first area that was singled out for state intervention in 'the industrial policy offensive' was the credit market. This was motivated by the need for large and long-term investments made necessary by technical development and the decreased ability of firms to finance investments out of profits. The formation of a state-owned investment bank in 1967 has to be seen in this context. The object of the new bank was to finance large and promising investment projects that were considered too risky by other actors in the credit market. The bank's instructions were somewhat contradictory. Individual investment projects had to be judged on the basis of their estimated future profitability, but a social economic rationale also had to be taken into account (Schäfer 1984: 42–6; Waara 1980: 160–3). To increase the supply of risk capital a new, fourth, general pension fund was formed in 1974. Unlike the three earlier pension funds, it was allowed to invest its capital in shares (Schäfer 1984: 134–8). The issue of collective capital formation received increased attention later in the 1970s when the Social Democrats adopted the controversial proposal of wage earners' funds, according to which the corporations had to set aside a portion of their profits to funds controlled by the trade union movement. In exchange for wage restraint the unions would thus have strengthened their influence over the allocation of investments. The wage earners' funds proposal was described as a 'creeping socialization' by the non-socialist parties and the employers' organizations and led to a heated political debate. A much diluted form of wage earners' funds was finally set up by a Social Democrat government in 1983 (Pontusson 1992: 196 ff.). It was later dissolved by the non-socialist Bildt government in the early 1990s.

Since technical change was considered of paramount importance for economic growth, research and development (R & D) received enlarged state support. While the principal role of the state in this context was considered to be its supply of higher education and research, it was also considered necessary to support R & D activities of the firms. A new state organ, the 'Technical Development Council' (Styrelsen för teknisk utveckling) was formed in 1968 through an amalgamation of five previous state-supported R & D institutes (Schäfer 1984: 46–8). At the same time a new state-owned company, Statens utvecklingsaktiebolag AB, was formed to promote innovations of social importance, e.g. in medicine, environmental development, and energy.

The new industrial policy also led to a more important role for the state-owned companies. State enterprises still accounted for only a minor share of the manufacturing industry. In the middle of the 1960s, less than 5% of employees were employed by state-owned firms (Pryor 1973: 46–7). If we disregard the transfer to state ownership of the remaining shares in the iron-ore company LKAB in 1955, there were no important nationalizations in the 1950s. Most of the firms that were added to the state company sector in the 1960s were small and were subsidiary companies to the state-owned quasi-corporations. There is, however, one exception to this rule. In 1963 the state took over 50% of Uddevallavarvet, a shipyard that otherwise would have had to close down because of lack of working capital (Waara 1980: 154–7).

In the late 1960s the extension of the state company sector took on a partially new character. State enterprises were now given a role in the implementation of industrial policy. The nationalization in 1965 of a company in the building material sector, in order to influence structural development within this sector, may be seen as the first example of the new role for state enterprises. In order to facilitate coordination between the state-owned enterprises, a holding company, AB Statsföretag, was formed in 1970 (Waara 1980: 166). The demands on the new holding company were somewhat contradictory. Profitability was stated to be the major concern, but the state-owned companies were also expected to stimulate employment in certain regions, further R & D, enhance competition, and contribute to the development of a more efficient firm structure in certain branches of manufacturing industry (Schäfer 1984: 48–52; Waara 1980: 166).

Among the sectors that were singled out for state interventions were high-tech industries such as nuclear energy production and the computer and microelectronics industries, where the state acquired new companies and entered into joint ventures with private firms. The retail distribution of pharmaceutical products was nationalized, and the new holding company of state-owned enterprises also

TABLE 6.2. *Net costs of state subsidies to manufacturing and mining divided in categories* (constant prices 1980 = 100, mill. kr)

	1975/6	1979/80	1982/3	1987/8
Regional policy	591	736	748	696
Firm and branch support	246	7,120	8,774	600
R & D	533	425	467	206
Export	−60	134	1,334	569
Small firms	84	237	217	74
Energy-saving measures	n.a.	43	314	114
Other measures	n.a.	n.a.	n.a.	360
TOTAL	1,394	8,695	11,854	2,619

Sources: Ds I 1982:5 (1982); NU 1985:8 (1986); Pontusson 1992:143.

took an active part in the restructuring of the pharmaceutical and brewery industries by taking over substantial shares of these.

The formation of AB Statsföretag was seen as part of an offensive industrial policy aimed at restructuring. When the state holding company substantially enlarged its share of the Swedish industry in the second half of the 1970s, however, this was the result of defensive actions to safeguard employment in branches hit by structural crisis, mainly the shipbuilding, steel, forestry, and textile industries.

The state took over majority ownership in three textile companies in the middle of the 1970s. In 1977 the state-owned textile firms were amalgamated into a concern, in order to facilitate their reconstruction. The state also bailed out two forest-product firms and took over substantial ownership shares in these companies.

The Swedish shipbuilding industry was heavily specialized in the production of oil tankers and was consequently severely hit by the oil crisis in 1974–5. Between 1975 and 1978 all of the major shipyards were taken over by the state. They were amalgamated to form the new state-owned shipbuilding concern, AB Svenska Varv.

The shipbuilding crisis had repercussions in the steel industry. The crisis within the steel industry led to the formation in 1978 of a new state enterprise, Svenskt Stål AB, when the state-owned NJA merged with the two largest private raw steel producers.

The structural crisis in shipbuilding, steel, and some other branches of manufacturing brought forward a massive increase in industrial subsidies in the second half of the 1970s. Due to some public investigations on industrial support policies, we have detailed data for the 1970s and 1980s (Carlsson, Bergholm, and Lindberg, 1981; SOU 1981:72; Ds I 1982:5; NU 1985:8). In Table 6.2 subsidies are calculated according to the 'net cost principle', i.e. only the subsidization elements in loans and guarantees are added to the figures. Subsidies are dated as to the actual date when payments occurred.

As can be seen from Table 6.2, there was an explosion of industrial subsidization in the later half of the 1970s. The net cost of subsidies was multiplied in the late 1970s and increased by another 50% between 1979/80 and 1982/3 when they reached their peak. A perspective on the importance of subsidies can be gained if we compare them to value added in manufacturing and mining as a whole. Between 1975/6 and 1980/1 the share of subsidies (net costs) in the value added of the manufacturing and mining industries was 5.4%. The corresponding figure for the period 1979/80–1983/4 was 7.8%.

The greater part of the increase in subsidization can be explained by rescue operations to help companies in economic distress. These subsidies mostly ended up in the shipbuilding and steel industries. The shipbuilding industry received 40% of the support in the 1970s while the steel industry received 30% (Carlsson, Bergholm, and Lindberg 1981). The growth in export subsidies after 1980 can also to a large extent be explained by the structural crisis in shipbuilding and steel.

Ironically the rapid increase of industrial subsidization took place in 1976–9 under the first non-socialist government since the early 1930s. In general there was a parliamentary agreement behind the industrial subsidization. What prompted the government, whether Social Democrat or non-socialist, to pay out these huge sums? A basic reason was a concern to preserve employment. In many instances the firms that received the subsidies were the dominating employers in the region. The outlay on industrial subsidies was also motivated by the thought that the receiving firms would be viable if the crisis was 'overbridged' and the companies reconstructed. A closure would have meant massive destruction of human and material capital.

While most of the increase in subsidies from the middle of the 1970s can be explained by 'extra-ordinary' firm support, the regular industrial policy measures also increased. Of these regional policy was the most important. The regional policy instruments included loans as well as grants. In the 1970s about one-half of the outlay on regional policy consisted of loans. The net cost of the regional subsidies grew about 10% per year in real terms during the second half of the 1970s and about 5% per year during the first half of the 1980s.

The net cost for R & D support more than doubled in real terms between 1975 and 1983. Support for small companies was mostly given in the form of loans on commercial terms, which accounts for the relatively small role played by small firm support in total subsidies when measured in net costs.

6.4. THE REORIENTATION OF INDUSTRIAL POLICY IN THE 1980S AND EARLY 1990S: THE RETURN OF MARKET SOLUTIONS

In the beginning of the 1980s the heavy subsidization of firms in crisis was critically evaluated. Insofar as industrial reconstruction under state guidance was one of the objectives of the subsidization policy, it must be considered to have been a failure in most cases. Only in the steel industry did reconstruction succeed, at the cost of massive investments and a drop in employment. The shipbuilding industry, on the other hand, could not survive in the long term and in 1984 the government decided to halt the production of merchant ships (Stråth 1987: 114). While most observers agreed that the state had an obligation to preserve full employment, critics asserted that this could have been achieved without bailing out companies on such favourable terms. The owners of these firms and the banks were thus insulated from normal risks in a competitive market economy. In many cases the financial situation of the former owners actually improved as a consequence of the state takeovers (Pontusson 1992: 141). The fiscal deficit and increase in state debt that resulted from the subsidization programme would have been considerably less without such generosity towards the former owners.

The policy of 'extra-ordinary' firm subsidization was phased out by the Social Democrat government that entered office in 1982. Actual payments peaked in 1983/4 as a consequence of earlier decisions; after this firm subsidies diminished rapidly (Table 6.2). In the end of the 1980s state subsidies to firms were less than one-third of its amount in the beginning of the decade, measured in constant price. 'Extraordinary aid' to firms now accounted for less than 20% of the total. Employment was no longer to be upheld by subsidizing firms and sectors in crisis. Instead state support was directed to the individuals concerned and local communities. The competitive edge of Swedish industry was temporarily strengthened by a devaluation of the currency in 1982 rather than by selective state subsidies. The ambitions to actively influence the pattern of industrial restructuring by means of industrial policy were reduced (Pontusson 1992: 147–9).

The reorientation of industrial policies in the 1980s also implied a reassessment of the role of state enterprises. In 1982 the state enterprise sector was reorganized. LKAB (iron-ore mining), ASSI (forestry), and SSAB (steel) were taken out of the state holding company and formed independent concerns. At the same time these corporations were reconstructed financially by the government. The state holding company was thus relieved of its most problematic companies and could concentrate on the profitable lines of production. It was now clearly stated by the government that profitability should be the sole guiding line for the state holding company, renamed Procordia in 1984. Its production activities became gradually specialized in food processing and pharmaceuticals through a process of buying and selling companies in the 1980s (Pontusson 1992: 147–8; 1988: 135–6). The reorganization of the state enterprise sector also set the stage for a process of partial privatization. In the 1980s privatization mainly occurred through the issuing of new shares by state companies, while outright sales of state assets were much less common. Most of the share issues were specifically directed towards institutional investors such as insurance companies, pension funds, and the wage-earners funds. Only a minor share were directly offered to the general public. Privatization as practised by Social Democrat governments in the 1980s was not motivated by any changed ideological conceptions regarding the benefits of private vs. public property. Rather the motive seems to have been to infuse new capital into the state enterprises from the buoyant stock market at a time when budgetary consideration did not allow the state to make any contribution. Nevertheless the privatization measures mark the end of the use of state enterprises as a tool for industrial policy (Pontusson 1988: 138–9; 1992: 148–50).

The market-oriented approach of industrial policy also led to a new role for the state-owned companies producing public utilities. The new infrastructure policy was initiated by a Social Democrat government in the late 1980s and carried forward with great zeal by the non-socialist coalition government headed by Carl Bildt in 1991–3. The state-owned quasi-corporations were if possible reorganized into one part administering the network and another part that was to compete with private companies in the actual provision of services. In order to further competition and prevent the state-owned companies from using their dominating market position to influence prices, the legislation regulating competition has also been sharpened. To strengthen the efficiency of the state-owned companies competing with private firms some of them were transformed to joint-stock companies. This happened with Vattenfall (electricity generation) in 1992 and Televerket (telecommunications) under the new name of Telia in 1993 (Kaijser 1994: ch. 7). Telia is now facing competition from privately owned companies, especially in the mobile telephone market. The quasi-corporation providing postal services (and also some financial services) was incorporated in 1994. Its legal monopoly of distributing mail has been abolished and in many cities it is now facing competition from private mail distributors. The state-owned railway company, SJ, has not yet been formally incorporated, but on the other hand it has been split into separate divisions that are supposed to be guided by profitability in their operation. In some regional railways SJ is now facing competition from private firms.

The incorporation of the utility-producing quasi-corporations has been seen as a step towards their complete or partial privatization, but so far they remain in state ownership. Otherwise privatization was one essential ingredient in the industrial policy of the Bildt government. The most spectacular privatizations were the sales of substantial shares in Celsius (the remnants of the former state-owned shipbuilding concern, now diversified to defence materials and telecommunication technology), SSAB (steel), ASSI-Domän (forestry), and Pharmacia (pharmaceuticals). While these sales can no doubt be partially explained by attempts to mitigate public deficits, they also express an ideological preference for private ownership in a market economy.

The return of the Social Democrats to government in 1994 may have slowed down the privatization process somewhat, but has not led to any significant change of industrial policy.

6.5. SUMMARY AND CONCLUSIONS

In this overview of Swedish industrial policy since the late nineteenth century we have broadly distinguished four separate phases. In the first period, stretching from the 1870s to the First World War, the Swedish economy was transformed to a modern industrial economy. This period also saw an increased role for the state in the economy. In order to improve the general conditions for economic progress, the state made large investments in railways, telecommunications, and electricity generation. The activities of the private companies in these sectors were regulated so that they fitted in with the emerging national infrastructure policy. The state-owned companies constructed and operated main lines, while regional lines were initially left to private capital. In the first half of the twentieth century the state gained a de facto monopoly over at first the telephone and later the railway network. The national system of electricity generation, on the other hand, has always been characterized by a mixture of public and private producers. In its fundamental traits the infrastructure model that was formed in the late nineteenth and early twentieth centuries remained unchanged until the 1980s.

Several studies on the determinants of economic growth have emphasized the importance of a well functioning infrastructure. Insofar as it contributed to a nationwide extension of infrastructural utilities, industrial policy in this period seems to have been beneficial for economic development. Much more controversial is the protectionist trade policy, introduced in the 1880s and early 1890s, which was another means by which the state tried to foster national industry around the turn of the century. The protectionist system had some effects on the industrial structure insofar as it stimulated the home market industries. It has been criticized because it subsidized 'unfit' industries at the expense of others where Sweden had a comparative advantage. The supporters of protectionism, on the other hand, argued that industrial tariffs made possible a period of learning and a subsequent catching up on the advanced industrial nations within sectors where Sweden did not have a 'natural' disadvantage. The exact role of protectionism in the two crucial decades of the Swedish industrialization process before the First World War remains to be evaluated by economic historians.

In the inter-war period protectionism as a means to further industrial progress was repudiated. In contrast to many countries in Europe, Sweden did not raise its tariffs on manufactured goods in the 1930s. The relatively fast growth of the Swedish economy in this period probably made demands for increased protection seem superfluous. Among the present-day OECD countries Sweden had the fastest growth in GDP per capita between 1913 and 1950 and in this period Sweden developed from a relatively poor country to one of the richest countries in the world. Within Europe its GDP/capita level in 1950 was only surpassed by Switzerland and the UK (Maddison 1991: 51, 67).

Successful economic performance was accompanied by important institutional changes within Swedish society. In the 1930s an almost fifty-year long period of unbroken Social Democrat governmental rule was ushered in. From a theoretical point of view the Social Democrats considered state interventions legitimate in order to improve the coordination and efficiency of the capitalist economy. In the 1930s and 1940s there was also much discussion of industrial planning and restructuring under state guidance. This did not lead to any practical results, however. From the 1930s to the 1960s industrial policy in practice relied on general instruments, such as an investment-inducing company taxation system, the introduction of export guarantee systems, and the formation of special credit institutes for business firms. The central thrust of industrial policy in the 1950s and the early 1960s was to reinforce and facilitate the structural change spontaneously generated by the market economy. It did not attempt to direct structural change through selective policies. The role of the state in the economy increased in this period, but this was primarily due to the growth of the welfare state and the exigencies of stabilization policy, rather than a 'dirigiste' industrial policy. The reinforcement of structural transformation by policies in the 1950s and 1960s had a favourable influence on productivity growth in these decades, but it also contributed to an increased specialization of Swedish industry which probably enhanced its vulnerability to structural crises in the 1970s.

In Sweden as in other countries the post-war golden age of rapid economic growth was petering out in the late 1960s. At the same time the prevailing form of economic growth was criticized for its adverse consequences in the form of regional imbalances, bad working conditions, etc. In order to tackle the structural problems of many branches within manufacturing as well as to mitigate the negative side effects of economic growth, industrial policy was lifted to the centre stage of economic policy. From the late 1960s industrial policy became more interventionist and ambitious. Its objective was to promote the growth of technically advanced sectors and at the same time to diminish the social costs of structural transformation. Subsidies were introduced in order to further R & D and regional balance. Institutions were also created to facilitate the financing of risky but promising investments. The most striking feature of the new industrial policy was perhaps that the state enterprise sector, hitherto relatively unimportant in the manufacturing industry, was given a key role in industrial restructuring. In practice industrial policy in the 1970s turned out to be not offensive, as envisioned in the policy formulations, but dominated by defensive actions to save companies hit by the structural crisis in the shipbuilding and steel industries in the middle of the 1970s. Subsidies to firms in these industries proliferated in the late 1970s. It was also in these sectors that state ownership increased dramatically in this decade.

The subsidization of firms hit by structural crisis was critically evaluated and sharply reduced in the 1980s. This decade also marks a general retreat from ambitious plans of industrial restructuring under state guidance. Since the late 1980s many formerly state-owned firms within the manufacturing industry have been privatized. A new infrastructure policy characterized by increased competition within unregulated markets has been initiated. The prevailing view now is that industrial policy should be confined to improve the general conditions for business. In the late nineteenth century this notion was the starting point for increasing state interventions. Today, a hundred years later, it is motivating an industrial policy that gives lesser weight to selective state interventions and where privatization and deregulation are the key words.

REFERENCES

ANDERSSON-SKOG, L. (1993). 'Såsom allmänna inrättningar till gagnet, men affärsföretag till namnet'. *SJ, järnvägspolitiken och den ekonomiska omvandlingen efter 1920*. Umeå: Umeå Studies in Economic History.

AXELSSON, R., LÖFGREN, K. G., and NILSSON, L. G. (1987). *Den svenska arbetsmarknadspolitiken under 1900-talet*, 4th edn. Stockholm: Prisma.

BERGSTRÖM, W. (1969). *Den ekonomiska politiken i Sverige och dess verkningar*. Stockholm: IUI.

BLADH, M. (1991). *Bostadsförsörjningen 1945–1985*. Gävle: Statens institut för byggnadsforskning.

BOHLIN, J. (1989). *Svensk varvsindustri 1920–1975: Lönsamhet, finansiering och arbetsmarknad*. Göteborg: Meddelanden från ekonomisk-historiska institutionen.

—— (1996). 'Nominella och effektiva tullar i Sverige 1888–1913'. Unpublished manuscript, Dept. of Economic History, Gothenburg University.

CARLSSON, B., BERGHOLM, F., and LINDBERG, T. (1981). *Industristödspolitiken och dess inverkan på samhällsekonomin*. Stockholm: IUI.

DAHMÉN, E. (1950). *Svensk industriell företagarverksamhet*. Band I. Stockholm: IUI.

Ds I 1982:5 (1982). *Induststristödets nettokostnader: En rapport upprättad inom industridepartementet*. Stockholm: Industridepartementet.

GÅRESTAD (1987). *Industrialisering och beskattning i Sverige 1861–1914*. Uppsala: Uppsala Studies in Economic History.

GLETE, J. (1983). *ASEA under 100 år 1883–1983 en studie i ett storföretags organisatoriska, tekniska och ekonomiska utveckling*. Västerås: EHF.

GUSTAFSSON, B. (1993). 'Unemployment and fiscal policy in Sweden during the 1930's', in W. R. Garside (ed.), *Capitalism in Crisis: International Responses to the Great Depression*, 56–69. London: Pinter.

HECKSCHER, E. (1957). *Svenskt arbete och liv*. Stockholm: Bonniers.

HEDBORG, A., and MEIDNER, R. (1984). *Folkhemsmodellen*. Stockholm: Rabén & Sjögren.

HEDIN, L. E. (1972). 'Finansiering av den svenska järnvägen 1860–1914', in R. Adamsson and L. Jörberg (eds.), *Problem i svensk ekonomisk historia*, 123–40. Lund: Gleerup.

HIBBS, D., and LOCKING, H. (1997). 'Den solidariska lönepolitiken och produktiviteten inom industrin', in Bergström (ed.), *Arbetsmarknad och tillväxt: Tio års forskning med facket*, 34–53. Stockholm: FIEF.

IVEROTH, A. (1943). *Småindustri och hantverk i Sverige*. Stockholm: IUI.

JAKOBSSON, E. (1995). 'Industrialized rivers: The development of Swedish hydropower', in A. Kaijser and M. Hedin (eds.), *Nordic Energy Systems: Historical Perspectives and Current Issues*, 55–74. Canton, Mass.: Science History Publications/USA.

JOHANSSON, A. L. (1989). *Tillväxt och klassamarbete—en studie av den svenska modellens uppkomst.* Stockholm: Tiden.

JOHANSSON, J. (1991). *Offentligt och privat i regionalpolitiken.* Lund: Statsvetenskapliga inst. Lund University.

JONSSON, B. (1969). *Staten och malmfälten: Studier i svensk malmfältspolitik omkring sekelskiftet.* Stockholm: Almqvist & Wicksell.

JÖRBERG, L. (1961). *Growth and Fluctuations of Swedish Industry 1869–1912: Studies in the Process of Industrialisation.* Stockholm: Almqvist & Wicksell.

KAIJSER, A. (1994). *I fädrens spår: Den svenska infrastrukturens historiska utveckling och framtida utmaningar.* Stockholm: Carlssons.

KATZENSTEIN, P. J. (1985). *Small States in the World Market: Industrial Policy in Europe.* Ithaca, NY and London: Cornell University Press.

KILANDER, S. (1983). 'Staten byter ansikte—om statsuppfattning och samhällssyn i sekelskiftets Sverige', in K. Abrahamsson and D. Ramström (eds.), *Vägen till planrike: Om stat, sektor och sammanhang,* 179–200. Lund: Studentlitteratur.

—— (1991). *Den nya staten och den gamla: En studie i ideologisk förändring.* Stockholm: Almqvist & Wicksell.

LEWIN, L. (1967). *Planhushållningsdebatten,* 2nd edn. Stockholm: Almqvist & Wicksell.

LINDBECK, A. (1975). *Svensk ekonomisk politik,* 2nd edn. Stockholm: Aldus.

LOCKING, H. (1996). *Essays on Swedish Wage Formation.* Göteborg: Ekonomiska studier, nationalekonomiska institutionen.

LUNDBERG, E. (1983). *Ekonomiska kriser förr och nu.* Stockholm: SNS.

MADDISON, A. (1991). *Dynamic Forces in Capitalist Development: A Long-Run Comparative View.* Oxford: Oxford University Press.

MÅRTENSSON, T. (1994). *Bantågens gång: Järnvägens godstrafik och dess anpassning till näringslivets rumslighet, branschstruktur och transportefterfrågan 1890–1985.* Göteborg: Meddelanden från ekonomisk-historiska institutionen.

MJØSET, L. (1986). *Norden dagen derpå: De nordiske økonomisk-politiske modellene og deres problemer på 70-og 80-tallet.* Oslo: Universitetsforlaget.

MONTGOMERY, A. (1921). *Svensk tullpolitik.* Stockholm: Almqvist & Wicksell.

—— (1947). *Industrialismens genombrott i Sverige.* Stockholm: Almqvist & Wicksell.

MYHRMAN, J. (1994). *Hur Sverige blev rikt.* Stockholm: SNS.

NORDLUND, S. (1989). *Upptäckten av Sverige: Utländska direktinvesteringar i Sverige 1895–1945.* Umeå: Umeå Studies in Economic History.

NU 1985:8 (1986). *Industristöd och offentliga finansieringsordningar i Norden: Nordiska rådet/Nordiska ministerrådet.* Stockholm: Liber.

OHLIN, B. (1965). *Utrikeshandel och handelspolitik,* 8th edn. Stockholm: Natur & Kultur.

OLSSON, K. (1983). *Från pansarbåtsvarv till tankfartygsvarv: De svenska storvarvens utveckling till exportindustri 1880–1936.* Göteborg: Svenska Varv AB.

OLSSON, U. (1982). 'The state and industry in Swedish rearmament', in M. Fritz, I. Nygren, S.-O. Olsson, and U. Olsson (eds.), *The Adaptable Nation: Essays in the Swedish Economy during the Second World War,* 59–78. Stockholm: Almqvist & Wicksell.

PONTUSSON, J. (1988). 'The triumph of pragmatism: Nationalisation and privatisation in Sweden'. *West European Politics,* 11(4): 129–40.

—— (1992). *The Limits of Social Democracy: Investment Politics in Sweden.* Ithaca, NY and London: Cornell University Press.

PRYOR, F. L. (1973). *Property and Industrial Organization in Communist and Capitalist Nations.* Bloomington and London: Indiana University Press.

SANDBERG, L. G. (1978), 'Banking and economic growth in Sweden before World War I'. *Journal of Economic History*, 3: 650–80.

—— (1979). 'The case of the impoverished sophisticate: Human capital and Swedish economic growth before World War I'. *Journal of Economic History*, 1: 225–41.

SCHÄFER, J. (1984). *Från tillväxt till trygghet: Tio års debatt om strukturpolitikens mål och medel*. Stockholm: Almqvist & Wicksell.

SCHÖN, L. (1989). 'Kapitalimport, kreditmarknad och industrialisering 1850–1910', in E. Dahmén (ed.), *Upplåning och utveckling*, 227–73. Stockholm: Allmänna förlaget.

SÖDERSTEN, J. (1977). 'Bolagsskattens verkningar', in SOU 1977:87, *Beskattning av företag: Bilagor*, 107–93. Stockholm.

SOU 1924:37 (1924). *Betänkande angående tullsystemets verkningar i Sverige före världskriget del I*. Stockholm.

SOU 1981:72 (1981). *Att avveckla en kortsiktig industripolitik: Betänkande av inustristödsutredningen*. Stockholm.

STRÅTH, B. (1987). *The Politics of Deindustrialisation: The Contraction of the West-European Shipbuilding Industry*. London: Croom Helm.

WAARA, L. (1980). *Den statliga företagssektorns expansion: Orsaker till förstatliganden i ett historiskt och internationellt perspektiv*. Stockholm: Liber.

WIBBLE, A. (1971). 'Selektiv och generell ekonomisk politik', in E. Lundberg (ed.), *Svensk finanspolitik i teori och praktik*, 39–75. Stockholm: EFI.

WICKMAN, K. (1980). *Makro-ekonomisk planering orsaker och utveckling*. Stockholm: Almqvist & Wicksell.

7

The Netherlands: The History of an Empty Box?

JAN L. VAN ZANDEN
University of Utrecht

7.1. INTRODUCTION

Since its creation in the final decades of the sixteenth century, the Netherlands has arguably been the most liberal country in Europe. In the seventeenth century its policy of 'free trade' was based on the very open character of its economy and superiority in manufacturing and international trade. In the eighteenth century, with industry in decline as a result of foreign competition, the strong interests of the Dutch bourgeoisie in international trade and finance ruled out the possibility of a switch to a more protectionistic trade policy. In the nineteenth and twentieth century this tradition basically has remained unchanged. For the wealthy and politically dominant bourgeoisie of a small open economy, with strong interests in export industries and an important part of its capital invested abroad, a policy of non-intervention into the development of industry and international trade seemed to be the most beneficial. The strong laissez-faire orientation of the Dutch ruling classes was not shaken by the fact that during periods of increased protectionism in the world economy—for example in the first half of the nineteenth century and in the 1920s and 1930s—the Dutch economy was the first to be hurt. Only in case of dire necessity, with its economy in ruins after a devastating war—in fact only after 1813 and 1945—were experiments with more interventionist policies adopted.

This chapter aims to give an account of industrial policies during the twentieth century. I have chosen a chronological ordering of their development. Section 7.2 contains a brief discussion of liberal economic policies during the nineteenth century, followed by a sketch of the changes experienced during the inter-war period (Section 7.3). The major part of this chapter deals with the period after 1945, when:

(1) between 1948 and 1963 a policy of industrialization was implemented; this was the second break in the Dutch tradition of economic liberalism;

(2) between 1963 and 1983 the government actually intervened in the development of (declining) industries much more actively than it did between 1948 and 1963;

(3) after 1983 these policies were discredited and non-intervention once again became the norm (and industrial policies were succeeded by policies aimed at promoting R & D).

TABLE 7.1. *Average aggregate tariffs*[a] *in the Netherlands, Belgium, Great Britain, and France, 1816/20–1911/13* (%)

	Netherlands	Belgium	Great Britain	France
1816–20	3.2	—	—	—
1821–5	3.7	—	53.1	20.3
1826–30	3.9	—	47.2	22.6
1831–5	2.9	—	40.5	21.5
1836–40	2.5	4.8	30.9	18.0
1841–5	2.4	5.1	32.2	17.9
1846–50	2.2	5.2	25.3	17.2
1851–5	2.2	4.4	19.5	13.2
1856–60	1.5	3.2	15.0	10.0
1861–5	1.1	2.5	11.5	5.9
1866–70	1.1	2.3	8.9	3.8
1871–5	1.0	1.7	6.7	5.3
1876–80	1.1	1.5	6.1	6.6
1881–5	1.2	1.8	5.9	7.5
1886–90	1.2	2.0	6.1	8.3
1891–5	1.3	2.1	5.5	10.6
1896–1900	1.7	2.4	5.3	10.2
1901–5	1.7	2.0	7.0	8.8
1906–10	1.6	1.6	5.9	8.0
1911–13	1.5	1.5	5.4	8.8

[a] Customs revenue as a percentage of the value of imports.
Source: Horlings 1995: 136.

7.2. LIBERAL DOMINATION (1848–1914)

The failure of the interventionist economic policies of William I resulting in the near bankruptcy of his regime in 1840 further cemented the 'laissez-faire' consensus in Dutch public life (Brugmans 1969: 214–25). Trade policy offers something of a 'proof' of this liberal orientation. Estimates of the degree of protection offered by import tariffs, presented in Table 7.1, clearly show the liberal orientation of trade policy during the nineteenth century. Throughout the century tariffs were lower in the Netherlands than in any other European country. With a few exceptions, tariffs were only levied for fiscal purposes. On this score only Belgium became almost as liberal as the Netherlands (Horlings 1995: 135–7), which is ironic because strong differences about the desirability of industrial protection had divided both parts of the former United Kingdom of the Low Countries during the 1820s.

Especially between 1848 and the 1890s, when a new group of 'radical' politicians gained influence, this consensus dominated political debate. However, for a number of reasons policies which affected the development of industry were still a matter of concern. One reason was the apparent failure of the market to supply the economy with basic infrastructure, i.e. railways and new canals; another was the regulation of the institutional setting for industrial development.

One example of the importance of the institutional setting was the patent law. The 1817 patent law, which was generally considered to be ineffective, was abolished in 1869, during the high point of laissez-faire. In spite of some international pressure on the Dutch government, mainly by the International Union for the Protection of Industrial Property, of which the Netherlands was in fact a member, it took until 1912 before a new law was introduced. Between 1869 and 1912 there was no restriction on the imitation of new inventions; however, Dutch inhabitants could get their inventions patented abroad. For a small economy, which was heavily dependent on the diffusion of foreign technology and with an almost negligible amount of research of its own, this was probably an optimal solution.

At least two big firms have profited greatly from this exceptional situation. The margarine industry was created in the 1870s by two families of entrepreneurs, Jurgens and Van den Bergh. They used the ideas of the original patent of Mège Mouriès, and copied each other's inventions without any restrictions, which certainly contributed to the large success of the industry (Wilson 1954: 29 ff., 55 ff.). Both firms decided to work closely together in 1908 and were later amalgamated with the English Lever company into Unilever. The start of the Dutch industry of incandescent lamps, by Gerard Philips in 1891, was also greatly facilitated by the fact that, at least for production for the domestic market, he did not have to worry about the Edison patents. The development of the metal filament lamp after 1907 was also greatly facilitated by the absence of a patent law (Heerding 1986: 174–7). After 1910 the company set up a laboratory, perhaps in anticipation of the Dutch patent law (Schiff 1971: 66).

Eric Schiff, who studied the effects of the absence of patent law on industrialization in the Netherlands and Switzerland (where a modern patent law was introduced in 1907), concluded that in general industrial development was not stifled by its absence; in a few cases 'this absence has, on balance, furthered rather than hampered development' (Schiff 1971: 67). He also noted that in the decade after 1912 there was a big increase in the number of applications for patents from Dutch inhabitants in four large countries (Great Britain, Germany, United States, and France), which points to an increase in industrial R & D after the introduction of the law. This increase, however, did not occur in Switzerland (after 1907), but the Swiss output of international patents was already relatively high (compared with the level of the Netherlands, Denmark, Norway, and Sweden).

The most obvious market failures which led liberal governments to take actions were in the field of infrastructure. During the 1860s and the 1870s the government was more or less forced to organize and finance the construction of a national railway system and to subsidize the digging of new canals to the two main ports, Rotterdam and Amsterdam (Voort 1994: 145–70). In order to stimulate competition a private firm was created to manage the railway network. It had to compete with the two private companies which already operated older parts of the railways (in Holland and between Holland and Germany). In this way government-financed railway construction was combined with a maximum degree of competition and private enterprise.

In the 1890s a comparable debate took place about the (lack of) progress in the exploitation of the coal fields in the province of Limburg. A few private firms were already active in the region, but it was generally felt that much more could be done (in view of the large Dutch imports of coal). The government decided to take the initiative; with the Mining Act of 1901 a large public company was created which came to dominate the mining industry (Brugmans 1969: 350). Unlike the railways, no attempt was made to privatize the company. In 1913 however, it was decided that Staatsmijnen was to be managed as a private enterprise, which gave its management a relatively large degree of freedom to pursue independent policies. This decision was the result of the Bedrijvenwet (Company Law) of 1912, which ruled that every (semi-) public firm had to be run along commercial lines, and that its financial administration had to be independent of government finances. This law became the legal basis of the relatively independent development of many (semi-) public companies in the Netherlands during the twentieth century (Ru 1981: 30–1).

In the second half of the nineteenth century the most intense public debate in the field of industrial policy related to the ownership of public utilities, and especially the gas companies (Vries 1994). In a few big cities the British Imperial Continental Gaz Company had acquired a monopoly in the manufacturing and distribution of gas, which (according to its left-wing critics) resulted in high prices for consumers and enormous profits for its owners. In Leiden in 1848 the first municipal gas company had started, which became an important source of income to the city. The question whether or not to 'nationalize' the British (and other private) gas factories became a major bone of contention between the orthodox liberals and the left-wing 'radicalen', resulting in the victory of the latter. In the 1880s and 1890s almost all private gas companies were acquired by the municipalities (Brugmans 1969: 349). The same process occurred with the growth of the electricity industry: the pioneers of the 1880s and 1890s were after 1900 rapidly overtaken by municipal, and after 1913 by provincial firms, which came to monopolize the industry.

In these debates the interests of consumers loomed very large, but also the fact that Dutch industries had to pay high prices for these inputs as a result of the monopolization of gas production by private interests, played a role in the decision to 'nationalize' them (Zadoks 1899).

7.3. THE INTER-WAR PERIOD (1914–1945)

The First World War forced the government to intervene much more actively in the national economy, but this did not result in a consistent set of policies aimed at stimulating industrial progress. Some measures were taken, however. For example, the Minister of Economic Affairs, the 'radical' Treub, decided to finance part of the establishment of the first Dutch blast furnace, NV Hoogovens, in 1917. Moreover, a detailed agreement with Staatsmijnen secured the delivery of (relatively cheap) coal to the new industry (Dankers and Verheul 1993: 27–30). Government support for the plan to set up this basic industry was aimed at reducing dependency of imports of iron and steel. In the same year government participated in the formation of another basic industry, Nederlandsche Zoutindustrie (Dutch salt industry), which began the exploitation of rich subterranean salt deposits in the eastern part of the country (Ru 1981: 32).

A few other firms profited from the increased willingness of government to subsidize new strategic industries. Antony Fokker, who switched his production of airplanes from Germany to Amsterdam in 1919, and Albert Plesman, the founder of KLM (Royal Dutch Airlines) both profited from government support during the inter-war years to compensate for the large deficits on current operations. The strategic importance of KLM especially was related to the close relationship with the colonies; the government wanted to control the means of communications with the Dutch East Indies and was prepared to subsidize KLM to that purpose. In 1927 the state was more or less forced to buy a majority holding in KLM because no other sources of share capital could be found (Brugmans 1969: 486–7). But, like de Staatsmijnen and other semi-public companies, KLM remained in essence managed as a private enterprise.

But these were the exceptions; other big firms which expanded rapidly after 1914, such as Philips, Jurgens & Van den Bergh, Royal Dutch, and AKU (later to become AKZO), did not profit from particular government support (and the subsidies for KLM and Fokker dwindled in size compared with the enormous funds going to agriculture during the 1930s).

During the inter-war period tariffs became more important as a source of government income and instrument of protection. In 1921 and 1923 two special laws were introduced to protect Dutch industries against the dumping of German cigars and shoes, respectively. In 1924 a general upward revision of tariff levels was introduced, officially for fiscal reasons, but a special tariff for cars was introduced as the price-ticket from Ford to establish an assembly plant in the Netherlands (Zanden and Griffiths 1989: 126). As a result, the ratio between the value of imports and customs revenue went up in the 1920s (Table 7.2).

During the 1930s a number of instruments were used to protect some Dutch industries against the vagaries of the Depression. Trade policy was the most important: tariffs were raised once again, but much more important were quantitative import restrictions directed at reducing the dumping of foreign products on the Dutch market. As a result, Dutch industry succeeded in significantly increasing its market share in national demand (Schaik 1986). These import controls meant an important break in Dutch trade policy, but it was realized that a government, even one headed by an orthodox liberal such as Colijn, had no other options to protect industry.

In general, industrial policy in the 1930s was very defensive: its aim was to prevent the further decline of industrial production and employment. A few

TABLE 7.2. *Customs revenue as a percentage of imports and as a percentage of total taxes, 1910/14–1935/9*

	Percentage of imports	Percentage of taxes
1910–14	1.5	9.2
1920–4	2.5	6.4
1925–9	3.5	10.2
1930–4	4.8	15.9
1935–9	7.4	17.5

Source: *Jaarcijfers*.

politicians from the Catholic party, who were influenced by ideas about the restructuring of the economy along corporative lines, experimented with setting up new institutions (local development institutes) to assist industry in certain regions (de Hen 1980). In the depth of the Depression the Social-Democratic party presented a programme to end it, the Plan van de Arbeid (Plan of Labour), in which a detailed planning of the economy was proposed. But both initiatives were outside the mainstream of Dutch academic and political debate.

7.4. INDUSTRIALIZATION POLICY (1945–1963)

The war made a big change. The newly appointed government of 1945 was dominated by social democrats; one of the authors of the Plan van de Arbeid, Hein Vos, became Minister of Economic Affairs. Socialist and Keynesian ideas about the desirability of government intervention became much more fashionable, although leading politicians outside the Labour party generally mistrusted these experiments. As if to confirm their suspicions, Hein Vos set up the Centraal Planbureau (Central Planning Agency), which had to develop forecasts and plans for the reconstruction of the economy. In the same year, 1945, he proposed a radical restructuring of the economy in which central planning would play a large role (Liagre Böhl, Nekkers, and Slot 1981: 62–73).

The first elections after the war, in 1946, proved to be a test case for these ambitious plans. The Labour party lost the elections; the Catholic party regained a majority position and it demanded that Vos be succeeded by the conservative Huysmans. Willem Drees, the leader of the Labour party, gave in; his ambitions were 'restricted' to measures concerning welfare and social security (he would become the founder of the Dutch welfare state). During the years in which Huysmans was in control of economic policies, nothing happened (apart from the purging of his ministry of the most ardent followers of Vos) (Hen 1980: 274). The rapid recovery of the Dutch economy between 1945 and 1948 was realized with minimal assistance from the Centraal Planbureau (which was still suspected of sympathy for the ideas of Vos). In 1946–7 all plans for a more systematic industrial policy seemed dead and Dutch politics had returned to its tradition of laissez-faire.

So it is difficult to understand why in 1949 a formal policy of industrialization was implemented, consisting, amongst others, of a five-year plan for investments in industry and specific targets for the growth of output and employment in the different industrial sectors in the period 1948–52. In 1948 Huysmans was succeeded by the more flexible Van den Brink, again from the Catholic party and again a real proponent of the market economy. But a number of developments seem to have moved him away from the dogmatic position of Huysmans. To get funds from the Marshall Plan, schemes for future spending of this money had to be made. During this exercise, it was acknowledged that in spite of the rapid growth of the Dutch economy during the period 1945–8 long-term economic problems were not yet solved. According to the predictions of 1947–8, structural unemployment would rise rapidly as a result of the acceleration of the growth of the labour supply, and the deficit on the balance of payments seemed to run out of control. The only solution that could be offered was a further acceleration of industrial growth; especially those industries that exported a large part of output had to be stimulated. This would create employment and in the long run (after the ending of the Marshall plan) solve the external problem (Liagre Böhl, Nekkers, and Slot 1981: 196–212).

These problems were discussed widely in 1947–8. Politicians from the Labour party attacked the Minister of Economic Affairs for not taking any actions and fell back on the still rather popular ideas of the Plan van de Arbeid. Between 1945 and 1958 Dutch governments were based on a coalition between the Labour party and the Catholic party, and Van den Brink could not completely ignore the criticism of his partner in government. His solution, the industrialization plan of 1949, was brilliant. The plan he put forward set out the desired development of Dutch industry between 1948 and 1952, with detailed targets for employment, exports, and output. At first sight it was an impressive and ambitious scheme to solve the major problems of the economy. But when it came to specific measures its contents were very meagre: the starting point of the plan was that government would not interfere with the autonomy of private enterprise. Policies would be restricted to the creation of a favourable climate for investment and growth; for example, tax reductions for investing firms were enlarged. In fact, apart from some tax cuts no new measures were suggested (Zanden and Griffiths 1989: 243–5).

Industrial policies between 1949 and 1963—when the official policies in this field were terminated—were a typical product of Dutch policy-making. It was a compromise between the Labour party (or at least its left wing) which persisted in its wish for a more active, 'planning' government, and the other parties who resisted any interference with private enterprise. Industrial policies were implemented by Ministers of Economic Affairs (Van den Brink, Zijlstra) with very strong preferences for the free market economy. As a result, actual policies were restricted to financing the expansion of no more than two large companies, to regional subsidies (aimed at industrializing the 'underdeveloped' parts of the country), and to the encouragement of technical education, etc. (Liagre Böhl, Nekkers, and Slot 1981).

The two firms that received substantial direct capital transfers from government were Hoogovens, which was able to enlarge its operations and form an integrated steel mill, and the new firm Koninklijke Nederlandse Soda Industrie (Royal Dutch Soda Industry), which became part of AKZO in 1969. One of the reasons for investing in these firms was that they were 'basic industries', which made the Dutch economy less dependent on imports of semi-finished manufacturers. Both were highly successful and are good examples of a strategy of 'picking the winners'. Others, especially the smaller firms, were supported by the Herstelbank—a new bank set up in 1945 by government, the large commercial banks, and insurance companies to finance small-scale industry. The state was a 51% majority shareholder and guaranteed the payment of a dividend of 3.5% on the rest of the shares of the Herstelbank, which channelled its funds into the industries that were specially favoured by the industrialization policy (Hen 1980: 258–9).

Another instrument was used to stimulate the creation of a Dutch aluminium industry: cheap energy. During the early 1960s government promised to supply very cheap gas (with which equally cheap electrictricity was generated) to a new firm (Aldel), a joint enterprise of Hoogovens and Shell subsidiary Billiton, set up to build a large aluminium plant in the northern part of the country. This cheap gas was set apart from the rest of the gas reserves in order to stimulate the industrialization of this part of the Netherlands, where the huge gas reserves were found. In 1967 the big French aluminium firm Péchiney got almost the same privileges for the start of another plant in the province of Zeeland (Dankers and Verheul 1993: 280–97).

Herstelbank and the industrialization policies were part of a new institutional structure that was set up after 1945 in order to organize the reconstruction of the Dutch economy (which was relatively badly hit by the Second World War) and to improve its long-term economic performance. Probably the most important part of this new setting was the institutions in which trade unions and employers' organizations under the strong guidance of the government negotiated the yearly increase in wages. After 1945 this 'guided wage policy' was the cornerstone of reconstruction policy. Its aim was to improve the competitive position of Dutch industry in the long run and, by restraining internal consumption, to contribute to the growth of exports. It was accompanied by a strict policy to keep down the cost of living; for example house rents and the rents of agricultural land were frozen until about 1950 (in spite of a threefold increase in the general price level) and the prices of agricultural products were controlled by the government. Both policies—to control wages and prices—were highly successful until the early 1950s (Zanden and Griffiths 1989: 45–7). After about 1953 its success, i.e. increased shortages on the labour market as a result of the economic boom of the mid-1950s, gradually seems to have undermined its effectiveness.

An econometric study of wage formation by Noé van Hulst has shown that wage policy did not significantly affect wage increases any more during this period (Hulst 1984).

At the local and regional level governments became much more involved with the furthering of industrial development than before the Second World War. Every province set up its institute for economic development (Economisch technologisch instituut) after the model developed during the 1930s, with the explicit aim to increase industrial employment in the region. The development of the Rotterdam port was stimulated by ambitious schemes to attract new industries (oil refining and chemical processing) and to enlarge its harbour (Goey 1990). Schiphol, which in 1945 was designated as the national airport, profited from large subsidies by the state to increase its facilities and improve its position vis-à-vis other continental airports. In both cases, Rotterdam and Schiphol, municipal bodies were responsible for the rapid development of infrastructure and the efficient organization of international services in a strongly competitive environment. In 1958 Schiphol became a joint stock company (because the city of Amsterdam could not afford any more to finance the investment necessary for its development), with national government and Amsterdam as the main shareholders (Ru 1981: 68). The long-run success of both 'public enterprises' was lasting; in the 1990s both are still considered main engines of economic growth in the western part of the Netherlands.

In the public mind the industrialization plans of the years between 1949 and 1963 became much more important than they were in practice. The myth that the recovery and growth of the Dutch economy after the war should be attributed to the benificial effects of this policy was given new life in the 1970s and 1980s when reasons for the decline of Dutch industrial employment were widely discussed. In fact, in his memoirs even Van den Brink fell into the trap he himself had created (Brink 1984; also Griffiths 1986); Zijlstra, on the other hand, hardly mentioned industrial policies in his memoires (Zijlstra 1992). The reason why the industrialization plan made such a big impact on the public mind is that it changed the definition the Dutch had traditionally given of their nation. They used to think of themselves as a nation of farmers and merchants which could prosper thanks to its large colonial empire. In 1949 this idea was shattered by the independence of Indonesia. At that same moment Van den Brink formulated a new 'destiny' for the Dutch nation: to become an industrial economy (a process which, of course, had started way back in the nineteenth century). In such a way the industrialization plan of 1949 was important: it helped to foster a new identity (Zanden and Griffiths 1989: 245–6).

7.5. INDUSTRIAL POLICIES WITHOUT A PLAN (1963–1983)

In 1963 the industrialization policy was officially terminated: balanced growth became the government's new aim in this field. In the same year industrial employment peaked; after 1965 a slow but consistent decline started, which until 1975 was concealed by the strong expansion of tertiary employment. Industrial policies after 1963 were connected with this trend: declining industries—textiles, leatherwork, shipbuilding, mining—were the main focus. A period with brilliant industrialization plans but no real steering of industrial development was followed by years without a plan but with many, sometimes far-reaching interventions in the development of these declining industries.

Perhaps the most far-reaching decision was taken in 1965, when the socialist Minister of Economic Affairs Den Uyl decided to gradually close down the Dutch coal mines during the next ten years. The long-term prospects of the industry were very meagre, in spite of the fact that they were among the most modern and productive mines of Europe. During the 1950s Staatsmijnen had already started large-scale activities in chemicals and related activities (in fact, the production of fertilizers dated back to 1930). Coal was still the most important basis for its chemical division, but it wanted to switch to cheaper oil and gas and increase these very profitable activities (Messing 1988: 65–6). As a result, it had begun to see its mines as a liability, and was in fact putting pressure on the government to start closing down the first mines (Messing 1988: 281).

Finally, the discovery of enormous reserves of natural gas in the northern part of the Netherlands around 1960 made it clear that coal would not be able to compete much longer with this new, and very cheap, source of energy. In 1963, after a number of requests by Staatsmijnen for subsidies for their mining activities, on which it was making losses since the 'coal crisis' of 1958/60, the government decided to give the company a share in the exploitation of the gas reserves (Voogd 1983: 162). The firm set up to exploit these reserves, the Nederlandse Aardolie Maatschappij, was reorganized to include, besides Shell and Esso (with a share of 30% each), Staatsmijnen, which was allotted a share of 40% (Messing 1988: 276). The enormous income from natural gas made possible the heavy investment in new chemical activities and the gradual closure of the mines after 1965. Part of the money was also used—under strong pressure from the government— to invest in other industrial ventures, for example a new automobile factory of DAF in Born (Smidt and Wever 1987: 160). As a result of the expansion of DSM, which was the new name of De Staatsmijnen after it became a joint stock company in 1967, total employment fell by one-third between 1958 (44,411) and 1974 (29,500), when the last mine was closed. Much less successful was the support given to the three private coal mines, which also closed down after 1965. It aimed to reinvest their capital in other activities in order to create new employment, but the effects of the policy were quite limited (Messing 1988: 485–6).

On a smaller scale the government became involved with other declining industries. The main goal of industrial policy became the restructuring of these activities in order to create larger, more competitive firms and to close down surplus capacity. In 1972 the Nehem (Netherlands Reconstructuring Company) was created as an independent body to carry out this policy (Vrolijk 1982). During the 1970s subsidies for declining industries grew rapidly. After 1973 attempts were made to stem the downturn of the economy by large (Keynesian) plans to stimulate employment; part of this money was also used to subsidize these industries. According to OECD statistics, the industrial subsidies as a percentage of sectoral GDP went up from 1.2% in 1970/74 to 2.1% in 1975/79 and 2.6% in 1980/84; a more or less comparable increase was found in most other OECD countries (Ford and Suyker 1990).

The industry that profited most from these measures was shipbuilding; between 1975 and 1979 more than 64% of the expenditure on 'measures to restructure industry' went to this sector. After having donated large subsidies to a number of shipbuilding firms in the years 1967–71 because of their urgent financial problems, the Minister of Economic Affairs forced them to form one large company, Rijn-Schelde-Verolme (RSV). After a few rather prosperous years, the depression of 1974/75 led to new rounds of subsidies, during which RSV got ample funds to develop new activities outside shipbuilding (ranging from the manufacture of nuclear power stations to platforms for drilling oil). But in spite of massive subsidies (totalling 2,700 million guilders), the company was almost bankrupt in 1983. This led to a public scandal, which resulted in an official inquiry by the Dutch Parliament into the allocation of this money and the management of the RSV (the first official Parliamentary inquiry since 1946). The inquiry was broadcast on television in 1984/85 and became a media event; MPs exposed the follies of captains of industry, high-ranking public servants, and (former) Ministers of Economic Affairs. In general the inquiry showed the lack of planning of government and RSV management and the absence of control of the spending of large government funds (Zanden and Griffiths 1989: 79–85). Others have noted, however, that the results of the inquiry were too negative for the management of RSV. Its problems were, in view of the worldwide decline in shipbuilding during this period, unsolvable and the strategy to develop new activities was the only alternative (Voogd 1993: 230).

With hindsight the criticism of the relatively generous policies towards companies in need seems to have been somewhat exaggerated. Numerous firms which went through a difficult period between 1973 and 1983 were probably helped very much by these funds; some of them (Akzo, DSM, Hoogovens) are still considered to be jewels in the crown of Dutch industry. Dercksen and Schenk (1982/83: 142) calculated that the average subsidy per job that was saved for at least one year thanks to these subsidies—including the money spent on firms that went bankrupt—was not excessive (see Table 7.3). This average subsidy per job was less than the average annual sum paid by employers for social insurance and taxes. If all those jobs had been lost and if all employees had become unemployed—two big 'ifs', of course—total government expenditure would have probably been higher.

On the other hand, a lot of the criticism seems to have been justified. The aims of these policies were very defensive, i.e. to secure employment and restore competitiveness in 'old' industries, whereas almost no attention was paid to the possibilities of creating new employment in emerging industries. Although one of

TABLE 7.3. *Results of government support to industrial companies,*
1975–1978 (situation end 1979)

Position of firms	Number of firms	Total subsidy (f million)	Number of jobs
Bankrupt	91	155	9,183
Hopeless	26	40	2,461
Unclear	70	1,369	76,689
Reasonable	112	541	32,634
Recovered	58	67	5,822
TOTAL	357	2,172	126,789

Source: Dercksen and Schenk 1982/3.

the conditions of government support was that it was to be given only once, many firms were 'repeaters' and became addicted to subsidies (Wijers 1982; Ru 1981: 109). The Nehem, the 'independent' body which was established to carry out the policy of reconstruction, was not very successful. The Ministry of Economic Affairs in fact refused to delegate authority and the power to spend the large sums involved to the Nehem, as a result of which the Nehem remained ineffective (Vrolijk 1982).

The RSV debacle and the parliamentary inquiry into it meant that the policies of ad hoc support for industries and companies in need had to be terminated. It ended an almost 'un-Dutch' period of generous subsidies for and active intervention in the development of industries and companies in decline. In a way the media event of 1984/85 led Dutch industrial policy back into the tradition sketched in the first paragraph of this chapter; after the follies of the 1970s and early 1980s non-intervention again became the norm.

Another, more subtle experiment with the steering of the economy did not fare better. In 1975 the Minister of Economic Affairs, Lubbers, introduced the WIR, a law regulating premiums for investment which were to replace the tax reductions for investing companies which dated back to the first Industrialization Plan of 1949. By introducing a number of criteria for these premiums—e.g. the employment effect and the effect on the environment of the new plant or production line—the WIR was supposed to stimulate 'selective growth', i.e. growth in 'desired' directions.

It was an immediate success in the sense that businessmen succeeded in profiting enormously from the complex system that was introduced. As a result it proved to be much more expensive than was expected. According to non-official sources the WIR allowed the big Dutch multinationals to receive far more premiums than they paid for corporate taxes (Schenk 1987). Moreover, it became increasingly clear that the premiums as such were not very effective in monitoring the direction of economic growth (Spierenburg 1982: 119). In 1988 the WIR was terminated and the system of tax reductions was introduced again.

7.6. TECHNOLOGY POLICY IN THE 1980S AND 1990S

During the short-lived second cabinet led by Van Agt (1981–2), Jan Terlouw, one of the most consistent critics of policies to subsidize declining industries, became Minister of Economic Affairs. He initiated the switch to a more 'offensive' industrial policy aimed at stimulating technological change and the 're-industrialization' of the country. Moreover, in 1982 the MIP (Maatschappij voor Industriële Projekten; Society for Industrial Projects) was set up as a joint venture between the government and a number of large banks and insurance companies to supply innovative firms with venture capital.

Between 1981 and 1985 industrial policy was gradually transformed into technology policy; only subsidies for shipbuilding remained more or less intact. A number of special arrangements were created to stimulate R & D, to subsidize innovative firms, and to contribute to technological change in general. In nominal terms the sums involved show a declining trend from about the peak of almost 2.4 billion guilders in 1983 to 1.8 billion in 1991; its share in GDP was almost halved (from .60 to .33%) as was its share in government expenditure (figures from Wijers 1985 supplemented with data from the government budgets published in the *Handelingen der Staten-Generaal*). According to Ford and Suyker (1990) support to manufacturing declined from 4.1% of sectoral GDP in 1981 to 3.3% in 1986. These figures include the rise in government support for R & D, which went up from 5.6% of total R & D expenditure in 1979 to 12.5% in 1985. (The OECD estimates of total subsidies to industry published by Ford and Suyker show a continued increase in subsidies in the 1980s, which can probably be attributed to the increase in money spent on railways and housing subsidies.) With its increase in industrial subsidies in the 1970s and the (modest) decline in the 1980s, the Netherlands fits very well into the general OECD pattern in this period.

In spite of the changes in official policies much remained the same. Large subsidies for Hoogovens within the framework of European plans to restructure the steel industry were given in 1984 and 1985. Until 1980 Dutch subsidies to this sector had been negligible (between 1975 and 1979 these amounted to about 20 million guilders or less than 0.1% of total subsidies to the steel industry of the EC (Voogd 1993: 193). The restructuring of Hoogovens after 1982 was (again) made possible by new capital transfers from government. However, as soon as the profitability of Hoogovens was re-established, the Minister of Economic Affairs decided to sell a large part of its shares again (Dankers and Verheul 1993: 565). The small Dutch automobile industry also received large sums on a number of occasions. The restructuring of Hoogovens and of DAF-trucks and Volvo Car during the 1980s and early 1990s now seems to have resulted in efficient firms which can face international competition. The fate of Fokker is less clear; after huge subsidies to restructure the firm and develop new planes, the company was 'sold' to Dasa/Daimler Benz. But its integration in Europe's biggest industrial company has not solved the problems of Fokker, which is continually making large losses. Before 1995 new subsidies were given again and again because the 'national champion' Fokker was regarded a 'leading edge company', in which new products and technologies were developed for rapidly growing markets. But this myth has faded, as losses have piled up and detailed studies of the effects of Fokker on the rest of Dutch industry have shown that these were and are quite modest. It was finally closed down in 1996.

A few large companies have profited the most from the switch to 'technology policy'. Wijers calculated in 1985 that seven big firms would get about 80% of all available funds; Volvo Car, DAF-trucks, Fokker, and Philips (with a project to develop megabyte chips together with Siemens) were among the happy seven (Wijers 1985: 186). This suggests that firms which already have close ties with government for other reasons—acute financial problems—have a big chance to profit from the special R & D subsidies. The case of Fokker makes clear that 'defensive' and 'offensive' subsidies in practice cannot easily be distinguished. The big difference from the 1970s was that after 1984 financial problems were concentrated in a few very large companies, whereas the majority of (small- and medium-sized) firms prospered and were happy enough not to have to ask for government support. Another difference was that production capacity of the big spender of the 1970s, shipbuilding, was closed down at an accelerated pace in the early 1980s.

The MIP, which was expected to develop into an investment bank, did not become a success. Few firms applied for its mediation, simply because the supply of venture capital from other parties—the big commercial banks, insurance companies, and pension funds—was elastic. In 1989 the government decided to sell its share in the MIP to one of the big banks.

This was one of the many steps towards privatization taken during the 1980s and 1990s. According to De Ru already during the 1950s and 1960s (semi-) public companies like KLM, Staatsmijnen, and others became increasingly independent from direct government control, and were gradually transformed into private enterprises, with a declining participation of the state. Hoogovens is another case in point; the Minister of Economic Affairs had already in 1961 decided to sell a large part of its shares in the company (Ru 1981: 79). Moreover, compared with the rest of Europe, the share of public enterprise in the economy was relatively small in the Netherlands. De Ru estimated its share in total GDP at 7.6% in 1970; in the other countries in his sample this share was much larger: Great Britain 10.8% (1968), France 12.2% (1967), and Italy 13.9% (1967) (Ru 1981: 342).

After 1980 privatization became in vogue again, also because government was desperately looking for money to finance its large deficits. Part of its participation in KLM, DSM, and in Hoogovens was sold (again), the privatization of government-owned banks and savings institutes (NMB and the Postbank), of the postal services (KPN) and a number of smaller public firms was implemented (Davids 1995). At the time of writing, KPN, the former government monopoly, has just been listed on the Wall Street stock exchange and the privatization of the railways (which were nationalized in 1937) is being discussed in Parliament.

In 1992–3 the debate on industrial policy flared up again. The background to this debate included the problems of a number of large industrial companies (Philips, Fokker, DAF-trucks); and the question of whether the Minister of Economic Affairs Andriessen should not formulate more aggressive policies to stop the decline of these big firms was central to it. Almost instinctively, so it seems, Andriessen came up with the same solution that was proposed during the debates of the early 1970s and 1980s, when the NEHEM and the MIP were created. He proposed the establishment of a separate fund, the Industriefaciliteit, for the supply of venture capital. In 1993 this was set up, again in cooperation with the big banks. Until now two firms have made use of its facilities. One, Océ van der Grinten, recently complained that it was pressed by the Ministry to borrow money from the new Industriefaciliteit (it would have preferred to borrow it from its regular bank). After its creation in 1993 the debate calmed down. If history repeats itself, and industrial policies seem to suggest that it will, we will have to await the early years of the twenty-first century, after the liquidation of this Industriefaciliteit, for another round in this discussion.

7.7. CONCLUSION: IS INDUSTRIAL POLICY AN EMPTY BOX?

The most fierce critic of all these attempts to formulate something like an industrial policy, a policy aimed at steering the direction of industrial development, H. W. de Jong (1985), has called it an empty box. In his opinion in a small open economy that is largely dominated by cartels and large multinational firms, industrial policy cannot do anything but implement what businessmen have already decided upon and is therefore superfluous. This review of the development of industrial policy shows that this view is at least one-sided. Of course, the long-term development of Dutch industry during the twentieth century was in the first place shaped by the development of world markets, its competitive position, the ingenuity of its entrepreneurs, the moderation of its trade unions and so on and so forth. The effectiveness of the 'offensive' industrialization policy of the period 1948–63 is largely a myth and the 'defensive' industrial policies of 1963–83 did not do much more than to assist declining industries in closing down their factories. But this is only part of the story. The new institutional structure that was created after 1945 and the policies directed at keeping down wages and prices were fundamental for the economic success of the Netherlands after 1945. Moreover, the Dutch government was on various occasions involved with the creation of new basic industries for the production of coal, steel, aluminium, salt, and soda, which all have been relatively successful. In coal it took the initiative itself, after a failure of the market to develop Dutch mining industry. The other basic industries were set up by private enterprise, but it needed, because of the large funds that were involved and the very risky nature of these ventures, support from the government to launch the new industries successfully. In this way government at least assisted in the creation of highly successful corporations such as DSM, Hoogovens, and one of the precursors of AKZO. Other 'infant industries' that profited from heavy government involvement were Fokker and KLM.

A characteristic feature of the institutional framework of Dutch industrial policy was the relative independence of the management of public and semi-public enterprises, which probably dates back to the Bedrijvenwet of 1912. Party politics did not play a role in the management of these enterprises, nor were managers in general selected on the basis of party membership. The Staatsmijnen could, for example, develop into a chemical company and put pressure on the Minister of Economic Affairs to close down the coal mines. Other semi-public enterprises like Schiphol and the Havenbedrijf Rotterdam were basically run along commercial lines and were focused very much on improving its international position. The (partial) privatization of DSM, KLM, and other smaller firms was therefore a relatively small step. In general, the Dutch public sector seems to have been rather efficient during the past century, although it is not easy to test this notion. The fact that the public sector has contributed effectively to the rise of at least a number of Dutch multinationals, is perhaps a small piece of evidence in its favour.

If there is a lesson to be learned from the Dutch success in industrial policies (in the period before 1963)—its ability to pick winners and to develop a number of efficient market-oriented public enterprises—it may be that this was the result of a relatively strong aloofness of the Dutch elite towards government intervention in general. But this was coupled to the political necessity to reach consensus and to integrate (former) opposition parties—the 'radicals' after 1890 and the social democrats after 1945—into the system of government. The compromise that was reached allowed for a certain degree of direct government intervention: the establishment of Staatsmijnen and Hoogovens, for example, or the formulation of the Industrialization Plan of 1949. But in all these cases the elite saw to it that the discipline of the market was not really affected, that new public enterprises were run along commercial lines and that industrialization plans did not reduce the autonomy of private enterprise.

REFERENCES

BRINK, J. R. M. VAN DEN (1984). *Zoeken naar een 'heilstaat': Opbouw, neergang en perspectief van de Nederlandse welvaartsstaat*. Amsterdam: Elsevier.

BRUGMANS, I. J. (1969). *Paardenkracht en Mensenmacht*. 's-Gravenhage: Martinus Nijhoff.

DANKERS, J. J., and VERHEUL, J. (1993). *Hoogovens 1945–1993*. Den Haag: SDU.

DAVIDS, M. (1995). 'The relationship between the state enterprise for postal, telegraph and telephone services and the state in the Netherlands in historical perspective'. *Business and Economic History. Journal of the Business History Conference*, 24/1: 194–205.

DERCKSEN, W., and SCHENK, H. (1982/3). 'Industriepolitiek als gevangene van de internationale konkurrentiestrijd'. *Tijdschrift voor Politieke Ekonomie*, 6: 129–49.

FORD, R., and SUYKER, W. (1990). 'Industrial subsidies in the OECD economies'. *OECD Economic Studies*, 15: 37–84.

GOEY, F. DE (1990). *Ruimte voor industrie*. Rotterdam: Eburon.

GRIFFITHS. R. T. (1986). 'Enkele kanttekeningen bij de eerste industrialisatienota's van J. R. M. van den Brink'. *Bijdragen en mededelingen betrefffende de geschiedenis der Nederlanden*, 101: 110–17.

Handelingen der Staten-Generaal (1982–94).

HEERDING, E. (1986). *Een onderneming van vele markten thuis*. Leiden: Martinus Nijhoff.

HEN, P. E. DE (1980). *Actieve en re-actieve industriepolitiek in Nederland*. Amsterdam: De Arbeiderspers.

HORLINGS, E. (1995). *The Economic Development of the Dutch Service Sector 1800–1850: Trade and Transport in a Premodern Economy*. Amsterdam. NEHA.

HULST, N. VAN (1984). *De effectiviteit van geleide loonpolitiek in theorie en praktijk*. Amsterdam: Economische Fakulteit VU.

Jaarcijfers van het Koninkrijk der Nederlanden (1925–40).

JONG, H. W. DE (1985). 'Industriepolitiek: Een lege doos'. *Economisch-Statistische Berichten*, 70: 192–7.

LIAGRE BÖHL, H. DE, NEKKERS, J., and SLOT, L. (1981) (eds.). *Nederland industrialiseert!* Nijmegen: SUN.

MESSING, F. A. M. (1988), *Geschiedenis van de mijnsluiting in Limburg*. Lieden.

RU, H. J. DE (1981). *Staatsbedrijven en staatsdeelnemingen*. Nijmegen: Stichting Ars Aequi.

SCHAIK, A. VAN (1986). *Crisis en Protectie onder Colijn*. Amsterdam.

SCHENK, H. (1987). *Industrie en technologiebeleid: Analyse en perspectief*. Groningen.

SCHIFF, E. (1971). *Industrialization without National Patents*. Princeton: UP.

SMIDT, M. DE, and WEVER, E. (1987). *De Nederlandse industrie*. Assen: Van Gorcum.

SPIERENBURG, R. J. (1982). 'Staatsinterventie en noodlijdende bedrijven', in H. Vrolijk and R. Hengeveld (eds.), *Interventie en vrije markt*, 93–123. Amsterdam: SUA.

VOOGD, C. DE (1993). *De neergang van de scheepsbouw en andere industriële bedrijfstakken*. Vlissingen.

VOORT, R. VAN DER (1994). *Overheidsbeleid en overheidsfinanciën in Nederland 1850–1913*. Amsterdam: NEHA.

VRIES, H. DE (1994). *Nederlandse economen over een ondernemende overheid, 1850–1940*. Leiden.

VROLIJK, H. (1982). 'Opkomst en neergang van de Nederlandse herstructureringsmaatschappij', in H. Vrolijk and R. Hengeveld (eds.), *Interventie en vrije markt*, 49–92. Amsterdam: SUA.

WIJERS, G. J. (1982). *Industriepolitiek*. Leiden and Antwerpen: Stenfert Kroese.

—— (1985). 'Een pleidooi voor industriepolitiek'. *Maandschrift economie*, 49: 175–91.

WILSON, C. (1954). *The History of Unilever*. London: Cassell & Co.

ZADOKS, S. (1899). *Geschiedenis van de Amsterdamse consessies*. Amsterdam.

ZANDEN, J. L. VAN, and GRIFFITHS, R. T. (1989). *Economische geschiedenis van Nederland in de 20e eeuw*. Utrecht: Het Spectrum.

ZIJLSTRA, J. (1992). *Per slot van rekening: Memoires*. Amsterdam: Contact.

8

Belgium: Liberalism by Default

LUC HENS AND PETER SOLAR

Vesalius College, Vrije Universiteit Brussel

During the last century Belgium has rarely had a clearly articulated industrial policy. Perhaps the only occasion was around 1960 when a series of measures designed to liberalize economic activity and to encourage physical capital formation, particularly that by foreign enterprises, was implemented. During the rest of the century one can only search the actions and inactions of successive governments for coherent patterns, and such coherence often proves difficult to find.

This lack of coherence, as well as a serious shortage of empirical work by historians and economists on the effects of particular policies, makes it difficult to judge the overall impact of Belgian industrial policy. But it will be suggested here that, especially since the 1930s, state policy towards industry has often been counterproductive and at best ineffective.

8.1. THE CONTEXT FOR INDUSTRIAL POLICY

Certain features of Belgium's economic situation provide the context for *any* industrial policy. One is its early industrialization. Developing an industrial base has not been Belgium's problem during the twentieth century. Already in 1896, 38% of total employment was in industry and by 1910 this had reached 47%; the twentieth-century peak would be only slightly higher, at 47.5% in 1973 (De Brabander 1983). Before the First World War, Belgian producers were highly competitive on world markets, dominating international trade in some products (zinc, glass, linen yarn) and exporting mainly to developed countries. Belgium's problem during the twentieth century has been to sustain this high level of activity as industrial development took place elsewhere in Europe and the rest of the world. When existing industries did lose ground, the problem became that of renewing an old industrial structure.

Belgian policy has also been shaped by the country's small size and by its location at what, until recently, has been the industrial heart of Europe (Duquesne de la Vinelle 1963). On its own Belgium would have a hard time restricting flows of goods and capital across its borders. In practice, it has rarely wanted to. Since the 1860s the country has favoured free trade and sought to benefit from its central location by handling transit trade and by developing subcontracting

We gratefully acknowledge helpful comments on a previous version of this paper from Erik Buyst, Patricia Van den Eeckhout, Michelangelo Van Meerten, Guy Vanthemsche, and Jef Vuchelen.

and supplier relationships with producers in neighbouring countries. Belgium has also been relatively open to direct investment by foreigners, though Belgian investment abroad has tended since the First World War to be for portfolio rather than direct investment. This openness to goods and factor flows has given a strong international dimension to Belgium's industrial policies.

Belgium's small size and its early start led to the development of a mix of industries that has been particularly sensitive to shifts in its neighbours' commercial and industrial policies. In the late nineteenth century Belgian industry specialized in standardized, semi-finished manufactures with relatively high import content (Drèze 1961). In textiles, for example, its major exports were cleaned Australian and South American wool, high-quality prepared flax that had been grown in France, the Netherlands, and Belgium, and medium counts of linen yarn produced from imported Russian flax. The large Belgian steel industry specialized in rails and other standard items.

The products of Belgian industry have also had a high energy content, the heritage of an early industrialization based on abundant coal resources. Iron and steel, bricks and glass, cement, nonferrous metals and chemicals (mainly fertilizers) are all energy-intensive industries in which Belgium has had a persistent revealed comparative advantage (Crafts 1989). Not surprisingly, the domestic coal industry on which these industries depended has been a focus of industrial policy during the twentieth century.

The political context for policy-making has been a stable but weak parliamentary government. Belgian politics in the twentieth century have been shaped by strong, long-standing ideological differences among anti-clerical conservatives, anti-clerical socialists, and Catholics on both the right and the left. These differences have been increasingly overlaid with linguistic and territorial quarrels between speakers of French and Dutch. The results of these cross-cutting divisions have been a very stable party system, a thorough politicization of public services, and the prevalence of coalition governments able to act only on the basis of complex compromises (Lijphart 1981; Frognier 1988). This political structure has both impeded the formation of coherent policy and been particularly susceptible to capture by existing industrial interests.

The political context for industrial policy changed significantly in the 1980s. Internally, responsibility for industry was devolved to the Flemish, Walloon, and Brussels regions as part of the continuing regionalization of Belgium. Externally, European Union competition directives started to limit the scope for assistance to industry, though governments have often found ways to circumvent these constraints.

8.2. INDUSTRIAL STRUCTURE, CONTROL, AND POLICY: THE MAIN LINES

The Belgian state has, in general, not chosen to pursue its aims through the ownership and control of firms. Throughout the century Belgian industry has

TABLE 8.1. *Control regimes*

	1896	1937	1960	1980
Coal mining	P	P	R	N
Other extractive	P	P	P	P
Basic metals	P	P	P	N/P
Engineering	P	P	P	P
Glass, ceramics, plastics	P	P	P	P
Chemicals, petroleum	P	P	P	P
Textiles, clothing, shoes	P	P	P	P
Woodworking	P	P	P	P
Paper, printing	P	P	P	P
Food, drink, tobacco	P	P	P	P
Electricity, gas, water	R	R	R	R
Railways, waterways	N/P	N	N	N
Post, telephone	N	N	N	N
Other	P	P	P	P
Regime by employment (%)				
Private	88	89	82	77
Regulated	1	1	9	3
Nationalized	12	10	9	20

Intellectual Health Warning: These classifications, based on a variety of sources, are intended only to give a general idea of sectoral distribution and changes over time. The distributions by employment simply count each sector by its broad classification; they do not take account of the mix of regimes within sector.

N = state ownership and control
R = mainly private ownership and control; regulated
P = mainly private ownership and control; unregulated

remained overwhelmingly in private hands (Table 8.1). The only true national-ized industries have been in the transport and communications sectors (and in water supply). These industries came into public hands during the nineteenth cen-tury and most remain there today. The state also acquired some industrial lame ducks in the 1960s and 1970s: many of these have died long and costly deaths. The regulated sector of the economy has also been small, being largely confined to energy production.

Private firms, the norm in Belgian industry, have operated during the last cen-tury within a highly permissive legal framework. Since the Companies Act of 1873, the formation of limited liability enterprises has been cheap and relatively unrestricted (Stevens 1995). Accounting and financial reporting requirements for limited and other companies have been rudimentary, at least until the 1970s and 1980s when the implementation of European directives led to major changes. The protection of shareholders' rights has been, and remains, minimal (La Porta *et al.* 1996). The lack of protection for minority shareholders and poor informa-tion on companies have limited active trading on the stock exchange to utilit-ies and holding companies. These holding companies, a distinctive feature of the Belgian economy, have been able to control a large part of heavy industry

TABLE 8.2. *Market structure and protection from foreign competition*

	1896	1937	1960	1980
Coal mining	CU	OP	OP	MP
Other extractive	CU	CU	CU	CU
Basic metals	CU	OP	OU	OU
Engineering	CU	CU	CU	CU
Glass, ceramics, plastics	CU	CU	CU	CU
Chemicals, petroleum	CU	CU	OU	OU
Textiles, clothing, shoes	CU	CP	CP	CU
Woodworking	CU	CU	CU	CU
Paper, printing	CU	CU	CU	CU
Food, drink, tobacco	CU	CU	CU	CU
Electricity, gas, water	MP	MP	MP	MP
Railways, waterways	MP	MP	MP	MP
Post, telephone	MP	MP	MP	MP
Other	CU	CU	CU	CU
Market structure by employment (%)				
CU	88	48	51	66
OU	0	0	12	16
CP	0	26	19	0
OP	0	15	7	0
MP	12	11	11	18

Intellectual Health Warning: These classifications, based on a variety of sources, are intended only to give a general idea of sectoral distribution and changes over time. The distributions by employment simply count each sector by its broad classification; they do not take account of the mix of regimes within sector.

C = competitive
O = oligopoly or weak cartel
M = monopoly or strong cartel
P = protected on domestic market
U = unprotected on domestic market

through cascades of majority holdings in subsidiary companies (Daems 1978). The remainder of Belgian industry has been composed of closely held companies dependent on retained earnings or bank credit for finance.

The Belgian state has been reluctant to use tariffs or quotas as instruments of industrial policy (Table 8.2). Before the First World War, the country was an ardent free trader. Between the wars, it moved away from free trade, as did most European countries, but its departures were quite limited (Hogg 1986). Coal mining was the main industrial beneficiary of protection, with lesser help going to textile producers. Protection of these industries continued to a certain extent into the 1950s. For the rest of Belgian industry, foreign competition has simply been a fact of life for most of the century.

Free trade has limited the power of Belgian firms on the domestic market, which may account for the generally permissive stance the state has taken towards cartels of domestic producers. Most Belgian industries have been highly competitive, with cartels being relatively shortlived (Table 8.2). Even in industries

TABLE 8.3. *Subsidy regimes*

	1896	1937	1960	1980
Coal mining	N	L	H	H
Other extractive	N	N	N	N
Basic metals	N	N	N	H
Engineering	N	N	N	N
Glass, ceramics, plastics	N	N	N	L
Chemicals, petroleum	N	N	N	N
Textiles, clothing, shoes	N	N	N	H
Woodworking	N	N	N	N
Paper, printing	N	N	N	L
Food, drink, tobacco	N	N	N	N
Electricity, gas, water	N	N	N	N
Railways, waterways	L	L	H	H
Post, telephone	L	L	L	H
Other	N	N	N	N
Subsidy regimes by employment (%)				
Heavily subsidized	0	0	13	32
Lightly subsidized	12	20	3	10
Not subsidized	88	80	84	58

Intellectual Health Warning: These classifications, based on a variety of sources, are intended only to give a general idea of sectoral distribution and changes over time. The distributions by employment simply count each sector by its broad classification; they do not take account of the mix of regimes within sector.

H = heavily subsidized
L = lightly subsidized
N = not subsidized

where there has appeared to be a high degree of concentration, like chemicals or glass, Belgian firms have often been more oriented towards export markets and there have been substantial imports as well as exports of these products.

Until quite recently the Belgian state has not made extensive use of subsidies to promote or sustain particular industries. During Belgium's early industrialization, state support for industry was quite common, but from the 1870s existing subsidies were reduced and few new subsidies were given. Until the government became involved from the 1930s in the long death of the coal industry, only the few nationalized industries benefited from modest capital subsidies. The coal industry would prove to be a bottomless pit, absorbing vast sums until, and even after, the final mine closed in 1992. During the 1970s the difficulties faced by the steel and textile industries, as well as a certain laxness in the nationalized industries, led to a major increase in state subsidies. By the early 1980s among the EC countries only in Luxembourg did government support constitute a larger share of industrial output (Ford and Suyker 1990). This degree of support was unsustainable and was cut back somewhat in the late 1980s and early 1990s.

Except for its aid to lame ducks, the Belgian state has pursued general rather than selective industrial policies. Although in a few contexts it has favoured domestic over foreign firms, it has rarely singled out individual industries or firms for promotion. Its policies have been industry-wide though in practice particular programmes have favoured certain sorts of industries. For example, general investment subsidies in the 1960s were of greatest use to capital-intensive industries such as petrochemicals. Belgium's policies have also tended to be passive, rather than active: they have been applicant-driven, with the available resources then being divided among the many applicants, rather than concentrating them on a few carefully selected candidates.

Given these general features of policy, it is possible to break the last century into two broad periods. Up to the 1930s Belgium had what could be called a *passive businessman's state*. The government sought to provide a stable monetary and legal environment for business. It put relatively few constraints on businessmen's freedom of action in input or output markets. It sought to keep the costs of labour, purchased inputs, and taxes as low as possible. These policies, it was hoped, would bring success on export markets, profits, and prosperity (Van den Eeckhout 1996).

From the 1930s the changing configuration of political power within Belgium turned the businessman's state into a *producer's state*. Profits had to share priority with wages and employment. This period can, in turn, be broken down into three subperiods. In the first, from the 1930s to the 1950s, the state's ambitions were quite limited. Policies did not change markedly from the earlier period, but protection of existing interests took priority. The second subperiod, during the 1960s and 1970s, was characterized by great ambitions backed by significant resources. Initially the focus was on promoting growth by attracting new firms from abroad and by stimulating investment by existing firms; later it shifted to maintaining the level of employment. The last subperiod, during the 1980s and 1990s, has been one of great ambitions but very limited resources, a direct consequence of the extravagances of the preceding subperiod.

It is worth noting that the two world wars had little lasting effect on Belgian industrial policy. State intervention in industry did increase markedly but the state was German. When the wars ended, the policies under the occupation were quickly dismantled.

The next three sections take up Belgian industrial policies in greater detail, dealing successively with nationalized, regulated, and unregulated industries. The last section returns briefly to the political economy of industrial policy in Belgium.

8.3. STATE-OWNED INDUSTRY

Some enterprises have been under state control and management throughout the century. Full-fledged *nationalized* industries have consistently been confined to transport and communications sectors. (The state has also owned and managed financial institutions, the role of which is discussed later in the chapter.) Local and regional governments, by contrast, have at various times been involved in supplying electricity, gas, water, urban transport, and cable television, though only in water and urban transport has government control ever been the norm (electricity, gas, and cable television will thus be treated as regulated industries). A miscellany of other enterprises have come under full or partial state ownership but not under full-fledged state management. These have mainly been lame ducks acquired since the Second World War, especially since the late 1960s.

8.3.1. Transport and Communications

Despite many private initiatives in the nineteenth century, during the twentieth century most communications and transport services have been supplied by the state. Telegraph and telephone services had been brought within the long-standing postal monopoly by 1900. The state had also acquired most private railways and waterways, though not as part of a well-developed strategy. In some cases it was manoeuvred into purchasing them at great cost to the Treasury (Kurgan-van Hentenryk 1978); in others bureaucrats and state railway officials were seeking to eliminate competition from private companies (Van der Herten and Van Meerten 1994). Air transport was effectively monopolized by SABENA, created by state initiative in 1923 as a joint-stock company with a minority of private shareholders.

From the 1850s and 1860s, when liberal governments first began to reduce prices in order to promote greater use of railways and telegraphs, low prices for transport and communications services, especially to industrial customers, have been a substantial element in Belgian industrial policy. Before the First World War, the Belgian railways were well known for their low passenger fares, especially for workers' seasonal tickets. Freight rates, particularly for bulk goods used by heavy industry, were also low by international standards and remained low into the inter-war years (Hogg 1986). Low prices helped extend the use of the telephone (Verhoest, Vercruysse, and Punie 1991). During the 1950s and 1960s prices of transport and communications services remained relatively low by international standards, but sometime during the 1970s and 1980s Belgium seems to have lost this advantage.

The implicit goal of pricing policy in the nationalized industries seems to have been to keep prices as low as was consistent with the enterprise not constituting too great a drain on the state budget. Although the conflation of current and capital expenditures in their accounts makes precision illusory, the state industries seem to have required only modest capital subsidies up to the 1930s. This began to change from the 1930s when the railways, already hit by the fall in traffic during the Depression, started to face competition from road transport. By the late 1950s large and growing subsidies were being given to the railways. The postal service and the internal waterways, both facing greater competition, also received more and more state help (Baudhuin 1970; Robert *et al.* 1983). So, too, in air transport as SABENA absorbed larger subsidies from the late 1960s. By the end of the 1970s the state industries were receiving 60% of all state aid to industry, a sum equivalent to 3.5% of GNP (Gilot 1987).

The policy of keeping prices low without straining the state budget depended on increasing the efficiency and so keeping down the costs of providing transport and communications services. But it appears that, particularly after the Second World War, these state enterprises have faced a relatively soft budget constraint. They were able to maintain a very high level of investment, at least until the budget constraint tightened significantly in the 1980s. Throughout most of the century roughly one-quarter of all Belgian investment (excluding dwellings) has gone into transport and communications, by far the greater part of it into the state industries. Railways took most of this investment between the wars and their share remained high into the 1950s. Major investments undertaken in the late 1940s and 1950s, ostensibly to modernize the railways, have been criticized as ill-conceived and extravagant: the railway system was essentially restored to its pre-war structure and electrified at great cost (Baudhuin 1958). Since the Second World War, the state has made very large investments in water transport and port development. While those in the port of Antwerp probably yielded a respectable return, many others, notably at the port of Zeebrugge and on canals in Wallonia, are unlikely ever to yield positive private or social returns (Baudhuin 1970: 161–2). Such investments were probably encouraged by the favourable terms on which the state and state industries have been able to borrow.

Another manifestation of the soft budget constraint is that labour costs may have been pushed up unduly since the Second World War. Strong unions with allies in government have been able to keep employment in the state industries at a high level. To make matters worse, in the 1970s the government encouraged the railways and other state industries to take on workers in order to keep down the growth in unemployment (Robert *et al.* 1983; De Borger 1993).

The state industries have not made particularly good use of the resources available to them. Belgium ranks consistently near the bottom of the table in international productivity comparisons made in the 1980s and 1990s (Moesen 1990). Moreover, productivity growth in the sheltered sector of the Belgian economy, in which state (and regulated) industries figure prominently, has been notably slow by European standards (Cassiers, De Villé, and Solar 1996).

Belgium has come late and only half-heartedly to privatization. Politicians have been loath to let go of client firms, especially as large job cuts would inevitably result. Even when SABENA and Belgacom (the renamed telephone monopoly) were privatized in the 1990s, the state initially sold only minority shares. The real impetus for privatization has come from the parlous state of the public finances (Vuchelen and Van Impe 1987). Not only have asset sales helped keep down government deficits, the state's unwillingness to finance new investment in its enterprises during the 1980s and 1990s has led managers to lobby for freedom from state control.

8.3.2. Water and Urban Transport

During the nineteenth and early twentieth centuries some municipalities entered into the business of providing water, gas, electricity, and urban transport. Before the First World War municipal ownership was widespread in water, less common for gas, rare for electricity, and rarer still for tramways. The city of Brussels was the most enterprising, supplying its own water, gas, and electricity. But in general municipal ownership was less widespread in Belgium than in England and other European countries. Except in the case of water, concessions to private enterprises were the norm (Brees 1906).

Municipal participation in industrial enterprise increased from 1922 when legislation made it easier for *communes* (the basic administrative unit, rural or urban) to form joint enterprises with each other and with private firms. The *intercommunale* form of organization was particularly important since many urban areas in Belgium were divided into several *communes*. For private firms there were tax advantages to this form of organization and it was a way of protecting their assets. In electricity and gas, the *communes* were generally minority shareholders.

The provision of water has largely been in public hands throughout the century, although there has been increasing concentration as *intercommunales* have merged. The number of different water authorities makes it difficult to generalize about pricing, but many appear to have sought to keep water prices as low as possible, sometimes with the help of capital subsidies from local and national governments. The lack of coordination among these local authorities led the central government to become involved in the water industry from the late 1960s. It initiated the construction of large dams that served several localities and pushed for more consolidation of local water authorities (Baudhuin 1970).

Urban transport tended to come into public hands as it became less profitable or as concessions granted in the late nineteenth century expired. In most large urban areas trams were run by private firms on concession until after the Second World War, when they gave way to *intercommunales* owned predominantly by local governments. During the 1960s, 1970s, and early 1980s subsidies from local and national government increased, until the national government's financial difficulties led to a reduction in subsidies and investment and a rise in prices in the late 1980s (Delmelle 1981).

8.3.3. Lame Ducks

Until the 1960s the Belgian government occasionally helped firms in difficulty but was reluctant to take on the responsibilities of ownership and control. In the early 1930s, for example, instead of intervening directly to save Minerva, the remaining indigenous automobile producer, it pressured the *Société Générale*, the dominant holding company, into doing so (Hogg 1986). Indeed, in the interwar period it was usually the holding companies that were left to deal with the reorganization of problem industries.

After the war the situation was reversed: the government instead took problem industries off the hands of the holding companies, though only as a last resort. In 1967 it acquired the rump of the coal industry, but only after some three decades of state assistance and after the last mines in the south of the country had closed. The steel industry's continuing problems in the 1970s and early 1980s turned the state's initial minority interest into majority control of Cockerill-Sambre, the largest producer, and of several smaller mills. During the 1970s and 1980s central and regional governments ended up with controlling interests in firms in a miscellany of other industries.

State ownership has in most cases only slowed firms' demise at considerable cost to the taxpayers. The Limburg coal mines, in the north of country, are a major case in point. The national government subsidized these mines directly and indirectly from the late 1960s to the early 1980s, the subsidies increasingly seen as the compensation to Flanders for help given to the Walloon steel industry. When industrial policy was regionalized in 1983, the Flemish regional government quickly realized the cost of keeping the mines open and accelerated their closure, though in the end the last Belgian mines closed almost twenty years after comparable ones in neighbouring Dutch Limburg had been shut down.

State ownership of lame ducks has had only one notable 'success'. After pouring vast sums into Cockerill-Sambre, the government persuaded a top French manager to make one last attempt to reorganize the steelmaker. With large subsidies and an explicit promise of no government interference in the restructuring programme, Cockerill-Sambre was severely thinned down and by the late 1980s had become a reasonably competitive firm in a still troubled European industry (Gandois 1986).

8.4. REGULATED INDUSTRIES

All industry in Belgium has from time to time been subject to some regulation. Until the 1980s the Ministry of Economic Affairs retained formidable powers to review price changes. Similarly, in the 1970s and 1980s tripartite agreements among business, labour, and government often committed firms to investment, employment, or other targets. But here regulation will be taken to mean sustained monitoring of an industry's pricing and other policies, usually with the purpose of protecting consumer interests in the face of market power. The only true regulated industries in Belgium have been those in the energy sector, mainly electricity and gas, though oil to a lesser extent.

8.4.1. Gas and Electricity

Until after the Second World War, the gas and electricity industries were controlled at local rather than national level. This stemmed from the authority over lighting given to the *communes*. During the nineteenth century, development of these industries was diverse: some *communes* went into production and/or distribution; others gave concessions to private firms. Alongside these municipal initiatives, industrial users often generated their own electricity or gas, or purchased them from private firms. In the electricity industry these *autoproducteurs* accounted for more than half of output until the late 1920s (Kurgan-van Hentenryk 1987).

During the inter-war years, the utility industries became significantly more concentrated. The major forces behind concentration were technical, as regional and national distribution networks were being developed, and financial, as the holding companies consolidated their various interests and acquired other firms. By the late 1930s the production of gas and electricity had become highly concentrated, whereas distribution to residential and commercial users was largely in the hands of *intercommunales*. This form of association had tax advantages for private firms, though they had to share control and profits with the affiliated *communes*. *Communes* seem generally to have preferred monopoly rents to lower prices, so that by the end of the 1930s concern was being expressed about the effects of the monopolization of gas and electricity supplies. Industrial users, however, still benefited from relatively low electricity prices, in part because of the continued importance of *autoproduction* (Kurgan-van Hentenryk 1987).

After the Second World War, the concentration of the utility industries continued apace but the basic structure of private producers and *intercommunale* distributors has not changed fundamentally. The major change was the introduction in 1955 of a national regulatory body for the electricity industry. This *comité de contrôle* was a peculiarly Belgian creation: it resulted from negotiations, under the auspices of the national federation of employers and with the tacit approval of the government, between the electricity producers and distributors and the major national trade unions. The resulting private regulatory commission was composed of producer and trade union representatives, along with government observers. In 1963 the gas industry was also brought under this regulatory commission.

National regulation made possible greater coordination of investment and production. It also permitted the establishment of national prices for electricity, and later gas. These prices were relatively high by international standards (De Staercke 1963), and the utilities have been able to pass along cost increases fairly easily. Prices were also kept high during the 1960s and early 1970s in order to keep inefficient coal-burning power plants in business and hence provide an indirect subsidy to the coal industry (Bosman and Proost 1981).

This private regulatory system broke down in the 1970s when the socialist trade union withdrew from the commission. The only result was that the committee was given legal status as an independent regulatory board in 1983. The way it operated changed little.

8.4.2. Other Regulated Industries

The petroleum sector has been regulated from the 1950s, with the government fixing maximum prices that move in line with the world market oil prices.

These maximum prices have incorporated abnormally high distribution margins and tended to serve as reference points for retailing pricing by the oligopoly (Bosman and Proost 1981).

8.5. UNREGULATED INDUSTRIES

The great bulk of Belgian industry has been in private hands and not subject to close regulation by the state. State policies towards this sector of the economy can be grouped into those directed at particular industries and those directed at industry generally. Industry- or firm-specific policies have been less common than general policies (Gilot 1987).

Selective policies can be active or reactive. Active policies seek to promote the development of particular firms or industries. Reactive policies usually try to deal with the problems faced by existing firms or industries. In Belgium reactive policies have prevailed.

8.5.1. Active Industry- or Firm-Specific Policies

As large purchasers of certain goods, governments necessarily have a substantial influence on some industries. The impact of Belgium's procurement policies on industrial development has been limited by the small size of the country. Moreover, what impact they might have had has been dissipated by a lack of focus.

The industries on which government purchasing has had the largest potential impact have been arms and transport and telecommunications equipment. Whereas a large Belgian government contract did lead to the amalgamation in 1889 of several Liège arms-makers into the *Fabrique Nationale*, in the firm's subsequent development the Belgian government tended to buy new models only after they had already been developed on contract for other governments (Francotte and Gaier 1989). Army orders for jeeps and other small vehicles kept Belgium's small indigenous automobile industry alive until after the Second World War. Since the war Belgium, because of its small size and its international commitments, has purchased aircraft, tanks, and other weapons from foreign firms, though it has usually negotiated for some of the work to be subcontracted to Belgian firms. Such work has been distributed among several firms, so that it has been costly to execute and that most of the firms involved have remained dependent on such contracts.

The state railways and urban transport companies have generally bought their rolling stock from Belgian firms. Before the First World War transport equipment was a Belgian speciality. There were many firms producing for both home and foreign markets, and the state railway kept down its costs by spreading its orders among these firms. When foreign markets contracted after the war, the industry was left with excess capacity. Although the Belgian state railway did try to rationalize its purchasing, it still distributed orders among 10–15 firms, probably keeping too many of them in business. After the Second World War railway equipment producers became almost completely dependent on state contracts (Vandeputte 1985). Urban transport companies have usually bought buses from Van Hool, a Belgian assembler which has had some success on export markets. One perverse effect of regionalization in the 1980s has been that Walloon authorities have tried to create, from nothing, a Walloon alternative to the Flemish company.

The state telephone company, unlike the railways, has had a dominant supplier: Bell Telephone Manufacturing Co., a subsidiary of ITT until it was purchased by Alcatel in the 1980s. The main result has been that equipment costs have been high by international standards, though having the domestic market may have helped give the firm credibility on Third World markets (Verhoest, Vercruysse, and Punie 1991).

Until the 1980s one must search hard for instances of other policies designed to promote particular firms or industries, and even harder for policies that were effective. There have been several general efforts to modernize Belgian industry but these had little impact. After the First World War, the government set up the *Société Nationale pour le Crédit à l'Industrie-Nationale Maatschaapij voor Krediet aan de Nijverheid* (SNCI-NMKN) to help finance reconstruction and especially to aid small firms. Its policies towards reconstruction proved to be extremely conservative and it was later captured by the holding companies, with the result that over two-thirds of its loans went to the coal and steel industries (Hogg 1986). In the late 1930s, the *Office de Redressement Économique* (ORÉC) was established to find and promote new industries but it was never given the authority or the resources to do so.

After the Second World War, the Belgian government, like other European governments, considered how scarce resources for investment might best be used. During the late 1940s, it published annual investment programmes, though these were quite conservative in character and, in any case, only indicative. Belgium received little from the Marshall Plan; most of what it did receive went into the coal industry (Kurgan-van Hentenryk 1993). In 1959 a Planning Office was set up to do medium-term planning but again the plans were only indicative and had little effect, even on the state's own investments. During the 1950s and 1960s the best example of an effective industry-specific policy was probably the use of public infrastructure investments to promote the development of petroleum refining and petrochemical industries in the ports of Antwerp and, to a lesser extent, Ghent and Zeebrugge.

The limits on public resources in the 1980s led national and regional governments to try to be more selective in their assistance to industry. State investment funds were set aside for specific industrial development, particularly in electronics. But these selective policies lacked continuity and their industrial impact was limited (Boelaert 1993: 429–30). The regional governments set up holding companies to manage their existing assets and to provide venture capital, though their success as venture capital funds has been at best limited. Finally, the central government has used tax advantages to encourage multinational enterprises to locate staff functions in Belgium. This last policy was not, strictly speaking, industry-specific, but it did target certain sorts of activities—management, research, and development—that the state wanted to encourage.

8.5.2. *Reactive Industry- or Firm-Specific Policies*

Most state aid for specific industries has been given to stem decline. The major beneficiary has been the coal industry. In the 1930s coal from some parts of Wallonia was already more expensive than imports from elsewhere in Europe. After the war Belgian coal faced heightened competition first from coal producers outside Europe, then from oil. During the 1930s the industry obtained, successively, quotas on imported coal, import duties, an industry cartel, and export subsidies (Hogg 1986). After the war the Belgian government subsidized wages and investment, then brought its European partners to the aid of the industry in the 1950s (Milward 1992). The coal industry was able to extract so much assistance thanks to the political weight of its large and militant workforce and of the major banks and holding companies with important interests in the mines.

The textile and clothing industries have received state assistance since the 1930s but only became large-scale recipients during the 1970s. Weavers benefited from import quotas in the 1930s and during the 1950s quotas and other measures were used to limit the impact of the Benelux agreement on Belgian producers (Boekestijn 1990). But protection has been difficult to implement because of conflicts of interest among spinners, weavers, and clothing manufacturers and because of the importance of export markets for many producers. As a result, during the 1950s and 1960s the government allowed a large share of the industry to run down and disappear (de Vylder 1992). The Belgian textile industry of the 1970s was, in general, much more modern and more specialized. While it did face serious competition from producers in the Far East and elsewhere, that it received as much aid as it did in the 1970s and early 1980s resulted from the need to compensate Flanders, where most of the textile industry was located, for the assistance given to the Walloon steel industry (Bataillie 1989). The regional compromises of the 1970s also involved the small Flemish shipbuilding industry (Peeters 1983) and some Walloon glass producers.

The overall effect of these reactive policies was that state aid to enterprises grew by 9–13% per annum between 1975 and 1984 (Gilot 1987). Most of this went to the nationalized industries and the so-called 'national sectors'—steel, coal, textiles, shipbuilding, and glass. During the 1980s these 'national sectors' received over one-third of all direct assistance to private industry (Boelaert 1993).

The Belgian government has also been sensitive to the threatened departure of successful, but potentially highly mobile industries. A prime example is the Antwerp diamond industry, which, as rising labour costs in the 1960s and 1970s made it vulnerable to competition from India and Israel, was given special tax treatment and several other forms of assistance.

8.5.3. General Policies Directed at Output and Input Prices

The Belgian state has pursued a wide range of policies not intended for benefit of specific industries or firms, but aimed at providing general support for industry. These may be classified by the ways in which they have sought to affect firms' profits.

In a small open economy such as Belgium's it is crucial to distinguish between open and sheltered sectors. Much of Belgium's industry is in the open sector and has generally been a price-taker for both its exports and its imported inputs. But open sector industries also buy inputs from sheltered sector firms which may have some market power.

Since Belgian producers have largely been price-takers on export markets, the state has had relatively little scope for export promotion. Its principal role has been to push for freer access to foreign markets, which it did at economic conferences and in bilateral negotiations between the wars and in the context of Benelux and the European Union after the war. Direct subsidies to exports have been rare, though exports have been subsidized indirectly through insurance and credit schemes. Belgium has not been particularly lavish in this regard. Until the 1930s the Export Credit Guarantee Department could only deal with states or public institutions abroad, so most of its guarantees were for railways (Hogg 1986). Its mandate was then widened and from 1973 additional credit facilities were provided.

Belgian producers joined international cartels before the First World War and between the wars. The state neither opposed such initiatives nor did much to facilitate them (Vanthemsche 1983). Even the ostensibly powerful holding companies had a difficult time keeping Belgian firms from being loose cannons in the International Steel Cartel (Gillingham 1991).

In the open sector, prices could only be increased on the home market by protection. Except for modest increases in tariffs in the 1930s and quotas in the 1930s and 1950s, this was generally avoided. Even with protection, the scope for exercising market power in most industries was limited and the state has done little to restrict competition.

A major thrust of Belgian industrial policy, at least until the 1970s, has been to keep down firms' input costs. During the late nineteenth century, Belgium was known for its cheap labour. High fertility, particularly in Flanders, and low emigration made for an abundance of workers. There were few restrictions on hours or on work by women and children. The cost of living was kept low through free trade and low prices for rail transport. Governments have also pursued hard currency policies, notably in the 1950s and 1980s and 1990s, in order to prevent import price increases from being translated into higher wage costs through indexation. The textile and mining industries were particular beneficiaries of low wage policies.

Over the Second World War, Belgium's position with respect to labour costs changed (Cassiers, De Villé, and Solar 1996). From the 1950s it has been a country with relatively high labour costs, not least because of a major extension of the social welfare system and because agriculture became a pampered sector. During much of the post-war period an explicit policy of keeping down wages could not be pursued. Only with increasing economic difficulties in the late 1970s and early 1980s did reductions in wages and social security charges become a policy option. Incomes policies followed after the devaluation of 1982 were explicitly intended to restore firms' profits by restraining wage growth. The competitivity law of 1989 set an international standard for Belgian wage growth.

Belgium's general commitment to free trade, as well as its resistance to currency devaluation, has served to keep down the prices of imported inputs throughout the century. Up to the 1930s prices of many domestically produced inputs were also kept as low as possible. This was the case for transport and communications services, thanks to pricing policies in state industries, and for energy, where competition kept down coal and electricity prices.

Over the Second World War the relative prices of domestically produced inputs rose. Energy prices increased significantly after the war as the result of policies towards the coal industry. The costs of many other inputs tended to rise with labour costs and with the introduction of anti-competitive measures in some service industries. With the liberalization of the economy from around 1960, increased competition in the sheltered sector of the economy helped restrain input cost increases during the 1960s. But in the 1970s another sharp rise took place as the state industries passed their increased labour costs through to industrial users (Cassiers, De Villé, and Solar 1996).

8.5.4. General Policies Directed at Factor Accumulation

Only after the Second World War, and especially after 1960, has the state become particularly active in encouraging capital formation. (Sufficient domestic savings has never been a problem since the country has long had one of the highest savings rates in Europe.) Assistance has been directed more to investment in physical capital than to training or research and development (Gilot 1987: 20–4). But Belgian policies have not been characterized either by clear objectives or by careful execution.

Direct subsidies to investment by private sector firms were rare before the First World War, though the state did try to reduce the cost of finance to certain sorts of firms by creating a number of specialized credit institutions. These institutions persisted through the inter-war period and after the Second World War, and some additional ones were created, but their contribution to the finance of industry has been relatively small. By contrast, until the banking reform of 1934, Belgium's mixed banks were intimately involved in financing industrial

investment, especially that in heavy industry. The reform imposed a separation
of investment and banking activities. After the Second World War, the resulting
commercial banks were increasingly regulated and used by the government to
finance its own activities. In return, the banks were sheltered from foreign competition and tacitly allowed to cartelize the domestic market, so that until the late
1980s there were frequent complaints about the cost and availability of bank credit
to industry.

During the 1950s governments at different levels began to experiment with
investment incentives. These experiments were unified and greatly augmented
in the so-called Expansion Laws of 1959. These laws—one national in scope,
the other directed at regions in difficulty—provided loan guarantees, interest subsidies, tax relief, and other benefits to investors. Originally intended as medium-
term measures to get the economy out of recession and relaunch growth, they
were repeatedly prolonged until the late 1970s. More than one-third of gross capital formation in the 1960s benefited from some assistance under the Expansion
Laws. But the efficacy of this aid has been questioned. The total amount of aid
may not have been large enough to increase the rate of investment significantly
(De Brabander 1981; Gilot 1987). Aid was also given unselectively and tended
to favour capital-intensive projects, often by existing firms (Camu 1961; Van den
Broeke 1984; Boelaert 1983).

Until the 1960s state spending on education was relatively low in Belgium.
Ideological conflicts over control of the schools slowed development of the system until the late 1950s, when the conclusion of a 'School Pact' opened the way
for massive, parallel expansion of Catholic, state, and local systems. By the 1970s
Belgium had by European standards become a heavy spender on education. But
these resources were not used very efficiently. The spending increase was concentrated in the secondary schools and paid for compulsory schooling until the
age of 18, for large numbers of students who had to repeat one or more years
and for a proliferation of programmes. Spending on primary and university education has remained low by northern European standards, and vocational education has been the poor stepchild of the expansion. In any case increased spending
on education has been driven only very indirectly, if at all, by considerations of
industrial development.

8.5.5. General Policies Directed at Industrial Efficiency

State support for research and development has been modest by international
standards (Tharakan and Waelbroeck 1988). Before the 1960s the government
gave some assistance to research centres set up at industry initiative, though
these were few in number and relatively small. During the 1960s state spending
increased, both for university research and for direct subsidies to industry, but
its level has remained low relative both to the large European countries and to
small countries such as the Netherlands, Sweden, and Switzerland. Moreover,

the allocation of funds for research and new product development has been criticized for being unselective.

Although Belgium has undertaken relatively little research and development during recent decades, it has probably benefited disproportionately from that done elsewhere (Coe and Helpman 1995). This is because so much of Belgian industry has become foreign-owned: on one estimate 59% of value added in manufacturing in 1990 (Daems and Van de Weyer 1993). Although large multinationals such as General Motors and Siemens have been active in Belgium since the 1920s, the real boom in foreign investment came during the 1960s and early 1970s. This influx was due in large part to Belgium's situation in the nascent European Union but foreign firms were actively recruited by central and local governments and may have been encouraged by the Expansion Laws. If anything, Belgium has tipped the playing field in favour of foreign firms.

Belgium's openness to foreign investment and ownership has certainly had efficiency effects beyond technology transfers. During the 1960s multinationals introduced new management methods, which then passed to domestic firms by example and by movements of managers. Foreign control has also imposed stiffer standards for efficiency: loss-making subsidiaries have probably been closed down faster than domestic firms in similar situations.

8.6. CONCLUSION

At the risk of oversimplification the main features of Belgian industrial policy over the last century might be summarized as follows:

- outside a small core of nationalized industries, the state's role in industry remained quite limited until the 1960s;
- among active policies, the state has preferred general to industry- or firm-specific measures;
- its industry- or firm-specific policies have been primarily reactive;
- among general policies, assistance to industry has been given without much selectivity, either across industries or across firms within industry.

Why until relatively recently has industrial policy been largely non-interventionist? Belgium started the century with a well-developed and confident industry that was heavily oriented to foreign markets. What this industry, and its politically powerful leaders, expected from government was free trade, a stable currency, low taxes, and no measures that would push up costs. In any case business could hardly expect more active policies from a weak state largely preoccupied with non-economic issues. When the state did reluctantly become more involved in industry, from the 1930s, it was because weaknesses began to appear in industrial sectors associated with powerful business interests, interests whose influence was augmented by the growing political power of organized labour. The major increase in government intervention, from the 1960s, arose from the crisis of confidence in traditional industry associated with the demise of the coal industry and with relatively slow economic growth in the 1950s.

The Belgian state has preferred general to selective policies because favouring particular industries or firms would have meant trying to pick winners. Belgium has not had a public administration with the confidence and authority to do this. Talent has not been drawn into public service for several reasons: low wages, the state's lack of authority, and, especially after the Second World War, widespread politicization. The exigencies of coalition government in Belgium have also made it difficult to favour particular industries or firms. There have been too many claimants with political backing. Governments have thus preferred general policies with benefits distributed either first come, first served (*politique de guichet*) or by linguistic, regional, or ideological quotas. Such policies have tended to favour existing interests and to dissipate scale economies or spillovers that might arise from an active industrial policy. But insofar as it is difficult for any government to pick industrial winners, Belgium's reliance on general subsidies may have been less damaging than the use of more interventionist policies.

Despite a preference for general policies, the Belgian state has still been drawn into supporting particular industries or firms. The structure of Belgian politics, with its need for regional and ideological compromises, has made this a costly endeavour, from the 1930s to the 1950s for the coal industry (and agriculture) and in the 1970s and 1980s for the 'national sectors'. That all of these industries were under Belgian ownership suggests the importance of local connections in rent-seeking activity.

These costly interventions have probably done more harm than good. Subsidies and anti-competitive practices slowed industrial redevelopment and made for relatively poor growth performance from the 1930s to 1950s. The turnaround in growth that came in the 1960s owed much to the influx of foreign investment, drawn not so much by the investment subsidies as by labour supply conditions and Belgium's location at the heart of the nascent European Union. The increase in subsidies to the nationalized industries and to the 'national sectors' in the 1970s and early 1980s contributed to the deterioration of the public finances and cast a shadow over future growth.

REFERENCES

BATAILLIE, M. (1989). 'Het Textielplan: ontstaan, werking en evaluatie'. *Economisch en Sociaal Tijdschrift*, 1: 53–80.

BAUDHUIN, F. (1946). *Histoire économique de la Belgique 1914–1939*, 2nd edn. Brussels.

—— (1958). *Histoire économique de la Belgique 1945–1956*. Brussels.

—— (1970). *Histoire économique de la Belgique 1957–1968*. Brussels.

BOEKESTIJN, A. J. (1990). 'The formulation of Dutch Benelux policy', in R. T. Griffiths (ed.), *The Netherlands and the Integration of Europe 1945–1957*, 27–48. Amsterdam.

BOELAERT, R. (1983). 'Het budgettaire beleid 1953–1980'. *Bulletin de documentation du Ministère des Finances*, 7: 5–38.

—— (1993). 'Steun aan ondernemingen en overheidsinstellingen: de steeds maar magerder jaren', in M. Frank *et al.* (eds.), *Histoire des finances publiques en Belgique, la période 1980–1990*, 407–40. Ghent.

BOSMAN, E., and PROOST S., (1981). 'Studie van enkele interventiemechanismen in de energiesector', in *Overheidsinterventies: Effectiviteit en Efficientie*, 46–48. Leuven.

BREES, E. (1906). *Les Régies & les concessions communales en Belgique*. Brussels.

CAMU, A. (1960). 'Essai sur l'évolution économique de la Belgique'. *La Revue Nouvelle*, 32/11: 397–418.

—— (1961). 'Essai sur l'évolution économique de la Belgique-II'. *La Revue Nouvelle*, 33/5: 481–500.

CASSIERS, I., DE VILLÉ, P., and SOLAR, P. (1996). 'Economic growth in postwar Belgium', in N. Crafts and G. Toniolo (eds.), *Economic Growth in Postwar Europe*, 173–209. Cambridge.

COE, D., and HELPMAN, E. (1995). 'International R & D spillovers'. *European Economic Review*, 39: 859–87.

CRAFTS, N. F. R. (1989). 'Revealed comparative advantage in manufacturing, 1899–1950'. *Journal of European Economic History*, 18: 127–37.

DAEMS, H. (1978). *The Holding Company and Corporate Control*. Leyden and Boston.

—— and VAN DE WEYER, P. (1993). *L'Économie belge sous l'influence*. Brussels.

DE BORGER, B. (1993). 'The economic environment and public enterprise behaviour: Belgian railroads, 1950–86'. *Economica*, 60: 443–63.

DE BRABANDER, G. (1981). 'La création d'un état d'abondance', in *L'Industrie en Belgique: Deux siècles d'évolution 1780–1980*, 207–42. Brussels.

—— (1983). *Regionale structuur en werkgelegenheid*. Brussels.

DELMELLE, J. (1981). *Histoire des tramways et vicinaux belges*. Brussels.

DE STAERCKE, J. (1963). 'La Structure de la distribution de l'électricité en Belgique'. *Reflets et perspectives de la vie économique*, 2: 431–40.

DE VYLDER, G. (1992). *Trade Policy and the Search for Textile Markets: The Case of the Benelux and India 1945–1992*. Tilburg.

DRÈZE, J. (1961). 'Quelques réflexions sereines sur l'adaptation de l'industrie belge au marché commun'. *Comptes rendus des travaux de la Société Royale d'Economie Politique de Belgique*, 275: 3–37. Translated and reprinted in A. Jacquemin and A. Sapir (eds.), *The European Internal Market*, 13–32. Oxford, 1989.

DUQUESNE DE LA VINELLE, L. (1963). 'Study of the efficiency of a small nation: Belgium', in E. A. G. Robinson (ed.), *Economic Consequences of the Size of Nations*, 78–92. London.

FORD, R., and SUYKER, W. (1990). 'Industrial subsidies in the OECD economies'. *OECD Economic Studies*, 15: 37–81.

FRANCOTTE, A., and GAIER, C. (1989). *FN 100 ans: Histoire d'une grande entreprise liègeoise 1889–1989*. Brussels.

FROGNIER, A.-P. (1988). 'The mixed nature of Belgian cabinets between majority rule and consociationalism'. *European Journal of Political Research*, 16: 207–28.

GANDOIS, J. (1986). *Mission acier*. Paris-Gembloux.

GILLINGHAM, J. (1991). *Coal, Steel and the Rebirth of Europe, 1919–1955*. Cambridge.

GILOT, A. (1987). 'Les Aides publiques aux entreprises privées: Essai d'évaluation'. *Bureau de Plan, Planning Paper*, DS 713.

Hogg, R. L. (1986). *Structural Rigidities and Policy Inertia in Inter-War Belgium*. Brussels.

Kurgan-van Hentenryk, G. (1978). 'Industriële ontwikkeling', in P. Blok *et al.* (eds.), *Algemene Geschiedenis der Nederlanden*, xiii. 18–28.

—— (1987). 'Le Régime économique de l'industrie électrique belge depuis la fin du XIXe siècle', in F. Cardot (ed.), *1880–1980: Un siècle d'électricité dans le monde*, 119–33. Paris.

—— (1993). 'Le Plan Marshall et le développement économique de la Belgique', in E. Aerts *et al.* (eds.), *Studia Historica Economica: Liber Amicorum Herman Van der Wee*, 157–72. Leuven.

La Porta, R., Lopez-de-Silanes, F., Shleifer, A., and Vishny, R. (1996). 'Law and finance'. *NBER Working Paper*, 5661.

Lijphart, A. (1981). 'Introduction: The Belgian example of cultural coexistence in comparative perspective', in A. Lijphart (ed.), *Conflict and Coexistence in Belgium: The Dynamics of a Culturally Divided Society*, 1–12. Berkeley.

Milward, A. S. (1992). *The European Rescue of the Nation-State*. London.

Moesen, W. (1990). 'The need for performance auditing in the public sector and the best practice frontier'. *Bulletin de documentation du Ministère des Finances*, 4: 274–89.

Mommen, A. (1994). *The Belgian Economy in the Twentieth Century*. London.

Peeters, C. (1983). *Staatssteun en scheepsbouw*. Leiden.

Robert, F., de Donnea, F., Marchard, M., and Tulkens, H. (1983). 'Entreprises et services publics: Évolution institutionnelle générale et dix-neuf études de cas (1950–1980)'. *Bulletin de documentation du Ministère des Finances*, 9: 5–126.

Stevens, F. (1995). 'Vie et mort des sociétés commerciales en Belgique', in M. Moss and P. Jobert (eds.), *Naissance et mort des entreprises en Europe XIXe–XXe siècles*, 3–16. Université de Bourgogne.

Tharakan, P. K. M., and Waelbroeck, J. (1988). 'Has human capital become a scarce factor in Belgium?'. *Cahiers économiques de Bruxelles*, 30/118: 159–79.

Van den Broeke, C. (1984). 'L'Incidence sur l'économie des aides d'expansion économique'. *Bulletin de documentation du Ministère des Finances*, 1: 33–73.

Van den Eeckhout, P. (1996). 'Geschiedenis van het sociaal-economisch beleid', in H. Matthijs and F. Naert (eds.), *Sociaal-economisch beleid*, 27–85. Brussels.

Vandeputte, R. (1985). *Economische geschiedenis van België 1944–1984*. Tielt.

Van der Herten, B., and Van Meerten, M. (1994). 'De spoorlijn Antwerpen-Gent, 1841–1897: De wisselwerking tussen privé-initiatief en overheidsinterventie in de Belgische spoorwegen'. *Revue belge de philologie et d'histoire*, 72: 861–912.

Vanthemsche, G. (1983). 'De Belgische overheid en de kartels tijdens het interbellum: Situering en analyse van de wetgeving op de verplichte kartelvorming'. *Revue belge de philologie et d'histoire*, 61: 851–94.

—— (1987). 'De economische actie van de Belgische Staat tijdens de crisis van de jaren 1930'. *Res Publica*, 29/2: 127–52.

Verhoest, P., Vercruysse, J.-P., and Punie, Y. (1991). *Telecommunicatie en beleid in België 1830–1991: een reconstructie van de politieke besluitvorming vanaf de optische telegraaf tot de oprichting van Belgacom*. Amsterdam.

Vuchelen, J., and Van Impe, W. (1987). *Privatisering van macht naar markt*. Antwerp.

9

Ireland: From Inward to Outward Policies

EOIN O'MALLEY

Economic and Social Research Institute, Dublin

9.1. INTRODUCTION

Under the Act of Union of 1800, all of Ireland was an integral part of the United Kingdom (UK) throughout the nineteenth century and it remained so until the independent Irish Free State (later the Republic of Ireland) was established in the early 1920s. Northern Ireland continued as part of the UK. This chapter deals with the industrial policies of the independent Irish state since 1922. Although there was little scope for Ireland to take independent action on matters of industrial policy prior to that time, it will be useful to start with a few brief remarks about the situation of Irish industry before the 1920s.

Ireland had experienced the beginning of an Industrial Revolution in the late eighteenth century and by the early nineteenth century it had a fairly substantial industrial sector by the standards of many countries at that time. According to the 1821 Census, one-third of the Irish counties, including 6 out of 23 outside the northern province of Ulster, had a greater number of people engaged in manufacturing, trade, or handicraft than in agriculture. In the Belfast area in the north-east, in what is now Northern Ireland, industrial growth continued into the twentieth century in a manner similar to that of large industrial centres in Great Britain. In the rest of Ireland, however, early industrial growth turned into industrial decline during much of the nineteenth century.

The data on industrial output for this period are less than satisfactory, but it is now considered that industrial production may not have declined for Ireland as a whole, and that there may in fact have been some increase between the 1840s and the second decade of the twentieth century. However, with rapid growth occurring in sectors such as linen, shipbuilding, and engineering which were increasingly concentrated in the north-east, there must have been decline in industrial output in the rest of Ireland (Ó Gráda 1994: 309–13). Certainly, industrial employment declined substantially in the rest of Ireland.

As industrial employment outside the north-east declined, while large numbers were leaving agriculture, the total labour force fell. From the 1840s onwards, emigration rose to levels which led to continuous population decline. The labour force of the area which is now the Republic of Ireland dropped from 2.7 million in 1841 to 1.3 million in 1911, which represents a decline from 38% of the size of the British labour force in 1841 to just 7% in 1911 (Crotty 1986: 2). The population of the same area fell from 6.5 million in 1841 to 3.0 million in 1926, while other European countries which had smaller populations in the 1840s—such as Belgium, the Netherlands, and the Nordic countries—doubled or more than doubled their populations in the same period (Kennedy 1994: tab. 1).

Against this background, there developed a nationalist movement which held the view that political integration with Great Britain was the cause of Ireland's economic difficulties, and that political independence would be necessary to generate economic development. As regards industry, it was felt that Irish industries had been disadvantaged by having to compete under free trade with the more advanced industries of Great Britain.[1] While the nationalist movement did not spell out a very explicit agreed economic programme before independence, its thinking on this matter generally seemed to favour a policy of protection against imports in order to regenerate Irish industry (Girvin 1989: ch. 2). And indeed the question of protection did become a major issue in the first few decades of independent Irish industrial policy.

9.2. THE 1920S

When the Irish Free State was established in the early 1920s, it had a very small industrial sector. According to the Census of Industrial Production of 1926, just 56,400 people, or less than 5% of the labour force, were employed in manufacturing. The Census of Population for the same year indicates a higher figure of 9% of the labour force being engaged in manufacturing, but either way these are small percentages. By comparison, about 25% or more of the labour force was engaged in manufacturing in other small European countries such as Denmark, Sweden, Belgium, and the Netherlands at around that time, although the situation in Finland was more comparable to Ireland.

In Ireland, almost half of manufacturing employment and three-quarters of manufacturing gross output was concentrated in the food and drink sectors in the 1920s. Thus other sectors of industry were of little significance for the economy. Industry, having been shaped by a free trade environment, was quite highly export-oriented. In 1929, 45% of industrial output went to export markets—very largely to the UK. In the food sector 56% of output was exported, in drink and tobacco the figure was 38%, and in the rest of industry combined it was 27% (O'Malley 1989: tab. 4.2).

9.2.1. Objectives and Policies

From various statements made by representatives of the national independence movement before independence was attained, it might have been expected that

---

[1] For reviews of possible causes of the failure of industry in most of Ireland in the nineteenth century, see O'Malley (1981) and Ó Gráda (1994: ch. 13).

an early step to be taken by a new Irish government would be the introduction of a protectionist policy to foster industrial development. However, in practice, the governments of the 1920s were cautious about taking this or any other radical step in economic policy. Thus there was a strong element of continuity with the past rather than radical change in the first decade of Irish economic policy under governments formed by the Cumann na nGaedheal party.

These governments concentrated on establishing stable political and economic conditions. They had inherited, and they maintained, the British-based legal structure for business. They sought to keep taxes and public borrowing for capital purposes low, to balance budgets, and to establish confidence in the currency. The post and telecommunications services were retained as part of the public sector, as they had been under the British administration. The governments of the 1920s did take some steps to improve the economic infrastructure, by promoting the merging of private railway companies and by establishing the Electricity Supply Board as a public enterprise responsible for the national electricity supply. But economic policy in the 1920s remained predominantly passive and 'orthodox', with a considerable reliance on free trade and market forces. It was argued that a radical break with free trade policies could endanger the agricultural and food exports which were the key earners of foreign exchange for the economy at that time. And policy in the 1920s looked primarily to growth of agricultural production to stimulate the development of the economy. Within this context, there was rather little in the way of an explicit industrial policy in the 1920s.

The reason for this general approach was partly that it was grounded in orthodox economic theory which was favoured by many civil servants, particularly those in the influential Department of Finance, and by economic advisers. But the political background was also of relevance.

When the the Anglo-Irish treaty, which ended the War of Independence, was signed in 1921 and ratified by the Dáil (the Irish Parliament) in 1922, a substantial minority of the formerly united independence movement rejected the terms of the treaty. There followed a civil war between the anti-treaty group and the pro-treaty government, which ended in victory for the government in 1923. The civil war was quite localized and brief, but it did have lasting effects in creating entrenched political alignments.

The pro-treaty party, Cumann na nGaedheal, which was to remain in government until 1932, came to draw much of its core support from the bigger farmers and from the urban middle class, which was a narrower socio-economic grouping than the broader group of supporters of the formerly united independence movement. Thus the objectives and policies of that party were not necessarily going to be the same as those espoused by the broader nationalist movement before independence. The rather conservative economic policies which were implemented by Cumann na nGaedheal governments can in fact be seen as suiting the interests of its core supporters in the externally-oriented commercial middle class and the large commercial farmers. But apart from this, a tendency towards caution in economic policy was perhaps not surprising in a government which was seeking as a priority to establish stability and normality following an armed conflict. The administrations of the 1920s did not completely rule out the use of protection against imports as a means to encourage industry, without considering the merits of the issue. In fact, there was quite an amount of discussion of this issue within and between government departments, and formal structures were established to assess the merits of protection and to canvass the opinions of industrialists on this matter (Girvin 1989: ch. 2). But given a primary emphasis on the objective of developing export agriculture and the need to keep costs competitive, only a rather limited number of protective tariffs were approved selectively as a result of this process.

It may be concluded that the primary objective of economic policy in the 1920s was to establish stability and to safeguard competitiveness, particularly of the agricultural sector. Within that general context, there was relatively little in the way of an explicit industrial policy. But industrial policy, such as it was, used a limited range of protective tariffs with the objective of increasing employment in certain selected industries.

9.2.2. Effects on Industry

There was a modest increase in industrial employment in the 1920s. Employment in 'transportable goods' industries[2] increased from 61,300 in 1926 to 67,900 in 1929, with a slight decline to 66,500 in 1931 (Kennedy 1971: tab. 2.2). This increase occurred particularly in the newly protected industries. Lyons (1976: 601) says that over a hundred new factories had opened in the protected industries by 1930. And data presented by Girvin (1989: tab. 3.4) indicate that employment in the protected sectors of industry increased by almost 8,000 from the year of introduction of the relevant tariffs up to 1927. This increase occurred mainly in clothing (2,700 jobs), confectionery (1,600 jobs), tobacco (1,400 jobs), and bootmaking (700 jobs). Thus there was a correspondence between the introduction of protection for certain sectors and employment increases in those sectors.

9.3. THE PROTECTIONIST PHASE: 1930S–1950S

Following the general election of 1932, there was a change of government, which brought about significant changes in economic and industrial policy. The new government party, Fianna Fáil, was the party of the anti-treatyites of the 1920s and it was associated with strong nationalist sentiments. Fianna Fáil remained in government for 16 years until 1948.

---

[2] 'Transportable goods' industries are almost the same as total manufacturing, except that they include a few thousand jobs in mining.

9.3.1. Objectives and Policies

In certain respects there was a degree of continuity in economic policy after 1932. For example, parity was maintained between the Irish pound and sterling which ruled out an independent monetary policy, and budgets remained balanced or nearly so under Fianna Fáil (Neary and Ó Gráda 1986). A major change in industrial policy, however, was the introduction of a much stronger and more wideranging policy of protection. In addition, restrictions were introduced on foreign ownership of new manufacturing ventures and a number of new state-owned enterprises were established.

The objective of Fianna Fáil's protectionism was stated to be the development of national self-sufficiency. Thus in 1928, Sean Lemass of Fianna Fáil had said in the Dáil: 'we believe that Ireland can be made a self-contained unit, providing all the necessities of living in adequate quantities for the people residing in the island at the moment and probably for a much larger number' (quoted in Meenan 1970: 319). Whereas the limited experimenting with tariffs in the 1920s might be interpreted as support for 'infant industries' which would have the potential to develop a real competitive advantage over time, this could hardly be said of protectionist policy after 1932 (Ó Gráda 1994: ch. 16). For the policy was applied in a rather indiscriminate fashion and indeed in the 1930s, until 1938, the use of protectionist measures was partly tied up with the 'economic war' with Great Britain. (The 'economic war' began with the Irish government's refusal to transmit the remaining land annuities accruing under the Irish Land Acts to the UK government, and it involved successive impositions of penal tariffs by both governments.) In the application of Irish protectionist measures, there was generally little sign of a longer term concern to have the protected 'infant industries' develop to a competitive maturity (Kennedy, Giblin, and McHugh 1988: chs. 2, 11). Rather, the primary focus was on having more Irish people employed in Ireland producing goods required by the domestic market.

It has been estimated that between 1931 and 1936 the average tariff rose from 9 to 45% (Ryan 1949).[3] The number of products which were subject to tariffs increased more than fourfold. In addition to this, there were numerous new import quotas and other restrictions (Meenan 1970: ch. 5). Of course, a marked increase in protectionism at that time was not peculiar to Ireland, since many countries resorted increasingly to protective measures in response to the impact of the Great Depression. However, such a policy shift in Ireland would probably have occurred in any event, since it reflected clear policy differences between the parties in government before and after 1932. The protectionist policies implemented by Fianna Fáil after 1932 corresponded closely to their earlier statements of policy between 1926 and 1932 (Girvin 1989: ch. 4). Under the Cumann na nGaedheal government, in contrast, Ireland had been relatively slow, by international standards, to introduce more protectionist measures in the early 1930s,

---

[3] Ó Gráda (1994: ch. 16) questions the accuracy of Ryan's estimates, but he does not doubt that there was a marked strengthening of protection.

although it did move in that direction. Thus by later 1931 and early 1932, it was possible to describe Ireland as one of the last predominantly free-trading economies in the world. Some years later, on the other hand, Ireland was one of the most protected economies (Meenan 1970: ch. 5).

The protectionist policy of the 1930s and later was not simply a matter of imposing tariffs and quotas and then passively awaiting developments. Rather the policy has been described as an active 'drive to industrialize'. Thus the Department of Industry and Commerce invited proposals from companies to establish or expand industries. The department became involved in consultations and negotiations with industrialists about matters such as the degree of protection which would be required in order to induce particular investments in industrial expansion. In some cases, further inducements were agreed such as the award of a monopoly of the Irish market to a specific company. And in some cases, the department sought to influence the location of proposed new industries, or it sought to have companies purchase specific material inputs in Ireland by its controls over imports. A state-owned Industrial Credit Company was also established to underwrite share issues by approved industrial companies (Girvin 1989: ch. 4; Ó Gráda 1994: chs. 15, 16).

From the early 1930s, the Control of Manufactures Acts were used to restrict and control the presence of new foreign-owned industries in Ireland. These Acts did not rule out foreign investment, but they could be used to enforce certain criteria before foreign investment would be approved. In general, if foreign companies proposed to produce new products with no Irish competitors, or if they proposed to produce for export, such proposals were favourably considered. Thus in activites in which investments were not forthcoming from Irish enterprises, foreign enterprises could be an acceptable substitute. And in a few industries in which investments were not forthcoming from private enterprise, the state itself established some large public enterprises to further the policy of developing national self-sufficiency; examples were large-scale peat extraction, processing of sugar beet, and the national airline and shipping line. The railways and principal bus services were also nationalized by the early 1950s.

To summarize on objectives and policies after 1932, the stated objective of policy was to develop national self-sufficiency, essentially with a view to widening the range of production so as to increase employment opportunities in Ireland. The major type of policy instrument used was strong protectionist measures, with an active approach to ensuring that these would induce industrial investment and expansion. Less important supplementary instruments were state financial guarantees for some companies and the establishment of some new state enterprises. The recipients or beneficiaries of these policies were a wide range of industries, with priority for Irish-owned ventures.

9.3.2. *Effects on Industry*

Following the introduction of strong protectionist policies, industrial employment (in 'transportable goods', see note 2) increased from 66,500 in 1931 to 103,200 in 1938 (Kennedy, 1971: tab. 2.2).[4] This growth was interrupted by the difficulty of importing fuel and material inputs during the Second World War, but industrial employment stood at 116,300 by 1946 and it then increased further to 148,000 by 1951.

This experience of considerable growth in industrial employment beginning during the international depression of the 1930s was rather unusual among Western European countries. But it corresponds quite well with the contemporary experience of some of the less-developed countries (e.g. Argentina, Brazil, Chile, and Mexico) which were independent at the time and also experienced a process of import-substituting industrialization. By 1951, 15% of total employment in Ireland was in manufacturing. This was distinctly higher than in the 1920s but was still little more than half the level of many Western European countries, although it was comparable to some Latin American countries such as Mexico and Brazil (Furtado 1976: ch. 11).

It seems reasonably clear that the protectionist measures which were used in Ireland were responsible to a significant degree for bringing about the increase in industrial employment. Ó Gráda (1994: tab. 15.9) presents data which show that employment in 'those protected industries which expanded considerably since 1932' increased by almost 35,000 between 1932 and 1939, which accounts for almost the whole increase in industrial employment in that period. Similarly, data presented by Girvin (1989: tab. 4.1) indicate that employment in the protected sectors of industry increased by 51,000 from the year of introduction of the relevant tariffs (which in some cases would be before 1932) up to 1939. Thus industrial employment growth was very much concentrated in the protected sectors, indicating that protection had the intended effect of causing employment growth.

A less desirable trend, however, was the very low rate of growth of labour productivity in industry. In fact, in the period 1926–38, output per worker declined by –0.8% per year for total 'transportable goods', although it increased by a very modest 0.8% per year if brewing and malting are excluded (Kennedy 1971: ch. 2). This strongly suggests that protection allowed a degree of inefficiency and uncompetitiveness to prevail in many of the protected industries, and this impression is strengthened by the export statistics. In 1929, as was noted above, 45% of industrial output was exported, while the figure for industries other than food, drink, and tobacco was 27%. But by 1951, only 16% of industrial output was exported and, if food, drink, and tobacco are excluded, the figure was just 6% for the rest of manufacturing (O'Malley 1989: ch. 4). Thus protection probably fostered growth in industrial employment for a couple of decades, but it did not develop an internationally competitive industrial sector.

The fact that output per worker declined in total transportable goods in 1926–38, while there was a small increase for industries other than brewing and malting, came about because brewing was a particularly important industry which experienced a decline in both output and output per worker in the 1930s. In 1926,

---

[4] These figures probably overstate the rate of growth of employment to some extent, since the Census of Industrial Production increased its coverage in this period. Nevertheless, it is clear that there was substantial expansion in industrial employment at this time; see Daly (1988), Johnson (1988), and Girvin (1989: 108–11).

brewing accounted for 30.6% of total net output of transportable goods, and most of this was accounted for by the Guinness company, a major brewing firm by world standards. Irish brewing was a successful exporting industry at that time, with 70% of its output being exported, mostly to the UK.

Guinness had emerged as the dominant Irish brewer as the growing importance of economies of scale in brewing had brought about a process of increasing concentration into a smaller number of firms during the nineteenth century. In Ireland, this process proceeded to the point where there was one highly dominant firm. But in Great Britain the process of concentration was less extreme, apparently because the market share attainable by individual brewing firms was ultimately limited by their practice of buying up public houses and thus cornering limited markets. Consequently, Guinness was large even by British standards and it had advantages of economies of scale which helped to make it competitive in the British export market. In the 1930s, however, Guinness felt that its export trade was threatened by the climate of protectionism. Although the British did not impose a specific penal duty on imports of Irish beer as part of the 'economic war' of the 1930s, beer was subject to a general 10% import duty imposed in Britain in 1932. Guinness apparently decided that it needed to safeguard its market in Britain by having a brewery there. It opened its first brewery outside Ireland at Park Royal, near London, in 1936, and the subsequent sharp decline in Irish beer production and exports between 1936 and 1938 closely matched the output of the Park Royal brewery (Kennedy 1971: ch. 2).

Against the background of a general failure to develop competitive exporting industries, the phase of protectionist expansion of Irish industry eventually ran into a crisis in the 1950s. There was virtually no further increase in manufacturing employment between 1951 and 1958. Since this occurred while the large agricultural labour force continued to decline in accordance with a long-established trend, the total labour force declined quite rapidly and emigration rose to exceptionally high levels.

The difficulties of the 1950s were basically due to the emergence of a chronic balance of payments constraint. This arose partly from the near exhaustion of the 'easy' stage of import-substituting industrialization, which meant that there was little further replacement of imports by new domestic production. At the same time, imports of goods which had not been replaced by domestic production, including many of the materials and capital goods required to sustain production, had to continue to grow as long as the economy was growing. Thus the cost of imports of goods which had not been substituted by domestic production eventually grew to exceed the cost of all imports before the process of import-substitution began. Since there was a continuing failure to achieve adequate growth of exports, serious balance of trade deficits became inevitable, leading to recurring balance of payments problems and prolonged recession in the 1950s (O'Malley 1989: ch. 4). Arguably, the balance of payments constraint on further growth could have been eased for a time in the 1950s by using the country's external reserves and/or foreign borrowing to finance more expansionary fiscal policies (Kennedy,

Giblin, and McHugh 1988: ch. 3), but ultimately the balance of payments was going to be a major constraint in the absence of more significant export growth.

Thus Ireland in the 1950s experienced a fairly typical conclusion to a process of import-substituting industrialization, in which rather indiscriminate protectionism was the main policy instrument used. Other late-industrializing countries using the same approach commonly ran into a similar problem eventually with a balance of payments constraint on further growth, although many of them went through the sequence rather later than Ireland, since they only acquired the independence necessary to adopt protection in the 1950s or 1960s.

9.4. OUTWARD-LOOKING POLICIES: LATE 1950S TO MID-1980S

In view of the difficulties experienced in Ireland in the 1950s, a number of related and quite fundamental changes in industrial policy were introduced. A more 'outward-looking' approach evolved in the 1950s and the 1960s. This meant that the emphasis shifted to developing industrial exports, that active steps began to be taken to attract foreign enterprises to produce in Ireland for export markets, and that the protectionist measures against imports were gradually dismantled.

9.4.1. The Shift in Objectives

This general change in the strategy for industrial development reflected a growing acceptance of the need to develop industries that would be internationally competitive. Thus international competitiveness became an objective of industrial policy, although the ultimate purpose of this was generally still stated to be creation of employment and reduction of emigration. This view of the objectives of industrial policy—international competitiveness in order to enhance employment—gradually became established and has remained in place up to the 1990s.[5]

A number of factors combined to bring about the change in the orientation of industrial development strategy. To start with, there was an obvious motivation for some sort of policy change arising from the economic crisis of the 1950s, and this motivation was heightened by an awareness of the more favourable situation in other countries. For the 1950s was not generally a period of international recession or slow growth. Thus the existence of a widespread receptiveness to the idea of changes in policy was not surprising. The need for new solutions was also given political urgency by the succession of defeats of outgoing governments in the four general elections from 1948 to 1957.

It was notable that there was a fair degree of consensus among the main political parties about the reorientation of industrial policy, with no great resistance

---

[5] For example, the Department of Industry and Commerce (1990: 15), in setting out the objectives of policy, said: 'The primary objective of industrial policy is to promote the development of a strong internationally competitive industrial and international services sector in Ireland which will make the maximum contribution to employment growth and higher living standards.'

to the change by any of them. This reflected a change of attitude particularly in Fianna Fáil. With the passage of time since the War of Independence and with the decline in importance of the civil war issues, there was a decline in the strength of nationalist feeling in Fianna Fáil which had initially at least partly motivated the adoption of protection and restrictions on foreign investment (O'Malley 1989: ch. 5).

In these circumstances, there was a greater political receptiveness to the orthodox economic advice from economists and public servants in favour of a more outward-looking policy. Besides, the need to develop exports at least was clear from the nature of the crisis of the 1950s, although there was some dis-agreement with the removal of protection. In addition, the new strategy was geared to take advantage of newly emerging opportunities—both to secure more satisfactory export markets for the country's important agricultural sector, and to attract export-oriented foreign direct investment which was a phenomenon that first became significant in the world economy in the 1950s. Apart from some positive attractions of the new policy, from the late 1950s onwards it was in-creasingly felt that there would be some necessity to follow the UK into the EEC or whatever international free trade arrangements might emerge involving the UK, in view of Ireland's overwhelming dependence on the British market for exports.

A final point which should be made about the objectives of policy is that from the 1950s these came to include more specific objectives concerning regional development.

9.4.2. Changes in Policy Measures

The reorientation of industrial policy towards a more outward-looking approach has sometimes been associated with the year 1958, since that was the year of publication of two important policy documents, *Economic Development* and the *Programme for Economic Expansion*; these included re-evaluations of earl-ier economic policies and proposals for future policy directions. However, the actual change in policy was an evolutionary process which took some time.[6] In 1949, the Industrial Development Authority (IDA) was established, initially to review the operation of tariffs and quotas; subsequently, in 1952, it was given the task of seeking to attract foreign industries to Ireland, although this activity was at that time still subject to the restrictions of the Control of Manufactures Acts. In 1952, also, the government established Coras Tráchtála (the Irish Export Board), a promotional and advisory body to assist firms attempting to develop exports.

During the 1950s, by a number of stages, a scheme of financial grants was introduced to support capital investment in new and expanding industries. These grants included a regional policy dimension since higher grant rates were offered

---

[6] Further details on the changes in policy measures which are outlined in this section can be found in O'Malley (1989: ch. 5).

in the less developed regions than elsewhere. The investment grants scheme encouraged the development of export-orientation in industry, since grant-aided firms were required to be internationally competitive and to have favourable growth prospects; in practice this usually meant that only export-oriented firms qualified (McAleese 1971: ch. 2).

Export development was further encouraged by changes in taxation of industrial profits in 1956 and 1958. After these changes, no tax was charged on manufacturing profits earned from increases in exports sales over the 1956 level. This tax relief meant that there was no tax on profits arising from all exports of firms starting up after 1956, including new foreign-owned establishments. New investment by foreign firms in export-oriented industry was further encouraged by the weakening in 1958 and the repeal in 1964 of the Control of Manufactures Acts, leaving no restrictions on foreign firms.

Following the measures outlined above, the main elements of the policy package to promote exports and to encourage foreign direct investment for that purpose were in place by the end of the 1950s. Further changes in the incentives and supports for industry over the next two decades tended to strengthen this general approach, rather than changing it radically. Such later changes in financial supports included the introduction in the 1960s of a grants scheme tailored specifically for small firms, and the introduction of grants to support research & development and training of workers. Also, since the 1970s, firms involved in internationally traded services have been eligible for industrial policy supports.

In the area of tax policy, more favourable depreciation allowances were introduced to reduce the after-tax costs of industrial investment or leasing of capital equipment. The tax relief on export profits remained in place during the 1960s and 1970s. But no new firms were allowed to qualify for this relief since 1981 and it was abolished completely ten years later. Instead, a new low rate of corporation profit tax of only 10% has applied to all industry (not only exporters) and to certain internationally traded services since 1981. A number of observers in the 1970s and early 1980s concluded that the Irish package of tax and grant incentives for investment in industry and in exports particularly was one of the most attractive available in Europe; and they concluded that the efforts to market Ireland as a location for export-oriented foreign industries were also among the most effective (O'Malley 1989: ch. 5).

As regards regional policy, there was some debate in the 1960s about the merits of a more concentrated 'growth centre' policy as opposed to a policy of spatial dispersal. But in effect, a policy of dispersal came to be favoured, most explicitly in the 1970s (Breathnach 1982). The policy was implemented by offering higher grant rates in less developed regions and by building industrial estates for new industries in many locations around the country.

The issue of dismantling protection and returning to free trade was considered in Ireland in the late 1950s, and steps in this direction began in 1963 and 1964 with minor reductions of all tariffs. This was followed in 1965 by the signing of the Anglo-Irish Free Trade Area agreement, which removed the few UK tariffs on Irish manufactured products and the more severe British restrictions on imports of Irish agricultural products and foods. In return, Ireland was to remove protection against imports of British manufactured products by ten annual reductions of 10% each. When Ireland and the UK, together with Denmark, joined the EEC in 1973, Ireland agreed to remove protection against other EEC manufactured products by five annual tariff cuts of 20% each.

To prepare for freer trade, the government set up structures in the 1960s to encourage firms in each industry to specialize more, to consider mergers, and to cooperate in areas such as purchasing materials and marketing—all with a view to improving economies of scale and hence competitiveness. 'Adaptation grants' were also made available to help meet the costs of necessary structural change, and such grants were eventually paid to most of Irish industry.

9.4.3. Industrial Development (1960s–1980s)

Under the new outward-looking strategy, industrial growth picked up considerably in the 1960s and 1970s compared with the 1950s. Whereas manufacturing output grew by just 1.7% per annum in 1951–8, it increased to 6.7% per annum in 1958–73 and 5.1% per annum in 1973–9. The annual rate of growth of manufacturing employment increased from just 0.2% in 1951–8 to 2.4% in 1958–73, and 0.8% in 1973–9.[7] This phase of industrialization was characterized by particularly rapid growth of exports. Whereas just 19% of manufacturing output was exported in 1960 (only marginally higher than the figure of 16% in 1951), this rose to 41% in 1978 and further to 64% by 1988. This trend helped to ease the balance of payments difficulties which had caused major problems in the 1950s, and thus it facilitated overall growth of the economy. In the 1980s, however, unfavourable new aggregate trends emerged, particularly a decline in manufacturing employment by one-fifth between 1979 and 1987, which prompted some significant rethinking on industrial policy.

Even during the 1960s and 1970s, however, Irish industrial performance had a significant weak spot. It was new investment by foreign-owned multinational companies that made the major contribution to the growth of industrial employment, output and exports, while native Irish-owned or indigenous industry did not fare so well. Indigenous industry was apparently not able to take much advantage of the new incentives and opportunities to export, while at the same time it was quite rapidly losing market share to competing imports in the home market as the protectionist measures were dismantled after the mid-1960s.

In this context, there was no employment growth in indigenous industry from the mid-1960s to the end of the 1970s and then in the 1980s its employment fell sharply by 27% in just seven years. It is very likely that by the mid-1980s employment in indigenous industry was lower than at any time since the 1940s. Essentially, what happened was that indigenous industry was just about able

---

[7] The source for these data is the *Census of Industrial Production*.

to maintain its overall employment level while domestic demand was growing sufficiently strongly, in the late 1960s and the 1970s, to compensate for the loss of market share to competing imports. But when domestic demand weakened considerably in the 1980s for a variety of reasons, its employment slumped.[8]

The performance of foreign-owned or overseas industry in Ireland was a good deal more satisfactory. Many highly export-oriented foreign firms were attracted to Ireland, which they saw particularly as a suitable location in which to produce goods for the UK and EEC markets. Compared with other potential European locations, Ireland had exceptionally low taxes on profits, attractive financial grants and generally competitive labour costs. By 1988, foreign firms came to account for 44% of Irish manufacturing employment, 55% of manufacturing output, and 75% of manufacturing exports. However, while employment in foreign-owned manufacturing grew almost continuously in the 1960s and 1970s, it reached a peak at 88,400 in 1980 and then fell to 78,700 by 1987. While this was a distinctly lower rate of decline than in indigenous industry, it still amounted to a decline of 11% over seven consecutive years.

In the 1980s, therefore, there was continuous decline in total industrial employment until 1987, while unemployment was rising from 7% of the labour force in 1980 to almost 18% in 1987, and there was substantial emigration as well. In this context, there was a growing feeling that there was a need for some significant revisions to industrial policy, and indeed quite a number of policy changes were made.

The pattern of regional location of industry became a good deal more even and less centralized between the late 1950s and the mid-1980s. In 1961, 17.0% of total employment in the state as a whole was in manufacturing industry. But the percentage of total employment which was in manufacturing ranged from 27.2% in the East region to just 5.6% in the West region. By 1986, the range was reduced very substantially from a maximum level of 25.0% in the North-East to a minimum level of 16.1% in the West. This was brought about mainly by getting the new incoming foreign industries to go disproportionately to the least industrialized regions, while employment decline in the formerly protected indigenous industries had the greatest negative impact in the regions which initially had the greatest concentrations of industry (Drudy 1991; O'Malley 1994).

9.5. INDUSTRIAL POLICY FROM THE MID-1980S TO THE EARLY 1990S

Beginning in the mid-1980s, a number of changes were made in industrial policy. These did not transform the nature of policy as radically as the switch to comprehensive protectionism in the 1930s or to an outward-looking strategy in the late 1950s and 1960s. Irish industrial development strategy certainly remained

---

[8] See O'Malley (1989: ch. 6) for details on the performance of Irish indigenous industry.

'outward-looking' in the sense outlined earlier. But within the broad parameters of that strategy, there were changes of emphasis and policy instruments which arguably defined the beginning of a distinctive phase of policy.

9.5.1. Shifts in Objectives

The basic or ultimate objective of industrial policy remained as it was, namely, the development of an internationally competitive industrial sector which would make the maximum contribution to employment growth and higher living standards. And policy remained committed to free trade (within the context of EU membership), promotion of exporting or internationally trading industries, and an active approach to attracting foreign direct investment. In these respects there has been no change from the objectives and approach of the 1960s and 1970s. But some of the more specific aims of policy have changed since the early 1980s.

In particular, since the White Paper on *Industrial Policy* (1984), there has been a somewhat increased emphasis in official policy statements on the aim of developing Irish indigenous industry.[9] This arose, not from a rejection of foreign-owned industry, but more from a recognition that there were limits to the benefits that could be expected from foreign investment and that the relatively poor long-term performance of indigenous industry called for a greater focus on addressing that problem. More specifically, policy statements since 1984 have referred to a need for policy towards indigenous industry to be more selective, aiming to develop larger and stronger firms with good prospects for sustained growth in international markets, rather than assisting a great many firms indiscriminately. Policy was intended to become more selective, too, in the sense of concentrating state supports and incentives more on correcting specific areas of disadvantage or weakness which would be common in indigenous firms (but not so common in foreign-owned firms), such as technological capability, export marketing and skills. It was intended to shift expenditures on industrial policy from supporting capital investment towards improving technology and export marketing (*Industrial Policy* 1984: chs. 1, 5; Department of Industry and Commerce 1987: ch. 2).

Another prominent theme in statements of industrial policy objectives after the early 1980s, in a context of mounting concern about the growing public debt at that time, was a strong emphasis on the need to make spending on industrial development more cost-effective so as to obtain better value for money. And a further notable element in statements of policy objectives after the early 1980s was the objective of promoting greater integration of foreign-owned industry into the Irish economy, e.g. through stronger purchasing linkages with Irish industry, rather than simply encouraging more new first-time foreign investment.

---

[9] An increased emphasis on developing indigenous industry had earlier been recommended by the report of the Telesis Consultancy Group (1982) to the National Economic and Social Council, and by the National Economic and Social Council (1982) itself.

9.5.2. Changes in Policy Measures

The introduction of policy changes in pursuit of the objectives mentioned above was in some respects rather hesitant and gradual, and indeed there was some questioning about the real strength of commitment to the objectives. For example, in 1992, the Industrial Policy Review Group (1992: 67) recognized that greater efforts had been undertaken by then to promote indigenous industry, but still considered that there had not been a 'full commitment' to this process. The group called for a more decisive shift in the focus of policy towards developing indigenous industry, and this objective has since been re-emphasized. However, even going back to the mid-1980s, there were quite a number of relevant policy changes, of an incremental rather than a radical nature, introduced over a period of some years.[10]

For example, the Company Development Programme was introduced in 1984. This involved staff of state development agencies with a range of expertise working with selected relatively promising indigenous companies on formulating and implementing strategic development plans. And the National Linkage Programme commenced in 1985 with the aim of building on selected indigenous sub-supply companies which could supply components to the foreign multinational companies; this programme also involves participation by development agency staff with a range of expertise. The role of the state agencies in these programmes is to act as catalysts, sharing opinions, acting as information brokers and making suggestions on how they can assist a company's long-term development through their range of financial supports and services.

After the mid-1980s, too, efforts were made to award capital investment grants more selectively to those firms which would have the best prospects for growth in international markets; furthermore, the award of such grants was increasingly made dependent on firms having prepared overall company development plans. With a view to obtaining better value for state expenditure, the average rate of capital grant was reduced after 1986, performance-related targets were applied as conditions for payment of grants, and there was the beginning of a move towards repayable forms of financial support such as equity financing rather than capital grants. Given these constraints, together with a more selective focusing on relatively promising indigenous firms, the share of the industrial policy budget going to support capital investment declined from 61% in 1985 to 47% in 1992.

In this context, there was a shift in emphasis towards measures other than capital grants. From 1985, a range of new initiatives were introduced to strengthen export marketing capabilities of Irish firms, and the share of the industrial policy budget going to support marketing increased from 11% in 1985 to 17% in 1992. Assistance to improve marketing was redirected from short-term operational support towards developing companies' long-term potential. And this support for marketing was focused more selectively on indigenous firms. Science

---

[10] The relevant policy changes are summarized very briefly here. Further details can be found in official documents such as *Industrial Policy* (1984), and Department of Industry and Commerce (1987, 1990).

and technology policies for industry were also reorganized considerably after the mid-1980s, and new technology policy measures were introduced such as technology acquisition grants and subsidized technology audits of firms. The share of the industrial policy budget going to science and technology measures increased from 11% in 1985 to 21% in 1992. Other new measures since 1986 included management development grants to enhance the management strength of indigenous firms.

These policy changes were accompanied by substantial reorganization of the institutional arrangements for implementing policy. In particular, administrative responsibility for promoting indigenous industry was separated from the task of encouraging foreign direct investment, so as to ensure that there would be a body of state agency staff giving their full attention to the indigenous sector.[11] Another type of initiative since the mid-1980s has been the formulation of sectoral development strategies or plans for a number of selected sectors. The purpose of such strategies was to identify development opportunities, and to help to focus the support of state agencies on building on areas of actual or potential competitive advantage and on correcting identified weaknesses.

9.5.3. Effects of Policies after the Mid-1980s

As was noted above, manufacturing employment in Ireland declined by as much as one-fifth between 1979 and 1987. After that, it grew by 13% in the period 1988–96. An increase in new foreign investment, leading to employment growth in foreign-owned industry after 1987, was a large part of the reason for this recovery. However, there was also a noticeable improvement in Irish indigenous industry. Employment in indigenous manufacturing had declined by 27% between 1980 and 1987, but it declined no further in 1988 and then increased by 7% between 1988 and 1996 (Forfás Employment Survey). This was quite a modest increase but it represented a distinct improvement over previous experience, and it was also a relatively strong performance by international standards, since industrial employment in the European Community and the OECD declined in the same period.

An important aspect of the long-term weakness of indigenous industry had been its failure to make much progress in developing exports. *Census of Industrial Production* (CIP) data show that 26.6% of the output of indigenous manufacturing was exported in 1986, which indicates little or no change from estimates of about 26 or 27% in 1973 and 1976 (O'Malley 1989: ch. 6). However, the CIP data show an increase from 26.6% in 1986 to 33.4% in 1990 and 35.3% in 1993. The value of indigenous manufacturing exports, in current dollar terms,

---

[11] This was done first in 1988 by means of an internal reorganization within the Industrial Development Authority (IDA), which involved the establishment of separate divisions for the promotion of indigenous and overseas industry. Since 1993, there have been separate agencies for these two functions—the Industrial Development Agency of Ireland (or IDA Ireland) for overseas industry, and Forbairt for indigenous industry.

increased by an average of 11.1% per year in 1986–93, compared with an annual average increase of 8.5% for the manufacturing exports of the European Community, also valued in current dollars.[12]

Thus the export performance of Irish indigenous industry after 1986 was relatively strong by European standards and quite unprecedented in indigenous industry's own experience. The employment performance of indigenous industry after 1988 was also better than previous experience and relatively strong by European standards, although there was not very strong employment growth in absolute terms. These improved trends in indigenous industry are probably not sufficiently strong or sufficiently long-established to show that indigenous industry is on a new long-term growth path. But there is at least some indication here that the policies introduced in the 1980s to give a new impetus to the development of a stronger, internationally competitive indigenous sector were meeting with some success.

---

[12] The data on the EC's manufacturing exports are from the OECD's *Historical Statistics*; they include SITC categories 0, 1, and 5–9.

REFERENCES

BREATHNACH, P. (1982). 'The demise of growth-centre policy: The case of the Republic of Ireland', in R. Hudson and J. R. Lewis (eds.), *Regional Planning in Europe*, 35–56. London: Pion.

CROTTY, R. (1986). *Ireland in Crisis: A Study in Capitalist Colonial Undevelopment*. Dingle: Brandon.

DALY, M. E. (1988). 'The employment gains from industrial protection in the Irish Free State during the 1930s: A note', *Irish Economic and Social History*, 15: 71–5.

Department of Industry and Commerce (1987). *Review of Industrial Performance 1986*. Dublin: Stationery Office.

—— (1990). *Review of Industrial Performance 1990*. Dublin: Stationery Office.

DRUDY, P. J. (1991). 'The regional impact of overseas industry', in A. Foley and D. McAleese (eds.), *Overseas Industry in Ireland*, 152–69. Dublin: Gill & Macmillan.

Economic Development (1958). Dublin: Stationery Office.

FURTADO, C. (1976). *Economic Development of Latin America: Historical Background and Contemporary Problems*. Cambridge: Cambridge University Press.

GIRVIN, B. (1989). *Between Two Worlds: Politics and Economy in Independent Ireland*. Dublin: Gill & Macmillan.

Industrial Policy (1984). Government White Paper. Dublin: Stationery Office.

Industrial Policy Review Group (1992). *A Time for Change: Industrial Policy for the 1990s*. Dublin: Stationery Office.

JOHNSON, D. (1988). 'Reply', *Irish Economic and Social History*, 15: 76–80.

KENNEDY, K. A. (1971). *Productivity and Industrial Growth: The Irish Experience*. Oxford: Clarendon Press.

KENNEDY, K. A. (1994). 'The national accounts for Ireland in the 19th and 20th centuries', paper for N. W. Posthumus Institute Seminar on *Comparative Historical National Accounts for Europe in the 19th and 20th Centuries*, University of Groningen.

—— GIBLIN, T., and McHUGH, D. (1988). *The Economic Development of Ireland in the Twentieth Century*. London and New York: Routledge.

LYONS, F. S. L. (1976). *Ireland since the Famine*. London: Fontana.

McALEESE, D. (1971). 'Import demand, protection and the effects of trade liberalisation on the Irish economy'. Ph.D. thesis, Johns Hopkins University.

MEENAN, J. (1970). *The Irish Economy since 1922*. Liverpool: Liverpool University Press.

National Economic and Social Council (1982). *Policies for Industrial Development: Conclusions and Recommendations*. NESC report no. 66. Dublin: NESC.

NEARY, J. P., and Ó GRÁDA, C. (1986). 'Protection, economic war and structural change: The 1930s in Ireland'. Working Paper, University College Dublin, Centre for Economic Research, 40.

Ó GRÁDA, C. (1994). *Ireland: A New Economic History 1780–1939*. Oxford: Clarendon Press.

O'MALLEY, E. (1981). 'The decline of Irish industry in the nineteenth century'. *Economic and Social Review*, 13/1: 21–42.

—— (1989). *Industry and Economic Development: The Challenge for the Latecomer*. Dublin: Gill & Macmillan.

—— (1994). 'The impact of transnational corporations in the Republic of Ireland', in P. Dicken and M. Quevit (eds.), *Transnational Corporations and European Regional Restructuring*, 29–44. Utrecht: Netherlands Geographical Studies, 181.

Programme for Economic Expansion (1958). Dublin: Stationery Office.

RYAN, W. J. L. (1949). 'The nature and effects of protective policy in Ireland'. Ph.D. thesis, University of Dublin.

Telesis Consultancy Group (1982). *A Review of Industrial Policy*. NESC report no. 64. Dublin: NESC.

10

Spain: Industrial Policy under Authoritarian Politics

PEDRO FRAILE BALBÍN
Universidad Carlos III, Madrid
University of Texas, Austin

10.1. INTRODUCTION

In contrast to most cases of Western European post-war industrial development, Spain was the only country to successfully establish a substantial manufacturing sector under a stable political regime of autocracy. Neither the inter-war
Fascism, nor the Mediterranean dictatorships of the post-war period, succeeded
as dictatorial industrial regimes. In the first instance, the Allied victory did away
with the political structure of Fascism, and in the second, the Portuguese and
Greek authoritarian leaders never pursued an industrial policy meant to transform
their countries into leading industrial powers. Only Spain combined authoritarianism with a political ideology of intense and large-scale industrialization. The
nationalist political structure that started to develop at the turn of the century and
served as a frame for the state's economic intervention, became a paradigm of
what political scientists describe as state corporatism. Philippe Schmitter, for example, identifies the Iberian Peninsula as the homeland of the ethos of corporatism, and Howard Wiarda points at the Iberic-Latin historical tradition as an
optimal antecedent for dictatorial state intervention in social and economic life
(Schmitter 1979; Wiarda 1973).

Yet, despite the pervasive control of industry by the Franco regime, the Spanish tradition of state intervention prior to the 1936–9 Civil War was only indirect,
and often limited to the creation of a nationalist environment for business—
especially, through tariff protection—that practically eliminated foreign competition
from domestic industrial markets. This does not mean that the Spanish state did
not assert a strong influence on industry before the Franco era. Quite the contrary,
industrial activity in Spain was progressively cartelized under an umbrella of state
protection. An all-encompassing network of councils, commissions, boards,
chambers, committees, associations, delegations, and consultation groups pervaded
every aspect of national economic life. However, in all the corporatist structure
there lacked any distinctive strategy for industrial growth, and the amount of public resources allocated to industrial encouragement was limited by a fiscal system which in itself was always insufficient for the creation of infrastructure or

the subsidization of manufacturing. Direct public involvement in industry was undertaken on a large scale only after the Franco regime founded the National Institute of Industry (INI) in 1941 in an attempt to break the cartelized structure of specific sectors—especially basic industries—that were blocking industrialization on a grander scale. But even then, most cases of public intervention through state-owned enterprises had a limited scope when compared to other European countries, and ended up, in most cases, supporting specific industrial groups within the private sector. After Franco's death in 1975, the transition to democracy triggered a process of profound transformation of the Spanish economy. In addition to wider reforms, such as the tax system and financial markets, the two main industrial policy goals were to deregulate labour markets and the modernization of public industries inherited from the past. For both of these objectives, a new pressure group—organized labour—would prove to be a formidable obstacle that delayed basic reforms after Spain joined the EEC in 1985.

Following this introduction, Section 10.2 of this chapter surveys the pre-Civil War state intervention in industry, agriculture, and infrastructure in the context of the nationalist economic policies launched at the turn of the century. Section 10.3 outlines the basic instruments and sectors of the Franco regime's industrial policy, and focuses on the Spanish state's increasing intervention in steel, electricity, and coal from tariffs to subsidization, indirect regulation, direct production, and nationalization in the 1980s. This part of the essay describes the capture of the state regulatory agencies by the managers and engineers of the regulated sectors by focusing on the special relations between the industries' associations (UNESID for steel and UNESA for electricity) and the state regulatory agencies. Section 10.4 surveys the changing conditions for state intervention created by the transition from dictatorship to democracy after 1975, and the new role of organized labour in the implementation of industrial policy. The final section compares the extent of state intervention in basic industry in Spain with the rest of Europe. It also analyses the peculiar political nature of the Franco regime as a framework for industrial policy, and the consequences of government action brought about by democracy at the end of the 1970s.

10.2. INDUSTRIAL POLICY BEFORE THE CIVIL WAR

As in the rest of the peripheral countries of Europe, industrial backwardness became one of the main stimuli for government intervention in Spain at the turn of the century, and it was precisely in the strategic sector of shipbuilding that the first industrial encouragement took place. After the destruction of the navy in the Spanish-American War of 1898, the Maritime League—a lobby formed in 1903 by Basque shipbuilders, navigation companies, and steel makers—launched a campaign that eventually gave birth to the 1907 Naval Programme, meant to rebuild the fleet and at the same time encourage domestic steel mills, shipyards, and engineering firms (Harrison 1976), which were further aided by the 1909

Law for the Protection of Maritime Industries and Communications. Other basic sectors also received special treatment. Coal mining, in particular, was considered of strategic importance. A series of corporatist offices under the control of mining interests—the National Coal Consortium (1917), the National Fuel Council (1926), and its offshoot, the Central Sales Office—coordinated an extensive network of state protection: in addition to high tariffs, mandatory use of domestic coal and direct production subsidies were granted to coal producers (Coll 1987). The electric industry was also granted extensive privileges. Despite the presence of economies of scale in production and distribution, and the scarcity of input sources (waterfalls), the state abstained from any effective rate regulation until after the Civil War. In fact, the generous granting of waterfall rights to some companies created a monopolistic regional structure dominated by large banks (most of them from the Basque country) that survives until today. During the first third of the century, the main regional generating and distributing companies, discussed in the second part of this chapter, were formed in the absence of any significant regulation on the part of the state. In 1918, an attempt to control distribution on a national network never materialized, and the role of the state was reduced to a generous policy of concessions and obstacles to foreign investment (Hernández Andreu 1986). In the context of a free rate policy, technical progress and large scale did not translate into drastic reductions of energy prices. Rather, excess capacity, discriminatory rates, and high prices in Spain slowed down the transition from coal to commercial electricity that had contributed in other countries to widespread factory reorganization and manufacturing growth (Antolín 1989).

An extensive sectoral policy of direct subsidies, tax exemptions, and public purchases was also followed in the cement, steel, and chemical sectors (García Delgado 1984). However, the attempts to stimulate manufacturing reached all industrial activities (Castel 1936). The first law for the promotion of general manufacturing is the 1907 Act of Industrial Protection. It established a strict procedure for state purchases of domestic products, and set up the Commission for the Protection of National Production for its implementation. A series of other laws and decrees tried to extend state protection and impose import substitution on every front. In 1917, a law granting special tax, tariff, and credit privileges for the promotion of new industries was enacted. It also provided for the creation of a public Industrial Bank. The Royal Decree of 1924, establishing a New Regime for the Aid of Complementary Enterprises, attempted to encompass every possible area of manufacturing overlooked in the previous legislation. The 1907 Commission for the Protection of National Production was replaced in 1925 by the National Economic Council, and a subsequent series of additional Acts and decrees grew into a thick web of protective legislation and corporatist institutions.

Indeed, manufacturing was not the only field of industrial policy experiments in Spain. A long regenerationist tradition aimed at rescuing rural life from poverty materialized under the new nationalism of the turn of the century in several proposals for agrarian reform. An Agricultural Repopulation Act was passed in 1907, and the Central Council for the Internal Repopulation and Settlement was set up the same year. At least four different plans for the promotion of new agricultural settlements designed to alleviate the endemic unemployment of the landless campesinos in the southern latifundia were proposed by the Central Council between 1911 and 1921 (Monclús and Oyón 1986). Irrigation—a central element in the economic regeneration of nationalist ideology—also became the focus of many plans for state intervention. The Gasset plan of 1902 envisaged the construction of a network of reservoirs, dams, and canals for the irrigation of almost a million and a half hectares. The hydrologic policy became a symbol for state involvement in agricultural reform, and gave place to the more encompassing programmes of Hydrologic Confederations of the 1920s, the Irrigation Works Act (OPER) of 1932, and the 1933 Plan of Hydrological Works that sought a more coordinated use of irrigation-and-electricity water resources in different river basins, and even the whole country (Velarde 1973).

Infrastructure was also the object of state intervention in other areas as well as agriculture. In 1926, a massive highway plan called for the construction of an extensive network of 7,000 kms to be built in four years. In addition to the public support—tax and tariff exemptions and guaranteed minimum profits— that railroad companies (many of them foreign) had received during the initial construction phase in the second half of the previous century, a special Railroad Fund and a Railroad Policy were launched in the 1920s for the modernization and new network construction. The 1924 Railroad Ordinance allowed for higher transportation prices, provided for a good deal of new construction and the replacement of most of the old infrastructure. The railroad network was 'rescued' (Tamames 1980) from private foreign interests by the Franco regime in 1941 with the new state-owned enterprise RENFE.

Despite the relative accomplishment in railroad construction during the 1920s, the public attempts to create infrastructure in Spain were very seldom successful during the first half of the twentieth century. Less than half of the highway mileage projected in 1926 had actually been built in 1930. Lack of fiscal resources and political commitment guaranteed that the irrigation plans and the agrarian repopulation programmes of the beginning of the century would never materialize. Only the Ebro river Hydrologic Confederation enjoyed a relative success during the 1920s, and the settlement programmes were able to settle just a few thousand labourers on a little more than thirty thousand hectares. The more ambitious agrarian reform of 1932, which for the first time entailed a large-scale land redistribution scheme was interrupted by the 1936–9 Civil War and later reversed by the Franco regime.

As in agriculture, direct measures for the encouragement of industry lacked the political commitment and the necessary coordination and selective nature for a carefully designed industrial policy. Inefficiency and corruption plagued every programme, and it is doubtful that intervention served as a clear incentive for the creation of a modern manufacturing sector. For J. L. García Delgado, the policy of direct encouragement 'was no part of the rise of a public sector as found then in many modern economies, but part of the traditional "paternalistic" approach of the Spanish state' (García Delgado 1987). This negative view is also shared by J. Velarde, another expert in the economic nationalism of this period: 'In summary, the outcome was an increase in the economy's degree of monopoly and a stronger rigidity of the production mechanisms' (Velarde 1973).

It is doubtful, however, that efficiency and industrial growth are the only— or even, the best—criteria by which to judge the success of an industrial policy. As becomes apparent in the second part of this chapter, it could be argued that state intervention, whether subsidizing or regulating manufacturing activity, could be to the industrialists' advantage, since in many cases it promotes, as it did in Spain, the elimination of competition. The degree of monopoly and the absence of competition could, alternatively, be a mark of success for government intervention.

Nowhere was this clearer in Spain than in the case of indirect industrial policy. The elimination of foreign competition was achieved through a policy of drastic tariff protection, that, as in most countries, was controlled and stimulated by well-organized industrialists and farmers. Despite the well-known difficulties in measuring tariff levels, all evidence suggests that Spanish customs rates had always been very high during the nineteenth century, even before the end-of-century general protectionism (Prados and Tena 1994). Tariff rates were subsequently increased in 1891, 1906, and 1922, and in 1927, the League of Nations' Preparatory Committee declared Spain the most protected country in the world (League of Nations 1927). Based on Heinrich Liepmann's concept of potential tariff levels, Table 10.1 compares Spanish industrial protection with other European countries for all industries, and for steel and textiles (Carreras 1989).[1]

Regardless of the reasons for the unique intensity of Spanish tariff protection,[2] its effectiveness in isolating domestic industry from international competition is difficult to question. Openness of the Spanish economy consistently declined from the 1880s to the 1940s (Tena 1989, 1992), and industrial growth, which up to the turn of the century had been partially based on international markets,[3] became inward oriented and autarkic in nature (Molinas and Prados 1989).

In any case, Spanish manufacturing output did grow substantially. The intensive treatment of import-substitution industrial policy doubled the country's industrial index during the first third of the century. However, increases in manufacturing output were a general phenomenon in all European economies, including those on the periphery. When analysed in comparison to other countries

---

[1] In the 1920s, the textile sector accounted for almost one-third of all industrial income, and together with steel accounted for almost half of all industrial value added (Carreras 1989).

[2] The height of industrial tariffs in Spain and the rest of Europe during the first third of the century have been analysed in terms of the specific manufacturing sector's geographical concentration, the relative backwardness of the non-industrial sector, the strength of direct (income) taxes, and the degree of parliamentary development in each country (Fraile 1991).

[3] Exports accounted for a significant proportion of output of the two leading sectors—steel and cotton textiles— at the end of the nineteenth century, but progressively declined since (Fraile 1991).

238					*Pedro Fraile Balbín*

TABLE 10.1. *Industrial protectionism in Europe, 1913–1931* (most favourable minimum tariffs as a percentage of the international prices of leading manufacturing exporters, rank in parenthesis)

Country	1913			1931		
	General	Steel	Textiles	General	Steel	Textiles
Poland[a]	79.0(1)	59.0(1)	43.0(2)	43.0(3)	48.4(3)	83.0(3)
Finland	36.4(2)	16.0(6)	26.4(3)	19.1(13)	17.2(12)	39.0(5)
Spain	35.7(3)	36.4(2)	45.0(1)	55.0(2)	56.5(2)	81.5(4)
Romania	22.5(4)	22.7(3)	18.3(6)	40.4(4)	24.3(9)	110.0(2)
Sweden	22.5(4)	16.6(5)	16.6(8)	21.0(11)	13.5(13)	28.8(8)
Bulgaria	18.7(5)	10.7(10)	19.2(5)	70.4(1)	36.0(5)	149.0(1)
Yugoslavia	15.0(6)	14.0(7)	16.8(7)	27.2(8)	31.2(6)	27.7(9)
Austria[b]	14.6(7)	17.0(4)	16.0(9)	21.5(10)	28.4(7)	22.6(11)
Hungary[b]	14.6(7)	17.0(4)	16.0(9)	29.7(6)	67.5(1)	30.4(7)
Czechoslovakia	14.6(7)	17.0(4)	16.0(9)	29.2(7)	38.0(4)	32.4(6)
France	12.9(8)	7.0(12)	21.0(4)	23.6(9)	18.6(11)	21.3(12)
Italy	12.6(9)	11.6(8)	15.6(10)	33.8(5)	21.8(10)	19.6(13)
Belgium	8.7(10)	11.0(9)	12.3(11)	9.2(15)	11.0(15)	14.4(14)
Germany	8.5(11)	6.7(13)	10.0(12)	15.0(14)	12.5(14)	26.0(10)
Switzerland	7.6(12)	8.2(11)	4.7(14)	20.3(12)	24.5(8)	10.4(15)
Holland[c]	5.0(13)	5.0(14)	5.0(13)	8.0(16)	8.0(16)	8.0(16)
GB[d]	0.0(14)	0.0(15)	0.0(15)	0.0(17)	0.0(17)	0.0(17)
AVERAGE	19.34	16.22	17.75	27.43	26.90	41.41

[a] Russia for 1913.
[b] Austria-Hungary for 1913.
[c] Liepmann's highest estimate for Holland (p. 36).
[d] *idem* 36–7 and 131–3.

Source: Liepmann 1938: 383–98.

with similar per capita income levels and less protection, the Spanish case is less than brilliant: excluding the war period, the Italian industrial index grew between two and three times faster than Spain's for the entire half century prior to 1940 (Carreras 1992). While the 1910 ratio between per capita industrial output in other European countries and Spain was 3.5 in the case of Britain, 1.6 in the case of Sweden, and 1.2 in the case of Italy (Prados 1988), the 1930 League of Nations calculations of industrial product per person were 40 dollars for Spain, 50 for Hungary, 80 for Italy, 90 for Austria, 110 for Czechoslovakia, 160 for Sweden, and 190 for Britain (League of Nations 1945). According to these estimates then, Spain's manufacturing during the first thirty years of the century had lost ground not only with respect to the old industrial countries but also to the late comers from the periphery. Taking into account that the relative industrial backwardness came associated with the withdrawal from international markets, the Spanish experience could be described not as a traditional ISI (import-substitution industrialization) process, but rather as an ESDI process, that is, a trend towards export-substitution de-industrialization (Fraile 1991).

10.3. INDUSTRIAL POLICY UNDER DICTATORSHIP: THE FRANCO ERA

Rigid autocracy characterized Spain's politics during the 1940s and 1950s. Within the framework of a stern dictatorship, the Spanish state extended its influence in the economy, and heavy industry and energy became the prime targets. Rapidly declining costs, capital lumpiness, abundant externalities, and strong linkages with other sectors made state intervention in the iron and steel industry, electricity, and coal mining a basic strategy for the new dictatorial regime that emerged victorious from the 1936–9 Civil War. Intervention in these three sectors was proclaimed by the new regime as its 'trilogy of industrialization', and was undertaken with the central purpose of removing the obstacles to output growth in the basic industries. As was mentioned in the previous section, steel, electricity, and coal production were controlled by cartelized oligopolies operating in protected markets since the late nineteenth century. Notably, the INI, Instituto National de Industria (National Institute of Industry), a holding company clearly patterned after Mussolini's IRI, became the state's main intervention and regulation instrument. In addition to regulatory policies of price controls and subsidies to capacity expansion, INI created its own integrated steel mill, Ensidesa, and a series of electric companies, Endesa, Enher, and a large coal mining concern, Hunosa.

During the second post-war period, all Western European countries expanded their interventionist industrial policies, especially through state-owned enterprises. But the peculiar nature of Spain's political system implied three significant differences with respect to the rest of Western Europe. In the first place, the need to rely on supporting coalitions during the uncertain initial stages of the new regime conditioned the dictatorship's industrial policy to a larger extent than in the case of the democratic regimes of other European countries, and this became a permanent feature of the Franco regime even in later stages of its political development. The numerous failed attempts to reform coal production, for example, were always marred by the regime's desire to minimize confrontation in the politically sensitive mining region of Asturias, where organized labour posed a continuous threat to the regime's stability.

In the second place, Spain's industrial backwardness translated into a lack of an ample pool of managerial and engineering skills necessary to carry out the regulatory policies, and this, in turn, gave the technicians and managers of the private oligopolies, which the state policies were supposed to regulate, an advantageous position to control the interventory agencies. Asymmetrical information between the regulator/intervener and regulated/intervened, and a continuous flow of personnel from the industry to the agencies, made the regulatory bureaux progressively fall under the control of private industrialists and their representatives. This became specially evident in the case of steel and electricity, so that to the extent that INI's intervention agencies in other heavy industry sectors were also captured by the interests of the intervened industries, the pre-war cartelized structure of the Spanish basic industry was perpetuated and reinforced, and consequently, the transition to a modern, more open and competitive industrial growth was postponed in Spain.

Finally, the ideological background of the regulators was also a crucial element. Although with declining intensity, the need to industrialize in isolation was felt by most policy-makers in charge of industrial policy. This was specially true during the autarkic two decades that followed the Civil War. But even after the 1957–9 reorientation in the state's strategies, Spanish industry remained heavily protected against foreign competitors. Economic nationalism, therefore, underlay Spain's industrial policy from the late nineteenth century, and particularly for the half a century since the Civil War to EEC membership. Nationalism became one of the main obstacles to real reform in the country's industrial markets: on the one hand, fostering rapid industrial growth—especially in basic industries —was the state's primary economic goal. On the other hand, however, industrialization had to occur in isolation. As opposed to the regime's enthusiasm for industrial growth, the established oligopolies felt reluctant to abandon their comfortable positions in the protected domestic markets. In addition, the new regime's uncertain future and the supply problems created by the World War further inhibited private industrialists from joining the state's plans for industrial expansion, and this confrontation led in many cases—especially in basic industries—to the state's direct intervention through publicly owned enterprises.

10.3.1. A State Intervention in Three Basic Sectors

At the end of the 1936–9 Spanish Civil War, a coalition of nationalist and Fascist bureaucrats undertook a determined industrial policy programme to foster rapid growth in basic industries and energy considered 'strategic' for the purpose of autarky. As was mentioned above, economic isolation had been a goal for industrial and agricultural lobbies for a long time, and a formidable tariff barrier had been erected during the inter-war years. The industrial growth plans of the new regime's bureaucrats, however, were in conflict with the interests of their own political allies, the industrialists, whose protected oligopolies had prospered during the first third of the century (García Delgado 1987). Despite their opposition to the relatively left-wing economic programmes of the Spanish Second Republic (1931–6), industrialists gave but an ambiguous endorsement of the new Fascist industrial strategy. Uncertainty about the viability of the new regime, its precarious international standing, and the threat of state intervention in private industrial matters made industrialists reluctant to support the ambitious industrial programmes of the early Franco regime (Cabrera 1983; Linz 1988; de Miguel 1975; Viver 1978).

The long process of industrial policy initiated under the dictatorship of General Franco can be divided into two distinct periods: from the end of the Civil War in 1939 to the First Development Plan of 1963, and from this date to the end of the dictatorship and the transition to democracy during the late 1970s. Although economic nationalism has always been a strong tendency in industrial policy-making in Spain, it was during the early years of the Franco regime that it completely conditioned the state's economic strategy. Import substitution and tight internal controls were developed in almost all sectors. A Junta Superior de Precios (High Council for the Control of Prices) was set up in 1941 for the purpose of price intervention in almost every market. The Junta was reorganized in 1959, and again in 1973, and has survived until today as yet another instrument of state control (Montes 1993).

Indirect state intervention in industry gained its legal base in the Ley de Ordenación y Defensa de la Industria Nacional (Industrial Regulation and Defence Law) of 1939. It established the requirement of the state's previous permission to enter any industrial activity, erected barriers against foreign investment, and mandated the public sector's purchases to be domestically produced. Another basic law was promulgated the same year: Ley de Protección a las Nuevas Industrias de Interés General (Law for the Protection of the New Public-Interest Industries) which extended subsidies and preferential treatment to public capital for undertaking new industrial activities declared of 'public interest'. But the reluctance of private entrepreneurs mentioned above, made indirect industrial encouragement scarcely effective. Direct intervention made a much stronger impact. Under the leadership of J. A. Suances—a personal friend of General Franco with ample political support—INI assumed the responsibility for reconstruction and industrial expansion over almost a quarter of a century. During its first decade, INI created the nucleus of its enterprises in the basic sectors and energy: Adaro and Encasa (mining, 1942), Endasa (aluminium, 1943), Elcano (shipping, 1943), Endesa and Enher (electricity, 1944 and 1945), Iberia (air transport, 1944), Enasa (vehicles, 1945), Bazán (shipbuilding, 1947), Repesa (oil refining, 1949), and Ensidesa (steel, 1950). By 1959 INI controlled 56 firms in more than twenty industrial sectors (Martín Aceña and Comín 1990).

The second period of industrial policy started when the autarkic industrialization process reached its limits at the end of the 1950s. Inflation, acute balance of payments problems, and a new political team of 'technocrats' put an end to the attempt to industrialize in complete isolation. Although very limited in scope, a series of reforms were enacted during the 1950s, and a Stabilization Plan approved in 1959. A timid liberalization of the rigid previous autarchy translated into more diversified and competitive industrial growth, and into a clear change in the instruments for public intervention in industrial policy. Even though Spain maintained a high level of industrial protection (Gamir 1972), some protective measures against foreign competition were lifted, and foreign investment allowed under certain (restrictive) conditions. Previous entry permits to start industrial firms were abolished, and a new sectoral approach (as opposed to individual firms) was used to identify 'public interest' industrial activities.

Under the new orientation of the 1960s, the strategy of direct public intervention was also altered. INI was detached from its privileged connection to the

Presidency of the Government. Suances resigned in 1963. INI was put under the control of the Ministry of Industry, and its role was redefined as subsidiary to private investment in a context of indicative planning. From that moment INI lost part of its political independence and, in the words of Martín Aceña and Comín, 'became progressively kidnapped by its own enterprises' (Martín Aceña and Comín 1991).

The First Development Plan (1964–7) included the sectoral Acción Concertada (Coordinated Action) plans by which firms and the state reached agreements to increase efficiency and competitiveness through capacity expansion with subsidized loans and special tax treatment. Together with Acción Concertada, the Planes de Reestructuración Sectorial (Sectoral Reorganization Plans) tried to save sectors in crisis by encouraging subsidized mergers to attain economies of scale. With the Planes Especiales (Special Plans) the state tried to inform private sector industrialists of its investment projects in order to dissolve the potential uncertainty created by public intervention.

The implementation of these instruments reached almost every industrial sector in Spain. Between 1964 and 1977 state subsidies were channelled in one way or another to 2,514 firms in electronics, shipbuilding, mining, oil refining, electricity, engineering, steel, chemicals, paper, appliances, cars, dairy products, processed vegetables, pastas, wines, tobacco, and plastics (Buesa and Molero 1988). Finally, when in the 1970s decreasing industrial demand coincided with higher energy costs and the uncertainty of Spain's political transition to democracy, the state launched several Programas de Reconversión Industrial (Programs of Industrial Reconversion) aimed to subsidize capacity, payroll, and costs reductions, and to promote the competitiveness of a sector in crisis. Table 10.2 summarizes the instruments of industrial policy and the sector where they were applied during this second phase of public intervention.

Direct and indirect state intervention reached almost every sector of Spain's industry. However, the principal industrial goal of the Franco regime—to develop a strong nucleus of basic industries—remained almost unchanged until the end. As late as 1989, the three sectors initially intervened in accounted for almost three-quarters of INI's total investment and supplied about half of all steel, electricity, and coal produced in Spain (Martín Aceña and Comín 1991). Yet, their importance is not only quantitative. They also represent two of the basic problems of the Franco regime's industrial policy: the proclivity of the regulatory agencies to fall under the influence of the intervened sector (steel and electricity), and the political weakness of intervention under dictatorship (coal). The rest of this section describes the Spanish state intervention in these three sectors from the end of the Civil War up to the transition to democracy at the end of the 1970s.

10.3.1.1. Iron and Steel   The Spanish steel industry had grown around the iron-ore mining region of Bilbao in the Basque Country and in the coal-mining fields of Asturias, both on the coast of the Bay of Biscay. Protected from

TABLE 10.2. *Instruments and sectors of Spanish industrial policy, 1964–1982*

A. Planes de Acción Concertada (Coordinated Action Plans) 　Integrated steel (1964–73) 　Leather (1964–77) 　Processed vegetables (1964–80) 　Paper (1965–74) 　Bituminous coal (1965–73) 　Iron-ore mining (1967–73) 　Shipbuilding (1967–75) 　Non-integrated steel (1974–81) 　Coal (1974–9) 　Electricity (1975–85) C. Planes de Reestructuración y reconversión (Restructuring and Reconversion Plans) 　Cotton textiles (1969) 　Linen textiles (1973) 　Wool textiles (1975) 　Flour processing (1973) 　Special steel (1980) 　Appliances (1980) 　Zinc (1981) 　Oil refining (1981) 　Electronics (1974) 　Integrated steel (1981) 　Electric engines (1981) 　Copper products (1982) 　Shipbuilding (1982) 　Steel (1982) 　Shoes (1982)	B. Sectores de Interés Preferente (Preferential Interest Sectors) 　Integrated steel (1969) 　Nuclear generators (1972) 　Automobiles (1972) 　Automobile parts (1974) 　Defence industries 　Ethylene/polyethylene (1965) 　Sulphuric/phosphorus acid from 　　domestic pyrites (1973) 　Pharmaceutical products (1976) 　Food processing (1974) 　Gas (1976) 　Electronics (1974) D. Planes Especiales (Special Plans) 　Iron and Steel Programme 　Refrigeration Network 　Electronics Plan (PEIN) 　Cement Plan 　Sectoral R & D plans

Sources: Martín Aceña and Comín 1991: 316; Buesa and Molero 1988: 237–53.

foreign competition, by 1907 the steel industry had organized itself into a well-coordinated cartel, Central Siderúrgica (CS), dominated by the largest firm in the industry, Altos Hornos de Vizcaya (AHV) founded in 1902. During more than three decades CS kept prices high and confronted accusations from other industrial sectors of obstructing Spain's industrial growth by restricting the supply of steel (Fraile 1991). Removal of the obstacles to growth in the steel sector became a major goal of the new political regime that emerged from the Civil War, and plans for an active role in the industry were initiated from the very beginning.

In addition to protection from foreign competition, the bureaucrats of the new regime tried every possible intervention strategy to regulate prices and output in a cartelized industry with rapidly declining average costs (Rowley 1971). They set up a regulatory agency in an attempt to keep prices close to minimum average costs allowing firms in the industry just to break even. They entered the industry as a state-owned enterprise to challenge the cartel's leader by increasing supply and reducing prices. They later tried to subsidize capacity expansion to the socially optimum price and output, through agreements with individual firms in the industry. And finally, when international competition had reduced domestic demand, they nationalized the whole industry and internalized the difference between costs and revenues (Navarro 1988).

Even before the end of the Civil War, plans were devised to control prices and regulate inputs and output, and in December of 1940 the government established the Delegación Oficial del Estado en la Industria Siderúrgica (DOEIS), or State Delegation in the Steel Industry, as a price-regulating agency within the Ministry of Industry. DOEIS's attempts to control orders and input purchases forced steel producers to evade official rules in order to carry on their own production plans, and it also gave place to a very active parallel market in which firms sold as much as 50% of their output. DOEIS disappeared in 1959, but the legal aspects of steel price controls became especially complicated after the government's attempt to harmonize Spain's rate structure with that of the European Coal and Steel Community. In any case, certain price controls—such as authorized or allowed prices—lasted until very recently. Direct intervention in industry had always been one of INI's favourite strategies in the chemical, energy, and iron and steel sectors. Plans for a large-scale integrated steel mill in cooperation with the existing private firms had been considered from the very beginning of INI, but the refusal of the private sector to go along with the government's project prompted INI to build Ensidesa as a fully state-owned enterprise to compete in the domestic market against the cartelized steel oligopoly led by Altos Hornos de Vizcaya (AHV) (INI 1941–58). The refusal of private steel producers to engage in the INI's early plans for steel expansion has produced an abundant amount of literature in recent Spanish economic history. In the immediate post-war period, the scarcity of steel and the cartelized structure of supply produced a remarkable increase in profits for the cartel members. In addition, they did not share the state bureaucrats' optimism about the new regime's political and economic viability (Navarro 1988). Ensidesa fired its first two high furnaces in 1957 and 1958, and became the country's largest steel producer by the mid-1960s. Following orders from the Ministry of Industry, Ensidesa absorbed Uninsa in 1973. A relatively large integrated mill, Uninsa had been formed by the merger of three nineteenth-century steel companies in the northern Asturian coal region. The absorption of Uninsa increased Ensidesa's capacity by more than one million tons and pushed the public share of total production close to 50% (see Table 10.3).

Agreements between the government and private firms for capacity expansion through state subsidies was a central element of the French model of indicative planning. It was adopted in Spain in the Acción Concertada plans (Coordinated Action) from 1964 to 1972, and 1973 to 1977, and resulted in an increase of more than six million tons of new capacity. Expansion through state intervention continued in Spain even after the international crisis of the 1970s had set in. The uncertainty created by domestic political problems—General Franco's death and

TABLE 10.3. *Public sector share of steel production in Spain, 1958–1980*
(figures in 000s of tons)

Year	Total production	Ensidesa	Uninsa	Public share (%)
1958	1.560	80	—	5.1
1959	1.823	287	—	15.8
1960	1.919	417	—	21.7
1961	2.349	641	—	27.4
1962	2.311	648	—	28.1
1963	2.765	685	342	24.7
1964	3.150	681	376	21.6
1965	3.515	650	486	18.4
1966	3.847	803	472	20.8
1967	4.512	1.171	553	25.9
1968	5.083	1.307	563	25.7
1969	5.981	1.727	572	28.8
1970	7.392	2.170	631	29.3
1971	8.025	2.402	760	29.9
1972	9.525	2.856	1.399	29.9
1973	10.808	4.021	—	38.3
1974	10.473	5.187	—	45.2
1975	11.137	5.145	—	46.1
1976	11.002	4.992	—	45.3
1977	11.102	4.980	—	44.8
1978	11.269	4.907	—	43.5
1979	11.269	4.884	—	41.4
1980	12.841	4.866	—	36.5

Sources: Martín Aceña and Comín 1991; UNESID 1973; Ministerio de Industria, Delegación Oficial del Estado en las Industrias Siderúrgicas, *Monografía 1958*; Navarro Arancegui 1989; UNESID 1976.

the transition to democracy—added a further difficulty for restraining expansionary plans. A fourth integrated mill had been projected in the late 1960s in cooperation with AHV, to be constructed on the Mediterranean coast near Barcelona. The first stage of the new plan began in the early 1970s but further expansion projects were abandoned in the following decade. During the 1980s, however, the indebtedness of the leading private steel firm, AHV, to public banks led to its nationalization, so that by the time Spain joined the EEC the whole of the country's integrated steel sector was in public hands.

10.3.1.2. Electricity As was mentioned above, from the beginning of the century the Spanish electric industry was also highly concentrated. A small number of regional companies served most of the country: in Catalonia, the Barcelona Traction (1911) group, linked to AEG and GM. In the rest of Spain, a small number of concerns like Hidroeléctrica Española (1907), and Hidroeléctrica Ibérica (1901) were linked to financial groups from the Basque country. By the eve of the First World War, the sector's basic nucleus was already in place, and in the

1940s seven companies[4] produced half of total output (de la Sierra 1953). Despite attempts to build and bring under public control the distribution grid during the 1920s (Antolín 1994; Núñez 1994), these regional electrical monopolies operated in a basically unregulated market with free rates and private distribution. However, the outcome of the Civil War started a process of tight state control. Rates were frozen until 1953, and a set of controls were implemented to coordinate production and distribution. In 1944 the Ministry of Industry created a corps of Special Technical Delegates to cooperate with the newly organized Unidad Eléctrica SA (UNESA), the industrialists' association, in the task of managing the distributing network to guarantee an adequate level of output (Buesa 1986).

However, as in the case of steel, the supply of electricity became one of the major economic bottlenecks of the new regime's first decade. The dependence on hydraulic generation, and the lack of rain and new private construction were in clear contradiction to the programme of industrial expansion, and led to frequent confrontations and threats of boycotting new construction unless the state rate policy was changed (Muñoz Linares, Gutierrez, and Velarde 1953). The change in pricing policy occurred in 1952. Based on the high marginal cost of the sector's smaller firms (Buesa 1986) a new rate system was approved that allowed for generous annual increases and for the establishment of a supplemental 'factor R' to cover expenses in the firms' fixed costs (del Val 1983), and a new electricity clearing house, Oficina Liquidadora de Energía (OFILE) was established to administer these funds.

But the state's main concern was to expand production, so efforts were channelled to the construction of new thermal facilities that would guarantee output regardless of rain precipitation. Several decrees urged private investors to accelerate construction and the state extended preferential treatment for new projects by classifying most electric companies as Enterprises of National Interest. But the 'lack of private initiative' persuaded policy-makers to pursue a strategy of direct intervention. As in the case of steel, INI was to undertake production of electricity on behalf of the state. One year after starting operations, INI set up the Consejo Técnico de Electricidad (Technical Council of Electricity) as a specialized INI office whose mission was to increase electric output in the short run (Martín Aceña and Comín 1991). The consequence of this strategy was the creation of Empresa Nacional de Electricidad (Endesa) in 1944, and Empresa Nacional Hidroeléctrica de Ribagorzana (Enher) in 1946. Other projects followed, and INI's installed capacity went from 26,000 to 122,000 kw during the second half of the decade. By 1963, the six enterprises owned by INI had an installed capacity of 680,000 kw (hydraulic) and 980,000 kw (thermal).

As Table 10.4 shows, INI's share of output increased from 1% in 1946 to one third in 1970. After some privatizations in 1971, public output of electricity went down to about one sixth of total production. However, the subsidized

---

[4] Iberduero (formerly Hid. Ibérica), Hidroeléctrica Española, Riegos y Fuerza del Ebro, Electra del Viesgo, Energía Eléctrica de Cataluña, Sevillana de Electricidad, and Mengemor.

TABLE 10.4. *INI's output of electricity as a percentage of Spain's total, 1946–1987*

Year	Gwh	%	Year	Gwh	%	Year	Gwh	%
1946	32	1	1960	2,285	12	1974	12,107	15
1947	101	2	1961	3,678	18	1975	12,920	16
1948	122	2	1962	4,453	19	1976	20,671	23
1949	287	5	1963	3,810	15	1977	16,335	17
1950	543	8	1964	5,379	18	1978	16,476	17
1951	411	5	1965	6,850	22	1979	20,416	19
1952	611	7	1966	7,729	21	1980	27,657	25
1953	1,008	10	1967	9,653	24	1981	31,299	28
1954	1,277	13	1968	11,776	26	1982	36,268	33
1955	1,780	15	1969	16,714	32	1983	36,389	31
1956	1,666	12	1970	18,984	33	1984	36,750	31
1957	2,504	17	1971	18,553	30	1985	36,764	29
1958	2,631	16	1972	12,077	18	1986	41,500	32
1959	2,206	13	1973	11,839	16	1987	42,800	32

Source: Martín Aceña and Comín 1991: 647.

expansion of the Acción Concertada plans (*Coordinated Action*) accelerated growth during 1975–85. INI's output tripled during these years and it again accounted for one third of total production at the end of the 1980s.

10.3.1.3. Coal Mining State protection of coal mining is one of the oldest and best known features of Spanish economic history (Coll 1987). Despite high tariffs, subsidies, and preferential public purchases, Spanish coal could not compete in quality and cost with imports and accounted for two-thirds of domestic consumption. The World War restricted supply, and Franco's support to the Axis resulted in a post-war embargo. After the Civil War, nine large enterprises,[5] most of them located around the northern region of Asturias, produced more than half of all output, while more than 300 small producers accounted for the rest (de la Sierra 1953). The New Regime started a policy of domestic output control and expansion. Yet, supply became very inelastic, and although output went up it was not enough to cover total demand and to compensate for the increasing inefficiency and obsolescence of the coal-burning equipment.

The public industrial strategy to avoid supply scarcities, however, was different this time. Despite several studies and explorations of INI's Technical Council for the Fossil Fuels, possibilities to exploit new deposits were almost nil, and efforts were directed to price controls and synthetic fuels.[6] In 1941 the Commission for the Distribution of Coal was created, and since then Spanish coal prices have been directly or indirectly controlled. Minor INI participation

[5] Duro-Felguera, Minero-Metalúrgica de Peñarroya, Hulleras de Turón, Hullera Española, Minero Siderúrgica de Ponferrada, Fábrica de Mieres, Hullera Vasco-Leonesa, Minas de Langreo y Siero, and Carbones Asturianos.

[6] The Empresa Nacional Calvo Sotelo de Combustibles Líquidos y Lubricantes (ENCASO) was established by INI in 1942 to obtain petroleum from bituminous slate (Sudriá 1992).

TABLE 10.5. *Losses of Spanish state-owned enterprises, 1980–1981*
(in millions of pesetas)

Enterprise	Sector	Sales	Exports	Employment	Losses
Hunosa	coal	30,673	—	20,999	20,774
Astilleros Españoles	shipyards	60,383	31,088	17,846	21,702
Astilleros del Noroeste	shipyards	10,025	8,424	5,913	3,646
AIIM	steel	24,562	9,471	4,364	8,890
Seat	autos	116,394	31,624	28,202	25,917
Babcok Wilkox	metal	15,457	5,328	4,301	4,969
Other		30,260	2,418	11,934	10,208

Source: García Fernández 1985: 197.

in coal companies took place during the 1950s (Sudriá 1992), but the subsequent liberalization of the Spanish economy allowed for the importation of oil, and coal lost its importance as a 'strategic' sector. INI's share of total output remained below 10% until the mid-1960s, and it was not until 1967 that INI became directly involved in a large-scale operation of coal production. But this time it was not with the purpose of breaking a monopoly, but rather to save a sector in crisis. INI nationalized eight mining companies[7] and created Hullera del Norte SA (Hunosa) with the purpose of maintaining employment in the Asturian region. Hunosa soon became the largest company in the sector, and since its creation it has accounted for about half of all national production.

Coal nationalization did not solve the sector's basic problems. Spanish annual output per worker at the end of the 1980s was less than half the European average, while the productivity of Hunosa's workers was one-third lower than the Spanish average (Vázquez and del Rosal 1995). In fact, the figures of annual output per person were lower in the public company than in any of the smaller private coal mines (Marrón 1994). The drastic employment and output reduction that took place in other European economies after the initial protectionist reaction to the rise of oil imports—the EEC-10 coal production and employment was more than halved from 1970 to 1990—never happened in Spain. Actually coal production expanded since the 1960s, and employment fell only after the application of the EEC coal directives of 1990 (Vázquez and del Rosal 1995). From 1965, several Acción Concertada (Coordinated Action) plans extended capital subsidies, tax exemptions, and soft loans. In exchange, the mining industry committed itself to several schedules of productivity increases, consolidation, and cost-cutting. The continuous failure of these programmes made coal mining one of the many endemic problems of the Spanish public sector. While public subsidies have kept growing (Marrón 1994), losses in the coal sector are among the largest in all public enterprises (see Table 10.5).

---

[7] Metalúrgica Duro-Felguera, Asturiana Santa Bárbara, Fábrica de Mieres, Hullera Española, Cía. de Carbones, Industrias y Navegación, Industrial Minero Astur, Carbones Asturianos, and Nueva Montaña Quijano.

10.3.2. The Government and Private Interests

The presence of private sector technicians in the regulatory agency DOEIS was common from the beginning of the post-war regulation of the steel industry. Information on input prices, costs, demand conditions, and foreign trade was often obtained directly from producers or from their association, CS. The shift of managers and engineers from private firms to the regulatory agencies continued throughout the post-war period and reached a crucial moment in 1962 when one of them, Gregorio López Bravo, an engineer and manager associated with the leading private firms, was appointed Minister of Industry. From that moment on, a regular stream of steel managers originating in AHV or its subsidiaries became first leaders of the entrepreneurial association and then General Directors in charge of steel regulation or even Ministers. INI was disengaged from the Presidency of the Government and put under the direct control of the Ministry of Industry. The Ministry, in turn, was subdivided into Undersecrctariats (General Directorates) each specialized in individual industrial sectors. The original steel association, CS, was reorganized and renamed UNESID. It included the state-owned Ensidesa, and maintained from then on a close link with the General Directorate for the Steel Industry and the Ministry itself. They shared personnel on a regular basis, and the managers of UNESID doubled as advisers to the General Directorate and the Ministry. From the 1960s to the early 1980s every General Director for the Steel Industry had previously been associated with the private sector's leader, AHV and/or the steel-makers association, UNESID. In 1970 the President of the largest private mill, AHV, became President of the INI, the institution in control of Ensidesa (Interviews 1992).

The capture by private interests of the regulatory bodies, INI, the Ministry, and its General Directorate, put Ensidesa in a peculiar situation. Ensidesa was supposed to be the strongest intervention instrument to challenge AHV's leadership in the industry, yet its position in the market was severely conditioned by two factors. First, once the leader had captured the regulatory agencies, Ensidesa became a clear follower in a relationship in which AHV maximized profits on its residual demand. And second, as a state-owned enterprise, Ensidesa had typical principal–agent problems that made its day-to-day management very difficult to control from Madrid. In particular, Ensidesa's managerial discretion translated into a tendency to maximize output regardless of demand conditions (Interviews 1992), and this translated into a tendency to accumulate a high volume of stocks (relative to the industry's average), and a high proportion of its sales in foreign markets at below-cost prices.[8]

In the electric sector, a series of producers' associations had been very influential from the very beginning of electricity in Spain. The Comisión Permanente Española de Electricidad (Spanish Standing Commission of Electricity) was created in 1912, the Asociación de Productores y Distribuidores de Electricidad

---

[8] For a more detailed account of Ensidesa's stocks and exports as an index of AHV's leadership, see Fraile 1992.

(Association of Producers and Distributors of Electricity) in 1920, and the Cámara Oficial (Official Chamber) in 1929 (Antolín 1994; Núñez 1994). After the Civil War, UNESA played the same role as UNESID did in steel. It was established in 1944 as a corporation led by the largest firm, Iberduero. The government's dependence on information from UNESA was obvious from the beginning, and the flow of personnel from the industrialists' group to the government was as active as in the case of UNESID. The Ministry of Industry's attempts to regulate production, and control distribution by the Comisión de Interconexiones Eléctricas (Commission of Electricity Exchange) were devised and implemented by private management. Based on UNESA's advise, capacity expansion plans assigned INI the thermal generation subsector, and kept the more profitable hydroelectricity in private hands (Buesa 1986). UNESA was also instrumental in the creation of the Oficina Liquidadora de Energía Eléctrica, OFILE (Energy Settlement Office). OFILE and UNESA helped in establishing the rate system of 1953, which included a surcharge (*recargo*), in addition to the price fixed by the tariffs (IBRD 1963). The *recargo* was credited to OFILE and distributed to power companies as contributions to the capital and operating costs of new generating plants. The system of allocating these funds in favour of private (hydraulic) and not public (thermal) plants is just another example of the subsidiary role played by public enterprise in this sector (Fraile 1992).

The main obstacle to the state, however, in controlling the private electric interest, was the lack of vertical integration of the public enterprises. In 1984 the distribution grid was nationalized, and in 1985 the public firm Red Eléctrica de España was established to exploit it in cooperation with the private companies (Martín Aceña and Comín 1991). But until that moment, the grid had been controlled by UNESA and its members with little participation of the Ministry. The government itself stopped several attempts of INI to build high-tension lines, but heavily subsidized new construction by private firms (Buesa 1986). As a result, most output produced in state-owned firms—between 70 and 100% in the early 1960s—was sold to the private grid controlled by UNESA (Buesa 1986; Boyer 1975).

As was mentioned before, the problem of coal mining was different in nature. The flow of imports after 1959, the shift to other energy sources, and the endemic shortcomings of productivity and high costs had all contributed to create the situation described in the previous section, with Hunosa being the heaviest and most long-standing financial burden for INI. The political antagonism to the Franco regime in the Asturian coal basin, and the well-organized labour movement of the miners were always the main threats to the political stability of the regime. The wave of strikes of the 1960s—with Asturias taking the lead of Catalonia and the Basque country in labour conflicts (Pérez and Raposo 1973)— caught the political leaders unprepared to follow the same rationalization programmes in the coal mining industry of other European countries at the time. Instead, wages were increased and employment maintained. The government decided 'to buy social peace . . . in a short-term maximizing strategy consistent with its political survival' (Gónzalez 1988). The coming of democracy and the legalization of unions in the late 1970s reinforced even more the bargaining power of the coal-mining labour. The socialist SOMA-UGT and the communist CCOO established in 1977 the influential Commission of the 16, to oversee not only collective bargaining but the running of HUNOSA as well, and started an active policy of opposition to any attempt on the part of INI to reduce capacity and employment (Madera 1994).

10.4. THE TRANSITION TO DEMOCRACY

The end of the Francoist authoritarian regime started a proccess of profound transformation of the Spanish economy. From the dictator's death in 1975 to the joining of EEC in 1986, the country's fiscal system, labour markets, financial structures, and industrial policy went through a process of convergence with the rest of Western Europe. This journey, however, was far from smooth, and to some extent it is yet unfinished. The shift from a political context of dictatorship to another one of democratic parliamentarism was initially fraught with the opposition of special interests from the old establishment, and the hard demands for higher wages and improved working conditions from the newly legalized trade unions and political parties of the left. Industrial policy under the new circumstances was heavily conditioned by the inheritance of an extremely uncompetitive and fragile productive structure whose transit towards an open market was in itself a menace to the country's delicate political equilibrium at the time.

In order to dismantle the old corporatist industrial structure inherited from the Franco times and make it able to compete in an open European market, a runaway process of wage and price increases had first to be controlled. Thus, fighting inflation became the prime objective of the newly elected policy-makers. As shown in Figure 10.1, the goal of restoring price stability, only partially achieved in the 1990s, was approached in three stages divided by two decisive events: the anti-inflation agreement of 1977 and the joining of EEC in 1985–6 (García Delgado 1990).

The decade of the 1970s brought an unprecedented increase in prices. In order to neutralize the international crisis's effects and avoid domestic political instability,[9] the government followed a compensatory policy of subsidizing energy prices, and wage increases (Fuentes 1990) that gave place to the wage outburst shown in Figure 10.2. In a climate of political emergency, the 1977 Moncloa Agreement (Pactos de la Moncloa) between all political and labour leaders established a negotiated framework for a progressive labour market deregulation and a wage bargaining system based on previous—rather than

[9] From the beginning of the 1970s, the belligerent attitude of the underground labour organizations became a political threat to the dictatorship. The assassination in 1973 of Admiral Carrero Blanco—General Franco's president of the government—and the dictator's ailing health became additional elements that contributed to the political uncertainty of the moment.

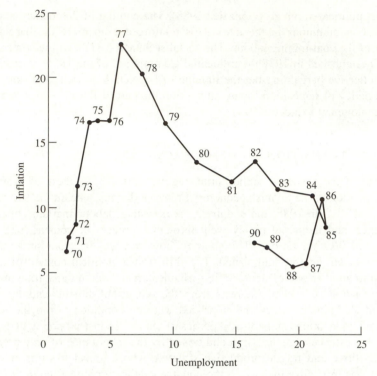

FIG. 10.1. The Phillips curve in Spain, 1970–1990

Source: Contabilidad Nacional de España, Instituto Nacional de Estadística;
Encuesta de Población Activa, Instituto Nacional de Estadística.

expected—inflation rates (Fuentes 1990). There followed a rapid drop in output growth and employment, but by the time of entry into the EEC the inflation rate had been halved from its peak of 1977. From the mid-1980s, EEC membership translated into a new period of rapid capital accumulation and foreign investment, with a rise in employment and rapid output growth.

State intervention in democratic Spain, therefore, has been conditioned by a framework of high inflation and high unemployment. As a consequence, each case of state industrial policy since the anti-inflation Moncloa Pact of 1977 has aimed to control the inflationary tendencies developed during the 1970s, and to bring the Spanish economy in line with the rest of Europe through a policy of reconversion and market deregulation. The fiscal system was reformed, and a new and, for the first time effective, income tax was introduced in 1977. Banking, insurance, pension funds, the stock market, and foreign exchange trading, all were to some extent liberalized in the early 1980s. Controls on foreign investment and domestic prices were softened (although not altogether lifted), and some, albeit timid, measures were taken to promote domestic competition through anti-trust legislation (Serrano and Costas 1989, 1990). From the first

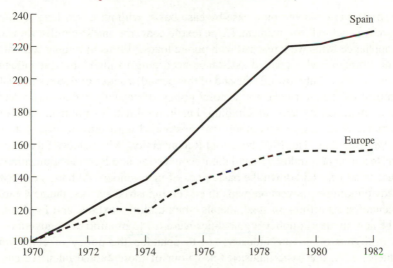

FIG. 10.2. Industrial real wages in Spain and in the rest of Europe, 1970–1982
Source: Maravall 1987: 28. Average of Britain, Belgium, Denmark, France, Germany,
Italy, and the Netherlands.

socialist cabinet of 1982 to the early 1990s four particular areas became of prime importance: labour market liberalization, industrial restructuring, public enterprise reform, and energy modernization (Segura 1990). Labour markets were deregulated to some extent. Despite the rigid legislation that still helps to generate Europe's highest unemployment rate, the coming of democracy brought the trade unions into legality, and provided a somehow more flexible framework of negotiation in industrial relations. During the Franco regime, all labour contracts were of indefinite duration, and its termination implied a very high compensation to labour. As a result, final demand increases translated into higher demand for overtime instead of larger payrolls. In addition, non-wage compensations, as opposed to wages themselves, became the main element in total labour payments. Under the new situation, a series of agreements—such as the Moncloa Pacts of 1977, the National Agreement for Employment (ANE) of 1982 or the Social and Economic Agreement (AES) of 1985—between the labour unions, employers' associations, and the government introduced new forms of labour relations—learning and practice, limited duration, and half-time contracts—that contributed to some extent to a more flexible market. As a consequence, the lag between labour costs and productivity—that had grown 42.2% between 1973 and 1979—started to narrow in 1980 (Malo de Molina 1991).

The attempts to reduce redundant industrial capacity and modernize manufacturing were undertaken in three distinct periods: from the Moncloa Agreements to 1982; during the first socialist cabinet; and from the joining of the EEC in 1986 (Navarro 1990). From the Moncloa Agreement to the first socialist government (1977–82), the first cases of industrial reconversion (Reconversión

Industrial) were enacted on a case-by-case basis, without a real long-term programme of sectoral readjustment. Large textile concerns and steelmills, shipyards,
and appliance firms were rescued with public loans. 'Firms in trouble approached
the government, who granted assistance according to their political influence'
(Navarro 1990). Only towards the end of this period, a series of decrees in 1980–2
attempted to sketch a coherent sectoral policy of capacity reduction in sectors
such as steelmaking and shipbuilding, but in a climate of political and labour
instability, large-scale intervention was postponed until the socialist victory in
the 1982 elections. The 1983 Industrial Reconversion White Book (Libro Blanco
de la Reconversión Industrial) and the Reconversion and Re-industrialization Act
of that same year laid down the basic lines of intervention. Although there were
already ongoing reconversion plans in eleven industrial sectors, the new cabinet
concentrated its efforts on steel, metals, shipbuilding, textiles, and fertilizers.[10]

The new industrial policy's guidelines were (*a*) to minimize the government's
role in favour of private industry; (*b*) to abandon the policy of employment
maintenance in the basic industries in favour of more capital-intensive activities; and (*c*) to concentrate public industrial intervention in small and mid-size
enterprises instead of large industrial projects (Martín Aceña and Comín 1991).
Unemployment, however, became the main obstacle to the new government's
plans, so despite the new industrial policy's austerity intentions, these guidelines
were only partially implemented. The new government applied a policy of regional re-industrialization with the ZURs (Zones of Urgent Re-industrialization)
where the capacity reduction of the old enterprises had created serious labour
redundancy problems, and a system of FPEs (Funds for the Promotion of Employment) provided generous assistance—especially in the form of early retirement—and some retraining, although it was considered insufficient by organized
labour and gave place to serious conflicts, particularly during 1984. After joining
the EEC in 1986, the general improvement in employment and output allowed
for another push ahead with the reconversion plans of steel, metal production,
and naval construction; under the supervision of the European Community
industrial reconversion became a programme of permanent adjustment that has
lasted until now. All in all, the policy of loans, subsidies, tax relief, and labour
compensation accounted for almost one-third of public deficits accumulated during the 1980s,[11] and had a doubtful effect as a re-industrializing instrument.

Political uncertainty and the government's desire to avoid confrontations
with organized labour are considered the main causes of the excessive cost of
the industrial reconversion programmes in democratic Spain (Segura 1990). The
generous schemes of unemployment compensation and early retirements were

[10] Although coal mining was not formally included within the general reconversion plans, many sectoral
schemes—the so-called Program-Contracts, the Plans for the Future, and the Enterprise Plans—were applied during the 1980s and early 1990s with the purpose of reducing capacity and increasing productivity (Marrón 1994).
[11] Annual public deficits grew threefold during the 1980 decade, reaching almost 7% of GDP in 1985 and recovering subsequently until a new downturn in the early 1990s. The accumulated public deficits from 1979 to 1988
were Pts 11.13 billion. One of the experts on the subject (Navarro 1990) estimates the public expenditures on the
reconversion programmes for the same period as Pts 3.66 billion.

aimed to avoid a confrontation *a la británica* with trade unions, especially in public industrial enterprises. The case of coal mining is a good example: labour unions in the northen coal region of Asturias were able to organize political parties, regional authorities, municipalities, and even the Catholic Church into a coalition to reject the reconversion programmes of Hunosa in the 1980s and early 1990s. Employment reductions in public coal mining, originally planned for 6,000 miners, were reduced to 2,000, and the age for early retirement went from 63 in 1991 to 57 in 1992 and 55 in 1993 (Vázquez and del Rosal 1995).

Public enterprises were indeed one of the main instruments of the industrial policy during the first democratic governments in the 1970s. Despite being one of General Franco's most symbolic institutions, nobody suggested INI's dismantling under the new democratic regime. Quite the contrary, INI was regarded as a powerful potential instrument to intervene in the basic industries in which it was specialized. INI became the central piece in the government's policy of labour appeasement launched in the late 1970s. It served as an enterprise hospital for a large number of private firms in trouble. Between 1976 and 1983 more than twenty large industrial enterprises—most of them in the engineering, metallurgy, naval construction, and capital goods sectors—were acquired by INI. In addition to their big financial losses, they brought to the public sector an obsolete overcapacity and a very low level of productivity (Martín Aceña and Comín 1991).

The INI's financial troubles grew with its size. To the nationalization of un-profitable industries were added the already heavy losses of the public steel-mills (Ensidesa) and coal mines (Hunosa). Thus, a programme of downsizing and reorganization was started in the mid-1980s. INI was divided into different sub-holding companies along sectoral lines. Petrochemical industries were ceded to another controlling institution, and a number of activities were progressively privatized or simply closed down. INI's size has since diminished, and eventually INI itself disappeared in June 1995, but the problem of the basic sectors it controlled—notably coal and steel—continue to be a heavy burden on the Spanish public finances.

10.5. THE POLITICAL FRAMEWORK OF INDUSTRIAL POLICY: SPAIN IN THE EUROPEAN CONTEXT

10.5.1. The Extent of Government Intervention

State intervention in industrial markets was a common feature of almost all European countries after the Second World War. Some governments, as in the case of Italy, had undertaken policies of direct intervention prior to the Great Depression, but it was after the war that an industrial policy of massive subsidies and state-owned enterprises became the pattern in Europe. This was particularly true in the case of basic industries. Almost all European economies followed a similar trend of direct state involvement. The French steel industry—including Usinor and Sacilor—was progressively nationalized at the end of the 1970s and early 1980s (Goudima 1980). In Belgium, the growing state intervention of the 1950s resulted in the control of Cockerill, Sidmar, Hainaut Sambre, and TMP in the early 1980s (Goudima 1980). Britain nationalized the steel sector under the post-war Labour government, and although the Conservatives returned it to private hands in the 1950s, they continued an active policy of direct intervention. Steel was again nationalized by the Labour government of Harold Wilson in 1967 when the fourteen largest private companies merged into the state owned British Steel Corporation (Kelf-Cohen 1969), and was again privatized by the Conservatives between 1988 and 1989. In Germany, direct state intervention has always been relatively unimportant. The state controls Peine Saltzgitter, but private combines such as Thyssen, Klöckner, Krupp, Mannesmann, Hoesch, and Saartahl account for most steel output. Nevertheless, a series of direct and indirect subsidies—for example, the bailing out of Krupp in 1967—have always been in place (Howell *et al*. 1988). The Austrian steel sector was nationalized after the Second World War. The Italian state has intervened in steel since the 1880s. The IRI founded Finsider in 1937, and its subsidiary Italsider (ILVA since 1988) created the large-scale coastal mills in the South (Hogan 1991). In Finland, the government has owned Outokumpu Oy since 1932, and in 1960 it created the country's largest steel concern, Rautaruukki Oy. Norway's only integrated mill, Norsk Jernwerk, is also government owned. The Swedish public-sector-owned Norbottens Jarneverk (NJA) merged with the other two principal steel producers—Stora-Koppargarg and Granges—into Svensk Staal Aktiebolag (SSAB) in 1977, extending state ownership to most of the industry (Howell *et al*. 1988). As shown in Table 10.6, by the end of the 1970s the state had a pervasive influence as a direct steel producer. With the exception of Germany and Denmark, all European governments had become major steel producers, especially in the integrated subsector of the industry.

The state involvement in coal dates back to the nineteenth century in most European economies. Before the wave of the post-Second World War nationalizations, most European countries had set up councils and specialized administrative groups to regulate and control coal production. In some cases—like the German state with the Hibernia company or Saargruben AG—the state became a direct entrepreneur. The government of the Netherlands had also been in coal mining before the First World War (Lister 1960), and the French and British coal mines were nationalized in the post-Second World War period. As Table 10.7 shows, the state increased its ownership in almost every country.

The case of electricity was not very different. The post-war nationalizations —France in 1946, Britain in 1947—started a trend towards a more direct control of electricity generation and its distribution (Frost 1991; BEA 1949). Given the nature of the electric industry as a network activity, and its implications for market competition, control and operation of the grid became a prime objective of public policy. Table 10.8 shows the degree of state ownership and indirect

TABLE 10.6. *Public sector share of steel output in Western Europe, 1978*

Country	Total output (Mt) (A)	State-controlled output (Mt) (B)	B/A %
Ireland	0.1	0.1	100.0
Austria	4.3	4.3	100.0
Portugal	0.6	0.6	100.0
Great Britain	20.3	16.0	78.8
Norway	0.8	0.6	75.0
France	22.8	15.8	69.3
Finland	2.3	1.5	65.2
Sweden	4.3	2.5	58.1
Italy	24.3	13.9	57.2
Spain	11.3	4.4	40.0
Belgium/Luxembourg	17.4	6.0	34.5
Netherlands	5.6	1.8	30.5
Germany	41.2	4.5	9.6
Denmark	0.9	0.0	0.0
EEC	132.5	58.14	43.9
Western Europe	156.2	72.00	46.1

Source: Goudima 1980: 54.

TABLE 10.7. *Public sector share of coal output in Western Europe, 1960*

Country	Total output (Mt) (A)	State-controlled output (Mt) (B)	B/A %
ECSC			
Germany	131.8	21.6	16
France	55.3	54.3	98
Belgium	30.0	—	—
Netherlands	11.9	7.5	63
Italy	1.1	0.9	94
Britain	225.1	225.1	100
Spain (1960)	14.5	0.5	4
Spain (1970)	10.3	5.4	52

Source: Lister 1960: 165; Martín Aceña and Comín 1991: 674.

participation in both generation and distribution in Western Europe during the post-war nationalization period.

10.5.2. *The Political Context*

The Spanish case of direct state intervention in steel, electricity, and coal was not, therefore, an exception. In fact, most other European governments had a larger

TABLE 10.8. *Public sector share of electricity output in Western Europe as a percentage of total production (P) and distribution (D), 1953*

Country	State enterprises		Mixed enterprises		Private enterprises		Total output (10^6 kwh)
	P	D	P	D	P	D	
Germany	40	52	54	42	6	6	57,750
Austria	90	93	—	—	10	7	8,764
Belgium	7	19	—	14	93	67	9,806
France	81	86	10	—	9	14	41,531
Greece	16	16	—	—	84	84	1,141
Ireland	100	100	—	—	—	—	1,235
Italy	10	10	30	—	60	90	32,618
Netherlands	100	100	—	—	—	—	9,104
Portugal	—	—	51	7	49	93	1,354
Norway	50	51	—	—	50	49	19,620
Sweden	46	25	—	—	54	75	22,434
Switzerland	53	62	9	7	38	31	13,465
Britain	100	100	—	—	—	—	74,100
Spain (1963)	6	—	9	—	85	100	25,959

Sources: OEEC 1957: 14; Martín Aceña and Comín 1991: 188.

role in production than the Spanish public sector.[12] What made Spanish industrial policy different was not the degree of state intervention, but rather the institutional context in which it took place. In the immediate post-war period, Spain was the only peripheral country in Western Europe to pursue a policy of intense industrialization through direct public intervention in heavy industries. Neither Portugal, Ireland, nor Greece placed such emphasis on steel, energy, chemicals, and engineering as a basis for growth as INI did in Spain. However, the endowment of regulatory resources—accumulated human capital in the field of management and engineering—was heavily conditioned by the country's general backwardness.

As shown in Table 10.9, the percentage of technical and professional workers per total active population in Spain as late as 1970 was only higher than that in

[12] The overall weight of government-owned enterprises in Spanish industry was also relatively small. Both as a percentage of occupied non-agrarian labor (L) and as a percentage of gross capital formation (K) the Spanish figures are rather modest:

	L	K		L	K
Italy	23.7	49.0	Belgium	7.0	14.0
France	11.5	28.6	Spain	6.1	13.7
Britain	7.9	26.3	Netherlands	10.0	6.8
Austria	18.7	20.9	Portugal	0.0	0.0
Ireland	10.0	16.0	Greece	0.0	0.0
Germany	10.4	13.8	AVERAGE	9.5	17.2

Source: Myro Sánchez 1985: 84–8.

TABLE 10.9. *Technical and professional workers as a percentage of total active population, 1970*

	Percentage		Percentage
Sweden	18.9	Belgium	11.1
Netherlands	13.3	Germany	9.8
Norway	12.3	Ireland	9.1
Denmark	12.2	Italy	7.3
Switzerland	12.1	Greece	5.7
Finland	11.9	Spain	5.5
France	11.4	Turkey	3.7
Great Britain	11.1	Portugal	3.6

Source: ILO 1990: 628–94.

Turkey and Portugal.[13] Although this is not perhaps the best indicator for the availability of the managerial and engineering skills necessary for industrial regulation, it is close enough to suggest the dilemma faced by the interventionist bureaucrats of the new Spanish regime. On the one hand, they regarded rapid growth of heavy industries as essential for national survival. And on the other, their intervention plans depended on the expertise of precisely those that were the managers and engineers in the intervened sector. With a scarce and inelastic supply of skills, the urge for rapid industrial growth made the demand for skilled personnel also very inelastic, and gave directors and technicians of private basic industries an advantageous position as sellers of their regulatory expertise to the public sector. Hence, the managers and engineers of the regulated oligopolies found from the very beginning of the post-war intervention easy access to the positions of control in the regulatory agencies, and this facilitated the rapid process of capture analysed before.

Capture was also made easier in the Spanish case by the very nature of the political system. The regime imposed on Spain by General Franco was a peculiar combination of Fascism and autochthonous authoritarian nationalism, that for decades has intrigued the analysts of political systems (García Delgado 1987). But the differential notes that separated the Franco regime from the rest of Europe was its dictatorial nature and the emphasis its policy-makers placed on economic autarky. The harsh autocracy that emerged from the Spanish Civil War progressively became a relatively permissive authoritarian regime after the late 1950s. But, for the first twenty years, General Franco's political system provided a very rigid dictatorial framework for state intervention of the economy, which heavily conditioned the new regime's industrial policy.

State intervention under dictatorship, however, presents special characteristics worth noting. Two opposing views of the relationship between despotism

---

[13] In addition to the country's general condition of backwardness, the 1936–9 Civil War resulted in a substantial exodus of intellectuals, scientists, technicians, and professionals that went into exile with the takeover of the Franco regime (López García 1991).

and economic growth regard dictators either as 'technocratic' or 'kleptocratic' (Alesina *et al.* 1992). The first is a well-established tradition in the field of political economy. It takes dictatorship as the optimum path to insulate political elites from interest group pressures, and therefore to achieve the necessary independence in establishing an active growth-fostering industrial policy (Haggard 1990), and to take on the necessary short-term sacrifices difficult to attain through an open and democratic voting process (Rao 1984). This view, however, assumes that, in addition to the insulating effect that protects dictators from rent-seeking lobbying groups, the dictatorship itself wants to assume the necessary short-term costs associated with the promotion of long-term growth (Przeworski and Limongi 1993). The second view, on the contrary, considers despots not necessarily as enlightened, altruistic, and benevolent reformers. Rather, dictators are constrained by specific circumstances, incentives, and preferences within which they try to maximize their own utility with little regard for society. In summary, 'history suggests that dictators come in two types, one whose personal objectives often conflict with growth promotion and another whose interests dictate a preocupation with economic development. The theory that determines which kind of dictatorship will prevail is presently missing' (Barro 1994).

In any case, the historical moment in which a dictatorship takes place seems to play an important role.[14] Most evidence in favour of the positive relation between dictatorship and growth has been associated with the experience of the new Asian industrial countries in which nationalism and prestige may have played an important role in the dictators' intentions (Przeworski and Limongi 1993), and where a relatively even income and wealth distribution may have had the double effect of fostering political and social stability conducive to investment and growth (Alesina and Perotti 1993), while at the same time precluding collective rent-seeking action by private interest groups (Bardhan 1993).

The prospects for long-term stability for a pro-Axis despot, however, were quite different at the end of the Second World War, and during the long post-war period that followed. For dictatorships that seized power through revolutionary means, such as Franco's coalition of nationalist forces that emerged victorious from the Spanish Civil War, uncertainty about the very survival and viability of the new regime must have implied a time preference biased in favour of the present and at the expense of the future. It is not surprising, then, that strategies for immediate political stability took precedence over long-run considerations, even if they implied inefficiencies in the allocation of resources that compromised future economic growth. The hypothesis of the dictator's priority for stability at the expense of growth has found ample support. Brough and Kimenyi suggest that stability is the crucial variable that conditions most dictators' economic strategies (Brough and Kimenyi 1986), and Mancur Olson (1991) stresses the importance for the dictator of credibility about his own survival, so that an insecure

---

[14] For a review of the quantitative comparative studies on the impact of dictatorship (or democracy) on economic growth see e.g. Przeworski and Limongi (1993) and Maravall (1995).

autocrat may be tempted to default in all of his commitments in exchange for stability. The dictator's short-term constraints and time preferences are conditioned by his need of support from the existing coalitions. In comparison with the wider support generated by democratic systems, the dictator usually relies on groups that already have some degree of power, so that the dictator's political support tends to be based on smaller coalitions than in the case of democracies. This has at least two economic consequences for the initial economic strategies of the dictator. In the first place, as Gordon Tullock has noted, potential participants in the new regime have an incentive to free-ride: the probability of the new order's failure is high, yet if it succeeds they can share the benefits (Tullock 1974). In the second place, in comparison to democratic systems, the dictatorship's supporting coalitions are in a particularly advantageous position to extract rents from the public sector and ultimately to control its economic strategy (Cao-García 1983).

In the case of industrial policy, a dictatorial regime's need to secure short-term stability implies a relative (with respect to a democracy) willingness to give up independence in exchange for support. If the dictatorship is assumed to make rational decisions based on its utility function, and it has a trade-off between stability and the size of the supporting coalition, then it is logical to assume that for each size of the coalition supporting a government's industrial policy, the democratic case shows higher levels of stability in comparison to a dictator. On the assumption that smaller coalitions of industrialists have an advantage over larger ones in their objective of turning the interventory policies in their favour, it is also plausible to assume that the independence of the public sector's policies—and consequently its efficiency—is greater under democracy. In summary, if intervention is meant to resolve market failures—such as monopolistic situations—whose solution involves stimulating competition either through regulation or direct participation with state-owned enterprises, democracies are more likely to succeed in their industrial policies.

In the case of heavy industries, the Spanish state relied on a smaller coalition of industrialists than the democratic regimes of other Western European countries. The need for support, in turn, could have generated a lower level of independence and a greater probability of capture of the state policy by industrial cliques (Fanjul 1987; Fuentes 1988; González 1979; Maravall 1995). These hypotheses imply that, as a result of dictatorship, industrial policy in Spain had a tendency to be less efficient than in the democratic post-war regimes. In addition, the conditions of backwardness and scarcity of human capital described above would have only worsened this outcome, as they accentuated the public sector's dependence on the coalition of industrialists to implement the regulatory policies. But equally important, the precondition of isolation of the Franco industrial policy-makers implied a serious constraint for the success of their regulatory plans. The 'anti-capitalist' approach to industrialization of the early Franco regime was not unique to Spain. The French Resistance and the early post-war projects for reconstruction blamed the capitalists' 'lack of initiative' for the crisis of the 1930s. This argument was implicit in many of the European industrialization plans of the post-war era (and in the pre-war, in the case of Italy), and contributed to create a wide consensus about the need for state intervention in the planning and controlling of industry in modern post-war Europe (Lieberman 1977, 1981). European planning and state intervention, however, was always conceived in a relatively open European economy based on international cooperation (Milward 1984). In contrast, the Spanish authorities implemented a rigid system of import substitution that, although partially justifiable until the end of the 1940s by the war conditions and the anti-Franco boycott, became superfluous in the following decade, and yet remained in place almost intact until the Spanish entry into the EEC in the 1980s, despite the timid liberalization of the 1960s.

The Spanish transition towards democracy that started in 1975 with General Franco's death had profound consequences for the institutional framework of industrial policy. Instead of an abrupt break with the past, the transition towards democracy in Spain became a paradigm of agreement and negotiation. During the late 1970s and early 1980s politics took precedence over economics in order to guarantee a smooth and gradual dismantling of the dictatorship without risking stability. This strategy, however, imposed a heavy toll on the Spanish economy. As J. M. Maravall has pointed out (Maravall 1995), the arrival of a new democracy—especially if it stems from the gradual evolution, rather than the defeat, of a dictatorship—increases societal expectations that diminish the new regime's ability to adopt unpopular austerity policies. Similarly, Robert J. Barro's empirical work suggests that starting from a situation of harsh dictatorship and low per capita income, loosening the dictator's power may be growth enhancing due to the limitations of government power. But a further increase in political rights from a situation of higher income may, on the contrary, intensify the concern with income redistribution and short-term consumption (Barro 1994).

The labour unions' political prestige and legitimacy, greatly enhanced by their decisive contribution to the dictatorship's undermining, proved to be formidable obstacles in implementing the reforms that had been postponed during the early 1970s in Spain, especially labour markets' flexibility and public industry downsizing. The evolution of Spain's industrial policy during its first decade of democracy seems, therefore, to follow the classical pattern (de Schweinitz 1959; Huntington 1968) of national income redistribution in favour of labour, and all-out immediate consumption at the expense of investment. In this way, organized labour acquired a new protagonism as yet another powerful pressure group for influencing the direction of industrial policy. As was mentioned before, organized labour's influence as a pressure group was especially strong in the sectoral reconversion plans that—as in coal mining and steel making—required a deep restructuring and capacity reduction. Economic reforms and a more realistic industrial policy had to be postponed. Overcoming the inertia of the long dictatorship required profound reforms in what Maravall (1995) calls the 'intellectual map of economic policy'. Not before the failure of the Labour strategy in England in the late 1970s, and the first Mitterrand policies in France in the early 1980s, a new generation of post-Keynesian Spanish economists (paradoxically, within the Socialist government's political cadres) was able to implement the long overdue reforms and a more rational industrial policy.

REFERENCES

ALESINA, A. *et al.* (1992). 'Political instability and economic growth'. Working Paper no. 4173, National Bureau of Economic Research. Cambridge, Mass.

—— and PEROTTI, R. (1993). 'Income distribution, political instability, and investment', Working Paper no. 4486, National Bureau of Economic Research. Cambridge, Mass.

ANTOLÍN, F. (1989). 'Electricity and economic growth: A view from Spain', paper given at the Second World Congress of Cliometrics, 24–27 June, Universidad de Cantabria, Santander, Spain.

—— (1994). 'Iniciativa privada y política pública en el desarrollo de la industria eléctrica en España', Universidad Internacional Menéndez Pelayo, Santander, Spain. Seminar 'Empresas y Empresarios en la Historia de España', 1–5 Aug.

BARDHAN, P. (1993). 'Symposium on democracy and development'. *Journal of Economic Perspectives*, 3.

BARRO, R. J. (1994). 'Democracy and growth', Working Paper no. 4909, National Bureau of Economic Research. Cambridge, Mass.

BEA (British Electric Authority) (1949). *First Report and Accounts, August 1947–March 1949*. London.

BOYER, M. (1975). 'La empresa pública en la estrategia industrial española: El INI'. *Información Comercial Española*, Apr.

BROUGH, W. T., and KIMENYI, M. S. (1986). 'On the inefficient extraction of rents by dictators'. *Public Choice*, 48: 37–48.

BUESA, M. (1986). 'Política industrial y desarrollo del sector eléctrico en España (1940–1963)'. *Información Comercial Española*, June.

—— and MOLERO, J. (1988). *Estructura industrial de España*. Mexico.

CABRERA, M. (1983). *La patronal ante la Segunda República: Organizaciones y estrategia*. Madrid.

CAO-GARCÍA, R. (1983). *Explorations toward on Economic Theory of Political Systems*. Lanham, Md.

CARRERAS, A. (1989). 'La industria', in Albert Carreras *et al.* (eds.), *Estadísticas Históricas de España. Siglos XIX y XX*. Madrid.

—— (1992). 'La producción industrial en el muy largo plazo: Una comparación entre España e Italia, 1861–1980', in L. Prados de la Escosura and V. Zamagni (eds.), *El desarrolo económico en la Europa del Sur*. Madrid.

CASTEL GONZÁLEZ AMEZÚA, J. (1936). *Legislación protectora de la producción nacional*. Madrid.

COLL, S. (with C. SUDRIÁ) (1987). *El carbón en España, 1770–1961: Una historia económica*. Madrid.

FANJUL, O. (1987). 'Política Industrial, Competencia y Crecimiento (1960–1980)', in F. Maravall (ed.), *Economía y Política Industrial en España*. Madrid.

FRAILE, P. (1991). *Industrialización y grupos de presión: La economía política de la protección en España, 1900–1950*. Madrid.

—— (1992). 'Interés Público y Captura del Estado: La Empresa Pública Siderúrgica en España, 1941–1981'. *Fundación Empresa Pública, Documento de Trabajo no. 9203*. Madrid.

FROST, R. L. (1991). *Alternating Currents: Nationalized Power in France 1946–1970*. Ithaca, NY and London.

FUENTES QUINTANA, E. (1988). 'Tres decenios de la economía española en perspectiva', in José Luis García Delgado (ed.), *España, economía*. Madrid.

GAMIR, L. (1972). 'El proteccionismo arancelario en la España actual'. *Información Comercial Española*, Mar.

GARCÍA DELGADO, J. L. (1983). 'Prosperidad y Crisis en la Industria Española entre 1914 y 1922: Una Reconsideración', in Gonzalo Anes *et al.* (eds.), *Historia económica y pensamiento social*. Madrid.

—— (1984). 'La industrialización española en el primer tercio del siglo XX', in Ramón Menéndez Pidal (ed.), *Historia de España: Los Comienzos del Siglo XX*, Vol. xxxvii. Madrid.

—— (1987). 'La industrialización y el desarrollo económico de España durante el franquismo', in J. Nadal, A. Carreras, and C. Sudriá (eds.), *La economía española en el siglo XX: Una perspectiva histórica*. Barcelona: Ariel.

—— (1990). 'Claves de unos años decisivos', in J. L. García Delgado (ed.), *Economía española de la transición a la democracia, 1973–1986*. Madrid.

—— (1992). 'Economic nationalism and state intervention, 1900–1930', in Nicolás Sánchez-Albornoz (ed.), *The Economic Modernization of Spain, 1830–1930*. New York.

GARCÍA FERNÁNDEZ, J. (1985). 'Política empresarial pública: Tiempos de capitulación (1974-V. 1984)'. *Información Comercial Española*, Feb.

GONZÁLEZ, M. J. (1979). *La Economía Política del Franquismo (1940–1970): Dirigismo, Mercado y Planificación*. Madrid.

—— (1988). 'Mineria, siderurgia y empresa pública en Asturias: El siglo XX', in Emiliano Fernández de Pinedo and José Luis Hernández Marco (eds.), *La industrialización del Norte de España (Estado de la cuestión)*. Barcelona.

GOUDIMA, C. (1980). *L'Industrie sidérurgique dans le monde*, Collection 'Analyses de secteurs', 2e trimestre, Dafsa-Analyse.

HAGGARD, S. (1990). *Pathways from Periphery: The Politics of Growth in Newly Industrializing Countries*. Ithaca, NY.

HARRISON, J. (1976). 'El coste de oportunidad del Programa Naval español de 1907: ¿pantanos o acorazados?', *Hacienda Pública Española*, 38.

HERNÁNDEZ ANDREU, J. (1986). *España y la crisis de 1929*. Madrid.

HOGAN, W. T. (1991). *Global Steel in the 1990s: Growth or Decline*. Lexington, Mass.

HOWELL, T. R., NOELLERT, W. A., KREIER, G. J., and WOLLF, A. W. (1988). *Steel and the State: Government Intervention and Steel's Structural Crisis*. Boulder, Colo.

HUNTINGTON, S. P. (1968). *Political Order in Changing Societies*. New Haven.

IBRD (International Bank for Reconstruction and Development) (1963). *The Economic Development of Spain: Report of a Mission of the International Bank for Reconstruction and Development at the Request of the Government of Spain*. Baltimore.

ILO (International Labor Office) (1990). *Yearbook of Labor Statistics (Retrospective Edition 1945–1970)*. Geneva.

INI (1941–58). *Memorias anuales del Instituto Nacional de Industria*.

Interviews (1992). Interviews with managers, engineers, and bureaucrats of the INI, Ministry of Industry, and UNESID conducted during 1992.

KELF-COHEN, R. (1969). *Twenty Years of Nationalization: The British Experience*. London.

League of Nations (1927). *Tariff Level Indices (International Economic Conference)*, ii. *Economic and Financial*. Geneva: Publications of the League of Nations.

—— Economic (1945). *Industrialization and Foreign Trade*, ii. *Economic and Financial*. Geneva.

LIEBERMAN, S. (1977), *The Growth of European Mixed Economies 1945–1970: A Concise Study of the Economic Evolution of Six Countries*. New York.

—— (1981). 'The ideologial foundations of Western European planning'. *Journal of European Economic History*, 10/2.

LIEPMANN, HEINRICH (1938). *Tariff Levels and the Economic Unity of Europe*. London.

LINZ, J. J. (1988). 'Política e intereses a lo largo de un siglo en España, 1880–1980', in M. Pérez Yruela and S. Giner (eds.), *El corporativismo en España*. Barcelona.

LISTER, L. (1960). *Europe's Coal and Steel Community: An Experiment in Economic Union*. New York.

LÓPEZ GARCÍA, S. (1991). 'La organización de la investigación científica y técnica tras la Guerra Civil (Contrastes y similitudes con los logros de las primeras décadas del siglo XX)', Encuentro de Historia Económica, UIMP, Valencia.

MADERA, J. R. (1994). 'La Minería de la Hulla Asturiana en el Período 1967–1980', in Juan A. Vázquez and Germán Ojeda (eds.), *Historia de la Economía Asturiana*. Madrid.

MALO DE MOLINA, J. L. (1991). 'Mercado de trabajo: empleo y salarios. Distorsiones y ajustes', in José Luis García Delgado (ed.), *España, economía*. Madrid.

MARAVALL, FERNANDO (1987). *Economía y política industrial en España*. Madrid: Pirámide.

MARAVALL, JOSÉ MARIA (1995). *Los resultados de la democracia*. Madrid.

MARRÓN JAQUETE, J. L. (1994). 'La Reconversión Minera (La Minería Asturiana del carbón en el Umbral de Siglo XXI)', in Juan A. Vázquez and Germán Ojeda (eds.), *Historia de la Economía Asturiana*. Madrid.

MARTIN ACEÑA, P., and COMÍN, F. (1990). 'Industrial Planning in Spain under the Franco Regime (1945–1958)', in Erik Aerts and Alan S. Milward (eds.), *Economic Planning in the Post-1945 Period*. Session B-4. Proceedings. Tenth International Economic History Congress. Leuven.

—— —— (1991). *INI: 50 años de industrialización en España*. Madrid.

MIGUEL, A. DE (1975). *Sociología del franquismo: Análisis ideológico de los ministros del Régimen*. Madrid.

—— and LINZ, J. J. (1966). *Los empresarios ante el poder público (el liderazgo y los grupos de interés en el empresariado español)*. Madrid.

MILWARD, A. S. (1984). *The Reconstruction of Western Europe, 1945–1951*. London.

MOLINAS, C., and PRADOS, L. (1989). 'Was Spain different? Spanish historical backwardness revisited'. *Explorations in Economic History*, 26/4.

MONCLÚS, F. J., and OYÓN, J. L. (1986). 'De la colonización interior a la colonización integral (1900–1936): Génesis y destino de una reforma agraria técnica', in Ramón Garrabou *et al.* (eds.), *Historia agraria de la España contemporánea*, iii. *El fin de la agricultura tradicional (1900–1960)*. Barcelona.

MONTES FERNÁNDEZ, J. (1993). 'La regulación de los precios en España'. *Información Comercial Española*, 723.

MUÑOZ LINARES, C., GUTIERREZ BARQUÍN, M., and VELARDE FUERTES, J. (1953/4). 'Monopolio y tarifas eléctricas', in FET–JONS (ed.), *Notas sobre política económica española*. Madrid.

MYRO SÁNCHEZ, R. (1985). 'Empresa Pública', in Juan Manuel Prado (ed.), *Enciclopedia Práctica de Economía*. Barcelona.

—— (1990). 'La evolución de la economía española a través de sus principales magnitudes agregadas', in José Luis García Delgado (ed.), *España, economía*. Madrid.

NAVARRO ARANCEGUI, M. (1988). 'La política de reconversión en España: El caso de la siderurgia'. Doctoral thesis. Department of Economics, Deusto University, Bilbao.

—— (1989). *Crisis y reconversion de la siderurgia española, 1978–1988*. Madrid.

—— (1990). *La política de reconversión: Un balance crítico*. Madrid.

NÚÑEZ ROMERO-BALMAS, G. (1994). 'Cien años de evolución en el sector eléctrico en España', in G. Núñez and L. Segreto (eds.), *Introducción a la Historia de la Empresa en España*. Madrid.

OEEC (1957). *Electricity Rates: Administrative Regulations Concerning the Supply of Electricity*. EL (56)4. Paris.

OLSON, M. (1991). 'Autocracy, democracy and prosperity', in R. J. Zeckhauser (ed.), *Strategy and Choice*. Cambridge, Mass.

PÉREZ MANRIQUE, A., and RAPOSO SANTOS, J. M. (1973). *Situacioón actual y perspectivas de desarrollo de Asturias*, Vol. ii. Madrid.

PRADOS DE LA ESCOSURA, L. (1988). *De imperio a nación: Crecimiento y atraso económico en España 1780–1930*. Madrid.

—— and TENA, A. (1994). 'Protectionism in Spain, 1869–1930', in P. Lindert, J. V. Nye, and J. Chevet (eds.), *Political Economy of Protectionism and Commerce: Eighteenth–Twentienth Centuries*. Proceedings of the Eleventh International Economic History Congress, Universitá Bocconi, Milan.

PRZEWORSKI, A., and LIMONGI, F. (1993). 'Political regimes and economic growth'. *Journal of Economic Perspectives*, 3.

RAO, V. (1984). 'Democracy and economic development'. *Studies in Comparative International Development*, 4.

ROWLEY, C. K. (1971). *Steel and Public Policy*. London: McGraw-Hill.

SCHMITTER, P. C. (1979). 'Still the century of corporatism?', in P. C. Schmitter and G. Lehmbruch (eds.), *Trends Toward Corporatist Intermediation*. London.

SCHWEINITZ, K. DE (1959). 'Industrialization, labor controls and democracy'. *Economic Development and Cultural Change*, 7.

SEGURA, J. (1990). 'Del primer Gobierno socialista a la integración en la CEE: 1983–1985', in José Luis García Delgado (ed.), *Economía española de la transición a la democracia, 1973–1986*. Madrid.

SERRANO SANZ, J. M., and COSTAS COMESAÑA, A. (1989). 'La reforma institucional de la economía española: Impulsos y resistencias'. *Revista de Economía*, 1.

—— —— (1990). 'La reforma del marco institucional', in José Luis García Delgado (ed.), *Economía española de la transición a la democracia, 1973–1986*. Madrid.

SIERRA, F. DE LA (1953). *La concentración económica de las industrias básicas españolas*. Madrid.

SUDRIÁ, C. (1992). 'El Instituto Nacional de Industria en el sector de la Minería: Orígenes y evolución', Fundación Empresa Pública, Documento de Trabajo 9202, Madrid.

TAMAMES, R. (1980). *Estructura Económica de España*, 13th edn. Madrid.

TENA, A. (1989). 'El comercio internacional', in Albert Carreras *et al.* (eds.), *Estadísticas Históricas de España: Siglos XIX y XX*. Madrid.

—— (1992). 'Protección y competitividad en España e Italia, 1890–1960', in Leandro Prados de la Escosura and Vera Zamagni (eds.), *El desarrolo económico en la Europa del Sur: España e Italia en perpectiva histórica*. Madrid.

TULLOCK, G. (1974). *The Social Dilemma*. Fairfax, Va.

UNESID (1973). *La Acción Concertada en la siderurgia española: Análisis y resultados*. Madrid.

—— (1976). *Estadísticas siderúrgicas*. Madrid.

United Nations Industrial Development Organization (1969). 'Iron and steel industry', Monograph no. 5, Vienna.

United Nations, Economic Commission for Europe (1968). *World Demand and Steel Demand in Developing Countries*. New York.

VAL, A. DEL (1983). 'Las tarifas eléctricas'. *Información Comercial Española*, Nov.

VÁZQUEZ, J. A., and DEL ROSAL, I. (1995). 'The effects and policy responses to pit closures in Asturias'. Unpublished manuscript, Universities of Sheffield, Barcelona and Oviedo.

VELARDE FUERTES, J. (1973). *Política Económica de la Dictadura*. Madrid.

VIVER PI-SUNYER, C. (1978). *El personal político de Franco, 1936–1945*. Barcelona.

WIARDA, H. J. (1973). 'Toward a framework for the study of political change in the Iberic-Latin tradition: The corporative model'. *World Politics*, 25/2.

11

Portugal: Industrialization and Backwardness

JOÃO CONFRARIA

Universidade Católica Portuguesa, Lisboa

11.1. INTRODUCTION

By the end of the nineteenth century Portugal was one of the poorest countries in Europe. One century later, the position is similar (excluding Eastern Europe), even if for most of the period after 1950 the income gap with Western European countries has decreased. During the same period industrialization was often considered a necessary condition for sustainable economic growth. Accepting this position, it is possible to suggest two basic constraints for Portuguese growth. First, it was difficult to build a domestic consensus for industrialization policies; the issue was settled only by the middle of this century. Second, the small dimension of the domestic market was a powerful constraint on some industrialization strategies, for instance, those based on import substitution. Actually, import-substitution policies were pursued until the late 1950s, as a result of domestic political processes and, also, of wider constraints related to international trade conditions. Later, following participation in the movements for European economic integration, export promotion became increasingly accepted. Meanwhile, the role of the state in fostering industrialization became particularly obvious after 1926. Since then, the policy framework has almost always led to state intervention not only in areas such as human resources and infrastructures but also in firms' investment and, less often, pricing decisions.

In this chapter, after a brief descriptive overview of economic growth in Section 11.2, main industrial policies are surveyed in Sections 11.3 to 11.6 according to four periods: the end of constitutional monarchy and the First Republic; the *Estado Novo*, as the political system set up in 1933 was known; the period of political and economic instability from 1974 to 1985; and finally, from 1986 onwards, after membership of the European Community. In Section 11.7 the possible effects of industrial policies on economic growth are briefly discussed and some concluding remarks are presented in Section 11.8.

11.2. PORTUGUESE GROWTH AND INDUSTRIALIZATION: AN OVERVIEW

From the mid-nineteenth century to the late twentieth century, it is possible to consider three main periods concerning the constitutional framework of economic activity in Portugal. The first one, ending in 1926–33, began with the Constitution of 1822, later followed by *Carta Constitucional* (1826) and by the Constitution of 1838. They laid the foundations of liberal forms of economic organization, as well as parliamentary democracy, even if with some exceptions, including a civil war from 1828 to 1834, between liberals and the supporters of absolute monarchy. They included the progressive elimination of restrictions on ownership of land, beginning with the reforms of Mouzinho da Silveira in 1832 and almost totally accomplished by 1863 (the exception being land belonging to Casa de Bragança, the royal house), the end of corporatist restrictions on entry into many industries, the confiscation of Church property, and the abolition of slavery, in 1869. The triumph of the Republicans in 1910, ending the monarchy, did not imply fundamental changes in these areas (Constitution of 1911).

In the second period, after the military coup of 1926, the Constitution of 1933 set the framework for a nationalist/authoritarian regime, the *Estado Novo*, deeply influenced by the political and economic thinking of Oliveira Salazar, who was to remain prime minister until 1968.[1] Concerning economic organization, the constitution set the foundations of corporatist institutions that were to be developed in the following decades according to areas of economic activity and regions and integrated in a 'pyramidal' form of organization.[2]

After the fall of *Estado Novo* in 1974, the new Constitution of 1976 was deeply influenced by socialist principles, concerning economic issues. However, it has been argued that it was set within a framework consistent with a 'mixed' economy, giving an important role to the private sector, despite the strong influence of the state as owner of productive assets. Several reforms enacted in the 1980s reinforced this interpretation, eliminating previous restrictions concerning the disposal and management of state-owned firms (Franco and Martins 1993).

Evidence about Portuguese economic growth during the first half of the twentieth century is scarce and not always consistent. Some estimates of GNP (for instance, Nunes, Mata, and Valério 1989; Lains and Reis 1991, for some comments) suggest that the economy grew from the late 1850s to 1900 at around 2% a year, but stagnated, or even declined, during the first 25 years of the twentieth century. However, accepting the lower bounds of the index of industrial production computed by Reis (1993), industry grew around 24% between 1890 and 1900 and 30% from 1900 to 1913.[3] Confusingly enough, census data

---

[1] There is some contention about the 'nature' of *Estado Novo*. It has been considered by some as a Fascist regime, notwithstanding the enormous differences, both in style and in substance, between Portugal and Fascist Italy. Lucena (1979) further suggests that from 1968 to 1974 the regime evolved from Fascism without a Fascist movement to some form of corporatism without Fascism.

[2] In practice there were differences among industries concerning the hierarchies of corporative organizations. The pyramidal form was probably more common in traditional industries, most of them located north of Lisboa; owners and managers of large firms in new industries, many of them in the Lisboa area, had probably direct access to government members and senior public servants (Makler 1979). There are some doubts about the effectiveness of corporative organizations in fostering cooperative behaviour among its members as well as about their real influence on government policy.

[3] Similar inconsistencies arise from an agricultural production index suggested by Lains (1995). The problem becomes quite obvious using the above-mentioned estimates to explain changes in an index of GNP at constant prices by the evolution of industrial and agricultural production (IP and AP). The results show either negative or not significant relationships for the periods 1890–1900 and 1900–1913 (t-statistics in parentheses):

TABLE 11.1. *Registered companies* (sociedades)

	1940		1960		1980[a]	
	Number	Statutory equity (10^3 contos)	Number	Statutory equity (10^3 contos)	Number	Statutory equity (10^3 contos)
Agriculture and fishing	1%	2%	2%	3%	2%	2%
Mining	1%	2%	1%	2%	0%	2%
Manufacturing	30%	35%	31%	35%	23%	40%
Construction	1%	1%	1%	1%	6%	3%
Electricity, water, and gas	0%	10%	0%	23%	0%	10%
Wholesale and retail trade	56%	24%	49%	13%	53%	22%
Transport and communications	3%	4%	3%	5%	8%	9%
Banking and insurance	1%	17%	1%	15%	1%	11%
Other services	6%	5%	13%	3%	8%	2%
TOTAL	100%	100%	100%	100%	100%	100%
TOTAL (number and value)	12,121	2,963	26,949	19,151	61,334	271,683

[a] Data include *sociedades* and state-owned firms with the legal status of *empresa pública*.

Source: *Estatísticas das Sociedades*, several issues, Instituto Nacional de Estatística.

suggest a decline in industrial employment between 1911 and 1930 but labour force surveys (Marques 1978) point to strong growth of manufacturing employment during the 1920s. By 1940 it was clear that some industrialization process had been going on. Manufacturing accounted for 15% of employment, up from 13% ten years before, and manufacturing companies accounted for a larger share of the total number of companies and total equity in the economy (Table 11.1).

$$1890-1900: \text{GNP} = 100,62 - 0,31 \text{ IP} + 0,91 \text{ AP } (R^2 = 0,47)$$
$$(-1,08) \quad (1,94)$$
$$1900-1913: \text{GNP} = 531,06 - 0,15 \text{ IP} - 1,95 \text{ AP } (R^2 = 0,64)$$
$$(-2,09) \quad (-3,60)$$

Other estimates of GNP (Marques and Esteves 1994) yield similar results for the same periods:

$$1890-1900: \text{GNP} = 79,80 + 0,48 \text{ IP} - 0,27 \text{ AP } (R^2 = 0,60)$$
$$(1,93) \quad (-0,66)$$
$$1900-1913: \text{GNP} = 776,26 - 0,26 \text{ IP} - 3,39 \text{ AP } (R^2 = 0,72)$$
$$(-2,38) \quad (-4,24)$$

It should be noted that the indexes of agricultural and industrial production are, basically, value added indexes, as the authors have assumed that the relationships between value added and production remained stable along the period under consideration.

TABLE 11.2. *Average annual growth rates of the capital stock* (%)

	1953–60	1960–70	1970–80	1980–7
Total[a]	4.2	6.4	5.4	2.9
Industry[b]	7.7	8.9	5.6	3.3

[a] 1977 prices.
[b] 1963 prices.
Source: Neves 1994.

Since then, growth proceeded smoothly until 1973 (perhaps with the exception of the period 1939–45); from 1967 to 1973 the economy grew at around 8% a year. However, in the following decade, average growth rate was around 2%, recovering, from 1986 to 1993, to a rate slightly above 3%. During this period, economic structure changed. From the 1930s to the late 1960s, industrialization and rapid growth of services provided the main impetus to economic growth: the share of manufacturing in employment increased to 26% in 1970 and the share of services from 25 to 33%. Since then, growth of services and the decline of agricultural production have been the main features of structural change in production. The share of services in employment increased to more than 50% in 1990, the share of manufacturing remained roughly stable and agriculture accounted for 10% of employment. By 1960 Portuguese GDP was around 33–35% of the EEC and OECD averages (US dollars, at current exchange rates). The income gap decreased from 1950 to 1973, remained stable (on average) in 1974–85 and decreased since then, being around 47–50% in 1993 (Neves 1994; Confraria 1995).

For the same periods there are different trends concerning the growth of the production factors. Capital stock has grown consistently since 1953, but at a decreasing rate for the last twenty years (Table 11.2). During this period, the country had investment and savings rates consistently above 20% of GDP (and often above 25%). Although available data is scarce, two previous periods have also been remarkable, at least concerning public investment: the second half of the nineteenth century, in investment in railways and roads, and the 1930s, when the state also led a programme of infrastructural investment in transport and communications networks.

Growth of the labour force, from 1890 to 1980, was around 0.5% a year, with several decades of negative growth (Table 11.3). This was mainly the result of migratory movements. For instance, the increase in the 1940s is the result of the Second World War, and the increase in the 1970s came from the slowdown in emigration following the crisis of 1973/75 and the inflow of refugees from the former colonies. The general outflow of active population from the country, including many young individuals, certainly harmed economic growth; on the other hand, emigrants' remittances were an important inflow of capital resources, reaching more than 10% of GDP in 1980, and made possible the relatively high savings rates recorded.

João Confraria

TABLE 11.3. *Average annual growth rate of the labour force* (%)

1890–1900	1900–10	1910–20	1920–30	1930–40
–0.3	0.3	–0.4	0.4	1

1940–50	1950–60	1960–70	1970–80	1985–90
1.4	0.4	–0.8	2.3	1.1

Source: 1890–1980, Nunes 1989; 1985–90, *Inquérito ao Emprego*, Instituto Nacional de Estatística.

TABLE 11.4. *Illiterates*[a] *as percentage of census population*

1890	76%
1911	69%
1930	60%
1950	42%
1970	21%
1991	10%

[a] Over 10 years old.

Source: *Recenseamentos Gerais da População*, several issues.

The slow growth of active population has been accompanied by a gradual improvement in its 'quality', as measured by illiteracy rates (Table 11.4). This fall in illiteracy, a result of a progressive widening of educational opportunities, raises a few questions concerning the type of education being provided. Secondary technical education was an option for (a reduced but increasing number of) students for most of the century, until the early 1970s. By then educational reforms aimed at providing uniform secondary education to all students, without specific technical objectives. This policy was reinforced after 1974 and only recently secondary and university level technical education became again widely available. There is some consensus that schools have not been providing the type of education most useful in the labour market. Similar doubts have been raised in relation to university education (Forum para a Competitividade 1995).

Technological progress was mainly embodied in imported capital goods, as the level of R & D activity in Portugal has been low. The number of patents granted by the Portuguese Patent Office has increased, from a low base, but most of the patents have been granted to foreigners (Table 11.5). It is not likely that Portuguese inventors had a much improved performance registering their inventions abroad; data for the 1980s, concerning patents granted by the US and European Patent Offices, suggest one of the lowest levels of inventive activity in Europe (Archibugi and Pianta 1992) and this is consistent with the relatively small amounts of resources allocated to R & D, slightly above Greece and Turkey (OECD 1993).

TABLE 11.5. *Patents granted by the Portuguese patent office*

	Total (number)	To Portuguese individuals/firms[a] (% total)
1880[b]	61	23%
1913[c]	409	13%
1928	423	17%
1962	950	7%
1969	1,384	6%

  [a] 1928–69: individuals/firms resident in Portugal, including subsidiaries of foreign-owned firms.
  [b] Portuguese according to nationality.
  [c] firms/individuals with a Portuguese name.

Source: *Boletim da Propriedade Industrial*, several issues.

11.3. A DISARTICULATED ECONOMY (1890–1926)

From the early nineteenth century, Portuguese manufacturing began to suffer the full impact of the British Industrial Revolution (Macedo 1982). Free access to the Brazilian markets granted to British traders and producers, during the Napoleonic wars, and the perceived lack of natural resources, such as coal and iron, further aggravated what was basically a technological problem. Meanwhile, for most of the nineteenth century, growth of agricultural production was considered to be a necessary condition for improving living standards and the construction of a transport network an almost sufficient condition for agricultural growth. It was assumed that roads, railways, and ports would lead to the integration of domestic regional markets or would increase export opportunities, thereby increasing investment and productivity. Technological improvements in agriculture, related to mechanization, increased use of fertilizers, improving farmers' knowledge about both demand conditions and the quality of land had a very limited role in economic policies pursued until the fall of the monarchy and during the First Republic.

There are some doubts about the economic effects of the investments in transport networks (from 1849 to 1910, 11,754 km of roads were built; the first railway, 36 km, was opened in 1856 and by 1910 there were 2,098 km of railways). Possibly they increased export opportunities and had a positive, but limited, influence on the integration of regional markets (Alegria 1990). However, it is not clear how much farmers benefited from increases in agricultural surpluses, because merchants in urban areas often controlled the access to the final users of the products. On the other hand, improvements in the transports increased import penetration, damaging local producers.

Other consequences relate to wider macroeconomic constraints. The development of railways and roads had been financed by state borrowing abroad.

TABLE 11.6. *Average nominal tariff rates on imports*

	1880	1892	1921	1923	1929
1. Average (%)	—	34	6	8	33
2. Coefficient of variation	—	1.60	8.95	9.29	2.8
3. Tariff revenues/imports (%)	28	32	4	7	22

Source: Lines 1 and 2: Author's estimates with Sónia Sousa, from the tariff schedules of 1892, 1921, 1923, and 1929, and including the changes resulting from trade treaties and special treatment of classes of products (other than particular exemptions granted to imports for specific projects). Line 3: Mata and Valério 1994.

Public debt increased from 37% of GNP in 1851 to 84% in 1892 and, by 1925 it was still 74%, showing the failures of successive governments in controlling the problem (despite a few successes in the first years of republican governments). Most of the debt was external: 54%, 58%, and 65% of total public debt in the same years. This led to a general decrease of investment in roads, railways, and ports, until the late 1920s; mail, telephones, and telegraphs were an exception (Marques 1981). The dismal state of the road network constrained the growth of road transport, then an important source of regional dynamics, probably more important than railways, improving the access of producers and rural middle classes to urban markets (Macedo 1979).

Industrial development had, in general, a secondary position in the framework of economic policy. The problem of technological backwardness, that was to be considered for most of the twentieth century as the main source of Portuguese industrial underdevelopment, was addressed mainly through protectionist policies. However, mention should also be made of protection of intellectual property rights (invention patents); since 1826 and, from 1892 to the end of the First Republic, exclusive rights of production (for less than ten years and, confusingly, also known as patents) were awarded for introduction of 'new industries', meaning not an invention but the manufacture of goods previously not produced domestically.

The tariff structure adopted in 1892, following the financial and economic crisis of 1891, reinforced previous protectionist trends, as higher nominal protection has been granted to consumer goods (textiles and clothing, shoes, beverages, cigarettes, and drugs), with lower tariffs being imposed (with a few exceptions) on raw materials, transport equipment, and machinery. The decrease in the average tariff rates after 1910 was accompanied by a strong increase in their dispersion, as measured by the coefficient of variation, again biased towards higher nominal protection of consumer goods (Table 11.6). The average global decrease was the result of several factors. Unit tariffs were the general rule and inflation accounted for a fall of around 60% in average nominal protection. An adjustment was tried, setting tariffs in a unit of account, the *escudo-ouro*, with a fixed value in sterling; however this did not compensate for British inflation and, anyway, many exemptions were granted. Preferential trade

TABLE 11.7. *Tariff rates as percentage of tax revenues*

1890	1900	1910	1920	1930
44	34	31	31	38

1940	1950	1960	1970	1980
29	28	32	18	6

Source: Mata and Valério 1994.

agreements with major trading partners and special treatment related to the preferences given to trade in the national merchant fleet led to further reductions in protection. Finally, the problem was eventually made worse by lack of effectiveness of government agencies in collecting tax revenues, as a result of the political instability and almost constant changes of governments.

The reform of 1929 imposed general increases in nominal levels of tariffs but, again, awarding larger protection to consumer goods. In a sense the government granted consistent protection to industries where domestic production was relatively developed—and, for that reason, these industries had larger political influence than infant industries. However this leads to the question, why tax imports of intermediate goods and raw materials? Part of the answer relates undoubtedly to import-substitution purposes, but it also happened that tariff revenues were a large part of state revenues, and even exotic products were taxed for fiscal reasons. This feature of the structure of tax revenues was to remain relevant until the 1970s (Table 11.7).

The process of import substitution had limitations, and considering only short-run static effects, was unlikely to lead to significant increases in economic growth. Actually, the best prospects for improving economic performance were probably based on the development of wine production, reinforcing the, until then, traditional pattern of exports (Reis 1993) (although wine was one of the goods benefiting from higher nominal protection and it is not obvious how domestic producers would be able to achieve the large increase in foreign market shares necessary to sustain a specialization in wine production).

Concerning the setting of development policies, it was remarkably difficult to build winning coalitions, in the political framework of the First Republic, given the difficulties of the political establishment adapting to new economic conditions, such as industrialization of Lisboa and Porto and, as mentioned above, the dynamics of local producers (Macedo 1979) and given the variety of conflicting interest groups economically isolated from each other in a 'disarticulated economy' (Schwartzman 1989). These groups included agro-based exporters (wine, olive oil, and cork), industrial exporters (canned fish, cork products), import-substitution industries, import-substitution agriculture (including grain producers in the south, that were to remain an import political force), and the special case of textiles. Textile firms developed on an import-substitution basis, but were increasing export capacity to the (protected) colonial markets, and were to become progressively integrated with colonial production of raw materials, as a result of deliberate policy initiatives designed to promote colonial development (Pitcher 1993).

One result of this was the relevance of a development policy based on agricultural growth until the 1940s—that had been defended assuming both that the country could not industrialize successfully because it lacked natural resources necessary to industrial development and that industrialization would increase the risks of social and political instability (Andrade 1902; and for criticisms of this view, Perdigão 1916; Jesus 1918; Dias 1946). It was the authoritarian/nationalist system led by Oliveira Salazar that, in the 1930s, proved successful in achieving some equilibria among different groups of agricultural and industrial interests (Rosas 1986). Grain and, later, production of other agricultural goods were supported through import restrictions, subsidies to production and technical advice (e.g. Campanha do Trigo, similar to some agricultural policies implemented in Italy). Incumbent industrial firms were protected from foreign competition by an increase in protection (Table 11.6), favouring import-substitution processes and from domestic competition by a general licensing system (see next section). Moreover, after several years of balanced budgets, infrastructural investments financed by the state recovered, grouped in Lei da Reconstituição Económica.

11.4. INDUSTRIAL POLICY IN PROTECTED MARKETS

The general approach to macroeconomic policy during *Estado Novo* was based on price stability and budget equilibrium at a low level of taxation. In these areas, economic policy has been generally successful, although since the late 1960s inflationary pressures were increasingly obvious. At the same time, concerning microeconomic policy, the state reserved for itself mainly the role of regulator of market processes, having a limited role as producer. Exceptions to this general rule were some infrastructures (roads, telephones) and services such as education and health, in most cases directly produced and provided by the state. However, regulatory policies implemented were deeply interventionist, both concerning the dynamics at each industry and the general pattern of allocation of resources.

11.4.1. Mobility Regulation

Import protection was consistently pursued until the late 1960s, notwithstanding membership of the European Free Trade Association. Under Annex G of the Stockholm Treaty, Portugal was granted a longer period for tariff liberalization, even if domestic producers benefited from rapid access to the markets of the other member countries; the effects of tariff liberalization in the EFTA framework were felt mainly from 1970 to 1974 (Table 11.8); meanwhile, competitiveness

TABLE 11.8. *Average tariff rates on imports*

	1950	1964		1970		1974	
		Nomin.	Effect.	Nomin.	Effect.	Nomin.	Effect.
1. Average for manufacturing (%)	—	21	58.7	16	58.4	8	37.0
2. Coefficient of variation	—	1.4	2.2	0.6	1.6	1.3	2.9
3. Tariff revenues/ imports (%)	14	10	—	11	—	4	—

Sources: Lines 1 and 2: Porto 1982; line 3: Mata and Valério 1994. Lines 1 and 2 are not comparable with those in the previous tariff table for differences in computation methods.

of domestic industries, as industrial growth was increasingly based on exports (Cravinho 1982) acted as a severe constraint on import-substitution projects, of textile machinery, for instance (Silva 1986).

In this closed economy, the government imposed since 1931 a regulation of investments in manufacturing, known as *condicionamento industrial*. It has been basically an investment licensing system: in regulated markets, entries and investments by incumbents were subject to discretionary approval by the regulatory agency. During the 1930s, almost every manufacturing market has been subject to this kind of regulation; by 1960, regulated industries accounted for around 60% of manufacturing employment (Dias 1960), a proportion that was maintained in the next decade (Martins 1970). In 1972 several policy reforms decreased the scope of regulation and the complexities of the regulatory process.

In several monopolistic and oligopolistic market structures the regulatory agency has mainly pursued a specific form of exit policies. It was considered that in those markets there was an excessive number of incumbents, with obsolete technologies and excess capacity; exit policies were based on the closure of plants and the building of new plant(s), owned by a new firm held by the previous incumbents according to their pre-merger market share.[4] The most obvious successes of this approach have been the restructuring of the flat glass markets, where a monopoly producer, Companhia Vidreira Nacional, with a single plant emerged in place of seven firms and in the production of some raw materials for hat producers, where a new firm with two plants, Cortadoria Nacional do Pelo, became the single supplier. Both cases happened in the 1940s; by then incumbents in many other industries were mounting increasing resistance to this type

[4] One may ask why did excess entry and excess capacity appear? A possible explanation, particularly attractive given the fact that *condicionamento* was imposed in 1931, is the world recession. However, there are some doubts about the effects of the 1929 crisis on the Portuguese economy, mainly because the country was very isolated from the international economy, concerning trade and capital flows, and also because aggregate demand was stimulated by the infrastructural public investments of the 1930s (Rosas 1986). Adaptive behaviour to entry by incumbents may well have a contribution to excess entry, defined as a situation where the number of incumbent firms is greater than the number of firms that maximizes social welfare (e.g. Mankiw and Whinston 1986).

of restructuring policy, probably for reasons related to the control of the post-merger firm. The regulatory agency ended up allowing for small increases of capacity by incumbents, that did not solve any of the technological problems. Survival of the firms was obviously dependant on tariff protection; although some officers at the regulatory agency argued that tariffs should be manipulated, threatening import entries into the domestic market, to persuade incumbents to accelerate the pace of restructuring. That did not happen, possibly because of political lobbying and lack of coordination among different ministries and agencies (as interested parties in the tariffs include industry agencies, trade agencies, the Ministry of Finance, as noted above, and the Ministry of Foreign Affairs). In the textile markets, most of them competitive, *condicionamento* has meant basic-ally a set of restrictions on the investments of smaller firms, both entrant and incumbents, that made exit easier and entry and internal growth more difficult. Licences were generally given to large-scale entry and large-scale investments ('large' meaning above legally set minimum levels and 'small', below those levels). In other industries the problem of the regulatory agency was considered to be avoiding excess entry, by the coordination of investments of entrants and incumbents; the pulp, cement, refining, and petrochemicals industries are inter-esting examples of this approach (Confraria 1992).

The approach of Portuguese policy-makers to problems of excess entry and inefficient exit has been quite ambitious, given the objectives of regulating mobility in so many manufacturing markets for so long, and contrasts with more selective approaches later followed in Taiwan or South Korea or, as in Spain, for a shorter time span.

Several factors can reduce or overturn inefficiency losses resulting from excess entry (Vickers 1995). They include the possibility of entry deterrence and the development of competitive processes. On the other hand, entry regulation helps to avoid these types of market dynamics and may lead to other distortions resulting from regulatory failures. At least in monopolistic and oligopolistic indus-tries, *condicionamento* often implied the protection of incumbents and avoided the potential restructuring effects that might have resulted from entry, both at the firm and at the industry levels. Until the middle 1960s, it was argued by policy-makers and senior officers at the regulatory agency that the benefits of regulation outweighed potential regulatory failures, but reforms undertaken in the early 1970s aimed explicitly at the reduction of such negative effects of regulation (Martins 1970; Confraria 1992). Policy-makers took a very critical view of the effects of entry on market dynamics, assuming that entry would in gen-eral reinforce collusive behaviour among inefficient firms (Dias 1960). This is consistent with the more general view of competition as essentially a destruct-ive process (Salazar 1935), that was at the basis of the wider institutional frame-work in place from 1931 to the early 1970s.

As a matter of fact, the main problems probably resulted from this wider institutional framework. Corporatist organizations have been developed, albeit slowly, with the stated aim of coordinating supply. Suggestions from several officers at the regulatory agency to use tariff reductions, or a credible threat of tariff reductions, as instruments of a competition policy have never been seriously implemented, possibly for the reasons mentioned above. This framework implied that competition was often legally blockaded; incumbents were protected from both domestic and external competition and this allowed them to avoid what might have been painful restructuring processes or to benefit from monopoly power (Dias 1960; Sobral and Ferreira 1985; Brito 1989; Confraria 1992). In the latter case, government agencies were not very critical, based on the idea that static costs caused by increases in producers' surpluses resulting from monopoly power, would be offset by dynamic gains arising from higher investment rates. The argument is not without merit, given the inefficiency of the banking system and the role of reinvestment of profits to finance internal growth, as stated by one of the main industrialists, A. Champalimaud (quoted by Ribeiro, Fernandes, and Ramos 1987).

11.4.2. Inter-Industry Allocation of Resources

Import substitution has been an objective of industrial policy consistently pursued at least until the late 1960s. The rationale was based mainly on the supposed benefits to economic growth coming from structural change and development of new industries. Import substitution was promoted through *condicionamento* (it was easier to get licences for import-substitution projects), as well as through other policy instruments: a ten-year monopoly has been granted to some import-substitution firms (e.g. tyres, steel, sewing machines), tariff protection has been reinforced in some cases and state organizations provided financing, both as lenders and equity holders. By the middle 1960s it was increasingly accepted by policy-makers that technologically efficient import substitution was limited by the small dimension of the domestic market—and that many of the import-substitution industries could hardly survive under international competition. It was argued that the development of new industries should depend on their export potential; otherwise the new industries would impose a large burden on (exporting) industries downstream and on consumers. However, it was also considered that government intervention was necessary to attract private investors as was happening in other countries such as Spain and Turkey (Pintado 1964; Martins 1970).

This kind of state involvement resulted, in part, from some peculiar institutional arrangements of the banking system. For reasons related to the stability of the financial system, several restrictions had been imposed from the late 1920s to 1959 on 'commercial' banks as providers of long-term finance. That role was given in 1929 to the national savings bank, Caixa Geral de Depósitos, through an autonomous organization, Caixa Nacional de Crédito, that shared staff and equipment with the savings bank. Reis (1994) suggested that this might be the best institutional arrangement because it was less costly, as it would not be necessary to fund another bank, duplicating staff and equipment, Caixa Geral de

Depósitos already had some experience of lending to 'productive' activities, had an extensive network of officers, and a private bank would probably be owned by banks that might not be too much interested in the development of a competitor (banks managed to give some 'long term' credit by the renewal of short-term loans). Finally, it is also possible that the state feared collusion and an increase in concentration. Reforms of the banking system enacted by 1957–59 made easier medium- and long-term lending by commercial banks but, at the same time, the state maintained a strong position in long-term credit concession. It did so not only through Caixa Nacional de Crédito (until the late 1960s) but also through a state-owned development bank, Banco de Fomento Nacional, created in 1958.

For economic policy-makers, state intervention in long-term credit was obviously considered necessary, not only because of the regulation imposed to safeguard the stability of the banking system, but also because it was assumed that the state could somehow select 'strategic' sectors. The private sector would avoid committing resources to large investments in (new) industries without the implicit guarantee provided by the participation of the state or of state-owned organizations.

State involvement, as provider of equity capital and long-term loans, was particularly obvious in the fertilizer, steel, pulp, and electricity industries (see Inspecção Superior do Plano de Fomento 1959, for a detailed account, for 1953–8, the period of the First Development Plan). With hindsight, one may question the wisdom of economic policies strongly protecting steel production, but it remains surprising that in profitable industries producing what was then a non-tradeable, such as electricity, state involvement was necessary to attract private capital to the producing and distribution companies. Perhaps the same could be said about the pulp industry. The state was directly involved from 1942, as provider of equity and loans, in the development of the second pulp firm in Portugal, Companhia Portuguesa de Celulose (the first being a small British-owned firm, Caima Pulp Company, in place since the late nineteenth century). The new firm was given several benefits, including a state guarantee on dividends, but not tariff protection, as it was considered that it was an industry where the country had comparative advantages resulting from the availability of cheap wood. Only in the late 1950s, when Companhia Portuguesa de Celulose achieved a dominant position in the domestic market and exported an important part of its production, did private capital become interested in the industry that developed strongly in the following decade.

Notwithstanding the policy-makers' beliefs about the ability of the state to take leading roles in new industrial projects, the development of relations between banking and industry grew rapidly during the 1960s. This led to a pattern of capitalist organization, common to many developing economies, that has been called 'the group', and that could well be an organizational form well suited to face the disadvantages coming from imperfections in capital markets, government regulation, and scarcity of managerial and entrepreneurial talent (Leff

1978). Some of these groups had an industrial origin, acquiring a bank in a later stage of their development (the most important was the group of firms controlled by A. Champalimaud, with origins in cement and the chemicals company Companhia União Fabril), others acquired industrial and agricultural stakes from a strong basis in banking (among others, Banco Espírito Santo, Banco Nacional Ultramarino, and Banco Português do Atlântico).

11.5. INDUSTRIAL POLICY IN TRANSITION (1974–1985)

The military coup of 1974, putting an end to *Estado Novo*, was followed by political and social upheavals with consequences still remaining in current economics and politics. They implied a reversal in macroeconomic policy, giving up the previous objectives of price stability and budget equilibrium and, as discussed below, the role of the state in economic activity increased enormously. On the other hand, they led to some changes in the availability of capital and labour. As mentioned above, labour supply declined during the 1960s but increased dramatically after 1974, following the fall in emigration, the inflow of refugees from the former colonies, and the reduction in military forces.[5] At the same time, budget and external deficits, restrictions on inward investment and capital flight, fearing the upheavals of domestic politics, increased the domestic scarcity of capital. Hence it was not surprising that the traditional pattern of specialization of the country based on labour-intensive industries was reinforced since 1974 and that real wages faced strong downward pressures. All this happened as the end of the authoritarian system allowed increasing influence in policy of previously neglected social groups (industrial workers, small farmers), increasing the difficulties of policy-making and the potential for social conflicts. In the end, labour markets proved to be remarkably flexible, and workers accepted declines in real wages following the macroeconomic stabilization packages agreed with the IMF in the late 1970s (Krugman and Macedo 1981) and in the early 1980s.

11.5.1. Protectionism and Nationalizations

Because of balance of payments constraints, the process of trade liberalization suffered a reversal (Table 11.9). Moreover, tariff protection was complemented

---

[5] The loss of assets in the former colonies, reduction of military forces, and inflows of refugees were probably the most important economic consequences of de-colonization. A few industries (wine, low-quality textiles, for instance) and individual projects, such as the Sines petrochemical complex, dependant on access to Angolan oil suffered a negative shock, but the colonies had a secondary role to Portuguese firms, as export markets—by 1973 they were the destination of around 15% of exports (down from 26% in 1960) and the source of 10% of imports (15% in 1960). Moreover, many consumers came to Portugal, as refugees, albeit with a reduced purchasing power. It is also possible that some firms were relieved to have free access to international markets of raw materials, previously restricted to reinforce economic integration in the Portuguese political area. Corkill (1993) probably overstates the shock to Portuguese industry resulting from de-colonization and suggests, intriguingly, that the burden imposed on post-1975 governments by the return of refugees was the fault of pre-1974 governments, because, in the first place, they sent people to the overseas territories.

TABLE 11.9. *Average tariff rates on imports*[a]

| | 1974 | | 1977 | | 1986 |
	Nominal	Effective	Nominal	Effective	
1. Average for manufacturing (%)	6	11	26	55	—
2. Coefficient of variation	0.8	1.1	0.7	1.1	—
3. Tariff revenues/imports (%)	4	—	7	—	1

[a] Average weighted by imports, including import surcharges in 1977 and the effects of preferential trade arrangements.

Sources: Lines 1 and 2: Silva 1986; line 3: Mata and Valério 1994. Lines 1 and 2 are not comparable with those in the previous tariff tables for differences in computation methods.

TABLE 11.10. *Share of the state in sector value added* (%)

| | 1938 | 1973 | 1976 | |
	State[a]	State[a]	State firms[b]	State[a]
Agriculture		0.5	0.1	0.6
Mining		1.1	0.3	1.9
Manufacturing	1.0	2.0	8.9	10.9
Construction		2.5	2.5	4.1
Electricity, gas, and water	15.8	12.2	98.5	99.9
Electricity and gas	11.6	7.3		
Water	37.1	57.5		
Wholesale and retailing		1.0	2.8	3.5
Banks, insurance and property		8.1	63.0	63.4
Banks	48.8	13.4		
Transport and communications	15.2	28.3	68.4	75.6
Oceanic transport	9.4	25.6		
Buses and electric	35.9	31.9		
Airlines		8.3		
Communications	67.5	92.8		
Education	78.2[c]	89.8		88.6
Health		68.4		69.5

[a] State firms and public agencies involved in the activities considered.
[b] Totally or majority owned by the state.
[c] In 1938, total for education and health.

Source: National Accounts, *Instituto Nacional de Estatística*.

by import licensing schemes, inherited from previous years and, from 1974 to 1985, by a compulsory deposit scheme that increased the costs of imports by around 3%.

Following a nationalization process involving the most important industrial and financial firms, the share of the state in value added has increased sharply (Table 11.10), even if to levels not uncommon in Western Europe. As noted by the OECD (1976), the share of the state in value added and gross fixed capital formation was in France 17% and 19% by 1975, and 26% and 30% in Italy, by 1974. However this new role of the state led to ambiguities concerning private property rights. Nationalizations resulted from the deep political and social instability, including the development of leftist revolutionary processes, prevailing in Portugal in 1974–5; former owners and managers left the country, compensations later set were much below the value of nationalized assets and, as noted above, the new Constitution implied that the development of a 'socialist' economy should be the final objective of economic and social policies.

By 1976, with greater political stability and the economic crisis, the role of the private sector in economic activity became increasingly reinforced, notwithstanding the fact that, under the new Constitution, previous nationalizations were considered 'irreversible'.

The problem of nationalized firms was seen as an absence of an appropriate institutional framework for its management. In many cases (cement, pulp, electricity, banking, insurance), horizontal mergers of nationalized firms were promoted, reinforcing the deep structural changes in industrial and financial markets initiated by the nationalizations (Table 11.11). In principle, this could lead to the implementation in firms' management of wider social objectives than

TABLE 11.11. *Changes in ownership and in market structure in the 1970s; manufacturing, banking, insurance, utilities, and transport*[a]

	c.1973–4	c.1977–8
Tobacco	duopoly (mainland)[b]	state monopoly (mainland)
Brewing	oligopoly	duopoly of state firms
Pulp	oligopsony[c] (majority stake of the state in one firm)[d]	mixed oligopsony; leading position by the state firm
Paper	oligopoly	mixed oligopoly (state firms' market share over 50% in some market segments)
Cement	duopoly (several firms, under the control of two groups)	one state firm and one majority state owned
Flat glass	monopoly	monopoly (state owned majority stake)
Crystal glass	mixed duopoly	mixed duopoly
Bottles and glass tableware	oligopoly	mixed oligopoly (market share of state firms less than 50%)
Basic metallurgy	oligopolies/monopolies with fringe firms; state stake in the steel producer	state ownership of several producers, including the steel producer
Refining and distribution	oligopoly; minority stakes of the state in some private firms	State monopoly of refining and mixed oligopoly in distribution: state firm with a market share c.80%.
Heavy chemicals	oligopolies/monopolies in different market segments	fertilizers: state monopoly basic petrochemicals: state monopolies

TABLE 11.11. *(Cont'd)*

	c.1973–4	c.1977–8
Shipbuilding (excluding military)	oligopoly in large- and medium-sized ships	state firms with a market share larger than 50%
Engineering (non-electrical)	state (sometimes majority) stakes in several producers	Majority state ownership of some of the main producers
Printing	Mixed oligopoly (one state firm)	Mixed oligopoly (one state firm)
Commercial banking	oligopoly	oligopoly of state banks with fringe private banks (c.2% of assets, loans, and deposits)
Insurance	oligopoly	mixed oligopoly, state firms market share above 75%
Electricity production and transport	monopoly partially state owned	state owned monopoly for production, transport and distribution (mainland[a])
Electricity distribution	regional and local firms; local authorities	
Water	local authorities; private firm in Lisboa until 1974	local authorities state owned firm in Lisboa
Telephones and telegraph	market partition[c] among three monopolies; one state owned; minority stake of the government in another	legal segmentation of the market; two state owned monopolies and the third operator majority owned by the state
Railways/trains		state monopoly
Road transport (interurban)	oligopolies with a regional basis	state firm with more than 50% of passenger traffic and less than 10% of freight transport
Airports	state organization	state monopoly
Airlines	monopoly, state minority stake	state monopoly

---

[a] Only the most important nationalizations. In other markets, oligopolistic and competitive, many firms became 'indirectly' owned by the state through the nationalization of banks, insurance, and holding companies, leading to 'mixed' market structures.
[b] Excluding Açores and Madeira.
[c] Most of the output being exported, competition among domestic producers related to purchases of wood.
[d] State stakes include equity directly owned by the state, by state organizations and by state firms.
[e] According to local, long distance domestic and international calls and geographic areas.

Sources: Martins 1975; Martins and Rosa 1979; António *et al.* 1983; nationalization laws.

profit maximization, eventually subject to a constraint on a minimum return to capital. The legal framework set in 1976 for the most important state firms considered explicitly this situation, stating that prices should be set to provide for an adequate return to capital, but if not, government subsidies should compensate the firms for any losses. These firms were given an exceptional status (*empresa pública*), including their exemption from bankruptcy rules applying to the private sector. Later, several of them, already operating industries more or less closed to foreign competition, became protected from potential domestic

TABLE 11.12. *State support for private and state-owned firms, 1952–1989*

	State subsidies as % of factor incomes				Capital transfers as % of gross fixed capital formation			
	State firms	Non-financial private firms	Banking and insurance	Total	State firms	Non-financial private firms	Banking and insurance	Total
1952				1.9				5.7
1960				0.8	23.6			1.5
1973				1.3	19.6			4.9
1976				2.2	51.9			8.1
1980	27.3	1.9	0.1	5.7	13.0	1.3	0.0	11.5
1985	17.9	1.6	0.0	4.1	7.7	2.8	0.0	7.9
1986	14.3	2.3	0.0	3.4	8.0	2.7	0.0	9.6
1989	7.0	1.8	0.4	2.1	2.2	6.5	0.2	11.4

Source: National Accounts, *Instituto Nacional de Estatística.*

competition. Entries by private firms were, in practice, forbidden in the following cases: cements, fertilizers, refining, basic petrochemicals, steel, production and distribution of electricity, water, gas, telegraphs and telephones, airlines, banking and insurance (Lei de delimitação dos sectores).

Detailed evidence on market performance of state firms is not available, but it seems possible to suggest that coherent strategies for the public sector have not been implemented and that there were no adequate rules for selecting and evaluating the performance of public managers. It has been suggested that serious inefficiencies accumulated in many state firms: pricing policies of public firms were systematically set according to macroeconomic short-run objectives related to reducing inflation, public firms were forced to borrow abroad to ease balance of payments constraints, state debts accumulated, employment policies and careers were possibly too much dependant on political considerations (Sousa 1988; MIE 1984). Not surprisingly, state subsidies accounted for a large share of incomes paid in state firms and capital transfers were an important source of resources to finance investment, although the problem was not the same in every market. For instance, from 1977 to 1984 the percentage of investment financed by the state has been below 10% in the state firms operating in the brewing, pulp, cement, refining, and electricity industries (MIE 1984) and banks and insurers received a small amount of subsidies. However, this process highlighted differences in conditions of access to capital among private and state firms (see Table 11.12). At least on capital transfers this was the case in the two previous decades, but the share of the state in investment was then much smaller.

11.5.2. Financing and Incentive Systems

Other distortions in the financial markets followed from macroeconomic stabilization policies, as credit has been rationed, interest rates fixed, and the banks forced to buy public debt in conditions favourable to the state. But banks were compensated by relatively high margins allowed for financial inter-mediation, which amounted to implicit taxation (Macedo 1990). In this context it was not clear that the banking system would support the most promising investments, as the interest rate could not be used as a selection mechanism. Labour and bankruptcy laws imposed further distortions on firms' mobility as they acted mainly as barriers to exit: restrictions to lay-off made restructuring of firms very difficult and complex legal requirements for bankruptcy proceedings implied that avoiding market exit was perhaps the best option for firms and creditors.

Several incentive systems were implemented, with the stated objective of supporting investment, employment, and exports. The bulk of these incentives, for which there are no reliable global estimates, came from tax exemptions and credit subsidies, although they also involved direct financial transfers. An agency to support small- and medium-sized businesses (Instituto de Apoio às Pequenas e Médias Empresas Industriais) was created and managed some of those programmes. Private exporting industry has also been fostered by the (nominal and effective) devaluation of the currency. Further benefits (*contratos de viabilização*) were awarded to several hundred firms that were considered to have been particularly hit by the political and social unrest of 1974–5 (e.g. owners and managers had been forced to leave by workers' committees).

The reversal of exchange rate policies after 1974, following four decades of nominal currency stability, was unavoidable given the increases in oil prices of the 1970s and the loss of Portuguese firms' assets in the former colonies, after their independence. Macroeconomic mismanagement in 1974–6, leading to increasing deficits in the trade and capital balances, reinforced the trend. The incentive systems showed a deliberate attempt to influence firms' decisions and, at the same time, to ease conditions of access of private firms to finance. No comprehensive evaluation of these incentives has been made, but it has been suggested that their effectiveness was hampered by cumbersome bureaucratic procedures as well as by government delays in paying incentives awarded. There are also some doubts about the selection process (Rendeiro 1984). On the other hand, they are part of a general pattern of government intervention in the allocation of financial resources. After crowding out private investment, through different means of supporting public firms and financing the state deficit, government regulated private access to capital, using bureaucratic selection processes, and favoured firms' strategies directed to employment creation, investment, and exports. Bankruptcy laws deepened the government-imposed distortions on market mobility and competition, as firms in trouble avoided exit and remained in the market, delaying the payments of wages, taxes, and social security contributions.

11.6. INDUSTRIAL POLICY AFTER MEMBERSHIP OF THE EUROPEAN COMMUNITY

11.6.1. Institutional Change and Privatizations

A more consistent approach to industrial policy began to emerge after 1986, following membership of the European Union and an improvement in macro-economic stability. The restrictions on banking and financial markets, as well as the preferential conditions of financing the state had designed for itself were removed. At the same time, liberalization of capital movements, according to European Union objectives, may well have had a different impact on different organizations. For the state and for big firms, conditions of access to finance improved, as it was easier to borrow abroad. But it is doubtful that small- and medium-sized firms experienced similar opportunities. Actually, liberalization of capital movements may have, in the short run, a negative impact on small firms' financing, as both domestic and foreign banks may take advantage of better investment opportunities elsewhere. Part of the problem has an informational basis from the banking system point of view. At the same interest rate it may be preferable to lend to a few large organizations, domestic or international, with relatively well-known risk ratings, than to a larger number of relatively unknown small domestic firms.

Meanwhile, privatization of major state firms was initiated in 1988, under a legal framework that only allowed for 'partial privatization', with upper limits on the stakes to be held by any individual investor or by foreign investors. In 1990, after a change in the Constitution, full privatization of state assets became legally possible. According to the privatization law, the objectives of privatization were related to improving firm and market performance, as well as to the development of capital markets. The receipts could only be used to reduce public debt, to cover interest costs arising from privatization or as capital transfers to the public sector. Prior to privatization, restructuring processes have been initiated at the state firms. Sometimes they included the merger of state-owned firms (telephones). In other cases they were broken up, including the sale of non-core assets (chemicals, pulp, steel) or assets transferred between firms in the same market, 'equalizing' the market shares (cement), supposedly to increase post-privatization competition (concerning industrial firms supervised by the Ministry of Industry and Energy, see Amaral 1991). In order to maintain some kind of domestic control over state assets, the government may, in some cases, retain 'golden shares' (telephones, refining, pulp) and, in other cases, has set on the stakes to be held by foreign firms (banking, later abandoned). Until 1994, major privatization processes occurred mostly in the financial sector; major industrial privatizations (yet partial) were in the cement, refining, and petrochemicals markets. Meanwhile, the state has been disposing of equity stakes in many firms, that had been a by-product of privatization.

Further change happened in the utilities markets. Production of electricity has been opened to the private sector and a production company, a main carrier (high voltage) and regional distributors have been created from the former state monopoly. They were grouped under a holding company. Water distribution and sewage industries, traditionally owned by local authorities (with the exception of Lisboa, where a state-owned company has been operating) are undergoing fundamental changes. Distribution companies have been set, each one providing water to the local authorities in a given region (again, Lisboa is the exception, where local distribution will be provided by the regional distributor). All these companies are at present grouped in a state holding, although the possibility of privatizing at least part of them is not excluded. Natural gas distribution is an entirely new industry, structured around a main carrier and regional distributors. The main carrier is the supplier of regional distribution companies, electricity generators, and large industrial clients; a state-owned company has equity stakes in all natural gas firms, but some of them are minority stakes, the remainder belonging to domestic investors and foreign firms. Finally, the main telecommunications operator was partially privatized and a mixed duopoly in cellular telephony has been formed. In most of these cases changes come from the need to make large investments, being assumed that the new framework will improve financing capabilities, as well as the current management of utilities.

11.6.2. Incentives to Mobility

From 1987 to 1993, policy-making emphasized investments in infrastructures (roads, telecommunications, and energy) as well as in education and training. Transfers from the European Community (amounting to around 3% of GDP in 1993, net of the national financial contribution to the EC) have been mainly used to finance those investments. Policy measures specifically related to industrial infrastructure and investment were structured in a different programme, the 'Programa específico de desenvolvimento da indústria portuguesa' (Pedip), financed by grants from the European Community (slightly above 5% of total grants) and from the state budget and by loans from the European Investment Bank.[6] This programme was divided in four main areas: technological infrastructures, training, investment support at the firm level, and improvements in the areas of productivity, quality, and industrial design (Table 11.13).

The development of technological infrastructures, an idea that had already been present in industrial policy but not always consistently pursued, was based on the creation of organizations, specialized in technological issues related to a given industry or clusters of industries, co-financed by firms, business associations, and universities, that should be able to develop increasing relationships

---

[6] A similar programme, 'Sistemas de incentivos de base regional' (Sibr), focused on the country's less developed regions, using criteria similar to Pedip, but with different supervision (Pedip was overseen by the Ministry for Industry and Sibr by the Ministry for Planning).

TABLE 11.13. *Grants and investment under Pedip, 1988–1992*

	Grants according to Pedip areas as % of total grants	Average grant (million *escudos*)	Grants as % of investment
Technological infrastructures	16	563	82
Training	15	47	70
Firms' investment	55	38	22
Management and productivity improvement	9	15	39
Quality and industrial design	4	15	73

Source: GEP 1994.

with firms, covering at least part of their expenses through contracts with them. The areas of productivity and management improvement, quality, and design related to the diffusion of information on technology, organization, and markets and to improve cooperation among firms. Support to investment at the firm level included not only investments related to gross fixed capital formation, but also R & D, environment, and internal restructuring of firms. Eligibility criteria were related to the financial structure of firms (minimum values for equity have been set) and to the nature of the project, emphasis being put on the introduction of new technologies, reinforcement of relations with industries upstream producing domestic natural resources, research and development, environment-related investments, and improvements in management (MIE 1992).

Given the eligibility criteria at the firm level, one might suggest that the objectives of incentive systems such as Pedip are to enlarge the opportunity set of supported firms, allowing for investments that otherwise would not have been made. An example is the case of investments that, without financial support, would violate the restrictions on the financial structure of the firm imposed by owners or managers. Grants should allow for increasing internal growth of firms benefiting from them. Different cases could also be considered. Some of the supported investments would have been made anyway, grants being used mainly to reduce debt, or some of the supported investments might not have been profitable (from private and social points of view) without some subsidies. With an efficient selection process, the latter case should be reduced to a minimum, as it cannot be avoided, failures being part of market processes. There is not yet detailed evidence on failures in Pedip-supported projects. However, at least concerning gross fixed capital formation, the subsidies awarded, up to 20% of investment value, left at least 80% of the project financing to be accomplished by equity and debt. This implied the involvement of the banking system in the selection process, helping to reduce bias that could result from bureaucratic project evaluation. Finally, it should be noted that, at least formally, minimizing adjustment costs in crisis industries was not an explicit objective of Pedip, except for provisions related to the restructuring in the wool textile markets and of some

TABLE 11.14. *Number of firms supported as percentage of total firms by size class defined by the number of employees, 1988–1992, average of 15 industries*

<10	10–49	50–99	100–199	200–499	500–1,000	>1,000
1	5	17	31	57	40	56

Source: Confraria 1995.

metallurgical firms. However, in the end, such considerations probably played a meaningful role in the decision-making process (GEP 1994).

Government support to R & D infrastructures and projects, much higher than in other cases, may be justified on the basis of the usual argument related to the positive externalities arising from R & D. However, some of these infrastructures have not been successful in developing relationships with the related industries, suggesting that the externalities have not been created. Although this is not common to every infrastructure, it has been noted that the R & D system remains rather fragmented, with very weak links between funding and performance of R & D. For instance, government finances more than 90% of R & D of government organizations and firms also finance most of their own R & D (OECD 1993). The rationale for this type of government support has not been questioned, the point being to devise ways to improve interaction between R & D organizations and firms. On the other hand, concerning firm level investments (Table 11.13, line 3), government financed R & D projects, on average, up to 42% of total investment, giving them higher grants than those awarded to investments in gross fixed capital formation (19%) and environment and management (40%). However, most of the projects submitted at the firm level were related to gross fixed capital formation (Confraria 1995). This has reinforced the impression that, because of firms' preferences, industrial policy-makers have basically addressed, with Pedip, the problem of technological backwardness that, for most of the century, has been at the core of Portuguese industrial policy.

Incentive systems such as Pedip can be seen as a way to protect domestic production and increase domestic market mobility, as policies traditionally used with this objective are not consistent with Community rules. Given the number of firms with individual investment projects supported (Table 11.14), the level of subsidies, as mentioned above, and the infrastructural investments made, these effects were potentially not negligible. However, the mechanisms at work are different from those of, say, tariff protection. In the latter case, the final result is a price increase that distorts relatives prices in the domestic market and, given the new price, a competitive process may develop domestically. Incentive schemes support a subset of firms that get a cost advantage or reduce a cost disadvantage for competition in an open market; distortions result from new taxation necessary to finance the system and, eventually, from bias in the bureaucratic selection process. From a national point of view, the costs from additional taxation have not been particularly high, as the domestic government has financed around 25% of grants awarded, 75% coming from EC sources, either under solidarity principles or as compensation to less developed regions for potential losses resulting from the single market. In the latter case, distortions imposed to finance the grants should be offset by Community-wide efficiency gains obtained through free movement of goods and factors of production.

11.7. INDUSTRIAL POLICIES AND ECONOMIC GROWTH

The global effects of industrial policies on industrial and economic growth are not obvious. During *Estado Novo*, earlier emphasis on infrastructures certainly had a positive effect. Most doubts come from the regulatory framework imposed on private firms and on the role of the state in financing industry. As suggested above, there was some potential for rent-seeking and for accumulating inefficiencies at the plant level. However, during that period, growth rates of income and of industrial output were higher than in developed Western European countries and similar to less developed Southern European countries. To argue that *Estado Novo* policies constrained economic growth is to assume that a different institutional framework could lead to higher economic growth (a different but related issue being the discussion of domestic capabilities to develop such a framework). In the long run, perhaps one of the biggest shortcomings relates to the (relatively low) level of investments in education, constrained by the principles of budgetary equilibrium and, possibly, by political reasons.

The deep changes in economic policy in 1974–6 had probably a negative effect on growth. Otherwise it would be difficult to explain the fall in the growth rate of the economy, notwithstanding the oil shocks of the 1970s. The emphasis on investments in infrastructure and education after 1986 should lead, in the long run to higher growth, although it is clear that some institutional changes are necessary to improve the allocation of financial resources as well as the performance of many organizations. The amount of subsidies involved created opportunities for rent-seeking put also helped in the implementation of many industrial projects. Overall, it should be stressed that the share of industry in value added has remained stable, at least until 1991 (since then detailed data is conspicuously missing), suggesting some capabilities of adjustment to competition within the EEC.

11.8. CONCLUDING REMARKS

Portuguese approaches to industrial policy have varied remarkably during the last century. Until the late 1920s, it seems possible to suggest that the general approach was of laissez-faire inside an area with some (declining) protection from foreign competition. By the early 1930s a very different approach was implemented, based on the assumption that the state could improve resource allocation by controlling competitive processes and promoting new industries, with increased protection from foreign competition. From 1970 to 1973 this framework was subject to reforms, interrupted in 1974. In the second half of the 1970s, policy focus shifted towards state ownership of firms, as well as to new constraints on competition, in this case to protect public firms. From 1986, through privatization, the state has been undoing the work of the previous decade. At the same time it has been implementing some policies with a renewed emphasis on infrastructures, education, and R & D, as well as on the traditional approach of trying to influence market mobility, this time through incentive systems. Many of these changes were not policy developments built on accumulated experience. They resulted from wider political change: the end of the First Republic in 1926, the fall of *Estado Novo* in 1974 and membership of the European Community in 1986. That is, at given moments, discontinuities in industrial policy were not necessarily related to their past effectiveness or to the distortions imposed.

It is also clear that the Portuguese state often promoted ambitious policies. They were obviously demanding with regard to the analytical capabilities of the civil servants and they probably required knowledge about technology, demand conditions, and firm behaviour that was not available to the regulatory or supervising agencies. On the other hand, for most of the time from 1926 to the early 1980s they implied, not always for the same reasons, a deep distrust of free markets as means to achieve efficient or fair allocations of resources. Successive governments have (implicitly) assumed that the costs of regulation would be negligible.

Finally, the problems of policy coordination among different agencies and ministries should be stressed. The previous discussion focused on external trade policies, but it is not difficult to find other examples (for instance, several agencies belonging to five different ministries are involved, without much success, in forestry management). In the case of tariff protection membership of the European Community solved the domestic conflicts. The same happened in other areas where Community or Union policies apply. However, that will not solve the domestic problem of trying to define concepts of public interest, for regions and communities, that must be part of domestic and Union policy-making.

REFERENCES

ALEGRIA, M. (1990). 'A organização dos transportes em Portugal (1850–1910): As vias e o tráfego'. *Memórias do Centro de Estudos Geográficos*, 12.
AMARAL, L. (1991). *Indústria e Energia: As Apostas Portuguesas*. Lisboa: IAPMEI.
ANDRADE, A. (1902). *Portugal Economico*. Lisboa: Manuel Gomes Editor.
ANTÓNIO, A., MOTA, A., and CARVALHO, A. (1983). *O Sector Empresarial do Estado em Portugal e nos Países da C.E.E.* Lisboa: Imprensa Nacional-Casa da Moeda/CEEPS.

ARCHIBUGI, D., and PIANTA, M. (1992). *The Technological Specialization of Advanced Countries*. Kluwer Academic Publishers.

BRITO, J. (1989). *A Industrialização Portuguesa no Pós-Guerra*. Lisboa: Dom Quixote.

CONFRARIA, J. (1992). *O Condicionamento Industrial: Uma Análise Económica*. Lisboa: Direcção Geral da Indústria.

—— (1995). *Desenvolvimento Económico e Política Industrial*. Lisboa: Universidade Católica Editora.

CORKILL, D. (1993). *The Portuguese Economy since 1974*. Edinburgh: Edinburgh University Press.

CRAVINHO, J. (1982). 'Sources of output growth in the Portuguese economy, 1959–1974'. *Estudos de Economia*, 2/3: 271–89.

DIAS, J. (1946). *Linha de Rumo*. Lisboa: Livraria Clássica Editora.

—— (1960). 'Política Industrial'. *Boletim da Direcção Geral dos Serviços Industriais*, XII/582.

Forum para a Competitividade (1995). *A Competitividade da Economia Portuguesa*. Lisboa.

FRANCO, A., and MARTINS, G. (1993). *A Constituição Económica Portuguesa*. Coimbra: Livraria Almedina.

GEP (1994). *O Pedip e a Evolução da Indústria Portuguesa: Perspectivas de uma Avaliação*. Lisboa: Gabinete de Estudos e Planeamento do Ministério da Indústria.

Inspecção Superior do Plano de Fomento (1959). *Relatório Final de Execução do I Plano de Fomento*. Lisboa: Imprensa Nacional.

JESUS, G. (1918). *Bases para um Plano Industrial*. Lisboa.

KRUGMAN, P., and MACEDO, J. (1981). 'The economic consequences of the April 25th Revolution', in J. Macedo and S. Sefarty (eds.), *Portugal since the Revolution: Economic and Political Perspectives*. Boulder, Colo.: Westview Press.

LAINS, P. (1995). *A Economia Portuguesa no Século XIX*. Lisboa: Imprensa Nacional Casa da Moeda.

—— and REIS, J. (1991). 'Portuguese economic growth, 1833–1985: Some doubts'. *Journal of European Economic History*, 20/2.

LEFF, N. (1978). 'Industrial organization and entrepreneurship in the developing countries: The economic groups'. *Economic Development and Cultural Change*, 26: 661–75 (reprinted in M. Casson (1990). *Entrepreneurship*. Aldershot: Edward Elgar Publishing Ltd.).

LUCENA, M. (1979). 'The evolution of Portuguese corporatism under Salazar and Caetano', in L. Graham and H. Makler (eds.), *Contemporary Portugal: The Revolution and its Antecedents*. Austin and London: University of Texas Press.

MACEDO, J. BRAGA (1990). 'External liberalisation with ambiguous public response: The experience of Portugal'. *CEPR Discussion Paper Series*, 378.

MACEDO, J. BORGES (1979). 'A problemática tecnológica no processo de continuidade República-Ditadura Militar—Estado Novo'. *Economia*, III/3.

—— (1982). *Problemas de História da Indústria Portuguesa no Século XVIII*. Lisboa: Querco.

MAKLER, H. (1979). The Portuguese industrial elite and its corporative relations: A study in compartmentalization in an authoritarian regime', in L. Graham and H. Makler (eds.), *Contemporary Portugal: The Revolution and its Antecedents*. Austin and London: University of Texas Press.

MANKIW, G., and WHINSTON, H. (1986). 'Free entry and social inefficiency'. *Rand Journal of Economics*, 117: 48–58.

MARQUES, A. (1978). *História da Primeira República Portuguesa*. Lisboa: Figueirinhas.
MARQUES, C., and ESTEVES, P. (1994). 'Portuguese GDP and its deflator before 1947'. *Banco de Portugal*, WP 4/94.
MARTINS, M. (1975). *Sociedades e Grupos em Portugal*. Lisboa: Editorial Estampa.
—— and ROSA, J. (1979). *O Grupo Estado*. Lisboa: Edições Jornal Expresso.
MARTINS, R. (1970). *Caminho de País Novo*. Lisboa.
MATA, E., and VALÉRIO, N. (1994). *História Económica de Portugal: Uma Perspectiva Global*. Lisboa: Editorial Presença.
MIE (1984). *O Sector Empresarial do Estado na Indústria e Energia: Análise e Propostas de Actuação*. Lisboa: Ministério da Indústria e Energia.
—— (1992). *PEDIP: Colectânea de Legislação (1988–1992)*. Lisboa: Ministério da Indústria e Energia.
NEVES, J. (1994). *The Portuguese Economy. A Picture in Figures*. Lisboa: Edições Universidade Católica.
NUNES, A. (1989). *População Activa e Actividade Económica em Portugal dos Finais do Século XIX à Actualidade*. Doctoral dissertation. Lisboa: ISEG.
—— MATA, E., and VALÉRIO, N. (1989). 'Portuguese economic growth 1833–1985'. *Journal of European Economic History*, 18/2.
OECD (1976). *Economic Surveys: Portugal*. Paris: OECD.
—— (1993). *Reviews of National Science and Technology Policy: Portugal*. Paris: OECD.
PERDIGÃO, J. (1916). 'A indústria em Portugal: Notas para um inquérito'. *Arquivos da Universidade de Lisboa*, III.
PINTADO, V. (1964). *Structure and Growth of the Portuguese Economy*. Geneva: EFTA.
PITCHER, M. (1993). *Politics in the Portuguese Empire: The State, Industry and Cotton, 1926–1974*. Oxford: Clarendon Press.
PORTO, M. (1982). 'Estrutura e Políticas Alfandegárias—o Caso Português'. *Separata do Boletim de Ciências Económicas*, vols. 25–27, Coimbra: Universidade de Coimbra.
REIS, J. (1993). *O Atraso Económico Português (1850–1930)*. Lisboa: Imprensa Nacional Casa da Moeda.
—— (1994). 'The national savings bank as an instrument of economic policy: Portugal in the interwar period', in Y. Cassis, G. Feldman, and U. Olsson (eds.), *The Evolution of Financial Institutions and Markets in Twentieth-Century Europe*. Aldershot: Scolar Press.
RENDEIRO, J. (1984). *Estratégia Industrial na Integração Europeia*. Lisboa: Banco de Fomento Nacional.
RIBEIRO, J., FERNANDES, L., and RAMOS, M. (1987). 'Grande indústria, banca e grupos financeiros—1953–73'. *Análise Social*, 23: 945–1008.
ROSAS, F. (1986). *O Estado Novo nos Anos 30, 1928–1938*. Lisboa: Editorial Estampa.
SALAZAR, A. (1935). 'Conceitos económicos da nova Constituição'. *Discursos*, I.
SCHWARTZMAN, K. (1989). *The Social Origins of Democratic Collapse: The First Portuguese Republic in the Global Economy*. Lawrence: University Press of Kansas.
SILVA, A. (1986). 'An Analysis of the Effects of Preferential Trade Policies through the Estimation of Quantitative Models: The Case of Portugal'. Doctoral dissertation. University of Reading.
SOBRAL, M., and FERREIRA, J. (1985). *Da Livre Concorrência à Defesa da Concorrência*. Porto: Porto Editora.
SOUSA, A. (1988). 'As estatizações de 1975'. *Economia*, XII/2.
VICKERS, J. (1995). 'Concepts of competition'. *Oxford Economic Papers*, 47/1: 1–24.

12

Greece: From Rent-Seeking Protectionism to Direct Intervention

IOANNA PEPELASIS MINOGLOU

Athens University of Economics and Business

12.1. INTRODUCTION

In the course of the last century, Greece has evolved from a poor[1] peasant quasi-mercantile society to a middle-income (quasi-industrial) economy.[2] Throughout this trajectory, industrial policy has at times been effective, but was always inefficient, failing to enhance the international competitiveness of Greek industry.[3] Two structural continuities have been responsible for this outcome.

First, the protection of Greek industry has led to growth but not development. The size of the country and consequently the market are small. Also, an 'infant industry' argument being absent, protection (in spite of a pro-light industry bias) has been all-embracing, non-selective, and perpetual (Dertilis 1993: 87–90). In fact neither market failure, know-how, or managerial skill have been used consistently as the basic criteria in the designing of any industrial policy tools. For example, the provision of soft loans by an oligopolistic and mostly state-controlled banking system has had distortive effects. It allowed for the creation and perpetuation of inefficient firms; and enhanced excess entry into the traditional sectors, while simultaneously creating disincentives for exit. Political favouritism in combination with the provision of plentiful collaterals in real estate (and not potential profitability) have been the most common criteria used in the disbursement of industrial credit. This pattern of behaviour was further

I wish to thank Dr Y. Caloghirou, Prof. G. Dertilis, Dr S. Ioannides, Prof. A. Lazaris. Dr C. M. Lewis, Prof. H. Louri, Prof. V. Panayotopoulos, Prof. A. Pepelasis for their comments on this essay, and Mr Y. Archontakis for guiding me through the legal texts. Also I thank the participants of the Thesis Workshop of the Economic History Department at the London School of Economics—and in particular the two discussants: Mr Dudley Baines and Dr Paul Johnson. Foremost, I am grateful to Dr J. Foreman-Peck for his painstaking remarks during the writing of the final draft.

[1] Per capita income in 1895 was 217.67 drachmas in constant 1914 prices. This was equivalent to roughly 218 French Francs (Dertilis 1993: 152–3). Per capita income was roughly $6,500 in 1990 (OECD 1992).

[2] For the coexistence of a large subsistence sector with an advanced mercantile community in the Greek economic formation of the nineteenth and earlier centuries, see Mouzelis (1978: 6–17). For the economic development of Greece during the last century, Dertilis (1984: 3–8, 19–46). Regarding the structure of the economy, the population census of 1879 gives the following picture: the Primary sector absorbed 57% of the active population, the Secondary 15%, and the Tertiary sector 28%. Moreover, according to this census, 73% of the population lived in rural communities (Hristopoulos 1977: vol. ID, p. 193). In 1988 the distribution of the active population was as follows: Primary sector, 25.3%, Secondary 27.5%, Tertiary 47.1% (OECD 1989/90).

[3] By 'effective' meaning that industrial policy has attained its goal whatever it may have been. (See general introduction of the book.)

repeated with the other two tools of industrial policy, namely tax allowances and direct grants.

The second structural continuity has been the absence of co-ordination between industrial policies and other areas of economic policy. Even during the interventionist 1980s, infrastructure did not expand in co-ordination with schemes designed to promote industrial investment. For the years prior to World War II, this disarticulation has been attributed to the fact that neither politicians nor the banking establishment ever really believed in the industrial potential of Greece —a view shared by most intellectuals and by the country's foreign economic supervisors.[4] But, this can only provide a partial explanation. For throughout the last century, in order to cover expenditure inflated by the pressures of the politics of 'patronage and populism', the state has consistently appropriated surplus capital, by floating high interest rate bonds (in particular during the 1880s, the inter-war period, and the 1980s). These bonds being an immensely popular form of investment with the public, credence could be given to an argument of a crowding-out variety.[5]

Greek political culture has been largely responsible for the existence of these two 'distortive' structural continuities. Constitutional parliamentarism, introduced in the 1860s, has functioned differently and less satisfactorily than in the West (Mouzelis 1978: 141–4). From the last quarter of the nineteenth century onwards, the public sector has been growing at a rate faster than National Income and accounts today for more than 50% of GNP. Notwithstanding its large size, the state was internally weak, i.e. it was to a significant degree a 'porous' institution. Public finances have been under tight external management for long periods (1898–circa 1940, 1947–60). This factor in combination with the absence of a competent (and autonomous from political interference) bureaucratic cadre has made the state susceptible to immediate pressures posed by antagonistic vested interests. As a result, policy choices have often been inappropriate and measures that in other countries had positive outcomes, have had in the case of Greece a record of poor performance.

At this point it may be suggested that future research should concentrate on a sectoral analysis of industry and policy. It thus may be possible to measure the impact of policy on international competitiveness and the divergence between private and social returns. The manner in which the rent-seeking behaviour of the state and firms conspired to block change is also an unresearched territory. This is an oversight, as in the case of Greece the imposition of a participatory democratic system on an immature economy produced distributional coalitions instead of a strategy of capital accumulation.[6] The literature should also take into

---

[4] Or to put it otherwise, theirs was a belief that Greece could not become an industrial country with a heavy industry. A notable dissident viewpoint regarding the industrial potential of Greece was expressed in Zolotas (1964).

[5] Indeed, within the context of a crowding out argument, it could be argued that heavy public borrowing actually allowed only for the development of light industry as the latter (as opposed to heavy industry) had low capital requirements.

[6] Indeed, the existence of the twin disarticulation regarding the spread and application of the ideas of political and economic liberalism in Greece has largely remained unidentified in the literature.

1880–1918

Objective to raise revenues
Tool tariffs

The inter-war period

Objective to build a light industry so as
to narrow the trade deficit
and fight unemployment

Tools • tariffs
• general subsidies
• bank credits
• public procurements

Post-World War II: The era of international integration

Phase I **1953–1974**

Objective import substitution and
export-led industrialization
Tools • infrastructure building
• non-tariff barriers
• general (fiscal) subsidies
• price controls
• special concessions to
foreign direct investment
• bank credits
Macroeconomic
framework monetary and fiscal stability
within an open economy
framework

Phase II **1974–1990**

Objective industrial restructuring and
regional development
Tools • investment incentives
• non-tariff barriers
• bank credits
• nationalization of banking
sector
• public procurements
• direct state ownership of
industries
Macroeconomic
framework demand management
within an open economy
framework

FIG. 12.1. A summary of Greek industrial policy

account the impact of external interventions and menaces on the nature of the Greek state in general and industrial policy in particular.

More specific work needs to be done on property rights. Surprisingly little has been written on how political and cultural factors have affected entrepreneurship. Greek entrepreneurs, being 'footloose capitalists', have shied away from enduring industrial ventures. They have avoided vertical and horizontal organizations, preferring instead to pull up roots and move into new areas (Thanopoulou 1996).[7]

The survey that follows delineates the rationale of Greek industrial policy and its transition from a revenue-seeking protectionism to supply-side policies and eventually direct state intervention. (See Fig. 12.1 above.) The effect of policy on industrial performance in discussed.[8] Throughout emphasis is laid on the internal contradictions of policy, its interplay with political culture and the permanence of institutional constraints.

12.2, THE NINETEENTH-CENTURY LEGACY (1880–1918)

Throughout the 'long' nineteenth century, industry occupied an insignificant position in the economic life of Greece (Haritakis 1927: 42–8; Agriantoni 1986: 117, 129–30). In 1889 there were only 145 industrial establishments with a horsepower of 5,568 units and only 21% of the population lived in urban communities (Haritakis 1927: 30, 1930: 13, 27). State intervention in railway construction and banking neither aimed at industrialization, nor induced it. Furthermore, heavy foreign borrowing and tariffs were not linked to an infant industry argument, as they had a purely revenue-seeking character. Yet, indirectly—by default one might argue—tariffs contributed to industrial expansion. They widened the size of the local market and theoretically enhanced the supply of capital by supporting industrial profits. Ironically, however, their impact was undermined by other forms of state intervention, such as the system of tolls and the appropriation of surplus funds from industry, via the public flotations of government bonds.

In the Greek case, there was no conscious effort to assist industry through supply-side policy devices such as direct subsidies and procurements, both of which were popular in other more advanced European countries. Indicative of the weak interest in industry is that the one and only agency set up in the nineteenth century 'for the encouragement of industry', was not allowed to support the production of any manufactured good 'if it was more expensive than a

---

[7] In the bibliography Greek shipowners have also been exemplified as typical asset players. Also, it should be noted that an interesting area of enquiry would be to examine the insecurity experienced by industrialists because of frequent changes in government regulations and war adventures. Another issue of a cultural nature which has not been analysed is why industrial engagement being largely a family affair, the overall motivation has been conservative, i.e. to retain family control often at the cost of innovation and expansion.

[8] Because the literature largely focuses on the legal aspects of positive action, and given the limited statistical information available (as for example regarding the interindustry distribution of tariff rates), it is not possible to quantify precisely the impact of industrial policy on economic performance.

foreign product of the same quality' (Psalidopoulos 1994: 17). Most of its funds were spent on agricultural ventures, although the state agreed to participate in the share capital of three firms (the cotton spinning factory of Fotinos in Patras in 1846; the Forge factory of Vassiliades in Piraeus in 1868; the cotton thread factory of Agathokleous in Stylis in 1869) (Hadjiiossif 1993: 269, 271–2).

Historically speaking, 'indifference towards industry' was a phenomenon typical of agricultural countries that espoused Western parliamentarism (Hadjiiossif 1993: 271). However, in nineteenth-century Greece, apathy towards industry in particular, and economic development in general, was not so much a case of dedication to the principles of economic liberalism, but rather a reflection of an underlying belief that the country had no industrial potential. Furthermore, a drive towards industrialization was not perceived as a tool that could facilitate either political consolidation or territorial expansion, the two primary goals of state policy. Although Greece was declared independent in 1830, additions to its territory were made in 1864, 1881, 1912–13, and 1919–20. The last irredentist war adventure was carried out in 1919–22. High military expenditures and the existence of a permanent budget deficit in order to secure universal consent for parliamentarism drained the meagre resources of the Treasury (Dakin 1972: 261–70, 318–21; Dertilis 1993: 23–46). Public investment in the real economy did not surpass 1.7% of GNP and was devoted almost exclusively to the creation of a national railway system. It was through railways (and not for example the establishment of a local armaments industry) that the state sought to enhance its military strength.[9] Rails also had the additional advantage of helping the state to centralize the administration of the country and undermine the long tradition of communal rule (Dertilis 1984: 98).

When the railway effort began in 1882 Greece had only 11kms of rails. By 1902, when the boom in construction petered out, 1,065kms had been built. Half of the railways were pure foreign direct investments and the other half were constructed with public funds and were run by the state. Railways did contribute, albeit slowly, towards the monetization of the economy and the curtailment of the subsistence sector. However, Greece having no coal or iron deposits, railways did not act as a stimulus to the development of a heavy industry. The lines were built by foreign contractors with foreign machinery. All materials were imported; even those that could be produced locally. For example, foreign wooden rods were employed, although they could be provided by local industry. In addition, the network, being basically a coastal line uniting rural markets and not linking isolated areas with urban centres, did not substantially enlarge the domestic market for industrial goods (Papayiannakis 1982: 203–6). Not only railways, but tariffs also failed in the Greek case to initiate industrialization. The tariff system which was initially set up in 1830 placed a 6% duty on all imports and a 10% duty on all exports. In 1856 and 1867 this tariff system was revised

---

[9] In 1888 Greece had only one state arsenal factory and one private gunpowder production plant (Anastassopoulos 1947: ii. 599).

and it became less obtrusive for exports and more supportive towards Greek industry.[10] As the century came to a close, repeated revisions were made to tariffs,
not because there was any initiation to the infant industry argument, but in order
to further increase government revenues.[11] Industrialization was a secondary,
if not minor, aim of the tariff system and there was not even a perception of
an infant industry argument for consumer goods. Duties were heaviest on
luxury goods. For cotton textiles (a basic sector of Greek industry) the tariff
rate was 7%, whereas that on cotton threads was 20%.[12] Mostly tariffs were raised
on an ad hoc basis due to the pressure exerted on the government by specific
industrialists—those applicants having the greatest political power benefiting
the most from tariff revisions (Anastassopoulos 1947: ii. 573, 681, 683, 687).
But if tariffs somewhat increased the demand for native industrial goods, just
the opposite was achieved by the division of the country into regional protected
markets by a national network of toll stations and communal taxes. Both of these
revenue-raising measures, by impeding the creation of a unified domestic market, contributed to the perpetuation of barter trade, self-sufficiency, and cottage
industry.

Another factor working against industrial development was the strong bent
towards classicism of the educational system, which in Greece has always been
under close supervision. In fact, technical education was consistently neglected
and considered of inferior status 'unworthy of government guidance and support'. This acted as a bottleneck in the supply of technicians and skilled personnel. Notably, engineers and technicians were imported from Spain, Italy, and
France for railway building and the Lavrion mines, the largest industrial enterprise in the nineteenth century (Pepelasis 1968: 21; Dakin 1972: 146; Dertilis
1988: 210).

State intervention impeded industrialization in one more way. From the
1860s, in order to cover its mounting budget deficits, apart from forcing on a
reluctant National Bank of Greece the inflationary printing of money, the state
flooded the capital market with high interest government bonds, mostly issued
to the public. Furthermore, it diverted banking funds away from the 'real economy', becoming for over thirty years the largest customer of the two most
important banks: the National Bank of Greece (henceforth NBG) and the Ionian
Bank. Between 1881 and the end of the century, the advances made by the
banking sector to the government surpassed the amounts they lent to the private
sector (Pepelasis Minoglou 1995).

Heavy public borrowing in combination with the absence of a specialized
industrial credit bank,[13] forced many Greek industrial firms to rely not on bank

---

[10] Specifically, the duty on exports was lowered to 1% and the duty on imports for raw materials and industrial
inputs was lowered to 5% whereas for industrial goods produced in Greece it was raised to 10% and for luxury
goods it was fixed at 15% (Psalidopoulos 1994: 15).

[11] As for example the tariff revisions of 1884 and 1894. It should be noted that Prime Minister Trikoupis in
1887 on the occasion of the revision of the tariff claimed that there existed no industry worth protecting
(Anastassopoulos 1947: ii. 574).

[12] The figure is for the 1880s (Anastassopoulos 1947: ii. 545).

[13] A bank by the name of Industrial Credit Bank was set up in 1873. But it remained a small institution and did
not concentrate on industrial credit despite its name.

credits, but on private moneylenders, paying interest rates which at best were 10%, but were usually nearer 25% in the urban centres or 50% in the countryside during periods of poor crops (Dertilis 1988: 121). Other latecomers were helped by massive intervention in the banking system which channelled investments into the 'right' sectors. However, in the case of Greece, outside intervention was for 'rent-seeking' purposes and blocked capital accumulation in industry (Pepelasis Minoglou 1995: 250–64). The opening of the twentieth century was marked by the subjection of public finances to foreign supervision. As a result of the tight monetary regime enforced with the 'Law of Control' of 1898, the NBG (which besides being the country's largest commercial financial institution also functioned as a bank of issue) was relieved from acting as State Treasurer. Indeed, for over a decade, the state was forced to make a speedy redemption of its large debt towards the National Bank. Thus, the latter was given the opportunity to release substantial funds to the private sector, some of which found their way to industry (Tsouderos 1939: 1–19). Another positive development of the early years of the twentieth century was that although a forceful argument in favour of industrial development did not emerge, import duties were imposed on cheap cloths, a major product of the Greek textile industry and a staple consumption item of the peasants. Also, duties on imported raw materials and inputs employed in the production of some industrial goods, most of which had an export orientation, were temporarily lifted (Hadjiiossif 1993: 275–6; Tsotsoros 1993).[14]

Between 1914 and 1918 industry (especially textiles and food processing) experienced a spurt. The number of industrial establishments by 1917 had risen to 2,213 with a total horsepower of approximately 70,000 (Haritakis 1927: 44, 1930: 172). The impression of contemporaneous and recent scholarship is that significant as the advantages stemming from foreign supervision may have been and in spite the dawning of an interest in industry, this acceleration was largely the product of historical circumstances. It has been seen as related to the sudden increase in the demand for local industrial products brought about, not by exports, but by the annexation of territories following the Balkan wars (1912–13); the presence of large allied armies in the country during World War I; and the cutting off of Greece from international trade due to the blow to Greek shipping of the allied blockades of the ports of Southern Greece for months on end (Anastassopoulos 1947: ii. 950–1). In sum: prior to the 1920s there was no clear perception of an industrial policy. Tariffs raised for revenue purposes allowed Greek industry to be protected from international competition, but unlike the case west of Greece there was no notion of an infant industry argument and comparative advantage. Whatever positive benefit was attained from this 'primitive' protectionism was erased by other government measures contributing to the shortage of supply-side factors (such as capital or a technically trained labour force). Overall, government policy was uncoordinated; the only unifying theme or principle being irredentism, the domestic consolidation of the state and the need to secure ever-increasing revenues.

---

[14] The few industries that exported their produce were of peripheral importance to the economy with the exception of the knitting industry.

12.3. THE INTER-WAR PERIOD: AN EMBRYONIC INDUSTRIAL POLICY

During the inter-war period, industry experienced marked quantitative growth. Taking 1928 as a base year, the index for industrial output was 70.5 in 1922 and 164.2 in 1938. National income on a constant price basis rose from 1,966,038 drs in 1922 to 2,870,073 drs in 1938 (Haritakis 1940: 188–265; Dertilis 1993: 152). With the return to peace in 1922,[15] there was a shift from revenue-seeking protectionism to deliberate import substitution. Protectionism became somewhat linked with an infant industry argument. More importantly some direct measures were taken to promote industry and it is possible to discern an incipient industrial policy. Divergence from the contemporary Western European pattern of industrial policy remained pronounced. The Greek rationalization effort of 1929–32 was weak. Also, there was an absence of industrial planning or the build-up of a war industry in the late 1930s. As in the past, industrial policy was effective in that it may have contributed to expansion (i.e. quantitative growth), but it was inefficient in that it encouraged the creation of a disarticulated industrial formation.

The significance of the emergence of an embryonic industrial policy should not be exaggerated, as it was just one facet of the growing involvement of the state machine in the economy during the 1920s. The main priority of the state at the time was, on the one hand, the productive absorption of the 1,200,000 refugees that had suddenly fled in 1922–3 into Greece from Asia Minor,[16] and on the other hand, the attainment of self-sufficiency in cereals, in which Greece had a large deficit. It should be remarked that the development of the country's resources and autarchy in basic foodstuffs were considered as a sine qua non for the consolidation of the international position of the state, allowing it to have a greater bargaining power on political issues vis-à-vis stronger nations (Pepelasis Minoglou 1993). The refugee settlement scheme undertaken under the supervision of the League of Nations was combined with a radical land reform and the drainage of large areas of land (Hristopoulos 1977: vol. IE; Pepelasis Minoglou 1993). Moreover, a system of price supports was set up to encourage the cultivation of cereals. Also, two public banks were created: the Agricultural Bank of Greece (1929) and the Bank of Greece (1928). The statutes of the second were drawn up by the Bank of England along the lines of the central banking principles of the time (Costis 1987: 251–66). It can be argued that the above measures (to the degree that they enhanced agricultural productivity, the creation of a more market-oriented peasant class, monetization, and the modernization of the banking sector) contributed in the longer run to industrialization.

Industry received far less attention than agriculture, and only two public works schemes concerned urban areas.[17] It should be underlined that industrial policy

---

[15] After World War I, Greece was engaged in military conflict with Turkey (1919–22).

[16] This inflow created a shock as most refugees were destitute and Greece at the time had a population of barely 5,000,000.

[17] These were the electrification and the provision of a modern water system for the greater Athens area.

was largely prompted not by any expectation that Greece would ever become an industrial nation, but by a conviction that industry could be a valuable source of employment and would help alleviate the permanent trade deficit. Under the new policy framework the scale of protection increased. Within a decade, the average tariff rate rose from 22–30% of the value of imported industrial goods to 35–40%. But, as in the past, Britain (a major exporter of industrial goods to Greece) maintained its traditional right of free access to the Greek market.[18]

Industrial policy becoming for the first time something more than tariffs, subsidies were introduced for investments, tax reliefs were granted for large companies making 'low' profits and public procurement was initiated so as to enhance demand.[19] These measures, by not differentiating among sectors or regions, had a general character, there not being an even indirect reference to comparative advantage or market failure. Investment was subsidized as follows: private and communal land could be expropriated and state lands could be 'freely' used for the purpose of expanding or building new industrial plants, under the condition that these factories produced goods 'important' for the national economy. The element of discretion left to the public authorities was large and political clientelism affected the application of this 'applicant driven' measure. This was inevitable, as it was not specified whether the word 'important' referred to demand —i.e. whether the goods were of a basic mass consumption type—or whether it implied goods in the production of which Greece had a comparative advantage, or in the last analysis whether it referred to heavy industry. In addition, a fiscal subsidy was granted by lifting for the first time ever import duties on raw materials, machinery, and equipment (not produced in Greece) that were necessary for building new factories or 'substantially' extending old ones (Tsotsoros 1993: 232; Haritakis 1927: 156–9). Tax exemptions were also provided on dividends for industrial companies with a share capital above 5,000,000 drs ($134,000) under the condition that the dividends were no higher than 5% of the nominal value of the shares (Hadjiiossif 1993: 283). As for the introduction of the principle of public procurement, it was specified that the government would be obliged in its purchases of goods to give preference to local industry—as long as the prices were no more than 5% over the prices of imported goods (tariffs and communal taxes inclusive). In 1925 this percentage difference for the preference of Greek goods was significantly raised to 20% and in 1930 to 30%.[20] Finally, in addition to setting up an incentives system, property rights became more defined, as for the first time patents were allowed to be registered without the provision of a guarantee and industrial trade marks were given protection (Haritakis 1927: 159–63).

In spite of the general character of the supply-side policies, there was discrimination in favour of industries that had a low value added.[21] Not only were

[18] The Anglo-Greek Commercial Treaty signed in 1886 gave preferential treatment to certain imports from Britain, such as textiles. This Treaty was renewed in 1926.

[19] Law 2948/1922. [20] Royal Decree of 6/10 Nov. 1925, Art. 29. Law 4536/1930, Art. 2.

[21] For example, paper production was protected with a 100% tariff rate.

tariffs higher for light industry, but also the policy of encouraging the expansion and building of new factories, by lifting duties on imported machinery and equipment not produced locally, decreased the competitiveness of the incumbent capital goods industry. Moreover, the principle of public procurement was in practice undermined. The Refugee Settlement Commission (which had at its disposal more than £10,000,000—a huge sum by the standards of the time) and public works contractors were exempted from any obligation to buy Greek goods. Actually, they were allowed to import free of duty whatever materials and equipment they required from abroad (Kitsikis 1947).

It can also be argued that the tariff and industrial incentives system introduced in 1922 enhanced excess entry into industry, encouraging the formation of a disarticulate industrial configuration. Small marginal 'factories' mushroomed simultaneously with the emergence of a few big firms. The common characteristics of these two different scales were an increasing concentration in light industry (Freris 1986: 93),[22] dependence on protection from the price mechanism and indebtedness to the National Bank. This large financial institution had already begun to establish close links with industry, largely as a result of the fact that it was relieved of its central banking functions in 1928 and of agricultural credit in 1929. All of these characteristics became more apparent as the decade progressed, emphasizing the inherent contradictions in economic policy and in particular in 'industrial policy'.

12.3.1. The 'Unproductive' Response to the World Financial Crisis

Though the need for rationalization was publicly recognized, the Greek rationalization effort was weak. An attempt to enhance industrial concentration basically consisted of a few half-hearted amendments to the industrial incentives introduced in 1922. Namely, small firms were deprived of the right to benefit from subsidies, and thus from 1929 onwards only large industrial firms were exempted from duties on imported machinery and equipment. Also, from 1930, land could be expropriated only for the building of large factories.[23] The only 'positive' incentive for 'rationalization' was the tax reliefs given to joint stock companies in the event of mergers (Tsotsoros 1993: 238–40). But two institutional blockages impeded substantial mergers. Most industrialists did not want to relinquish family control over their businesses and the long-term capital provided to industry through the NBG was meagre. It consisted of about 26 loans given between 1928 and 1931 to a small number of large firms in order that they convert part of their high-interest short-term obligations towards the National Bank of Greece to long-term low-interest debts (Pepelasis Minoglou 1993). Among the main recipients were the cement companies Erakles and Titan, the Chemical Industry SA, and the Distilleries SA. Effectively in the Greek context

---

[22] Up to the eve of World War II about 50% of the total value produced in manufacturing was in textiles, food, and tanning.
[23] Law 4536/1930. See also Laws: 545/1937, 1033/1938, 1298/1938.

the experiment in rationalization had nothing to do with a structural revamping of the industrial sector (in terms of management, the types of products produced, the technology employed, etc.) as may have been the case in the West. In essence, it merely consisted of tactics to weaken the incentives for exit by easing the liquidity crisis of the larger firms resulting from expanding the production of goods beyond the 'call of the market'.

Following the abrupt halt in foreign capital inflow and the collapse of the gold standard in 1931, rationalization as a policy issue receded to the background. The problem of the current account deficit drew the attention of the government and an attempt was made to solve it, not through enhancing productivity, but by keeping the prices of goods low through two types of defensive measures: namely, on the one hand, by controlling the level of wages and maintaining the external value of the drachma low, and, on the other hand, by reducing the volume of imports (Hadjiiossif 1993: 308).

The steepening of protectionism widened the size of the market for industrial products, but it also acted as a brake on investment. Starting in 1932, industrial firms were allowed to import tools and machinery only in order to replace worn-out equipment.[24] Also, from 1933 onwards, large firms were no longer permitted to import equipment free of duty.[25] Moreover, the permission of the Committee of Industry of the Ministry of National Economy was made obligatory for the establishment of new factories or significant extensions.[26] The policy of keeping the drachma 'undervalued' and curtailing industrial investment had a negative long-term impact: the mechanical equipment of Greek industry became even more ossified and the international competitiveness of this sector was further undermined.

Towards the end of the 1930s, most European governments initiated some sort of industrial planning and the building of war industries. Greece once again was an aberration. The attainment of autarchy in cereals had become by this time an accepted principle all over the political spectrum. But, the only ones to protest in favour of strengthening the position of heavy industry and attainment of strategic self-sufficiency in basic metallurgy and munitions were the military and a few prominent industrialists vocal in the Confederation of Greek industrialists. It was with cooperation of the latter that the authoritarian regime of Metaxas (1936–40) began to show some interest in the production of munitions. Close ties were established with Bodosakis, the Diaspora entrepreneur who practically monopolized this field in Greece. Also, in 1937 the state took over a factory that had been established in the 1920s by the British firm Blackburn for aircraft servicing and repair (Hadjiiossif 1993: 308–12; Koliopoulos 1985: 95–7). Undoubtedly, during the late 1930s, the most striking feature of industrial policy was its emphasis on labour issues. In a corporatist strain and imitating neighbouring Italy, a minimum wages level and a system of compulsory arbitration

---

[24] Law 5426/1932 'for the curtailment of the importation of goods'.
[25] Law 5843/1933.　　[26] Law of 29 May 1935.

were introduced whereby all collective bargaining took place under its auspices (Freris 1986: 97).

In conclusion, during the inter-war period the state strove to expand the economic resources of the country and attain self-sufficiency in certain basic agricultural goods. Although industrialization was not a top priority, for the first time an industrial policy was designed. But, the susceptibility of the government to various pressure groups and the credit policy pursued by the National Bank of Greece created an environment whereby inefficient (small and large) firms could survive.[27] The deliberate import-subsitution framework set up, in combination with the fiscal incentives system of the early 1920s, promoted excess entry especially in light industry. Growing international isolation in the 1930s and the brief 'rationalization' policy weakened incentives for exit or more efficient organization.

In the last analysis as what was to be the case throughout the post-war era, policy had a positive impact on the personal wealth of industrialists, but did not enhance competitiveness and productivity.

12.4. PETTY REGULATIONS WITHIN A 'FREE MARKET' FRAMEWORK (1953–1974)

For almost a decade (1965–73), Greece had one of the highest growth rates in the world.[28] The economy lost its strong agricultural character and by 1973 industry accounted for 21% of GDP.[29] Industrialization for the first time became a major policy objective. Within a context of enhancing private initiative a 'complex' industrial incentives system was set up. Greek industry expanded but its international competitiveness remained low. Perhaps this was so, because the supply-side measures, by weakening the incentive for exit, discouraged innovation. In spite of public declarations of a commitment to the liberalization of the economy, industry operated in an artificial environment riddled with distortions of the market mechanism. It may be argued that the reluctance of policy to rely on the criterion of 'market failure' contributed to what has been considered by some as the de-industrialization of the Greek economy in the 1980s (Lyberaki 1997).

Following World War II, there was turmoil due to civil war. Economic reconstruction was carried out under the Marshall Plan (1947–52). During this five-year transition period, Greece received substantial foreign aid for military purposes

---

[27] On the eve of World War II roughly £9,000,000 was owed by industry to the NBG. This was a large amount considering that at the time the annual value of industrial production in Greece was in the area of £25,000,000 (Anastassopoulos 1947: iii. 1581).

[28] The Greek economy between 1965 and 1973 experienced high growth rates both in terms of output and productivity. For example, among the eleven European countries of the OECD, Greece was first in terms of the rate of growth of labour productivity (Vaitsos and Yiannitsis 1987: 19).

[29] In 1970 for the first time the share of agriculture in the GDP was lower than that of industry (Freris 1986: 156).

and the construction of a nationwide network for electrification, telecommunications, and roads. However, the reconstruction of Greek industry took place with a limited use of external finance.[30] Originally the American Mission for Aid to Greece designed a substantial loan package to support industry, but only a small part was actually disbursed (half of the funds going to cement, chemical, and metallurgical firms).[31] The Mission was deterred by the absence of a free market environment and modern infrastructure. Notably, standardized accounting practices were non-existent in business activities (Stathakis 1990: 71). Furthermore, price distortions were ample as a result of price controls and the preponderance of indirect taxation in the fiscal system.[32] Also, banking credit was provided on the basis of personal/political connections rather than profitability. And, finally, Company Law required that shares transfered (i.e. which changed hands) should be taxed and made nominal.[33] Given all these domestic institutional constraints, the American Mission decided that to allocate large amounts of capital to industry would be a waste of resources, preferring instead to concentrate on expanding the country's physical infrastructure in the hope that the liberalization of the economy would eventually follow (Freris 1986: 128–32).

After the official termination of the Marshall Plan, the political forces that governed the country were influenced by preconceptions of economic integration in the world economy, as propagated by the American economic advisers appointed at the ministries and other public institutions well into the mid-1960s. Following a heated political debate regarding whether the country should rely on economic planning with emphasis on heavy industry (a strategy that had become identified with the political forces of the left), the government opted for a free market path of economic development based on foreign direct investment in industry and local private initiative.[34]

The 50% devaluation of the drachma in April 1953 is considered as the starting date for the new policy orientation. With this move, the exchange rate of the drachma was fixed at 30 drs per US dollar and the war-related hyperinflation and speculation in gold was finally put to an end. Monetary stability and fiscal prudence became the cornerstones of macroeconomic policy for the next twenty

---

[30] For a summary of the conflicting views regarding the reasons for the marginal contribution of the Marshall Plan to industrial reconstruction: Stathakis (1992: 133–5).

[31] The amount granted to industry was in the area of $5–6 million which was minuscule considering that the total amount of aid granted to Greece under the Marshall Plan amounted to $2 billion (Stathakis 1992: 133, 149).

[32] See Bitros (1985: 149–50) for the system of price controls set up in 1946. Regarding the importance of indirect taxes it should be noted that in 1948 industrial production was burdened with taxes which reached almost 50% of the value of goods (Stathakis 1990: 71). Also, for the late introduction and low returns of income tax and taxes on inheritance in Greece, see Dertilis (1993: 58–64).

[33] Greece acquired a law for joint stock companies in 1920—a late date considering that the Companies Act of England was passed in 1862. This law which was inspired by the German–French precedents remained unchanged until 1955. In 1955 for the first time semi-Greek companies were allowed to transfer their shares without the requirement that the shares be nominal (Georgakopoulos 1972: 19–34).

[34] The post-war framework for FDI in industry was provided by Law 2687/1953, which gave foreign firms tax concessions, free repatriation of profits and capital, and prohibited the confiscation of foreign-owned assets. It is notable that between 1953 and 1978 on the basis of this law $985 million was imported and invested in manufacturing. This amount represented 13% of the total industrial investments that materialized during this time period (Kintis 1982: 156–60).

years. The direct entrepreneurial role of the state was confined to public utilities
and participation in a few sugar refining, fertilizer, and oil refining plants. (State
participation in the net fixed assets of industry was small and decreased from
8% in 1954–5 to 3.5% in 1974–8.) In conformity with its Western neighbours,
and as a result of the Association Agreement with the EEC in the early 1960s,
tariffs were gradually lowered.[35] But, even within this more international background and in spite of public declarations of a commitment to trade liberalization, the institutional environment had not changed all that radically from the
days of the American Mission for Aid to Greece. The market was not allowed
to function smoothly. Falling tariffs were counterbalanced by the introduction of
non-tariff barriers such as quotas, invoice controls, and advance deposit requirements for importers. Price controls covered a fair number of goods.[36] And, finally
the political authorities continued to interfere in commercial banking.

Within this peculiar and confused economic environment, a plethora of regulations were issued with the aim of promoting industry.[37] From 1953 onwards
and for a period of twenty years, industrial policy consisted of two fiscal incentives, that were of a general character as they were not 'tied' to certain sectors.[38]
The first, tariff exemptions on the importation of capital goods to be employed
in large investment projects, was the most important, on average accounting for
70% of the total value of state assistance to industry. The second fiscal incentive consisted of tax deductions and increased depreciation allowances. This subsidy, requiring as a prerequisite the existence of profits, in practice benefited mostly
well-established firms.

In 1973 a new tool of industrial aid was introduced: the subsidization of interest rates on long-term loans granted to industry for fixed capital formation.[39] Once
introduced, this direct subsidy acquired a prominent position in the incentives
system. Already by 1974, one year after it was applied, it accounted for 69% of
total state assistance to industry. As was the case with the fiscal incentives, this
applicant-driven subsidy was of a general scope and did not discriminate among
sectors. However, as the eligibility conditions and the awards were set by the
'Currency Committee', which was under the direct authority of the prime minister, the disbursement of this subsidy was largely influenced by party politics
and not by strict economic criteria.

The figures regarding the net contribution of public funds to industry are
scant. However, it has been estimated that by 1975 the aforementioned fiscal and
financial subsidies granted were equivalent to 29% of the total net profits of

---

[35] The Greek economy became gradually more open. An indication of this is that exports and imports as a percentage of GNP increased from 22.5% in 1960 to 26.4% in 1970, to 47% in 1980 and 51.4% in 1985 (Vaitsos and
Yiannitsis 1987: 91).

[36] For the operation of the system of price controls over the years, see Bitros (1985: 149–53).

[37] Prior to 1982 it was estimated that the industrial incentives system set up consisted of around 50 laws and
legal decrees and 30 ministerial decisions.

[38] Law 2687/1953.

[39] A law was introduced in 1967 which provided for the covering of part of the interest rate for loans to be
employed in new investments. However, in the quantitative data provided, there is no evidence that this law was
applied prior to 1973.

industry. Not all sectors benefited equally. For consumer goods, the subsidies offered amounted to 44% of net profits, whereas for capital goods and consumer durables, state assistance was equal to 20% of net profits (Yiannitsis 1983: 107).

Thus, it can be argued that the incentives system set-up was geared towards enhancing import substitution in light industry. Indeed, in addition to being relieved of the 24% import duties which existed for capital goods, light industry enjoyed up to the mid-1970s an effective rate of protection of consumer goods equal to 367% (Vaitsos and Yiannitsis 1987: 101). Import substitution was after a point combined with some form of export promotion. Direct subsidies were offered to firms producing industrial goods for exportation largely through short-term soft loans.[40] This preferential treatment was followed by a rise in exports which helped to ease the problem of the trade deficit. However, it did not enhance the international competitiveness of Greek industrial goods. Apparently, there was no planned strategy of choosing specific sectors within light industry, be they winners or declining industries.

The repeated modifications regarding the regulations concerning these supply-side policies created a climate of uncertainty. Probably, the weakest point of industrial policy—apart from this factor and the entanglement of party politics in the allocation of the financial subsidies—was that by keeping costs artificially low, while simultaneously protecting the high level of domestic prices for consumer goods, profits (especially in the traditional low value added sector of industry) were supported at levels which would not have been possible under truly competitive conditions. Profits were supported in the hope that they would lead to a rise in productivity. But this was not the case. Reinvestment was low, never accounting for more than 35% of investment in industry, and remained restricted to traditional sectors.

From the mid-1960s the banking sector acquired a greater presence in industry, especially in big business. A specialized bank for the development of industry was set up which ironically allocated most of its funds to tourism. Nevertheless, long-term bank loans rose from 13% of industrial investments in 1960–6 to 27% in 1967–72 (Vaitsos and Yiannitsis 1987: 106). The generous banking policy towards industry was largely self-defeating and 'anti-developmental' in character. This was reflected in the criteria used by banks. The large collaterals demanded (and the fact that most collaterals took the form of land and buildings), on the one hand, assisted in eliminating from industry the entrepreneur 'who brings only his talent and ideas'. On the other hand, it led to general types of investment which were not use-specific and kept industry away from specializing in new areas. Moreover, political clientelism was an important factor in the decision-making process, for the government through the 'Currency Committee' directly controlled the distribution of a large part of commercial bank loans up to 1982 (Papandreou 1991: 9–12).

---

[40] These measures were introduced in 1963 and 1970, respectively, but it is not clear whether they were actually applied prior to the mid-1970s.

The other main source of capital outside self-finance was Foreign Direct Investment (FDI). Indeed, FDI peaked during 1960–6 amounting to 50.5% of gross fixed capital formation in manufacturing. This outcome was in part the product of the fact that Greece for the first time ever adopted an open door policy, granting foreign investors special privileges. However, there was a wider historical conjuncture as at a world level FDI in industry in less developed areas was at its highest point. Foreign Direct Investment was directed either towards the production of consumer goods for the home market or towards the processing of resource-based materials. The three largest FDI projects of the 1960s (the Esso Pappas refinery, the Hellenic Steel plant, and Pechiney-Aluminum) were among the most significant investments in heavy industry at the time. Overall, foreign investment took an enclave form failing to transfer its dynamism and high productivity to the rest of the economy. The influx of FDI did not last long. During the military dictatorship (1967 to 1974), the incentives granted to foreign firms became even greater. But, by 1973–80 FDI petered out, amounting only to 3.7% of total investment in manufacturing (Mouzelis 1978). The general trends in the world economy regarding the orientation of FDI were no longer favourable for Greece. However, it was also the case that a strong sentiment expressed in Greek society against foreign ownership developed during the latter part of the 1970s. In addition, it could also be argued, that an inhibiting contributory factor was the eventual realization by foreign investors that the irrationalities—distortions—of the Greek market system were a permanent phenomenon.

In short, after World War II in contrast to most Western European countries, there was limited demand management of the economy and direct intervention in the productive process.[41] In spite of the open market framework adopted, there were plenty of price controls and Greek industry through a host of ad hoc regulations continued to be protected from international competition. Industrial policy contributed to the perpetuation and preponderance of: (i) the phenomenon of ailing oligopolies operating in the midst of a plethora of numerous marginal small firms and (ii) traditional light industries (e.g. textiles), in which Greece was beginning to lose its competitive edge due to the rise of Far Eastern low-cost producers. Both of these weaknesses became more apparent after the massive inflow of FDI came to an abrupt halt.

Given the outstanding performance of the growth rate of the Greek economy during the mid-1960s, what is the verdict? It can be safely argued that to the extent that there was development (and not simply growth), it was fragile. Industrial policy did not initiate a sustainable industrialization and it actually contributed to the perpetuation of a number of institutional constraints. Nevertheless, one aspect of industrial policy had a strong positive impact on industrial performance. This was the economic and political commitment adopted towards the West, as exemplified primarily by the 1960 Agreement of Accession to the EEC

---

[41] For an account of the argument that Keynsianism was not practised in Greece during the 1950s and 1960s, see Psalidopoulos (1990: 48–64, 74).

and the adoption of an open door policy towards FDI. But, it should be under-lined that the inflow of foreign capital would not have been so impressive had this policy shift not coincided historically with the substantial increase of FDI in the industrial sector of backward countries in general.

12.5. INDUSTRIAL RESTRUCTURING WITH TRADE LIBERALIZATION (1974–1990)

In the mid-1970s the pace of industrialization petered out and in the beginning of the 1980s Greece entered a phase of falling rates of industrial activity. By 1990 manufacturing as a percentage of GNP was about 4 points lower than in 1974 (Yiannitsis 1993: 29). From a historical perspective, there is an explana-tion for this loss in momentum. For as already noted above, Greek industry had become over the years concentrated in areas of a growing international com-petition. Moreover, the slipping in the competitiveness of industry coincided with Greece's accession to the EEC in 1981 and a significant shift in the orientation of policy towards correcting social injustices. Namely, demand management was introduced and there was active state intervention in industry. This new twin pol-icy orientation set Greece apart from mainstream trends. In the 1980s most Western European nations experienced policies of deregulation and privatization within a framework which gave priority to the fighting of inflation.

The replacement of the stable 'monetarist' model of the preceding two decades with an expansionary credit, fiscal and incomes policy was undertaken in the conviction that through the enhancement of a demand-led growth, two things would be possible: on the one hand, to comply with the populist pressure that the economic position of no social group would worsen and, on the other hand, for development to follow automatically (Caloghirou, Ioannides, and Lyberaki 1993: 59–61, 81, 88–90).

But, in reality only the first aim was temporarily satisfied. Fiscal explosion fed the creation of a plethora of small firms displaying a low degree of special-ization and concentrated in the traditional branches of light industry, i.e. food, drinks, and textiles. Thus, by no coincidence these products accounted for 46% of the total value produced in manufacturing in the 1980s (Papandreou 1991: 8–9).

Shortly after the fall of a seven-year military dictatorship in 1974, and within a social climate of 'socialist renaissance' the state acquired a much larger stake in the economy. Public utilities (water, electricity, post, telecommunications), transport (railway, urban, plus air) and over 80% of the commercial banking sector came under its direct control.[42] Public ownership in industry increased

---

[42] The two largest banks (the National Bank of Greece and the Commercial Bank of Greece) were nationalized. These two institutions accounted for two-thirds of all deposits and 85% of all assets of the commercial banking sector (Papandreou 1991: 10).

significantly, largely through the industrial holdings of the commerical banks, but also as a result of the post-1982 effort of the state to salvage certain ailing firms. State ownership amounted to 18.4% in textiles, 50% in fertilizers, 55% in cement, and 100% in shipbuilding.[43]

A vast public investment programme has also been conceived for the building of large plants in the petrochemical and metallurgical industries. However, fiscal constraints loomed large and only one project materialized: the modernization of the Aspropyrgos refinery. In retrospect, the limited direct public investment undertaken resulted mostly from the new industrial incentives legislation of 1982 which made the provision of public assistance to large private investment projects conditional on equity participation of the state.[44]

Apart from aiming at massive public investment in industry, the new policy framework introduced between 1978 and 1990 had two other main objectives: (i) the industrial development of the more backward regions, most of which were in the border areas; and (ii) a rescue plan for the management of ailing firms and the enhancement of high-technology industries. But, the record regarding regional development and restructuring was even less impressive than the public investment programme. Special government bodies were set up for their implementation, but they were immobilized. Resistance to change and the use of 'structural tools' was expressed from within the apparatus of the state machinery. The basic shortcoming of regional policy was that the regions to benefit the most already had a large industrial base due to the existence of strong urbanization economies (Louri 1988: 433–8, 1989: 231–9).

Although some factories were built in the most backward regions, they either did not operate at all, or did so at a loss due to the absence of infrastructure facilities and 'producer services'. Thus, regional policy was eroded by the inability of the state to escape from the pressure of focusing exclusively on expanding the infrastructural base of the congested urban areas (Louri-Dendrinos 1985; Yuill, Tsoukalas, and Louri 1983: 13–25).

The rescue plan for ailing companies was no success story either, although it absorbed about 14.5% of industrial subsidies. About 44 companies, accounting for 4.5% of industrial output and 31,000 employees, came under the control of a state holding company set up in 1983.[45] These firms were all large-scale operations and important employers in their branch. (For example, they accounted for 45% of employment in basic metallurgy, and 36% in paper.) A defensive policy was pursued. The losses of these companies were transferred from their owners to the public as a whole without a restructuring of their capacity. Moreover, there was no consistent scheme to promote high technologies or widen the product base of Greek industry (Lyberaki and Travlos 1993: 81).

---

[43] State ownership (without taking into account the state-owned defence sector) and as measured by assets (Caloghirou, Ioannides, and Lyberaki 1993: 81).
[44] For a discussion of this project and those that were planned but never materialized, see Caloghirou, Ioannides, and Lyberaki (1993: 75–6, 78–80).
[45] This holding company was named the Organization for the Economic Reconstruction of Firms (OAE in Greek).

During this second post-war phase, the incentives system was simplified in an effort to bring Greek legislation in conformity with EEC practices. The number of industrial subsidies offered was cut down to only four, i.e. two financial (grants and interest rate subsidies) and two fiscal (tariff cum company tax allowances and increased depreciation allowances) (Louri-Dendrinos 1985).[46] Investment incentives persistently favouring capital cost suffered from an 'inherent bias' towards capital deepening. But, as in the past, the incentives offered had a general scope and did not aim at specific sectors.

With the gradual liberalization of trade from 1973 onwards there was a marked shift in emphasis away from fiscal and towards direct financial incentives. Thus, by 1980 fiscal incentives amounted to less than one-fifth of the total subsidies to industry. About 28% of the financial subsidies granted consisted of direct state participation, 36% of public grants and 36% of soft loans. The increasing financial stake of the state either directly or through the banks it controlled, allowed industry to maintain levels of self-finance below 20%.[47] A 1:9 ratio of equity to total debt became commonplace for many firms. This development was negative in the sense that this capital inflow was undertaken 'indiscriminately'. Loans were dispersed without reliable risk assessments or project analyses. The ample provision of soft loans by the banks (under the orders of the government-controlled Currency Committee) and the large public grants encouraged the fixed assets of industry to expand 'beyond the call of the market'. Inefficient firms, especially the larger ones, were allowed to survive. Between 1979 and 1986, the number of bankruptcies was less than 7%, although almost half of industrial firms constantly made losses.

In total, throughout this sixteen-year period subsidies offered to industry grew as a percentage of industrial profits. Indeed, the subsidization of industry by international standards reached a high level, Greece having after Ireland the highest rate of subsidization among the OECD countries, in the latter part of the 1980s (OECD 1991: 45). As in the past, although subsidies were mostly of a general character, the traditional light industries (food and textiles) due to their established position in the economy were able to absorb the lion's share. In fact, as time went by, the gap between light and heavy industry grew in terms of the amounts of assistance they received.

Finally, in an attempt to foster the widening of the industrial base, the public procurements policy was supposedly 'Hellenized' in the 1980s. The public authorities explicitly declared that they aimed at increasing the domestically produced content of industrial goods bought by the state (Caloghirou, Ioannides, and Lyberaki 1993: 77–8).[48] Those firms benefiting most from this policy reorientation were basically large 'older' firms that had developed an oligopolistic

---

[46] Law 1262/1982.

[47] More than half of the lending of the banking system was directed to manufacturing. It is notable that bank loans rose from 13% of industrial investments in 1960–6, to 27% in 1967–72, skyrocketing to 45% of the total by 1981–3 (Caloghirou, Ioannides, and Lyberaki 1993; Yiannitsis 1983: 94).

[48] Also, for a detailed presentation on public procurement, see Caloghirou (1993: 95–128).

position as suppliers to the state and which in spite of the intentions of the government remained entirely dependent on the importation of technology from abroad. Thus, in this area, as for example with regional policy, intervention helped to maintain the status quo and proved incapable of provoking radical changes in the output structure. It ended up maintaining the level of industrial profits, without inducing industrialists to improve the quality of the goods produced and take risks by turning to products with a dynamic comparative advantage. In the last analysis, it may be argued that, as a result of the continuing pursuance of policies which were inappropriate, EU membership was not allowed to make any effective difference apart from providing some revenue for Greece.[49] These policies perpetuated the twin problems of low productivity and specialization in areas of declining comparative advantage.

In short, after 1980 for the first time ever, industrial policy aimed at restructuring Greek industry. But as in the past, it failed to encourage innovation. Internal resistances to rationalization were strong, undermining the 'will' to induce a spatial and sectoral redeployment of capital across sectors. From 1990/1, under the impasse of the growing fiscal imbalance and mounting pressures from the European Union, there has been a new policy orientation. Demand management has been replaced by a policy of monetary stability and labour market flexibility. Also, price controls are becoming fewer than in the past. Regarding industry, new measures have been passed with the aim of enhancing the role of private initiative in the restructuring of industrial activity.[50] It is not yet clear how this policy shift and the (real but slow) privatization drive have affected the international competitiveness of Greek industry.[51]

12.6. CONCLUSION

The state from being a largely obstructive rent-seeking institution, evolved during the last century into a more autonomous benign institution with visions of grand projects. At a parallel level there was a shift from revenue-seeking protectionism to direct intervention. Furthermore, there was a transition from inward-looking trade policies to integration in the open market environment of the Western World. Nevertheless, in spite of these changes, industrial policy showed a degree of continuity. Protectionism and the 'manipulation' of the financial system were the most used instruments. Overall, policy in spite of the general character of the measures taken supported light industry. (This is just an observation and not an argument that it should have shown a pro-heavy-industry

---

[49] During 1989–93, under the first EEC 'Community Support Framework of Greece' infrastructure—i.e. transportation, telecommunications, and energy—absorbed 57% of the funds allocated for sectoral (i.e. not regional) development. Manufacturing benefited only from the 7.5% which was allocated for the improvement of the efficiency of business firms in general. Regarding the second package of 'Support' for 1994–9, about 13.4% of the approved funds are going to be made available to industry. Thus, the direct subsidization of Greek industry by the EU is still 'low' (Ministry of National Economy 1994: 46, 62).

[50] Law 1892/1990, Law 2234/1994.

[51] Privatization has proved harder than expected; the two major nationalized firms succeeding in finding private buyers have been Piraiki Patraiki and Halkis Cements.

bias.) The weaknesses of industrial policy lay elsewhere. Its basic flaw was that it allowed—and even encouraged—the sprawling development of inefficient firms both large and small. More specifically, political intervention impeded the capital market from operating efficiently. Notably, banking credit did not facilitate specialization in areas of more dynamic comparative advantage.

Moreover, the state being susceptible to the pressures levied by competing interest groups, rationalization was permanently postponed. When the need for 'restructuring' heightened, in the midst of the world financial crisis of 1931–3, short-run palliatives were resorted to. In the 1980s following the upheaval brought about by the oil crises, a consistent stimulation of efficient industries was once again postponed. It is argued that external shocks to the system have intensified distributionist actions and did not provoke economic change. As the participation of the banks and the state in industry grew, so did their stake in avoiding bankruptcy and evading rationalization. Any change in the status quo would have required a near elimination of the political system of spoils, favours, and short-run partisan considerations. Such institutional modernizations were neither welcomed by the labour unions, the confederation of industrialists, bankers, nor, of course, by the administration.

Another permanent feature of Greek industrial policy is the persistent divergence from Western Europe. There is a time lag in the application of certain tools in the case of Greece. This for example has been demonstrated in the deliberate protectionism for industrial development in the 1920s or demand management in the 1980s and the privatization drive of the 1990s. Or it could even be argued that Greek industrial policy was not a belated version, but a fundamentally different one from the Western European 'prototype'.[52] The embracing of the free market economy by the Greek authorities in the post-World War II era did not work 'efficiently'. Apparently the ground rules that were taken for granted in the West did not exist locally. Two major sources of inefficiency were: (i) collusion within the web of elites of politicians, civil servants, bankers, and the industrial establishment; and (ii) the absence of a favourable legal framework (i.e. a system of property rights) capable of stimulating entrepreneurship and innovation.

In sum, industrial support, being of a generalized character and perpetual, protectionism has defeated its purpose. Industry became clogged with too many over-capitalized firms working at suboptimal scales of production, there being no reference to the notions of market failure, dynamic comparative advantage, and profitability (Papandreou 1991: 3–5). What is more, the penetration of foreign industrial goods in the Greek market has increased and as result the balance of payments has worsened.[53]

---

[52] Although it cannot be unequivocally argued that the 'Western Model' regarding industrial policy was the optimum one for Greece, it would be a mistake to overlook the distortions involved in its 'imperfect' implantation in Greece. The notion that Greek industrial policy was in the last analysis a fundamentally different version of the Western prototype is related to the thesis that the Mediterranean pattern of industrial development is fundamentally different (Berend and Ranki 1982: 9–10).

[53] At the end of the 1970s the degree of penetration of foreign industrial goods in the Greek market amounted to 23% on average, by the second half of the 1980s it had risen to 35% (Lyberaki and Travlos 1993: 75).

In the last analysis, industrial policy, in itself an expression of Greece's peculiar socio-economic formation, has affected adversely the industrialization process. It was a case of being both inefficient and at times even ineffective.

REFERENCES

AGRIANTONI, CH. (1986). *The Beginnings of Industrialization in Greece during the 19th Century*. Athens: Educational and Cultural Foundation of the Commercial Bank of Greece. (In Greek)

ANASTASSOPOULOS, G. (1947). *A History of Greek Industry 1840–1940*. Athens: Greek Publication Company. (In Greek)

BEREND, I. T., and RANKI, G. (1982). *The European Periphery and Industrialization 1780–1914*. Cambridge: CUP.

BITROS, G. (1985). *Price Controls and their Repercussions*. Athens: IOVE. (In Greek)

CALOGHIROU, Y. (1993). 'Public procurements, industrial structures and state policies in Greece', in T. Yiannitsis (ed.), *Industrial and Technological Policy in Greece*, 95–129. Athens: Themelio. (In Greek)

—— IOANNIDES, S., and LYBERAKI, A. (1993). 'Crucial time-lags in the philosophy of the state's role in development'. *Journal of Modern Hellenism*, 10: 59–90.

COSTIS, C. (1987). *Agriculture and the Agricultural Bank: Facets of the Greek Economy in the Interwar Years (1919–1928)*. Athens: Cultural Foundation of the National Bank of Greece. (In Greek)

DAKIN, D. (1972). *The Unification of Greece 1770–1923*. London: Ernest Benn.

DERTILIS, G. B. (1984). *The Greek Economy (1830–1910) and Industrial Revolution*. Athens: Sakkoulas. (In Greek)

—— (1988) (ed.). *Banquiers, usuriers et paysans, resaux de credit et strategies du capital en grece (1780–1930)*. Paris: Fondation des Treilles.

—— (1993). *Taxation and Political Power in Modern Greece*. Athens: Alexandrie. (In Greek)

—— and COSTIS, C. (1996). 'Banking, public finance, and the economy: Greece, 1919–1933', in C. Feinstein (ed.), *Banking, Currency and Finance in Europe between the Wars*, 458–71. Oxford: OUP.

DRITSAS, M. (1990). *Industry and Banks in Interwar Greece*. Athens: Cultural Foundation of the National Bank of Greece. (In Greek)

FRERIS, A. F. (1986). *The Greek Economy in the Twentieth Century*. London: Croom Helm.

GEORGAKOPOULOS, L. (1972). *Company Law*, Vol. ii. Athens. (In Greek)

HADJIIOSSIF, H. (1993). *'The elderly moon'—Industry in the Greek Economy, 1830–1949*. Athens: Themelio. (In Greek)

HARITAKIS, G. (1927). *Greek Industry*. Athens: Estia. (In Greek)

—— (Selected years, 1929–40). *Economic Yearbook of Greece*. Athens: National Bank of Greece.

HRISTOPOULOS G. (1977) (ed.). *History of the Greek Nation*, Vols. ID and IE. Athens: Ekdotiki Athinon.

KINTIS, A. (1982). *The Development of Greek Industry*. Athens: Gutenberg. (In Greek)

KITSIKIS, N. (1947). 'Foreign private capital and reconstruction'. *I Nea Ikonomia*, 4: 191–6. (In Greek)

KOLIOPOULOS, I. (1985). *Restoration, Dictatorship and War 1935–1945: The British Factor in Greece*. Athens: Estia. (In Greek)

LOURI, H. (1988). 'Urban growth and productivity: The case of Greece'. *Urban Studies*, 25/5: 433–8.

—— (1989). 'Regional policy and investment behaviour—The case of Greece 1971–1982'. *Regional Studies*, 23/3: 231–9.

LOURI-DENDRINOS, H. (1985). 'Regional policy and investment in Greek manufacturing industry: 1971–1982'. D. Phil. thesis. Oxford University.

LYBERAKI, A. (1997). 'The dynamics of change under the surface of stagnation: Greek manufacturing in the post-1974 period', in M. Dritsas and T. Gourvish (eds.), *European Enterprise: Strategies of Adaptation and Renewal in the Twentieth Century*. Athens: Trochalia.

—— and TRAVLOS, S. (1993). 'State interventions in industry: Direct and indirect industrial policy in the 1980s', in T. Yiannitsis (ed.), *Industrial and Technological Policy in Greece*, 39–94. Athens: Themelio. (In Greek)

Ministry of National Economy of Greece (1994). 'Plan for regional development 1994–99'. Athens: Secretariat of Investments, Regional Policy and Development (Official Report submitted to the EU). (In Greek)

MOUZELIS, N. (1978). *Modern Greece: Facets of Underdevelopment*. London: MacMillan.

OECD (selected years, 1972–92). *Economic Surveys, Greece*. Paris: OECD.

—— (1991). *Strategic Industries in a Global Perspective: Policy Issues for the 1990s*. Paris: OECD.

PAPANDREOU, N. (1991). 'Finance and industry: The case of Greece'. *International Review of Applied Economics*, 5/1: 1–23.

PAPAYIANNAKIS, L. (1982). *Greek Railways (1882–1910): Geopolitical Economic and Social Dimensions*. Athens: Cultural Foundation of the National Bank of Greece. (In Greek)

PEPELASIS, A. (1966). 'Economic development and some antinomies of executive power: The case of Greece'. Unpublished paper.

—— (1968). 'The image of the past and economic backwardness'. *Human Organization*, 17/4: 19–27.

PEPELASIS MINOGLOU, I. (1992). 'The institutional morphology of foreign capital in Greece during the interwar period', in M. Dritsas (ed.), *L'Entreprise en Grèce et en Europe XIXe–XXe siècles*, 117–31. Athens: SO.FH.I.S.

—— (1993). 'The Greek state and the international financial community, 1922–1932: Demystifying the foreign factor'. Ph.D. thesis. LSE.

—— (1995). 'Political factors shaping the role of foreign finance in Greece', in J. Hariss, J. Hunter, and C. Lewis (eds.), *The New Institutional Economics and Third World Development*, 250–64. London: Routledge.

PSALIDOPOULOS, M. (1990). *Keynesian Theory and Greek Economic Policy: Myths and Reality*. Athens: Kritiki. (In Greek)

—— (1994). *Essays on Greek Industry in the 19th Century: Natural Evolution or Protection?* Athens: Technology and Cultural Foundation of the Greek Bank of Industrial Development. (In Greek)

SHERRARD, P., and CAMPBELL, J. (Dec. 1966–Feb. 1967). 'The historical revival of the Greek state'. *Synoro*, 40: 250–67. (In Greek)

STASSINOPOULOS, E. (1966). *A History of the National Bank of Greece, 1841–1966*. Athens. (In Greek)

STATHAKIS, G. (1990). 'The postwar industrialisation model'. *Ta Istorika*, 12/13: 57–74. (In Greek)

—— (1992). 'Finance and reconstruction: The case of the Marshall Plan in Greece', in M. Dritsas (ed.), *L'Entreprise en Grèce et en Europe XIXe–XXe siècles*, 133–50. Athens: SO.FH.I.S.

—— (1994). 'Economic policy of the USA in Greece, 1949–1953: Stabilisation and monetary reform', in M. Psalidopoulos (ed.), *Greek Society during the First Post War Period*, 41–56. Athens: Sakis Karagiorgas Foundation. (In Greek)

STAVRIANOS, L. S. (1958). *The Balkans since 1453*. New York: Rinehart and Co.

SVORONOS, N. (1976). *A Survey of Modern Greek History*. Athens: Themelio. (In Greek)

THANOPOULOU, H. J. (1996). 'Anticyclical investment strategies in shipping: The Greek case', in D. A. Hensher, J. King, and P. Oum (eds.), *World Transport Research: Proceedings of the Seventh World Conference for Transport Research*. iv. *Transport Management*, 209–19. Oxford: Elsevier Science.

TSOTSOROS, ST. (1993). *The Formation of Industrial Capital in Greece (1898–1939)*. i. *The Slow Moving Industrialization*. Athens: Cultural Foundation of the National Bank of Greece. (In Greek)

TSOUDEROS, E. I. (1939). *Stefanos Streit—Public Finances and the National Bank of Greece from 1896 to 1911*. Athens: Pyrsos. (In Greek)

TSOUKALAS, C. (1981). *Social Development and the State*. Athens: Themelio. (In Greek)

VAITSOS, K., and YIANNITSIS, T. (1987). *Technological Transformation and Economic Development*. Athens: Gutenberg. (In Greek)

YIANNITSIS, T. (1983). *Greek Industry: Development and Crisis*. Athens: Gutenberg. (In Greek)

—— (1993) (ed.). *Industrial and Technological Policy in Greece*. Athens: Themelio. (In Greek)

YUILL, D., TSOUKALAS, D., and LOURI, H. (1983). *Industrial Aids in Greece: Report Prepared for The Centre of Public Policy*. Glasgow: University of Strathclyde Centre for the Study of Public Policy.

ZOLOTAS, X. (1964). *Greece in the Stage of Industrialization*, 2nd edn. Athens: Bank of Greece, Department of Economic Studies. (In Greek.)

13

Russia: A Comparative Economic Systems Interpretation

CHRISTOPHER MARK DAVIS

Lecturer in Russian and East European Political Economy
University of Oxford and Fellow, Wolfson College

13.1. INTRODUCTION TO ECONOMIC SYSTEMS AND INDUSTRIAL POLICY IN RUSSIA

The industrial policies of the Russian Empire and its successor states during the twentieth century have been of considerable importance to Europe for several reasons.[1] First, until the 1990s Russia/USSR consistently occupied an extreme position in the spectrum of industrial policies associated with maximal state intervention. The success of these policies has varied over time, as have foreign perceptions. For many years, Soviet ideology and theories concerning industrial ownership, structure, priorities, and labour relations exerted powerful influences on debates and practices in Western Europe. Second, industrial polices appeared to have played a key role in transforming the backward Tsarist economy into a powerful, modern one capable of producing advanced civilian machinery and weapons. One result was that the USSR became a major market for European industrial exports. Another was that it increasingly posed political and military challenges that caused European states to allocate substantial resources to the development of their armaments industries in order to support aggressive wars (i.e. Germany in World War II) or to maintain deterrent military capabilities (i.e.

I would like to express my appreciation to the co-editor of this volume, James Foreman-Peck, for his constructive criticism of successive drafts, and to Duncan Allen of the Eastern Research Group, Foreign and Commonwealth Office, Wlodzimierz Brus of the University of Oxford, Robert W. Davies of the University of Birmingham, Peter Gatrell of the University of Manchester, Paul Gregory of the University of Houston, Mark Harrison of the University of Warwick, Michael Kaser of the University of Birmingham, and Byung-Yeon Kim of Essex University for providing me with comments, suggestions, and data. I also benefited from the comments made by participants in the Workshop on 'A Century of European Industrial Policy' in Pisa in April 1995, Joseph Berliner and Abrahm Bergson at a Harvard Russian Research Center Seminar in December 1995, the participants in a seminar at LATAPSEES in Sophia Antipolis in Provence in April 1996, and Sergei Bobylev, Sergei Glaz'ev, Vladimir Mau, Aleksandr Radygin, and Sergei Tsuklo during visits to Moscow in 1996 and 1997. This research was not funded by a specific grant, but benefited from the general support provided by the University of Oxford, especially the Institute of Economics and Statistics, and by Wolfson College.

[1] The meaning of industrial policy and the definition of its components (objectives, instruments, recipients of benefits, and effectiveness) are discussed in Ch. 1 of this volume written by James Foreman-Peck and Giovanni Federico. A comprehensive discussion of industrial policy is presented in Adams and Klein (1983). Chang (1994) reviews the definitions of industrial policy provided by a number of authors and on p. 61 offers his own narrow one: industrial policy is 'a policy aimed at particular industries (and firms as their components) to achieve the outcomes that are perceived by the state to be efficient for the economy as a whole'.

NATO in the Cold War era). Third, Russian industrial strategies and policies were imposed on other European countries.[2] In this century the Russian state has contained parts or all of the now independent nations of Belarus, Estonia, Finland, Latvia, Lithuania, Moldova, Poland, and Ukraine. The Soviet command economic system was forced upon six Eastern European countries (Bulgaria, Czechoslovakia, East Germany, Hungary, Poland, and Romania) after World War II and variants of it were adopted in Albania and Yugoslavia.

Although the general features of Russian industrial policy are known, there are many unanswered questions about it as well, especially since the collapse of the Soviet system has revealed previously hidden realities. How unique were Russian/Soviet policies with respect to goals, instruments, and beneficiaries? Were the interventionist policies of the Russian state necessary to overcome resistance to modernization in industry? Were Russian and Soviet economic theories of relevance to industrial policy different from those in Western Europe? Did the Russian state design and adopt industrial policies in accordance with ideologies and economic theories, or in response to circumstances? What roles have legal and informal markets played in an industrialization process in Russia apparently dominated by the state? How effective were Soviet industrial policies in achieving goals related to growth, innovation, military power, regional development, and international competitiveness? Did the Soviet autarkic development strategy hamper the industrialization process in all periods? Has the shift from state ownership and intervention to private property and reliance on the market in the 1990s generated efficiency gains, a more appropriate branch structure, and improved corporate governance in Russian industry?

In answering these questions, it should be recognized that although Russia has shared with other European countries some experiences of industrialization, it also has endured a series of shocks and revolutionary transformations that have given it political and economic systems that have been fundamentally different from those in Western Europe. Russian industrial policy has been inextricably related to these economic systems, in that the latter usually have been chosen to promote industrial objectives (e.g. the Stalinist model) and their features have pre-determined the instruments, beneficiaries, and effectiveness of industrial policy. Given this, a comparative economic systems methodology is used to evaluate changes in Russian industrial policies and their international uniqueness in different periods.

---

[2] In this chapter Europe is broadly defined to include European OECD countries, Eastern Europe including the Balkans, and the successor states to the USSR excluding those in the Caucasus and Central Asia. See the discussion of concepts of Europe in the 'Introduction' to N. Davies (1996). It should be noted that in the 1990s Czechoslovakia split into the Czech Republic and Slovakia and Yugoslavia fragmented into the Federal Republic of Yugoslavia (Serbia and Montenegro), Bosnia-Herzogovina, Croatia, Slovenia, and the Federal Republic of Macedonia. The German Democratic Republic has been absorbed by the Federal Republic of Germany. Although this volume does not contain studies of industrial policies in the twelve current Eastern European economies, it is hoped that the Russian chapter will provide some insights into common aspects of their experiences as command and transition economies. For information about industrial developments in Eastern Europe during the command period, see Kaser and Radice (1985, 1986). Their experiences during economic transition are analysed in EBRD (1994, 1995, 1996, 1997); ECE (1993, 1994, 1995, 1996, 1997, 1998); and UNIDO (1995, 1996, 1997).

TABLE 13.1. *Classification of economic systems*

System features	Type of economic system			
	Capitalism	Transition market economy	Market socialism	Command socialism
Decision-making structure	Decentralized	Chaotically decentralized	Decentralized	Centralized
Mechanisms for information and coordination	Primarily market, but with state regulation	Weak state and imperfect markets	Indicative plans and markets (but not for capital)	Compulsory plans, restricted labour and retail markets
Property rights	Primarily private ownership	State, legal private and illegal private (organized crime)	State and collective ownership	State ownership of all productive assets
Incentives	Material (primarily financial) and moral (based on capitalist ideology)	Predominantly material (cash), limited moral incentives due to weak ideology	Material (cash, privileges allocated by the state) and moral (based on socialist ideology)	Material (cash, privileges allocated by the state), moral (based on communist ideology), coercion (e.g. forced labour)

Source: Adapted by the author from Gregory and Stuart 1995: fig. 2.3 on p. 27.

Several concepts are used in this comparative analysis. Economic systems are defined according to four criteria: decision-making structure; mechanisms for information and coordination; property rights; and incentives.[3] Their main types are shown in Table 13.1: capitalism, transition market economy, market socialism, and command economy. Economic outcomes (growth, efficiency, income distribution, stability, attainment of objectives, and viability) are generated by the interaction of the economic system, environmental factors, and state policies. A transition is a revolutionary process that fundamentally alters the features and functioning of an economic system.[4]

---

[3] The definition of economic systems utilized in this chapter is based upon concepts outlined in Gregory and Stuart (1995). Table 13.1 is similar in structure to that of fig. 2.3 in this source, but has an added column for the transition economy. This is based on the assumption that it is possible to define a transition economic system. The text in the table cells is somewhat different.

[4] Until the 1990s the concept of transition of an economic system was neglected in mainstream literature; there are no definitions in the *Oxford Economic Dictionary*, the *Palgrave Economic Encyclopaedia*, or the *MIT Dictionary of Modern Economics*. Marxist economists made use of the concept in their writings about shifts from one 'mode of production' to another. See the entries on 'transition from feudalism to capitalism' and 'transition to socialism' in the *Dictionary of Marxism*. EBRD (1995: 2) states that 'Transition is the process through which open market-oriented economies are being established. It involves changing and creating new institutions . . . market-oriented transition is, as a concept, sharply different from economic development.'

On the basis of this methodology, it is possible to identify thirteen economic systems, generated by twelve transitions, in Russia and the Soviet Union during 1890–98 (see Table 13.2).[5] Russia began this period with twenty-eight years of a state-dominated capitalist economy that was similar in many aspects to others in Europe at that time. In subsequent periods it had a hybrid command-market socialist system for seven years (1921–7) and has had a transition market economy for seven years (1992–8). But the dominant system has been the command socialist economy, which existed in various forms for sixty-seven years (1918–20, 1928–91). None of the latter three systems is directly comparable with ones found in Western Europe.

Space constraints make it impossible to analyse Russian industrial policy in all the periods shown in Table 13.2. Instead, five of these economic systems, encompassing the four basic types, have been selected for detailed study: Tsarist Peacetime Economy 1890–1913 (capitalist); New Economic Policy 1921–7 (hybrid of command and market socialism); Stalinist Peacetime Economy 1928–41, and the Mature Soviet Command Economy 1965–85 (command socialist); and Russian Transitional Market Economy 1992–7 (transition market).

Each of the five sections reviews the features of the economic system of the period and then assesses industrial challenges, theories, debates, policies, instruments, and beneficiaries in accordance with the template of the Editors. This is followed by the examination of common topics of importance to industrial policy: the role and behaviour of the industrial enterprise; the evolution of the defence industry; the ability of industry to generate technological progress; the changing regional distribution of industry; and foreign economic relationships of industry. The performance of Russian industry has been determined not only by policies, but also by the economic system and environment. It is evaluated on the basis of production indices and growth rates, measures of productivity, the shifting balance between heavy and light industry, output of key commodities, and international competitiveness.[6] The final section presents conclusions concerning Russian industrial policies and industrialization in the twentieth century.

The text is supplemented with four appendices. The characteristics of Russian/Soviet industrial policies in all periods of the years 1890–2000 are summarized in Appendix A. Basic indicators of the role of industry in the economy are contained in Appendix B and statistics on the production of industrial commodities are presented in Appendix C. International comparisons of Russian industry in six key years are made in Appendix D.

---

[5] Davies (1994*a*) makes use of the concept of economic systems in tracing developments in the Russian economy during 1913–45. But his definition of economic systems is different from, and more general than, the one used in this study.

[6] In this chapter an attempt is made to adhere to a definition of industry that is consistent with that of the CIA index of Soviet industrial production, described in Converse (1982). It includes: industrial materials (ferrous metals, non-ferrous metals, fuels, electric power, chemicals and petrochemicals, wood, pulp and paper, and construction materials), machinery (producer durables, consumer durables, and military machinery), and consumer non-durables (light industry, food processing). However, at times the chapter discusses other economic activities, such as railway construction, that are not industrial but are directly related to industrial policy.

TABLE 13.2. *Russian economic systems and transitions, 1890–2000*

Years	Russian economy	Economic system	Transition
1890–1913	Tsarist state-dominated peacetime economy	Capitalism	
1914			Start of World War I
1914–17	Tsarist war economy	Capitalism	
1917–18			February and October (Bolshevik) Revolutions, Civil War
1918–21	War communism	Command socialism	
1920–1			End of Civil War and Kronstadt Uprising
1921–7	New economic policy	Hybrid of command and market socialism	
1928–9			Adoption of First Five Year Plan and collectivization
1928–41	Stalinist peacetime command economy	Command socialism	
1939–41			Militarization and Mobilization
1941–5	Stalinist war economy	Command socialism	
1945–6			Demilitarization and demobilization
1945–53	Late Stalin command economy	Command socialism	
1953–5			Malenkov's 'New Course' and its failure
1953–7	Transient post-Stalin command economy	Command socialism	
1957			Khrushchev's regionalization and the Seven Year Plan
1957–64	Khrushchev's regionalized command economy	Command socialism	
1965–8			Recentralization and failure of Kosygin reforms
1965–85	Mature Soviet command economy in the superpower arms race	Command socialism	
1985			Early Perestroika
1985–8	Soviet command economy with traditional priorities and timid reforms	Command socialism	
1989			Late Perestroika
1989–91	Malfunctioning Soviet command economy with weakening central control	Command socialism	

TABLE 13.2. *(Cont'd)*

Years	Russian economy	Economic system	Transition
1991–2			Disintegration of the USSR and 'Shock Therapy' policies in Russia
1992–2000	Russian transition capitalist economy	Transition market economy	

Source: Author's lectures at Oxford University on the economic history of Russia and the USSR.

Some qualifications should be made concerning the analysis in this chapter. It is primarily concerned with industrial policy, not industrialization. Although numerous important theoretical and empirical topics related to the industrialization process and industrial economics are neglected, most have been comprehensively covered in cited publications. The definition of industrial policy used in this study is the one elaborated by the Editors in Chapter 1, namely, 'every form of state intervention that affects industry as a distinct part of the economy'. The levels of industrial policy considered are those of 'creating a landscape', 'modifying the environment', and 'changing the relative importance of industry'. The features and problems of Russian/Soviet industrial statistics are mentioned in the text, notes, and tables but not examined in detail.[7] Authoritative Western studies of Russian industrial issues are the main sources of information for the period 1890–1991, although Soviet scholarly works and official statistics have been examined as well. Original analysis of Russian material by the author has focused on the period of transition to the market in Russia (1992–7), which has not yet been adequately analysed by other scholars. Finally, although archival documents on industrial policy in the Tsarist and Soviet periods are now available on an unprecedented scale, only a few are utilized in this study.[8]

13.2. INDUSTRIAL POLICY IN THE PEACETIME TSARIST ECONOMY (1890–1913)

The features, environment, policies, and performance of the Russian economic system during 1890–1913 are summarized in Table 13.3. In Tsarist Russia,

---

[7] Excellent studies of Russian and Soviet industrial statistics include: Grossman (1960); Goldsmith (1961); Nutter (1960, 1962); Powell (1963); Greenslade and Wallace (1966); Greenslade (1972); Converse (1982); Gatrell (1986); and Wheatcroft and Davies (1994). These have been used as sources for the text and appendix tables.

[8] The main repository of material on Soviet industry is the Russian State Archive of the Economy. RGAE (1994) is a guide to its collection. This author has worked in the archive on four occasions in recent years gathering material on the Soviet defence industry in the 1920s and the development of industry in regions (*oblasti*) of Russia during 1913–41. Due to space constraints, few archival documents were used in preparing this chapter.

TABLE 13.3. *Tsarist peacetime economic system, 1890–1913*

Features

Decision-making	Tsarist autocracy. Quite centralized. Key decisions made by state bureaucracy, large firms, and banks
Coordination mechanism	Bureaucratic directives establish parameters of markets. State orders important. Oligopolies dominate industrial markets. Most peasants engaged in subsistence farming
Property rights	Significant state ownership of industry and land. Private ownership of most industry, commerce, and urban property. Nobles own 60% of land. Peasants' land controlled by communes
Incentives	Material incentives: cash in cities, in-kind in countryside

Environment

International	Strained situation with arms races and war scares
Territory and resources	Stable borders with full access to natural resources. Population of Russian Empire: 171 m in 1913 (139 m in USSR inter-war boundaries)

Policies

Utilization of national income	High investment with significant state share. Moderate defence spending. Large consumption share
Sectoral priorities	State favours selected branches of heavy industry (engineering, railway, defence)
Foreign economic	State encourages foreign investment, protects industry using tariffs, and tries to acquire Western technology

Performance

Economic growth	Rapid GDP and industrial growth (of extensive nature) in absolute and relative terms. But growth modest on per capita basis. Industry grows faster than agriculture
Efficiency and technological innovation	Inefficient economy relative to Western Europe. Labour productivity about average. Little technological innovation
Income distribution	Substantial inequality. Upper income: Nobles, bureaucracy, bankers, merchants. Bottom income: Peasants, urban unemployed. Large share of the population lives in poverty
Consumer welfare	Slow increases in per capita consumption. Social and medical services poor for most, especially in the countryside. Infant mortality 237 deaths per 1,000 births in 1913
Stability	Fluctuations in ouput with large decline in 1905–6. Budget deficit low and financed by foreign capital. Low inflation and urban unemployment. Large rural underemployment
Foreign economic	Substantial success in export of wheat and oil. But few competitive manufactures. Chronic trade deficits. High foreign share of investment (40%)
National viability	Ineffectual government. Much popular dissatisfaction. Unstable political system

Sources: Lectures of the author at Oxford University; Davies 1990; Falkus 1972; Gatrell 1986, 1994; Gregory and Stuart 1994; and Nove 1989.

economists and government decision-makers concerned with industrial policies were influenced by four conflicting ideologies.[9] A liberal school advocated ideas consistent with those prevalent in Britain, such as private property, free trade, reliance on market mechanisms, and minimal state intervention in industry. Liberals were represented in the Duma by the Constitutional Democrats, but they had influence on state policy. Supporters of agrarian socialism argued that Russia should base its development on the rural commune (*obshchina*) and cottage industry (*kustarnichestvo*). They were opposed to the expansion of factory industry in Russia and any government policies that assisted it. The peasantoriented populist programme was supported by a number of opposition parties, notably the Socialist Revolutionaries. Marxism grew in influence in this period and spawned numerous studies of Russian industry, including that of V. I. Lenin (1908). Marxist economists and theoreticians in the Bolshevik Party argued that monopoly capitalism with imperialist tendencies had developed in Russia. They believed that Tsarist industrial policies supported the exploitation of the workers and called for a revolution to replace the existing capitalist system with a socialist one. The most influential ideology was Russian autocracy, which was based on the concepts of absolute power of the Tsar, service to a strong centralized state, collectivism, and Russian Orthodoxy.

The ideology of the Tsarist regime influenced its industrial policy. Economic leaders, such as Finance Minister Sergei Witte, believed that the state should play a decisive role in industrialization in order to remedy the technological backwardness that had contributed to Russia's military defeats in the Crimean War (1854–5) and the Russo-Japanese War (1904–5) (von Laue 1963; Portal 1965; Kaser 1978). Their general strategy was to promote the development of heavy and defence industry using interventionist policies and to finance this by extracting resources from agriculture and borrowing foreign capital. Although the resulting industrial policies in Russia gave a more prominent role to the state than did those of liberal countries, they were similar to those of other continental European powers, such as Germany and France. Despite this interventionism, market forces were allowed to determine industrial developments in all but a few critical sectors (Kahan 1967).

The Russian government employed a number of fiscal instruments to promote industrialization, especially state budget expenditures on infrastructure such as communications and transportation (Portal 1965; Kaser 1978; Gatrell 1986). State orders for railway goods stimulated the growth of the iron, steel, and engineering industries, especially in conjunction with the tariffs imposed in 1891 upon imports of competing manufactures. The rail network expanded fortyfold from 1860 to 1916 (Goldsmith 1961: 442). This improved links between regions with complementary products, opened up markets in Siberia and the Far East,

---

[9] Good sources on the ideologies underpinning industrial policies in the Tsarist period are: von Laue (1963); Portal (1965); Gatrell (1986); and Mau (1993).

and facilitated the transport of agricultural goods, extracted from the peasantry through taxation, from internal regions to international markets. The exports helped the government to finance imports of industrial goods and to service foreign loans. Expenditures from the state budget on railways fell by two-thirds after 1900, but the effects on industry of this reduction of government demand were offset by the growth of military procurement associated with the rebuilding of the army and navy after their defeats in the Russo-Japanese War and the arms race preceding World War I (Gatrell 1994).

The Tsarist state provided subsidies of capital investment and production to selected industrial enterprises engaged in work considered vital to national interests. Although the government's average annual share of national investment was a low 7% in the years 1909–13, much of this was directed into defence industry to significant effect. Civilian leaders, such as Witte, did not identify electrification as a significant component of industrialization (Coopersmith 1992). However, the Army and Navy recognized the strategic importance of electrotechnology and supported its development from the late nineteenth century onwards by funding research, purchasing electrical products and electricity, and subsidizing factories producing electrical equipment. The government tolerated, if not colluded in, the formation of cartels in the coal, oil, iron, and steel industries that divided up market shares in attempts to regulate demand and prices.[10] The central state did not have a coherent regional strategy for industry, but its policies of supporting railways, defence factories, and shipbuilding had differing geographical impacts.

The international components of industrial policy included tariffs and export promotion. The Tsarist government encouraged foreign direct investment and purchases of state bonds in order to gain access to entrepreneurship, managerial skills, and advanced technology in world markets. To this end it adhered to prudent fiscal, monetary, and exchange rate policies.

The main beneficiaries of Tsarist industrial policies were the railway, engineering, iron, steel, and defence industries. Light industry was neglected by the state but not penalized. Much of the burden of industrialization fell on the agricultural sector as a result of tax policies. Consumers were disadvantaged due to the heavy alcohol taxes, cartels, tariffs, and distortions caused by the state-directed expansion of heavy industry. The regions to benefit from state policies, albeit in an unplanned manner, were those located in the Central economic zone

---

[10] Gatrell (1986: 179) writes; 'Throughout the period immediately before the First World War (and during the War itself), Russian heavy industry became highly integrated. Typically, metallurgical plants would be united with coal and iron ore mines under the same corporate control. These industries were also associated formally or informally (through the medium of the major banks) with finishing industries, such as engineering firms producing industrial equipment, agricultural machinery, construction materials, shipbuilding and defence goods.' For example, by 1911 the Society for the Sale of Metallurgical Products of Russian Industry (*Prodmeta*) 'controlled 90 per cent of the sales of assorted and sheet iron, 96 per cent of girders and channels, and 74 per cent of pig iron production'. See Lyashchenko (1949: ch. 32) and Kaser (1978: 477–82) for evaluations of syndicates (cartels). These cartels have a number of features that are similar to the Financial-Industrial Groups that are developing in the contemporary transition period in Russia (*Finansovo* 1996) (see section 13.6).

(Moscow, Vladimir, Tula), the North West (St Petersburg), Ukraine, and the Urals (Portal 1965).[11]

In the Tsarist era, industrial enterprises were owned by the Russian state, domestic businessmen, and foreign companies and banks. The corporate governance mechanisms of the private firms tended to be bank-based, even when companies made use of equity markets.[12] On the whole, firms operated in a market environment and were responsive to consumer demand and prices. But markets for heavy industry were imperfect due to oligopolistic conditions, price-fixing, and state subsidies. The average Russian factory was larger than its equivalents in the West, had lower labour productivity and relied upon oppressive measures to maintain worker discipline. Russian firms were more protected from foreign competition than were their equivalents in Western Europe due to the large size of the economy, the underdeveloped transportation system, poor weather, and state policy.

The military-industrial complex provided one of the pillars of the Tsarist regime and therefore obtained significant allocations of resources from the state, especially after 1905 (Pinter 1984). As in most European countries, Russian defence industry enterprises predominantly were state-owned, although there were some private ones of significance (Gatrell 1994). These firms faced minimal competition and were dependent upon government procurement and subsidies for their survival. The technological level of the defence industry was low by international standards and its production capacity was insufficient to meet the needs of the large Russian military. Tsarist Russia exported insignificant quantities of weapons and relied upon the import of Western technologies for the modernization of armaments production.

The international economic policies of the Tsarist state were successful in encouraging foreign involvement in Russian industry (McKay 1970). By the end of this period foreigners held about one-half of both government debt and joint-stock capital and they supplied 57% of the total equipment flowing into Russian industrial firms (Gatrell 1986; Nove 1989).

The performance of Russian industry in the pre-war period reflected the interactions between the economic system, state policies, and the unstable political situation.[13] The index of gross industrial output increased from 31 in 1890 to 100

[11] According to Davies (1994*b*: 134), industry was concentrated in the Central, North, and North West (including the Baltic states) economic zones of Russia, which accounted for 51% of production. Other regional contributions were: Ukraine 21%, the South and Eastern (including Russian Poland) zones of Russia 11%, the Urals and West Siberia 6%, and the Transcaucasus 7%.

[12] Corporate governance refers to the mechanisms that exist in an economic system to ensure that agents managing firms behave in an optimal manner with respect to advancing the interests of their principals (the owners). In a market economy this entails profit maximization. The main alternative corporate governance models in market economies are bank-based control, as in Germany, and equity market control, as in the USA. See Estrin (1994) and EBRD (1995).

[13] Gerschenkron (1965*a*, 1965*b*) and others have argued that consumer demand was important as well as state orders in stimulating industry in the late Tsarist period, especially cottage (*kustar*) production in the branches of textiles, household products, and agricultural machinery. According to Gatrell (1986), by the turn of the century cottage industry accounted for about one-quarter of manufacturing output.

in 1916 (see Figure 13.1). However, production stagnated in 1901–2 and the output index dropped to 60 in the revolutionary year of 1905. The subsequent recovery was stimulated by the armaments procurement programme of the state. The annual average rate of industrial growth over 1900–13 was a relatively low 3%, but it accelerated to 5% for the years 1908–13. The production of most key commodities rose over time (Appendix C).

Industrial output grew faster than did the economy as a whole, with the consequence that its share of national income by sector-of-origin rose to 21% (Appendix B). Nevertheless, in 1913 agriculture still produced one-half of GDP. Factories generated three-quarters of industrial production, but only about 40% of the commodities came from heavy industry. Industry's share in the national capital stock went up from 8% in 1900 to 17% in 1913 (Kahan 1978: 290). There were improvements in production technology and the quality of industrial goods. Labour productivity growth in industry fluctuated over 1900–13 with an upward trend (Crisp 1978).

By the turn of the century, Russia was the largest producer of oil in the world and ranked fourth in the output of iron and steel and in its share of world manufacturing. However, despite interventions by the Russian state little progress was made over 1890–1913 in closing the gaps between technological levels in Russian industry and those in more advanced countries (Appendix D). The industrial sector in Russia had a low share of heavy industry and a high one of light industry relative to Western Europe. A large proportion of Russian industrial goods was produced by hand in small-scale units, whereas mass production was rare. Russia's engineering was about a generation behind that in Germany and Britain and its industry generated negligible amounts of technical innovation. Its electricity production was similar to that of France and Italy, but it was only one-quarter of theirs per capita. Factor productivity in Russian industry was comparatively low. Finally, Russian industrial commodities remained uncompetitive with those of more advanced nations. In 1913 manufactures accounted for only 4.5% of Russian exports. Most were from light industry and were sold in non-European markets, such as China and the Caucasus (Gatrell 1986).

The seven years following the outbreak of World War in August 1914 were turbulent for Russia, with the Bolshevik Revolution in October 1917 marking a decisive shift in political and economic systems. Appendix A outlines the features and effects of industrial policy in the Tsarist War Economy (1914–17) and War Communism (1918–21). As a result of the revolutions and wars, Finland, the Baltic states, Poland and Bessarabia seceded from the Russian Empire; these territories accounted for about one-quarter of Russian industrial capital equipment and output in 1914 (Gatrell and Davies 1990; Gilbert 1993; N. Davies 1996). By the end of 1920 the Bolsheviks had decisively defeated their internal and external enemies. But acute crises in agricultural and industrial production and in the distribution of goods threatened the political viability of the regime and forced the Bolsheviks to launch the New Economic Policy (NEP).

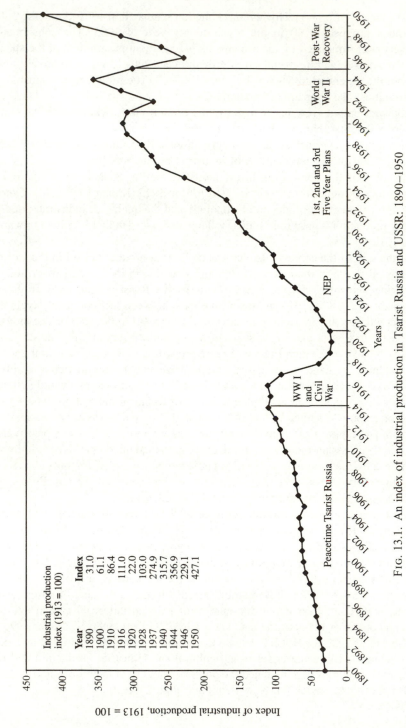

FIG. 13.1. An index of industrial production in Tsarist Russia and USSR: 1890–1950

Sources: This figure was generated from an index of industrial production with a base year of 1913 that was calculated using the sources outlined below.

1890–1913   Derived by the author from a Russian industrial production index with a base year of 1900 covering the years 1860–1913 that was constructed by Goldsmith 1961. See Table 7 on pp. 462–3. This index chains together links that are calculated using outputs of 19 industrial material products for 1890–9 and 26 for 1900–13 and imputed value added weights for 1897, 1900 and 1908. Nutter 1962, Table A-19 (p. 344) presents five different production indices (1913 = 100) for selected years in the period 1860–1913 that have slightly different values from those of the series used for this figure. For example, the range of 1900 values is 59.4–63.6, whereas this author's calculation based on Goldsmith is 61.1.

1913–28   The index numbers of industrial production for individual years are identical to those in an index (1913 = 100) of industrial materials output with 14 to 31 main products (the number varies by time period) and 1913 weights calculated by Nutter 1962. The index is presented in Table 47 and discussed in Appendix A, Technical Note 3. An alternative analysis of industrial production trends is provided in Gatrell and Davies 1990.

1928–40   The index numbers for 1928–37 were derived by chaining to the previous series values from an index (1937 = 100) calculated from data on civilian and munitions industry output in 1937 and index numbers from Moorsteen and Powell 1966, Table P-1 (pp. 622–4). Index numbers for 1938–40 are based on estimates of total industry value added in 1937 roubles made by Harrison (1998). These are lower than those of Moorsteen and Powell and reflect more reliable information on quantities and prices now available from archives. The Harrison index (1928 = 100) gives a 1940 value of 307, whereas that of Moorsteen and Powell is 318. A third authoritative index of total military and civilian industrial production is that of Nutter 1962, Table 53 (see also Appendix A, Technical Note 3). The index is estimated from the output of 101 to 119 civilian products, moving weights (1928, 1955), and limited information on military production. The 1940 value of this index (1928 = 100) is 312. This index shows lower growth in the early 1930s than Moorsteen and Powell and higher growth later in the decade.

1940–50   1941–5 values were estimated by chaining in the Harrison index presented in Harrison 1996. This index incorporates new archival information about hidden inflation, which results in higher values for all years than those of TsSU (presented in Harrison 1985) or previous Western analysts. For example, the 1943 values (1940 = 100) are 101 for Harrison, 90 for TsSU and 70 for Powell. The 1946–50 values are estimated from the index of Moorsteen and Powell 1966. It is quite similar to the index for these years of final industrial product in 1937 prices in Powell 1963, p. 179.

13.3. INDUSTRIAL POLICY IN THE NEW ECONOMIC POLICY
PERIOD (1921–1927)

Bolshevik policy-makers were confronted by severe industrial challenges in early
NEP. Factory production had fallen to catastrophically low levels (12% of the
1913 level), there were acute shortages of fuel and raw materials and the transportation network was barely functioning. The capital stock had been adversely
affected by years of insufficient investment, negligent maintenance, and war
damage. All industrial enterprises had been nationalized during War Communism, were financed by the state budget, and operated in accordance with government directives, rationing, and barter (Malle 1985). For four years managers
and workers had been more concerned with survival than with improving the
quality of output, efficiency, or technological levels in industry.

The economic strategy and policies of Bolshevik leaders during NEP were
influenced by Marxist-Leninist theory. But there was some confusion initially
because the ideological justifications for the money-less command economy of
War Communism were being replaced by ones more supportive of the market-
oriented reforms.[14] The modified ideology called for the Bolshevik state to retain
monopoly political power, ownership of most productive assets, and control over
the 'commanding heights' of the economy: banking, large-scale industry, wholesale trade, and foreign trade. However, it allowed some price liberalization, privatization, and decentralization of routine economic decision-making to managers
of state industrial trusts, peasants, and private entrepreneurs. The market resumed
its role as a coordination mechanism, but administrative instruments remained
dominant. A hybrid socialist command-market economic system gradually
evolved with features outlined in Table 13.4.

In early NEP, industrial policy was neither a top priority issue nor coherently
formulated. To the extent that the government had goals, they were to reduce
the fiscal burden of the state sector and to promote the recovery of the output
of industrial commodities needed for the relief of production bottlenecks and
exchanges with the peasants. In its drive to achieve a balanced budget and stabilize the currency the central government severely cut all major spending programmes, such as defence, and divested itself of direct financial responsibility for
most industrial and welfare institutions (Davies 1958; Davis 1983). It attempted
to minimize subsidies to state factories, although this policy was modified as the
1920s progressed because of the side effects of the price controls discussed below.

Industry was reorganized so that virtually all large-scale, state-owned enterprises (4,144 in number) were grouped into 430 trusts that operated on an independent commercial basis (*kommercheskii raschet*). The 172 trusts that produced

---

[14] Szamuely (1974) provides an evaluation of the development of Bolshevik ideologies underpinning economic
policies in the War Communism and NEP periods. The Bolsheviks generally agreed that the NEP economic system was a temporary, intermediate one that would be replaced by a proper socialist economy as soon as political
and economic conditions allowed. However, there was considerable difference of opinion concerning the length
of the period, with proposals ranging from 3 to 20 years.

TABLE 13.4. *Soviet economic system during NEP, 1921–1927*

System features

Decision-making — Bolshevik dictatorship, but relatively tolerant. State controls 'commanding heights' of economy. Decentralization of decision-making in industry to monopolistic trusts and syndicates

Coordination mechanism — Reliance on administrative methods to coordinate economic activities, especially in heavy industry. But significant role for markets and prices in retail and wholesale trade. Large second economy (black market). By late 1920s indicative planning (control figures) becomes influential

Property rights — State owns most of industry and all land. Some private ownership of small-scale industry and retail trade. Peasants have rights to use land and dispose of its products

Incentives — Mostly cash incentives. Some in-kind benefits in state sector and party apparatus. Limited reliance on coercion

Environment

International — Peaceful period. No serious external threats, but Bolsheviks experience war scare in 1927

Territory and resources — Stable borders and full access to natural resources. Population of USSR: 153 m in 1928

Policies

Utilization of national income — Defence share falls to historic low level. Investment share low relative to 1913 and most finance comes from the state. Consumption share increases

Sectoral priorities — Priorities of the state become less important. Defence industry cut back radically. Heavy industry developed to serve civilian economy. Favourable conditions created for agriculture, light industry, and trade

Foreign economic — Government tries to open up economy while maintaining the state monopoly of foreign trade. Acceptance of foreign investment and establishment of 'concessions'. Energetic efforts made to obtain Western technology

Performance

Economic growth — Rapid recovery of output in industry and agriculture after 1922 through better utilization of existing capacity. GDP back to 1913 levels by 1927. Concern about sustainability of growth generates the industrialization debate

Efficiency and technological innovation — Reliance on markets and competition results in improved coordination and efficiency. But lack of investment constrains technological progress. Most technology in industry is outmoded and inferior to that in the West

Income distribution — Growth of inequality in pay and privileges. Upper income: Party elite, businessmen (NEP-men), rich peasants (kulaks). Bottom income: Poor peasants, urban inhabitants without social insurance. Large share of population lives in poverty

TABLE 13.4. *(Cont'd)*

Consumer welfare	Due to economic recovery and tolerance of private initiative there are substantial improvements in the food supply and nutrition. The provision of medical services by the state increases, but they are distributed unequally. Intensifying shortage of urban housing
Economic stability	Initial instability (hyperinflation 1921–3). But this is corrected by an effective fiscal and monetary stabilization programme. Despite this, open price inflation remains a problem in the 1920s. Gradual shift to a classical unemployment disequilibrium state (excess demand for goods, excess labour supply)
Foreign economic	Foreign trade recovers slowly. By 1927 the index (1913 = 100) of exports reaches 33 and that of imports 38. State encounters growing problems exporting industrial and agricultural goods
National viability	No serious internal or external threats to the Bolshevik regime

Sources: Lectures by the author at Oxford University; Davies 1990; Davies, Harrison, and Wheatcroft 1994; Dobb 1960; Erlich 1960; Gladkov (1960); Gregory and Stuart 1994; Zaleski 1971.

the most important commodities were supervised by the Supreme Council for the National Economy (VSNKh). The others were subordinated to local governments. Some of the trusts subsequently were formed into syndicates (cartels) with the goals of limiting competition and guaranteeing market shares (Kaser 1978: 489–90). However, after 1926, the trusts lost their powers and enterprises regained their financial autonomy.

A significant number of medium-sized state firms were leased to entrepreneurs and cooperatives for profit-oriented operations, while a few were returned to their owners. Small industrial enterprises (employing 10–20 workers) were denationalized and the creation of small private firms was legalized. By 1927 three-quarters of small-scale industry was private.

The Bolsheviks initially removed most price controls. Due to the existence of repressed demand, this liberalization resulted in substantial open inflation that was dealt with through a fiscal and monetary stabilization programme (Davies 1958). Industrial prices in 1921–2 fell relative to agricultural ones because of the greater demand for food products in a time of famine. By 1923, however, the 'scissors crisis' had emerged as a result of a rapid rebound in real industrial prices (their index relative to 1913 = 100 rose to 190 in October 1923) and a drop in agricultural prices (their index fell to 60).[15] Bolshevik leaders thought that this would strain relations with the peasantry and disrupt food supplies in cities. They therefore intervened to drive down industrial prices and to raise those

[15] The main factors causing the rise of industrial prices were the slow recovery of industrial output relative to that of agriculture, inefficiency of industrial production, manipulation of markets by cartels, and weaknesses in the trade system. See analyses of the 'scissors crisis' in Dobb (1960) and Nove (1989).

of agriculture. This resolved the immediate crisis, but the long-term consequences of this intervention were considerable. Throughout the 1920s the prices that trusts could charge for their goods, especially in heavy industry, were tightly controlled and kept low relative to rising demand in the recovering economy. This caused growing shortages in markets for industrial products (the 'goods famine'). The state attempted to compensate for this through the rationing of scarce supplies and, rather counter-productively, the imposition of tighter restrictions on private traders to prevent them from taking advantage of market disequilibrium. Another side effect of price controls was that trusts producing capital goods became unprofitable. Since they were vital for the economy and could not go bankrupt, the state softened their budget constraints by providing them with subsidies and loans.

Physical controls were employed by the Bolshevik state to regulate industry throughout the NEP period. The core of industry subordinate to VSNKh was managed using administrative methods, such as state procurement and centrally-directed exchanges between firms producing key commodities (iron, steel, weapons, fuel).

One feature of Soviet industrial policy in the 1920s that distinguished it from that of Tsarist Russia or Western Europe was its growing reliance on national economic planning (Zaleski 1971). The 'Electrification Plan for the RSFSR' produced by GOELRO in December 1920 constituted an initial, utopian long-term national economic plan (Zaleski 1971; Coopersmith 1992: ch. 6). In early NEP indicative planning methods were refined, leading to the annual publication of 'control figures' that were meant to influence, but not command, economic developments. By the second half of the 1920s, planning of industry became increasingly directive in nature and administrative control over the whole economy intensified (Mau 1993).

Investment in industry was different in character to that of the Tsarist period, because foreign sources were unavailable, constraints existed on the extraction of surpluses from the peasants, and entrepreneurs were reluctant to commit private capital to industrial projects given the unstable political situation. This meant that the state had to be the main provider of investment for the less profitable branches of industry, notably capital goods, and that it had to be financed primarily through taxes on industry and trade. Most central investment in heavy industry was allocated by VSNKh through increasingly sophisticated plans that relied on financial regulators. Special banks were established to channel credits to industry, such as Prombank and Elektrobank. In contrast, profitable state-owned consumer industries tended to finance their investment out of earnings (Gatrell and Davies 1990).

The government was constrained in its capability to alter the inherited geographical distribution of enterprises due to the lack of investment. Nevertheless, it launched a number of major projects in transportation (e.g. the Turkestan–Siberian and Urals–Kuzbas railway lines) and in branches of industry (e.g. the Dniepr hydrostation) that constituted an uncoordinated regional industrial policy. In the late 1920s the Soviet regime formulated plans to develop interior regions for national security reasons that ignored economic considerations (North and Shaw 1995). Overall, though, little progress was achieved in changing industrial location.[16]

The state monopoly of foreign trade regulated exports and imports using direct physical controls rather than indirect ones, such as export taxes and tariffs. Soviet Russia was forced to maintain a balance in its trade with the West, and therefore needed to offset its imports of industrial raw materials and machinery with exports of foodstuffs and energy products. One market-oriented innovation in the foreign trade sphere was the 'concession', which was an industrial enterprise involving Western investment and management. Throughout the 1920s attempts were made to obtain military-related technologies from leading industrialized countries through covert programmes involving trade and the 'concessions'.[17] Secret military cooperation agreements allowed Germany to establish bases in the USSR for aviation and tank training and factories for the production of munitions and weapons, in contravention of the Versailles Treaty, in exchange for some financial payments and the sharing of military experiences and products.

The main beneficiaries of NEP industrial policy were quite different from those of the Tsarist period or War Communism. In the 1920s the only heavy industries favoured were those necessary for the recovery process. The state promoted the production of agricultural machinery and the market rewarded light industry producing for consumers.

Most large- and medium-size industrial firms in NEP were state-owned and financially subordinate to their trust. This model was unusual by the international standards of the time. State enterprises in light industry and private small-scale firms in all sectors operated in reasonably competitive market environments, were responsive to consumer demand and prices, and possessed hard budget constraints. In contrast, heavy industry firms functioned in imperfect, cartelized markets. As mentioned above, they were subject to tight price controls, operated in sellers' markets, and had soft budget constraints. Managers and firms began to adopt behavioural patterns that were typical of those found in a shortage economy.[18] Capital goods firms increasingly relied upon the central government for investment funds, subsidies, and allocations of supplies. The vertical relations of these firms with their bureaucratic superiors became more important than horizontal, market-related ones.

---

[16] Although state policies did not change the geographical distribution of industrial enterprises within the USSR during NEP, the regional pattern of industrial employment and output in 1927 was different from that of Tsarist Russia. This was primarily due to the war-related alterations in international boundaries. The shares of output and employment of the Central, North-West, and Southern regions increased whereas those of the others declined (Gatrell and Davies 1990: 131).

[17] General features and results of Soviet policies aimed at acquiring military-related technology are assessed in Sutton (1968: chs. 15, 20). Erickson (1962) provides an early assessment of Soviet–German cooperation. His study has been amplified by D'yakov and Bushueva (1992), based on newly released, previously secret documents. This author has obtained additional archival documents on technology acquisition in the Russian State Archive of the Economy (RGAE).

[18] The concepts of the shortage economy model were developed by Janos Kornai and used to analyse the mature command economies (Kornai 1980, 1992). The model is evaluated in Davis and Charemza (1989a,b).

During the initial years of NEP, the size of the Red Army was cut from 5.3 million to 560,000.[19] State orders for weapons and munitions were reduced, which caused a large decline in the military output of the defence industry. Less important defence enterprises were transferred to trusts and ordered to convert to civilian production. The core of the defence industry was placed under the VSNKh Chief Administration for the Armaments Industry. Defence firms operated in accordance with state orders, military regulations, investment plans, and central rationing; market forces had only modest impact on their conditions and behaviour.

In the NEP period, the Soviet regime reorganized scientific research institutions and maintained a strong formal commitment to technological innovation, which it believed would be more rapid in a socialist economy than in a capitalist one (Cooper and Lewis 1990). The state awarded high priority status to programmes designed to develop selected technologies, such as electroenergy and metallurgy. However, there was only modest actual technical progress in industry, due to the existence of sellers' markets, closed nature of the economy, lack of investment, and absence of state orders for high-technology commodities, such as weapons. Nevertheless, Soviet Russia began to produce some industrial goods for the first time, such as oil extraction equipment, turbines, and tractors.

Developments in Soviet foreign economic relations of relevance to industry were not notably positive in the 1920s (Sutton 1968; Dohan 1990). The concession policy resulted in a mere 42 agreements with foreign firms and only three-quarters of these were still functioning by the end of the decade, when they accounted for 1% of industrial output. The state gave imports of machinery and industrial raw materials a relatively high priority and consumer goods a low one. Machinery accounted for 27% of Russian imports in 1927 versus 15% in 1913. Imports were responsible for 30–40% of machinery installed, but in real terms these foreign supplies to industry reached only 75% of their 1913 level.

During NEP, market forces and government policies generated a recovery of the output of Soviet industry by 1927 to that of 1913 (Figure 13.1 and Appendices B and C). Most heavy industry branches, but not defence, achieved pre-war production levels before those of consumer goods due to preferential treatment by the state. But the NEP recovery was based primarily on the growing utilization of existing capacity. Although real investment in industry was greater in 1927 than it had been in 1913, as was industry's share of the total, much of it was devoted to the renovation of existing capital stock. The commercialization of industry resulted in a rise of urban unemployment from close to zero in 1921 to 14% in 1927 (Shapiro 1990). By the end of NEP, labour productivity was 10% above its 1913 level.

---

[19] Military developments in the 1920s are authoritatively analysed in Erickson (1962). Recent studies of defence industry in this period include Samuelson (1996) and Simonov (1996). In 1991 this author wrote two discussion papers on the economics of the Soviet defence sector in the 1920s using published sources. More recently he has obtained numerous archival documents from RGAE and the Russian State Military Archive related to defence spending, weapons procurement, defence industry production, logistics and military foreign trade. These are being analysed in a British Academy project and an article on this subject is in preparation.

The NEP economic system did not generate increases in the share of industry in GDP or the technical quality of industrial products significantly above those of the Tsarist economy. Soviet industry in 1928 was still dominated by the textile and food-processing branches and a substantial share of output was produced by small-scale enterprises using manual labour. It possessed insignificant production capabilities in technically advanced branches (machine building, electrical engineering, chemical).

Soviet industry remained backward relative to the standards set by major world powers. Due to its low level of mechanization, the consumption of energy per worker in Soviet industry was 41% of that of Germany and 13% of the US standard. Although industrial labour productivity improved over time, it remained lower than that achieved in all Western countries and one-seventh that of the USA. The technological gap between Russia and the West widened from 1917 to 1928 and the USSR's share of world manufacturing output declined.

In the second half of the 1920s the Bolshevik leadership became worried that the existing economic system would not generate the investment needed for the rapid industrialization of the backward Soviet Union on socialist principles and for the development of high-technology defence industries to support a modern Red Army. These concerns provoked a debate on industrialization strategy between the left and right wings of the Bolshevik Party.[20] The leftists were in favour of a rapid industrialization, with emphasis on heavy branches, that was to be financed through an extraction of resources from the agricultural sector on the basis of 'primitive socialist accumulation' (Preobrazhensky 1926). The right forces, led by Nikolai Bukharin, advocated a more gradual and balanced development involving the maintenance of market relationships, efficiency improvements in industry, and expansion of ties with the capitalist world. There also were related disputes over whether economic planning should be compulsory, goal-oriented (teleological) and unbalanced in favour of heavy industry or indicative, equilibrium-oriented (genetic) and demand-responsive. By 1928 the dominant Stalin faction in the party had appropriated a modified version of the left's strategy and introduced the overly ambitious First Five Year Plan for 1928–32 that had as its primary objective the rapid growth of heavy and defence industries. Collectivization of agriculture commenced in 1929 with the goal of bringing the peasants under the tighter state control needed for the extraction of a surplus to provide investment resources for the industrialization drive.

13.4. INDUSTRIAL POLICY IN THE STALINIST PEACETIME COMMAND ECONOMY (1928–1941)

In the Stalinist economic system, decision-making became highly centralized, quantity-oriented central plans were utilized as the main coordination mechanism,

---

[20] The industrialization debate is analysed in (Erlich 1960) and Carr and Davies (1974).

and the state owned all productive assets (see Table 13.5). Stalinist incentives included moral rewards linked to socialist ideology, differentiated privileges and cash payments, and physical coercion. Within several years this system of inconsistent plans, non-monetary exchanges, chronic shortages, sellers' markets, and hierarchy generated the prototype of the socialist shortage economy analysed in Kornai (1980, 1992).

The choice of the main Stalinist industrial goals, the rapid growth and modernization of heavy and defence branches, was influenced by several factors. Marxist-Leninist ideology called for the construction of socialist industry on the basis of state ownership and centralized administrative controls. Industrialization was viewed as a process leading to a victory in the class war through the expansion of the urban proletariat and the reduction in the power of the peasantry. The Marxist development model of that time postulated that high shares of national income invested in heavy industry ('the means of production') would generate the fastest long-term growth of the economy, which eventually would benefit 'the means of consumption' and living standards.[21] National security justifications for rapid industrialization were based on a war scare in 1927, Japanese military activity in Asia, and the rise of Fascism in Europe (Erickson 1962; Samuelson 1996).

Due to the interconnections between institutional arrangements, goals, and policies in the Stalin period, it is difficult to evaluate industrial policy as an independent issue. In reality, the Stalinist economy was an expression of industrial policy and specific resource allocation decisions were almost predetermined by systemic factors. Taking these qualifications into account, one can observe that the Stalinist regime used a number of industrial policy instruments that were unusual by European standards of the day. Most obvious were mandatory state planning and the linked central rationing of supplies to industries (Zaleski 1980). However, Soviet plans were over-ambitious with respect to targets for industrial outputs and productivity improvements and consequently were inconsistent (Rutland 1985). Party and state organizations intervened regularly to revise output targets and redistribute supplies in attempts to rectify demand–supply imbalances that arose during plan implementation.

The priority system was another instrument the Stalinist regime used to promote its variant of industrialization.[22] The leadership realized that the backwardness of Russia and the scarcity of resources meant that only a limited number of goals could be achieved in any given period. They therefore established rankings of programmes and outputs and developed institutions and mechanisms in planning, supply (rationing), and administration to ensure that the most important branches of the economy, defence and heavy industry, received preferential treatment to maximize their possibilities of fulfilling plans.[23] Low priority sectors,

---

[21] An influential Marxist model of unbalanced rapid industrialization was developed in mathematical terms by G. A. Fel'dman in papers in *Narodnoe Khozyaistvo* in 1928–9. English translations of them are provided in Fel'dman (1928). His model was reformulated and its implications evaluated in Domar (1957).

[22] Discussions of Soviet industrial priorities in the 1930s can be found in Nutter (1962: 64) and Zaleski (1980).

[23] A mathematical (algebraic and geometric) exposition of concepts of priority related to the defence sector can be found in Ericson (1988). These ideas have been adapted and supplemented by Davis (1989, 1990a, 1997) in

TABLE 13.5. *Stalinist peacetime economic system, 1928–1941, 1945–1953*

Features

Decision-making	Harsh Stalinist dictatorship that strives for complete centralization. But some limited decentralization of decision-making due to the need for managers to cope with inconsistent plans
Coordination mechanism	Emergence of centralized, teleological planning. Money and budgets become passive. Firms rely on central rationing for their supplies. Constrained legal retail and labour markets exist. Black markets survive, especially for food. Some illegal barter between firms
Property rights	State assumes ownership of all productive assets. Collectivization of agriculture
Incentives	Combination of moral campaigns (e.g. Stakhanovite movement), benefits rationed by the state, cash wages and bonuses, and coercion (e.g. purges)

Environment

International	Stalinist regime feels acutely threatened by Germans and Japanese in the 1930s and Americans in the post-war period (1945–53)
Territory and resources	Borders expanded through conquests in 1939–40, 1944–5. Full access to natural resources. Population of USSR: 194 million in 1940 (post-war border), 188 million in 1953

Policies

Utilization of national income	Rapid industrialization requires high investment and militarization entails high defence spending. Consumption squeezed down to 55% of GDP
Sectoral priorities	Defence and heavy industry given top priority. Light industry, agriculture, and services neglected
Foreign economic	Autarkic policies and drive for self-sufficiency in pre-war period. USSR develops state monopoly trading system using inconvertible currencies with Eastern European communist states in post-war period

Performance

Economic growth	Rapid growth on extensive basis of GDP (about 5% p.a.). Industry share GDP grows rapidly from 20% in 1928 to 31% in 1940, whereas the share of agriculture falls
Efficiency and technological innovation	Inconsistent planning and the emergence of a shortage economy result in poor static and dynamic efficiency. Sluggish technological innovation except in high priority branches of industry
Income distribution	Significant, but disguised, inequality. Upper income: Communist Party elite, managers, scientists, defence workers. Bottom income: Peasants, workers in services, elderly. Substantial poverty
Consumer welfare	State induced famine in 1932–4. Food supply adequate later in 1930s. But another famine in 1946. Real wages do not reach 1928 levels until 1953. Under-investment in welfare and medical services, housing

TABLE 13.5. *(Cont'd)*

Stability	Substantial microeconomic instability due to imperfect planning, but only modest macroeconomic fluctuations. Shift to a repressed inflation (chronic shortage) disequilibrium state
Foreign economic	Trade turnover drops from 6% GDP in 1928 to 1% in 1937. Growth in trade with Nazi Germany in 1939–41. Little post-war trade but subtantial forced war reparations from occupied territories in Eastern Europe
National viability	Rapid economic growth, victory in World War II, totalitarian ideology, and repressive controls ensure the security of the Stalin regime

Sources: Lectures of the author at Oxford University; Baykov 1947; Davies, Harrison, and Wheatcroft 1994; Dobb 1960; Gregory and Stuart 1994; Nove 1989; Zaleski 1980.

such as light industry and the medical system, were residual claimants of scarce resources.

A third distinctive instrument was state coercion. Soviet managers in industry were placed under severe pressure to fulfil plans irrespective of conditions by real threats of arrest and execution for imagined acts of 'sabotage'. Throughout the 1930s two–three million Soviet prisoners worked on major industrialization projects in the GULAG system, primarily in mining and on construction of factories, railways, and canals (Swianiewicz 1965; Bacon 1994; Davies 1998). Although it is possible to show that the forced labour system was effective in accomplishing specific objectives in inhospitable regions of the USSR, there is debate over whether it made an overall net contribution to industrialization.

Stalinist industrial policy minimized the role of markets. Legal wholesale markets were virtually eliminated and exchanges between firms were primarily governed by central rationing. Informal processes continued to exist, however, and there was some inter-firm black market trade and bartering. Industrial consumer goods were distributed to the population through regulated retail markets characterized by excess demand and domination by sellers. Collective farm (*kolkhoz*) markets for food existed throughout the 1930s and in periods of less intense state repression, consumer demand spilled over into flexible-price black markets, resulting in sales of deficit commodities at higher prices.[24]

order to analyse the high-priority defence sector and low-priority health sector in the Soviet economy. Indicators of priority during plan formulation include weight in planners' objective function, degree of responsiveness of decision-makers to past problems in a sector, wage rates and norms used in planning and budgeting. Priority indicators during plan implementation include degree of commitment to fulfilment of plans (output, supply, and investment), hardness of budget constraints, tolerance of inventories, existence of reserve production capacity, and intensity of shortages in a sector.

[24] The role and features of the Soviet second economy in the 1930s are discussed in Zaleski (1980). Davis (1988) presents a model of the second economy in a command economic system that describes its institutions (such as industrial firms) and markets (such as that for illegal producer goods). It also contains a review of the literature on the second economy, including that on the informal activities of industrial enterprises.

The price mechanism was an industrial policy instrument of secondary importance. In the initial years of the First Five Year Plan, the state attempted to keep
industrial prices stable and anticipated that they would be reduced as efficiency
improvements lowered costs of production. However, the low inflexible prices
contributed to the chronic shortages of industrial goods and undermined incentives for technological innovation. In some later periods in the 1930s price
policy became more realistic (Davies 1998). As a general rule, though, industrial
prices tended to be low relative to demand.

One enduring consequence of the Stalinist practice of arbitrarily setting prices
and exchange rates was that domestic prices of industrial goods diverged from
world market relative prices. Domestic rouble prices usually were set so that most
industrial enterprises were profitable. But if the outputs and inputs were to be
measured using world market prices, the possibility existed that some firms and
sectors of industry in the closed Soviet economy could generate negative value
added.[25]

Stalinist fiscal policy was influenced by ideas of non-price control and the
slogan that 'the budget should follow the plan'. Given that the over-ambitious plans
had to be financed, state budgets became equally unrealistic documents. At lower
levels of the industrial hierarchy decision-makers came to realize that it was most
important to fulfil plans in quantitative terms at any cost and that budgets would
be adjusted *ex post*. Over time this practice resulted in the phenomenon of the
soft budget constraint (Kornai 1992: 140–5).

Banking and monetary policies were passive and of minor significance to industrial development. Banks funded industrial investment projects through grants or
soft loans in accordance with central directives, irrespective of risks and returns.
Attempts were made to finance the state budget deficit through compulsory bond
sales to the population. But the residual was covered by printing money.

The Five Year Plans in the 1930s adopted ambitious industrialization targets
for backward regions and launched large projects to develop steel and machine-
building industries in the Urals, the textile industry in Uzbekistan, the engineering industry in Georgia, and mining in Kazakhstan (Davies 1994*b*). Some of these

---

[25] Numerous Western studies have discussed Soviet price policy and the consequences for industry of arbitrary,
sticky prices. McKinnon (1991) argues that protectionism and distorted domestic relative prices in the Soviet-type
system can produce a situation in which manufacturing generates negative value added when measured at world
market prices. Let gross output of finished goods industry i be represented by the production function: $Z_i = Z_i (L_i,
M_i)$, where L_i = primary factors such as land and labour, M_i = intermediate material inputs. Assume one interme-
diate input and one domestic factor. Value added in domestic prices of the ith finished goods industry is equal to
gross value minus the cost of intermediate inputs: $V_i = P_i Z_i - P_m M$, where P_i and P_m are the domestic currency
prices of the finished product and material input. Now reformulate in terms of world prices, which are assumed to
be fixed. Let t_i represent the implicit tariff protecting domestic production of the finished product, the gap between
the foreign and quality-adjusted domestic price: $P_i = (1 + t_i)P_i^*$, $P_i > P_i^*$ and let t_m represent the similarly calculated
implicit export tax on material inputs: $P_m(1 + t_m) = P_m^*$, where $P_m < P_m^*$. Express the ratio of the finished product
and material inputs in terms of foreign relative prices: $P_i/P_m = (1 + t_i)(1 + t_m)(P_i^*/P_m^*)$. This equation captures
the dual aspect of the overall protection of the gross output of finished goods: the effect of restricting competing imports and of subsidizing the use of material inputs. Domestic value added at world prices is determined
by: $V_i^* = P_i^* Z_i - P_m^* M$. Although V_i usually is positive, there can be no presumption that domestic value added at
world prices is positive. If either t_m or t_i is sufficiently high, and if the relatively cheap M is substituted for other
factors of production, then it is possible for $V_i^* < 0$.

could be justified on economic grounds, such as the ones that located industries near resources. Others were supported for national security reasons because they created vital industries far from vulnerable borders.

Industry was influenced as well by foreign economic relations. The Stalinist state became strongly committed to the principle of economic self-sufficiency and import substitution. In doing so, it was pushing to the extreme trade-related industrial policies that were prevalent in continental European economies. The domestic economy was tightly insulated from international influences through the state monopoly of foreign trade. The state authorized the import of critical machinery, metals, and industrial raw materials from Western countries and financed their purchase by exporting agricultural products. The government also allowed foreign engineers and managers to provide direct technical assistance by working in the USSR.

The main beneficiaries of Stalinist industrial policies were heavy industry, especially steel and engineering, and the defence industry. Textiles, food processing, and chemicals were neglected, as were agriculture and social services. The geographic regions that contained high priority industrial enterprises received preferential treatment by the central authorities.

Government policies and the related changes in the environment and functioning of state-owned industrial firms during the early 1930s established patterns that were maintained throughout the Soviet period (Granick 1954; Berliner 1957, 1976). Although individual enterprises were given formal responsibility for their economic performance, in reality they were completely subordinated to industrial commissariats (later renamed ministries). Soviet firms tended to be large in scale, monopolistic in regionally segmented markets, vertically integrated and protected from international competition. Their main objectives were to fulfil centrally planned output targets set by their superiors in the ministerial hierarchy, not to maximize profits or satisfy customers. On their output side, firms operated in sellers' markets, attempted to expand the volume of production (the quantity drive), and were inattentive to the quality of their goods.[26] On their input side, they possessed soft budget constraints, encountered chronic shortages of labour and supplies, and made excessive demands for investment goods. Within the firm the shortage conditions generated production bottlenecks, forced substitution, inappropriate product mixes, excessive inventories, low factor productivity, high energy and material intensity of production, sluggish technological innovation, and low technological levels.

The Stalinist leadership was committed to the rapid growth of military power and to this end attempted to expand and modernize the existing defence industry (Sapir 1990; Davies 1994*b*; Samuelson 1996; Simonov 1996; Harrison and Davies 1997). Supra-ministerial bodies were created to coordinate the defence programme and military departments were established in the planning and

---

[26] The seminal works on the market situation and behaviour of industrial firms in socialist shortage economies are Kornai (1959, 1980, 1992).

supply agencies and in the Communist Party's central bureaucracy (Harrison 1985). The high priority status of defence institutions guaranteed them preferential access to resources and favourable operating conditions. Special organizational arrangements were made to promote an above average quality of military production (e.g. basing military inspectors in factories) and more rapid technological innovations (e.g. creating powerful weapons design bureaux). The defence industry share of investment increased from 3% in 1928 to over 30% in 1940. Defence spending rose from a modest 1% of national income in 1928 to 18% in 1940, with procurement and military R & D expenditure increasing more rapidly than wages and operations and maintenance.[27] The annual output of main weapons systems rose as follows: tanks from 170 to 2,794; combat aircraft from 204 to 8,232; and artillery pieces from 952 to 15,000.

The Soviet government attempted to accelerate technological progress in industry by improving the organization of science and increasing investment in R & D (Lewis 1994). Notable technological advances were achieved in the chemical industry and in machine building (Holloway 1982). The quality of weapons systems increased and by 1941 some of them (e.g. the T-34 tank) were at the forefront of world military technology. Domestic innovation was supported by the import of advanced Western technologies and by the participation of foreign engineers and scientists in Soviet programmes (Sutton 1971).

As a result of the state's technology acquisition policy, the value of legal imports of machinery and equipment trebled from 1925 to 1930 (when they accounted for 47% of total imports) before falling to about one-fifth of its peak by 1940 (MVT 1967: 27). Heavy industry's share of total imports rose from 36% in the mid-1920s to 85% in the early 1930s (Gaidar 1997: 129). The main sources of technology supplies were the USA and Germany. Soviet intelligence services intensified their efforts to obtain Western military technologies using covert methods. The secret programmes of cooperation with Germany in the military and defence industry fields continued through 1932 and resumed again in the period of the Soviet–Nazi Pact, 1939–41 (Erickson 1962; D'yakov and Bushueva 1992).

The general and targeted policies of the state changed the territorial structure of Soviet industry during 1928–40. The drive for self-sufficiency meant that seaport cities, such as Odessa and Leningrad, and regional industries dependent upon imports declined in importance (North and Shaw 1995). Industrial output in the Moscow region grew relatively slowly due to its domination by the low priority textile industry. In contrast, the capital stock and production of heavy industry in Ukraine's Donets Basin and Krivoi Rog complexes, the Volga region, the Urals–Kuznetsk combine, and Siberia increased rapidly.[28]

---

[27] Although some Western countries were engaged in similar rearmament drives in the 1930s, the Soviet pre-war effort was distinguished by its large-scale mobilization of resources, detailed organization, high-priority status, and rapidity in generating substantial outputs of weapons systems (Milward 1977; Harrison 1985, 1996).

[28] This author initially intended to present an assessment of changes in the regional distribution of Russian and Soviet industry over the century. To this end he obtained statistical material on gross industrial output in 1926/7 prices for 49 regions of the Russian Federation for the years 1913, 1927/8, 1932, 1936, and 1937 (RGAE *fond* 4372, *opis'* 35, *delo* 158, pp. 18–19). It confirms the general observations made in the text. However, it is not possible to report in more detail in this chapter due to space constraints.

Stalinist industrial policies dramatically expanded the capacity and output of Soviet industry and transformed its branch structure. According to official Soviet estimates, the average annual growth rate of gross industrial production in 1928–40 was 17%. Western scholars have demonstrated that the official record is exaggerated and most would accept estimates of growth rates in the 8–10% range (Nutter 1962; Moorsteen and Powell 1966; Davies 1994*b*). However, some scholars, notably Selyunin and Khanin (1987), have argued that industrial output grew at a lower annual rate of about 5%.[29] The index of production (1913 = 100) shown in Appendix B, which is based on conventional Western estimates, increases from 103 in 1928 to a pre-war peak of 316 in 1940. The production of key industrial commodities is shown in Appendix C.

Industry's share of GDP climbed from 20% in 1928 to 31% in 1940. But the unbalanced Stalinist industrialization resulted in uneven development across sectors; plan targets for heavy and defence industries were consistently over-fulfilled, whereas those of the low priority consumer goods industry were not achieved (Zaleski 1980). The share of producer goods in total industry output rose from 40 to 61% from 1928 to 1940 (Appendix B). The defence share of total industrial output increased from 3% in 1930 to 6% in 1932 to 23% in 1940 (Davies 1994*b*: tables 28–29).

The issue of whether the Stalinist collectivization policy actually extracted the resources from the agricultural sector needed to support this rapid industrialization has proved to be controversial. Some Soviet and Western economists have challenged conventional wisdom by arguing that although confiscation and taxation generated a large outflow of commodities from collectivized agriculture, the inputs from industry to agriculture were much greater than anticipated because of the need to compensate for the destruction of livestock, the main source of productive power, that accompanied collectivization.[30] By using different prices (1928 or 1913) to value the flows, it is possible to show that there was a net outflow of resources from or inflow to the agricultural sector. Despite this alternative analysis, the consensus remains that agriculture was an important source of accumulation for the industrialization drive. Furthermore, collectivization contributed to the large-scale flow of labour from the countryside into construction and industry.

Another question to be considered is whether Stalinist policies enabled the USSR to improve the international standing of its industrial sector. Due to the rapid growth of industrial output and the Great Depression in the West, the Soviet share of world manufacturing increased from 5% in 1929 to 18% in 1938 (Kennedy 1988: 330). By the end of the 1930s the Soviet Union had become the third largest producer of steel in the world and the largest one of weapons (Appendix D). However, Soviet per capita indicators of industrial development remained low by European standards, as did measures of the intensity of production, mechanization in industry, efficiency, and labour productivity.

---

[29] The Khanin-Selyunin critique is thoroughly evaluated in Ericson (1990) and Harrison (1993). See also Davies (1998).

[30] The debate over the net contribution of collectivization to industrialization is reviewed in Ellman (1975, 1988) and Nove (1989). See also Gregory and Stuart (1994: ch. 5).

The outbreak of war between Nazi Germany and the USSR in June 1941 resulted in a shift of the economic system to the Stalinist War Economy (1941–5). This was followed, in sequence, by transitions to: the Late Stalin Peacetime Command Economy: 1945–53; the Post-Stalin Interregnum Command Economy: 1953–7; and Khrushchev's Regionalized Command Economy: 1957–64. All of these were variants of the basic Stalinist economic system discussed above. Industrial policies and performance in these four periods are summarized in the Appendix tables and Figures 13.1 and 13.2.

In a comprehensive study of Soviet industrial policy, the Khrushchev period would be examined more thoroughly due to its importance in the industrialization process. During 1957–64 gross industrial output grew at an average rate of 8% per annum and its production index doubled. The military R & D programme generated numerous world-class space and defence technologies, such as the Sputnik satellite and ICBMs. However, there were serious underlying problems. Industrial growth remained 'extensive' in nature and decelerated from 10.2% in 1951–5 to 8.3% in 1956–60 to 6.6% in 1961–5.[31] As before, the quality of manufactures and the technological levels of industries remained low by world standards. Plan targets continued to be over-fulfilled in heavy industry and under-achieved in the consumer sector. The poor industrial performance and the related stagnation in living standards contributed to the weakening of Khrushchev's political position and thereby to his removal as leader in October 1964.

13.5. INDUSTRIAL POLICY IN THE MATURE SOVIET COMMAND ECONOMY DURING THE SUPERPOWER ARMS RACE (1965–1985)

The CPSU leadership under Leonid Brezhnev and his successors significantly altered key components of the Khrushchev programme and over the next two decades managed a command economy with the features, policies, and performance shown in Table 13.6. Economic decision-making was re-centralized, state ownership of productive assets was maintained, and mandatory planning remained the primary coordination mechanism. Although only labour and retail markets were legal, the influence of the second economy in the industrial sector increased.[32] The effectiveness of economic incentives diminished due to the weakening influence of socialist ideology, the narrowing of wage differentials, and the decreased reliance on coercion.

In this period the goals and features of Soviet industrial policy were influenced more by pragmatic considerations than by Marxist-Leninist ideology.[33]

---

[31] According to Gregory and Stuart (1995: 321): 'Extensive growth is the growth of output from the expansion of inputs, land, labour, and capital. Intensive growth is the growth derived from increasing output per unit of factor input—that is, from the better use of available inputs.'

[32] Grossman (1977), Davis (1988), and Treml and Alexeev (1993) contain information about the second economy in the Brezhnev period and references to numerous other related works.

[33] Official Soviet interpretations of the role of industry in the socialist economy can be found in the textbook *Politicheskaya Ekonomika*, which was revised several times in the Brezhnev period. Independent assessments of orthodox Marxist-Leninist political economy in the USSR and Eastern Europe and its propositions concerning industrial policies can be found in Brus (1975, 1988) and Sutela (1991).

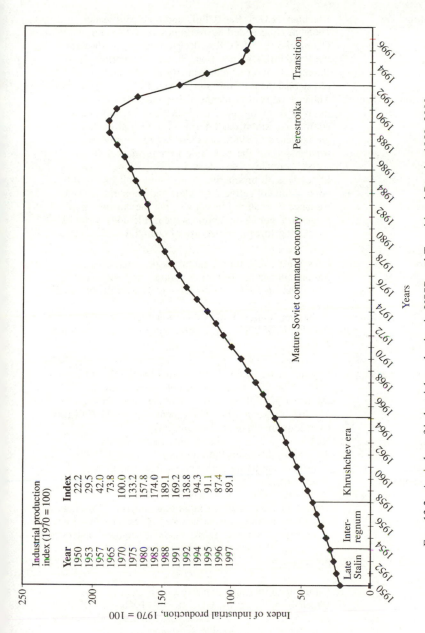

Industrial production index (1970 = 100)	
Year	**Index**
1950	22.2
1953	29.5
1957	42.0
1965	73.8
1970	100.0
1975	133.2
1980	157.8
1985	174.0
1988	189.1
1991	169.2
1992	138.8
1994	94.3
1995	91.1
1996	87.4
1997	89.1

FIG. 13.2. An index of industrial production in USSR and Transitional Russia: 1950–2000

Sources: This figure was generated from an index of industrial production with a base year of 1970 that was calculated using the sources outlined below.

1950–80 Index numbers for industrial production in the USSR from Converse 1982, pp. 191–2. Calculated from data on the production of 312 industrial products and 1970 value added weights.

1980–91 Chain estimate from an index of industrial production in the USSR (1980 = 100) calculated using data on industry value added in 1982 roubles and annual growth rates from CIA 1990, Table C-1 and Noren and Kurtzweg 1993, p. 15.

1992–7 Chain estimate based on an index of industrial production in the Russian Federation (1989 = 100) from ECE 1998, Appendix Table B.4.

TABLE 13.6. *Soviet command economic system, 1965–1985*

Features

Decision-making	Brezhnev is Gen. Sec. CPSU and dominant leader 1965–82. Succeeded by Andropov (d. 2/84) and Chernenko (d. 3/85). Key decision-making bodies are the Politburo, Defence Council, CC Secretariat. Re-centralization of the economy in 1965 and re-establishment of ministerial system
Coordination mechanism	Reliance on central planning. Repeated attempts to improve planning using mathematical economics and computers. Ambitious reforms of industrial management are launched in 1965, but these fail to improve the performance of the economic system. Market-driven second economy expands in 1970s
Property rights	State owns all productive assets. Some relaxation of controls on collective farm plots and cooperative flats
Incentives	Reliance on material incentives, but the narrowing of wage differentials undermines them. Ideology loses its motivating force. Limited use of coercion

Environment

International	East–West conventional and strategic arms races throughout period. But more political and economic interaction in 1970s due to detente. Tense relations with China
Territory and resources	Stable boundaries. Full access to natural resources. Population of USSR: 230 million in 1965, 276 million in 1985

Policies

Utilization of national income	Defence share of GDP rises from 13% in 1965 to 16% in 1985. A broader definition of defence and smaller estimates of GDP generate defence burdens in the 25–40% range in 1985. Investment reduced in 10th FYP. Consumption share held down
Sectoral priorities	Defence and heavy industry obtain top priority. Agriculture becomes more important in early 1980s. Consumer industries and social services neglected
Foreign economic	Ambitious plans for intra-CMEA integration. In the 1970s the USSR uses detente with West to pursue a growth strategy based on large-scale import of Western machinery and equipment financed by exports of oil and natural gas. Energetic efforts made to acquire Western technology through covert (spetzinformatsiya) programmes

Performance

Economic growth	Failure to shift from extensive to intensive growth. Deceleration of annual GDP growth: 1966–70 5.2%; 1971–5 3.2%; 1976–80 2.2%; 1981–5 1.9%. Years after mid-1970s became known as 'stagnation era'
Efficiency and technological innovation	Economy remains energy inefficient. Problem of negative value added in industry grows. Sluggish technological

TABLE 13.6. *(Cont'd)*

	innovation in civilian sectors. Major advances in weapons and space systems, but technological gap with West increases
Income distribution	Growth in disposable income and reduction in differentials among working population. Significant in-kind benefits for those working in high-priority sectors. Upper income: Communist elite, top scientists and intelligentsia, managers. Bottom income: elderly women, collective farmers, large families
Consumer welfare	Improvements in supplies of food, housing, consumer goods. But deceleration of growth of living standards. Problems of alcoholism, poor medical care, rising mortality
Stability	Continuing instability in agricultural production. GDP growth steadily decelerates, but no cycles. Insignificant unemployment and low open inflation. But increasing repressed inflation and shortages
Foreign economic	General expansion of trade. Turnover with West grows 10 times during 1973–85 due to rising revenue from energy exports. But as a result of deteriorating competitiveness, USSR share of world trade of manufactured goods declines
National viability	Soviet system appears solid. No serious external threats. Internal dissidence increases but is kept under control

Sources: Lectures of author at Oxford University; Ellman 1988; Gregory and Stuart 1994; Hewett 1988; IMF *et al*. 1991; JEC 1966, 1973, 1976, 1979, 1983, 1987.

Soviet industry was supposed to demonstrate its superiority over other forms based upon capitalism, Maoism, and market socialism. Technological innovation was to be accelerated and the production of sophisticated weapons was to be expanded. More consumer goods were to be produced in order to provide better material incentives. Finally, there was to be a shift from extensive to intensive growth in industry. These multiple, conflicting goals were supposed to be achieved while preserving the existing system and remaining within resource constraints.

State planning was retained as the key industrial policy instrument and attempts were made to enhance its effectiveness through reforms introduced in 1965, 1973, and 1979 (Ellman 1973; Sutela 1991). Plans for industry tended to be less ambitious and more scientifically based than those of the past. But they continued to be inconsistent and therefore subject to continual revisions during plan implementation. The priority system became more formalized in organizations such as Gosplan and military industries were awarded the highest priority status (Davis 1990*a*). Civilian industries considered vital for progress (e.g. natural gas, agricultural machinery) also had preferential access to resources. Consumer industries and social services kept their low priority status (Davis 1989).

Although industrial wholesale prices were changed in relative terms and raised several times, they continued to be set in an arbitrary manner by the state. Soviet and world relative prices increasingly diverged after 1973, primarily because free market energy prices rose more substantially than did domestic prices. Due to the lack of incentives in Soviet industry to economize on energy usage, by 1985 industrial technologies were significantly less energy efficient than those in the OECD region. A growing number of branches of Soviet industry generated negative value added according to world market prices.[34]

The state budget played an important, if largely reactive, role in the industrial sphere. Its share of total industrial investment declined from 60% in 1965 to 46% in 1985, whereas that of enterprises rose to 51% (Kim 1996: 288). The budget provided substantial subsidies to cover the differentials between output and input prices in industry, especially in food processing, which rose from about 3 billion roubles in 1965 to 66 billion roubles in 1985 (Kim 1996). Rising expenditures on subsidies, social welfare, and defence generated budget deficits of about 2% of GDP per annum that were financed by an expansion of the money supply. Price controls ensured that this did not cause open inflation, but they intensified repressed inflation and shortages of industrial goods.

The Brezhnev regime introduced numerous policies to accelerate scientific-technological progress (Amann and Cooper 1982). The State Committee of Science and Technology was established to coordinate R & D activities in civilian sectors of the economy. A national programme of certification of the quality of industrial products (the *znak kachestva*) was launched. Scientific-production associations were formed through the amalgamation of industrial enterprises, R & D institutes, and construction bureaux. The government put greater pressure on high-priority defence industries to accelerate technological progress and to 'spin off' some of it to the civilian sector (Cooper 1987).

Although the Soviet Union retained the state monopoly of foreign trade and a preference for self-sufficiency, changing international conditions impelled it to expand trade in the industrial sphere. Close links were developed with Eastern European countries in the Council for Mutual Economic Assistance (CMEA) and elaborate programmes of socialist economic integration were formulated (van Brabant 1980). With respect to the capitalist world, the government adopted a strategy of 'import-led growth', which called for the large-scale importation and diffusion of Western technology to promote the modernization of industry and the shift to intensive growth. However, in contrast to the Polish practice of paying for technology imports from loans, the USSR attempted to cover its costs by exporting energy and other natural resources to hard-currency markets (Hanson 1982; Gomulka 1986).

In the Brezhnev period the main regional policies were to expand defence production capacity in selected areas, to construct the Baikal Amur Railway, to

---

[34] The concept of negative value added is explained in n. 25 above. The statement is offered as a hypothesis on the basis of backward extrapolation of findings of negative value added in Soviet industry in the studies of Hughes and Hare (1992) and IEPPP (1993).

extract more oil and natural gas from fields in West Siberia, to expand the mining of raw materials, and to modernize port and transport systems (roads, railways, pipelines) connected with foreign trade operations. The government created a new economic organization, the territorial production complex (TPK), to facilitate integrated development in regions of special importance (Kammerling 1983; North and Shaw 1995). Enterprises that were formally subordinated to a variety of ministries were placed under the operational control of the TPK in order to improve inter-ministerial coordination, achieve economies of scale, and promote balance between extraction, production, transportation, and social activities.[35]

The main beneficiary of Soviet industrial policy in this period, unlike in the Khrushchev years, was the military-industrial complex. High-priority branches of the civilian economy also did well. Consumers experienced some advances in the late 1960s due to a temporary surge in output of light industry and again in the 1970s as a result of imports of consumer goods.

Repeated attempts were made to improve the functioning of industrial enterprises. The 1965 Kosygin reforms called for fewer plan targets, new market-linked success indicators (e.g. sales and profits) and bonuses, decentralization of investment financing, interest rates on loans, and direct horizontal links between firms (Hewett 1988; Sutela 1991). However, these reforms never had the potential to correct the systemic deficiencies that were generating the key problems in industry and, in any event, were undermined by hostile bureaucrats and their own inconsistencies before being reversed after 1968 (Schroeder 1979, 1983). Thus, Soviet firms continued to function in a shortage economy, but with weakened Party and ministerial control over them.[36] Soviet managers took advantage of softening budget constraints to make high wage and bonus payments, launch excessive numbers of investment projects, and neglect the task of improving energy efficiency. Firms also participated more actively in second economy transactions and illegally 'siphoned' consumer goods from retail markets into closed shops for their workers, thereby exacerbating the shortages in the public sphere (Kim 1996).

The government's policies resulted in significant technological progress in high priority sectors, but did not improve performance overall (Berliner 1976; Amann and Cooper 1977, 1982; Feinstein 1997). Incentives neither sufficiently

[35] According to Kammerling (1983), the number of TPKs rose from four in the 9th Five Year Plan (1971–5) to 12 in the 11th Five Year Plan (1981–5). They included: Timan-Pechora (petroleum, natural gas, forest products), Kursk Magnetic Anomaly (iron ore, steel), West Siberia (petroleum, natural gas, petrochemicals), Kansk-Achinsk (coal, electric power), Sayan (hydroelectric power, aluminium), South Yakutia (coal, iron ore), Bratsk-Ust-Ilimsk (hydroelectric power, aluminium, forest products), Orenburg (natural gas, petrochemicals), Mangyshlak (petroleum, natural gas), Karatau-Dzhambul (phosphates, chemical fertilizers), Pavlodar-Ekibastuz (coal, electric power), and South Tajik (hydroelectric power, aluminium).

[36] Whitefield (1993) provides a thorough analysis of the re-centralization of economic decision-making in the Brezhnev period and the role of the industrial ministries in the Soviet economy. He argues that the ministries became dominant economic and political actors, eclipsing even higher CPSU bodies. This hypothesis appears to be inconsistent with findings of some other scholars, such as Almquist (1990), that party and state bodies in the security field (Defence Council, Defence Industry Department of the Central Committee Secretariat, Military-Industrial Commission) had substantial power relative to ministries. It also conflicts with the argument of Kim (1996) that ministries were weakened relative to enterprises in the post-1965 period due to unintended decentralizing consequences of successive economic reforms.

rewarded success in innovation nor penalized failure. The lower rates of investment in this period constrained the completion of projects. Scientific production associations proved unable to co-ordinate the work of industrial firms and research institutions that were subordinate to different ministries and academies.

The Brezhnev regime achieved considerable success in improving the capabilities of the defence industry (CIA 1986; USDOD 1987; Almquist 1990). The Military Industrial Commission was given greater powers to coordinate military R & D, weapons production, and the covert collection of Western military-related technology (CIA 1985). Real defence spending doubled from 1965 to 1985 and the share of GNP devoted to defence rose from 13 to 16% (Steinberg 1990; Firth and Noren 1997). Defence industry enterprises substantially expanded their production capacity, improved the technical quality of conventional and nuclear weapons systems, and increased their output in quantitative terms. Despite these achievements, the defence industry and military research institutes became increasingly unable to satisfy the demands of the Soviet armed forces for world-class weapons systems. One problem was that defence industry enterprises operated in sellers' markets in a shortage economy and did not have strong enough incentives to raise technologies to the highest levels achieved in NATO countries (Davis 1997). Another was that the growing complexity of weapons production made the defence industry increasingly reliant on civilian branches with low-quality standards in a period when the effectiveness of the priority system was diminishing.[37]

Regional policies did not significantly shift the territorial distribution of industry, but changes were important in absolute terms. North and Shaw (1995) point out that a 1% redistribution of industrial output in 1976–80 involved 70 times more production than it would have in 1928–32. Industry in defence-dominated regions continued to grow, although the share of total industrial output of the Urals declined. The expansion of foreign trade boosted industrial activities in coastal and border cities. The Volga region's share of industrial output expanded due to the growth of its chemical, petrochemical, and automotive industries.

Foreign trade policies had major impacts on industry. The value of Soviet imports of 'machinery, instruments and transport equipment' from the socialist countries increased from 3 billion foreign trade roubles in 1970 to 20 billion roubles in 1985, which was 47% of socialist imports (TsSU 1989: 636, 648). In return, CMEA partners predominantly received energy and raw materials. The CMEA pricing mechanism tended to overvalue substandard Eastern European machinery in world market prices and undervalue energy products that were easily saleable in the West. Due to rising world energy prices, Soviet implicit subsidization of Eastern European countries increased from $5.3 billion in 1975 to a peak of $18.6 billion in 1981 before declining to $13.7 billion in 1985 (Marrese and Vanous 1983*a*, 1983*b*; McIntyre 1987).

---

[37] This military–civilian interdependence existed in the West as well. But there the open, competitive civilian economy was the source of most of the advanced technologies used by defence enterprises, so these linkages benefited the military sector.

The pro-trade policies of the detente era, rising hard-currency earnings, and credit from the West resulted in an increase of the USSR's imports of machinery and equipment from the West from $900 million in 1970 to a peak of $11.8 billion in 1981 (McIntyre 1987: 478). This legal trade was supplemented by the large-scale covert acquisition of military-related Western technology by the Soviet *spetsinformatsiya* programme involving the KGB Directorate T, Soviet military intelligence (GRU), and other agencies (CIA 1985). But the unreformed Soviet civilian industrial enterprises experienced difficulties in assimilating foreign technology. In the 1980s the demand for Western machinery declined, energy-related export earnings diminished, and Western controls on technology trade tightened. These factors caused legal Soviet imports of machinery and equipment to drop to $4.8 billion in 1985.

The Brezhnev regime's industrial policies were successful according to some performance indicators. The output of Soviet industry increased threefold in this period (Appendix B) and the production of key commodities grew substantially (Appendix C). Industry's share of GDP increased from 32% in 1965 to 37% in 1985. The state's civilian branch priorities generated the highest growth in the oil and natural gas industries. Each year the defence industry produced about 3,000 tanks, 1,200 fighter aircraft, and 10 submarines (USDOD 1987). Nevertheless, several key goals were not achieved. Despite plans to increase the importance of the consumer goods industries in relative terms, their share of total industrial production remained around 25%. There were failures in programmes to accelerate technological progress, improve industrial efficiency, and shift to intensive growth. The average annual growth rates during 1981–5 of output in total industry (1.8%) and machine-building and metal-working (MBMW) (1.3%) were far below their values in 1966–70 (6.3 and 7.1%) (CIA 1988*a*; Kurtzweg 1987: 14). The dynamic efficiency of Soviet industry, measured by labour and capital productivity, worsened.[38] Total industry factor productivity growth decelerated from 0.1% in 1966–70 to −2.3% in 1981–5.

Soviet industrial policies enabled the USSR to catch up with the major industrial countries in terms of manufacturing capacity and output during 1965–75, but this surge was not sustained and the USSR fell behind in later years (see Appendix D).[39] The Soviet Union was second to the USA in primary energy production and was third in its output of trucks and buses and machine tools (CIA 1991*b*). Although the USSR was the world's leader in the production of crude steel (155 million metric tons) in 1985, this could be interpreted as an indication of backwardness given trends in the restructuring of industry in the West.

---

[38] Dynamic efficiency is measured by productivity indicators, which are the differences between the growth of real output and that of inputs of labour (labour productivity), of capital (capital productivity), or of their weighted average (total factor productivity) (Gregory and Stuart 1995: 321–6). The accelerating negative growth of capital productivity in the USSR implies that the leadership persisted in expanding the capital stock despite evidence of a falling rate of return on investment that in a market economy would signal the need for contraction.

[39] A comparison of GNP reveals a similar trend. According to CIA estimates, the ratio of Soviet GNP to US GNP (both expressed in US dollars) rose from 50% in 1965 to a peak of 58% in the mid-1970s, but then dropped back to 53% in 1985. Over the same period, the Soviet Union's share of world GNP declined from 15.3 to 13.8% (Davis 1990*b*).

On the negative side, the USSR lagged behind the USA in the sophistication of its manufacturing technologies: by 4–6 years in microprocessors; by 3–5 years in computer-operated machine tools; and by 5–10 years in software (USDOD 1987). It was able to achieve technological superiority over the USA in only four of 29 deployed weapons systems. The declining competitiveness of the USSR was reflected in the drop in the small Soviet share of total OECD imports of manufactures from 0.8% in 1965 to 0.4% in 1985. In sum, by the mid-1980s the Soviet Union was a declining world power in industrial and military terms (Davis 1990*b*).

The CPSU elite selected Mikhail Gorbachev as General Secretary in March 1985 in the hope that he would implement reforms that would correct the many problems of the 'stagnation era', thereby accelerating technological progress and economic growth, while maintaining the communist system (Brown 1996). Soviet industrial policies in Early Perestroika (1985–8) were conventional (high defence spending, substantial investment in heavy industry) and reforms were timid (Appendix A). Attempts at change became more energetic and radical in Late Perestroika (1989–91), but the central state had diminishing power to implement its policies (Noren and Kurtzweg 1993). As the economy unravelled, industrial performance and living standards deteriorated throughout the country. In 1991 the growth of industrial output ranged from 5% in Azerbaijan to −8% in Russia to −23% in Georgia. Economic difficulties combined with long-standing ethnic and regional grievances to generate powerful nationalist and separatist movements and centre–republic disputes. The resulting political chain reaction provoked the coup attempt in August 1991 and the subsequent dissolution of the USSR. The remainder of this chapter will focus on industrial policy during 1992–2000 in the largest successor state, the Russian Federation.

13.6. INDUSTRIAL POLICY IN THE RUSSIAN TRANSITIONAL MARKET ECONOMY (1992–2000)

Since 1992 the Russian government's policies of marketization, price and trade liberalization, macroeconomic stabilization, and privatization have transformed the economy into a hybrid market system with the features shown in Table 13.7.[40] The federal government still has considerable power, but there has been both intentional and involuntary decentralization of economic decision-making to banks, firms, and economic regions. Most transactions are carried out in evolving, inefficient markets.

At the start of transition, Russia was the dominant industrial power among the Soviet successor states, with approximately two-thirds of industrial assets that

[40] During 1992–8 the Russian President has been Boris Yeltsin and Prime Ministers have been Yegor Gaidar (1992–3), Viktor Chernomyrdin (1994–8), Sergei Kiriyenko (March–August 1998), and Yeugenii Primakov (1998–present). The transition programmes of the governments have been comprehensive and have included reforms of all aspects of the economy ('Programma' 1992; Aslund 1995). Specific policies of relevance to industry are discussed in the text.

TABLE 13.7. *Russian transitional market economic system, 1992–2000*

Features

Decision-Making	Constitution of 1993 gives the President (Yeltsin 1992–8) a dominant role. Central government is headed by the Prime Minister (Gaidar 1992, Chernomyrdin 1993–8, Kiriyenko March–August 1998, Primakov September 1998–present) and plays an important role in economic decision-making. Nevertheless, it remains weak relative to regions and enterprises and has difficulty in implementing its economic policies
Coordination mechanism	The government rejects state planning and initiates 'big bang' transition to the market. But market institutions do not develop rapidly. State bodies intervene in the economy in a pervasive, if often uncoordinated, manner. Rapid growth of second economy and rampant corruption
Property rights	Government implements auction and voucher programmes to privatize state property at a rapid pace. By 1997 private shares of assets are: retail trade (75%), personal services (77%), industrial firms (80%). Limited progress achieved in privatizing housing, farms, and land
Incentives	Almost exclusively material incentives. No motivating ideologies or reliance on coercion

Environment

International	End of Cold War and radical cuts in weapons. Beginning of integration of Russia into world capitalist system. No serious external threats, but tense relations with some FSU states
Territory and resources	Central government experiences some difficulties in controlling resources in regions due to economic collapse, nationalism, localism, crime. Population of Russian Federation in 1998: 148 million

Policies

Utilization of national income	Drastic cuts in GDP shares of defence (to 5%) and investment (to 24%). Index of investment (1989 = 100) falls to 22 by late 1998. Consumption share of GDP increases
Sectoral priorities	Priorities of the state become less important. Main goal of government in 1994–8 is macroeconomic stabilization. It imposes tight constraints on budget-financed institutions, such as education and health, and offers special protection to only a few sectors of the economy
Foreign economic	Trade liberalization and shift to currency convertibility. Foreign direct investment and joint ventures encouraged

Performance

Economic growth	GDP growth is negative during 1992–8. Industrial production index (1989 = 100) falls to 30 in 1998. Increasing differentiation in growth rates between branches of industry. Reductions in investment hamper recovery and shift to intensive growth

TABLE 13.7. *(Cont'd)*

Efficiency and technological innovation	Distortions of market signals and lack of investment hinder improvements in efficiency and technological progress. In most sectors, the technological gap with the West continues to widen. But some are upgraded through the import of Western equipment and expertise
Income distribution	Growing wage and income inequality. Communist nomenklatura obtains control of a significant share of privatized state assets. Upper income: bankers, traders, managers of firms with marketable assets, state officials. Bottom income: workers in bankrupt firms, farmers, state employees in low priority institutions, elderly. 40% of population lives in poverty in late 1998
Consumer welfare	Initial large drop in real wages and consumption for majority of population. But shortages of goods and queues in shops are eliminated. Real income grows from 1992 to 1997, but falls in 1998. All social services deteriorate. Rising illness and mortality rates in 1992–5
Stability	Government initially unable to control budget deficit (19% of GDP in 1992) or money supply. Annual CPI rises from 100 in 1991 to 1,529 in 1992. But in 1994–8 tight fiscal and monetary policies reduce both deficits and inflation (CPI is 15% in 1997). Economic collapse after August 1998. Chaotic markets and trade shocks cause severe micro imbalances. Unemployment rate rises from 3% in 1992 to 11% in 1998
Foreign economic	Trade turnover drops in 1992–3 due to disruptions in the economic system, collapse of CMEA, and intra-CIS tensions. Exports and imports recover in subsequent years, but fall in 1998. Surpluses are maintained in balance of trade and current account. Exchange rate drops from $1 = R193 in 1992 to R5,785 in 1997. Large devaluation in August 1998. Russia has problems in servicing its debts and remains dependent upon IMF assistance
National viability	Several non-Russian nationalist groups demand independence for their territories and a war is fought in Chechnya. Although the government remains weak, it holds the nation together

Sources: Lectures by the author at Oxford University; Aslund 1995; Blasi, Kroumova, and Kruse 1997; ECE 1993 . . . 1998; EBRD 1994 . . . 1997; Yergin and Gustafson 1993; OECD 1995, 1997*c*.

generated a similar share of output. But its firms had old capital stock, used energy inefficiently, maintained excessive inventories of inputs, were over-manned, and were unable to produce internationally competitive manufactures.[41] By OECD

[41] The features of and conditions in Russia's industry at the start of transition can be extrapolated from the analysis of USSR industry in Section 13.5. Specific sources on Russian industry include Noren and Kurtzweg (1993); ECE (1993 . . . 1997); CIA (1994*a*); EBRD (1994 . . . 1997); GKS (1995*d*, 1996*b*); OECD (1995, 1997*c*); Gaddy (1996); and Blasi, Kroumova, and Kruse (1997).

standards the industrial sector was too large for the economy and it was dominated by a huge military-industrial complex and by civilian heavy industries.

There was general agreement among economists and policy-makers in 1992
that all branches of industry needed to be restructured fundamentally to make
them competitive. But there were disputes over whether this monumental task
should be managed by the state or left to the market.[42] The reformers in the Gaidar
government were in favour of a minimalist industrial policy as a result of their
negative experiences with Soviet bureaucracy, study of the Western industrial
policy debate, and liberal ideology. They did not believe that the weak Russian
state could either pick winners or control the rent-seeking behaviour of managers
and officials. More interventionist programmes were put forward by centrist and
leftist business and political groups, such as Civic Union.[43] Due to the patronage of President Yeltsin, the Gaidar strategy prevailed. During 1992–3 the government focused its attention on other components of transition and assumed
that industrial restructuring would take place as a result of cuts in state orders,
privatization, decontrol of markets, defence industry conversion, foreign competition, and private investment (Programma 1992). Over the subsequent five years
centrist forces have gained more political influence and have attempted to
enhance the role of the state in the management of structural change.[44] Due to
these differences of opinion and changes in economic leadership, Russia's
industrial policy has had neither stability nor coherence in the transition period.

One of the industrial policy instruments used by the Russian government has
been denationalization (privatization).[45] Small firms (under 200 employees) were
privatized by local government through open auctions and employee buyouts.
The 20,000 eligible medium and large enterprises (30% of the total number were
excluded) initially were transformed into open joint stock companies. In the
first phase of privatization, beginning in December 1992, their shares were distributed through three schemes to employees and managers by closed sales, to
the government, and to outsiders by voucher auction. By July 1994, 80% of these
firms had been corporatized and 75%, employing 17 million workers, had
been privatized (GKS 1995*a*). The second phase of privatization has had the

---

[42] This reflected the Western debate on industrial policy. Those in favour of intervention believed that the state
could play useful roles in correcting externalities, competition-reducing economies of scale and imperfections in
financial markets. Opponents argued that state agencies were incapable of picking winners and losers and diverted
resources in a wasteful manner due to their rent-seeking behaviour and bureaucratic empire-building. See Chang
(1994); Nuti (1994); Ellman (1995); and World Bank (1997).

[43] Civic Union rejected the shock therapy strategy and the goal of an open laissez-faire economy and advocated
instead a gradual transition to a state-regulated market economy with price and income controls, cautious privatization, government investment and promotion of industrial production, and a centralized industrial supply system.
See Aslund (1995).

[44] An informative discussion of the debates in Russia during 1993–5 on industrial reform strategies and policies can be found in Glaz'ev (1995). Plans by the Yeltsin government to increase the role of the state in the economy were unveiled in a Presidential address to the Council of Federation in Sept. 1997. The move toward greater
state intervention was accelerated by the appointment of Primakov as Prime Minister in September 1998.

[45] Privatization in Russia has been well covered in the literature. Among the useful sources are: Radygin (1994);
Aslund (1995); OECD (1995); and Blasi, Kroumova, and Kruse (1997). The legal basis for this process was pro-
vided by the July 1991 'Law on Privatization of State and Municipal Enterprises in the RSFSR' and the July 1992
'State Programme for the Privatization of State and Municipal Enterprises of the Russian Federation for 1992'.

objectives of divesting the state of its shares for cash through auctions and investment tenders and increasing the participation of outside private investors. By 1995
the share of the 137,000 firms of all types owned by state, municipal, and social
organizations had fallen to 8.6% (GKS 1996*b*: 29).

Price liberalization can be viewed as an instrument of industrial policy in the
Russian case. It has had the goals of making price-setting by firms more responsive to market conditions, correcting relative prices to make them consistent with
those in world markets, forcing firms to minimize costs, and reducing the heavy
subsidy burden on the state budget. The general pattern of adjustment has been
for relative prices of manufactures to decline and those of energy and raw materials to rise. However, the government has maintained controls on energy, which
has prevented a full realignment of relative prices (in 1994 domestic energy prices
were only 40% of world prices).

The liberalization of prices and foreign trade transformed the problem of negative value added from a hidden into an open one (see note 25). According to
Russian calculations, in 1992 the profitable sectors of industry at world market
prices included oil, gas, ferrous metals, and non-ferrous metals (IEPPP 1993:
85–8).[46] All others were unprofitable. Those generating negative value added
included coal, timber and wood-processing, and food. However, even within the
latter sectors some enterprises were potentially viable after restructuring.

The Gaidar government established a State Committee on Anti-monopoly Policies and introduced various measures that were intended to promote competition in industries with high concentration of market power (OECD 1995: 92–4).
However, its efforts were unsuccessful due to an incorrect focus on production
monopolies rather than trade monopolies, excessive state involvement in regulation, and the opposition of vested interests in crucial sectors of the economy,
such as energy (Aslund 1995: 152–6). During 1994–7 the government has tried
to encourage competition in accordance with its 'Programme for Demono-
polization of the Economy and the Development of Competition'. But it has
possessed neither the political will nor the economic power to ensure its successful implementation. In February 1997 the head of the State Committee was
dismissed, an action he blamed on pressure from a powerful financial oligarchy
that was in favour of a monopolized state capitalist economic system.

Since 1993 the Russian government has supported the development of 'national
champions' called Financial-Industrial Groups (FIGs), which are collections of
vertically integrated firms, research institutes, and financial institutions in particular industrial sectors (OECD 1995: 94–5; Glaz'ev 1995; Finansovo 1996).
The FIG is supposed to have similarities with the Japanese *keiretsu* and the Korean
chaebol, although these two institutions differ in fundamental characteristics.
Business units within FIGs are supposed to pool their resources to finance industrial restructuring while maintaining output and employment. By 1996, 35 FIGs
(including 550 enterprises, 75 banks, and 2.5 million workers) had been created

---

[46] In the Western literature, Hughes and Hare (1992) provide parallel estimates of negative value added and
domestic resource costs of branches of Russian industry.

'from above' by Presidential decree or 'from below' by business interests. Liberal critics of FIGs have warned that powerful conglomerates established with the patronage of the state bureaucracy could evolve into cartels similar to those in the Tsarist and NEP periods that will impede restructuring. But FIGs created from below could play useful roles if they are effectively regulated.

Fiscal policies have exerted considerable influences on industrial developments by design and accident. The government has drastically reduced the procurement of military and civilian industrial products and capital expenditure. By 1996 the state share of total investment had dropped to 19% (GKS 1996*b*: 43). But it has had significant localized influence due to its concentration on high priority projects in specific sectors. The government has made public commitments to reduce direct subsidies to industrial regions and individual firms, but these remained substantial through 1997. Industry as a whole has been indirectly subsidized as a result of the state financing the gap between world and domestic energy prices.

The basis of taxation of industry has shifted from the hidden turnover tax to corporate profits, value added, excise and import/export taxes. However, the weakened state bureaucracy has experienced severe difficulties in collecting them. Federal budget revenues during 1992–6 were only 40–60% of planned. In the first half of 1997 the government was able to collect only 19% of budgeted profits taxes and 29% of value added taxes (CEAGRF 1997: 22). Firms have complained that tax rules are applied arbitrarily and corruptly.

Monetary and banking policies have had considerable, if sometimes unintended, influences on industrial restructuring. In 1992–3 the Russian government authorised the banking system to provide industry with large-scale soft loans to settle inter-enterprise debts because it was unprepared to impose hard budget constraints that would lead to mass bankruptcies and unemployment. 'Pocket banks' continued to allocate loans to their parent industries independently of risk-evaluation and often at negative real interest rates. This accommodating monetary policy contributed to high inflation rates, and thereby to the disruption of production and investment in industry. However, from November 1994 through summer 1998 the Russian banking authorities adhered to tight monetary policies that reduced credits flowing to industry in accordance with IMF agreements (ECE 1998).

In 1992 Russia's defence industry contained about 1,500 major enterprises, 800 R & D institutions and five million workers (Gaddy 1996). The government has attempted to reorganize and downsize this sector and to increase significantly the civilian share of its output through national and regional conversion programmes.[47] It initially decided to privatize 65% of defence industrial enterprises using procedures similar to those in the civilian sphere, but then adopted a more restrictive policy. During 1994–8 the strained financial situation of defence firms has been worsened by the practices of the government of not paying

---

[47] Western literature on Russian defence industry conversion includes Cooper (1991, 1993); Gaddy (1996); and Davis (1997).

bills or sequestering budgeted funds. But the state has prevented insolvent defence firms from going bankrupt through the emergency provision of subsidies, loans, and tax relief.

The regional industrial policy of the central Russian government has been driven by attempts to deal with crises in critical regions and industries, rather than by a commitment to restructuring. Numerous ad hoc power-sharing arrangements have been made between federal and local authorities concerning the management of large industrial enterprises. Subsidies have been provided to territories that are of political or strategic importance, located in inhospitable geographic zones, or are highly dependent upon economically unviable industries. Some branches of industry, such as coal, have benefited from national subsidy programmes, which have differential geographic impacts.[48] Regions possessing high concentrations of defence establishments (e.g. Leningrad, Moscow, Nizhny Novgorod, Perm, Urdmutiya) and closed military cities (e.g. Arzamas 16) have obtained federal transfers and foreign assistance connected with conversion programmes (Gaddy 1996). In contrast, no special help has been provided to regions dominated by light industry.

With respect to international policies, the government has removed administrative restrictions on imports and established low tariffs in order to encourage foreign competition for monopolistic Russian industries. Most export controls have been lifted, even on previously secret military technologies, and state support has been provided to firms attempting to sell manufactures abroad, such as weapons producers. The Russian currency has been made convertible. But the government's policy of defending an 'exchange rate corridor' in 1995–8 has led to an appreciation of the rouble, to the detriment of industrial exporters. Numerous laws and decrees have been introduced to encourage foreign institutions to establish joint ventures and purchase shares of Russian companies.

There have been beneficiaries of industrial policies in Russia, despite the fact that most branches have suffered severe depressions and policies have been poorly coordinated, usually ineffective, and often reversed. Selected defence and civilian industries and their associated regions have received substantial government support through state orders, subsidies, and loans that have enabled them to survive despite market conditions. The branches of energy and metals have done well, usually by taking advantage of the state rather than benefiting from its policies. In all sectors of industry, workers have been partially protected by government measures designed to hold down unemployment by propping up uncompetitive enterprises.

By 1998 Russia's reforms had changed significantly the operating conditions and behavioural characteristics of industrial enterprises from those of the Soviet period. On the output side of firms, there has been a partial shift from sellers' to buyers' markets, which means that they have been put under pressure

---

[48] In 1994 subsidies amounting to 1.2% of GDP were provided to enterprises of the coal industry, which has labour productivity one-tenth that of the one in the USA.

to adjust product composition to demand, pay greater attention to quality, and become more energetic in marketing. However, the restructuring of production to make it more competitive often has been hampered by ineffective corporate governance, which is related to the fact that the majority of private firms are controlled by insider owners (managers and workers) who have more conservative objectives than do outside investors (Radygin 1994; Blasi, Kroumova, and Kruse 1997). Insufficient investment has constrained technological innovation in processes and products and has contributed to poor maintenance of existing capital stock. The average age of equipment in Russian industry rose from 10.8 years in 1990 to 14.1 years in 1995 (GKS 1996*b*: 70). The continuing softness of budget constraints has meant that market signals have not been as influential in determining the survival of firms as they are in Western economies. Nevertheless, there have been significant savings in the usage of energy, metals, and labour in production processes. The composition of inventories of enterprises has altered, so that there is a higher share of unsold finished goods and a lower one of hoarded inputs.[49] Despite marketization, much of the trade between enterprises has been conducted using barter.

The government's defence industrial policies have required radical adjustment by military enterprises because of the abrupt change in their status from one of privilege to low priority during transition (Davis 1997). Defence enterprises have experienced demand shocks due to severe cuts in procurement of military commodities (by 80% during 1991–7) and in R & D expenditures and substantial drops in foreign purchases of arms. In response, the production of military goods fell by 42% in 1992, and by large amounts in subsequent years (GKS 1996*b*: 11; CEAGRF 1997: 117). Despite national and regional conversion programmes, relatively little progress has been made in producing competitive civilian products (Gaddy 1996). But the output of civilian goods fell more slowly than that of military products, so the civilian share of defence industry output grew from 50% in 1991 to 80% in 1996. Conditions within defence enterprises increasingly have come to resemble those found in 'sunset' civilian industries. This has been reflected in the decline in the ratio of defence to all industry wages to 0.66 by 1995 and continued outflows of skilled labour to non-military sectors (GKS 1995*b*: 15–16).

The primary determinants of regional changes in Russian industry have not been state policies, but rather market-related factors such as endowments of natural resources (e.g. oil, natural gas, gold, diamonds), distances from suppliers and customers, and the performance of dominant industries. Price liberalization and the removal of subsidies have raised transportation costs to the extent that industries in remote regions have become financially unviable, such as coal mining in Vorkuta in the Komi Republic. Trends in regional industrial output have been influenced by the differential growth of branches of industry. For example,

---

[49] Kornai (1994) argues that one of the characteristic adjustments of firms in economies experiencing transformational recession is to reduce the ratio of input to output inventories. In Hungary the ratio fell from 6.1/1 in 1985 to 2.7/1 in 1991. The norm in a market economy is about 1/1.

in the Tyumen region the fuel share of industry was 80% in 1994 and the output decline was 34%, versus the Russian average of 44%, whereas in the Ivanovskaya region the light industry share was 50% and the output drop was 63%.[50]

On the whole, foreign economic developments have adversely affected most branches of industry during 1992–8. Russian firms have lost traditional export markets due to cuts in subsidized credits for Third World countries and the collapse of the CMEA in 1991. Sales to the former Soviet republics from 1992 onward have been constrained by the difficulties associated with conducting transactions in unstable and depressed markets. Enterprises have been unable to make compensatory sales to OECD countries markets due to the uncompetitiveness of their manufactured goods, which is linked both to low quality and the appreciation of the rouble. Exports of Russian civilian machinery, equipment, and vehicles to non-CIS countries declined from $12.5 billion (17.6% of total exports) in 1990 to a low of $2.9 billion in 1993, and then rose to $5.2 billion (7.3%) in 1996. Despite export promotion programmes, sales of military equipment abroad during 1992–8 have been in the $2.7–$3.5 billion range, or about one-half of the 1991 USSR level and one-ninth of the peak value of military exports in 1987 of $29 billion.[51]

In the case of imports, the opening up of Russia has enabled firms to purchase advanced Western technologies more easily. The value of non-CIS imports of machinery, equipment, and vehicles declined from $36.3 billion (44.3% of total imports) in 1990 to a low of $9.1 billion in 1993 before recovering slightly to $12.8 billion (30.3% of imports) in 1996. Furthermore, the Russian intelligence services have continued to supplement legal imports with covert acquisitions of military-related technologies in Western countries.[52] Nevertheless, the volume of Western machinery imports has remained low relative to the requirements of Russian industry and the technology has been focused on a subset of branches, notably energy. Imports of machinery and equipment from Eastern Europe and the CIS fell substantially during 1991–3, which contributed to the collapse of output of all branches of Russian industry. In recent years these imports have recovered somewhat, but are well below peak levels.

A different consequence of trade liberalization policies has been the large-scale influx of cheap foreign consumer goods, often with higher quality standards than equivalent domestic products. The technologically backward Russian industries have found it increasingly difficult to compete in domestic markets.

---

[50] The branch shares of industry in regions are from GKS (1994*a*: 616–21) and the production declines are from GKS (1994*b*: 220–2).

[51] Basic information about Soviet and Russian arms exports can be found in the annual reports of the US Arms Control and Disarmament Agency entitled *World Military Expenditures and Arms Transfers* (see ACDA 1996) and the International Institute for Strategic Studies entitled *The Military Balance* (see IISS 1997). Assessments of this trade are presented in Gaddy (1996) and Davis (1997). In the Soviet period actual receipts from arms exports were only about one-tenth their paper value, so in real revenue terms Russia has not suffered a great loss.

[52] In the post-Cold War period Western intelligence officials repeatedly have issued warnings of continued Russian technological espionage and OECD nations have expelled numerous alleged spies. It was reported in 1997 that Russia had illegally acquired an IBM supercomputer for its nuclear weapons establishment despite US government prohibitions of such exports.

This has been especially true of the textile, food processing, and consumer electronics industries. The Russian government has come under growing pressure to increase tariffs and physical controls over imports in order to prevent the devastation of industries that are engaged in restructuring.

State policies to encourage foreign direct investment did not yield good results prior to 1997. Cumulative FDI in Russia during 1989–96 of $5.8 billion was $40 on a per capita basis, compared with $1,300 for Hungary, $692 for the Czech Republic, and $140 for Poland (EBRD 1997: 126). Furthermore, FDI has had an unbalanced branch distribution; in 1994, 68% of it flowed into the energy industry, whereas MBMW obtained 3% of the total (GKS 1994*b*: 53). The major causes of the hesitancy of foreign firms and banks in providing investment have been political instability, uncertainty over property rights, and corruption.[53]

Given the leading role that the state has played in managing the economic transition in Russia, it is appropriate to hold its policies partially responsible for developments in industry. Measured by any conventional indicators, industrial performance has been poor. The combined effects of the demand and supply shocks discussed above generated negative growth of gross industrial output for six years in a row, which has resulted in its index (1989 = 100) dropping from 75 in 1992 to 48 in 1997. Most of the production decline has been real, rather than a by-product of faulty measurement.[54] Industry's share of GDP declined from 37.6% in 1991 to 31.3% in 1995 (GKS 1996*b*: 5). Such a large-scale collapse of industrial output in a major country in peacetime conditions is unprecedented in this century.

All branches of industry have experienced substantial drops in output, but there have been significant variations in sectoral performance that have reflected both state policies and market conditions. The industries experiencing the least loss in production during 1990–5 were electricity (–20%) and fuels (–33%). Those more adversely affected were chemicals and petrochemicals (–53%), machine-building (–59%), and light industry (–81%). The branch shares of electricity, fuel, and metals have increased, whereas those of machine-building, chemicals, and petrochemicals have declined. Contrary to initial expectations that industrial output in the transitional economy would be more consumer oriented, light industry has experienced the largest fall in output and negative growth accelerated over time. Its share of total industrial production dropped from 8.4% in 1990 to 3.1% in 1996, which was its lowest since the late Stalin period (GKS 1996*b*: 8).

[53] Sources of information on FDI in Russian industry include GosKomStat reports (e.g. GKS 1995*b*); OECD (1997*c*); and the annual reports of the ECE entitled *Economic Survey of Europe*. Corruption in the Russian economy is analysed comprehensively in Handelman (1995). According to a 1996 *Financial Times* article, a ranking of countries from least corrupt at 1 to most at 53 placed Russia at 47.

[54] It is generally recognized that there exist significant problems associated with the measurement of GDP and its components in transitional economies because of difficulties in monitoring private activity in services, agriculture, and foreign trade. In the case of Russia, debates have arisen over the magnitude of GDP decline. The initial GosKomStat series of real GDP showed it dropping by 49% from its 1989 level by 1994. Alternative estimates and the revised GosKomStat series indicate that the decline was 37% (OECD 1997*c*: 30). This fall in aggregate output is substantial, but some of the lost output might not have been saleable in a competitive market environment. Estimation of output trends in industry in Russia is less uncertain because of the greater reliability in data collection and the possibility of checking for consistency with sales and input statistics.

Trends in the production of key commodities, shown in Appendix C, reflect those of their industrial grouping. The outputs of a number of goods were higher in 1995 than in 1990, such as hydroelectric power and packages of heart disease medicine (GKS 1996*b*: 156, 179). Those with 1995 output less than 15% below 1990 included natural gas, buses, sugar cubes, and vodka. The production of many important consumer goods (fabrics, knitwear, shoes, washing machines, and television sets) has declined by 70–80%. Those commodities with production falls of 85% or more include forging-pressing machines, high-tensile boring pipes, textile looms, trailers for automobiles, and children's shoes.

During 1992–8 the output of industry declined at a faster rate than either officially-registered employment or capital stock, primarily due to soft budget constraints and insider privatization. In consequence, labour, capital, and total factor productivity growth rates in Russian industry have been negative. Capacity utilization in manufacturing industry in Russia declined from 62% in 1993 to 44% in 1996 (ECE 1997).

By 1996 investment in Russia had fallen to 25% of its 1990 level (Le Houerou 1996; OECD 1997). There were declines in the machinery and equipment shares of total investment from 38% in 1990 to 24% in 1995 and of total capital stock from 41% in 1992 to 30% in 1995 (ECE 1996: 80).

The international standing of Russian industry has worsened in the 1990s. Its share of the manufacturing output of the top 20 industrial countries dropped from 9.0% in 1990 (assuming Russia had a 64% share of USSR manufacturing) to 1.9% in 1995 (see Appendix D). Despite this, Russia remains a major producer of energy, metals, machine tools, and weapons, especially by European standards. Contrary to expectations, the technological gaps between Western and Russian industries in the 1990s have widened from those of the Soviet era due to the acceleration of technological progress in the former and the retardation of it in the latter. The competitiveness of Russian manufactures has declined from its poor state in the Soviet period. This is reflected in the current problems of the light and consumer electronics industries in Russia, which have experienced difficulties both in defending their shares of domestic markets and in exporting their products. In sum, the transition to a market system during 1992–8 has resulted in a deterioration of the position of Russian industry in the world and its relative performance from the standards established by the stagnating Soviet command economy.

The future industrial policies in Russia during 1999–2000 are likely to be more interventionist than those in the early transition period. President Yeltsin's election manifesto in 1996 promised an array of liberal reform policies: development of market institutions, fiscal reform, defence of price stability, creation of incentives for private investment, encouragement of small businesses, promotion of competition, regulation of monopolies, and full convertibility of the rouble. In 1997, the Charnomyrdin government attempted to introduce the promised measures. However, by the autumn of 1997 the spill-over effects of the Asian financial crisis and mounting domestic problems convinced Russian leaders that the central state had to be strengthened relative to private financial-industrial group-ings and regions, and had to play a more active role in the economy. This posi-tion was reinforced during 1998 by Russia's experiences with falling tax revenue, inability to service domestic and foreign debt, currency devaluation, collapse of the banking system, and further deterioration of the real economy. In September 1998 Prime Minister Primakov appointed Yuri Maslyvkov, former Chairman of Gosplan USSR, as his deputy for economic affairs. This new government will place much greater emphasis than did its liberal predecessors on having a strong state direct the economic transition process in general and industrial restructur-ing in particular.

Actual developments in the industrial sphere, however, will be a function not only of policies, but also existing problems, resource availability, and beha-vioural patterns. Considerable political uncertainties exist, that are associated with the health of President Yeltsin, the evolving succession struggle, and conflicts between the Presidency and legislature (State Duma and Council of Federation). It is probable that in the near future government policies will have minimal beneficial influence on industrial developments. Output probably will not stabilize until 1999 and may grow slowly and unevenly in subsequent years. Restructuring will depend upon many factors, such as guarantees of property rights and availability of invest-ment. It therefore is likely to lag behind the output revival. Only a small share of Russian industry will be competitive internationally by the year 2000.

13.7. CONCLUSIONS ABOUT RUSSIAN INDUSTRIAL POLICY

Over the twentieth century Russia's industrial policies and pattern of indus-trialization have had both distinctive features and similarities with those in other European countries. The divergences can be explained partially by the differ-ences in economic systems. Russian economies have been based on the principles of Tsarist state capitalism, the Stalinist command economy and its variants, and transitional state capitalism. These systems have reflected the leaderships' goals and have pre-determined subsequent industrial policies, behavioural patterns of industrial institutions, and the results of industrialization. Only the Tsarist sys-tem had direct equivalents in contemporaneous Western Europe.

Although there has been considerable diversity in the features of Russian eco-nomic systems, there have been regularities as well. The state always has played an important role in the industrial sector and decision-making has tended to be centralized. This has been true not only in the years of the command economy (1918–21 and 1928–91), but also when the market has been of significance: the Tsarist economy, NEP, and the current transition economy. Related to this has been state ownership of productive assets. In the command era it owned every-thing, which was an extreme case of the nationalization policies then prevalent in Europe. Despite the substantial private ownership of industrial enterprises in the Tsarist and transition economies, the Russian government has owned greater shares of land and production facilities in both periods than did its equivalents in Western Europe. Another constant feature, unusual by European standards, has been the reliance of Russia on non-market methods of coordination in industry. Throughout the century Russian product, labour, and capital markets have been distorted, inefficient, and constrained by the state. Quantity signals expressed through central plans, rationing, and barter usually have been more significant than price signals.

The incentives used in Russian economic systems to motivate decision-makers in industry have had some similarities to those employed in West European market economies, but fundamentally have been different. Although capitalism in the West relies upon ideologically-based moral incentives, they have tended to be individualistic (except in Fascist periods), whereas the Russian ones, based upon Tsarism/Orthodoxy or communism, have been collectivist. The power of moral incentives diminished significantly in the years of stagnation, *perestroika*, and early transition (1976–94), but in more recent years there appears to have been a reaction in Russia against 'Western' materialism and individualism and some reversion to nationalism as a motivating factor. Russia has relied heavily upon material incentives, as in the West, but they usually have not been linked to the market performance of managers and workers and expressed in cash terms. Instead, they have depended upon satisfaction of the state bureaucracy (e.g. by fulfilling plans) and have been provided 'in kind' (e.g. access to state housing or closed shops) by the state. Finally, Russia's reliance on state coercion should be recognized as an important deviation from twentieth-century European norms, although not a unique one given practices in the empire of Nazi Germany. The Tsarist system exploited the majority of industrial workers and peasants and made limited use of the forced labour of convicts. In the periods of War Communism and Stalinism, state terror was used to discipline and motivate workers, while millions of arrested Russians were forced to work in the OGPU/NKVD GULAG in slave-like conditions. Despite the reduction of coercion in the post-Stalin Soviet period, it remained illegal, according to various 'anti-parasite' laws, for most adults not to work.

Russian economists have made original theoretical contributions in the field of industrial policy and have tended to be strongly in favour of state intervention. In the Tsarist period, agrarian socialists and Marxists developed distinctive recommendations. Those of the former, such as the suppression of factory industry, were unusual by European standards of the time. In contrast, Russian Marxists called for the revolutionary transformation of industry and its expansion under state direction. From the Bolshevik revolution until 1991, most writings of Russian economists on industrial issues were based upon Marxist-Leninist political economy and favoured state ownership, mandatory central planning, rationing, and national self-sufficiency. Soviet concepts and policy recommendations exerted strong influences, if sometimes indirectly, on the European left throughout this period, and were broadly consistent with, if exaggerations of, prescriptions of interventionists. The gap between mainstream continental European and Soviet thinking about industrial policy did not widen fundamentally until the 1980s, when the former increasingly adopted Anglo-American liberal ideas. In the early transition period, Russia's reformers favoured a liberal industrial policy. However, since then most influential Russian economists concerned with industrial policy have developed rationales for greater state intervention, using instruments such as subsidies, state investment, tariffs, and exchange rate policy. So differences have been widening again between the liberal West and interventionist East.

Successive Russian governments have had six major goals of industrial policy: increase the share of industry in the economy; raise the share of heavy industry in total industry; expand the capacity and improve the technical sophistication of the defence industry; accelerate technological progress and raise the technical level of industry to the world standard; improve the efficiency and competitiveness of industrial enterprises; and alter the regional distribution of industry to satisfy state-determined economic and military criteria. The instruments used in the effort to achieve these objectives are described in the different sections of the chapter and in Appendix A. As a general rule, they were reliant upon central planning, state priorities, government investment, rationing of key commodities, state budget expenditures on military programmes and subsidies, government campaigns and directives, protectionism using tariffs and the state monopoly of foreign trade, and acquisition of Western technology.

The pattern of Russian industrial policy has been consistent with the hypothesis advanced by the Editors that states in large countries, such as Germany and France, tend to be more interventionist than do those in small ones, such as Belgium. However, it should be noted that the US government has adhered consistently to a liberal position, despite the country's large size, whereas the Netherlands at times has favoured state intervention (e.g. in the period of Tinbergen). In this century Russia has been the biggest country in Europe and has possessed abundant natural resources. But its vast domestic markets have been underdeveloped institutionally and not well integrated into the global economic system. These factors, combined with the prevalent anti-Western ideologies (Tsarist autocracy and Soviet Marxism-Leninism), have encouraged the state to play a leading role in the industrialization process.

The Russian government has tended to be confident of its ability to identify the main directions of industrial development and to pick winners. In the Tsarist period the state had clear ideas about the industries that were needed to enable Russia to become a major regional power, which were in part determined by its observations of trends in leading countries. The Soviet Communist leadership considered itself infallible in most areas, had pro-active industrial policies and almost by definition picked winners, since all firms grew and modernized in accordance with central plans. The shift to world market prices after 1991 has revealed that a large number of Russia's industrial enterprises were unprofitable, if not generating negative value added. This suggests that the earlier confidence in the correctness of the state's industrial policy was not well founded. In the early transition period the government became more passive and sceptical about its ability to contribute to the restructuring of industry. In recent years, though, the Yeltsin government has reasserted its right to direct economic development and has expressed confidence in its ability to intervene successfully and identify national champions.

If Russian industrial policies over this century are evaluated on the basis of their effectiveness, then the conclusion should be reached that they were partially successful. The economy became more industrialized, the share of heavy industry rose significantly, the Soviet defence industry became the second largest in the world, technological progress accelerated, and Russia was transformed from a weak regional power into a military superpower.

When the costs of Russian industrialization are considered as well, the record becomes less impressive. Throughout the Soviet period, growth in industrial output was achieved on an extensive basis and many sectors of industry would have generated negative value added had their inputs and outputs been measured by world market prices. Accordingly, resources have not been used in an optimal manner and industrial goals have been achieved by incurring substantial opportunity costs. Technological standards in Russia have remained lower than those of the major capitalist economies, systemic deficiencies have generated chronic inefficiency in the industrial sector, and Russian manufactures have failed to achieve competitiveness in open markets. The Stalinist model of forced industrialization imposed heavy burdens on the population in the forms of low living standards, massive loss of life through state oppression, and dictatorial rule.

The features of Russia's economic systems and specific industrial policies have meant that its industrial enterprises have operated in environments fundamentally different from those prevalent in Western Europe for 80 years of this century. The vertical relationships of Russian firms with the state bureaucracy have been more important than their horizontal ones with customers. For over seventy years firms have functioned in shortage economies, with their characteristic quantity drives, inattention to product quality, disincentives for innovation, soft budget constraints, and chronic shortages of inputs. During most of that time, enterprises have not been forced to face much domestic or foreign competition and have operated in sellers' markets for their outputs. In contrast, virtually all Western firms have been confronted by significant competition and have conducted transactions in buyers' markets. Shortage phenomena in the Soviet economy were self-reproducing and resistant to attempts by the government to alter the behavioural pattern of subordinate units. This systemic inertia explains both the repeated failures of Soviet regimes to reform the behaviour of industrial firms and the reluctance of enterprises to adapt to the new market environment of the transition period.

As a result of tenacious pursuit of governments' highest priority objective, to achieve dominant military power in Eurasia, the Russian economy always has contained a large defence industry. In the period 1928–91, Soviet defence industry was state owned, reliant on government procurement and subsidies, the beneficiary of numerous high-priority protection policies and mechanisms, and dominated the command economy. Despite its favoured status, Soviet defence industry was increasingly afflicted by the systemic deficiencies of the shortage economy after the mid-1970s. As a result it remained inefficient, lagged behind its Western counterparts in most fields of technology, and produced weapons systems that were not fully competitive by world standards. Russian defence spending and military production have declined substantially since 1989 and defence industry is no longer the favoured sector of the economy. However, military cutbacks have occurred in 1917–18, 1921–5, 1945–8, and 1957–61. In the light of recent political developments and military difficulties, it is probable that the Russian government will enhance the status of the defence industry in the years ahead.

Corporate governance has been a recurrent problem in Russian industry. For most of the century firms have been managed by the state on the basis of crude performance criteria and ineffectual incentive schemes. Severe principal–agent problems were evident in the Soviet economy. From the mid-1970s the power of the central bureaucracy gradually weakened, but in the Soviet period no progress was achieved in developing alternative, market-based corporate governance mechanisms. One of the main industrial policies of the Russian government since 1992 has been the denationalization of industrial enterprises in order to force them to restructure in accordance with market signals. However, the privatization process allowed insiders to gain control of firms and only modest success has been achieved in developing equity markets and an independent banking system. Thus, the governance of Russian industrial enterprises remains exceptionally weak by Western standards.

Russian governments have had clear ideas about the optimal geographical distribution of industry, which often have been influenced by national security considerations. The Tsarist state made use of a variety of policy instruments to open up Siberia, develop the iron and steel industry in Ukraine, and promote the growth of defence industry in interior regions. Due to wars and resource constraints, little was done to alter regional patterns during 1914–27. In contrast, the Stalin regime used forceful methods to create industrial capabilities in previously neglected inner regions, both in peacetime and during World War II. Subsequent Soviet governments adopted regional development strategies with varying objectives, resource commitments, and success. As a general rule, regional industrial policies had diminishing impacts on established patterns. In the transition era, the shift to the market has revealed large discrepancies between the actual distribution of industry and an economically viable one. Yet regional policy has become more reactive, fragmented, and ineffectual.

Another distinctive feature of Russian industrial policy has been its goal of insulating the economy from the world system and achieving self-sufficiency. The beginning and end of the century have been periods of relative openness. The Tsarist government relied upon the outside world for loans and supplies of technology and allowed substantial foreign direct investment. On the other hand, it protected its industry through tariffs and quantity controls and foreign trade accounted for a small share of national income, even after adjusting for the large size of the country. The repudiation of the Tsarist debts to governments, banks, and firms in the West ushered in a period of isolation for the Soviet economy that lasted until 1991. The government controlled foreign transactions through the state monopoly of foreign trade, and inconvertible currency, imposition of secrecy on indigenous technological developments, and prohibition of foreign investment. It encouraged the general development of industry, instead of participating in international specialization. As a result, many branches of industry enlarged in size beyond what would have been appropriate in a market environment, remained inefficient, and became unused to competing on a world level on the basis of product quality.

In the post-Stalin period the Soviet Union became involved in elaborate CMEA scientific-technological exchange, industrial trade, and economic integration programmes with the countries of Eastern Europe. However, since the USSR had imposed shortage economies on these nations, socialist trade did not solve many of the problems plaguing Soviet industry. Despite the general policy of self-sufficiency, the Soviet state was forced to import advanced Western technology for industry through legal and covert channels. Only a small share of this was successfully assimilated and led to significant improvements in the performance of enterprises. Over the final two decades of the command era, the international competitiveness of Soviet industry declined markedly.

The current transition economy has been opened up in an uncontrolled manner, without coordinating trade policies with the industrial restructuring process. As a result, there has been a substantial penetration of its markets for manufactures by foreign competitors and a failure of Russian industrial enterprises to export civilian or military commodities. Due to the chaos in the Russian economy and uncertainties surrounding property rights, only a small amount of foreign direct investment flowed into Russia during 1992–6. Although the volume of FDI grew significantly in 1997, influential Russians have questioned the benefits of openness and have argued for greater protection of industry. Their disquiet increased after large volumes of Western funds were withdrawn from Russia in late 1997 and 1998 due to the adverse impacts on all emerging financial markets of the banking and exchange rates crises in Asian countries. It is likely that Russia's economy will remain closed relative to Western European ones in the foreseeable future.

A final issue is whether Russian interventionist industrial policies have enabled the country to catch up with the West. At the start of century the Russian industrial sector was similar to those in Europe in many respects, although it possessed some unique features and was comparatively backward. The establishment of the Soviet regime initiated a process of divergence that peaked in the late Stalin period. Over the subsequent decades the common adoption of technological processes and models of industrial organizations in the East and West stimulated theories of inevitable convergence. However, these ignored the distinctive features of the Soviet shortage economy, the Communist Party dictatorship, and the underlying Slavic-Orthodox civilization.[55] By 1991 significant and widening gaps existed between industry in the collapsing USSR and that in the more dynamic Western Europe. At the start of transition in Russia, liberal reformers in the Yeltsin–Gaidar government committed Russia to the dominant Western model of a competitive open market economy and democracy. They attempted to reform in a radical manner the ownership and structure of Russian industry, and to alter behavioural patterns of managers and workers. However, progress in industrial restructuring has been modest and the existing transitional economic system remains quite distinct from those in Western Europe. In both Russia and the West there is growing debate over the proposition that all systems in the world will converge to the universal Western liberal democratic political and economic model.[56] The most likely outcome is that Russia will develop a unique pattern of industrial organization, policies and performance that will be consistent with historical traditions and will deviate significantly from those in Western Europe and North America.

[55] Huntington (1996) observes that during the twentieth century the major international wars originated in conflicts between Western nations over the balance of power (World War I) and/or ideological differences (World War II). His main hypothesis is that in the post-Cold War world conflict will arise from differences between the main civilizations, which he identifies as Western, Confucian, Japanese, Islamic, Hindu, Slavic-Orthodox, Latin American, and African. According to him, Russia is the leading country in the Slavic-Orthodox civilization and, as such, is different culturally, politically, and economically from Western European nations.

[56] In *The End of History and the Last Man*, Fukuyama (1992) argues that there is a 'coherent and directional universal history of mankind' and that liberal democracy, with its associated free market economic system represents the endpoint of mankind's ideological, political, and economic evolution. Huntington (1996) takes issue with these ideas, stating that 'The very notion that there is a "universal civilisation" is a Western idea . . . For the relevant future there will be no universal civilisation.' His critique is echoed by Gray (1998), who writes: 'Against Fukuyama, I will argue that what he calls "democratic capitalism" has no prospect of becoming universal. A world consisting only of liberal democratic regimes is not an inevitability: it is a utopia, a state of affairs made unrealizable by some of the most powerful forces of the age.' In Russia, only a shrinking minority of liberals consider it inevitable, or even probable, that their country will converge to the Western model. See also Davis (1996).

APPENDIX

APPENDIX A. Features of Russian industrial policy in different economic systems and periods, 1890–2000

Time period	Economic system	Industrial objectives and priorities	Industrial policy instruments	Beneficiaries of industrial policy	Industrial performance
1890–1913	Tsarist state-dominated peacetime economy	Improve national security through development of defence industry (DI), transportation, and communications. Tolerate growth of consumer industry. Protect domestic industries. Obtain advanced foreign technology and direct investment	State orders, investment, credits, subsidies. Tariffs to protect industry. Liberal laws and prudent fiscal and monetary policies to encourage foreign direct investment (FDI) in industry. Foreign loans to finance imports of machinery	Railways, iron and steel industry, DI. Main region to benefit was European Russia	Industry grows rapidly, but accounts for small share of GDP. Small-scale industry generates 1/3 of output. Capital goods share of industry low relative to W. Europe. Minimal high technology output or innovation. 1/3 industry capital stock is foreign owned. Low competitiveness of manufactures
1914–17	Tsarist war economy	Support the war effort. Increase state control. Give heavy and defence industry (HDI) top priority. Neglect consumer industry. Obtain technology from allies	State orders, investment and credits focused on railways and DI. Central control of supplies and production. DI concentration and standardization	DI and heavy industry (railways, munitions, engineering, chemicals)	Industrial output grows 17% 1913–15. Producer goods up by 62%, consumer down by 15%. DI share of production up from 5% to 30%. Drop in investment and imports of industrial goods. Little technological innovation. Growing chaos in economy in 1917 causes production decline
1918–21	War communism	Sole objective to win wars with internal and external enemies. Give DI top priority. Neglect	Non-market instruments (central rationing, barter, in-kind wages). Nationalization and	DI and war-related branches of heavy industry. Central regions in Russia	Catastrophic drop in industrial output to about 20% of 1913 level. Decline in efficiency and labour productivity. DI focuses on repairs of weapons

Period	System	Objectives	Policy instruments	Priority sectors	Outcomes
			militarization of DI and other key industries. Minimal investment, mainly repairs		not new production. Deterioration of capital stock. Loss of advanced industries in Poland and Baltic states. Blockades prevent imports
1921–7	New economic policy (hybrid command-market economy)	Promote rapid recovery of economy. Severely cut army and DI. Reduce industry subsidies and investment and focus them on heavy industry. Group firms into trusts and make them self-financing. No special regional goals. Obtain foreign technology	State control of banking, foreign, and wholesale trade, HDI. Use of administrative methods and market-related instruments to govern state-owned firms. Extensive intervention in price determination. Privatization of small firms. Trade 'concessions' to attract foreign investors and inflows of technology	Non-DI branches of heavy industry, agriculture, light industry	Rapid recovery of output to 1913 level by 1927. Light industry grows faster than heavy. Little net investment or expansion of capital stock. Minimal foreign investment despite 'concessions'. Slow, partial recovery of exports and imports. Insignificant technological progress
1928–39	Stalinist peacetime command economy	Promote rapid growth and modernization of HDI. Award DI increasingly high priority. Develop new industries in interior regions. Achieve industrial self-sufficiency	Mandatory planning, Gosplan (1st, 2nd, 3rd FYP), priority system, rationing, price controls, state investment and subsidies, regional plans, state monopoly of foreign trade, imports of foreign technology	Heavy and defence industries. Regions containing critical industrial raw materials and high priority projects	High investment rates and ambitious plans result in rapid growth of industry (8% p.a.). HDI increase relative to light and account for 64% of output. Significant technological advances due to domestic R & D and imports of machinery and technical expertise

APPENDIX A. *(Cont'd)*

Time period	Economic system	Industrial objectives and priorities	Industrial policy instruments	Beneficiaries of industrial policy	Industrial performance
1939–45	Stalinist war economy	Mobilize all resources to support the war effort. Award DI top priority. Neglect consumers. Evacuate industry in European regions and develop it in interior. Obtain technological assistance and equipment from allies	State Committee on Defence, hyper-centralization, short-term evacuation and output plans, rationing, militarization of civilian industry, use of GULAG labour, Lend Lease aid, technological espionage, use of captured personnel and equipment	Heavy and defence industries. Central/East Russian and Central Asian regions	Industrial output index 1940 = 100 declines to 77 in 1942. Large losses in European regions (58% of steel). Evacuate 1,500 big factories. Output share of East of Urals rises. DI output index up to 186 in 1942 (251 in 1944). HDI have 90% share of industrial output. Light industry neglected. Military innovation and mass production of new weapons
1945–53	Late Stalin command economy	Set ambitious reconstruction targets. Give heavy high priority and 88% of industry investment. Convert most DI to civilian production. But develop advanced weapons. From 1948 raise DI priority due to Cold War and Korean War. Develop Eastern regions. Establish CMEA. Obtain reparations	Central planning, Gosplan (4th and 5th FYP), rationing by Gossnab, administration by ministries, priority system, state investment and subsidies, regional plans. Expropriation of industrial equipment from East Europe	Heavy and defence industries	Industrial output index 1940 = 100 recovers to 96 in 1945 (114 heavy, 61 light) on extensive basis. Exceed targets of 4th FYP. By 1955 heavy index 392 and light 103. Substantial acquisition of foreign equipment and personnel from East Europe. Striking progress in weapons development (atomic bomb, missiles, aircraft). Minimal innovation in consumer industries

| 1953–7 | Transitional post-Stalin command economy | Malenkov 'New Course' shifts priorities from HDI to light industries. Ambitious output targets and more investment for consumer goods. But after 1955 Khrushchev shifts priorities back in favour of HDI. Encourage trade with Eastern Europe through CMEA | Central planning (6th FYP), priority system, rationing, cuts in prices of industrial goods, state investment, regional plans, state monopoly of foreign trade, CMEA socialist integration | Unclear situation due to shifts in priorities within time period. Overall, heavy and defence industries retain privileged positions | Continuing recovery of industrial production at high but decelerating rates. Disruptions in industry due to priority shifts and instability of plans. Consumer goods output above 6th FYP targets but below Malenkov ones. Growing excess demand and shortages in retail markets. Continuing advances in military technology (e.g. hydrogen bomb) |
| 1957–64 | Khrushchev's regionalized command economy | Accelerate growth. Adopt goal of overtaking USA in industrial output by 1970. Increase investment and improve capital productivity. Lower priority of DI and raise that of chemicals and fuels. Decentralize decision-making from ministries to regions. Develop East of Urals. Promote CMEA trade and integration | Regional Economic Councils, central coordination by Gosplan, seven-year plan (1959–65), rationing of inputs, regional plans, state investment and subsidies, new success indicators and incentives for enterprises | Chemical, oil, natural gas, space/missile, agricultural machinery, and pre-fabricated building industries. Eastern regions | High but decelerating extensive growth of industry (8.3% 1956–60 to 6% 1961–5). Inconsistent plans, production bottlenecks, and chronic shortages of goods. Big increases in output of consumer durables from low base, but underfulfillment of plans (growth of 5.4% instead of 7.4%). Quality of most goods remains low. Successful development of weapons (ICBMs) and space technology (sputnik) |

APPENDIX A. *(Cont'd)*

Time period	Economic system	Industrial objectives and priorities	Industrial policy instruments	Beneficiaries of industrial policy	Industrial performance
1965–85	Mature Soviet command economy in the superpower arms race	Accelerate intensive growth and technological innovation. Expand DI to support USSR as superpower. Raise priority of agriculture, energy, and consumer goods. Lower investment, but improve its efficiency. Reform regional management of industrial projects. Promote socialist integration and import-led growth based on Western technology	Central planning, Gosplan (8th, 9th, 10th, 11th FYP), Military Industrial Commission (MIC), Gossnab rationing, ministries, incentives for enterprises, price reforms, state investment, and subsidies, Territorial Production Complexes, state monopoly of foreign trade, technological espionage (MIC spetsinformatsiya programme)	Heavy and defence industries, fuels complex, agricultural machinery. Regions with DI, fuels, foreign trade links	Industrial output triples on basis of decelerating extensive growth (6.3% in 1966–70 to 1.8% in 1981–5). Stagnation era. Failure of reforms and conflicting priorities causes underfulfilment of plans and shortages. Negative growth of capital productivity. Increases in the quantities of weapons and improvements in their quality. But sluggish technological innovation and low quality outputs in civilian sphere. Manufactures remain uncompetitive and have small declining share of Soviet exports
1985–8	Soviet command economy subject to timid reforms	Accelerate intensive growth (uskorenie) and technological innovation. Improve planning, management and productivity. Raise investment and focus it on DI, MBMW, fuels. Low priority for consumer industries.	Plans with fewer indicators, Gosplan (12th FYP), MIC, Gossnab, super-ministries, new incentives and more autonomy for firms, quality control (Gospriemka), reduced state orders	Defence, MBMW, fuels, metals industries. Regions with these industries and foreign trade links	Industrial output expands at 2.5–3.0% p.a. Defence and heavy do better than light. Investment and supply plans are inconsistent and underfulfilled. Decentralized decision making of firms and lack of market signals causes growing confusion. Priority protection becomes less

		Give regions more power. Improve efficiency of foreign trade. Attract Western investment	and more wholesale trade, price reforms, state investment and subsidies, reformed state monopoly of foreign trade, joint ventures, technological espionage			effective, so civilian problems spill into DI. No improvement of efficiency or technological innovation. Technological gap with West widens
1989–91	Malfunctioning Soviet economy with weakening central control	Shift to indicative planning, lower growth targets, raise priority of consumers goods, cut military spending, DI conversion, decentralize decision-making to firms, increase private initiative through cooperatives, give regions greater powers, decentralize foreign trade	Central planning, Gosplan (12th, 13th FYP), MIC, rationing and wholesale trade, state and decentralized investment, self-financing of firms, price reforms, reduced subsidies, financial regulators (taxes, interest rates), decentralized foreign trade	Confused situation because state priorities have little influence and all branches collapse in 1990–1		Negative growth of industry (−0.6% in 1989, −2.8% in 1990, −10.5% in 1991). Output in all branches declines, especially in MBMW, metals, and food. Plans underfulfilled and acute shortages. Big drops in investment and capital productivity. Cuts in R & D and minimal technological innovation, even in DI. Unplanned cuts in imports undermine production

APPENDIX A. *(Cont'd)*

Time period	Economic system	Industrial objectives and priorities	Industrial policy instruments	Beneficiaries of industrial policy	Industrial performance
1992–2000	State-dominated unstable market economy in Russia	Shift ownership of most industrial firms (not DI core) to private, abolish planning and branch ministries, decentralize decision-making to firms, let market forces drive restructuring, break up monopolies, abolish state monopoly of foreign trade, expose industry to foreign competition, attract foreign and domestic private investment	Cuts in state orders, reduced state investment and subsidies, price liberalization, privatization, positive real interest rates on loans, anti-monopoly policies, Financial-Industrial Groups, DI conversion programmes, new taxes (profits, VAT), minimal export controls, low tariffs, new laws to attract FDI	Branches of industry producing for foreign markets (oil, gas, metals). Regions with natural resources and successful industries. Big cities	Collapse of industrial output; index 1989 = 100 to 41 in 1998. Industry share of GDP declines. Fuels, metals decline and recover. MBMW, food, light decline through 1998. Heavy share of total industry output rises. Reductions in R & D, DI, and weapons exports. Little investment. Low capacity utilization. Minimal technological innovation. Imported manufactures drive out domestic producers. Little FDI through 1997. Insignificant exports of manufactures

Sources:
This table is based on material from lectures of the author at Oxford University on 'From Revolution to Revolution: The Economy of Russia and the Soviet Union, 1917–1997'. The basic sources for each period are listed below.

1890–1913: Davies 1990; Gatrell 1986, 1994; Nove 1989; Portal 1965; von Laue 1963. See Section 2 of this chapter.
1914–17: Davies, Harrison, and Wheatcroft 1994; Gatrell 1994; Nove 1989.
1917–21: Davies, Harrison, and Wheatcroft 1994; Dobb 1960; Lokshin 1956; Malle 1985; Nove 1989; Rozenfel'd and Klimenko 1961.
1921–7: Davies 1990; Davies, Harrison, and Wheatcroft 1994; Dobb 1960; Lokshin 1956; Rozenfel'd and Klimenko 1961; Zaleski 1971. See Section 3 of this chapter.
1928–39: Carr and Davies 1974; Davies, Harrison, and Wheatcroft 1994; Lokshin 1956; Nove 1989; Rozenfel'd and Klimenko 1961; Zaleski 1980. See Section 4 of this chapter.
1939–45: Davies, Harrison, and Wheatcroft 1994; Harrison 1985; Lokshin 1964; Nove 1989; Rozenfel'd and Klimenko 1961; Zaleski 1980.
1945–53: Dobb 1960; Lokshin 1964; Nove 1989; Rozenfel'd and Klimenko 1961; Zaleski 1980.
1953–7: Berliner 1957; Dobb 1960; JEC 1960; Lokshin 1964; Nove 1989; Rozenfel'd and Klimenko 1961.
1957–64: Amann and Cooper 1977; Gregory and Stuart 1994; Lokshin 1964; Nove 1989, JEC 1962.
1965–85: Amann and Cooper 1977, 1982; Gregory and Stuart 1994; JEC 1973, 1976, 1979, 1983; Nove 1989. See Section 5 of this chapter.
1985–9: Aslund 1991; CIA 1987, 1988b, 1990; Ellman and Kontorovich 1992; IMF 1991; JEC 1987, 1993.
1989–91: Aslund 1991; CIA 1991a; Ellman and Kontorovich 1992; IMF 1991; JEC 1993.
1992–2000: Aslund 1995; EBRD 1994 . . . 1997; ECE 1993 . . . 1998; OECD 1995, 1997c. See Section 6 of this chapter.

APPENDIX B. *Industry in the economies of the Russian Empire, USSR, and Russian Federation, 1890–1995*

Indicator	Units	Russian Empire				USSR				
		1890	1900	1913	1921	1928	1940	1945	1950	1960
Industrial output index	1913 = 100	31.0	61.1	100.0	24.0	103.0	315.7	302.3	427.1	1038.5
Industry share of GDP	%	11.9	18.1	21.3	11.0	20.1	31.2	34.6	30.0	32.0
Industry share of investment	%	19.0	19.0	20.0	30.0	25.0	33.5	33.8	43.5	36.0
Industry employment	Millions	2.6	4.2	5.9	2.1	4.9	12.7	11.7	15.3	22.6
Civilian labour force	Millions	58.8	68.6	85.1	66.4	78.6	83.8	76.0	97.6	110.1
Industry share of labour force	%	4.4	6.1	6.9	3.2	6.2	15.2	15.4	15.7	20.5
Producer goods share of industrial output	%	25.0	28.0	35.1	30.8	39.5	61.2	74.9	68.8	72.5
Consumer goods share of industrial output	%	75.0	72.0	64.9	69.2	60.5	38.8	25.1	31.2	27.5

Indicator	Units	USSR				Russian Federation				
		1970	1980	1985	1990	1990	1992	1993	1994	1995
Industrial output index	1970 = 100	100.0	157.8	174.0	184.1	184.1	138.8	119.1	94.3	91.1
Industrial output index	1989 = 100	47.2	74.4	87.8	99.9	99.9	75.4	64.7	51.2	49.5
Industry share of GDP	%	32.0	36.8	37.1	36.9	37.8	33.8	34.4	33.0	33.7
Industry share of investment	%	35.2	35.3	36.5	34.3	35.9	39.9	36.3	30.3	33.6
Industry employment	Millions	31.6	36.9	38.1	40.0	22.8	21.3	20.8	18.6	17.2
Civilian labour force	Millions	125.6	147.3	153.3	157.5	75.3	72.1	70.9	68.5	67.1
Industry share of labour force	%	25.2	25.1	24.9	25.4	30.3	29.5	29.3	27.2	25.6
Producer goods share of industrial output	%	73.4	73.8	74.8	72.4	72.2	70.7	70.9	73.6	76.0
Consumer goods share of industrial output	%	26.6	26.2	25.2	27.6	27.9	29.3	29.1	26.4	24.0

Sources:

Industrial output index 1913 = 100 for years 1890–1960

Industry is defined to include Mining (quarrying and mining), Manufacturing and Utilities (gas, water, electricity) (MMU). Construction is excluded. See detailed notes for Figure 13.1. 1890–1913: Goldsmith (1961: 462–3); Nutter (1962: 185). 1921: Nutter (1962: 185). 1928–60: Moorsteen and Powell (1966: Table P-1); Harrison (1996). See also Nutter (1962: Table 53); Powell (1963: Table IV.9).

Industry share of GDP for years 1890–1960	An attempt has been made to estimate the MMU share of GDP. Most of the estimates presented for specific years are based upon cited works of other scholars. There are inconsistencies between the shares in the table and those implied by GDP and MMU growth indices. 1890, 1900: Estimated using the 1913 share and GDP and MMU indices. 1913: It is assumed that the 1913 share is the same as the 1912 share given in Gregory (1970: 28–9). A re-calculation of the MMU/NNP share in DHW (1994: 272) for GDP gives 20.3%. 1921: Estimated from the 1913 share using GDP and MMU indices. 1928: Gregory (1970: 28–9). The re-calculated DHW 1994 share is 19.4%. 1940: Re-calculation of the MMU/NNP share in DHW (1994: 272). 1945: It is assumed that the 1945 share is the same as the 1944 share given in DHW (1994: 321). 1950, 1960: Estimations using the 1940 share and the MMU and GDP growth rates give 32.0% for 1950 and 36% for 1960. These are significantly inconsistent with those of Converse (1982) of 25% and 28%. The shares in the table are compromise estimates that are in a range between the 1940 and 1970 shares.
Industry share of gross fixed capital investment for years 1890–1960	1890: Author's estimate based on fragmentary evidence in several sources. 1900, 1913: Gatrell (1986: 192); Gatrell and Davies (1990: 128). 1921: Author's estimate based on fragmentary evidence in several sources. 1928: Bergson (1961: 388) gives the sum of (new machinery outlays) + (capital repairs to machinery) as a share of all investment in fixed capital. 1940: TsSU (1986: 366). 1945: Bergson (1961: 388) for 1944. 1950: Bergson (1961: 388). 1960: TsSU (1986: 366).
Industry employment in millions for years 1890–1960	Employment in MMU where possible. 1890, 1900: Large scale industry employment of 1.44 million and 2.2 million from Lyashchenko (1949: 526). Calculate total industry employment on the assumption that artisan industry shares are 45% in 1890 and 47% in 1900. Nutter (1962: 509–13) gives estimates of employment in large and small scale enterprises in 23 branches of industry (bcth 2.95 million) for a total of 5.9 million. Alternative estimates of industry employment in this year are given in Davies (1990: 251–3, 294–6) without providing a definitive assessment. 1921: Industrial employment assumed to be 35% of 1913 level, whereas output was 25%. 1928: Employment in small scale industry in 1927/28 was 1.88 million according to Davies (1990: 296). Assume ratio of small to total is the same as 1926/27 of .384 calculated using small and large scale employment for that year (Davies 1990: 294, 296). This implies employment in large scale industry of 3.0 million and total industrial employment of 4.8 million. 1940: Weitzman, Feshbach and Kulchyka (1962: 620); 1945: DHW (1994: 322). 1950, 1960: Rapawy (1987: 202–3).
Civilian labour force in millions for years 1890–1960	1890, 1900: Estimated as 51.8% (1913 share) of populations of Tsarist Empire of 113.0 million and 132.0 million from Nutter (1962: 519). 1913: Ratio of economically active population of 51.8% calculated from 72.5 million employed (Davies 1990: 251) out of a pre-1939 borders population of 139.9 million (DHW 1994: 269). Population within Tsarist borders was 164.2 million (Nutter 1962: 519) so the labour force was 85.1 million. 1921: Population was 135.4 million (Nutter 1962: 519) and assume ratio of economically active fell to 0.49. 1928: Population was 153.2 million (DHW 1994: 269) and assume labour force ratio was same as that of census year 1926 of .513 (76.1 million economically active out of a population of 148.5 million according to DHW (1994: 273, 277). 1940: Weitzman, Feshbach and Kulchyka (1962: 611) state that census labour force in 1939 was 87.2 million (51.1% of population), of which 83.8 million was civilian. 1945: DHW (1994: 322). 1950, 1960: Rapawy (1987: 202–3).

Variable	Source / Notes
Industry share of labour force for years 1890–1960	Divide industry employment by civilian labour force.
	1890, 1900: Author's estimates. 1913: TsSU Prom (1964: 37). 1921: TsSU (1959: 147). 1928–60: TsSU Prom (1964: 37).
Producer goods share of industrial output for 1890–1960	As for producer goods share above. See Gregory (1970: 28–9) and Nutter (1962: 364) for shares of consumer goods (light and food) industry for the years 1912/13 and 1928.
Consumer goods share of industrial output for 1890–1960	1970–80: Index numbers from Converse (1982: 191–2). 1980–90 USSR: Chain estimate from an index 1980 = 100 calculated using data on industry value added in 1982 roubles and annual growth rates from CIA (1990: Table C-1), and Noren and Kurtzweg (1993: 15). 1990–95 RF: Chain estimate based on 1989 = 100 index of gross industrial output of the Russian Federation from ECE (1998: Appendix Table B.4). 1970–90: Chained to 1970 = 100 industrial output index for USSR. 1990–95 RF index from ECE (1998: 201).
Industrial output index 1970 = 100 for years 1970–95	1970, 1980: Pitzer (1982: 61). 1985, 1990 USSR: The shares were calculated by dividing USSR industry value added by GNP in 1982 roubles estimated on using 1980 values and growth rates from CIA (1990: Table C-1), and Noren and Kurtzweg (1993). 1990–95 RF: The shares are from GKS (1996b: 5).
Industrial output index 1989 = 100 for years 1970–95	1970–85: TsSU (1986: 366). 1990: GKS SSSR (1991: 551). 1990–94: RF share from GKS (1995a: 380). See also Le Houerou (1996: 61). 1995: GKS (1995b: 59) states that industry had a 60.1% share of productive investment in the RF, which in turn was 56% of total investment. CEAGRF (1997: 127) gives an industry share of 34.4%.
Industry share of GDP for years 1970–95	1970–85: Feshbach and Rapawy (1976); Rapawy (1987: 202–3). 1990: Estimate industry employment from a projection of the non-agricultural labour force for that year given in Rapawy (1987: 195) by using 1985 ratio of the two. 1990–95: RF employment from GKS (1996b: 5).
Industry share of gross fixed capital investment for years 1970–95	1970–85: Rapawy (1987: 202–3). 1990: Estimate average annual employment in USSR from projection of total labour force for that year in Rapawy (1987: 195) by using 1985 ratio. 1990–95: RF employment from GKS (1996b: 5).
Industry employment in millions for years 1970–95	1970–90: Divide industry employment in USSR by civilian labour force. 1990–95: RF share from GKS (1996b: 5).
Civilian labour force in millions for years 1970–95	1970: TsSU (1979: 117). 1980–90: GKS SSSR (1991: 353). 1990–95: RF share calculated by subtracting the consumer goods share shown in next row from 100.
Industry share of labour force for years 1970–95	1970: TsSU (1979, 117). 1980–90: GKS SSSR (1991: 353). 1990, 1992: RF shares calculated by assuming that the RF had the same 1985 share as the USSR and then applying producer and consumer goods production indices (1985 = 100) given in GKS (1993: 366) of 110 and 126 in 1990, and 82 and 101 in 1992. 1993, 1994: Calculated from 1992 share on assumption that consumer goods share changed in the same manner as that of light and food industry given in GKS (1996b: 8), which was 17.4% in 1992, 17.3% in 1993 and 15.7% in 1994. 1995: GKS (1996b: 10) gives a 1995 index of production of consumer goods relative to 1994 of 88 versus an all industry index of 97. Calculate 1995 RF share by multiplying the 1994 share of 26.4 by .88 and dividing by 97.
Producer goods share of industrial output for 1970–95	
Consumer goods share of industrial output for 1970–95	

APPENDIX C. *Physical production of industrial commodities in Russia and the USSR, 1890–1995*

Indicator	Units	Russian Empire				USSR						
		1890	1900	1913	1917	1921	1928	1932	1937	1940	1945	1950
Steel	Mill Tons	0.4	2.2	4.3	3.1	0.2	4.3	5.9	17.7	18.3	12.3	27.3
Iron ore	Mill Tons	1.7	6.0	9.5	5.3	0.1	6.1	12.1	27.8	29.9	15.9	39.7
Cast iron	Mill Tons	0.9	2.9	4.6	3.0	0.1	3.3	6.2	14.5	14.9	8.8	19.2
Oil	Mill Tons	4.0	10.4	10.3	8.8	3.8	11.6	21.4	28.5	31.1	19.4	37.9
Coal	Mill Tons	6.0	16.2	29.2	31.3	8.9	35.5	64.4	128.0	165.9	149.3	261.1
Electricity	Bill KwHs	0.2	0.8	2.0	2.2	0.5	5.0	13.5	36.2	48.3	43.3	91.2
Natural gas	Bill M Cu	0.0	0.0	0.0	0.0	0.0	0.3	1.1	2.3	3.4	3.4	6.2
Automobiles	Thousand	0.0	0.0	0.0	0.0	0.0	0.1	0.1	18.3	5.5	5.0	64.6
Tractors	Thousand	0.0	0.0	0.0	0.0	0.0	1.3	48.9	51.0	31.6	7.7	116.7
Cement	Mill Tons	0.1	0.8	2.1	0.9	0.1	1.8	3.5	5.5	5.7	1.8	10.2
Cotton fabrics	Bill M Sq	0.6	1.1	1.8	0.8	0.1	1.8	1.8	2.4	2.7	1.1	2.7

Indicator	Units	USSR						Russian Federation				
		1960	1970	1975	1980	1985	1990	1990	1992	1993	1994	1995
Steel	Mill Tons	65.3	115.9	141.0	148.0	155.0	154.0	89.6	67.0	58.3	48.8	51.3
Iron ore	Mill Tons	105.9	195.5	233.0	245.0	248.0	236.0	107.0	82.1	76.1	73.3	78.3
Cast iron	Mill Tons	46.8	85.9	103.0	107.0	110.0	110.0	59.4	46.1	40.9	36.5	39.2
Oil	Mill Tons	147.9	353.0	491.0	603.0	595.0	571.0	516.0	399.0	354.0	318.0	307.0
Coal	Mill Tons	513.2	624.1	701.0	716.0	726.0	703.0	395.0	337.0	306.0	272.0	262.0
Electricity	Bill KwHs	292.3	740.9	1039.0	1295.0	1544.0	1726.0	1082.2	1008.5	956.6	875.9	862.0
Natural gas	Bill M Cu	47.2	197.9	270.0	406.0	599.0	759.0	641.0	641.0	618.0	607.0	595.0
Automobiles	Thousand	138.8	344.2	1201.0	1327.0	1332.0	1259.0	1103.0	963.0	956.0	798.0	835.0
Tractors	Thousand	238.5	459.0	550.4	555.0	585.0	495.0	214.0	137.0	89.1	28.7	21.2
Cement	Mill Tons	45.5	95.2	122.0	125.0	131.0	137.0	83.0	61.7	49.9	37.2	36.4
Cotton fabrics	Bill M Sq	4.8	6.2	6.6	7.1	7.7	7.8	6.3	3.6	2.5	1.6	1.2

Sources:
1890, 1900, 1913, 1917: Lyashchenko (1949: 528–9); Mitchell (1992); NBER (1956: Supplement, Table 4); Nutter (1962: 411–96); TsSU Prom (1964: 38–9). Electricity production for 1890 and 1900 was estimated by the author using data in Coopersmith (1992).
1921, 1928, 1932, 1937, 1940, 1945, 1950, 1960: Akademiya (1976: 326); Nove (1989: 84); Nutter (1962: 411–96); TsSU Prom (1964: 38–9).
1970: TsSU (1976: 235, 240, 241, 244, 247, 265, 266, 277).
1975: TsSU (1976: 132–5, 265)
1980: TsSU (1981: 68–71, 171).
1985: TsSU (1986: 588–91); GKS SSSR (1991: 407).
1990: USSR: GKS SSSR (1991: 676–8).
1990–5: RF: GKS (1995d: 125, 129, 132, 136, 140, 141, 162, 163); GKS (1996b: 24, 29, 35, 46, 50).

APPENDIX D. *International comparisons of industrialization in the Russian Empire, USSR, and Russian Federation in selected years, 1913–95*

Country	Population	GDP per capita index	Industry share of GDP	Industry share employment	Steel output	Oil production	Electricity production	Cotton fabrics	Automobile production	Share of manufacturing of top 20 countries	Ratio of manufacturing output
	Millions	US = 100									USA = 100
		%	%	%	MMT	MMT	BKwHr	Bill M Sq	Thousands	%	
Russian Empire and leading industrial powers in 1913											
Russia	170.9	28.0	21.3	6.9	4.3	10.3	2.0	1.8	0	8.6	25.9
USA	97.2	100.0	27.2	28.0	31.8	34.2	24.7	5.7	485	33.4	100.0
Japan	51.3	44.0	20.2	19.2	0.3	0.3	1.5	NA	0	2.8	8.4
Germany	37.8	72.2	44.0	33.3	17.6	0.1	8.0	NA	20	15.5	46.4
France	41.5	65.0	41.0	30.2	4.7	0.0	1.8	NA	45	6.4	19.2
Italy	37.2	47.2	24.0	21.3	0.9	0.0	2.0	NA	7	2.6	7.7
UK	42.6	94.8	38.0	45.4	7.8	0.0	2.5	7.4	34	14.3	42.7
USSR and leading industrial powers in 1939											
USSR	180.6	34.1	31.0	16.1	17.6	30.3	43.2	2.6	20	9.8	28.8
USA	130.9	100.0	29.5	21.5	28.8	170.9	161.3	7.9	2,889	34.0	100.0
Japan	71.4	41.2	32.3	23.3	7.0	0.4	34.1	2.9	2	5.7	16.7
Germany	43.4	84.5	50.0	35.4	23.7	0.7	61.4	1.9	275	13.8	40.7
France	41.9	72.3	36.0	27.1	8.0	0.0	22.1	1.4	182	4.8	14.0
Italy	43.9	52.4	31.0	22.8	2.3	0.0	18.4	1.1	59	3.0	8.9
UK	48.0	91.0	36.0	29.7	13.4	0.0	35.8	3.5	305	11.7	34.3
USSR and leading industrial powers in 1970											
USSR	242.8	37.5	32.0	26.6	115.9	353.0	740.9	6.7	344	18.0	59.6
USA	205.1	100.0	29.5	26.8	119.3	475.3	1,742.7	6.8	6,547	30.2	100.0
Japan	104.3	63.6	32.5	27.7	93.3	0.8	359.5	2.6	3,179	8.7	29.0
FR Germany	60.7	80.3	39.6	41.2	45.0	7.5	242.6	0.9	3,528	8.4	27.7
France	50.8	77.8	31.3	28.6	23.8	2.3	147.0	1.4	2,458	5.8	19.2
Italy	53.7	64.0	34.5	27.7	17.3	1.4	117.4	0.8	1,720	3.5	11.5
UK	55.6	72.0	32.1	37.2	28.3	0.1	249.1	0.7	1,641	4.2	13.9

USSR and leading industrial powers in 1980

USSR	265.5	35.2	36.8	27.1	147.9	603.0	1,293.9	7.1	1,327	15.4	70.4
USA	227.7	100.0	29.0	22.5	101.5	430.0	2,437.8	4.0	6,376	21.9	100.0
Japan	116.8	71.8	39.4	24.9	111.4	0.5	577.5	2.1	7,038	14.5	66.1
FR Germany	61.6	84.0	37.5	34.5	43.8	4.7	368.8	0.7	3,512	10.8	49.2
France	53.9	82.5	31.7	25.5	23.2	1.4	243.3	0.9	3,487	6.3	28.9
Italy	56.5	71.9	36.5	25.7	26.5	1.8	185.7	0.9	1,445	5.2	23.9
UK	56.0	69.9	31.6	29.4	11.3	78.4	284.9	0.4	924	5.0	22.9

USSR and leading industrial powers in 1990

USSR	289.4	31.4	32.7	27.6	154.0	575.0	1,082.2	7.8	1,259	14.1	63.5
USA	250.0	100.0	26.5	18.6	89.7	373.9	2,997.4	3.7	6,052	22.2	100.0
Japan	124.0	84.8	31.1	24.1	110.3	0.5	808.0	1.8	9,948	18.3	82.7
Germany	79.4	85.5	32.8	31.1	44.0	3.6	440.0	0.9	4,802	11.5	51.6
France	56.7	81.3	24.1	19.6	19.0	3.0	400.0	0.8	3,295	5.5	24.8
Italy	57.7	72.9	27.5	20.8	25.4	4.6	217.0	1.8	1,963	5.3	23.8
UK	57.6	74.6	27.8	23.1	17.9	88.0	317.0	0.2	1,296	4.4	19.6

Russian Federation and leading industrial powers in 1995

Russia	148.2	16.6	33.7	25.6	51.3	307.0	862.0	1.2	835	1.9	7.1
USA	263.1	100.0	22.0	16.9	95.2	330.8	3,550.0	3.7	6,351	26.4	100.0
Japan	125.2	81.9	30.3	22.6	101.6	0.5	975.0	1.2	7,786	19.2	72.7
Germany	81.9	74.4	25.4	26.4	42.1	2.9	525.0	0.6	4,538	11.3	42.7
France	58.1	77.9	23.3	16.9	17.9	2.5	490.0	0.7	3,176	5.6	21.3
Italy	57.2	73.6	27.9	21.2	27.8	5.2	240.0	1.6	1,756	5.9	22.4
UK	58.5	71.4	26.8	18.5	17.4	121.8	335.0	0.2	1,532	4.5	17.2

Sources:

Population 1913, 1939: Russia/USSR Mitchell (1992: 83–5); USA USDC (1975: v. 1); Japan JSA (1987: v. 1, 48–9); Other countries Maddison (1995: 104–7); 1970, 1980: CIA (1984: 54–5); 1990: CIA (1991*b*: 48); 1995: World Bank (1997: 214–15).

GDP per capita index The index was calculated from GDP per capita figures from the following sources: 1913, 1939, 1970, 1980, 1990: Geary-Kravis estimates in Maddison (1995: 194–201); 1995 $ PPP GNP per capita estimates in World Bank (1997: 214–15).

Industry share of GDP Share of GDP of Mining (mining and quarrying), Manufacturing, and Utilities (electricity, gas, water) (MMU). 1913, 1939: Russia/USSR for 1940 Appendix B; USA calculated from data in USDC (1975: v. 1, 239, 240); Japan calculated from data in JSA (1987: v. 1, 239, 240); Other countries Mitchell (1992: 913, 915, 917). 1970, 1980, 1990, 1995: USSR/Russia Appendix B; other countries except USA and UK in 1995 calculated from data on GDP and MMU in OECD 1984 and OECD 1997*c*; USA 1995 from USDC (1997: 448); UK 1995 from UK ONS (1996: table 2.2).

Industry share of employment 1913, 1939	Employment in MMU as share of civilian labour force and MMU employment in USDC (1975: v. 1, 137, 139); Japan assume the same share as for 1920 calculated from data in JSA (1987: v. 1, 389); Assume shares are the same as 1907 for Germany and 1911 for France, Italy, and UK calculated from data in Mitchell (1992: 145, 149, 156); 1939: USSR for 1940 Appendix B; USA as for 1913; Japan calculated from data on labour force and MMU employment in JSA (1987: v. 1, 365); Germany for 1939 and France, Italy for 1936 calculated from Mitchell (1992: 145, 146, 149); Assume UK share the same as that for 1935 calculated from data on MMU in UN DESA (1963: 790).
Industry share of employment 1970, 1980, 1990, 1995	USSR/Russia Appendix B. For other countries shares were calculated from data on civilian labour forces and employment in MMU branches of industry that were obtained for 1970 from OECD 1991, for 1980, 1990, 1995 from OECD 1997a, and for France 1995 from OECD 1997b: 303.
Crude steel production	1913, 1939: Russia/USSR NBER (1956) and Nutter (1962); Other countries Mitchell (1992: 457). 1970, 1980: USSR Appendix C; Other countries CIA (1984: 148). 1990: CIA (1991b: 113). 1995: Russia Appendix C; Other countries CIA (1996, table 72).
Oil production	1913, 1939: Russia/USSR NBER (1956) and Nutter (1962) USA Nutter (1962: 587); Japan estimated from data in JSA (1987: v. 2, 250–1); Other countries Mitchell (1992: 426–7). 1970: USSR Appendix C. Other countries UN YIS (1978: v. II, 4–5) and CIA Handbook (1985) with production in thousands of barrels per day of oil converted into million metric tons using factor of one TBPD = 50 metric tons per year. 1980: TsSU (1981: 68–9). 1990: GKS SSSR (1991: 676–7); Other countries UN ICSY (1997: 5–6). 1995: Russia Appendix C; Other countries UN ICSY (1997: 5–6) and CIA (1996, table 48 with conversions as for 1970).
Electricity production	1913, 1939: Russia/USSR Appendix C and Nutter (1962); USA Nutter (1962: 585); Japan JSA (1987: vol. 2, 450); Other countries Mitchell (1992: 546–8). 1970, 1980: CIA (1984: 137). 1990: CIA (1991b: 97). 1995: Russia Appendix C; Other countries CIA (1996, table 58).
Cotton fabrics production	1913: Russia Appendix C; USA and UK from TsSU Prom (1964: 116–17); Information on other countries not available. 1939: USSR Nutter 1962); Other countries calculated from the figure given for the USA in TsSU Prom (1964: 116–17, of 7.9 billion square metres and an index with the USA as 1.0 based on statistics on cotton fabrics in millions of metres for 1938 given in Woytinsky and Woytinsky (1953: 1070). 1970: UN YIS (1978: v. II, 185–6) and CIA (1984: 170). 1980: TsSU (1981: 70–1). 1990: GKS SSSR (1991: 676–7); Other countries UN ICSY (1997: 262–3).
Automobile production	1913: Russia Appendix C; Other countries Foreman-Peck (1995) and Laux (1992); 1939: USSR Nutter (1962: 432); USA Nutter (1962: 593); Japan JSA (1987: v. 2, 387); Other countries Mitchell (1992: 535). 1970, 1980: USA USDC (1997: 627); Other countries CIA (1984: 178) and Mitchell (1992: 535). 1990: CIA (1991b: 126). 1995: Russia Appendix C; Other countries CIA (1996, table 88); USDC (1997: 627), and UN ICSY (1997: 819).
Shares of manufacturing output of top 20 countries, 1913, 1939	1913: Shares calculated from Bairoch (1982: 284), index of industrial output UK 1900 = 100 for top 20 countries. 1939: Ranking as for 1938. Bairoch (1982) gives shares of world manufacturing output for 16 countries in table 13 and indices of output UK 1900 = 100 for the USA and UK in table 2. The shares were converted to production indices for other countries by using ratios of their output share relative to that of the USA. Production indices (UK 1900 = 100) for other countries presented in table 16 indicated that six belonged in the top 20. Shares of the top 20 were calculated from the production indices.
Shares of manufacturing output of top 20 countries, 1970	1970: GDP generated by manufacturing in $ 1970 millions was calculated for 24 countries using GDP and manufacturing shares of GDP in 1970. World Bank (1993: 242–3) provided data for most countries. GDP for the USSR and East European countries was estimated by calculating their ratios of USA GDP in $ 1983 from CIA (1984: 32–3) and applying them to the World Bank USA GDP value. Missing shares of manufacturing were found for the USSR in Appendix B and for Eastern European countries and France in Alton (1977: 206–7). Shares for Sweden and Switzerland were estimated from data in UNIDO (1997). The top 20 countries were chosen and shares of their total output were calculated.
Shares of manufacturing output of top 20 countries, 1980, 1990	1980, 1990: The shares were calculated by obtaining estimates of manufacturing value added (MVA) in US $ 1990 for the top 20 countries from UNIDO (1997), aggregating and dividing. The 1990 figure for Germany is an aggregate of the FRG and GDR. The UNIDO estimates of industrial output in the USSR and East European countries seemed too low. New estimates of MVA in $ 1990 were made by calculating 1980 and 1990 values of GDP in UNIDO (1997) $ 1990 by using the same ratios of USA GDP as those given in Maddison (1995: 183, 187) and multiplying them by industry shares of GDP. Those for the USSR were 32.7% and 32.8% as in Appendix B. The 1980 shares of 39.2% for Czechoslovakia, 44.1% for the GDR, 33.9% for Poland, and 39.7% for Romania are from Alton (1985: 89), while the 35% for Yugoslavia was estimated from World Bank (1990: 183). The 1990 industry shares were estimated using values of GNP and industry shares for 1980 and respective indices of growth over 1980–8 given in Alton (1989: 87–8, 93). As a result, GDR, Poland, Czechoslovakia, Yugoslavia, and Romania were included in the top 20 in 1980 and Poland, Czechoslovakia, and Yugoslavia in 1990.
Shares of manufacturing output of top 20 countries, 1995	1995: Manufacturing value added estimates for the top 20 countries were obtained from UNIDO (1997) country tables and shares were calculated.
Ratio of manufacturing output	The ratios were calculated from either the indices of manufacturing output or manufacturing value added used to estimate shares of manufacturing output. See previous notes for sources.

REFERENCES

ACDA = US Arms Control and Disarmament Agency

ADAMS, F. G., and KLEIN, L. R. (1983) (eds.). *Industrial Policies for Growth and Competitiveness*. Lexington: Lexington Books.

Akademiya Nauk SSSR, Institut Ekonomiki (1976). *Istoriya Sotsialisticheskoi Ekonomiki SSSR: Sovetskaya Ekonomika v 1917–1920 gg.* Moscow: Nauka.

ALMQUIST, P. (1990). *Red Forge: Soviet Military Industry since 1965*. New York: Columbia University Press.

ALTON, T. P. (1977). 'Comparative structure and growth of economic activity in Eastern Europe', in US Congress, Joint Economic Committee, *East European Economies Post-Helsinki*. Washington, DC: USGPO.

—— (1985). 'East European GNPs: Origins of product, final uses, rates of growth, and international comparisons', in US Congress, Joint Economic Committee, *East European Economies: Slow growth in the 1970s*. Washington, DC: USGPO.

—— (1989). 'East European GNPs: Domestic final uses of Gross Product, rates of growth, and international comparisons', in US Congress, Joint Economic Committee, *Pressures for Reform in the East European Economies*, Washington, DC: USGPO.

AMANN, R., and COOPER, J. (1977) (eds.). *The Technological Level of Soviet Industry*. London: Yale University Press.

—— —— (1982) (eds.). *Industrial Innovation in the Soviet Union*. London: Yale University Press.

ASLUND, A. (1991). *Gorbachev's Struggle for Economic Reform*, 2nd edn. London: Pinter Publishers.

—— (1995). *How Russia Became a Market Economy*. Washington, DC: Brookings Institution.

BACON, E. (1994). *The Gulag at War: Stalin's Forced Labour System in Light of the Archives*. Basingstoke: Macmillan.

BAIROCH, P. (1982). 'International industrialization levels from 1750 to 1980'. *Journal of European Economic History*, 11/2: 269–333.

BAYKOV, A. (1947). *The Development of the Soviet Economic System: An Essay on the Experience of Planning in the U.S.S.R.* Cambridge: Cambridge University Press.

BERGSON, A. (1961). *The Real National Income of Soviet Russia Since 1928*. Cambridge, Mass.: Harvard University Press.

BERLINER, J. S. (1957). *Factory and Manager in the USSR*. Cambridge, Mass.: Harvard University Press.

—— (1976). *The Innovation Decision in Soviet Industry*. Cambridge, Mass.: MIT Press.

BLACKWELL, W. L. (1974) (ed.). *Russian Economic Development from Peter the Great to Stalin*. New York: New Viewpoints.

BLASI, J. R., KROUMOVA, M., and KRUSE, D. (1997). *Kremlin Capitalism: Privatizing the Russian Economy*. London: Cornell University Press.

BROWN, A. (1996). *The Gorbachev Factor*. Oxford: Oxford University Press.

BRUS, W. (1975). *Socialist Ownership and Political Systems*. London: Routledge & Kegan Paul.

—— (1988). 'Utopianism and realism in the evolution of the Soviet economic system', *Soviet Studies*, 40/3: 434–43.

CEAGRF = Centre of Economic Analysis of the Government of the Russian Federation

CARR, E. H., and DAVIES, R. W. (1974). *Foundations of a Planned Economy, 1926–1929*, Vol. i. Harmondsworth: Penguin.

Central Intelligence Agency (1984). *Handbook of Economic Statistics: 1984*. Washington, DC: CIA CPAS 84-10002.

—— (1985a). *Handbook of Economic Statistics: 1985*. Washington, DC: CIA.

—— (1985b). *Soviet Acquistion of Militarily Significant Western Technology: An Update*. Washington, DC: CIA.

—— (1986). *The Soviet Weapons Industry: An Overview*. Washington, DC: CIA DI 86-10016.

—— (1987). *Gorbachev's Modernization Program: A Status Report*. Washington, DC: Report submitted to the US Congress, Joint Economic Committee, 19 Mar. 1987.

—— (1988a). *The Impact of Gorbachev's Policies on Soviet Economic Statistics*. Washington, DC: CIA SOV 88-10049.

—— (1988b). *Revisiting Soviet Economic Performance under Glasnost: Implications for CIA Estimates*. Washington, DC: CIA SOV 88-10068.

—— (1988c). *Handbook of Economic Statistics: 1988*. Washington, DC: CIA.

—— (1990). 'The Soviet economy stumbles badly in 1989', Paper presented to the Technology and National Security Subcommittee of the US Congress, Joint Economic Committee, Washington, DC.

—— (1991a). *Beyond Perestroyka: The Soviet Economy in Crisis*. Washington, DC: Report submitted to the US Congress Joint Economic Committee, DDB-1900-164-91.

—— (1991b). *Handbook of Economic Statistics: 1991*. Washington, DC: CIA CPAS 91-10001.

—— (1993). *Handbook of International Economic Statistics: 1993*. Washington, DC: CIA CPAS 93-10004.

—— (1994a). *Rough Road to Markets in Russia and Eurasia*. Washington, DC: CIA.

—— (1994b). *Handbook of International Economic Statistics: 1994*. Washington, DC: CIA CPAS 94-10001.

—— (1995). *Handbook of International Economic Statistics: 1995*. Washington, DC: CIA.

—— (1996). *Handbook of International Economic Statistics: 1996*. Online edition at website http://www.odci.gov/cia/publications.

Centre of Economic Analysis of the Government of the Russian Federation (1997). *Russia—1997: Economic Situation*. Moscow: CEAGRF.

CHANG, H. J. (1994). *The Political Economy of Industrial Policy*. London: St Martin's Press.

CIA = Central Intelligence Agency

CONVERSE, R. (1982). 'An index of industrial production in the USSR', in US Congress, Joint Economic Committee, *USSR: Measures of Economic Growth and Development, 1950–80*. Washington, DC: USGPO.

COOPER, J. M. (1987). 'Technology transfers between military and civilian ministries', in US Congress, Joint Economic Committee, *Gorbachev's Economic Plans*. Washington, DC: USGPO.

—— (1991). *The Soviet Defence Industry: Conversion and Reform*. London: Pinter Publishers.

—— (1993). 'The Soviet Union and the successor republics: Defence industries coming to terms with disunion', in H. Wulf (ed.), *Arms Industry Limited*. Oxford: Oxford University Press.

—— and LEWIS, R. A. (1990). 'Research and technology', in R. W. Davies (ed.), *From Tsarism to the New Economic Policy*. London: Macmillan.

COOPERSMITH, J. (1992). *The Electrification of Russia, 1880–1926*. London: Cornell University Press.

CRISP, O. (1978). 'Labour and industrialization in Russia', in P. Mathias and M. Postan (eds.), *The Cambridge Economic History of Europe*. Vol. vii, Part 2. Cambridge: Cambridge University Press.

DAVIES, N. (1996). *Europe: A History*. Oxford: Oxford University Press.

DAVIES, R. W. (1958). *The Development of the Soviet Budgetary System*. Cambridge: Cambridge University Press. Reprint by Greenwood Press in 1979.

—— (1990) (ed.). *From Tsarism to the New Economic Policy*. London: Macmillan.

—— (1994a). 'Changing economic systems: An overview', in R. W. Davies, M. Harrison, and S. G. Wheatcroft (eds.), *The Economic Transformation of the Soviet Union, 1913–1945*. Cambridge: Cambridge University Press.

—— (1994b). 'Industry', in R. W. Davies, M. Harrison, and S. G. Wheatcroft (eds.), *The Economic Transformation of the Soviet Union, 1913–1945*. Cambridge: Cambridge University Press.

—— (1998). *Soviet Economic Development from Lenin to Khrushchev*. Cambridge: Cambridge University Press.

—— —— and WHEATCROFT, S. G. (1994) (eds.). *The Economic Transformation of the Soviet Union, 1913–1945*. Cambridge: Cambridge University Press.

DAVIS, C. (1983). 'Economic problems of the Soviet health service: 1917–1930', *Soviet Studies*, 35/3: 343–61.

—— (1988). 'The Second Economy in Disequilibrium and Shortage Models of Centrally Planned Economies'. *Berkeley-Duke Occasional Papers on the Second Economy in the USSR: No. 12*. Durham, NC: Duke University.

—— (1989). 'Priority and the shortage model: The medical system in the socialist economy', in C. Davis and W. Charemza (eds.), *Models of Disequilibrium and Shortage in Centrally Planned Economies*. London: Chapman and Hall.

—— (1990a). 'The high-priority military sector in a shortage economy', in H. S. Rowen and C. Wolf Jr. (eds.), *The Impoverished Superpower: Perestroika and the Soviet Military Burden*. San Francisco: Institute for Contemporary Studies.

—— (1990b). 'Economic influences on the decline of the Soviet Union as a Great Power: Continuity despite change', in D. Armstrong and E. Goldstein (eds.), *The End of the Cold War*. London: Frank Cass.

—— (1996). 'War and peace in a multipolar world: A critique of Quincy Wright's institutionalist analysis of the interwar international system'. *Journal of Strategic Studies*, 19/1: 31–73.

—— (1997). 'The economics of the defence sector in a declining superpower: The Soviet Union and Russia, 1975–2000'. Oxford: Oxford University Working Paper.

—— and CHAREMZA, W. (1989a). 'Introduction to models of disequilibrium and shortage in centrally planned economies', in C. Davis and W. Charemza (eds.), *Models of Disequilibrium and Shortage in Centrally Planned Economies*. London: Chapman and Hall.

—— —— (1989b) (eds.). *Models of Disequilibrium and Shortage in Centrally Planned Economies*. London: Chapman and Hall.

DOBB, M. (1960). *Soviet Economic Development since 1917*, 5th edn. London: Routledge & Kegan Paul.

DOHAN, M. R. (1990). 'Foreign trade', in R. W. Davies (ed.), *From Tsarism to the New Economic Policy*. London: Macmillan.

DOMAR, E. (1957). 'A Soviet model of growth', in A. Nove and D. M. Nuti (eds.), *Socialist Economics*. Harmondsworth: Penguin.

D'YAKOV, YU. L., and BUSHUEVA, T. S. (1992). *Fashistskii Mech Kovalsya v SSSR*. Moscow: Sovetskaya Rossiya.

EBRD = See European Bank for Reconstruction and Development

ECE = See Economic Commission for Europe

Economic Commission for Europe (1993, 1994, 1995, 1996, 1997, 1998). *Economic Survey of Europe in 1992–1993, 1993–1994, 1994–1995, 1995–1996, 1996–1997, 1997–1998*. New York: United Nations.

ELLMAN, M. (1973). *Planning Problems in the USSR: The Contribution of Mathematical Economics to their Solution 1960–1971*. Cambridge: Cambridge University Press.

—— (1975). 'Did the agricultural surplus provide the resources for the increase in investment in the USSR during the First Five Year Plan?' *Economic Journal*, Dec.

—— (1988). *Socialist Planning*, 2nd edn. Cambridge: Cambridge University Press.

—— (1995). 'The state under state socialism and post-socialism', in H. J. Chang and R. Rowthorn (eds.), *The Role of the State in Economic Change*. Oxford: Clarendon Press.

—— and KONTOROVICH, V. (1992) (eds.). *The Disintegration of the Soviet Economic System*. London: Routledge.

ERICKSON, J. (1962). *The Soviet High Command: A Military-Political History 1918–1941*. London: Macmillan.

ERICSON, R. E. (1988). 'Priority, duality and penetration in the Soviet command economy', Santa Monica, Calif.: RAND Working Draft WD-3445-NA.

—— (1990). 'The Soviet statistical debate: Khanin vs TsSU', in H. S. Rowen and C. Wolf, Jr. (eds.), *The Impoverished Superpower: Perestroika and the Soviet Military Burden*. San Francisco: ICS Press.

ERLICH, A. (1960). *The Soviet Industrialization Debate, 1924–1928*. Cambridge, Mass.: Harvard University Press.

ESTRIN, S. (1994) (ed.). *Privatization in Central and Eastern Europe*. London: Longman.

European Bank for Reconstruction and Development (1994, 1995, 1996, 1997). *Transition Report 1994, 1995, 1996, 1997*. London: EBRD.

FALKUS, M. E. (1972). *The Industrialisation of Russia, 1700–1914*. London: Macmillan.

FEINSTEIN, C. H. (1997). 'Technical progress and technology transfer in a centrally-planned economy: The experience of the USSR 1917–87', in C. H. Feinstein and C. Howe (eds.), *Chinese Technology Transfer in the 1990s: Current Experience, Historical Problems and International Perspectives*. Cheltenham: Edward Elgar.

FEL'DMAN, G. A. (1928). 'On the theory of growth rates of national income: I and II', in N. Spulber (ed.), *Foundations of Soviet Strategy for Economic Growth: Selected Soviet Essays, 1924–1930*. Bloomington: Indiana University Press, 1964.

FESHBACH, M., and RAPAWY, S. (1976). 'Soviet population and manpower trends and policies', in US Congress, Joint Economic Committee, *Soviet Economy in a New Perspective*. Washington, DC: USGPO.

Finansovo-Promyshlennye Gruppy v Rossii: Sostoyanie, Perspektivy, Normativno-Metodicheskoe Obespechenie (1996). Moscow: AFPI Ekonomika i zhizn'.

FIRTH, N. E., and NOREN, J. H. (1997). *Soviet Defence Spending: A History of CIA Estimates, 1950–1990*. Washington, DC: Manuscript of a forthcoming book.

FOREMAN-PECK, J., BOWDEN, S., and MCKINLAY, A. (1995). *The British Motor Industry*. Manchester: Manchester University Press.

FUKUYAMA, F. (1992). *The End of History and the Last Man*. New York: Free Press.

GADDY, C. (1996). *The Price of the Past: Russia's Struggle with the Legacy of a Militarized Economy*. Washington, DC: Brookings Institution.

GAIDAR, E. (1997). *Anomalii Ekonomicheskogo Rosta*. Moscow: Izd. Evraziya.

GATRELL, P. (1986). *The Tsarist Economy 1850–1917*. London: B. T. Batsford Ltd.

—— (1994). *Government, Industry and Rearmament in Russia, 1900–1914*. Cambridge: Cambridge University Press.

—— and DAVIES, R. W. (1990). 'The industrial economy', in R. W. Davies (ed.), *From Tsarism to the New Economic Policy*. London: Macmillan.

GERSCHENKRON, A. (1965*a*). 'Agrarian policies and industrialization: Russia 1861–1917', in H. J. Habakkuk and M. Poston (eds.), *The Cambridge Economic History of Europe*, Vol. vi. Cambridge: Cambridge University Press.

—— (1965*b*). *Economic Backwardness in Historical Perspective*. New York: Praeger.

GILBERT, M. (1993). *The Dent Atlas of Russian History*. London: J. M. Dent.

GKS = Gosudarstvennyy Komitet Rossiiskoi Federatsii po Statistiki

GKS SSSR = Gosudarstvennyy Komitet po Statistiki SSSR

GLADKOV, I. A. (1960) (ed.). *Sovetskoe Narodnoe Khozyaistvo v 1921–1925 gg.* Moscow: Izdatel'stvo Akademii Nauk SSSR.

GLAZ'EV, S. (1995). *Poltora Goda v Dume*. Moscow: Gals Plyus.

GOLDSMITH, R. (1961). 'The economic growth of Tsarist Russia 1860–1913', *Economic Development and Cultural Change*, IX/3: 441–75.

GOMULKA, S. (1986). 'Growth and the import of technology: Poland 1971–80', in S. Gomulka. *Growth, Innovation and Reform in Eastern Europe*. Oxford: Harvester.

Gosudarstvennyy Komitet Rossiiskoi Federatsii po Statistiki (1993). *Rossiiskaya Federatsiya v 1992 godu*. Moscow: Statistika.

—— (1994*a*). *Rossiiskii Statisticheskii Ezhegodnik: 1994*. Moscow: GosKomStat Rossii.

—— (1994*b*). *Sotsial'no-Ekonomichekoe Polozhenie Rossii 1994 g.* Moscow: Goskomstat.

—— (1995*a*). *Rossiiskii Statisticheskii Ezhegodnik: 1995*. Moscow: Goskomstat.

—— (1995*b*). *Sotsial'no-Ekonomichekoe Polozhenie Rossii 1995 g.* Moscow: Goskomstat.

—— (1995*c*). *Stroitel'stvo v Rossii: Statisticheskii Sbornik*. Moscow: Goskomstat.

—— (1995*d*). *Promyshlennost' Rossii: Statisticheskii Sbornik*. Moscow: Goskomstat.

—— (1996*a*). *Sotsial'no-Ekonomichekoe Polozhenie Rossii 1996 g.* Moscow: Goskomstat.

—— (1996*b*). *Promyshlennost' Rossii: Statisticheskii Sbornik*. Moscow: Goskomstat.

Gosudarstvennyy Komitet Statistiki SSSR (1991). *Narodnoe Khozyaistvo SSSR v 1990 g.* Moscow: Finansy i Statistika.

GRANICK, D. (1954). *Management of the Industrial Firm in the USSR*. New York: Columbia University Press.

GRAY, J. (1998). 'Global utopias and clashing civilizations: Misunderstanding the present'. *International Affairs*, 74/1: 149–64.

GREENSLADE, R. V. (1972). 'Industrial production statistics in the USSR', in V. G. Treml and J. P. Hardt (eds.), *Soviet Economic Statistics*. Durham: Duke University Press.

—— and ROBERTSON, W. E. (1973). 'Industrial production in the U.S.S.R.', in US Congress, Joint Economic Committee, *Soviet Economic Prospects for the Seventies*. Washington, DC: USGPO.

—— and WALLACE, P. (1966). 'Industrial production in the U.S.S.R.', in US Congress, Joint Economic Committee, *Dimensions of Soviet Economic Power*. Washington, DC: USGPO.

GREGORY, P. (1970). *Socialist and Nonsocialist Industrialization Patterns: A Comparative Appraisal*. London: Praeger.

GREGORY, P. R. (1982). *Russia's National Income, 1885–1913*. Cambridge: Cambridge University Press.

—— and STUART, R. C. (1994). *Soviet and Post-Soviet Economic Structure and Performance*, 5th edn. London: HarperCollins.

—— —— (1995). *Comparative Economic Systems*, 5th edn. Boston: Houghton Mifflin.

GROSSMAN, G. (1960). *Soviet Statistics on Physical Output of Industrial Commodities*. Princeton: Princeton University Press.

—— (1977). 'The "second economy" of the USSR'. *Problems of Communism*, 26/5: 25–40.

HANDELMAN, S. (1995). *Comrade Criminal: The Theft of the Second Russian Revolution*. London: Michael Joseph.

HANSON, P. (1982). 'The end of import-led growth? Some observations on Soviet, Polish and Hungarian experience in the 1970s'. *Journal of Comparative Economics*, 6/2: 130–47.

HARRISON, M. (1985). *Soviet Planning in Peace and War 1938–1945*. Cambridge: Cambridge University Press.

—— (1993). 'Soviet economic growth since 1928: The alternative statistics of G. I. Khanin'. *Europe-Asia Studies*, 45/1: 141–67.

—— (1996). *Accounting for War: Soviet Production, Employment and the Defence Burden*. Cambridge: Cambridge University Press.

—— (1998). 'Soviet industrial production, 1928–1950: Real growth, hidden inflation and the "unchanged prices of 1926/27"'. University of Warwick, Department of Economics, Discussion Paper.

HARRISON, M. and DAVIES, R. W. (1997). 'The Soviet military-economic effort during the Second Five-Year Plan (1933–1937)', *Europe-Asia Studies*, 49/3: 369–406.

HEWETT, E. A. (1988). *Reforming the Soviet Economy*. Washington, DC: Brookings Institution.

HODGMAN, D. R. (1954). *Soviet Industrial Production 1928–1951*. Cambridge: Harvard University Press.

HOLLOWAY, D. (1982). 'Innovation in the defence sector', in R. Amann and J. Cooper (eds.), *Industrial Innovation in the Soviet Union*. London: Yale University Press.

HUGHES, G., and HARE, P. (1992). 'Industrial policy and restructuring in Eastern Europe'. *Oxford Review of Economic Policy*, 8/1: 82–104.

HUNTINGTON, S. P. (1996). *The Clash of Civilizations and the Remaking of World Order*. New York: Simon and Schuster.

HUTCHINGS, R. (1971). *Soviet Economic Development*. Oxford: Basil Blackwell.

IEPPP = Institut Ekonomicheskikh Problem Perekhodnogo Perioda

IISS = International Institute for Strategic Studies

IMF/World Bank/OECD/EBRD (1991). *A Study of the Soviet Economy*. Paris: OECD.

Institut Ekonomicheskikh Problem Perekhodnogo Perioda (1993). *Rossiiskaya Ekonomika v 1993 Godu: Tendentsii i Perspektivy*. Moscow: IEPPP.

International Institute for Strategic Studies (1997). *The Military Balance 1997/98*. London: IISS.

JASNY, N. (1961). *Soviet Industrialization 1928–1952*. Chicago: University of Chicago Press.

Japan Statistical Association (1987). *Historical Statistics of Japan*. Vols. 1–5. Tokyo: Japan Statistical Association.

JEC = US Congress, Joint Economic Committee

JSA = Japan Statistical Association

KAHAN, A. (1967). 'Government policies and the industrialization of Russia'. *Journal of Economic History*, 27/4: 460–77.

—— (1978). 'Capital formation during the period of early industrialization in Russia, 1890–1913', in P. Mathias and M. Postan (eds.), *The Cambridge Economic History of Europe*, Vol. vii, Part 2. Cambridge: Cambridge University Press.

KAMMERLING, D. S. (1983). 'The role of territorial production complexes in Soviet economic policy', in US Congress, Joint Economic Committee, *Soviet Economy in the 1980's: Problems and Prospects*. Washington, DC: USGPO.

KASER, M. C. (1978). 'Russian entrepreneurship', in P. Mathias and M. Postan (eds.), *The Cambridge Economic History of Europe*, Vol. vii, Part 2. Cambridge: Cambridge University Press.

—— and RADICE, E. A. (1985, 1986) (eds.). *The Economic History of Eastern Europe, 1919–1975*, 3 vols. Oxford: Clarendon Press.

KENNEDY, P. (1988). *The Rise and Fall of the Great Powers: Economic Change and Military Conflict from 1500 to 2000*. London: Unwin Hyman.

KIM, B. Y. (1996). 'Fiscal Policy and Consumer Market Disequilibrium in the Soviet Union, 1965–1989'. D. Phil. dissertation. University of Oxford.

KORNAI, J. (1959). *Overcentralization in Economic Administration: A Critical Analysis Based on Experience in Hungarian Light Industry*. Oxford: Clarendon Press. Reprinted in 1994.

—— (1980). *Economics of Shortage*. Amsterdam: North-Holland.

—— (1992). *The Socialist System: The Political Economy of Communism*. Oxford: Clarendon Press.

—— (1994). 'Transformational recession: The main causes'. *Journal of Comparative Economics*, 19/1: 39–63.

KURTZWEG, L. (1987). 'Trends in Soviet gross national product', in US Congress, Joint Economic Committee, *Gorbachev's Economic Plans*. Washington, DC: USGPO.

LAUX, J. M. (1992). *The European Automobile Industry*. New York: Twayne Publishers.

LE HOUEROU, P. H. (1996) 'Investment policy in Russia'. *World Bank Studies of Economies in Transformation: No. 17.*

LENIN, V. I. (1908). *The Development of Capitalism in Russia*, 2nd edn. Moscow: Foreign Languages Publishing House. Reprinted in 1956.

LEWIS, R. (1994). 'Technology and the transformation of the Soviet economy', in R. W. Davies, M. Harrison, and S. G. Wheatcroft (eds.), *The Economic Transformation of the Soviet Union, 1913–1945*. Cambridge: Cambridge University Press.

LOKSHIN, E. YU. (1956). *Ocherk Istorii Promyshlennosti SSSR (1917–1940)*. Moscow: Gosudarstvennoe Izdatel'stvo Politicheskoi Literatury.

—— (1964). *Promyshlennosti' SSSR (Ocherk Istorii 1940–1963)*. Moscow: Gosudarstvennoe Izdatel'stvo Politicheskoi Literatury.

LYASHCHENKO, P. I. (1949). *History of the National Economy of Russia to the 1917 Revolution*. New York: Macmillan.

McINTYRE, J. (1987). 'The U.S.S.R.'s hard currency trade and payments position', in US Congress, Joint Economic Committee, *Gorbachev's Economic Plans*. Washington, DC: USGPO.

McKAY, J. P. (1970). *Pioneers for Profit: Foreign Entrepreneurship and Russian Industrialization, 1885–1913*. Chicago: University of Chicago Press.

McKINNON, R. (1991). 'Foreign trade, protection, and negative value added in a liberalizing socialist economy', in R. McKinnon (ed.), *The Order of Economic Liberalization*. Baltimore: Johns Hopkins Press.

MADDISON, A. (1995). *Monitoring the World Economy 1820–1992*. Paris: OECD.

MALLE, S. (1985). *The Economic Organization of War Communism, 1918–1921*. Cambridge: Cambridge University Press.

MARRESE, M., and VANOUS, J. (1983*a*). *Soviet Subsidization of Trade with Eastern Europe: A Soviet Perspective*. Berkeley: Institute of International Studies.

—— —— (1983*b*). 'Soviet policy options in trade relations with Eastern Europe', in US Congress, Joint Economic Committee, *Soviet Economy in the 1980's: Problems and Prospects*. Washington, DC: USGPO.

MAU, V. (1993). *Reformy i Dogmy: 1914–1929*. Moscow: Delo.

MILWARD, A. S. (1977). *War, Economy and Society: 1939–1945*. Harmondsworth: Penguin.

Ministerstvo Vneshnei Torgovlyi SSSR (1967). *Vneshnyaya Torgovlya SSSR: Statisticheskii Sbornik 1918–1966*. Moscow: Mezhdunarodnye Otnosheniya.

MITCHELL, B. R. (1992). *International Historical Statistics: Europe 1750–1988*, 3rd edn. London: Macmillan.

MOORSTEEN, A. H., and POWELL, R. P. (1996). *The Soviet Capital Stock 1928–1962*. Homewood, Illinois: Richard D. Irwin.

MVT = Ministerstvo Vneshnei Torgovlyi SSSR

National Bureau for Economic Research (1956). *Statistical Abstract of Industrial Output in the Soviet Union, 1913–1955*. New York: NBER.

NBER = National Bureau for Economic Research

NOREN, J., and KURTZWEG, L. (1993). 'The Soviet economy unravels: 1985–91', in US Congress, Joint Economic Committee, *The Former Soviet Union in Transition*. Washington, DC: USGPO.

NORTH, R. N., and SHAW, D. J. B. (1995). 'Industrial policy and location', in D. J. B. Shaw (ed.), *The Post-Soviet Republics: A Systematic Geography*. Harlow: Longman.

NOVE, A. (1989). *An Economic History of the USSR*, 2nd edn. Harmondsworth: Penguin Books.

NUTI, D. M. (1994). 'The role of the state in post-communist economies'. London: London Business School Working Paper.

NUTTER, W. (1960). 'The structure and growth of Soviet industry: A comparison with the United States', in US Congress, Joint Economic Committee, *Comparisons of the United States and Soviet Economies*. Washington, DC: USGPO.

—— (1962). *Growth of Industrial Production in the Soviet Union*. Princeton: Princeton University Press.

OECD = Organisation for Economic Cooperation and Development

OFER, G. (1987). 'Soviet economic growth: 1928–1985'. *Journal of Economic Literature*, 25/4: 1767–1833.

Organisation for Economic Cooperation and Development (1984). *National Accounts 1970–1982*. ii. *Detailed Tables*. Paris: OECD.

—— (1991). *Labour Force Statistics 1969–1989*. Paris: OECD.

—— (1995). *The Russian Federation*. Paris: OECD Russian Federation: Economic Survey.

—— (1997*a*). *Labour Force Statistics 1976–1996*. Paris: OECD.

—— (1997*b*). *National Accounts 1983–1995*. ii. *Detailed Tables*. Paris: OECD.

—— (1997*c*). *Russian Federation*. Paris: OECD Russian Federation: Economic Survey.

PINTER, W. M. (1984) 'The burden of defense in Imperial Russia, 1725–1914'. *The Russian Review*, 43: 231–59.

PITZER, J. (1982). 'Gross National Product of the USSR, 1950–80', in US Congress, Joint Economic Committee, *USSR: Measures of Economic Growth and Development, 1950–80*. Washington, DC: USGPO.

PORTAL, R. (1965). 'The industrialization of Russia', in H. J. Habakkuk and M. Postan (eds.), *The Cambridge Economic History of Europe*, Vol. vi. Cambridge: Cambridge University Press.

POWELL, R. P. (1963). 'Industrial production', in A. Bergson and S. Kuznets (eds.), *Economic Trends in the Soviet Union*. Cambridge, Mass.: Harvard University Press.

PREOBRAZHENSKY, E. (1926). 'Socialist primitive accumulation' (Translation into English), in A. Nove and D. M. Nuti (eds.), *Socialist Economics*. Harmondsworth: Penguin.

'Programma Uglubleniya Ekonomicheskikh Reform Pravitel'stva Rossiiskoi Federatsii' (1992). *Voprosy Ekonomiki*, 1992/8: 3–192.

RADYGIN, A. D. (1994). *Reforma Sobstvennosti v Rossii: Na Puti iz Proshlogo v Budushchee*. Moscow: Izdatel'stvo Respublika.

RAPAWY, S. (1987). 'Labor force and employment in the U.S.S.R.', in US Congress, Joint Economic Committee. *Gorbachev's Economic Plans*. Vol. i. Washington, DC: USGPO.

RGAE = Rossiiskii Gosudarstvennyy Arkhiv Ekonomiki

Rossiiskii Gosudarstvennyy Arkhiv Ekonomiki (1994). *Putevoditel': I. Kratkii Spravochnik Fondov*. Moscow: Blagovest Ltd.

ROZENFEL'D, Y. S., and KLIMENKO, K. I. (1961). *Istoriya Mashinostroeniya SSSR*. Moscow: Izd. Akademii Nauk SSSR.

RUTLAND, P. (1985). *The Myth of the Plan: Lessons of Soviet Planning Experience*. La Salle, Ill.: Open Court.

SAMUELSON, L. (1996). *Soviet Defence Industry Planning: Tukhachevskii and Military-Industrial Mobilization, 1926–1937*. Stockholm: Stockholm Institute of East European Economics.

SAPIR, J. (1990). *L'Économie Mobilisée*. Paris: Éditions La Découverte.

SCHROEDER, G. E. (1979). 'The Soviet economy on a treadmill of "reforms"', in US Congress, Joint Economic Committee, *Soviet Economy in a Time of Change*. Washington, DC: USGPO.

—— (1983). 'Soviet economic "reform" decrees: More steps on the treadmill', in US Congress, Joint Economic Committee, *Soviet Economy in the 1980's: Problems and Prospects*. Washington, DC: USGPO.

SELYUNIN, V., and KHANIN, G. (1987). 'Lukavaya tsifra'. *Novyy Mir*, 63/2: 181–201.

SHAPIRO, J. (1990). 'Unemployment', in R. W. Davies (ed.), *From Tsarism to the New Economic Policy*. London: Macmillan.

SIMONOV, N. S. (1996). *Voenno-promyshlennyy Kompleks SSSR v 1920–1950-e Gody: Tempy Ekonomicheskogo Rosta, Struktura, Organizatsiya Proizvodstvo i Upravlenie*. Moscow: ROSSPE.

STEINBERG, D. (1990). 'Trends in Soviet military expenditure'. *Soviet Studies*, 42/4.

SUTELA, P. (1991). *Economic Thought and Economic Reform in the Soviet Union*. Cambridge: Cambridge University Press.

SUTTON, A. (1968). *Western Technology and Soviet Economic Development: 1917–1930*. Stanford, Calif.: Stanford University Press.

—— (1971). *Western Technology and Soviet Economic Development: 1930–1945*. Stanford, Calif.: Stanford University Press.

SWIANIEWICZ, S. (1965). *Forced Labour and Economic Development*. Oxford: Oxford University Press.

SZAMUELY, L. (1974). *First Models of the Socialist Economic System: Principles and Theories*. Budapest: Akademiai Kiado.

TREML, V. G., and ALEXEEV, M. V. (1993). 'The second economy and the destabilizing effect of its growth on the state economy in the Soviet Union: 1965–1989', *Berkeley–Duke Occasional Papers on the Second Economy in the USSR: No. 36*. Durham, NC: Duke University.

Tsentral'noe Statisticheskoe Upravlenie SSSR (1964). *Promyshlennost' SSSR: Statisticheskii Sbornik*. Moscow: Statistika.

—— (1959, 1973, 1976, 1979, 1981, 1986, 1989, 1990). *Narodnoe Khozyaistvo SSSR v 1958 g., 1972, 1975, 1978, 1980, 1985, 1988, 1989*. Moscow: Ekonomika i Statistika.

TsSU = See Tsentral'noe Statisticheskoe Upravlenie SSSR, *Narodnoe Khozyaistvo*

TsSU Prom = See Tsentral'noe Statisticheskoe Upravlenie SSSR, *Promyshlennost' SSSR*

UK ONS = United Kingdom, Office for National Statistics

UN DESA = United Nations, Department of Economics and Social Affairs

UN ICSY = United Nations. *International Commodity Statistics Yearbook*.

UN YIS = United Nations. *Yearbook of Industrial Statistics*.

UNIDO = United Nations Industrial Development Organization

United Kingdom, Office for National Statistics (1996). *United Kingdom National Accounts 1996*. London: HMSO.

United Nations, Department of Economics and Social Affairs (1963). *The Growth of World Industry 1938–1961*. New York: UN.

United Nations (1997). *International Commodity Statistics Yearbook 1995*. New York: UN.

United Nations (1978). *Yearbook of Industrial Statistics 1978*. Vol. ii. *Commodity Production Data 1969–1978*. New York: UN.

United Nations Industrial Development Organization (1995, 1996, 1997). *Industrial Development: Global Report 1995, 1996, 1997*. Oxford: Oxford University Press.

US Arms Control and Disarmament Agency (1996). *World Military Expenditures and Arms Transfers 1995*. Washington, DC: USACDA.

US Congress, Joint Economic Committee (1960). *Comparisons of the United States and Soviet Economies*. Washington, DC: USGPO.

—— (1962). *Dimensions of Soviet Economic Power*. Washington, DC: USGPO.

—— (1966). *New Directions in the Soviet Economy*. Washington, DC: USGPO.

—— (1973). *Soviet Economic Prospects for the Seventies*. Washington, DC: USGPO.

—— (1976). *Soviet Economy in a New Perspective*. Washington, DC: USGPO.

—— (1979). *Soviet Economy in a Time of Change*. Washington, DC: USGPO.

—— (1983). *Soviet Economy in the 1980's: Problems and Prospects*. Washington, DC: USGPO.

—— (1987). *Gorbachev's Economic Plans*. Washington, DC: USGPO.

—— (1993). *The Former Soviet Union in Transition*. Washington, DC: USGPO.

US Department of Commerce, Bureau of the Census (1975). *Historical Statistics of the United States: Colonial Times to 1970*. Vols. 1 and 2. Washington, DC: USGPO.

—— (1997). *Statistical Abstract of the United States 1997*. Washington, DC: USGPO.

US Department of Defense (1987). *Soviet Military Power 1987*. Washington, DC: USGPO.

USDC = US Department of Commerce

USDOD = US Department of Defense

VAN BRABANT, J. (1980). *Socialist Economic Integration*. Cambridge: Cambridge University Press.

VON LAUE, T. H. (1963). *Sergei Witte and the Industrialization of Russia*. New York: Columbia University Press.

—— (1974). 'The state and the economy', in W. L. Blackwell (ed.), *Russian Economic Development from Peter the Great to Stalin*. New York: New Viewpoints.

WEITZMAN, M. S., FESHBACH, M., and KULCHYCKA, L. (1962). 'Employment in the U.S.S.R.: Comparative U.S.S.R.–U.S. data', in US Congress, Joint Economic Committee, *Dimensions of Soviet Economic Power*. Washington, DC: USGPO.

WHEATCROFT, S. G., and DAVIES, R. W. (1994). 'The crooked mirror of Soviet economic statistics', in R. W. Davies, M. Harrison, and S. G. Wheatcroft (eds.), *The Economic Transformation of the Soviet Union, 1913–1945*. Cambridge: Cambridge University Press.

WHITEFIELD, S. (1993). *Industrial Power and the Soviet State*. Oxford: Clarendon Press.

WHITEHOUSE, F. D., and CONVERSE, R. (1979). 'Soviet industry: Recent performance and future prospects', in US Congress, Joint Economic Committee, *Soviet Economy in a Time of Change*. Washington, DC: USGPO.

World Bank (1990). *World Development Report 1990: Poverty*. Washington, DC: World Bank.

—— (1993). *World Development Report 1993: Investing in Health*. Washington, DC: World Bank.

—— (1997). *World Development Report 1997: The State in a Changing World*. Oxford: Oxford University Press.

WOYTINSKY, W. S., and WOYTINSKY, E. S. (1953). *World Population and Production: Trends and Outlook*. New York: Twentieth Century Fund.

YERGIN, D., and GUSTAFSON, T. (1993). *Russia 2010: And What It Means for the World*. New York: Random House.

ZALESKI, E. (1971). *Planning for Economic Growth in the Soviet Union, 1918–1932*. Chapel Hill, NC: University of North Carolina Press.

—— (1980). *Stalinist Planning for Economic Growth, 1933–1952*. London: Macmillan.

14

A Cultural Theory of Industrial Policy

MARK CASSON

University of Reading, Department of Economics

14.1. INTRODUCTION

The preceding country case studies supply a rich variety of policy experiences to be interpreted. This chapter offers a theory that explains why such a range of industrial policies have been pursued over the last century or more in the various European economies. As in the earlier studies, a broad interpretation of industrial policy is adopted: an industrial policy is any policy designed by government to improve coordination between different sectors of the economy. Coordination is defined here with respect to the political aims of the ruling elite. Industrial policies are chosen, it is assumed, because they are expected to increase the economic efficiency with which the policy objectives of the elite are achieved.

Coordination is not defined in terms of the more usual criterion of Pareto-efficiency. To employ this criterion to explain the actual choice of industrial policy would be to assume implicitly that it represented the political objective of the ruling elite, which is clearly not the case in many countries. As we have seen, the political objectives of many elites are usually not principally economic; military considerations are often important as well, whether to support aggressive expansion or self-defence. With this broad definition, industrial policy includes not only competition policy and regulation but also technology policy, government procurement policy, tariff policy, and, indeed, any economic or financial policy which is targeted on selected industrial sectors of the economy —normally, but not exclusively, high-technology manufacturing industries and utilities.

Interventionist industrial policies attract most attention. These entail regulating, or even superseding, the market system. Sometimes the intervention is based on rules or procedures systematically applied across the economy, and sometimes it is selective or even arbitrary. The concept of industrial policy used here encompasses both interventionist and non-interventionist policies, including the extreme non-interventionism of laissez-faire.

The aim of this chapter is not to express approval or disapproval for particular industrial policies. As indicated above, this means that the Pareto criterion is not directly relevant to the analysis. The criterion remains indirectly pertinent

This chapter draws on my book *Entrepreneurship and Business Culture*.

though, because it helps to explain why some policies succeed in satisfying the preferences of the population as a whole while others do not. A politically powerful elite—or dictator—may be able to sustain a policy which performs badly on the Pareto criterion, but if they lack widespread acquiescence in their rule they may find that the unpopularity of their policies forces them out of office. Systematic and extreme violation of the Pareto criterion may therefore precipitate a change of government, although that may not improve matters for the population as a whole.

Neoclassical political economy suggests that various elites will tend to pursue different kinds of policy simply because of the different vested interests that they represent (Tullock 1967; Tollison 1982; Becker 1983). Thus in a traditional society agriculture may be protected to preserve the value of aristocratic landholdings, while in a democratic industrial society manufacturing may be protected to maintain the wages of the urban working class. A cohesive intellectual elite may succeed in subsidizing technological research, whereas party electoral competition in a pluralistic society is more likely to eliminate subsidies in the interests of consumers and taxpayers as a whole.

Historically, though, it is difficult to explain all industrial policy regimes in terms of the material self-interests of organized groups. Why are some European industrial democracies persistently more inclined to protectionism than others? Why have some European countries made a much stronger commitment to subsidize long-term R & D than others? These policies often transcend the agenda of any one political party and are perpetuated with only minor revisions when an opposition party comes to power. All the major political parties in the country may agree that the interests of certain groups enjoy a moral legitimacy because these groups serve to advance some higher objective of national policy (Hagen 1964; Hoselitz 1960). Shared beliefs about such matters constitute the culture of the society. This chapter shows how the explicit introduction of cultural factors into the discussion of industrial policy can complement the more conventional kind of strictly economic approach to the subject.

Section 14.2 reviews the various routes by which industrial policy can impact on national economic performance. It presents a 'systems view' of the economy and shows how different industrial policies impinge selectively on different linkages in the system. Section 14.3 indicates how the neoclassical political economy framework must be extended if cultural factors are to be introduced, contending that culture offers a collective vision of the economic system and its goals, which legitimates the policies of the elite. The population as a whole identifies with the elite sufficiently to share in emotional rewards, as well as material rewards, that are generated by industrial policy. Section 14.4 considers from this perspective the rationale for intervention in general and for protectionism in particular. A governing elite may be able to exploit its insight into the nature of collective emotional rewards by funding activities that generate such rewards—for example, the mastery of a new technology. These activities would not be profitable for private firms because the emotional rewards cannot be appropriated by them. Given the potential benefits of industrial policy, Section 14.5 considers why the intensity of industrial policy interventions varies over time. Many industrial policies can be interpreted as ideological experiments, which confer emotional benefits not only on the public in general but more particularly on the members of the elite that carry out these experiments. The propensity to engage in such experiments is dependent on the amount of 'new thinking' on which the elite can draw. New thinking is in turn often derived from technological advances which provide new metaphors for understanding the structure of the economic system, and indeed the structure of society. Sections 14.6 and 14.7 examine cross-country differences in industrial policy, distinguishing countries both by their tendency to engage in radical experiments and their propensity to adopt strongly interventionist policies.

Section 14.8 argues that the success of an industrial policy in meeting the aims of the elite depends on the level of trust in a society. The private sector is more likely to comply willingly with an industrial policy if it trusts the government that implements it. Conversely a government that trusts the private sector will perceive less need for potentially hostile interventions and, when it does intervene, will do so in a more informal and less bureaucratic way.

Section 14.9 argues that there is a feedback from industrial policy to ideological change, in the sense that failed industrial policies stimulate the search for an explanation. The feedback mechanism only explains very long-term changes in ideology because in the short run the natural explanation by a committed ideologist for the failure of his policy is that the policy has not been 'pure' or 'radical' enough. Failed policy experiments may therefore be pursued almost to the point of absurdity before ideological change takes place.

The preoccupation of European society with the ideological conflict between capitalism and socialism throughout the twentieth century can be understood as a consequence of the collapse of the idea of a society built upon customs and traditions which are endorsed by religious authority. This has not only sanctioned many wasteful ideological experiments but also experiments that have been 'one-dimensional' in the sense that they were predicated on a low level of trust within society. The real lesson of the failures of intervention in the inter-war and early post-war periods is that intervention is costly and ineffectual when organized in a bureaucratic low-trust manner, whatever the aims of the elite (Casson 1993). The lesson that ought to have been learnt from the failure of these policies is that a high-trust society works better than a low-trust one.

The analysis suggests that the most successful industrial policies, whether interventionist or not, are pragmatic rather than theoretical, and are implemented through high-trust mechanisms that represent the legacy of tradition within modern industrial societies. The low-trust legalistic attitudes of the 'new right' politicians currently in power in many countries do not meet these criteria. The analysis therefore predicts that further policy failures are in store for many countries. Further ideological change, reinforced by greater understanding of Europe's own historical experience will undermine the perceived legitimacy of low-trust 'new right' policies, just as the legitimacy of low-trust socialist policies has already been undermined. Only if a transition can be effected back to the high-trust atmosphere of the more traditional society will the cycle of ideological change be broken, for then the implementation of industrial policy, of any reasonable kind, will stand a good chance of success.

14.2. A SYSTEMS VIEW OF THE ECONOMY

Figure 14.1 offers a simple schematic view of a modern national industrial system. The figure identifies various types of activity and illustrates the network of linkages between them. For simplicity, some of the minor linkages have been suppressed. Furthermore, because of the high level of aggregation, each 'activity'

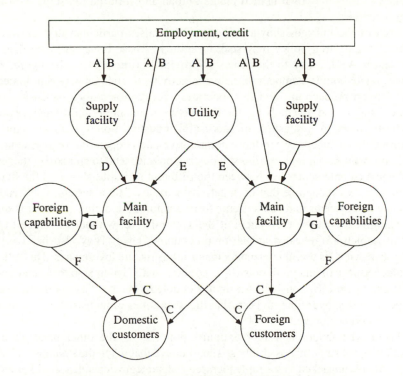

A Employee motivation; efficiency of the labour market
B Creditor confidence; efficiency of the market for ownership and control
C Effectiveness of competition in product markets
D Good supplier relations
E Harmonious sharing of utility output
F Harmonious trade relations
G Harmonious foreign ownership relations

FIG. 14.1. A national industrial system with international linkage
Source: Casson 1991.

is in fact a sub-system in its own right (for further details see Casson 1990: ch. 2). Indeed, it is possible to visualize a lengthy regress in which each activity in each sub-system is itself a sub-system, and so on. A successful industrial policy is one that takes account of this inherent complexity of the system to which it is applied.

Factor markets for labour and capital—particularly risk capital—appear at the top of the figure. These factors flow into both upstream and downstream production activities. The upstream activities include utility operations (energy, transport, and so on) and the supply of raw materials and components to downstream manufacturing and assembly activities. Downstream producers in turn sell to customers (both private and government) at home and abroad. At the same time foreign firms can sell into domestic markets. Furthermore some domestic plants may be owned by foreign firms, or license technology from them, whilst domestic firms may own branch plants abroad and form partnerships with foreign licensees.

Each of the linkages shown in Figure 14.1 raises particular strategic issues which an industrial policy may seek to address. These issues are identified by the letters A–G; a key to the issues is provided at the foot of the figure. The issues relate both to competition between activities—such as between domestic and foreign production—and to cooperation between activities—such as component supply and assembly, or the link between an energy utility and a manufacturing plant. A key aspect of successful industrial policy is to maintain an appropriate balance between these competitive and cooperative requirements.

Those who favour interventionist industrial policies tend to emphasize the technological complementarities between the different activities shown in the figure. Although they recognize that each activity may itself be a system, they tend to assume that systems and sub-systems form a natural hierarchy, so that it is quite meaningful to analyse the system at the sectoral level without reference to the details which are revealed at the microeconomic level. They also believe that a 'systems view' is useful in planning major infrastructure investments. This reflects another aspect of interventionism—a concern with dynamic rather than static efficiency gains. This vision of a tightly coupled system whose performance is to be optimized over time suggests that the institutions of industrial policy should be based on centralized control.

Those who favour non-interventionist policies, on the other hand, tend to emphasize substitution possibilities. They believe that when the systems and sub-systems are 'unpacked', no simple hierarchy of strategic dependence will emerge. Simultaneity and interdependence among a myriad of small activities is the key characteristic of the system, giving rise to intricate chains of substitution possibilities which only a market organization can detect. Non-interventionists regard dynamic efficiency simply as an inter-temporal analogue of static efficiency and believe that infrastructure projects should be evaluated by exactly the same criteria as those applied to ordinary manufacturing projects. The role of industrial policy should be to 'complete the market' by refining and extending property rights and not to weaken existing property rights by extending the realm of arbitrary government fiat.

Since a regime of free trade applies not only to finished products but to intermediate products too, free trade increases the substitution possibilities within the industrial sector by allowing surplus intermediate products to be exported and deficiencies of intermediate products to be made good by imports. Conversely, by denying firms open access to international markets in intermediate products, protectionism reduces the substitution possibilities within the industrial sector. This indicates an important reason why protectionism and central planning tend to be linked. It is not just that the planners like to intervene in everything, including trade, but also that the restriction of trade increases the effective degree of complementarity within the domestic industrial system, and so makes planning more worthwhile. In this sense the tendency for planners to regulate trade creates positive feedback in favour of planning because complementarities within the industrial system increase as a result.

14.3. EMBEDDING INDUSTRIAL POLICY IN A CULTURAL CONTEXT

Debate over interventionism tends to focus on issues such as economies of scale, sunk costs, technological spill-overs, environmental externalities, and the like, and the possibility of dealing with these successfully through the market mechanism. The central issue addressed in this chapter is not, however, whether the logic on one side of this debate is better than on the other, but rather why the concepts that dominate debate on industrial policy, and the assumptions that are most commonly made, vary over time and across countries.

The short answer to this question is that not everyone sees the world as an economist does. Different people see the same issue from different perspectives—indeed, in extreme cases they may not even be able to agree on what the issue is. Differences of this kind may not only be individual but also collective. One group of people may share a view which is quite different from that of another group. Where different social groups correspond to different nation states (or, more precisely, to the governing elites of these nation states) different perceptions of the same industrial issue may lead to very different national policies being used to address it.

Differences of interpretation are not the only kind of difference that can prevail between two groups. The objectives or missions of the groups may differ too. One group, for example, may believe that its social institutions are superior to those of other groups and may seek to impose these institutions by conquest. In this context technology policy may be driven by military ambition. Another group may be more concerned with material issues such as the standard of living, and view technology instead in terms of its civilian use in consumer goods industries.

A conventional economist might object to these remarks about groups on the grounds that groups exist, if at all, only in the minds of their members, and certainly do not have minds or wills of their own. This is a valid criticism—but only up to a point. Groups are objective in the sense that members of the same group normally interact more frequently with fellow members (insiders) than with non-members (outsiders). The group concept is also institutionalized in a wide variety of forms, from the family, school, and club on the local level to the church, trade union, and political party at the national level. It is also useful, for certain purposes, to consider firms and governing elites as social groups, rather than just as production units and legislators, respectively.

It is, however, correct to insist that the objective or mission of the group exists in the minds of its members and has no independent reality outside them. One of the features of a group, however, is that its members are likely to be standardized on their mission. This is because the mission is usually articulated by a leader who emerges from a division of labour within the group (Casson 1991). Pursuit of a collective mission can be a source of satisfaction (and hence of economic value) to the followers, and so the mission becomes a kind of intangible public good that is produced by the leader and is consumed by the members of the group.

Leaders do not operate in isolation, however. A leader with the ambition to seize political power needs a group of supporters who can occupy key administrative positions. These people must be committed to the leader, and competent in the performance of their tasks. Because the leader is dependent on them, they have influence over the leader as well, at least regarding issues that fall within their appointed domain. This group constitutes the elite.

There are several striking examples of the influence of elites on the formation of industrial policy in recent European history. A clique of bankers and industrialists supported the imperialist aims of Benjamin Disraeli in late Victorian Britain. Indeed, City of London financial interests continued to be important in Britain in fashioning the 'Treasury view' of economic policy during the inter-war period. At the other end of the political spectrum, an intellectual elite provided support for Lenin and the Bolshevik Revolution. The major impact of European intellectual elites, however, was in the early post-war period, 1945–70: the polytechnicians in France, the social planners in Sweden, the economic planners in the Netherlands, and so on. The military, too, have often been an important element of elites, particularly in the Fascist regimes of Nazi Germany, Mussolini's Italy, and Franco's Spain, where they combined with business interests to establish military-industrial complexes designed to further aggressive nationalistic policies.

In most societies there are a number of potential leaders, and there may be rivalry between them. Sometimes the leaders and their elites may divide along functional lines. One elite may represent industrial interests, another financial and commercial interests, while others may represent the professions, the landed aristocracy, and so on. In post-war Britain, for example, the Labour Party was largely controlled by intellectuals, who considered themselves to be the natural leaders of an inarticulate working class. The Conservative Party, on the other hand, was dominated by financial and industrial interests who feared the adverse impact on profits of trade union wage bargaining and working practices. In other cases the elites may divide along ideological or religious lines instead. Intense rivalry between elites can cause a society to disintegrate into rival factions. In this case the government of the country simply represents the particular faction that happens to be in power. In the British case, the alternation of Conservative and Labour governments exacerbated the stop-go tendencies of the political trade cycle, and jeopardized long-term investment plans in the major utility industries.

The governing faction will tend to pursue policies that benefit itself at the expense of other factions. Under these conditions industrial policy may have profound distributional implications. There is, however, a limit as to how far an elite can go in this direction, as indicated above. Ruthless pursuit of factional self-interest will tend to unify opposition forces and eventually cause the elite to lose political office. An elite must therefore make some attempt to buy off opposition if it wishes to remain in power.

It is a mistake to suppose that the aims of an elite are purely materialistic. The elite can generate emotional satisfactions not only for the followers it seeks to manipulate, but for itself as well. Elites often strive to win power out of ideological commitment. Even if they become tarnished by corruption later, members of elites may be very idealistic when they first come to power. Unaware of the complexities and difficulties that governments face, members of a new elite believe that some simple set of principles—economic, legal, moral, or whatever—is guaranteed to achieve success. Their initial period in office is a live experiment designed to demonstrate to themselves, and to others, the superiority of the policies that embody their principles over the policies that went before. The emotional rewards to the elite come both from the self-indulgence of carrying out such an exciting experiment, and the anticipated vicarious pleasure of seeing other people made better off as a result.

The search for emotional rewards can explain many of the special features of industrial policy. For example, mastery of a new advanced technology may confer an enormous feeling of national pride in which both the elite and the ordinary citizen can share. Mastery of technology then becomes, not merely a means to an end, but an end in itself. The specific direction taken by industrial policy can then be understood as a rational response to the pursuit of emotional benefits of this kind. This point is taken up in more detail in Section 14.7.

14.4. INTERVENTIONIST ELITES

Does the pursuit of emotional rewards necessarily warrant an interventionist industrial policy, though? There are two related grounds for believing that it may do so. The first is that the emotional rewards generated by the collective pursuit of common goals can be difficult for a private firm to charge for. This suggests that the government should charge instead, through taxation. But this makes the government responsible for procuring the rewards. There may be several methods of procurement, some of which involve more intervention than others. For example, the activity that generates the rewards could be either nationalized, protected, or subsidized. The second ground for intervention is that where transaction costs are high, measures involving limited intervention may be subject to considerable abuse. The abuse arises because the private sector exploits the fact that the government has only limited information about the way that its payments are used. Measures involving greater intervention may on balance prove more efficient because they provide the government with greater information and are therefore subject to less abuse.

There are, of course, objections to this line of argument. Where small-scale activities generate localized collective benefits, clubs and societies can be employed as exclusion mechanisms (Buchanan 1965; Olson 1965). Those who do not pay their membership fees do not benefit from emotional participation in the collective activity. Where national achievements are concerned, however, every patriotic citizen benefits, whether they belong to the particular firm or group responsible or not. In this case it is only reasonable that everyone who benefits emotionally makes a contribution, which means that the nation itself behaves effectively as a club. To avoid free-riding, it is appropriate that the club be financed out of taxation. The government, having an effective monopoly of the power of taxation, therefore becomes involved.

While a Paretian liberal might accept the argument so far, they would almost certainly argue that a policy of taxes and subsidies would be the appropriate response to a situation of this kind. The argument certainly does not provide carte blanche for selective intervention. It suggests instead that the emotional externalities should be internalized through taxes and subsidies in a systematic way.

In designing taxes and subsidies, however, transaction costs must be taken into account. The most obvious form of tax or subsidy may not be the best because it creates incentives for people to cheat. This is where the second aspect of the argument comes into the picture. Although the government knows that a certain kind of collective emotional reward is desired (or believes that it is), it does not know exactly which firms are best equipped to produce it, nor can it easily monitor the quantity and quality of what is produced. It may therefore need to intervene in a subtle way, rewarding activity which is not directly related to the production of the satisfactions but only indirectly related instead. The indirect output, which is positively correlated with the desired emotional output, is easier to monitor, and therefore a better object of policy action.

To illustrate the point, consider the case alluded to above where the mastery of an advanced technology has become an end in itself. The mastery of the technology by domestic firms generates emotional satisfaction for every citizen. It is difficult to see how in this case a private firm that mastered the technology could directly appropriate rewards from the general satisfaction that its mastery produced. Yet without such rewards it may be unprofitable for the firm to master the technology at all. To encourage the requisite investment, a government subsidy of some kind may be required.

A direct subsidy could be subject to abuse, however. It might well be claimed not only by those who had truly mastered the technology but also by those who had adopted the technology only to obtain the subsidy. In order to focus the subsidy on firms that have genuinely mastered the technology, a market test could be applied. Only firms that could sell the product made with the new technology in highly competitive and sophisticated markets would be eligible to receive the subsidy. Since export markets normally satisfy the requirements of competition and sophistication more readily than home markets, this suggests that an export subsidy may be more effective than a direct subsidy to production.

If the foreign price-elasticity of demand for the high-technology product is relatively low, however, then a high proportion of this subsidy may simply be passed on to overseas consumers. This is particularly likely when there is intense competition between home-country exporters. In order to redistribute income to the home country rather than away from it, protection of the domestic market may be preferred instead. This is a viable alternative, however, only if the domestic market is almost as sophisticated as the export market, and nearly as competitive too. If domestic customers are well informed and the market is large enough to support several producers, then protectionism may be an adequate measure. But if customers are ill-informed, the market is small, and firms have a tendency to collude, then it is unlikely to succeed.

In any case, to mitigate the obvious disincentive effect of restricting competition from overseas producers, protection must be offered for a strictly limited period. If this short-term protection is implemented in an even-handed way, then it will benefit not only incumbent firms but also other firms entering the industry, either as start-ups, or by diversification from other industries. In this sense a general policy of protection may prove more effective than a selective policy of subsidizing national champion firms because established national champions may be more strongly attached to the old technology, and less prepared than new entrants to experiment with the new one instead. It may also prove more effective than nationalization because owners of private firms have stronger incentives to control costs than do the managers of state-owned enterprises.

This example shows that deviations from free trade policy can be rationalized when there are external effects that need to be internalized. Because of its powers of taxation, the government is the natural agent to do this. Protection is the appropriate means of internalization when alternative policies would incur much higher transactions costs, and are more likely to benefit foreign citizens instead of domestic ones. In the example considered above, collective emotional benefits are the source of the externalities, but in other cases the externalities could arise from economies of scale, knowledge diffusion, or environmental effects instead.

14.5. LONG WAVES IN IDEOLOGICAL EXPERIMENTATION

It has been argued so far that the key to understanding industrial policy lies in recognizing the role of ideological experiments run by a governing elite. The elite wins support for such experiments by offering emotional benefits to citizens from the achievement of specific national goals such as the mastery of a new technology. But this still leaves unanswered the question of why elites at certain times and in certain countries favour one kind of ideological experiment and in other circumstances another (Hirschman 1982).

To address this question rigorously, two key distinctions must be made. The first is between the propensity for ideological experiments of any kind to occur and the propensity for these experiments to take a specifically interventionist line. For much of the last one hundred years, ideological experiments in Europe have been experiments with collectivism rather than with individualism. The socialists rather than the liberals have been in the vanguard of ideological innovation, and arguments for protectionism, allied to 'catch up' industrialization, have been fashionable in many countries (Gerschenkron 1968). This was not the case in the late eighteenth century and early nineteenth century, however, when liberals were much more in the vanguard of ideological change. Nor is it true of the last decades of the twentieth century, when the liberalism of the 'new right' has been ascendant. What needs to be explained, therefore, is both why ideological experiments occur at particular times and in particular places, and why in some cases the experiments take an interventionist turn and in other cases they do not.

The second distinction is between the variation of industrial policy over time and its variation across countries. There is undoubtedly a tendency for industrial policies in different countries to move in step with each other. This can be explained in terms of general factors which vary over time but impact on all countries fairly equally. At the same time, there are persistent differences between countries in their propensity to engage in ideological experiments and, when experiments occur, there are differences in the direction they are likely to take. These differences are most naturally explained in terms of country-specific factors. The main factors—both general and specific—which are responsible for the pace and direction of industrial policy change are summarized in Table 14.1.

The factor noted on the first line of the table is intellectual fashion. At any given time there are certain new ideas around for how a society should be organized—state socialism, market socialism, liberalism, and so on. Elites that consider themselves to be in the vanguard of progress will tend to identify with the latest intellectual fashion. Ideas travel internationally, particularly since members of elites often speak foreign languages and travel abroad quite frequently. Thus ideas taken up by an elite in one country may quickly set a fashion for elites in other countries to follow. The relative status of different countries will tend to influence the path by which ideas diffuse. New ideas adopted in the highest status country will first diffuse to the other high-status countries through socialization amongst their elites, and gradually 'trickle down' to lower-status elites. Lacking the intellectual insights of the innovatory elite, the imitators may

TABLE 14.1. *Summary of factors governing industrial policy over time and across countries*

Type of factor	Propensity to	
	Experiment with new policy	Intervene
General time-varying	Intellectual fashion Fundamental technological change Climate of international relations	Intellectual fashion
Country-specific and relatively time-invariant	Cultural factors (see Tables 14.2, 14.3)	Entrepôt potential (see Table 14.4) Stage of development (see Table 14.5) Cultural factors (see Table 14.6)

not fully understand the rationale of the policies they take up. Imitation often leads to error because the circumstances of the imitator differ from those of the innovator in a way that the imitator does not appreciate. Imitation can also be premature: failed policies can be imitated as well as successful ones, because in their haste to follow, imitators do not wait for the results of the innovator's policies to become clear.

New technology often provides a superficial rationale for ideological change. In the nineteenth century the technologies of steam and iron provided a rationalist and mechanistic metaphor of organization which encouraged the growth of scientific socialism. In the inter-war period the engineering of large production units to realize economies of scale encouraged the idea of planning by a centralized bureaucratic state. More recently, advances in computer technology have created a vision of a decentralized 'network society'. Indeed, it can be suggested that modernizing elites in particular countries have often seized on a particular technology as the key to their country's development. Steam railways represented a key technology in early Victorian Britain. Electricity later emerged as a key technology in France, and telecommunications in Sweden. Chemistry was a key technology in Germany, and the allied development of the internal combustion engine in Germany and France led a number of countries to champion their emergent motor industries as masters of a key technology.

It seems, therefore, that the recognition of an opportunity for technological innovation, allied to a belief in their nation's ability to master the technology, has often led elites to link technological and ideological change. The particular forms of intervention they have adopted reflect the particular technology involved and the ideological metaphors associated with it. Conversely, the ideological predisposition of the elite may incline it to championing one kind of technology rather than another.

The particular way that technology and ideology combine is influenced by a third factor—namely the climate of international relations. Nothing has been said about this so far, although it is an important influence on the direction that ideological change can take. So far as industrial policy is concerned, three climates can usefully be distinguished.

The first is one of overt hostility, where countries are arming themselves, either to carry out an attack, or to deter an aggressor. Such a climate favours an ideology of nationalism, emphasizing solidarity, and inculcating suspicion of foreigners. It highlights the military implications of technology and encourages self-sufficiency in strategic industries. Engineering, heavy industry, and energy emerge as key sectors, and centralized planning is perceived as the natural form of organization.

The second is one of peaceful rivalry, in which nations negotiate bilateral or multilateral arrangements with each other. Success in such negotiations tends to go to the highest status nations—those who are least dependent on others and have the widest choice of partners with whom they can trade. A nation which has a monopoly of key high-technology products clearly enjoys high status under these conditions. Mastery of technology thus acquires a strategic significance in international bargaining, over and above the collective emotional benefits that it confers. A climate of peaceful rivalry therefore encourages competition between nations to master prestigious technologies; in the latter half of the twentieth century, for example, national status has often been judged by technical mastery of rocket science, advanced computing, and nuclear power.

The third climate is one of institutionalized free trade. A free trade system is often presided over by a dominant power, who finds it to be in its own commercial interest to effect a division of labour in industry on a global basis. In the nineteenth century the dominant power was the UK, and in the second half of the twentieth century it has been, of course, the USA. A free trade regime makes it difficult for individual elites to invest in new technologies purely as a source of emotional reward. It also makes it difficult for them to run major ideological experiments. The problem is not only that a free trade regime rules out most forms of protection, but that in order to maintain a 'level playing-field' it rules out many other kinds of intervention too. Of course, free trade is never complete—services are often excluded, and non-tariff barriers usually remain. Nevertheless, a free trade regime encourages elites to concentrate on delivering material satisfactions to their citizens rather than emotional ones, and also encourages them to avoid ideological experiments other than laissez-faire. Free trade also discourages the designation of key technologies according to military criteria and encourages the use of strictly economic criteria for technological investments, such as cost reduction and quality improvement, instead.

The state of international relations, together with the ideological change and technological change, constitute the principal factors which impinge on all countries at any given point in time. All elites are susceptible to new ideas, they are all interested to some extent in the latest technology, and they are all aware of the climate of international relations. The combined effect of these three factors on the propensity to engage in ideological experiments is summarized in

TABLE 14.2. *Factors influencing the timing of ideological experiments*

Factor	1850–79	1880–1914	1918–39	1945–59	1960–79	1980–
Pace of ideological change	L	M	H	H	L	H
Pace of fundamental technological change	L	M	M	H	L	M
Degree of hostility in international relations	L	M	H	L	L	L
Index of overall propensity to experiment	0	1.5	2.5	2	0	1.5
Type of experiment		Socialist intervention			Deregulation	

Table 14.2. The table ranks each of the three factors as either low (L), medium (M), or high (H) for each of the periods 1850–79, 1880–1914, 1918–39, 1945–59, 1960–79, and 1980 to date. An index of the propensity to experiment is constructed by assuming that the effects of the three factors are additive. This is quite a strong assumption because there are significant interactions between the factors, as the preceding discussion has made clear. Nevertheless it is a useful approximation to make. The index is calculated by giving a value of one-half to a medium rating and a value of unity to a high rating. This generates a time-series for the index which is bi-modal. The index peaks initially in the inter-war period, which for most countries marks the high-point of centralized planning and organized intervention in the economy under peacetime conditions. After the period of the Keynesian consensus, during which little ideological innovation took place, the index begins to rise again in the final period, from 1980 to the present.

In practice, of course, there are leads and lags between different countries because some elites are more attuned than others to the latest thinking. But there is plenty of historical evidence to suggest that movements in industrial policy in different countries do occur broadly in step. For many countries the period 1850–79 was one of relatively free trade, deregulated industry, and, in some cases, laissez-faire. The period 1880–1914 was one of emergent national rivalries. This was associated with increasing protectionism, and growing experimentation with municipal socialization, often in connection with utilities (Foreman-Peck and Millward 1994). The inter-war period was even more protectionist, particularly after the world depression beginning in 1929, and saw the rise of powerful national and international cartels. The post-war period began with national rivalries in the commercialization of new technologies, and has moved fairly steadily towards free trade. The difficulties caused by stagnating productivity growth and rising government deficits in the 1960s and 1970s attracted many governments to the pro-market libertarian politics of the 'new right'.

Despite these commonalities, there remain significant differences between countries in their propensity to experiment with new ideologies and in the direction that these experiments take. In some countries the elite is normally persuaded to experiment by purely theoretical arguments, whilst in other countries pragmatic considerations dominate. For example, a modernizing elite dominated by politically partisan intellectuals is likely to seek highly abstract and theoretical grounds for policy change. A more traditional elite, however, reflecting the interests of commerce or of the landed aristocracy, is likely to be suspicious of abstract ideas, and to favour a more pragmatic approach instead. This pragmatic approach will involve a cautious attitude to ideological change.

A theoretical approach often suggests radical solutions. Theory raises intellectual possibilities that have never been put into practice before. At the same time the simplifying assumptions distract attention away from the complications that may be encountered. The mathematical elegance and logical consistency of the theory create a sense of confidence that nothing unexpected is likely to happen when implementation occurs. By contrast, a pragmatic approach favours incremental change. The pragmatist lacks the theorist's confidence that change is necessarily for the better, and so proceeds by trial and error in a sequence of small steps. The pragmatist, in other words, is much more averse to the risks involved.

The major building block of the modern world-view is natural science. A modern elite will therefore seek to present intervention as a scientific process based, for example, on the optimal control of the economic system. Intervention will involve large-scale data gathering, the formulation of computable models, and the setting of explicit targets. In addition to this mimicry of scientific method in the intervention process, intervention is likely to involve subsidies for experimental work in natural science too. The overt rationale may be long-term investment in new technology for economic growth, although the real motivation may simply be to subsidize the intellectual pursuits of the elite.

By contrast, a traditional elite is more likely to be interested in artistic pursuits. Support for traditional arts and crafts is likely to be favoured above radical experiments with new forms of expression. Scientific research will not necessarily be ignored, but is likely to be regarded purely instrumentally, as a means to an end (Wiener 1981). It is unlikely to be subsidized for reasons of enjoyment or prestige.

A final aspect of modern attitudes is a belief in the importance of formal and impersonal administrative structures. Traditional attitudes tend to favour informal personal arrangements instead.

Personal orientation is institutionalized in economic organizations, such as family firms, which are based on informal relationships between members of small, compact, and stable social groups (Ellickson 1991). Relationships are governed by traditional factors such as age, gender, paternity, and so on. Impersonal orientation, on the other hand, is institutionalized in large formal organizations in which a clear distinction is drawn between an office and the person who holds it. Relationships are defined in terms of offices, and office-holders are supposed to behave quite impartially. Showing favouritism towards family and friends is not acceptable, as it is with personal orientation, but is condemned as corruption instead. Impersonal orientation is reflected in a desire for transparency of structures and external accountability in organizations, whereas personal orientation involves an acceptance that relationships within an organization may well be opaque to outsiders and that secrecy will be maintained.

There is a paradox however, in the attitude of a modern elite which sets up impersonal institutions to implement its interventionist policies—namely that elites of any kind often function best when they operate traditionally through frequent face-to-face contacts amongst their members. The methods of coordination that the members of a modem elite employ amongst themselves are therefore often ones whose efficiency they ostensibly deny. Their commitment to formal and impersonal structures means that they do not understand the informal and personal mechanisms on which the cohesion of their elite depends. It is perhaps for this reason that intervention by elites so often fails in practice. Instead of informally diffusing their enthusiasm for intervention to the administrators they employ, the elite reduces intervention to formal bureaucratic routine and thereby alienates the very people who are directly responsible for making it work.

The four dimensions of culture described above are summarized in Table 14.3. The column headings show firstly the characteristic most conducive to radical policy experimentation, and below it the opposite characteristic that tends to inhibit radical change. To clarify the interpretation of these concepts, popular stereotypes are reported for each of the countries reviewed in this book. To place Europe in a global context, stereotypes are reported for Japan and the USA as well. Stereotypes are, of course, never completely accurate and are almost invariably out of date. They do, however, often contain an important germ of truth, albeit a simplified and exaggerated one. In the present context the stereotypes should be taken as indicative of the 1960–79 period, before the recent resurgence of ideological change. This period was a relatively stable one in terms of cultural attitudes to industrial policy (see Table 14.2) and is therefore particularly useful for benchmarking inter-country differences. The stereotypes represent the culture of the elite, rather than that of the country as a whole: they may be quite different from the culture of the poorer citizens in particular.

The table suggests that during this period France and Russia were the two countries most susceptible to radical policy experiments, whilst the UK, Ireland, and Portugal were the most oriented to only incremental change.

TABLE 14.3. *Four dimensions affecting the propensity for radical policy experimentation*

	Theory (T) Pragmatism (P)	Radical (R) Incremental (I)	Dimension of culture		Propensity for radical policy experimentation
			Scientific (S) Artistic (A)	Impersonal (M) Personal (P)	
Japan	P	R/I	S	P	1.5
US	T/P	I	S	M	2.5
UK	P	I	A/S	M/P	1
Ireland	P	R	A	P	1
France	T	R	S	M	4
Germany	P	I	S	M	2
Sweden	P	R	S	P	2
Russia	T	R	S	M	4
Italy	T/P	R	A/S	P	2
Spain	T/P	R	A	P	1.5
Portugal	P	R/I	A	P	0.5
Greece	T/P	R	A	P	1.5

France and Russia both have theoretical, radical, scientific, and impersonal cultures, which are reflected in their emphasis on a powerful bureaucratic state as the initiator of policy experiments. Although Ireland has political groups with a rather similar outlook, they have never gained sufficient political power to impose their values on the country as a whole. The strong grip of traditional religion and the absence of a large urban working class has forced nationalism to adopt a more personal and artistic cultural form in the Irish case, which has in turn engendered a more cautious approach to policy experiments. The same is true of Portugal where, in addition, the legacy of maritime enterprise has favoured a less radical and more incremental approach to industrial policy as well. The influence of commercial interests on national culture is even more striking in the UK, where a pragmatic and incremental approach to industrial policy has generally been favoured, except by the post-war Labour government, 1945–51.

Overall, it seems that the countries which have performed best in the post-war period are those with a moderate tendency for radical policy experimentation—Japan, USA, Germany, Sweden, Spain, and Italy. Amongst these countries it is scientific and pragmatic ones—Japan, Germany, Sweden, and to some extent the USA—which seem to have done best of all.

14.7. INTER-COUNTRY DIFFERENCES IN THE PROPENSITY TO INTERVENE

There are also significant differences between countries in the direction that industrial policy experiments are likely to take. In some countries there is a distinct bias towards experimenting with interventionist policies and to resisting fashions for liberal reforms. Other countries seem, by contrast, to be enthusiastic about movements for liberalization, and resistant to proposals for greater intervention.

To explain these differences, three further factors need to be taken into account. They are the country's geography, its stage of development, and its cultural traditions. The particular traditions that are relevant to its industrial policy are its disposition to individualism or collectivism. Although specific to a country, none of these factors is immutable. Like the other cultural factors discussed in Section 14.6, they can change in the long run. Compared to the general factors discussed in Section 14.5, however, their pace of change is likely to be relatively slow.

The geography of a country is obviously immutable in a number of important respects, such as climate and terrain. These govern the natural resource base of the country, which in turn affects the composition of its output and its comparative advantage in international trade. Climate and terrain can affect a country's institutional structure as well (North 1981). For example, by affecting the kind of crops that can be grown, they influence the type of commercial institutions that emerge to handle the distribution of agricultural products. This in turn determines the kind of institutional infrastructure on which later industrialization builds. Mountainous country encourages small self-sufficient groups of peasant farmers to practice a varied agriculture, whereas wide river valleys and plains encourage more specialized grain production with larger farms, long-distance transport, more sophisticated urban markets, and so on. Flatter countries therefore tend to commercialize earlier than hilly countries, and tend to develop a more modern outward-looking culture. Although mountainous country is often rich in mining activities, mining communities are often short-lived, because of the rapid depletion of resources. Moreover much of the downstream processing activity is carried on, not in the hills, but down near the coast, where skilled labour and other specialized inputs are more readily available. Mining activities may therefore do little to alter the traditional inward-looking culture of mountainous areas.

In another sense, however, geographical factors can alter as a result of external events. In particular, the entrepôt potential of a country can change as trade routes alter in its vicinity. Thus the entrepôt potential of Southern African countries was severely damaged by the opening of the Suez Canal, as was the potential of South American countries by the opening of the Panama Canal. Conversely, the entrepôt potential of Singapore has been strengthened by the growth of international trade through the Straits between Europe and Japan (and now with China as well).

The development of a major entrepôt centre, like the evolution of large-scale arable farming, does much to promote an outward-looking individualistic culture. Conversely, the absence of an entrepôt centre can create an inward-looking collectivist culture, which perpetuates itself by forcing the more enterprising individuals to emigrate overseas.

Qualitative estimates of the entrepôt potential of the major countries identified above are reported in Table 14.4. Island economies such as the UK and Japan score highly, as do countries which have major borders with the Mediterranean

TABLE 14.4. *Estimates of the entrepôt
potential of selected countries*

Country	Estimate
Japan	High
US	Low
UK	High
Ireland	Low
France	Low
Germany	Medium
Sweden	Medium
Russia	Low
Italy	High
Spain	Medium
Portugal	Low
Greece	High

TABLE 14.5. *Influence of protectionism on economic performance at
different stages of development*

Stage of development	Probable effect of protectionism
Pre-modern	Generates revenue for elite. High cost of living for ordinal people. Institutionalizes inequality
Transitional	Protects 'infant industry' and allows high-technology export sector to develop
Young modern	Retaliation by other countries inhibits export growth. Bilateral and multilateral tariff reductions are needed, generating momentum towards free trade
Maturity and stagnation	Protection of jobs in declining export industries inhibits structural change

Sea. Sweden benefits from its strategic position in the Baltic, while Germany occupies a key position on land-based routes in Europe, and benefits from the navigability of the Rhine. The USA and Russia have limited entrepôt potential because of their large land masses and their relative remoteness from trading routes between other countries. The limited entrepôt potential of the USA may partly explain the paradox that US governments have often been isolationist and protectionist despite their apparent ideological commitment to laissez-faire and free trade.

To many elites intervention seems a natural policy response to certain crucial stages of the development process. In particular, a leader who is determined that his country shall 'catch up' on its strongest rivals may well regard protectionism as crucial at a particular stage of the process. A possible rationale for this view was outlined in Section 14.4, and is expanded in Table 14.5. In a premodern economy protectionism is simply an excuse for perpetuating the social and economic inequalities which are often (though not invariably) characteristic of the traditional way of life. As an economy becomes ripe for development, however, on account of the increasing competence of its workforce, protectionism can acquire a more positive role in assisting the transfer of technology from overseas. If it succeeds in this objective, however, then protectionism sows the seeds of its own destruction, since a world-class exporter cannot realize its full potential if it is excluded by retaliation from major foreign markets. A switch to free trade is, in this context, a hallmark of success. But as other countries in turn learn from its example, the exports on which it built its industrial strength may lose their competitive edge. Vested interests in the declining export industries then unite to protect both jobs and profits, and protectionism threatens national economic performance by placing more and more resources into industries that have no future (Olson 1982). An intelligent elite that has the national interest at heart will therefore adapt its policy stance to the stage of development, building up protection as development gets underway and quickly running it down again thereafter. A self-interested elite may, however, commit itself to protectionism at other stages too—to maintain its status in a pre-modern economy, or to buy off the vested interests that keep it in power in a mature economy.

The third and final factor to be considered in this section is whether the elite takes an individualistic or collectivist view of society. An individualistic view may be characterized as atomistic, democratic, and consumer-oriented, whilst a collectivist view may be characterized as organic, elitist, and producer-oriented.

An atomistic view of society suggests that an individual's emotional satisfactions stem from his own behaviour—the morality of his own actions and his own personal achievements. The organic view, on the other hand, suggests that it is the individual's participation in the collective mission of the group that is really satisfying. It is the sense of having contributed in a small way to something very significant—so significant that only a group and not an individual could achieve it—that carries the greatest emotional weight.

The atomistic view suggests that emotional rewards are very much like material rewards, in the sense that they relate more to what the individual himself consumes than to what other people do. It encourages belief in the autonomy of each individual, and offers a vision of the group in which these autonomous individuals themselves create the group through a social contract. Because the individual is morally prior to the group, the role of the social contract is to secure the initial rights of each individual to property, privacy, and so on.

The organic view, on the other hand, emphasizes that members share in the emotional rewards of collective activity, and so the analogy between emotional rewards and material rewards suggests that material rewards should be shared as well. From this perspective, the private appropriation of material resources seems like an attempt to deny other people the opportunity to share in their enjoyment. Thus social ownership, or ownership in common, is preferred to private ownership.

This stance is further supported by the view that the group has moral priority over the individual, since without the support of the group the individual could not survive. The emphasis of law, therefore, is on the obligation of the individual to the group, rather than on the right of the individual to isolate himself socially from the group when he desires to do so. Since the generation of emotional rewards hinges crucially on collective activity, and the efficiency of such activity often requires conformity in behaviour, the organic view offers less scope for personal freedom than does the atomistic view.

The organic view influences not only the perception of society—it affects the perception of the industrial system too. Writers who incline to an organic view emphasize the relatedness of the technologies employed in different industries. They recognize, for example, that the innovation of a new technique in one industry may have to wait on the innovation of a different technique in another industry. Capital goods industries are often crucial constraints in this respect— a process innovation in a consumer good industry may have to wait upon a product innovation in a capital goods industry. Relatedness also involves the exploitation of economies of scope in basic technologies. An emphasis on relatedness, for example, encourages efforts to discover and exploit generic physical principles which, when applied in different fields, will generate a whole family of engineering solutions to specific problems.

Those who incline to an atomistic view, on the other hand, often perceive different aspects of technology as separable. They are concerned that each particular innovation should be assessed in terms of its calculable effects, and not in terms of ill-defined spillovers. While the organicist believes that technological appraisal must be carried out within the framework of an integrated industrial policy, the atomist favours decentralizing appraisal to individual entrepreneurs within a market system.

Another important distinction is between elitist cultures, which assume that the distribution of intelligence and managerial ability is very unequal, and democratic cultures, which assume intelligence and ability are fairly evenly spread. Modern Western culture strongly endorses the democratic view—certainly a key assumption is that the general standard of intelligence is sufficiently high to warrant a universal franchise. It is also reflected in a general distrust of government, and of the governing elite.

There is a tendency for atomistic attitudes to be linked with democratic ones, because the moral autonomy of an individual is normally assumed to rest on a certain minimum level of intelligence. There is also a link between organic attitudes and elitism—thus the organic metaphor suggests that the elite should act as a 'brain' to control the 'body' of the state. This attitude is less evident today, though, than it was amongst the late nineteenth-century intellectuals, who lived before European Fascist dictators came to power.

Having said this, it is not unreasonable to suggest that even today those who favour interventionist industrial policies tend to exhibit organic and elitist values, whilst those who dislike intervention incline to individualist and democratic values. Thus while many contemporary interventionists would deny any elitism, it is noticeable that they often appeal to academic authorities with strong elitist views—Schumpeter (1934) being the most noticeable example.

It is a mistake to suggest, though, that atomistic democratic cultures are opposed to intervention of all kinds. They are only opposed to the kind of active interventionism in which, for example, state control of strategic industries is seen as crucial for long-run national growth. When it comes to the regulation of utility prices, say, an atomistic culture may actually favour intervention because it is required to protect individual consumers against monopoly power. An organic culture, on the other hand, might see the high profits of unregulated monopoly as providing a boost to further large-scale investment, and hence consider it better not to intervene.

This suggests a third dimension along which cultures differ—namely consumer orientation and producer orientation. Consumer orientation means that people are visualized principally as shoppers, and the role of the industrial system is seen as being to fill the shops with exciting value-for-money products. Competition is seen as important both in maintaining low prices for standardized products and in encouraging variety through the continued innovation of novel products. Natural monopoly due to economies of scale in the utilities is perceived as an awkward exception to the beneficial rule of competition. Because unregulated competition would drive down prices to marginal cost and result in persistent losses in the utilities, intervention is required—but only for this limited purpose.

Producer orientation, on the other hand, means that people are visualized principally as workers, and industry is seen as a valuable source of employment. The larger the scale of the enterprise, the more jobs are created. Intervention is required to subsidize the investment which is needed to create sufficient jobs. Conversely, the desire to preserve existing jobs may encourage the subsidization of declining industries. Indeed, once created, large enterprises may be very difficult to close down, for neoclassical political economy indicates that industrial workers concentrated in large plants are more likely to mobilize political support than are consumers and taxpayers who are dispersed throughout the economy (Olson 1982).

The three dimensions of culture identified above are listed in Table 14.6. The format is similar to that of Table 14.3. Each line of the table corresponds to a different country. The column headings identify the opposing characteristics which define the dimension along which the culture may vary. In each case the characteristic favouring intervention appears at the top. The degree of intervention is calculated by attaching a unit weight to each of the pro-intervention characteristics, and a half-weight to cases where both characteristics are present, and then summing the weights. France, Spain, and Russia are identified as the most interventionist societies, and the USA as the least interventionist one. The UK is also fairly low on intervention, whilst Sweden is fairly high.

TABLE 14.6. *Three dimensions of culture that explain country-specific differences in the degree of intervention*

Country	Organicism (O) Atomism (A)	Elitist (E) Democratic (D)	Producer (P) Consumer (C)	Degree of intervention
Japan	O	E	P/C	2:5
US	A	D	C	0
UK	A	E/D	P	1:5
Ireland	O	D	P	2
France	O	E	P	3
Germany	O/A	E/D	P	2
Sweden	O	E/D	P	2:5
Russia	O	E	P	3
Italy	O	E/D	P/C	2
Spain	O	E	P	3
Portugal	O/A	E	P/C	2
Greece	A	E	P	2

14.8. TRUST AS THE KEY TO SUCCESSFUL INTERVENTION

A striking feature of Table 14.6 is that there seems to be no strong connection between the propensity to intervene and economic success. Both the USA and the UK are low-intervention societies, but the USA has performed significantly better than the UK. The fact that intervention is lowest of all in the USA cannot account for this success, because Germany and Japan, which have been more successful than either, tend to intervene more. This suggests that if it is not the degree of intervention that matters, then it is perhaps the underlying culture that counts instead. There must be some other missing aspect of culture which determines, not whether intervention occurs, but whether it works when government tries to carry it out. This missing element, it is suggested, is the level of trust in society.

Highly personalized societies are good at generating trust within small groups, such as the family firm and local community (Fukuyama 1995). Whether trust exists between members of different groups within the society is another matter, though. If it does, then we have a high-trust society. High trust exists when other members of society are expected to be honest whatever specific allegiance they may have (Polanyi 1944, 1977).

High trust encourages spontaneous cooperation and hence reduces the need for intervention to prevent, or correct for, dishonesty of various kinds. Conversely low trust undermines spontaneous cooperation. It creates a need for intervention because it encourages people to behave dishonestly.

The need for intervention is difficult to meet satisfactorily in a low-trust society. The problem is that in a low-trust society people not only cannot trust each other—they cannot trust the government either. Indeed, since the government has more power than anyone else, it is more to be feared than ordinary people. Although there are evils that need correcting therefore, they cannot be tackled because the solution—namely intervention—is feared more than the problem itself.

Fear of intervention means that trust becomes focused, not on people, but on processes instead. Intervention, when it occurs, is governed by rules: discretionary intervention is disliked because it is believed that discretionary powers are easier to abuse. Rules make is easier to detect when the intervener cheats.

Formal rules do not, however, offer complete security against cheating. Dishonest judges, false witnesses, and other forms of corruption are always possible in a low-trust society. As a result, a low-trust society with no discretionary intervention is always potentially inferior to a high-trust society with discretionary intervention.

14.9. CONCLUSION

Intellectual fashion has been a major driving force of cultural change, but over the last century has achieved little real progress. Further changes will be required before an adequate ideological framework for industrial policy is reached. The missing ingredient in twentieth-century ideological debate is the trust factor. Figure 14.2 presents a simple model of cultural change in which the legitimacy of existing leadership depends on its ability to meet its own performance norms. The elite sets the culture, which is expressed in two main ways. The first is through the values and beliefs of people, as determined by the leader's example and by his rhetoric. The second is through the institutions—firms, markets, the state—by which individual incentives are mediated. It is these institutions that determine the constraints that optimizers face.

Elites disseminated the culture they have chosen in order to achieve their own particular goals. The culture is set in the light of the leader's perception of the environment, and in the light of the lessons which the leader draws from comparing past performance with his own performance norms. Past performance reflects the collective outcome of previous individual behaviour, as determined by the interplay of values, beliefs, and institutional constraints.

An elite can normally remain in power so long as its past failures do not catch up with it—that is, so long as the performance for which it is deemed responsible meets the cultural norms the leader has set. There is always potential competition for leadership—in democracies it is institutionalized in the electoral process, whereas in dictatorships military mutiny and revolutionary insurgency are the most common threats.

Ideologies are crucial to leaders in legitimating their position: the survival of a leader may well depend on his having a convenient ideology which allows him to lay the blame for failure on other people. Throughout much of the twentieth century Western European countries have been dominated by a single

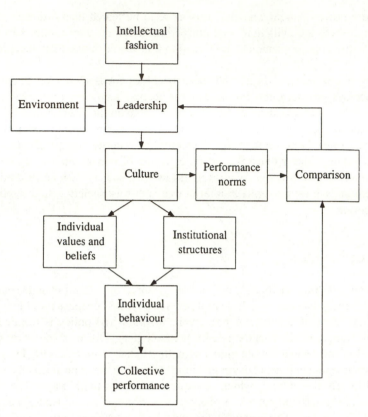

FIG. 14.2. Culture, conduct, and performance
Source: Casson 1991.

ideological struggle—between capitalism and socialism (Hobsbawm 1995). Capitalism articulates an atomistic, democratic, and consumer-oriented view of society and is essentially non-interventionist in its approach. Socialism represents an organic, elitist, producer-oriented view of society and is essentially interventionist.[1]

The First World War marks a turning point in this ideological struggle. Prior to 1914 capitalism had largely held its ground against trade union agitation and increasing socialism in urban government. Because of the war pro-capitalist leadership groups in several countries were discredited, and experiments in practical socialism became common—the most extreme being those in Russia after the 1917 revolution. Intellectual fashion increasingly favoured the Marxist interpretation of history, which suggested that industrialization was the key to economic growth. Rapid growth in turn depended on producing capital goods rather than consumer goods, which suggested an emphasis on heavy industries.

---

[1] Some socialists would dissent from this elitist characterization, but intellectual elites have played a prominent role in the formulation of socialist policies, and many socialist countries have lacked democracy.

Nationalist sentiments, promoted by the perceived injustices of the Versailles Treaty, encouraged countries to import technology in heavy industries so that they could master the technology themselves. A sense of military insecurity engendered by the war encouraged self-sufficiency in armaments-related industries. To secure a market for domestic producers, protectionism was introduced—especially in strategic industries such as steel and vehicles. On the European continent support for heavy industry for military purposes had begun well before, but the war completed the process.

After the slump of 1929–33, these trends were reinforced by liberal democratic thinkers such as Keynes, who favoured an increased role for government in achieving full employment. Maintaining investment levels became a government responsibility, and this financial commitment, combined with nationalist and socialist ideologies, strengthened the case for nationalization of industry. Keynes regarded the Second World War as a transitory period of high employment, after which the West was liable to stagnate. Capitalism could only continue as part of a mixed economy in which the state had a major role. This fitted in well with demands for a 'welfare state'. Keynesianism supplanted Marxism as the intellectual fashion in much of Western Europe. As a result government became an employer of last resort, with much employment being created by overmanning in the public services. This ideological shift was less obvious in Germany in the early post-war decades, with Chancellor Erhard's convenient formula of the 'social market economy', as we have seen in Chapter 4.

Unfortunately the commitment to full employment allowed trade union leaders to independently pursue another item on the socialist agenda—raising wages. But in countries where productivity growth was comparatively limited (notably Britain), higher money wages merely fuelled inflation and real wages did not rise much at all. At the same time the value of 'take home' pay was being eroded by the increasing levels of taxation needed to fund the public sector. Many other European economies in the 1980s began to experience similar difficulties of the British economy from the later 1960s. Following the first of the oil price shocks, wages needed to fall in some industries in order to compensate for the much higher price of energy inputs, but the necessary adjustments did not occur. Unemployment rose as a result or, as in Italy, the state bailed out the faltering firms, and expanded its share of the national economy. Either way, these trends greatly increased state expeditures. Social security payments became an increasing burden on the budget, and fears grew that the tax increases needed to fund them had created a serious disincentive to enterprise and hard work. The Keynesian compromise between socialism and capitalism became discredited, and it seemed as though it was the socialist component that was to blame.

During the 1980s the reaction against state intervention in the economy gathered momentum, most rapidly in Britain again. Privatization replaced nationalization as the key element in industrial policy. Monetary stability, and labour market flexibility engendered by curbs on trade union power, replaced fiscal policy as the mechanism of macroeconomic management. In Britain, the pendulum of intellectual fashion had swung back to its pre-1914 position, close to the capitalist extreme. Continental Europe followed this movement only later, and only to some extent. Privatization was much delayed and nowhere has it reached the British levels. In Italy the process of privatization started really only after a big political upheaval (second only to the fall of Communist regimes) and anyway the power of the trade unions was not broken. In France and Germany privatization was even less pervasive than in Italy, and was designed to minimize the impact on the existing balance of economic power.

In addition to the swing of intellectual fashion, something else happened as well. The ideological concept of capitalism was different in one crucial respect. The contemporary concept of capitalism has much more emphasis on interpersonal competition, and on the importance of the 'rule of law' in sustaining the competitive market system. Superficially it could be said that this is because contemporary notions of capitalism are borrowed from the USA, which is a legalistic low-trust society, rather than from the UK, which in the late-Victorian period was very much a high-trust society instead. But the enthusiasm with which the new concept of capitalism has been embraced suggests that the explanation goes deeper than that. For the UK itself has now become a more low-trust society than it used to be. Intellectual fashion has driven Western culture as a whole away from the high-trust view of society which was prevalent a century ago. What is so noticeable today is the deeply pessimistic view of human nature on which the ideological case for capitalism is based.

If society is to improve industrial policy-making, then the dimension of trust should be recognized explicitly—turning ideological debate into a two-dimensional affair. Politicians must appreciate that a successful industrial policy requires not only a suitable balance between individualism and collectivism, but an adequate degree of trust as well.

REFERENCES

BECKER, G. S. (1983). 'A theory of competition amongst pressure groups for political influence'. *Quarterly Journal of Economics*, 98: 371–400.

BUCHANAN, J. M. (1965). 'An economic theory of clubs'. *Economica*, NS, 32: 1–14.

CASSON, M. C. (1990). *Enterprise and Competitiveness: A Systems View of International Business*. Oxford: Clarendon Press.

—— (1991). *Economics of Business Culture: Game Theory, Transaction Costs, and Economic Performance*. Oxford: Clarendon Press.

—— (1993). 'Cultural determinants of economic performance'. *Journal of Comparative Economics*, 17: 418–42.

ELLICKSON, R. C. (1991). *Order without Law: How Neighbours Settle Disputes*. Cambridge, Mass.: Harvard University Press.

FOREMAN-PECK, J., and MILLWARD, R. (1994). *Public and Private Ownership in Britain, 1800–1990*. Oxford: Clarendon Press.

FUKUYAMA, F. (1995). *Trust: New Foundations of Global Prosperity*. London: Hamish Hamilton.

GERSCHENKRON, A. (1968). *Continuity and Other Essays in History*. Cambridge, Mass.: Harvard University Press.

HAGEN, E. E. (1964). *On the Theory of Social Change: How Economic Growth Begins*. London: Tavistock Publications.

HAYEK, F. A. VON (1960). *The Constitution of Liberty*. Chicago: University of Chicago Press.

HIRSCHMAN, A. O. (1982). *Shifting Involvements: Private Interest and Public Action*. Princeton: Princeton University Press.

HOBSBAWM, E. (1995). *Age of Extremes: The Short Twentieth Century, 1914–91*. London: Michael Joseph.

HOSELITZ, B. F. (1960). *Sociological Aspects of Economic Growth*. New York: Free Press of Glencoe.

NORTH, D. C. (1981). *Structure and Change in Economic History*. New York: W.W. Norton.

OLSON, M. (1965). *The Logic of Collective Action*. Cambridge, Mass.: Harvard University Press.

—— (1982). *The Rise and Decline of Nations*. New Haven: Yale University Press.

POLANYI, K. (1944). *The Great Transformation*. New York: Holt, Rinehart and Winston (reprinted 1975 by Octagon Books, New York).

—— (1977). *The Livelihood of Man*, ed. H. W. Pearson. New York: Academic Press.

POPPER, K. (1975). *The Poverty of Historicism*. London: Routledge & Kegan Paul.

ROSTOW, W. W. (1952). *The Process of Economic Growth*. New York: Free Press.

SCHUMPETER, J. A. (1934). *The Theory of Economic Development*, trans. R. Opie. Cambridge, Mass.: Harvard University Press.

TOLLISON, R. D. (1982). 'Rent seeking: A survey'. *Kyklos*, 35/4: 575–602.

TULLOCK, G. (1967). 'The welfare costs of tariffs, monopolies and theft'. *Western Economic Journal*, 5: 224–32.

WIENER, M. (1981). *English Culture and the Decline of the Industrial Spirit*. Cambridge: Cambridge University Press.

15

European Industrial Policy: An Overview

JAMES FOREMAN-PECK AND GIOVANNI FEDERICO

University of Oxford, Universita di Pisa.

How much have European industrial policies mattered? We begin this overview by assessing their impact. Since differences between national industrial policies have persisted for long periods of history, we go on to look at some of the institutions, events, and characteristics that underlie their durability and which may give rise to the distinctive national cultures discussed in the preceding chapter. There are also family resemblances among European industrial policies, thanks to intellectual climates, technology, common shocks, and the prevalent style of international relations. Because family resemblances change with the epoch, we divide the account into four periods—the end of the 'long nineteenth century', the inter-war years, the great post-war boom, and the aftermath of the oil price shocks. For each of these we compare across countries the causes and effects of policy instruments and the objectives. Among the greatest shifts in the climate of international relations and in European institutions have been the formation of the Common Market and the evolution of the European Union. We integrate explanations of the scope and limitations of supra-national European industrial policies with the accounts of the epochs in which they were implemented. Finally we offer some predictions and prescriptions.

15.1. THE IMPACT OF INDUSTRIAL POLICY OVER THE TWENTIETH CENTURY

Comparing the geographical dispersion in Europe of particular industries among a considerable number of nations with their concentration in the United States, it is difficult not to believe that national policies have played a vital role in creating the European pattern. Language and other differences must have contributed to this fragmentation but the principal causes were undoubtedly conscious decisions. As discussed in Chapter 1, unless there were market failures that warranted such policy interventions, then the political goals at which they were normally targeted must have imposed economic costs. A simple and imperfect measure of policy impacts on the efficiency, extent, and location of European industry is then the divergence between patterns of twentieth-century European and United States economic activity and population (Krugman 1991).

   The European industrial belt of Map 15.1, containing the Ruhr, Northern France, and Belgium (originally coal-related) accounted for a large proportion

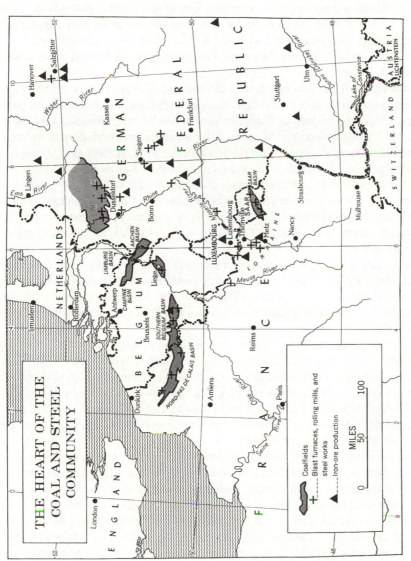

MAP 15.1. The centre of the Coal and Steel Community

of Western European industry—outside Britain—for the first half of the century with which we have been concerned. But US manufactured industry was much more concentrated, in a relatively small part of the Northeast and the eastern part of the Midwest, from the mid-nineteenth century to the 1960s. Three-quarters of US manufacturing employment at the turn of the century and two-thirds in 1957 was based there, even though by then most raw materials were drawn from other regions. We may infer that in a nineteenth- or twentieth-century United States of Europe the Ruhr–Northern France–Belgium industrial zone would have been bigger and more prosperous.

Although coal lost importance as a determinant of location over the twentieth century, European industry reconfigured surprisingly little, thanks to national pressures. Specialization among European economies has not increased very much over 1913 levels, at least for the more easily measured products, despite the technological and political changes in the intervening years. Almost every European country paid to support its steel and coal industries, and its national airline in the 1980s and 1990s. An 'American' distribution of European car production in, say, 1985 would have entailed the concentration of half the industry within 150 kilometres of Wolfsburg in Germany, a very different distribution from the historical pattern. In exchange, Germany would probably have lost its textile industry to Italy.

Such radical changes would require considerable political skills to implement. But judging by the continuing US productivity lead, there would be a substantial pay-off. Alternatively, Europe might choose to maintain its national policies and forgo greater international competitiveness and higher living standards.

Other evidence that the interventionist national industrial policies generating European industrial geography have been costly is the adverse side-effects. Even supposing these policies when directed to raising investment did so without offsetting reductions in productivity of capital, they promoted corruption, and corruption deterred investment (Ades and Di Tella 1997). Hence the net effect on investment of interventionist industrial policies may have been between one-half and four-fifths of the direct impact.

Despite, rather than because of interventionist industrial policies then, industrial performance since the Second World War has been unprecedentedly successful, both for leaders and followers. Italian manufacturing productivity caught up with the rest of the industrialized world most spectacularly, and France achieved a good second place. Britain and Germany, on the other hand, had not radically altered their relative productivity by the end of the 1980s. The industrial sectors in the small open economies of Netherlands and Sweden, subject to greater stimuli to efficiency from international competition boosted by falling transport and communications costs, increased their advantage in the course of the twentieth century. The creation of a European single market, in contrast to the strangulation of international specialization in the 1930s, must have contributed. However the bracketing of Sweden (outside the EC in 1989) with the Netherlands (one of the original 'six') suggests that formal membership of the single market cannot take all the credit for 'catching up' and 'overtaking'.

15.2. INDUSTRIAL POLICY PERSISTENCE

As the pattern of European industry suggests, industrial policies have been persistent, and national styles have survived across epochs and apparent shifts of ideology. French 'liberal' industrial policy entailed spending a far higher proportion of GNP on subsidies than Britain in the same period. Such continuity has led a number of writers to consider the contribution of 'national culture' to policy (e.g. Dobbin 1994; Temin 1997, as well as Mark Casson in Ch. 14).

'Culture' offers the ultimate historical explanation, for culture itself can only be explained by institutions and events that began far in the past. Sometimes it is helpful to think of cultural elements as means by which a society has come to avoid mutually destructive forms of behaviour and instead selected collectively beneficial actions. In these cases social interaction can be represented as repeated plays of the prisoner's dilemma game (with an infinite horizon). For instance, a national economy may reap the highest immediate reward by refusing a patent to an inventor, and allowing everyone to use the invention without charge. On the other hand, the inventor may then cease devoting time to research if it is not expected to pay. The best solution for the inventor would be a permanent monopoly, maintained perhaps by secrecy. In either case technical progress will be slower than necessary. This is the non-cooperative solution to the 'game', in which everyone is worse off than they need be.

'Culture' may help attainment of a cooperative solution. If, on the playing fields of Eton, or elsewhere at a formative stage, policy-makers have been inculcated with notions of fairness, they may prevent mutually harmful strategies being played. They may create institutions to bring about cooperation. A compromise, or cooperative solution, to the above game is to grant a fixed period patent, allowing the inventor the possibility of recovering the investment costs from higher sales prices or from royalties, only for a prescribed number of years. Frequency of play is a major consideration in choosing cooperation or conflict. In a large impersonal economy, with a great deal of personal and positional mobility, we might expect less cooperation and trust than in smaller economies with a slower pace of change. Western European economies have been, and are small, by comparison with the United States. The extent of competition has been less and traditional behaviour more supported by durable institutions. Culture is therefore perhaps more of an influence for persistence in industrial policy.

Of course there are other, possibly more fundamental, major constraints and motivators. The clearest pattern of national policies depends on the size of the economy. Large countries, Britain, France, Germany, Italy, Russia, could afford more interventionist stances if they chose; protectionism or policies intended to support the largely fixed costs of hi-tech defence. But there were limits to what even these economies could pay. The French Freycinet and Baudin Plans were perhaps the most extreme examples of the later nineteenth/early twentieth century interventionist industrial policies and, like many successor initiatives, were prematurely abandoned for lack of money. Policies aimed at non-economic goals, such as national security or glory, or at economic objectives but with ineffective, and expensive, instruments, were likely only to be persistently followed even by large countries, to the extent that they could ignore the costs.

Small countries could not indulge themselves with the industrial policies of the large, although that was not always recognized. Manufacturing businesses in the Netherlands, Belgium, Denmark, and Sweden were obliged to be internationally competitive or they could not survive. Domestic markets alone were inadequate to support high productivity manufacturers. Specialization was therefore essential, such as in telecommunications equipment in Sweden and small arms in Belgium.

The historical evidence on political sources of national policy continuity shows that neither the 'benign politicians' assumption nor the strict public choice approach, discussed in Chapter 1, are sufficient to understand fully the design of actual industrial policy. Industrial policy was certainly influenced by ideologies and party politics, and among ideologies nationalism has proved especially robust. At the end of the nineteenth century, nationalism made aggressive policies for development of military capabilities much more acceptable to the general public than they might be nowadays. But even in the 1950s, security was the supposed justification for an extraordinarily wide range of British import quotas, raising the spectre of a bizarre 'future war fought with yeast, jewels, sporting guns and silk cloth' (Milward and Brennan 1996: 194). 'Capture' by vested interests may well be the correct explanation for the policy. Blatant nationalism was no longer so acceptable in Western Europe by the 1990s, but it still crept in as the 'defence of national interests'. This apparently required that an advanced country produce certain goods (including coal in Germany as a 'national source of energy), and that it possess large companies, 'national champions', in 'strategic' industries. Again the public choice approach often helps us pass behind the veil of 'national interest'.

Linguistic or religious divisions can supply another basis for policy persistence, as in Belgium after 1945, where resources distributed to Flanders and Wallonia were necessarily equally balanced. In authoritarian states bureaucracies often gave continuity to industrial policy. Admittedly industrial policy might be slanted by the personality of the ruler, and by his interest and competence in economic affairs. Although Mussolini and Franco delegated most decisions to technocrats and their bureaucracy, they did intervene when they felt that important political questions were at stake. Stalin had his own ideas on industrial policy and central planning allowed him to be more interventionist. Russia was the most extreme authoritarian case, and, though the Tsars were not central planners like their successors, industrial policy continuity of a sort has been identified in the coercive styles of the two regimes. However in most of Europe over the last century, the climate for authoritarianism has not always been propitious.

15.3. NINETEENTH-CENTURY LIBERAL INDUSTRIAL POLICIES

Our study began when 'intellectual fashions' and other circumstances were not. Nineteenth-century European economic liberalism favoured markets and 'hands-off' policies. They were generally underwritten by limited political franchises and the accompanying respect for private property. Though Italy and France pursued economic strategies that were liberal by comparison with earlier stances, when compared with other countries they were interventionist. Already high, the French subsidy/government expenditure ratio, at 0.12–0.15 in the 1870s, and the proportion of GNP spent on industry, were to rise substantially in later years.

The exemplar of liberalism was British industrial policy, the model for nineteenth-century Belgium and Netherlands. Scandinavian policies by and large encouraged trade and free enterprise also. That Britain's average income per head was the highest in Europe seemed a good indication that British policies worked well.[1] There is no doubt that Britain was an industrial leader in Europe in 1913, even though it is possible to question whether it was *the* leader. Productivity in British and German manufacturing industries was similar in 1870, with Germany drawing ahead after 1900 (Broadberry 1994). At the outbreak of the First World War, Germany tended to dominate Europe in steel and sulphuric acid and in chemicals more generally. France was pre-eminent in the still tiny motor and aircraft industries. But French industrial productivity apparently lagged behind that in Britain and Germany.

Britain's high income per head stemmed as much from redirecting resources out of low productivity agriculture and into industry, for its industrialization had proceeded much further than other European economies. Free trade ensured that British industry was highly specialized. In a relatively open world economy, specialization may be expected to encourage excellence in particular national industries, especially where resource endowments are particularly favourable. World shipbuilding and cotton textiles were dominated by British businesses; as the principle of comparative advantage suggests, some other industries, such as electrical engineering, were small in comparison with those elsewhere.

One supporting piece of evidence that a small country could make gains by 'working with the grain' of the market, like Britain, (and a possible caveat) is that Belgium's very permissive company law attracted investment and encouraged the headquartering in Brussels of firms interested in secrecy. But much of continental Europe leaned against the wind of international competition towards the end of the nineteenth century, initially in agriculture, but subsequently in industry as well.

---

[1] Though historians and social scientists need evidence that the policy was not a response to this favourable position, rather than a cause.

Possibly nineteenth-century industrial policy was a little more intervention-ist the more backward the economy, but recent research has cast doubt on this earlier accepted wisdom. Where railway development and the definition or rede-finition of property rights were concerned the proposition may hold, but national traditions remain a competing explanation (Gerschenkron 1962; Sylla and Toniolo 1991: 16–18). Railway technology required unprecedentedly heavy investment less available in poorer countries, and more radical changes in property rights were needed for markets to work well in backward economies—such as the abolition of serfdom. But viewed from the end of the twentieth century what is most noticeable is that before 1913 all European governments were usually rather modest in their peacetime industrial policy aspirations, and in their selection of policy instruments, by comparison with the years after 1945.

15.3.1. Infrastructure Policy

Direct state spending focused on communications and transport infrastructure, a vital influence upon the competitiveness of manufacturing and the effect-iveness of national armies. Nineteenth-century technology determined that the scale of manufacturing enterprises was dwarfed by infrastructure business, and of these industries the most expensive was railways. Railways and roads were needed to carry troops to the frontiers, and telecommunications to tell them what to do. The state therefore was interested as a user of services in which private monopolies were likely to emerge. Communication networks, the postal service, and roads, were traditionally state monopolies for security reasons, which the electric telegraph and telephone hardly disturbed, except when finance was not available.

By the end of the nineteenth century, this monopoly was being extended to railways in much of continental Europe. The German government saw railways as a source of state revenue and nationalized them, to capture the advantages of their 'natural monopoly' position. French railway investment in Russia from the 1880s was intended to improve the pace and effectiveness of Russian mobiliza-tion against Germany. Commitment to free trade did not rule out state owner-ship of infrastructure. Despite a generally liberal stance on economic policy, as we have seen in Chapter 6, Swedish state railways in 1913 transported 60% of goods travelling by rail. Sweden established a state-owned electricity generator to exploit hydroelectricity as well. Other liberal states, notably Britain, opted for arm's length regulation of railways. Even so, that did not necessarily leave the cheaper telegraph and telephone networks safe for private enterprise in these countries.

Local government imitated national infrastructure policy, supplying water, elec-tricity, and gas in European cities. Dissatisfaction with private monopoly was a prominent motive in Stuttgart and in Stettin. As the most essential service, water was most likely to be municipalized, but the 28 largest German cities also took over gas supply between 1860 and 1896 (Batson 1933).

15.3.2. Manufacturing Industry: State Ownership and Purchasing

Many states acquired some small direct interest in manufacturing industry for military purposes. Their nineteenth-century foundries became a later basis for private metallurgical development. Bavaria owned mines and foundries in the Palatinate. There were eight state blast furnaces in the mid-nineteenth-century Wurtemberg, and in Hanover, six. Shipbuilding was among the most advanced of the nineteenth-century manufacturing industries. Dutch shipbuilding bene-fited from the requirement that shipping companies receiving government help should buy Dutch-built ships wherever possible. But the French subsidy policy may have encouraged investment in obsolete sailing ship technology. Backward but aspirant modern states, like Spain after defeat by the USA, and Russia after defeat by the Japanese, felt obliged to acquire and support a modern shipbuild-ing industry, by subsidy when necessary. By contrast, the advanced British eco-nomy easily built Dreadnought battleships for the arms race up to the First World War, with the state operating only as buyer. As a technological or pro-ductivity 'leader', it had less need of a security-based industrial policy, and could preach laissez-faire to 'follower' economies.

State buying, like that of Spain and Russia, was a long established and vital element of national demand for advanced technology industries. Later in the twentieth century, a common argument was that civilian 'spin-offs' from such purchasing benefited—and modernized—the economy. Four major arms manu-facturers employed 2,000 men in Turin in 1862, working with the most advanced machinery. Later they were the source of skilled labour for Ansaldo and Fiat (Saul 1978: 53). The weakness of many spin-off claims is that the opportunity-cost of the resources expropriated is ignored. What useful things might these men have produced other than armaments, and how rapidly might 'raw' labour have been trained for civilian manufacture when the demand arose?

Supplementary questions are whether these favoured industries could attain a minimum efficient size merely supplying one national market, and those arising from the contractual relations with the state purchaser. Sweden's L M Ericsson, now a world player in the telecommunications market, failed to receive Swedish state telephone contracts in the later nineteenth century and was forced to look abroad, especially to Russia, for buyers. A generation earlier, Siemens had been obliged to do the same after missing out on Prussian telegraphy equipment con-tracts. An absence of national 'featherbedding' ultimately stood these companies in good stead. By contrast the Belgian state telephone company's cosy rela-tionship with the Bell Telephone Manufacturing Company raised its costs and reduced competitiveness.

15.3.3. Technology and Patents Policy

Such armaments, telecommunications, and electrical engineering companies were in the vanguard of the technological advance that is usually reckoned to drive economic growth and rising living standards. Later, policy intended to accelerate technical progress encouraged research and development expenditures, usually by large corporations, but in the nineteenth century the individual inventor generated most innovations. A classic liberal industrial policy was therefore protection of technological property rights with patents.

Nineteenth-century Netherlands and Switzerland took a free ride on the innovative efforts of those in larger countries to the advantage of some of their manufacturers. Switzerland lacked any patent law until 1887, and thereafter left all processes unprotected (covering only inventions that could be represented by a model). Because German firms were unable to patent their processes in Switzerland, the Swiss chemical industry could employ German technology without payment in the production of speciality dyes. The Netherlands lacked any patent law at all from 1869 to 1910. This helped the Jurgens brothers develop a French process for the manufacture of margarine after 1870. It was also very useful for Gerard Philips, who established an incandescent lamp factory at Eindhoven in 1891, making essentially Edison's carbon filament lamp with only minor modifications. By 1913 he was one of the largest manufacturers in Europe. One element in his success was that in the early years he was the only maker in Western Europe not burdened with royalty payments to Swan/Edison (Schiff 1971).

Since Britain was a signatory of international patent agreements from the first, British experience was very different. British dyestuffs lobbyists worried about German blocking patents before the First World War. But Germany also had its problems. Aluminium manufacture in Germany made little progress before 1914 because of difficulties in upholding the patents for the Herault process against the claims of a less efficient American technology. So the AEG group, which owned the Herault patents, established their plant at the Rhine Falls in Switzerland where all process patents for aluminium were ineffective. Once domestic technical progress in these sectors became self-sustaining in the early twentieth century, both Switzerland and the Netherlands chose to join the International Patent Agreement so as to gain protection for their own technologies (Saul 1978: 55–6).

15.3.4. *Trade Controls as an Industrial Policy Instrument*

Another influence on the location of European industry was trade controls. These reduced international specialization and thus constrained productivity. Tariffs, rather than subsidies, were more highly favoured instruments of nineteenth-century industrial policy simply because they did not consume tax revenues but brought money into state treasuries. Moreover those who appeared to bear their burden were foreigners.

If we are to assess the impact of trade controls on industry, we must be able to measure tariff barriers, but that is no unambiguous matter, as discussed in Chapter 1. Table 15.1 adopts the simplest approach, the ratio of tariff revenues

TABLE 15.1. *Average European tariffs, 1860 and 1910*
(revenue/imports)

	1860	1910
Austria Hungary	0.157	0.060
Belgium	0.031	0.015
France	0.071	0.082
Germany	*	0.074
Italy	0.071	0.077
Netherlands	0.016	0.004
Portugal	*	0.229
Russia	0.214	0.278
Sweden	0.121	0.090
Spain	*	0.169
UK	0.109	0.049

Source: Calculated from Mitchell (1980) and UK *Statistical Abstract for Foreign Countries* (various).

to the value of imports.[2] The higher were tariffs and subsidies the more resources were switched to the protected sector and away from less privileged industries. Under conditions of constant returns to scale and full information any such reallocation must lower productivity. Does historical experience suggest there were market failures that would warrant such diversions?

Table 15.1 shows the richest countries, Britain, Belgium, and the Netherlands maintained low tariffs, and the poorest economies in Europe, Portugal and Russia, were the most protected.[3] Possibly the causal direction of policy ran from level of development, to availability of alternative taxes, to use made of tariffs, rather than from high tariffs to low productivity. But matching export taxes were an alternative policy for a poor country that was rarely tried because domestic interest groups would be penalized. In the years immediately after independence Greece employed export taxes, but dropped them as lobbies became more organized. Spain's falling behind between 1900 and 1930 stemmed from increasing insulation from the outside world and competition, consistent with protective industrial policies being harmful to living standards. Other things being equal, the damage of protectionism is usually less in a big country, measured by area and population such as Russia, than in a small country, such as Portugal. In the large economy there is a greater free trade area, and hence more competition behind the tariff walls.

[2] This approach can be misleading when tariffs are so high on selected products that they exclude virtually all imports in these categories, while allowing other products in virtually free. Under these conditions the ratio of tariff revenue to import value is low. However, as the Portuguese case study shows, in 1892 the ratio of tariff revenue to import value at 0.32 was close to the average tariff of 0.34. Federico and Tena (1998) show that trade weighted and unweighted duties in Italy were very similar.
[3] A statistical analysis (Foreman-Peck 1995b) suggests that Spain might have raised output per head by perhaps one-fifth if it had adopted tariffs at British levels.

15.4. WARS AND WORLD DEPRESSION: THE SPREAD OF INTERVENTIONISM

The continuity of many national European industrial policies was fractured in 1914. World war and a world depression indelibly marked policies with interventionism by the 1930s. Military demands and bankruptcy of large employers, coupled with a discrediting of free markets, raised the proportion of national income that the state directly influenced. Nationalism continued to be such a pervasive basis for industrial policy as to be taken for granted and nationalist policy-makers sometimes imitated each other. Like other European countries, the newly independent Republic of Ireland expanded industrial employment and reduced exports during the 1930s by adopting strongly protectionist policies favoured by economic nationalists everywhere. Import quotas assumed prominence as policy instruments in the early 1930s because, with falling prices, tariffs could not be guaranteed to secure the desired quantity of imports. The quotas remained when more prosperous times returned. Whereas tariffs allowed more imports as an economy grew, quotas permitted no such elasticity and were therefore more pernicious in their effects.

The collapse of the nineteenth-century liberal economic order in a welter of trade and currency controls was matched by political changes. Dictatorships in Germany, Italy, perhaps Portugal, Spain, and Russia aimed at economic control by governments, but so did democratic France. While private property and peace persisted, dictators' industrial policies were unlikely to differ markedly from those that might be pursued by a corporatist democracy. In Soviet Russia during the 1930s private property was virtually abolished and Stalin's industrial policy, based on central direction rather than markets, was therefore far more draconian than elsewhere. Wealthier countries were more likely to be policy leaders but strong ideology—in the case of Russia between 1917 and 1991 or perhaps Portugal in the mid-twentieth century—could still allow policy-makers to eschew the example of their richer neighbours. The Soviet avoidance of the Great Depression that began in 1929 added prestige to central planning as an industrial policy, and encouraged milder imitations later. In Southern Europe Mussolini's IRI holding company for large bankrupt manufacturers, bailed out by the state in the 1930s, became the model for Franco's INI, at the core of Spanish industrial policy from the 1940s for a generation.

More liberal states tried to deal with the impact of the world economic crisis by moral suasion, rather than by nationalization. Thus the Belgian government put pressure on the Société Générale to save the bankrupt car maker Minerva, and the formally independent Bank of England began an anaemic interventionist industrial policy to prevent the Labour government of 1929–31 from taking more forceful action.

Electricity in the early twentieth century, like steel in the later nineteenth century, was a basic industry for any state that aspired to military independence. That electricity transmission and distribution networks, like railways, looked as if they were natural monopolies, offered another reason for state intervention, often at the municipal level. Lenin's famous 1920 claim to the All-Russia Congress of Soviets 'Communism is Soviet Power plus electrification of the whole country' reflected the belief in a number of states that industrial development and competitiveness required the full exploitation of the new power source.

The European legacy of the traumatic period 1914 to 1945, or perhaps to 1953,[4] was a far greater role for the state in directing national resources. Industry was affected both intentionally and unintentionally by the extension of governmental economic power. Industrial policy in the Soviet Union remains an exception to the preceding rule, since by the end of the 1930s there was little economic space that the state had not already occupied. In Britain and France, greater social spending went hand in hand with higher peacetime military outlays after 1945 as they tried to resume their traditional roles as world powers. The 'displacement effect' of the war is most apparent in these, the most heavily taxed, countries. Their defence industries, especially aircraft and shipbuilding, accordingly gained. Britain also gave specific help to cotton and nationalized a considerable proportion of industry. Ambitious state finance for investment in France under the Monnet Plan was as nationalistic as any earlier policy, an attempt to restore France to pre-eminence in Western Europe. The German Federal Republic's policy was not so different in intention. But unlike France, Germany showed no tax increase as a proportion of income, because central and local taxes in 1938 were already so high.

Generally, subsidies in all countries tended to fall by 1950, though their course was more erratic in Greece and Ireland. The Italian state by 1950 controlled 80% of shipbuilding, 40% of rolling stock production, 60% of pig iron, and 43% of steel, mainly as an inter-war period inheritance. Unlike Britain's newly nationalized industries, Italy's state enterprises were run as if they were separate private businesses, and priced accordingly (UNECE 1953: 69, 76, 266–7).

15.5. THE GREAT POST-WAR BOOM: THE HUBRIS OF INDUSTRIAL POLICY

During the third quarter of the twentieth century, until the oil crises 1973/4 and 1979/80, the European economies boomed and each became increasingly open. International capital, trade and migration flows increased and the scope for independent national economic policies was apparently circumscribed. Moreover, the cost of military and defence-related technologies—jet aircraft, computers, nuclear reactors—soared. All these pressures were strong reasons for European cooperation and coordination. At one level, the 1957 Treaty of Rome and subsequent enlargements of the Community were recognition of these facts. Yet

---

[4] The later date allows the inclusion of the Berlin Blockade, the beginning of the Cold War, and the Korean War as economically traumatic events that should be included with the World Wars and the Great Depression.

TABLE 15.2. *Relative labour productivity in manufacturing* (UK = 100)

	France	Germany	Italy	Netherlands	Sweden
1913	79	119	59	—	102
1938	76	107	49	117	100
1973	114	119	95	133	128
1989	115	105	111	128	121

Source: Calculated from Broadberry (1994).

national industrial policies remained distinctive and far more pervasive than ever before in peace. The nation state was still paramount. European institutions and policies, such as the Coal and Steel Community, were generally means for the pursuit of national objectives (Milward 1992). Hence the history of European industrial policy, to which the case studies in this book are a contribution, may be written hardly noticing Europe as a political entity, at least until the drive for the Single European Market, as will be discussed below.[5]

It was the United States that favoured a single European market with supranational institutions as a bulwark to hold back Soviet influence (Hogan 1987; Foreman-Peck 1995*a*: 245–8). To ensure that Marshall Aid was spent in accordance with US intentions, the first European organizations after the Second World War were brought into existence; the Organisation for European Economic Cooperation (later the OECD) and the European Payments Union. Thereafter a succession of treaties widened and deepened supranational arrangements in Western Europe. Formally, these treaties curtailed industrial policy powers of national governments but, in practice, national policies and policy objectives were awarded priority. European industrial policies could serve those ends on occasion though, when they were convenient means of defusing domestic, as well as international, conflicts.

15.5.1. *The European Coal and Steel Community*

Purely national policies came closest to the self-defeating 'prisoners' dilemma' where European coal and iron-ore resources were concerned. Map 15.1 clearly shows the conflict between European national boundaries, on the one hand, and geology and economics, on the other. A supranational coal and steel community was the obvious answer—if almost a century of hostility on different sides of frontiers could be put aside. In 1950, the French Foreign Minister, Robert Schuman, advanced a proposal that did exactly that: 'The French Government proposes that the entire French–German production of coal and steel be placed under a common High Authority, in an organization open to the participation

---

[5] More detail on the European Union is to be found in Artis and Lee (1994) and El-Agraa (1994).

of the other countries of Europe.' The treaty that created the European Coal and Steel Community (ECSC) was less satisfactory than the political rhetoric. Article 17 was contradictory in a manner that was to become a distinctive feature of European Union policy. The Community was to 'eliminate the falsification of competitive conditions' at the same time as enforcing identical delivery terms, equalizing wages, and introducing common working conditions (Gillingham 1991: 240).

Under certain conditions, the ECS High Authority could impose minimum prices, determine production quotas, and order import restrictions. Supposedly the Authority enforced competition, but this commitment was honoured more in the breach than in the observance. The Authority never managed to dismantle the Ruhr coal cartel under Article 65 of the treaty, nor was it able to put an end to collusive practices in the steel industries (Spierenberg and Poidevin 1994: 653). Government subsidies were 'supervised' and mergers and agreements among companies required Authority approval. Through control of investment, the Authority was empowered to develop a 'sound' structure for the industry. Only two cross-border businesses were formed however; Arbed (Luxemburg/ Saar/Lorraine) and Estel (German/Dutch, which proved merely temporary). Nonetheless, when the Authority finally merged with the European Economic Community in 1968, it employed 1,000 staff.

What difference did the ECSC make? In an early appraisal, Diebold (1959: 574 et seq.) commented on the difficulty of discovering any influence of the Community in the investment record, which was largely determined by individual countries' recoveries. Intra-Community trade in steel nearly doubled in the four years after 1953, whereas production rose by only one-half. Intra-Community trade in non-treaty products increased by almost as much as steel however, which at first sight suggests little effect. But considering the wrangling over these coal and steel resources that had bedevilled international relations earlier, the implicit counter-factual, or base case scenario, may be too optimistic. If so, a greater impact must be ascribed to the ECSC.

15.5.2. *The European Economic Community*

Unlike the ECSC, the 1957 Treaty of Rome unambiguously embraced economic liberalism.[6] Underlying the Treaty is the doctrine that free movement of goods, services, and factors will enhance competitiveness. Industrial policy was not mentioned explicitly. Reduction of formal trade barriers between members— France, Germany, Italy, Belgium, Netherlands, and Luxembourg—was the major achievement of the early years of the Community. Britain remained outside the EEC and formed a free trade area (EFTA),[7] without a common external tariff and supranational elements of the Treaty.

---

[6] The Treaty also established the European Atomic Energy Community.
[7] The original partners with Britain were Norway, Sweden, Denmark, Switzerland, Portugal, and Austria.

Implicit in the Treaty was the proposition that markets are largely self-regulating so long as they are in their competitive, 'natural' state. The policy implications of this idea are enshrined in three Articles:

- Article 85(1) on collusive behaviour, which prohibits agreements in restraint of trade (such as price-fixing, market sharing, and restrictions on supply);
- Article 86 which prohibits the abuse of dominant position where it affects trade between Member States through the imposition of unfair trading conditions; and
- Article 92 on state aid and exceptions which asserts that distorting competition by favouring certain undertakings is incompatible with the Common Market.

Enforcement of these principles during the heyday of interventionist industrial policy was minimal and even afterwards was erratic, to say the least (Wright 1995). The Commission could not run counter to the will of the most powerful national governments (Woolcock and Wallace 1995). Through the 1970s much of the industrial subsidies went to state industries which were key policy instruments of Western European states. To attack the subsidies would have been to confront the powers behind the Commission.

In addition to sensitivity to key national governments, EC policy was subject to internal pressures and contradictions. The Industry Directorate (DG III) favoured big European companies as means of strengthening European industries and hence there was always some potential tension with DG IV.

15.5.3. Trade Controls as an Industrial Policy Instrument

The principal impact of the European Common Market in the early years was on taxes and controls on trade between Western European states. From 1958 six European countries formally surrendered their external trade policy to the European Commission, over a twelve-year transition period. Article 3 of the Treaty of Rome specifies that the European Community shall include a Common External Tariff and a Common Commercial Policy towards third countries. In the late 1950s and 1960s there were notable tariff reductions as components of Common Market ('the six') and EFTA ('the seven') policy. Intra-European trade both among the six and larger groupings of European states, such as the twelve eventual members of the EU, grew faster than total European trade (Tsoukalis 1997: 15–20; Foreman-Peck 1995a: 268–9). Although the theory of customs unions predicts only small gains from this liberalization, models based on different assumptions —scale economies and imperfect competition—generate larger benefits, more consistent with the strong industrial growth of the period.

Much of the momentum of trade liberalization immediately after 1945 actually came from the United States, one of the most protectionist countries in the world until then. Under the US-driven General Agreement on Tariffs and Trade of 1947, to which all Western European countries were signatories, import quotas were forbidden. Voluntary restraint agreements (VRAs) or voluntary export restraints (VERs) therefore began to replace unilateral quotas. These usually bilaterally negotiated arrangements were politically rather easy to implement because the restricted exporters could earn more profits. In addition they were popular with import-competing industry pressure groups. The cost to the consumer was never made public or included in the measurement of industrial support. To protect their textile industries against competition from newly industrializing countries, many European countries restricted imports through the biggest Voluntary Restraint Agreement, the Multi-Fibre Arrangement (MFA). The EC's first Multi-Fibre Arrangement was signed in 1974. Although these policies were not conducive to industrial efficiency, Brussels, or the European ideal, may have played a role in preventing even more restrictive policies within Europe. The quotas, prohibitions, and currency controls of the 1930s testify to the much greater disruption of economic life entailed by the untrammelled pursuit of national policies in the face of world demand collapse.

The USSR and rest of Eastern Europe used the state monopoly of foreign trade to achieve similar ends as these restraints and quotas. The Council for Mutual Economic Assistance (CMEA) was intended to mimic cooperative institutions in Western Europe, enhancing economic integration in the communist bloc. Soviet satellite economies had no choice but to continue with the Soviet model of industrial policy. But, like Western European states, they resisted specialization within the CMEA bloc when required to lose, rather than to gain, industrial capacity.

15.5.4. State Ownership and Purchasing as Policy Instruments

The Soviet example influenced French corporatist industrial policies in the 1950s. This was particularly so for economic planning and the Commissariat General au Plan which were at their zenith in the 1950s and 1960s. The views of Jean Monnet, the first Commissaire du Plan in 1946, on the necessity for raising business expectations of growing markets eventually spilled over into Britain in the mid-1960s. The First French Plan however was focused on heavy industry, which was largely state-owned anyway, so plan implementation merely required directives. Even during the Second Plan of 1954–7, the state wielded considerable direct influence through control of finance and fiscal incentives (Ch. 3 and e.g. Denton, Forsyth, and Maclennan 1968). Most other Western European states also had nationalized substantial proportions of industry, especially those with supposed 'natural monopoly' characteristics, like the utilities.

By the end of the 1970s, the high tide of interventionism as Figure 15.1 shows, in most of Western Europe, electricity, gas, coal, airlines, and steel were likely to be owned by the state (see also Tables 10.6–10.8). Governments held stakes in the motor industries in Austria, France, Britain, Italy, the Netherlands, and West Germany. State ownership of railways and the postal service was complete

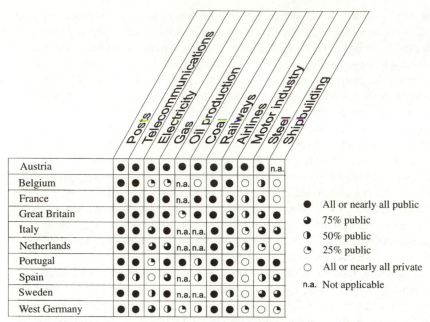

FIG. 15.1. The extent of state ownership in EU countries, 1978

in Europe, and only Spain broke the otherwise 100% nationalization of the tele-communications sector. These businesses rarely operated on commercial criteria, but were employed to achieve social and political objectives. In some countries jobs in state industry became means of rewarding party faithfuls.

National security continued to motivate a good deal of 'hi-tech' development, often by state industry, in Europe during the great post-war boom. Military tech-nology drove the costly British and French nuclear power generating industry. When the German government felt the time was ripe for their nuclear programme in the 1970s, their SNR 300 Fast Breeder Reactor lost DM 11 billion without ever entering service. Eventually privatization curtailed nuclear supply in Britain, by bringing into the open the risks and the expense of the technology.

Computers and aerospace absorbed vast sums of state money in the only two European states that still saw themselves as 'great powers' in the 1950s and 1960s, Britain and France. French computer policy was stimulated by President Johnson's refusal to allow the export of three large computers to France for mil-itary purposes. Twenty-two per cent of French state research funding in 1969 was spent on aerospace. British aircraft subsidies masqueraded as 'launch aid', but only one aircraft project ever managed to repay the aid from subsequent sales (Whitley 1976).

The enormous fixed costs of product development in aerospace singled out the sector as an obvious candidate for transnational collaboration. In the East there was the USSR's cooperation in R & D with its Warsaw Pact allies. A more equal distribution of the burdens and the benefits was specified in the Anglo-

French project, the supersonic commercial airliner, Concorde, begun in 1960. A remarkable technological achievement, the enterprise was commercially misconceived.[8] But at the same time the Americans spent an almost similar sum to that disbursed by Britain or France on a similar development and failed to end up with an operational aircraft at all (Gardner 1981: 266–77). Germany also had its Concorde, the VFW 614. By the time the project was cancelled, the German taxpayer had paid around DM 1 billion.

15.5.5. Formulas for Failure and Success

For all transnational cooperative ventures, the challenges of agreeing product specification, location of work, cost control, and charging were formidable. Cancelling transnational ventures that proved too expensive was more difficult than abandoning purely national projects. European governments did not see cooperative projects—Euratom, Concorde, Tornado—as alternatives to national projects but as means of strengthening domestic capabilities (Ergas 1992). Therefore each country had to receive from each programme an equivalent to what had been contributed. This requirement raised production costs, as the Airbus amply demonstrated.[9] Airbus, Concorde, and the Tornado were assembled in all partner countries. The duplication that cooperative ventures were intended to eliminate, remained.

Where elements of industrial policies after 1945 seem to have been most successful, in the Netherlands (the development of Schipol airport and Rotterdam port) and in Italy (Mattei and Sinigaglia in the 1950s), management was allowed a free hand and operated according to commercial criteria. In Mark Casson's terms (Ch. 14), there was sufficient trust not to hamper management with the range of checks and controls more typical of state enterprise in Europe.

Big projects, identified by government agencies and carried out by national champions have been very costly indulgences in all countries adopting this approach. Why then bother with state initiatives at all? Historical accident may explain, but not warrant, such policies. If some markets are absent or incomplete, a justification might be found. The commercial success of the British government-initiated Export Credit Guarantee Department in the 1930s, and after 1945, the 3i's, and predecessor investment banks or sources of enterprise capital, specifically intended to bridge an institutional gap, could support such an interpretation.

---

[8] Gardner puts the development costs of the project over 14 years at £1,000 million, 500% more than the 1962 estimate. By 1971 the Americans had spent $1,000 million on their aborted supersonic transport project. Together with the Advanced Gas Cooled nuclear reactor the financial loss to the UK from Concorde amounted to more than $20 billion in 1990 prices, or nearly two years of all British R & D expenditure in the late 1980s, according to Ergas (1992).

[9] Manufacture began with the two fuselage sections and the vertical tail stabilizer made in six MBB factories in Germany. MBB then added the cockpit, the front and the central fuselage sections manufactured in four French factories. Seven other consortium factories supplied components for the wings, assembled by British Aerospace together with Spanish inputs. All the pieces were then sent to France for final assembly and Germany was able to insist on a separate German assembly line for the A320.

However, much European industrial policy has not been designed to compensate for missing markets or institutions, or even for big high-technology projects,
but has been reactive (when not 'accidental' like the French nationalization
of Renault after the Second World War). The recession following the first oil
crisis in the mid-1970s brought widespread state intervention in European
industry, just as in the 1930s. The classic reactive policies of the 1970s concerned the car industry. The numbers of independent car makers had fallen as European integration proceeded. As in many industries, adjustment to the oil shocks,
and the ensuing higher energy prices and lower growth rates, proved difficult
for the survivors. Volkswagen nearly foundered in the early 1970s but the West
German government cemented a consensus strategy that permitted recovery. This
rescue perhaps marks an exception to generalizations about the adverse impact
of state bailouts. The same can hardly be said of the creation of BL in the late
1960s and subsequent nationalization, widely hailed as a disaster for the British industry. Though supported by the government, the merger may well have
occurred anyway (if it had not been blocked by pro-competitive merger legislation), but that was not true of the later rescue.

15.5.6. The Politics of Industrial Support

Reactive policies such as these, in principle, can be justified by public opinion
(or whatever are the most powerful political forces in a society) only being willing to tolerate so much pain in the name of market freedom. There will always
be a point beyond which the willingness to accept the laws, customs, and conventions on which markets depend, breaks down. At that juncture, the conventional prescriptions of welfare economics cease to be relevant, and pure politics
takes over. In short, reactive policies might sometimes be warranted to maintain
public support for a market economy (Jacquemin 1984: 7). Or they might be justified
by the supposed difficulty that market economies have in coping with change
that is not gradual.[10] The closure of a dominant firm in a region undoubtedly has
substantial short-run multiplier effects through its backward linkages to labour
and component or raw material markets. A shutdown may also create considerable havoc through forward linkages to buyers (as was predicted if British
Leyland were allowed to collapse, Ch. 2).

In practice lobbying typically pushed industrial policy far beyond the limits
indicated by the foregoing arguments. Regional conglomerations of firms may
have influenced the policy response. Unemployment resulting from adverse
shocks to a particular industry will be concentrated and encourage protests. Close
proximity of a large number of firms facing similar problems will reduce the
costs of organizing a lobby. So regionally dispersed German textiles received
little industrial support in the face of intense foreign competition, in marked

---

[10] Those who favour the 'big bang' approach for the transition economies of Eastern Europe of course are not
in this group, but the evidence accumulating does not support them.

contrast to concentrated German coal. British cotton textile firms in the late 1940s were generally located in close proximity to each other in Lancashire, and were the subject of special legislation. (Russian textiles were also regionally concentrated and still received no special assistance, but more than one variable determines industrial support.)

The essential drawback of reactive industrial policies is moral hazard; if governments are expected to bail out, or nationalize, large firms in difficulties, managements and workforces may become slacker, requiring increasing subsidies and more rescues. When enormous businesses demanded subsidies, as they did in the 1970s, the burden on state budgets could become impossibly heavy.

15.6. THE NEMESIS OF INDUSTRIAL POLICY: EUROSCLEROSIS?

After spectacular growth of output and productivity in the 1950s and 1960s, industrial expansion in Western Europe slowed. The oil shocks of the 1970s were transitory reasons for deceleration. Some loss of momentum after post-war reconstruction was inevitable. But the rise of Japan and other competitors in the Far East, together with the continuing industrial lead by the United States, triggered concerns that the European slow down was excessive.

Very few of the largest European firms were particularly competitive in world markets by the 1980s. Instead they were 'sleepy giants', according to critics. Inevitably European industrial policies were accused of braking industrial change, for much more was being spent than ever before. German economic success allowed huge outlays on industrial subsidies. Before 1914 subsidies paid to German companies were less than 0.01% of NNP. By the 1930s the figure had risen to 0.3–0.5% and by the end of the great post-war boom expenditure reached some 2% of NNP, tilted markedly towards 'sunset industries' (Ch. 4 this volume; Giersch, Paque, and Schmeiding 1992).

At the same time some governments began to have doubts about the pay-offs from nurturing 'national champions'. Those believing that their 'champions' would repay favours or fulfil political obligations and behave differently from other firms should have been disabused of any such notion during the first oil crisis. Then France and Britain put pressure on 'their' oil companies to give their respective countries privileged access to now scarcer oil, but the businesses impartially rationed all their customers according to past consumption (Keohane 1984: 223). These firms were transnational and needed to keep a number of governments happy, not just those where their head offices were based.

15.6.1. Deindustrialization and Unemployment

A 'national champions' policy was no solution either to the rising unemployment that went hand in hand with fewer manufacturing jobs (Figs. 15.2 and

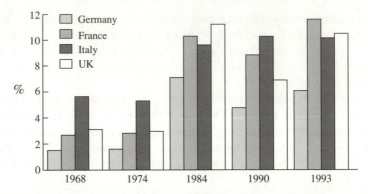

FIG. 15.2. Standardized unemployment rates, 1968–1993

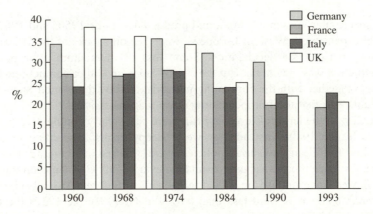

FIG. 15.3. Employment in manufacturing as a percentage of civilian employment, 1960–1993

15.3). In the 1980s Germany, France, and Italy, as well as Britain, employed a smaller proportion of their workforces in manufacturing than in the 1960s and experienced far higher unemployment—rates not seen since the 1930s. In the USA, a similarly timed structural break showed different characteristics: the stagnation or decline of unskilled wages.

Other shared European and world trends, also often linked in debate, were a rising ratio of trade to GDP and a decline in the share of manufacturing in total employment. Between 1968 and 1984 the expanding industries in the seven largest OECD countries were services, led by financial services, and technologically sophisticated manufacturing, particularly computers, telecommunications, and semiconductor equipment. Japan and the USA moved into these 'sunrise' sectors most rapidly, while France, Germany, and Britain followed at a medium pace. The purging of Britain's manufacturing industry with the rising exchange rate

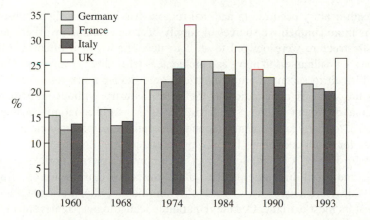

FIG. 15.4. Imports of goods and services as a percentage of GDP, 1960–1993

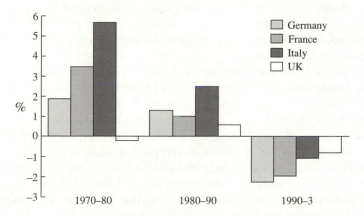

FIG. 15.5. Growth of manufacturing value added, 1970–1993

and tight money of 1980–1, gave the UK the second greatest structural change after Japan (OECD 1992).

In the European Union as a whole in the mid-1990s less than one worker in five was employed in manufacturing. For those who saw manufacturing as the fountainhead of prosperity, this last development was ominous. When associated with an absolute fall in manufacturing output for long periods, as in Britain, the trend was especially worrying. In the recession that began around 1990, manufacturing value added declined in the four largest Western European economies (Fig. 15.5). This is a large part of the explanation for the 1994 CEC White Paper's assertion that improved competitiveness was necessary to raise employment.

For the loss of jobs, globalization was a possible culprit; import penetration was considerably higher in the 1980s than in the 1960s (Fig 15.4). What in the nineteenth century occurred in national regions was now striking at sub-continents. As more competitive sources of supply became available, workers, capital, and infrastructure were obliged to shift to new employment often in different locations. Unwillingness to move and preferences for traditional ways were increasingly difficult to sustain. Large countries could devote more resources to tempering the wind of competition to the shorn industry without immediate and substantial detriment to living standards. But as the world economy became more integrated, formerly large countries found their options increasingly circumscribed, as those for small economies had always been.

Western Europe's economic worries were however mere pinpricks compared with the industrial difficulties of Russia and the rest of Eastern Europe from the later 1980s. Here above all was a test of a non-market, interventionist, industrial policy at its most extreme. Despite remarkable technological achievements, such as the Sputnik satellite launched in 1957 and the Mir space station, Soviet industrial policy failed to deliver across a broad range either sufficiently advanced products or consumer goods in volumes comparable with those of Western Europe. Moreover the record of environmental pollution in centrally planned economies was abysmal. By 1991 the Soviet empire collapsed under the weight of its misconceived economic policies.

In the 1990s Russian industry suffered massive disruption of an extent that Western Europe only faced at the end of world wars. Comparison with British switches from war to peacetime production in the twentieth century is instructive. In the demobilization after the First World War, policy was 'back to business as usual' as fast as possible. Unemployment remained high until the next world war. After that one, controls remained in place much longer. Unemployment remained low and the industrial growth rate was unprecedentedly rapid (Ch. 2). If, as seems likely, this association is causal, the 'big bang' approach to the Russian transition was mistaken (Ch. 13). The advantages of markets over command economies are likely to be greater when the shocks to which they are subject are mild.

15.6.2. Industrial Subsidies from the 1980s

The Western European response to collapses in sectoral demands or jumps in costs continued to be industrial subsidies. Germany and Denmark offered the lowest payments to manufacturing between 1981 and 1986, though they were by no means negligible (Table 15.3). They do not include the enormous coal mining subsidy (Ch. 4). Moreover German subsidies progressively increased after this period in contrast to the trend in the rest of Europe. Reconstruction of Eastern Germany in the 1990s was burdensome but the multiple layers of German policy-makers and implementers created more deep-seated problems. Germany pursued industrial policy at three different levels—federal, state (*Länder*), and

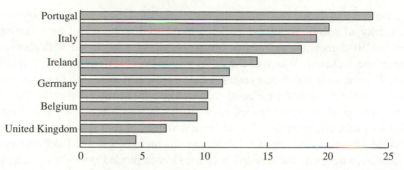

F IG. 15.6. Contribution to GDP of state-owned companies in EU countries, 1991

local. Policy-makers in each of the lower tiers supported declining industries to maintain jobs and tried to attract new employment at the expense of their neighbours. The Bavarian and the North Rhine–Westphalian state–bank–industry networks both appeared effective in this respect.

By the 1980s many manufacturing activities could afford to pick and choose their locations, especially when operating as subsidiaries of multinational companies. Hence, there was strong inter-government competition with subsidies to attract silicon chip or motor vehicle plants. These policies were 'pro-active' in contrast to the more usual 'reactive' industrial policies of European history. Probably more than 1,000 agencies in Europe competed to attract inward investment in the 1990s. Ireland's tax exemption for writers and musicians was the clearest consistent policy, but certainly not the most expensive. Britain implemented the most effective policy—in the sense that it drew in perhaps 40% of all foreign direct investment, and British policy-makers aimed for that goal. Whether intergovernmental and inter-regional competition to pay higher subsidies played much of a role is less clear. Siemens, offered a larger grant by Austria than by the United Kingdom to locate a new micro-chip plant in that country, nonetheless chose the north-east of England (*Financial Times, Survey*, 24 Oct. 1995: 1).

Subsidies were often directed at nationalized industries, which continued to account for a large proportion of GDP in most European countries. State-owned industries in Portugal and Greece produced over 20% of GDP, and France and Italy were not far behind. By contrast, Figure 15.6 shows how radically privatization altered Britain's position in 1991 relative to the 1970s. Most European governments disposed of some State assets in the 1980s, but only Britain and France (at a considerable distance) shifted the private–public industrial boundaries (Vickers and Wright 1988; 22 et seq.). The West German programme was essentially 'symbolic', and the Italians moved a labour force of only 100,000 into the private sector. Explanations for the unwillingness of much of the rest of Europe to follow the radical privatization lead include the fragility of coalition politics, and constitutional protection of state monopolies.

Even without these constraints, the initial electoral (or industrial lobbyist) un-popularity of ascetic industrial policies may need to be offset by some other 'success' if democratic politicians are to be allowed to persist with them. For Britain the Falklands War was the necessary antidote. Alternatively, conditions must deteriorate so much that voters demand radical change.[11] In the later 1990s, a strong desire to satisfy the budgetary requirements for membership of the European Monetary Union could be one motivation, as it was for Greece. The Greek Finance Minister planned to privatize 11 state firms and three or four state-controlled banks between 1998 and 1999, raising 300 billion drachmas (about £610 million) a year.

Such retrenchment was needed because Greece headed the subsidy league in the 1980s (Table 15.3). The payments reflected the operation of a weak state, large in relation to the size of the economy, the instrument of pressure groups, blocking economic growth by buying votes and with a fiscal imbalance which crowded out productive investment. In addition, the opening of the Greek mar-ket to EC imports of manufactured goods created a crisis of adjustment.

Greece was not unique, for all EC countries with smaller manufacturing sec-tors tended to offer higher subsidies, perhaps because they were more anxious to encourage them.[12] Steel was a major recipient of financial support everywhere, except in Germany and the Netherlands. Large subsidies were a disincentive to contract unprofitable activities and to search for new products and markets. Once international, and in particular Japanese, competition began to bite, the EC steel industry declined. Europeans failed to modernize adequately in the more pros-perous years before 1973 and suffered political difficulties of adjustment in the collapse after 1975. This was in part due to cartelization and restrictive practices persisting under the ECSC.

EC and national support for European steel firms had regularly provoked American anger. The United States maintained that large subsidies to EC steel exports supported unfair competition. In 1969 therefore, they placed an import quota on EC steel that expired in 1975. An even smaller quota was imposed the following year because the EC would not alter its policies. New tariffs and quotas on special steels were established in July 1983 with the overall goal of holding imports to 18.5% of the US market. EC retaliation against US restric-tions on imports followed in 1984. One more round began in January 1993, when steel subsidies triggered US antidumping duties of up to 100% on carbon steel imports from the EC.

Subsidies to Airbus Industrie seemed likely to precipitate a similar trade war over medium-range commercial jet aircraft. Airbus, a consortium of British Aerospace, Aérospatiale, Deutsche Aerospace, and Construcciones Aeronauticas SA was formed in 1970. By 1992 Airbus had captured 30% of the world mar-ket for airliners with over 100 seats. Aerospatiale and Construcciones were

---

[11] For Argentina, hyper-inflation, widespread and systematic political murders, and military defeat of military rulers proved to be catalysts.

[12] Statistical evidence of governments 'leaning against the wind'—or of an infant industry policy—is a rank correlation of –0.394. A similar result is also obtained for iron and steel alone (rank correlation –0.356).

TABLE 15.3. *Subsidy patterns in the EC, 1981–1986* (%)

	Manufacturing/GDP	Manufacturing subsidy	Steel subsidy	Steel/GDP
Germany	35.2	3.0	8.6	1.46
France	24.8	4.9	58.3	1.16
Italy	16.3	9.5	103.0	1.09
UK	27.6	3.8	57.6	0.94
Belgium	22.4	6.4	40.4	1.25
Denmark	17.8	2.8	18.0	0.20
Greece	16.7	12.9	n.a.	0.43
Ireland	30.7	7.9	107.2	0.17
Luxembourg	26.2	7.3	14.6	1.27
Netherland	17.1	4.1	4.3	0.81

Note: Columns 2 and 3 are calculated as a percentage of sector value added.

Source: Calculated from Ford and Suyker 1990; UN Industrial Statistics, EC.

TABLE 15.4. *R & D subsidies, EC and EFTA, R & D as percentage of industrial subsidies*

Germany	6.0	Netherlands	13.4
France	3.8	Portugal	1.4
Italy	2.8	Spain	2.8
UK	6.0	Austria	2.5
Belgium	2.4	Finland	12.8
Denmark	17.0	Iceland	16.4
Greece	5.3	Norway	6.5
Ireland	3.5	Sweden	8.0
Luxembourg	1.0	Switzerland	33.9

Note: EC 1986–8 av, EFTA 1984–7 av.

state-owned and each of the four partners' governments was represented on the Airbus Intergovermental committee.

The US industry and government objected to what they saw as tax-subsidized competition—with Boeing. Negotiations over this contention became increasingly acrimonious over the years 1980–8 (McGuire 1997). Yet a bilateral agreement was reached in 1992 without either side resorting to sanctions. Neither McDonnell-Douglas and Boeing nor Airbus wanted to lose the export sales that a trade war risked. They made their wishes plain to their respective governments. Since European governments wanted to reduce expenditures once Airbus was successfully launched, there was a happy convergence of interests.[13]

According to a US study, Europe lost by subsidizing the wide-bodied medium-range commercial aircraft, the Airbus A300, as a rival to the Boeing

---

[13] McGuire (1997) also invokes a European desire not to violate treaty obligations under the GATT, but that does not seem to have restrained them in other disputes.

767. Airbus competition lowered the price in that market and so conferred gains on consumers. But these benefits were insufficient to offset the subsidy paid by taxpayers (Baldwin and Krugman 1988).[14]

R & D subsidies remained a common form of industrial policy after the switch towards markets and competition in the later 1980s. EC and EFTA governments that provided lower industrial subsidy rates (Table 15.4) showed some (slight) tendency to emphasize research and development support in their total policy package. Small countries, Denmark, Switzerland, and Finland, favoured R & D subsidies over other forms. Most countries tended to focus assistance on specific new technologies: Norway and Denmark favoured biotechnology and information technology; the United Kingdom, microelectronics applications; Spanish policy favoured industrial robots among other fields; and Italy prioritized aeronautics (OECD 1986: 11–12).

The policy gains from R & D subsidies occurred in the early stages of product development and diffusion, such as in the use of computers by financial services between 1958 and 1972 or in the medical applications of scanners from 1972 to 1977. Measurement of R & D spillovers between firms and industries indicate that externalities are of major importance. But that still leaves open the questions of effectiveness and whether existing levels of state support were approximately correct.

The theoretical case for R & D subsidies is stronger than for most forms of industrial support, and they tend to be a more general industrial policy instrument, despite the national differences noted above. By contrast, sectoral support is more the concern of industry lobbyists. Lobbyists are unlikely to find general subsidies so worth pressing for; instead they push up sector- and firm-specific support. That smaller subsidizers focused more on R & D support, suggests some political systems were more prone to respond to lobbyists than others. In the 1980s fragmentation of Western European political parties was associated with higher state aid to manufacturing industry. Holding other factors constant, highly concentrated industries were apparently more successful at lobbying, but the timing of elections was irrelevant to the payment of industrial subsidies. Individual country peculiarities, associated with lax procedures and lack of transparency that made capture by business interests easy, were of greatest importance in explaining the pattern of state support (Nevens 1994). Belgium and Italy were among the countries that employed the least transparent procedures for allocating state aids.

Lack of policy transparency encouraged corruption. One cross-national measure is the World Competitiveness Report index of 'the extent to which improper practices, such as bribing and corruption, prevail in the public sphere'. This is based on surveys of between 1,800 and 3,300 managers and economic leaders in 32 countries between 1989 and 1992. A second index comes from the German

---

[14] The picture is further complicated by the payments to Boeing, for military contracts. On one interpretation such subsidies maintained a capability in civilian aircraft production, as well as in a vital defence industry. Hence, focusing only on this second function is misleading for assessing US gains and losses.

magazine *Impulse*, compiled by asking German businessmen in export trades to score countries on the basis of their experiences. The two measures are strongly correlated. Ades and Di Tella (1997) measure interventionist industrial policies by 'preferential procurement' indices and a fiscal index that shows the extent to which 'there is equal fiscal treatment for all enterprises', both from the same WCR survey. Another interventionist industrial policy index is the 1989 measure that WCR constructed from national accounts; the financial subsidy to private and public enterprises. Interventionist industrial policies and corruption were closely associated, however they are measured.[15]

15.6.3. Trade Controls and State Purchasing

Lobbying ensured that interventionist industrial policies in the form of trade controls varied markedly between Western European countries in the 1980s, despite the European common external commercial policy. VRAs on Japanese car imports in the 1980s were a clear violation of the policy. France allowed these imports no more than 3% of its car market, Italy limited imports to 2,500 cars, Spain to 1,000 cars, and Britain permitted them up to 11% of total domestic car sales. By 1988, of 261 VRAs in the world, 138 were imposed by the EC. Textiles were more regulated by VRAs than any sector in world, and, in the EC, were second only to agriculture in the extent of regulation. The most stringent restrictions were imposed on the cheapest imports. In Britain the cost of each textile job saved in 1988 was three to four times employee earnings.

International economic interdependence sometimes generated strange industrial policy spillovers. American restrictions on Japanese car imports in the 1980s allowed European exporters to charge higher prices than they would otherwise, conferring on them a very substantial gain at the expense of US consumers (Dinopoulos and Kreinen 1988).

Government procurement continued to support national defence industries or other 'strategic' suppliers, such as telecommunications. EC directives to open state purchasing to competitors from other countries seem to have been ineffective. The import content of purchases by governments of large members of the European Community was less than 4%. This form of barrier was of considerable importance, since public procurement accounted for 7–10% of Community GDP (Tsoukalis 1997: 65). 'Self-enforcement' of Commission 'fair contracting' procedures was rare; private businesses were loath to bite the hand that awarded contracts for fear that reprisals would ensure that they never received future business.

Differences in procurement policies could affect national competitiveness. British regulation of safety, pricing, basic research, and foreign direct investment created a demanding local competitive market for British pharmaceutical firms

---

[15] Statistical purists might object that the indices are only ordinal scale measures for which non-parametric techniques are appropriate, not ordinary least squares regression and Pearson correlation.

from the 1960s, training them in the necessary skills for international competitiveness. By contrast French pharmaceutical policy protected the local market and French firms therefore lost out internationally (Thomas 1994). Unusually, the Swedish Public Procurement Act required state tenders to be genuinely open to foreign businesses. This state recognition that a small country must specialize, and cannot hope to supply efficiently the full range of products, accounts for low prices in telecoms and electricity; 'the importance of this act for public sector efficiency and thus for Swedish welfare, can hardly be exaggerated' (Hjalmarsson 1991).

Undeterred by the expense and cost overruns of state cooperative ventures which they had not sanctioned, the European Commission tried to extend European technological cooperation. They sponsored pre-competitive research with the ESPIRIT programme of 1984, awarding very little funding. Similar programmes in other areas followed: Research in Advance Communications for Europe (RACE) and Basic Research in Industrial Technologies for Europe (BRITE). A possible drawback of such programmes however was the creation of European standards that could act as barriers more effective than the Common External Tariff.

15.6.4. The Single European Market and After

A wider market would enhance competitiveness and common voluntary standards, for instance on safety, could increase the effectiveness of cross-border trade as a stimulus to efficiency. But national standards—for electrical equipment, pharmaceuticals, and food—can be major barriers to transnational competition. They may also be an effective weapon of competition—by denying competitors access to networks for instance. The European Commission therefore faced a dilemma. If they tried to impose their own standards, they were in danger of creating 'angry orphans'—standards without business 'parents' and thus which no firms wished to use. On the other hand, a single European market would never be a reality if standards were not harmonized, as the 1985 White Paper on the single market acknowledged (CEC 1985). In the case of pharmaceuticals, firms interested in a position in the world's largest market, the United States, were bound to adopt US standards as a minimum, regardless of those of their country of origin. The Commission therefore attempted to achieve only mutual recognition of national standards. But the complexity and volume of business in enforcement of deregulation meant that officials needed to rely on greater transparency and on 'self-enforcing' regulations; those where for instance aggrieved firms themselves took legal action against governments not adhering to EC regulations.

During the 1980s the European Commission increasingly favoured competition and deregulation. But even when liberalization and privatization gained some momentum in Europe at the national level as a response to insupportable levels of public expenditure and debt, EC policies were obliged to bend pragmatically during recessions, such as that of the early 1990s. Pro-competition decisions in the cases of Rover, Perrier, and De Havilland remained exceptions (Menon and Hayward 1996). The Commission blocked a proposed De Haviland–Aérospatiale merger on the grounds that the French company would attain a dominant position by acquiring the Canadian small aircraft manufacturer. Nestlé tried to make the takeover of Perrier more palatable to the competition authorities by selling their Volvic brand. But the Competition Directorate, DG IV, argued that the proposed customer would create a position of 'joint dominance'. The British government was eventually forced to recover some of the 'sweeteners' paid to British Aerospace in return for taking the then state-owned Rover company off their hands. But these were unusual interferences. More common was the blind eye, as for instance turned to the French government's paying massive subsidies to Air France in 1996.

The Single European Market programme created a renewed interest in European-wide merger policy, in part through the accelerated tendency of European business to merge. In 1989/90 the 1,000 largest EC firms engaged in 622 mergers, 41.3% of them within the EC (Tsoukalis 1997: 82). Mergers came to be regulated late in Member States and at the European level. Britain only controlled mergers in 1965 and West Germany in 1973. By 1989 a division of competence was agreed between DG IV and Member States and in September 1990 the Commission proposal for regulating mergers and takeovers came into force. Of the 398 mergers notifiable to the Commission in the first five years, only four were forbidden.

What did the Single Market achieve? The Cecchini Report (CEC 1988) predicted a 4.5% higher GDP thanks to greater utilization of economies of scale, but the margin of error was likely to be large, especially since the research was financed by a Commission interested in showing big gains. Most of the measures proposed by the 1985 White Paper were in fact implemented, albeit with delays, and national differences of interpretation.

A number of the Commission's industrial policy White Papers tried to continue the 'deepening' of the European market in the 1990s. 'Industrial Policy in an Open and Competitive Environment' in 1990 originated in fears of declining European competitiveness. The White Paper necessarily tried to balance federalism and subsidiarity; the EC was only to become involved if the Member States' policies were ineffective or harmful to others. A very large number of areas were touched on, but all of them more symbolically than to achieve genuine change.

The term 'competitiveness' of CEC White Papers in 1994 (CEC 1994*a*, 1994*b*, 1994*c*) was less contentious than 'industrial policy'. Investment in tangible and intangible assets was to be promoted, transnational cooperative networks of firms were to be encouraged, fair competition would be ensured and public authorities were to be modernized. Small- and medium-sized enterprises were to be promoted through enterprise networks. But the main policy instruments remained in the hands of national governments which, on the basis of past experience, would continue to do what they considered expedient.

15.7. CONCLUSION

The supply of national European industrial policies of an interventionist kind has been constrained by the size and the level of development of the economy. A small country cannot hope to develop all industries and therefore is more likely—or at least has a greater need—than a large one to adopt outward-looking policies. With the globalization of the world economy, most countries are becoming 'small' in the sense that they must conform more closely to world market pressures.

The national level of development limits the feasible options by determining the available resources for intervention. Moreover a poor country cannot afford the large and efficient civil service needed to implement sophisticated policies involving tax concessions and planning. Throughout the nineteenth century, European national governments shaped industrial development—some more than others, and positively or negatively. But their tax bases were small and their desire to maintain the external value of their currency constrained state expenditure. The currency stability that joining the gold standard 'club' conferred, allowed poorer countries, such as Russia, access to foreign investment on a considerable scale. But it should not be forgotten that this was also a period of massive emigration from Europe. The most successful governments facilitated trade, investment, and interdependence. Other forces, such as language and custom, pulled in the opposite direction of economic nationalism. In the twentieth century, the greater contribution of legislation, taxation, subsidies, and state procurement to forming and maintaining custom, suggests the European distribution of industry has diverged more strongly from the pattern that would have pertained without those national policies.

Over the last hundred years or so, the instruments of European industrial policy have proliferated, and as the power of the state to raise taxes has increased, so too has expenditure on industrial support. Liberal industrial policy was, and is, distinguished by lacking specific policy objectives, such as security, or status, but instead attempting to create the framework or 'landscape'— for instance by establishing and enforcing property rights—which better allows industry to flourish. The most successful state-initiated activities have been those where they fill a gap in the market and management operates independently within commercial budget constraints. For both of these, the demand and the supply of industrial policy typically originate with political elites, rather than business. Grand projects, also initiated by governments, with long gestation periods during which no commercial monitoring is possible, have the greatest possibilities for becoming expensive mistakes.

With the formation of the European Community, the struggle for the control of industrial policy widened. Those such as the French and, before the 1980s, the British, who favoured 'national champions', vied in Brussels with the Germans and others who asserted that competition policy was the only industrial policy needed. In practice, as the different national quotas on Japanese car imports demonstrated, national interests continued to dominate a Community-wide industrial policy of considerable significance.

The greatest contribution of Brussels, or the European ideal, to industry is what has not happened in Western Europe over the last half century. That is the return to the general 'beggar my neighbour' industrial policies of the 1930s. Supranational European institutions have supported harmonization and dispute resolution, even though they have not eliminated reactive policies.[16] Anyway a case for such policies can sometimes be made in order to preserve the market from political reactions, when there are great unanticipated shifts in demand or in costs. Certainly that explains some European industrial policies. Confronted by wars, or oil or wheat price shocks, there is a demand for industrial policy from industry and the workforce. Governments try to ease, and sometimes direct, the transition to the new industrial equilibrium. Policy expenditures prove hard to maintain and, after some years, they are run down.

Institutions that accelerate this process are desirable. The 'tapered' subsidy, employed in Britain's railway privatization, may be worth extending to other cases where a state has incurred industrial financial obligations from which it wishes to withdraw. Such a scheme sends business clear signals as to how it should plan for the future and, to the extent that the taper is credible, gives an incentive to improve efficiency.

Scope remains for restrictions on 'sweeteners' to attract footloose plants to the competing economies of Europe. Competition in providing commercially better environments is much preferable to competition in subsidies. Where transnational projects for immensely expensive products like aircraft are concerned, it would be desirable to widen the areas over which states bargain. If three states cooperate over three aircraft, agreement on one nation each producing the lion's share of one aircraft would lower costs below those incurred when each economy shares equally in the production of all three. Of course this is easier said than done.

In 'landscaping' industrial policy, privatization and liberalization have spread only very slowly to continental Western Europe and Ireland. If these policies are effective, as many economists believe, then we must predict an improvement in British industrial performance relative to much of the rest of Western Europe over the next decade or more.

Future industrial policy will be less focused on the manufacturing sector. Manufacturing will account for a diminishing share of jobs, not (necessarily) because of 'Eurosclerosis' or other diseases, but because of rising productivity and consumers' tastes (Rowthorn and Wells 1987). As incomes rise, the demand for services will continue to expand disproportionately. This effect will be reinforced

---

[16] Of course the European Common Market is not unique in this respect. The North American Free Trade Area performs a similar function.

by productivity increases in manufacturing continuing to reduce the man hours needed to produce a given output more rapidly than in other sectors.[17]

Monetary union may well increase the demand for interventionist industrial policy. Unforeseen collapses of demand or price hikes in different parts of the new monetary area, no longer met by national monetary policy, could release pressure for subsidies to save jobs in particular firms or industries. How strong that force is will depend on the overall buoyancy of the European economy. Eastern Europe's new found faith in markets is likely to be tested if the economies continue to be traumatized by demand shocks, and politically sensitive industrial responses could be necessary to avoid apostasy.

---

[17] Even jobs in manufacturing are no longer what they seem; their classification can be arbitrary. In Siemens more than half of employment was indirect in 1997 and therefore could be considered as in services. But since Siemens is a manufacturing company, these jobs were classified as manufacturing (Freund *et al.* 1997 cited in Tomlinson 1997).

REFERENCES

ADES, A., and DI TELLA, R. (1997). 'National champions and corruption: Some unpleasant interventionist arithmetic'. *Economic Journal*, 107: 1023–42.

ARTIS, M., and LEE, N. (1994). *The Economics of the European Union: Policy and Analysis.* Oxford: Oxford University Press.

BALDWIN, R. E., and KRUGMAN, P. R. (1988). 'Industrial policy and international competition in wide-bodied jet aircraft', in R. E. Baldwin (ed.), *Trade Policy Issues and Empirical Analysis*. Chicago: University of Chicago Press.

BATSON, H. E. (1933). *The Price Policies of German Public Utility Undertakings.* London: Oxford University Press.

BROADBERRY, S. (1994). 'Technological leadership and productivity leadership in manufacturing since the Industrial Revolution: Implications for the convergence debate'. *Economic Journal*, 104: 291–302.

CEC (Commission of the European Communities) (1985). *Completing the Internal Market: White Paper from the Commission to the European Council.* Luxembourg: Office for Official Publications of the European Communities.

—— (1988). 'The Economics of 1992'. *European Economy* 35.

—— (1990). *Industrial Policy in an Open and Competitive Environment.* Com(90) 556. Brussels: CEC.

—— (1994a). *Growth Competitiveness, Employment: The Challenges and Ways Forward into the 21st Century.* White Paper. Brussels: CEC.

—— (1994b) *Integrated Programmes in Favour of SME's and the Craft Sectors.* Com(94) 207. Brussels: CEC.

—— (1994c) *An Industrial Competitiveness Policy for the European Union.* Com(94) 319. Brussels: CEC.

DENTON, G., FORSYTH, M., and MACLENNAN, M. (1968). *Economic Planning and Policies in Britain, France and Germany.* London: for PEP by Allen and Unwin.

DIEBOLD, W. (1959). *The Schuman Plan: A Study in Economic Cooperation 1950–1959*. New York: Praeger.

DINOPOULOS, E., and KREINEN, M. (1988). 'The effects of the US–Japan auto VER on European prices and US welfare'. *Review of Economics and Statistics*, 484–91.

DOBBIN, F. (1994). *Forging Industrial Policy: The United States, Britain and France in the Railway Age*. Cambridge: Cambridge University Press.

EL-AGRAA, A. M. (1994). *The Economics of the European Community*, 4th edn. Hemel Hempstead: Harvester-Wheatsheaf.

ERGAS, H. (1992). 'A future for mission-oriented industrial policies? A critical review of developments in Europe'. OECD unpublished.

Financial Times (1995). Survey 'Business Location in Europe'. 24 Oct.

FEDERICO, G., and TENA, A. (1998). 'Was Italy a protectionist country?'. *European Review of Economic History*, 2: 73–97.

FORD, R., and SUYKER, W. (1990). 'Industrial subsidies in OECD economies'. *OECD Economic Studies*, 15 (Autumn): 37–80.

FOREMAN-PECK, J. (1995a). *A History of the World Economy: International Economic Relations since 1850*. Hemel Hempstead: Harvester-Wheatsheaf.

—— (1995b). 'A model of later nineteenth century European development'. *Revista de Historia Economica*, 13: 441–71.

GARDNER, C. (1981). *British Aircraft Corporation: A History*. London: Batsford.

GERSCHENKRON, A. (1962). *Economic Backwardness in Historical Perspective*. Cambridge, Mass.: Harvard University Press.

GIERSCH, H., PAQUE, K.-H., and SCHMEIDING, H. (1992). *The Fading Miracle: Four Decades of Market Economy in Germany*. Cambridge: Cambridge University Press.

GILLINGHAM, J. (1991). *Coal, Steel and the Rebirth of Europe 1945–1955*. Cambridge: Cambridge University Press.

HJALMARSSON, L. (1991). 'The Scandinavian model of industrial policy', in M. Blostrom and P. Meller (eds.), *Diverging Paths: Comparing a Century of Scandinavian and Latin American Economic Development*. Washington, DC: Inter American Development Bank.

HOGAN, M. J. (1987). *The Marshall Plan*. Cambridge: Cambridge University Press.

JACQUEMIN, A. (1984). *European Industry: Public Policy and Corporate Strategy*. Oxford: Clarendon Press.

KEOHANE, R. O. (1984). *After Hegemony: Cooperation and Discord in the World Political Economy*. New Jersey: Princeton University Press.

KRUGMAN, P. R. (1991). *Geography and Trade*. Cambridge, Mass.: MIT Press.

MCGUIRE, S. (1997). *Airbus Industrie: Conflict and Cooperation in US–EC Trade Relations*. London: Macmillan.

MENON, A., and HAYWARD, J. (1996). 'State industrial policies and the European Union', in H. Kassim and A. Menon (eds.), *The European Union and National Industrial Policy*. London: Routledge.

MILWARD, A. (1992). *The European Rescue of the Nation State*. London: Routledge.

—— and BRENNAN, G. (1996). *Britain's Place in the World: A Historical Enquiry into Import Controls 1945–1960*. London: Routledge.

MITCHELL, B. R. (1980). *Abstract of European Historical Statistics*. London: Macmillan.

NEVEN, D. (1994). 'The political economy of state aids in the European Community: Some econometric evidence'. *CEPR Discussion Paper*, 945.

OECD (1986). *Industrial Policies, Developments and Outlook in OECD Countries: Annual Review*. Paris: OECD.

OECD (1992). *Structural Change and Economic Performance: A Seven Country Decomposition Study*. Paris: OECD.

ROWTHORN, R. E., and WELLS, J. R. (1987). *De-Industrialisation and Foreign Trade*. Cambridge: Cambridge University Press.

SAUL, S. B. (1978). 'The nature and diffusion of technology', in A. J. Youngson (ed.), *Economic Development in the Long Run*. London: Allen & Unwin.

SCHIFF, E. (1971). *Industrialisation without National Patents*. Princeton: Princeton University Press.

SPIERENBERG, D., and POIDEVIN, R. (1994). *The History of the High Authority of the European Coal and Steel Community*. London: Weidenfeld and Nicolson.

SYLLA, R., and TONIOLO, G. (1991) (eds.). *Patterns in European Industrialisation*. London: Routledge.

TEMIN, P. (1997). 'Is it kosher to talk about culture?'. *Journal of Economic History*, 57: 267–87.

THOMAS, L. G., III (1994). 'Implicit industrial policy: The triumph of Britain and the failure of France in global pharmaceuticals'. *Industrial and Corporate Change*, 3/2: 451–90.

TOMLINSON, M. (1997). 'The contribution of services to manufacturing industry: Beyond the de-industrialization debate'. *CRIC Discussion Paper*, no. 5. University of Manchester.

TSOUKALIS, L. (1997). *New European Economy Revisited*. Oxford: Oxford University Press.

UNECE (UN Economic Commission for Europe) (1953). *Economic Survey of Europe Since the War*. Geneva: UN Department of Economic Affairs.

VICKERS, J., and WRIGHT, V. (1988) (eds.). *The Politics of Privatisation in Western Europe*. London: Cass.

WHITLEY, A. (1976). *The Economics of Industrial Subsidies*. London: HMSO.

WOOLCOCK, S., and WALLACE, H. (1995). 'European Community regulation and national enterprise', in J. Hayward (ed.), *Industrial Enterprise and European Integration*. Oxford: Oxford University Press.

WRIGHT, V. (1995). 'Conclusion: The state and major enterprises in Western Europe: Enduring complexities', in J. Hayward (ed.), *Industrial Enterprise and European Integration*. Oxford: Oxford University Press.

INDEX

DATE DUE